Nordic Elites in Transformation, c. 1050–1250, Volume II

Nordic Elites in Transformation, c. 1050–1250, Volume II explores the structures and workings of social networks within the elites of medieval Scandinavia to reveal the intricate relationship between power and status.

Section one of this volume categorizes basic types of personal bonds, both vertical and horizontal, while section two charts patterns of local, regional, and transnational elite networks from wide-scope, longitudinal perspectives. Finally, the third section turns to case-studies of networks in action, analyzing strategies and transactions implied by uses of social resources in specific micro-political settings. A concluding chapter discusses how social power in the North compared to wider European experiences. A wide range of sources and methodologies is applied to reveal how networks were established, maintained, and put to use – and how they transformed in processes of centralizing power and formalizing hierarchies.

The engagement with and analysis of intriguing primary source material has produced a key teaching tool for instructors and essential reading for students interested in the workings of medieval Scandinavia, elite class structures, and Social and Political History more generally.

Kim Esmark is Associate Professor of Medieval History at the Department of Communication and Arts at Roskilde University. His main research interests lie within the historical anthropology of the Middle Ages, where he has published articles and co-edited books on dispute processing, rituals, kinship, gift-giving, and religious patronage.

Lars Hermanson is Professor of History at the University of Gothenburg. He has published many works on medieval political culture and has co-edited several anthologies on the subject. His latest book is *Friendship, Love, and Brotherhood in Medieval Northern Europe, c. 1000–1200* (Leiden, 2019).

Hans Jacob Orning is Professor of Medieval History at the Department of Archaeology, Conservation and History at the University of Oslo. He has written extensively on the political culture in medieval Scandinavia. His latest book is *The Reality of the Fantastic: The Magical, Geopolitical and Social Universe of Late Medieval Saga Manuscripts* (Odense, 2017).

Routledge Research in Medieval Studies

Medieval Hostageship c. 700–c. 1500
Hostage, Captive, Prisoner of War, Guarantee, Peacemaker
Edited by Matthew Bennett and Katherine Weikert

New Studies in Medieval and Renaissance Poland and Prussia
The Impact of Gdansk
Edited by Beata Możejko

The Colonies of Genoa in the Black Sea Region
Evolution and Transformation
Evgeny Khvalkov

The Plow, the Pen and the Sword
Images and Self-Images of Medieval People in the Low Countries
Rudi Künzel

Family, Work and Household in Late Medieval Iberia
A Social History of Manresa at the Time of the Black Death
Jeff Fynn-Paul

Nordic Elites in Transformation, c. 1050–1250, Volume I
Material Resources
Edited by Bjørn Poulsen, Helle Vogt, and Jón Viðar Sigurðsson

The Social Fabric of Fifteenth-Century Florence
Identities and Change in the World of Second-Hand Dealers
Alessia Meneghin

Nordic Elites in Transformation, c. 1050–1250, Volume II
Social Networks
Edited by Kim Esmarck, Lars Hermanson and Hans Jacob Orning

For more information about this series, please visit: https://www.routledge.com/Routledge-Research-in-Medieval-Studies/book-series/SE0452

Nordic Elites in Transformation, c. 1050–1250, Volume II
Social Networks

Edited by
Kim Esmark, Lars Hermanson,
and Hans Jacob Orning

NEW YORK AND LONDON

First published 2020
by Routledge
52 Vanderbilt Avenue, New York, NY 10017

and by Routledge
2 Park Square, Milton Park, Abingdon, Oxon, OX14 4RN

Routledge is an imprint of the Taylor & Francis Group, an informa business

© 2020 Taylor & Francis

The right of Kim Esmark, Lars Hermanson and Hans Jacob Orning to be identified as the authors of the editorial material, and of the authors for their individual chapters, has been asserted in accordance with sections 77 and 78 of the Copyright, Designs and Patents Act 1988.

All rights reserved. No part of this book may be reprinted or reproduced or utilised in any form or by any electronic, mechanical, or other means, now known or hereafter invented, including photocopying and recording, or in any information storage or retrieval system, without permission in writing from the publishers.

Trademark notice: Product or corporate names may be trademarks or registered trademarks, and are used only for identification and explanation without intent to infringe.

Library of Congress Cataloging-in-Publication Data
Names: Poulsen, Bjørn, 1955– editor. | Vogt, Helle, editor. | Jón Viðar Sigurðsson, 1958– editor.
Title: Nordic elites in transformation, c. 1050–1250 / edited by Bjørn Poulsen, Helle Vogt, and Jón Viðar Sigurðsson.
Other titles: Material resources.
Description: New York, NY : Routledge, 2019– |
Series: Routledge research in medieval studies ; 14 |
Includes bibliographical references and index.
Identifiers: LCCN 2019009726 (print) | LCCN 2019011560 (ebook) | ISBN 9780429262210 () | ISBN 9780367203054 (vol. 1 : hbk)
Subjects: LCSH: Elite (Social sciences)—Scandinavia—History—To 1500. | Social classes—Scandinavia—History—To 1500. | Scandinavia—Social conditions.
Classification: LCC HN540.Z9 (ebook) | LCC HN540.Z9 E457 2019 (print) | DDC 305.5/209368—dc23
LC record available at https://lccn.loc.gov/2019009726

ISBN: 978-0-367-90195-0 (hbk)
ISBN: 978-1-003-02300-5 (ebk)

Typeset in Sabon
by Apex CoVantage, LLC

Contents

List of Figures and Maps viii
List of Abbreviations x
Preface xii

1 Introduction 1
KIM ESMARK, LARS HERMANSON, AND HANS JACOB ORNING

SECTION I
Social Bonds, Social Resources 9

2 Kith and Kin: Ties of Blood and Marriage 11
KIM ESMARK, JÓN VIÐAR SIGURÐSSON, AND HELLE VOGT

3 Lords and Followers: Patron-Client Relationships 33
LARS HERMANSON AND HANS JACOB ORNING

4 Friends and Allies: Networks of Horizontal Bonds 54
LARS HERMANSON AND HANS JACOB ORNING

SECTION II
Patterns of Networks 77

5 Aristocratic Networks During the Late Viking Age in the Light of Runic Inscriptions 79
MAGNUS KÄLLSTRÖM

6 Nordic and Eastern Elites. Contacts Across the Baltic Sea: An Exiled Clan 104
JOHN H. LIND

vi Contents

7   Contact and Continuity: England and the Scandinavian
    Elites in the Early Middle Ages   125
    MARIE BØNLØKKE MISSUNO

8   Character Networks of the *Íslendinga Sögur* and *Pættir*   144
    RALPH KENNA AND PÁDRAIG MACCARRON

9   Angels in Scandinavia: Papal Legates and Networks of
    Nordic Elites, Twelfth–Thirteenth Centuries   169
    WOJTEK JEZIERSKI

10 Social Friendships Between the Dominican Order and
    Elite Groups in Thirteenth-Century Scandinavia   192
    JOHNNY GRANDJEAN GØGSIG JAKOBSEN

SECTION III
Networks in Action   213

11 Friends, Foes, and Followers: Power, Networks, and
    Intimacy in Medieval Iceland   215
    AUÐUR MAGNÚSDÓTTIR

12 Forming Bonds With Followers in Medieval Iceland:
    The Cases of Thordr kakali and Thorgils skarði   237
    VIÐAR PÁLSSON

13 Strength Through Weakness: Regent Elites Under Kings
    Inge, Sigurd, and Magnus Haraldsson   252
    IAN PETER GROHSE

14 The Politics of Exile in Northern Europe: The Case of
    Knud V of Denmark   271
    OLE-ALBERT RØNNING

15 Social Power and Conversion of Capital: Sune Ebbesen
    of Zealand   285
    KIM ESMARK

16 Constructing the Friendships and Hierarchies of
    the Clerical Elite: A Case Study of the Relationship
    Between Øm Abbey and Bishop Tyge   304
    SVEINUNG K. BOYE

17 Elites and Social Bonds – How Nordic Were the Nordic
   Medieval Elites? 325
   ARNOUD-JAN BIJSTERVELD, KIM ESMARK, AND HANS JACOB
      ORNING

List of Contributors 346
Index 348

Figures and Maps

Figures

5.1	The runestone Sö 338 from Turinge church in Södermanland	80
5.2	The rune-inscribed boulder U 11 at Hovgården in Adelsö parish, Uppland	82
5.3	The family tree of the Jarlabanke family in Täby, Uppland	86
5.4	The rock-inscription U 29 at Hillersjö in Hilleshög parish, Uppland	88
6.1	Lineage of the Riurikid dynasty	117
6.2	Lineage of the Hlaðir earls	118
6.3	Olof Skötkonung in the kinship web	118
6.4	Knut the Great's kinship web	118
7.1	Dynastic links between the Godwinsons and the Danish royal house	126
8.1	Small network of nodes and links	148
8.2	The character network for *Njáls saga*	150
8.3	The character network for *Laxdæla saga*	151
8.4	The character network for *Vatnsdæla saga*	152
8.5	The character network for the giant component of *Egils saga*	152
8.6	The character network for *Gísla saga*	153
8.7a	The degree distributions of *Njáls saga* and *Gísla saga*	156
8.7b	The degree distributions of *Vatnsdæla saga* and *Egils saga*	156
8.7c	The degree distributions of *Laxdæla saga*	156
8.8a	Assortative network	159
8.8b	Disassortative network	159
8.9a	Network with two communities	160
8.9b	Random network with no communities	160
8.10	Networks of five sagas amalgamated into one network	162
8.11	Networks of eighteen sagas amalgamated into one network	163
8.12	The degree distribution of the amalgamation of eighteen sagas	165

10.1	The social mix of donors behind the 268 recorded donations to the Friars Preachers in the province of Dacia in the period 1220–1349	200
15.1	Selective genealogy of descendants of Skjalm Hvide	287
15.2	Selective genealogy of the royal kindred	289

Maps

5.1	Map of distribution of carvings signed by or ascribed to the rune carver Ulv in Borresta	90
5.2	Map of distribution of rune carvings by the rune carver Torbjörn Skald	91
5.3	Map of distribution of rune carvings by the rune master Östen	97
6.1	Map of Kievan-Rus	107
10.1	Map of Dominican convents in the province of Dacia and its immediate surroundings around 1300	193

Abbreviations

Ágr	=	*Ágrip*. Edited and translated by Gustav Indrebø. Oslo, 1936.
AD	=	*Annales Danici medii aevi*. Edited by Ellen Jørgensen. Copenhagen, 1920.
ASC	=	*The Anglo-Saxon Chronicle: A Collaborative Edition*. Edited by David Dumville and Simon Keynes. Cambridge, 1983–.
CS	=	Helmold of Bosau. *The Chronicle of the Slavs*. Translated by Francis Joseph Tschan. New York, 1935.
DD	=	*Diplomatarium Danicum*. Edited by Niels Skyum-Nielsen et al. Copenhagen, 1938–.
DOPD	=	*Diplomatarium OP Dacie*. Edited by Johnny Grandjean Gøgsig Jakobsen. 2005–. Accessible at www.jggj.dk/DOPD.htm.
DR	=	*Danmarks runeindskrifter*. Edited by Lis Jacobsen and Erik Moltke. Copenhagen, 1941–42.
Gesta	=	Otto of Freising, *Ottonis et Rahewini: Gesta Friderici I. Imperatoris*. Edited by Georg Waitz. Hannover and Leipzig, 1912.
GH	=	Adam von Bremen. *Gesta Hammaburgensis Ecclesiae Pontificum*. Edited by Walter Trillmich and Richard Buchner. Darmstadt, 1978.
H	=	*Hirdloven til Norges konge og hans håndgangne menn: Etter Am 322 Fol*. Edited and translated by Steinar Imsen. Oslo, 2000.
Hkr	=	*Heimskringla* I–III. Íslenzk fornrit 26–28. Edited by Bjarni Aðalbjarnarsson. Reykjavík, 1941–51.
HOPD	=	"Historia Ordinis Predicatorum." In *Dacia*. Edited by Johnny Grandjean Gøgsig Jakobsen. 2007. Accessible at www.jggj.dk/HOPD.htm.
KLNM	=	*Kulturhistorisk leksikon for nordisk middelalder*. Edited by Finn Hødnebø et al. 22 vols. Oslo, 1956–78.

Abbreviations xi

KS	=	"Knýtlinga saga." Íslenzk fornrit 35. Edited by Bjarni Guðnason, 91–321. Reykjavík, 1982.
Msk	=	*Morkinskinna*. Íslenzk fornrit 23–24. Edited by Ármann Jakobsson and Þórður Ingi Guðjónsson. Reykjavík, 2011.
MUB	=	*Mecklenburgisches Urkundenbuch*. Various editors. Schwerin, 1863–1977.
NgL	=	*Norges gamle Love indtil 1387*, 3 vols. Edited by Rudolph Keyser, Peter Andreas Munch, Gustav Storm, and Ebbe Hertzberg. Christiania (Oslo), 1846–95.
PVL	=	*Povest' vremennykh let* "Ipat'evskaia letopis'." In *Polnoe sobranie russkikh letopisei 2*. Edited by Aleksei A. Shakhmatov. St. Petersburg, 1908.
Saxo	=	Saxo Grammaticus. *Gesta Danorum. The History of the Danes I–II*. Edited by Karsten Friis-Jensen. Translated by Peter Fisher. Oxford, 2015.
SDHK	=	*Svenskt diplomatarium*. Edited by Johan Gustav Liljegren et al. Stockholm, 1829–.
SM	=	*Scriptores minores historiae Danicae: Medii aevi*. Edited by M. Cl. Gertz. 2 vols. Copenhagen, 1917–20.
Sö	=	*Södermanlands runinskrifter*. Edited by E. Brate and E. Wessén (= SRI iii; Stockholm, 1924–36).
SRD	=	*Scriptores rerum Danicarum medii aevi*. Edited by Jakob Langebek et al. Copenhagen, 1772–1878.
SRI	=	*Sveriges runinskrifter*, Kungliga Vitterhets Historie och Antikvitetsakademien. Stockholm, 1900–.
Sturl	=	*Sturlunga saga I–II*. Edited by Jón Jóhannesson, Magnús Finnbogason, and Kristján Eldjárn. Reykjavík, 1946.
U	=	*Upplands runinskrifter*. 4 vols. Edited by E. Wessén and S. B. F. Jansson (= SRI vi–ix; Stockholm, 1940–).
Vg	=	*Västergötlands runinskrifter*. Edited by H. Jungner and E. Svärdström (= SRI v; Stockholm, 1940–70).
Vs	=	*Västmanlands runinskrifter*. Edited by Sven B. F. Jansson (= SRI xiii; Stockholm, 1964).
VSD	=	*Vitae sanctorum Danorum*. Edited by M. Cl. Gertz. 3 vols. Copenhagen, 1908–12.
Ög	=	*Östergötlands runinskrifter*. Edited by E. Brate (= SRI ii; Stockholm, 1911–18).
Öl	=	*Ölands runinskrifter*. Edited by Sven Söderberg and Erik Brate (= SRI i; Stockholm, 1900–1906).

Preface

The aim of the project *Nordic Elites in Transformation* is to examine elites in the Nordic countries (Denmark, Sweden, Norway, and Iceland) during the period c. 1050–1250. In order to avoid traditional divisions into "state," "church," and "aristocracy," the focus is on *elites* in a broad sense, encompassing powerful landowners as well as royal and ecclesiastical officials. The books seek to trace the dominance of this group in society, as well as to study changes and transformations occurring within the elite during this period. Moreover, the books adopt a Nordic perspective, on the one hand transcending national borders, on the other hand in an attempt to show how variable conditions were within the Nordic region.

The beginning of the period examined in the project is set to around 1050, when the Viking raids ended. By this time, Christianity had become the official religion in most parts of the Nordic countries, and the institution of kingship was well established in Denmark and Norway and possibly also in Sweden. The period covered ends in the middle of the thirteenth century, when royal and ecclesiastical power had been substantially strengthened and numerous monasteries and towns established. At this point, the position of the elites evolved into more formalized and institutionalized forms.

While the first book in the trilogy focuses on the material resources and economic basis of the Nordic elites, the social networks and how they anchored the rule of the elite both locally and internationally are dealt with in this volume. The final book explores the means of legitimacy and glorification that the Nordic elites employed to safeguard their dominance.

Along the way, we have received support from a number of institutions, whose generous funding has made it possible to organize workshops in Göteborg and Århus and to hire research assistants: Department of Archaeology, Conservation and History at the University of Oslo, Centre for Advanced Study at the Norwegian Academy of Science and Letters, the Research Council of Norway, the History Research Programme at History and Classical Studies, Aarhus University, Initiation

Grant from Riksbankens Jubileumsfond (RJ), Ernst Andersen og Tove Dobel Anders Fond, and finally Kaptajn, Ingeniør Aage Nielsens Familiefond. We would like to thank Eira Ebbs and Kate Gilbert for thorough proofreading, as well as Rein Amundsen and Torstein Bredal Jenssen for assisting us with a number of practical issues regarding the workshops and this publication.

1 Introduction

Kim Esmark, Lars Hermanson, and Hans Jacob Orning

Social Resources

This book is the second volume of the three-volume book project *Nordic Elites in Transformation*, c. 1050–1250. The first volume, *Material Resources*, treats the Nordic elites' economic sources of power (landed property, tribute, trade, taxation, etc.) and the third, *Legitimacy and Glory*, deals with cultural strategies used by the elites in order to justify their rank and rule. In the present volume, *Social Networks*, the aim is to analyze how the Nordic elites applied various forms of social resources in the creation of and competition for dominant positions in society. During the era under scrutiny, lordship, status, and hierarchy were to a large extent based on direct personal relations. Delegated authority through the holding of titles and offices certainly existed, but in an only vaguely institutionalized "face-to-face-society" even such authority tended to be based on and indeed merge with personal and social power. Thus, what we wish to highlight in this volume is the *variety and interplay of social bonds* connecting and empowering members of society's elites, including relations of both horizontal and vertical nature: family and kin, friends and followers, neighbors, patrons and clients, religious communities, intellectual networks, and so forth. Also closely connected to these relationships were various forms of delegated authority manifested by prominent titles and offices associated with political and religious institutions, such as church and monastic organization and kingship. How were these many different kinds of social bonds established, maintained, perceived, represented, challenged, or transformed, and first of all: How did people from the Nordic elites *make use* of such bonds in actual practice?

Elites

The choice of *elite* (from French *élite*, lit. "chosen person") as key analytical term throughout this book series is a conscious one. *Elite* is a modern sociological concept, flexible and open to neutral analysis of social power in a way that "native" categories such as nobility, aristocracy, and landed men are not. These and similar categories found in the medieval sources were themselves both products of and stakes in the social struggles that defined medieval society's hierarchies, and thus cannot be taken as analytical starting points. To get beyond the purely descriptive approaches of past discourses and stimulate sociological reflection one needs an exogenous concept – like "elite." That obviously doesn't mean we avoid speaking of *principes, magnates, milites, clerici, høvdinge,* and so forth. These were the terms by which medieval people described, distinguished, and indeed constructed the social divisions and leading groups within their own world. They are therefore all-important objects of study, but they are not analytical, scientific terms.

One important point of inspiration for this line of thought is the international collaborative project *Les élites dans le haut Moyen Âge occidental* (2002 to 2009).[1] Following some of the basic theoretical considerations underlying the research of this project, we define "elite" as those members of a society who hold a socially elevated position, whether in terms of wealth, political power, cultural prestige, social networks, knowledge, or some other relevant asset, and who are recognized by others as legitimately possessing such a position in a certain context.[2] Evidently, then, the elites included kings, queens, and members of the royal kin, but also men and women of the lay aristocracy; landowning magnates; castleholders and their knights; bishops, abbots, and other prominent ecclesiastics; learned clerics at royal, episcopal, and noble courts; leading townspeople and masters of guilds or other associations; influential elders at local *thing* assemblies; stewards and bailiffs; wealthy merchants; and well-to-do *bønder*. In other words, the elites included more than just those in control of political power in the narrow sense and should not be conceived of as a coherent or homogeneous class. Just like today, the elites in medieval Nordic society encompassed powerful people of many different sorts, who occupied a variety of positions and roles in social space, and who could often be at odds with one another. The analytical term *elite* is thus a relational one and may reach from the top echelons deep into local communities: It is really the specific context that determines whether a person or a group of persons can be considered "elite." Again, the inclusiveness – or vagueness – of such a definition is deliberate. As pointed out by Chris Wickham, the analytical utility of the concept of elite (as opposed to, e.g., aristocracy) "is precisely that it resists definition: it directs our attention to the 'minorité qui dirige', and asks us simply how that process of direction or domination worked – and how it changed."[3]

Networks: Practice and Strategy

In an attempt, nevertheless, to concretize what marked out medieval elites, Wickham suggests an ideal type (in the Weberian sense of *Idealtypus*) of nine elements: wealth, ancestry, public office or title, *Königsnähe* (nearness to the king), legal definition of elite status, peer recognition, wider societal prestige, display, and expertise/training.[4] What basically bound all these elements together, however, and made them operational, was social networks. This is forcefully underlined in a concluding remark of the *Élites dans le haut Moyen Âge occidental* project, according to which

> the history of the elites of the high Middle Ages, as we have tried to retrace it, is perhaps more than anything a history of connections and of networks. . . . It is certainly the possibility to belong to one of those networks, to be integrated in the more or less complex web that serves to support domination, which makes you a member – or not – of a certain elite.[5]

It is a central effort of our book to describe the history, structural composition, and geographical scope of Nordic elite networks, be they on a local, regional, or "transnational" scale. But more importantly than just mapping structures, we aim to analyze how social resources were *used*. To borrow a phrase of Stephen D. White's, bonds of kinship, like bonds of patronage, vassalage, and others, were "things that medieval nobles made (though not exactly as they pleased) and with which they did things – or tried to do things."[6] Such bonds functioned as *capital* in the sociological sense, *assets* that provided the necessary framework for almost any effective socio-political action, whether aiming at cooperation or at competition.[7] Great emphasis is therefore put on practice and agency: What did men and women of the elites actually *do* to shape and modify local hierarchies and power relations? How did individuals and groups make use of family, marriage, and/or friendship to enhance or defend their elevated status in society? How were personal ties and networks mobilized and adapted to changing contexts? How did "new" kinds of social capital (e.g., royal and clerical offices) interfere and interplay with "traditional" social resources (kinship, friendship) in particular micro-political constellations? Norms associated with various social bonds (loyalty, reciprocity, service, etc.) provided both a limiting framework for action *and* the necessary flexible tools to bend and negotiate this framework in actual practice. Analyzing the social resources of the elites therefore implies an appreciation of the strategic, creative element of socio-political action; of the ways people constructed and negotiated social bonds in a dialectic of action and discourse; of self-interested practical considerations and publicly avowable customs and norms.

A Nordic Perspective

The geographical scope of the book encompasses the Scandinavian kingdoms and Free State Iceland. Thus, the focus is on the Nordic world, but the socio-political perspective leads us to view this world in a wider cross-national context. Medieval elite networks often extended beyond the boundaries of individual realms, connecting royal and noble families, lords, friends, and members of ecclesiastical organizations and communities in Denmark, Sweden, Norway, and Iceland to social peers from neighboring regions and even beyond the Nordic world. In practice, power brokers of the upper layers of society operated in a vast political arena and rarely saw themselves restricted by conceptions of national or ethnic borders when looking for marriage partners, useful friends, or allies. Their scope for maneuvering was wide, and in communicating with one another, members of the Danish, Norwegian, and Swedish royal houses seldom addressed each other in their capacity as representatives of realms or dynasties. Instead they emphasized vocative forms linked to the social and emotional sphere such as "beloved brother" (*delectus frater*), "close relative" (*cognatus*), and "friend" (*amicus*). It was these kinds of obligatory relationships that influenced how power holders acted, or were supposed to act, in political matters. Local elites of lesser stature evidently did not connect across regions to the same extent, but bonds of patronage and practices of intercession "upwards" meant they were often linked up with larger cross-national networks nevertheless. All this hardly differed from conditions on the wider European continent. In trying to take systematic methodological account of this, the present book deviates from much previous Nordic research, which more or less unconsciously has taken national borders as a natural background for analyses of power and politics. In this book such borders are of minor importance – as they were back then.

Change and/or Continuity?

Another purpose of the book is to re-evaluate established interpretations regarding change and continuity. In most previous Nordic historiography the grand narratives of the eleventh to thirteenth centuries have been dominated by the themes of state building, christianization, and the diffusion of writing, and they have often tended towards a rather linear, progressive-evolutionary, almost "whiggish" transitional scheme. In focusing on interrelations and strategies of living actors rather than legal and institutional developments, the present book aims to arrive at a more nuanced view. To borrow a phrase of Fredric Cheyette's, our ambition is to study "first, the individuals in their particular, complex networks of relationships and, second, the systematic practices and transactions in which they engaged."[8] By approaching the transformations of elite social power in the period from this perspective, we hope to bring out more of the friction, conflict, ambiguity, dis-continuity and dis-connectedness that (also) formed part of the historical processes.

These processes were not utterly directionless, of course. Thus, an overarching structural context for the book's studies of particular actors and networks may be construed as processes of [1] transition from loosely unified kingdoms coexisting with local power bases to more organized polities wherein local power holders were gradually subordinated; [2] friction between loyalty based on reciprocity and consensus and loyalty founded upon a formalized hierarchy; [3] gradual formalization of socio-political relationships, promoted primarily by church and royalty; [4] centralization of power and concentration of social resources, implying reduction of the multiplicity of power bases and strengthening of royal and ecclesiastical authority.

With reference to these general trends and tendencies we specifically hope to explore the extent to which *in practice* traditional social resources were abandoned in favor of new ones during our period: Did the strengthening of royal and ecclesiastical power imply that traditional face-to-face ties of family, local patronage, and horizontal friendship lost their importance, or did inherited social structures continue to exist alongside new kinds of paid service and delegated office? Did gradual centralization and institutionalization alter hierarchies and privilege new groups, or did established elites continue to dominate by adapting to transformed conditions? How did new ways of reasoning about authority, service, and order influence established norms of honor and reciprocity and conventionalized practices of political communication and competition?

The Structure of the Book

The chapters of the book are organized in three sections. The first section, entitled "Social Bonds, Social Resources," aims to outline some basic features of kinship, patron-client relationships, and horizontal bonds – three main types of social ties that united and divided members of the medieval Nordic elites and constituted their sources of social power. The three chapters of section one will serve as framework and conceptual reference point for the studies presented in the following sections.

In section two, "Patterns of Networks," the structures of various elite networks are traced and mapped in six chapters. Applying a wide range of sources and methodologies, these chapters focus on runic evidence for aristocratic networks in late Viking Age Sweden; kinship webs between magnates in Scandinavia and Rus'; Anglo-Scandinavian connections and their transformation in the eleventh and twelfth centuries; local complex networks underlying the Sagas of Icelanders; the implications for elite networks of clerical education and papal legatine activities in the North; and bonds of friendship and patronage uniting Friars Preachers with religious communities and lay nobles in the thirteenth century.

6 *Kim Esmark et al.*

Section three then turns from wide-scope, longitudinal mappings of network patterns to "networks in action"; that is, case-studies of the ways social resources came into play in situated practice. How did particular groups and individuals within the lay and ecclesiastical elite apply social resources – "family, friends, and followers" – in competition for power and prominence in specific (micro-) historical settings? Six chapters explore the marriage strategies of a prominent Icelandic chieftain; the role of feasts and gifts in local patron–client relationships in late Free State Iceland; political elite groupings' exploitation of underage kings in mid-twelfth-century Norway; the politics of social obligations and political interests during an exiled Danish king's attempts to raise support outside his kingdom; sources of social power and strategies of capital conversion in the life of a twelfth-century Danish magnate; and conflictual perceptions of friendship and hierarchy in a prolonged intra-ecclesiastical dispute case from Denmark.

A final concluding chapter reflects on the main findings of the foregoing studies and discusses the possible "nordicness" of medieval Nordic elite networks: To what degree did structures and uses of social resources intersect with kingdoms and regions to form some kind of trans-regnal Nordic whole? And how did patterns, practices, and transformations of social power within the Nordic world compare to contemporary European experiences?

Notes

1. The project is documented in eight comprehensive edited volumes, focusing on the early and central Middle Ages and covering themes of crisis and change, mobility, stratification, culture, and wealth as well as discussions of historiography and methodology. For bibliographical details see Bougard, François, Hans-Werner Goetz, and Régine Le Jan, eds., *Théorie et pratiques des élites au Haut Moyen Age: Conception, perception et réalisation sociale* (Turnhout, 2011), 4.
2. Laurent Feller, "Introduction: Crises et renouvellements des élites au haut Moyen Âge: mutations ou ajoustements des structures?" in *Les élites au haut moyen âge: Crises et renouvellements*, ed. François Bougard, Laurent Feller, and Régine Le Jan (Turnhout, 2006), 5–21.
3. Chris Wickham, "The Changing Composition of Early Élites," in *Théorie et pratiques des élites au Haut Moyen Age. Conception, perception et réalisation sociale*, ed. François Bougard, Hans-Werner Goetz, and Régine Le Jan (Turnhout, 2011), 5–18 at 8.
4. Ibid., 9–13.
5. "l'histoire des élites du haut Moyen Âge telle que nous avons tenté de la retracer est peut-être avant tout une histoire de connexions et de réseaux . . . c'est sûrement la possibilité d'appartenir á l'un de ces réseaux, d'être intégré dans la toile plus ou moins complexe qui sert de support à la domination, qui fait qu'on est membre – ou pas – d'une certaine élite." Geneviève Bührer-Thierry, "Connaître les élites au haut moyen âge," in *Théorie et pratiques des élites au Haut Moyen Age: Conception, perception et réalisation sociale*, ed.

François Bougard, Hans-Werner Goetz, and Régine Le Jan (Turnhout, 2011), 373–84 at 382–83. Our translation.
6. Stephen D. White, *Re-Thinking Kinship and Feudalism in Early Medieval Europe* (Aldershot, 2005), vii.
7. Strategies of cooperation and competition in fact often overlapped in processes of what in an important recent study has been termed *coopetition* – a neologism borrowed from management studies for heuristic purposes of analyzing the specificities of early medieval socio-political rivalry, see Régine Le Jan, Geneviève Bührer-Thierry, and Stefano Gasparri, eds., *Coopétition: Rivaliser, coopérer dans les sociétés du haut Moyen Âge (500–1100)* (Turnhout, 2018).
8. Fredric L. Cheyette, "Review: Fiefs and Vassals: The Medieval Evidence Reinterpreted," *Speculum* 71, no. 4 (1996): 998–1006 at 1006.

Dedicated Bibliography

Bougard, François, Hans-Werner Goetz, and Régine Le Jan, eds. *Théorie et pratiques des élites au Haut Moyen Age: Conception, perception et réalisation sociale*. Turnhout, 2011.
Cheyette, Fredric L. "Review: Fiefs and Vassals: The Medieval Evidence Reinterpreted." *Speculum* 71 (1996): 998–1006.
Feller, Laurent. "Introduction: Crises et renouvellements des élites au haut Moyen Âge: mutations ou ajoustements des structures?" In *Les élites au haut moyen âge: Crises et renouvellements*, edited by François Bougard, Laurent Feller, and Régine Le Jan, 5–21. Turnhout, 2006.
Le Jan, Régine, Geneviève Bührer-Thierry, and Stefano Gasparri, eds. *Coopétition: Rivaliser, coopérer dans les sociétés du haut Moyen Âge (500–1100)*. Turnhout, 2018.
White, Stephen D. *Re-Thinking Kinship and Feudalism in Early Medieval Europe*. Aldershot, 2005.
Wickham, Chris. "The Changing Composition of Early Élites." In *Théorie et pratiques des élites au Haut Moyen Age: Conception, perception et réalisation sociale*, edited by François Bougard, Hans-Werner Goetz, and Régine Le Jan, 5–18. Turnhout, 2011.

Section I
Social Bonds, Social Resources

2 Kith and Kin
Ties of Blood and Marriage

Kim Esmark, Jón Viðar Sigurðsson, and Helle Vogt

Characteristics, Previous Research, and Sources

Family and kinship constituted the social backbone of medieval society's elite groups. "Of all the ties that bound a person in the Middle Ages," writes Gerd Althoff, "the most important was without doubt the bond to the family or kindred."[1] Other types of relationships obviously mattered as well, as will be discussed in subsequent chapters, but even they would often imitate the social and cultural matrix provided by family organization.[2] Few historians would thus contest Althoff's statement, which might in fact apply with particular weight to the Nordic realm, where generations of scholars have stressed the all-important role of kin. For many years medieval Nordic societies were defined quite simply as "kinship societies," i.e., traditional societies where the individual above all existed and acted as a member of an *ætt* (kin group) and where the *ætt* constituted a legal subject.[3] These societies were held to be essentially different from the supposedly "feudal" societies in other parts of Europe, still unspoiled by state, church, and foreign cultural influence.[4] To some historians these societies were also inherently violent: a "loosely knit conglomerate of shifting family alliances in perpetual mutual strife;"[5] a "mafia society," where individual legal rights were "rooted in a local, decentralized power institution, the kindred with its clients."[6] As comparative approaches have come to be used in recent years, however, the perception of family and kin in medieval Nordic society has become more complex, and increasingly tends to stress resemblances rather than differences between the Nordic and the wider European context.

The societal position of kin groups posed a recurrent problem in twentieth-century scholarly debates on the history of individualism in Europe. For Burckhardt and numerous historians after him the subjection of individuals to kinship interests was a predominant "traditional" or "pre-individualist" feature of medieval societies. Schemes and models developed by some of the founding fathers of sociology seemed to support the idea. According to Tönnies and Durkheim, for instance, one of the important effects of the modernization process was the gradual weakening of kinship loyalties in favor of relations of more contractual nature.[7] The traditional historiographical notion of medieval Nordic kinship society drew on this scheme, but empirically it often rested on the thin evidence of law texts and select episodes in Icelandic sagas. What exactly was implied by "kinship society" remained rather vague, and neither the structure nor the actual ways individuals supposedly subjected themselves to the kindred were investigated.

Only from the 1970s onwards did the medieval family become a central historical research topic, and in recent years it has become progressively clear that the roles and functions of kin groups are best analyzed by taking account of other types of relationships and group formations. Labelled alternately as "history of community," *histoire de la sociabilité*, or *Sozialgeschichte der Gruppen*, new research directions have looked at organizations of social life that stretch from family, friendship, and clientelistic relations to communal and other proto-state structures.[8] At the same time scholars have adopted new methodological approaches focusing on the everyday actions by which social actors established and maintained personal ties and group relations. Recognizing the processual nature of social bonds, the aim has been to reconstruct and understand the actual deeds and doings of medieval people, seen from an actor's perspective. This approach has proved to be an important inspiration for many of the studies in the present book.

In what follows we shall not present a general review of scholarship, carve out firm models of Nordic kinship, or try to establish which type of family organization dominated in this or that region or period. The aim, instead, is to outline the *interpretive framework for understanding the social dynamics of kinship*, which (in varying guises) informs the case studies in this volume, and to provide some select examples of ways kinship ties were conceptualized and put to work in practice.

Making Kinship: A Processual View of Family Relationships

For the elites of the Nordic world – just as for their counterparts elsewhere – bonds of kinship were a social asset and structuring capital of prime importance. Family and ancestry provided powerful idioms for claims to economic resources, political support, and symbolic legitimacy; they defined one's social status and identity, and regulated and safeguarded titles to property; they opened (or closed) the doors to political alliances and benefits; and they protected the individual, in principle at least, via threats of collective revenge. At the same time, rules, norms, and discourses related to kinship (inheritance, marriage, obligations to support or avenge one's kinsmen, etc.) might also be invoked to obstruct or constrain individual social action.

However, the kindred was never a permanent, objectively defined group. The fact that Nordic family organization was everywhere cognatic or bilateral meant that people traced their origins and relations through both paternal and maternal lines. Every individual would share blood with more than one descent group, and no two individuals (apart from full siblings) would have the exact same ancestors and relatives. In the resulting tissue of overlapping kin groups each link might be assigned different value, while the nuclear family held a central position.[9] Moreover, although the discourse of law as well as some narrative texts prioritized and idealized consanguinity, bonds of kinship were constituted not only by blood, but also by marriage (affinity) and relationships of custody or fosterage. Because of high mortality rates, kin groups would usually include several individuals who had remarried, adding ranks of stepchildren to the already highly composite family picture. Icelandic chieftains were sometimes said to possess *frændastyrk* or be *frændríkir*, meaning that their parents came from large families. For example, Gissur Thorvaldsson's father, one of the most powerful chieftains c. 1230–1270, had eight siblings, his mother had three, and Gissur Thorvaldsson himself had eight. A large, solid group of kinsmen like that not only provided support to its own members but also brought a large number of in-laws, who were often more important than the blood relatives.[10] On top of this, concubinage was widely practiced and accepted within the elite well into the thirteenth century despite increasing opposition from the Church. In Iceland again, many chieftains were born out of wedlock. In Norway children by concubines had fewer rights than their half-siblings born from regular marriages, but they were never wholly excluded.[11] In Denmark illegitimate children inherited from their mother and could inherit from their father, if he wished – they were therefore "potentially legitimate."[12]

Common descent from a particular noble ancestor (man or women) meant a great deal with respect to honor and status, if only in a somewhat unspecified sense, as the bilateral system obviously left considerable scope for tracing various links backwards in time.[13] The creation of "new families" was a more or less continuous and relatively rapid process. In the Icelandic genealogical texts *Ættartölur* and *Haukdæla þáttr*, probably written in the first half of the thirteenth century, none of the pedigrees for the eight most prominent families on the island reach further back than the early twelfth century. A key issue was producing sons. If there were no sons who could carry the family tradition, the family disappeared. Families in this sense usually only survived for three generations.[14]

In Iceland the family usually took its name from the farm where the "founding father" lived, as with *Borgarmenn*, the men of Borg. If a son moved away and established his household at the farm called, for instance, Laugar, he and his household would henceforward be known as the *Laugamenn*. The household name thus took precedence over the family name. Surnames were not used, but patronymics were.

If the so-called kinship society was thus really a complex mosaic of highly heterogeneous, overlapping groups, it is necessary to look for conceptualizations that are more sensitive to the fuzziness and fluidity of family structure.[15] For instance, in her work on the "predatory kinship" of the elite of Normandy, who originated from Scandinavian settlers, Eleanor Searle speaks of the "politics of kinship" and describes kinship as "not a matter of 'blood' or descent but a way of reckoning those who have a right to share in resources, and ... therefore also a way of identifying those upon whom each individual could depend."[16] In a specific Scandinavian context Lars Hermanson identifies "a relative conception of kin, variable and conditioned by socio-political circumstances,"[17] while Thyra Nors has proposed a conception of kin "primarily as a strategic, political field."[18] Other like-minded approaches, all pointing to the openness and malleability of kinship, could be added.[19] What they have in common is the assumption that the medieval kin group should be treated as a socio-cultural construct, a situated "imagined community" that not only structured social action, but was also constantly formed and re-formed by social action itself. Never a closed, stable unit, the kindred was the "fluid and multiform product of varied strategies and representations, which were continuously negotiated and adapted to different contexts and practical needs."[20] Hence, the meanings and practices of family and kin in the Nordic world not only varied chronologically and geographically (from the late Viking Age to the thirteenth century, from Iceland to Blekinge); even *within* each period and each region it was a matter of ongoing processes of constructing, performing, and representing kinship.

Official and Practical Kinship

Adopting the perspective that family relations were "things that medieval nobles made (though not exactly as they pleased) and with which they did things – or tried to do things"[21] entails a break not only with modern essentialist notions, but also with "native" representations in contemporary medieval sources. These were rarely objective descriptions, but stakes in political-discursive attempts to promote certain genealogical lineages or images of kinship at the expense of others.[22] Pierre Bourdieu's note on the existence of social groups in general is highly relevant in this regard:

> Whether they have an occupational basis as in our societies or a genealogical basis as in pre-capitalist societies, *groups are not found ready-made in reality*. And even when they present themselves with this air of eternity that is the hallmark of naturalized history, they are always the product of a complex historical work of construction.[23]

Some medieval scholars have found it useful to apply Bourdieu's twin notions of official and practical kinship – notions coined by the sociologist in his early work on kinship structures and matrimonial strategies among the Kabyles of colonial Algeria.[24] Official kinship, according to Bourdieu, is the formal representation of genealogical relationships made by outside observers (anthropologists or medievalists) or by social actors themselves (compilers of law, narrators of aristocratic family history, monastic chroniclers, etc.). It is the kind of abstract, quasi-legal representation that can be codified and systematized in a genealogical stemma without reference to actual use. It is well defined by law and norms, and primarily serves public purposes and the function of order. Practical kinship, on the other hand, points to those family connections that are actually kept in working order, the network of useful kinsmen, who are mobilized by specific actors for specific purposes at specific points in time. Thus, practical kinship is "private," situational, operational, strategic, and often blends with other types of relationships (lordship, friendship, clientage). Its boundaries are blurred and varied. Practical kinship, in short, is the *modus operandi* of family organization, "family in action."

According to Bourdieu (and the medievalists who have taken inspiration from his work) kinship strategies unfold in a *dialectic between official and practical kinship*.[25] In any given situation, the set of relatives one would or could call upon depended on context, function, and the prehistory of those involved. Did you need kinsmen for a revenge killing, to corroborate a land transaction, to negotiate a marriage, or to raise money for a pilgrimage? Who among the dead ancestors would it be profitable to commemorate and who should be forgotten? Which particular individuals among all those who *theoretically* could count as kin (through bonds of blood, marriage, or fosterage) were *socio-politically relevant* to declare as family in this or that situation? And how was practical kinship represented publicly so as to appear to comply with the protocol of official kinship?

The terminology used to describe family relationships in the North may serve to exemplify the point. Though the term *ætt* has been the basis for the scholarly discussion on kinship structures it features rarely in the sources, which more commonly use *frændi, frænde* for a man, *frændkona, frændkone* for a women, and *frændsemi, frændsæme* for the relationship between kinsfolk.[26] The Icelandic sources provide two different definitions of these words. The laws explain *frændi* and *frænka* in the same way as *ætt*, that is, as all persons whose kin relationship could be traced back five generations.[27] The saga narratives, on the other hand, which deal with people in action, use the terms in a narrower sense to describe the relationship between ego and sons, daughters, father, mother, brothers, sisters, nephews, nieces, uncles, aunts, cousins, grandfathers, and grandmothers.[28] The boundary for kin stops at cousins, except in chieftain families. In the North, as elsewhere in Europe at the time, there was no word for the nuclear family.[29] Instead, according to the sagas' terminology, the *frændr*-group, with all its overlaps, constituted the basic unit. *Mágr, magh* was used for in-laws.[30] Some family relationships were more essential than others, depending on the position of the family in local power structures. In Iceland, for instance, it proved more important to nurture a kinship relation with a powerful chieftain, even though he might be a rather distant relative, than, say, one with a brother.

The Workings of Kinship: Property, Marriage, and Conflict

How then did family ties come into play as a social resource in elite competitions for power and how and for what purposes did individuals mobilize their kinsmen? Turning to the actual workings of kinship we now take a look at three particular fields of activity where family bonds were continuously made, reaffirmed, and challenged.

Property

Bonds of kinship constituted the basic regulatory framework for possession and transfer of landed property within the Nordic elites (as within any group of householding freemen).[31] First of all, land was inherited within the kin group. When someone died his or her landed property passed to children, brothers, sisters, nephews, or other relatives according to customary practices or legal rules. From the outset, therefore, ownership and disposition of land was embedded in family structure. If someone's possessions were challenged, kinsmen were expected to step up as oath-helpers at the *thing* assembly to guarantee his or her title,[32] but kinsmen also restricted individual landowners' dispositions in various ways. Although land was held individually, it could not be bought, sold, granted, or received freely, as any property transfer potentially affected the status and prosperity of not only the vendor or donor, but also of heirs and relatives. These people would therefore often become involved in the transfer, especially when the land about to change hands was family land, i.e., farms, acres, woods, and so forth inherited from ancestors and relatives. Such property was distinguished from land acquired through purchase. It was associated with honor and distinction,[33] and protected throughout our period by various restrictions as to how it could be disposed of.[34]

Little is known about the specific norms governing transfer of family land before the advent of written law. The general impression remains that heirs to land that was granted or sold out of the kin retained some kind of moral right to reclaim the property or at least to have a say with regard to the alienation. Lawmen from mid-south Sweden for instance, instructed people that no pious gift of land be made by a dying person without the presence and consent of the heirs.[35] Such customary norms seem to have followed the same basic patterns as the *laudatio parentum* known from wider Europe. They did not form a coherent legal system, but should rather be conceived of as "a fluid set of general principles, characteristically formulated in the shape of proverbs and maxims," which, when applied to specific cases, "might easily support mutually contradictory solutions."[36] The bilateral kinship system further complicated things, as any marriage implied that property was being transferred to the new household from both contracting families, thus widening the circle of interested relatives.

Frustrated heirs' complaints about alienations could be acknowledged or refuted, depending on the arguments, pressure, and support they were able to mobilize, but at least in intra-class conflicts within the elite, disputants usually opted for some kind of compromise and compensation. The evidence, of course, is scarce for the early period, but scattered examples are found in charters recording donations and disputes. When in the early 1120s various "good men" donated land to the metropolitan church of Lund, the archbishop paid the donors' heirs to obtain their consent.[37] Some four or five decades later the newly founded Esrum Abbey in Denmark saw a series of gifts challenged by the donor's heirs, who were then allowed to donate the contested properties themselves; being thus given a share in the spiritual benefits of the initial grant, they renounced their claims.[38] In Scania heirs were allowed the right to object to pious gifts after the death of the donor.[39]

With the introduction of written law, compiled in the course of the twelfth and thirteenth centuries all over the Nordic regions by learned clerics backed by emergent royal power, fuzzy principles were superseded (or overlapped) by well-defined rules, less open to interpretation. In various forms, following various procedures and under various names – *lovbydelse* in Denmark, *bördsrätt* in Sweden, *odelsrett* in Norway – kinsmen were awarded a formal legal right of pre-emption for family land, and the exact group of relatives entitled to exercise this right was defined and delimited according to Canon law classifications of consanguinity. Thus, the process of law-making probably strengthened family ties in general, but also privileged certain official representations of kinship at the expense of other, less strict, more fluid conceptions.[40]

Marriage

The most important way for elites to create new family bonds was through marriage. Alliance and reproduction strategies always revolved around the unification of groups through exchanges of women and property. Cultural perceptions of marriage went through changes during our period as ecclesiastic reformers strove to transform the original social-secular institution, which allowed for divorce and concubinage, into a monogamous, indissoluble pact modeled on Christ's union with the Church. The function of marital strategies, however, did not change and remained a battleground of no less import than, say, property litigation or feuding. Unfortunately the all-important processes of negotiation that surrounded any contracting of marriage are rarely exposed in detail by the sources, perhaps because of the inherent nature of such processes: shrouded in secrecy, done by proxy, and so forth. A few examples are found in the sagas about Icelandic chieftains and Norwegian kings. In the winter of 1223–24, the chieftain Thorvaldr Vatnsfirding sent friendly words to Snorri Sturluson, one of the most powerful chieftains at that time, about creating an alliance (*samband*) and an in-law relationship. Snorri accepted this on condition that Thorvaldr should "undertake" whatever he "might ask of him, no matter against whom."[41] Discourses about marriage contracting were of course not all about politics and economy, but also about the beauty and cleverness of future wives.[42]

Success or failure in the marriage market easily decided the standing and fortune of a kin group, and heads of families were supposed to act with discretion and foresight, even to the degree of denying children the possibility of marriage.[43] What happened if a man had six sons? From Iceland we can see that some of them were allowed to marry while others had to content themselves with becoming members of their brothers' households. Likewise, not all daughters were invariably married off.[44]

With the gradual advance of clerical celibacy (from the twelfth century onwards) some members of the elite were formally prohibited from marrying, causing certain familial links to take on new meanings. Without children of their own, high-ranking ecclesiastics nurtured strong relations with their siblings' offspring in a kind of clerical dynastic structure. Bishops and canons were succeeded in their offices by nephews or second cousins, and written wills reveal how they built networks with nieces and their families.[45]

Members of the upper strata of the elite married across both geographical boundaries between realms and social boundaries between aristocratic and royal blood, ensuring considerable socio-political maneuverability.[46] The mightiest groups were capable of influencing royal power and reaping profits – material as well as symbolic – from their *Königsnähe* (nearness to the king), and occasionally even joined the competition for crowns and kingdoms.[47]

In other words, marriage – which in our time is associated with something "private" – was completely embedded in the "public" world of power and politics. Marriages were contracted both to seal settlements between contending factions and, preventively, to keep latent conflicts from breaking out. In case of feuding, individuals who were connected to both parties through marriage links could take the role of mediators (cf. Gluckman's *peace in the feud*).[48] The bilateral kinship system simply was not compatible with long-term warfare, since there would always be someone in the implicated networks with interests on more than one side. On top of this, Church prohibitions against marrying even distantly related blood relatives posed an ideological incentive to associating kindred and thereby promoting peace.[49]

The crucial role of marriage in kinship strategies left women with potentially great influence, even if this influence often had to be exercised "from within" or "behind the screen." Danish noblewomen were entitled to alienate land. A quarter of all donors registered in the obit book of Lund Cathedral are thus women.[50] Traditional historiography used to describe aristocratic women as passive objects in an all-male world of political competition, but recent research has stressed the active, participatory role of women in the power game, and has also pointed to the dependence of male political actors on conditions in the "private" family sphere.[51]

One particularly well-documented example is Queen Margrete Fredkulla ("Peace-Maiden") of Denmark, whose intricate marital politics during the reign of her husband King Niels (1104–34) for years managed to bridge rival branches of the royal family and thus maintain peace. Danish coins from the period bear her name along with that of the king, while foreign observers noted how the rule of Denmark was so dependent on the noble queen that it effectively lay in a woman's hand.[52] When Margrete died c. 1130, her carefully worked-out system of alliances collapsed and years of dynastic war followed.[53]

Conflict

With no centralized state power to uphold peace and monopolize prosecution and punishment of wrongdoers, medieval Nordic society was a "feuding society" in which protection of life and property relied on collective self-help and the threat or taking of revenge.[54] Even when lawbreakers were being judged at public assemblies, the wronged parties were left to carry out sentences themselves (by, for example, collecting fines). The primary group which the individual relied on here was the kindred. According to deep-rooted norms, which gradually came to be written down in law, kinsmen were held to be liable for each other. If someone suffered an insult or attack, his or her relatives were expected to help retaliate against the wrongdoer, and vice versa: If a member of a group violated someone, his or her kinsmen were all considered legitimate targets of the wronged party's revenge.

Yet exactly which relatives were obliged to take collective action in case of conflict remained unclear. Feuds therefore functioned both as tests of family solidarity and as occasions for actualizations of otherwise dormant relationships. According to the Danish chronicler Saxo one could claim assistance from both the paternal and the maternal side of the family.[55] In Iceland, where the sagas provide the most detailed view of things, sons and fathers had to give almost unconditional support to each other. The obligations between brothers were not as clear-cut as those between fathers and sons, but they usually stood up for each other. As regards more distant relatives, it is difficult to see any consistent pattern, but uncles and cousins were normally expected to help.[56] Although physical violence was the prerogative of men, women also shared responsibilities for defending the honor of the family or household. Women often took an active part in feuding processes and could even be seen acting publicly as heads of kin groups. At the same time women might also be specifically targeted as victims of rape or abduction aimed at casting shame on their group.[57]

It is important to note, however, that feuding groups were almost never family war bands, but highly composite factions, mobilized for the occasion, of not only kinsmen, but also friends, neighbors, patrons, dependents, and ad hoc allies.[58] Likewise, the (mostly small-scale) wars that were fought were not "blood feuds" in the archetypical-mythical sense, but political trials of strength that involved multiple parties and interests. As much as discourses of blood and honor might be invoked to justify claims and gather support, the kindred hardly ever acted like an organic fighting unit.[59] Speaking with Bourdieu, feuding was often legitimized by official kinship, but always carried out by practical kinship.

Once again, however, things got more formalized as they became codified in law. In all medieval Nordic laws (except the Icelandic) the collective paying and receiving of man's compensation (*ethebot*) among kinsmen in case of homicide was a fundamental principle. The provisions varied in their details, but generally all men related within the well-defined canonical degrees of consanguinity were legally obliged to participate in the giving and taking of man's compensation. One third of the compensation was to be paid by the killer himself, one third by his father's side, and one third by his mother's side.[60] In case of an intentional killing an additional fine was paid to the king for breaking the peace. Compensation payment was followed by the performance of an honor-restoring leveling oath (*javnetheed*): The killer's kinsmen swore in public that in the reverse situation they would do the same, i.e., accept payment in compensation for the killing of a relative of theirs. The logic behind the leveling oath was explained by Archbishop Anders Sunesen in his early thirteenth-century Latin paraphrase of the Law of Scania and points to the deeply honor-infused ethos of the elite:

> But the oath of equality is always enforced all the more diligently because by making those who are harmed equivalent to those who have harmed, the contempt appears to be taken away which is customarily stirred up by one who has suffered injury from oppression against those who have inflicted it. For prudent men always value the

integrity of their reputation and the restoration of the honor due to them more than pecuniary compensation.[61]

The strengthening of kinship implied by the formalization of collective responsibility between relatives also showed in legal provisions aiming to save individuals caught between public duties and family loyalty. According to the Frostathing Law from Norway, for instance, if a man was killed at the public assembly, all present were bound to pursue the killer. However, those related to the killer either by blood or by marriage were exempted and even allowed to help the fugitive – once and only once.[62]

Strength and Stability of Kinship Bonds

The relative strength and stability of kinship bonds was rooted in the socialization as a "family man/woman," which all members of the elite were exposed to. Socio-cultural norms and identities associated with belonging to a kindred were systematically inculcated through common upbringing, proverbs, songs, narratives, rites, and the manifold firsthand experiences of collective action at assemblies, ceremonies of property transfer, feuding activities, and so forth. The outcome of this comprehensive explicit and implicit pedagogical work was a distinct kinship habitus, a durable structure of embodied attitudes, inclinations, and abilities which guided the mental outlook and practical action of society's upper strata. On top of this, religious doctrines concerning love between blood relatives, between spouses, and between parents and their children posed a strong ideological reaffirmation of kinship norms.

The emotional aspect of family life within the elite should not be overlooked. Genuine affection for one's family members no doubt worked to cement relationships, at least among close relatives.[63] Even learned compilers of law took familial emotions into consideration. In the Law of Scania as explicated by Archbishop Anders Sunesen, for instance, custody of minors was always awarded to paternal relatives before maternal ones, with one exception: A mother's father had priority over a father's brother, because a maternal grandfather was assumed to possess more "affection" (*affectus*) towards the child than a paternal uncle.[64] Yet evaluating medieval discourses of love and loyalty between spouses and kinsmen remains a difficult task. How should we understand recurrent phrases in donation charters and written wills like "my beloved wife/husband"? Were such words expressions of subjective feelings as we think of them today, or standardized formulas?[65] Or what about kings who showed mercy to deadly rivals on account of distant family bonds: Did these otherwise ruthless rulers really hold feelings for their *propinqui*, or did their chroniclers simply invoke the norms of Bourdieu's official kinship to explain what in reality were calculated political decisions?[66]

In the last resort, strength and durability of kinship bonds depended on their usefulness. At times strong leaders succeeded in gathering both near and distant relatives around them, thus providing the impression of a truly united kindred.[67] Usually this had to do with the capacity of such leaders to *give* something, whether protection, wealth, offices, or access to other networks. When, for instance, a certain branch of the so-called Hvide family in twelfth-century Denmark became closely associated with the victorious line of kings that emerged from prolonged dynastic wars, they were able to attract distant cousins, nephews, and affines, who all wanted to share in their *Königsnähe*. The feeling of solidarity of this otherwise heterogenous network was strengthened through the erection of a *Hauskloster*, a family monastery, where individual members of the group were buried and commemorated in prayers. The collective activities implied by donations, prayer, and burial transformed the theoretical premise that all those involved were somehow related to each other by blood or marriage into a socio-politically relevant and recognized fact. In many respects, however, individual branches of the family network continued to operate by themselves, and as the leaders gradually lost their special tie to the throne, various branches of the family tended to look to other relationships and other cultic sites.[68]

Although norms warranted solidarity between kinsmen, intra-familial tension and disruption of kin groups was a built-in feature of the bilateral family structure. Competition between collateral branches overlapped with other, non-genealogical obligations; and internal strife between near relatives or parents and children were by no means uncommon as blood kin found themselves divided in terms of loyalty and socio-political interests.[69] Married couples might also experience split loyalties. In the mid-twelfth century the Danish magnate Peder Torstensen married into the powerful Hvide family, but he hesitated to support the monastery built by his wife's kindred and even restricted the size of her gifts to the family foundation. Decades later Peder's grandson continued to bother the monks who prayed for the souls of the family. In the end, the troublesome grandson was persuaded by mediating kinsmen to give up his stronghold and his lands around the monastery in return for more distant holdings.[70]

Turning to the laws again, various provisions reveal how the obligation to contribute collectively to the payment of *ethebot* in case of homicide might set kinsmen up against each other. Some killers' relatives simply refused to pay their installment, in which case killers might try to take it by violence. In other cases killers collected the installments owed by their blood kin, only to keep the money or goods for themselves – or just squander it.[71] The Norwegian chronicler Theodoricus equated kin-killings with crimes, murders, and false oaths, but in fact, much of what today is conceived of as "political history" in the Nordic realm was intra-dynastic or intra-familial quarrels.[72] Within royal dynasties examples of kin-slaying abound. The Danish king Erik II Emune ("the Unforgettable," r. 1134–7), for instance, was directly or indirectly responsible for the killing of one uncle, two cousins, a half-brother, and eleven children of his half-brother's. The Icelandic sagas provide unique evidence of conflict within non-royal kin groups, where kin strife seems to have been common, at least in some families. However, while wives might have their husbands killed, young men in the sagas never crossed the line of actually slaying their own parents or brothers. On the other hand, numerous examples from these same narratives show how kinsmen were often ready to betray and even sacrifice each other if need be.[73] To strengthen the somewhat precarious bonds of blood, kinsmen would often describe their relation concomitantly as "friendship" (*vinátta*) and "kinship" (*frændsemi*).[74]

Formalization and Strategy

Throughout our period, bonds of blood and affinity remained one of the most important types of social capital among the elites of all the Nordic realms. The main change was the introduction of canonical kinship in twelfth- and thirteenth-century legislation. Writing down law on kinship along the lines of learned law and canonical computation of blood relations meant that family structures and the rights and obligations associated with being a kinsman were defined in a hitherto-unseen systematic, coherent way. The fuzzy contours of the "old" kindred, with its elective elements and blurred lines between blood kin, friends, and allies, became more sharply delineated, and royal and ecclesiastical power slowly started to interfere in areas traditionally regulated by loosely structured, autonomous kin groups.

Ironically, more than anything else it was the strong emphasis on kinship in the Nordic law books that made generations of historians think of the medieval North as the archetypal "kinship society." But even if the legal provisions on such things as inheritance, land transfer, and compensation for homicide evidently echoed earlier norms and custom, they also (perhaps primarily?) represented a conscious and innovative attempt, led by Church and Crown, to *transform* kinship.

The introduction of canonical kinship was inspired by Christian peace ideology and aimed to limit the allegedly endless feuds and social conflicts among the elite, not only between rival aristocratic families but also internally between affines and blood relatives. Promoting ecclesiastical definitions of kinship was thus part of the Latin Church's "longstanding effort to use the logic of kin solidarity in the interest of social peace."[75] The goal was to "create a moral code according to which violence and murder of blood relatives was unacceptable."[76] As such the introduction of canonical kinship was as much a part of a moral or ideological campaign, "an attempt to influence the population's concept of right and wrong," as it was a judicial or political project.[77]

24 Kim Esmark et al.

Kings had every reason to support the program, which elevated them to a new, exalted position as legitimate upholders of societal peace. The motives for kings to co-promote canonical kinship and formalization of kinship norms may extend further than this, however. The purpose of legal provisions to secure kinsmen's rights to family land, for instance, may have been to "limit the extent to which individual aristocrats might reshape the economic hierarchy of the aristocracy on their own accord."[78] As the strength of royal power depended on a relative equilibrium between society's leading factions, un-regulated reshuffling of land among magnates was potentially destabilizing, and kings therefore had every incentive to try to contain and control the circulation of landed wealth – even, paradoxically, by strengthening kinship structures. In other words, it seems too simple to interpret the process of twelfth- and thirteenth-century formalization of kinship along the lines of traditional historiography as a weakening or even dissolution of old Nordic kinship society.

Exactly how and to what extent new maps of kinship really managed to transform strategies and behavior among the high medieval elite remains difficult to say. Did practices of feuding, marriage, or inheritance change significantly under the yoke of written law? Did new norms induce new family identities? Were kin structures consolidated? Did social hierarchies become more stable, less vulnerable to choice, individual enterprise, and the vicissitudes of an openly elective- and alliance-based system? With regard to social and political action, the logic of *practical kinship* obviously continued to rule. Yet, with the introduction of canonical conceptions of kin relations *official kinship* took on a new guise, which social actors evidently had to take into account and adapt strategies to – if only by finding ways to bypass it. In that sense canonical kinship and the general move towards formalization no doubt did make an impact. Whether it contributed to creating an overall more peaceful and socially just society is much more uncertain.

Notes

1. Gerd Althoff, *Family, Friends and Followers: Political and Social Bonds in Early Medieval Europe* (Cambridge, 2004), 23.
2. Ibid., 62; Alain Guerreau, *Lé féodalisme, un horizon théorique* (Paris, 1980), 184–91.
3. "Ætt," KLNM, vol. 20, cols. 587–98.
4. See for example Arne Odd Johnsen, *Fra ættesamfunn til statssamfunn* (Oslo, 1948); Helge Paludan, *Familia og familie: To europæiske kulturelementers møde i højmiddelalderens Danmark* (Aarhus, 1995).
5. Michael H. Gelting, "Magtstrukturer i valdemarstidens Danmark," in *Viking og hvidekrist*, ed. Niels Lund (Copenhagen, 2000), 179–205 at 196, critically summarizing characteristic views of Danish historians such as Ole Fenger, *Fejde og mandebod: Studier over slægtsansvaret i germansk*

og gammeldansk ret (Copenhagen, 1971); Carsten Breengaard, *Muren om Israels hus: Regnum og sacerdotium i Danmark 1050–1170* (Copenhagen, 1982); Niels Skyum-Nielsen, "Kvinde og slave: Danmarkshistorie uden retouche," *Historisk tidsskrift* (D) 13, no. 1 (1971): 398–405.
6. Carsten Breengaard, "Lund og den kirkehistoriske situation," in *Lund – medeltida kyrkometropol*, ed. Per-Olov Ahrén and Anders Jarlert (Lund, 2004), 27–46 at 34 and 42.
7. Ferdinand Tönnies, *Gemeinschaft und Gesellschaft: Grundbegriffe der reinen Soziologie* (Darmstadt, 1991[1889]); Émile Durkheim, *Über die Teilung der sozialen Arbeit* (Frankfurt am Main, 1977 [1930]). For a recent recapitulation of this narrative, see Francis Fukuyama, *The Origins of Political Order* (New York, 2011).
8. Jón Viðar Sigurðsson and Simon Teuscher, "Slektens rolle på Island og i Bern," in *Det europeiske mennesket*, ed. Sverre Bagge (Oslo, 1998), 106–30 at 106–07.
9. Robert T. Merrill, "Notes on Icelandic Kinship Terminology," *American Anthropologist* 66 (1964): 868–71; David Gaunt, *Familjeliv i Norden* (Malmö, 1983), 186–210; Preben Meulengracht Sørensen, *Saga og samfund* (Copenhagen, 1977), 30–36; Torben Anders Vestergaard, "The System of Kinship in Early Norwegian Law," *Mediaeval Scandinavia* 12 (1988): 160–93; Lars Ivar Hansen, "Slektskap, eiendom og sosiale strategier i nordisk middelalder," *Collegium Medievale* 7 (1994): 103–54; Lars Ivar Hansen, "'Ætten' i de eldste landskapslovene – realitet, konstruksjon og strategi," in *Norm og praksis i middelaldersamfunnet*, ed. Else Mundal and Ingvild Øye (Bergen, 1999), 23–55; Lars Ivar Hansen, "Slektskap," in *Holmgang: Om førmoderne samfunn. Festskrift til Kåre Lunden*, ed. Anne Eidsfelt et al. (Oslo, 2000), 104–32.
10. Jón Viðar Sigurðsson, *Chieftains and Power in the Icelandic Commonwealth* (Odense, 1999).
11. "Ætt," KLNM, 590.
12. Thyra Nors, "Slægtsstrategier hos den danske kongeslægt i det 12. århundrede: svar til Helge Paludan," *Historie* 1 (2000): 51–68 at 65.
13. Lars Hermanson, *Släkt, vänner och makt: en studie av elitens politiska kultur i 1100-talets Danmark* (Gothenburg, 2000), 181.
14. Jón Viðar Sigurðsson, *Skandinavia i vikingtiden* (Oslo, 2017), 16. We know from England in the period 1066–1327 that only 36 of 210 baronies "descended in a single male line for over 200 years" (Jennifer Ward, *Women of the English Nobility and Gentry, 1066–1500* (Manchester, 1995), 1–2). There is little reason to assume that the situation was significantly different in Scandinavia.
15. Hermanson, *Släkt, vänner och makt*, 8–10; Jón Viðar Sigurðsson, "Forholdet mellem frender, hushold og venner på Island i fristatstiden," *Historisk Tidsskrift* (N) 74 (1995): 311–30 at 328; William I. Miller, *Bloodtaking and Peacemaking: Feud, Law and Society in Saga Iceland* (Chicago, 1990), 139–78.
16. Eleanor Searle, *Predatory Kinship and the Creation of Norman Power, 840–1066* (Berkeley, 1988), 10, 105–6.
17. Hermanson, *Släkt, vänner och makt*, 181.
18. Nors, "Slægtsstrategier," 66.
19. Michael H. Gelting, "Odelsrett – lovbydelse – bördsrätt – retrait lignager: Kindred and Land in the Nordic Countries in the Twelfth and Thirteenth Centuries," in *Family, Marriage and Property Devolution in the Middle Ages*, ed. Lars Ivar Hansen (Tromsø, 2000), 133–65; Hansen, "Slektskap,

26 Kim Esmark et al.

eiendom og sosiale strategier"; Lars Ivar Hansen, "The Concept of Kinship According to the West Nordic Medieval Laws," in *How Nordic Are the Nordic Medieval Laws?* ed. Per Andersen, Ditlev Tamm, and Helle Vogt (Copenhagen, 2011), 177–206.
20. Kim Esmark, "Religious Patronage and Family Consciousness: Sorø Abbey and the 'Hvide Family'", c. 1150–1250," in *Religious and Laity in Western Europe 1000–1400: Interaction, Negotiation, and Power*, ed. Emilia Jamroziak and Janet Burton (Turnhout, 2006), 93–110 at 109.
21. Stephen D. White, *Re-Thinking Kinship and Feudalism* (Aldershot, 2005), vii, paraphrasing Pierre Bourdieu, *Outline of a Theory of Practice*, trans. Richard Nice (Cambridge, 1977), 35.
22. Nors, "Slægtsstrategier"; Esmark, "Religious Patronage."
23. Pierre Bourdieu, "What Makes a Social Class? On the Theoretical and Practical Existence of Groups," *Berkeley Journal of Sociology* 32 (1987): 1–17 at 8 (emphasis added).
24. Bourdieu, *Outline*, 33–38.
25. The Danish medievalist Thyra Nors points to essentially the same thing as she speaks of the interplay between "kin as ideology and as practically functioning kin groups" (Nors, "Slægtstrategier," 57).
26. Sigurðsson, *Chieftains and Power*, http://gammeldanskordbog.dk/ordbog.
27. *Grágás. Stykker, som findes i det Arnamagnæanske Haand skrift Nr. 351 fol. Skálholtsbók og en Række andre Haandskrifter*, ed. Vilhjálmur Finsen (Copenhagen, 1883): "frændsemi."
28. Sigurðsson, *Chieftains and Power*, 174–75.
29. David Herlihy, "Family," *The American Historical Review* 96 (1991): 1-16.
30. Sigurðsson, *Chieftains and Power*, 179.
31. See volume 1 of this series for a more comprehensive treatment of the kin as an economic unit or community.
32. Søren Lau Moeslund, "'Thet callum wi men alt fæthirnis iorth' – Slægtindivid relationer omkring jord," *Den jyske historiker* 42 (1987): 68–84 at 82–84.
33. For this mentality, see the classic study by Aron Gurevich, "Représentations et attitudes à l'égard de la propriété pendant le haut moyen âge," *Annales* 27 (1972): 523–47.
34. The classification of a given piece of land could become subject to both contention and change, of course: A farm successfully sold or donated out of the kin group would see its status as family land converted, just as purchased property would be turned into family land the moment the buyer died and left it to his or her heirs.
35. According to a letter from Pope Innocent III (*Svenskt diplomatarium*, vol. 1, ed. Johan Gustav Liljegren et al. (Stockholm, 1829), no. 131, 156–57). The provision also appears in the *Västgötalagen*: see *Corpus iuris Sueo-Gotorum antique: Samling af Sveriges gamla lagar*, vol. 1, ed. H. S. Collin and C. J. Schlyter (Stockholm, 1827), ch. 10, 27.
36. Gelting, "Odelsrett," drawing on Stephen D. White, *Custom, Kinship, and Gifts to Saints: The Laudatio Parentum in Western France 1050–1150* (London, 1988), ch. 3; See also Helle Vogt, *The Function of Kinship in Medieval Nordic Legislation* (Leiden, 2010), 192–94; Kim Esmark, "Godsgaver, calumniae og retsantropologi: Esrum kloster og dets naboer, ca. 1150–1250," in *Ett annat 1100-tal: Individ, kollektiv och kulturella mönster i medeltidens Danmark*, ed. Peter Carelli, Lars Hermanson, and Hanne Sanders (Lund, 2004), 143–80.
37. DD 1.2.56. Parallel examples of kinsmen compensated for consenting to gifts: DD 1.2.99 and the monastic chronicle of Øm Abbey, "Exordium monasterii Carø insula," in *SM*, 153–264 at ch. 10, 168.

38. Kim Esmark, "The Settlement of Disputes by Compromise According to Some Early Danish Charters," in *Denmark and Europe in the Middle Ages, c. 1000–1525: Essays in Honour of Professor Michael H. Gelting*, ed. Kerstin Hundahl, Lars Kjær, and Niels Lund (Dorchester, 2014), 11–26.
39. "The Church Law of Scania," ch. 5 of *The Danish Medieval Laws*, ed. Ditlev Tamm and Helle Vogt (London, 2016), 53. Complementary examples of consent by kinsmen to gifts of land from around 1200: DD 1.3.253 and 1.4.82.
40. Gelting, "Odelsrett"; Vogt, *Function of Kinship*.
41. Sturl I, 302: "skyldr þess at gera hvat, er Snorri legði fyrir hann, hverigir sem í mót væri."
42. Msk II, 56–58.
43. A micro-scale study of marital strategies in a Norwegian province in the later Middle Ages may give an impression of the social logic of the marital field in earlier periods as well: Lars Ivar Hansen, "The Field of Property Devolution in Norway During the Late Middle Ages: Inheritance Settlements, Marriage Contracts and Legal Disputes," in *Disputing Strategies in Medieval Scandinavia*, ed. Kim Esmark et al. (Leiden, 2013), 247–80.
44. See the contribution by Jón Viðar Sigurdsson and Helle Vogt in chapter 4 in volume I of this series.
45. Helle Vogt, "Protecting the Individual, the Kin and the Soul – Donation Regulations in Danish and Norwegian Medieval Legislation," in *Donations, Strategies and Relations in the Latin West/Nordic Countries from the Late Roman Period Until Today*, ed. Ole-Albert Rønning, Helle Sigh, and Helle Vogt (London and New York, 2017), 130–45.
46. John Lind, "De russiske ægteskaber: Dynasti- og alliancepolitik i 1130'ernes danske borgerkrig," *Historisk Tidsskrift* (D) 92 (1992): 225–63.
47. One famous example: The Danish magnate Ebbe Sunesen had his daughter Benedikta married to the Swedish prince Sverker, who became king of Sweden in 1196 but was then ousted by a rival. Ebbe Sunesen, however, insisted on pursuing the political promises of his daughter's marriage, and with his brothers he led an army into Sweden in an attempt to reinstate his son-in-law.
48. Sigurðsson, *Chieftains and Power*, 160–65.
49. Michael H. Gelting, "Marriage, Peace and the Canonical Incest Prohibition: Making Sense of an Absurdity?" in *Nordic Perspectives on Medieval Canon Law*, ed. Mia Korpiola (Helsinki, 1999), 93–124.
50. Skyum-Nielsen, *Kvinde og slave*, 97.
51. Lars Hermanson and Auður Magnúsdóttir, "Inledning," in *Medeltidens genus: Kvinnors och mäns roller inom kultur, rätt och samhälle – Norden och Europa ca 300–1500*, ed. Lars Hermanson and Auður Magnúsdóttir (Gothenburg, 2016), 11–26 at 16–17; Birgit Sawyer, "Women as Bridge Builders: The Role of Women in Viking Age Scandinavia," in *People and Places in Northern Europe 500–1600: Essays in Honour of Peter Hayes Sawyer*, ed. Ian Wood and Niels Lund (Woodbridge, 1991), 211–25.
52. "Historia S. Kanvti Dvcis et Martyris," in *Vitae Sanctorum Danorum*, ed. Martin Clarentius Gertz (Copenhagen, 1908–1912), 189–204 at 190.
53. Hermanson, *Släkt, vänner och makt*, 92–138; Ulla Hastrup and John Lind, "Dronning Margrete Fredkulla: Politisk magthaver og mæcen for byzantinsk kunst i danske kirker i 1100-tallets begyndelse," in *Medeltidens genus: Kvinnors och mäns roller inom kultur, rätt och samhälle – Norden och Europa ca 300–1500*, ed. Lars Hermanson and Auður Magnúsdóttir (Gothenburg, 2016), 29–72.
54. For a penetrating analysis of the social logic of vengeance see Miller, *Bloodtaking*.
55. Saxo, 14.5.3.
56. Sigurðsson, *Chieftains and Power*.

57. Auður Magnúsdóttir, "Förövare och offer: Kvinnor och våld i det medeltida Island"; Johan Zaini Bengtson, "De oäkta barnens rätt: Föreställningar om sexualbrott, barn och arv i svensk medeltida lagstifting"; Bjørn Bandlien, "I kjønnets grenseland"; all three in Hastrup and Lind, *Medeltidens genus*, at 111–44, 145–72, and 187–216, respectively.
58. Hermanson, *Släkt, vänner och makt*; John Danstrup, "Træk af den politiske kamp 1131–82," in *Festskrift til Erik Arup den 22. November 1946*, ed. Astrid Friis and Albert Olsen (Copenhagen, 1946); Birgit Sawyer, "The 'Civil Wars' Revisited," *Historisk tidsskrift* (N) 82 (2003): 43–73.
59. Cf. also Althoff, *Family, Friends*, 59–60.
60. Helle Vogt, "The Kin's Collective Responsibility for the Payment of Man's Compensation in Medieval Denmark," in *Wergild, Compensation and Penance: The Monetary Logic of Early Medieval Conflict Resolution*, ed. Stefan Esders, Han Nijdam, and Lukas Bothe (Boston and Leiden, forthcoming).
61. Anders Sunesen, "Liber Legis Scaniae," in *Danmarks gamle Love med Kirkelovene*, vol. I, ed. Johannes Brøndum-Nielsen and Poul Johs Jørgensen (Copenhagen, 1933–1961), ch. 46, 530: "Equalitatis autem tanto diligencius semper exigitur juramentum, quod per ipsum, lesis ledentibus adequatis, auferri videatur contemptus, qui perpessis iniuriam ex oppressione solet inferencium suscitari; pluris enim semper prvdentes faciunt integritatem fame et honoris debiti restitucionem quam pecuniariam satisfactionem." Translation kindly provided by Kate Gilbert.
62. According to the Frostathing Law (F) from the 1220s and the National Law (L) from 1274. *baugildemænd, neugildemænd*, and close *måger* (intermarried male relatives) were exempted. *Norges gamle Love indtil 1387*, 1–2 vols., vol. 1, ed. R. Keyser and P. A. Munch (Christiania (Oslo), 1846–48), F IV, ch. 9, 161: vol. 2, L, Mandhelgebolken, ch. 8, p. 214.
63. Cf. Amy Livingstone, *Out of Love for My Kin: Aristocratic Family Life in the Lands of the Loire, 1000–1200* (New York, 2010).
64. Sunesen, "Liber Legis Scaniae," vol. I, ch. 21.
65. Vogt, "Protecting the Individual."
66. See for example Saxo 14.19.17.
67. Cf. Regine le Jan, *Famille et pouvoir dans le monde franc (VIIe-Xe siècles)* (Paris, 1995), 407; Miller, *Bloodtaking*, 155–56.
68. Esmark, "Religious Patronage."
69. Miller, *Bloodtaking*, 160.
70. Michael Kræmmer, "Peder Torstensen af Borg," *Årbog for Historisk samfund for Sorø Amt* 88 (2001): 21–35.
71. Tamm and Vogt, *Danish Medieval Laws*, 99 (King Knud VI's Ordinance on Homicide); Sunesen, "Liber Legis Scaniae," vol. 1 ch. 47.
72. Sawyer, "The 'Civil Wars' Revisited," 70, n. 45; Nors, "Slægtsstrategier," 59.
73. Miller, *Bloodtaking*, 160–61. In Denmark Saxo, 14.26.9–10, likewise relates how Archbishop Eskil was prepared to let his own grandson, who was held hostage by the king, be executed rather than surrender his castle.
74. Sturl I, 386–87.
75. Gelting, "Odelsrett," 152.
76. Vogt, *Function of Kinship*, 265.
77. Ibid., 261.
78. Gelting, "Odelsrett," 151.

Dedicated Bibliography

Althoff, Gerd. *Family, Friends and Followers: Political and Social Bonds in Medieval Europe* [*Verwandte, Freunde und Getreue: Zum politischen Stellenwert*

der Gruppenbindungen im früheren Mittelalter]. Translated by Christopher Carroll. Cambridge, 2004.
Anders Sunesen. "Liber Legis Scaniae." In Danmarks gamle Love med Kirkelovene, vol. I, edited by Johannes Brøndum-Nielsen and Poul Johs Jørgensen. Copenhagen, 1933–1961.
Bandlien, Bjørn. "I kjønnets grenseland." In Medeltidens genus. Kvinnors och mäns roller inom kultur, rätt och samhälle. Norden och Europa ca 300–1500, edited by Lars Hermanson and Auður Magnúsdóttir, 187–216. Gothenburg, 2016.
Bengtson, Johan Zaini. "De oäkta barnens rätt. Föreställningar om sexualbrott, barn och arv i svensk medeltida lagstifting." In Medeltidens genus. Kvinnors och mäns roller inom kultur, rätt och samhälle: Norden och Europa ca 300–1500, edited by Lars Hermanson and Auður Magnúsdóttir, 145–72. Gothenburg, 2016.
Bourdieu, Pierre. Outline of a Theory of Practice. Translated by Richard Nice. Cambridge, 1977.
Bourdieu, Pierre. "What Makes a Social Class? On the Theoretical and Practical Existence of Groups." Berkeley Journal of Sociology 32 (1987): 1–17.
Breengaard, Carsten. Muren om Israels hus: regnum og sacerdotium i Danmark 1050–1170. Copenhagen, 1982.
Breengaard, Carsten. "Lund og den kirkehistoriske situation." In Lund – medeltida kyrkometropol, edited by Per-Olov Ahrén and Anders Jarlert, 27–46. Lund, 2004.
Corpus iuris Sueo-Gotorum antiqui. Samling af Sveriges gamla lagar. Edited by H. S. Collin and C. J. Schlyter. Stockholm, 1827.
Danstrup, John. "Træk af den politiske kamp 1131–82." In Festskrift til Erik Arup den 22. November 1946, edited by Astrid Friis and Albert Olsen. Copenhagen, 1946.
Durkheim, Émile. Über die Teilung der sozialen Arbeit. Frankfurt, 1977 [1930].
Esmark, Kim. "Godsgaver, calumniae og retsantropologi: Esrum kloster og dets naboer, ca. 1150–1250." In Ett annat 1100-tal: Individ, kollektiv och kulturella mönster i medeltidens Danmark, edited by Peter Carelli, Lars Hermanson, and Hanne Sanders, 143–80. Lund, 2004.
Esmark, Kim. "Religious Patronage and Family Consciousness: Sorø abbey and the 'Hvide family', c. 1150–1250." In Religious and Laity in Western Europe 1000–1400: Interaction, Negotiation, and Power, edited by Emilia Jamroziak and Janet Burton, 93–110. Turnhout, 2006.
Esmark, Kim. "The Settlement of Disputes by Compromise According to Some Early Danish Charters." In Denmark and Europe in the Middle Ages, c. 1000–1525. Essays in Honour of Professor Michael H. Gelting, edited by Kerstin Hundahl, Lars Kjær, and Niels Lund, 11–26. Dorchester, 2014.
Fenger, Ole. Fejde og mandebod: Studier over slægtsansvaret i germansk og gammeldansk ret. Copenhagen, 1971.
Fukuyama, Francis. The Origins of Political Order. New York, 2011.
Gaunt, David. Familjeliv i Norden. Malmö, 1983.
Gelting, Michael H. "Marriage, Peace and the Canonical Incest Prohibition: Making Sense of an Absurdity?" In Nordic Perspectives on Medieval Canon Law, edited by Mia Korpiola, 93–124. Helsinki, 1999.
Gelting, Michael H. "Magstrukturer i valdemarstidens Danmark." In Viking og hvidekrist, edited by Niels Lund, 179–205. Copenhagen, 2000.

Gelting, Michael H. "Odelsrett – lovbydelse – bördsrätt – retrait lignager. Kindred and Land in the Nordic Countries in the Twelfth and Thirteenth Centuries." In *Family, Marriage and Property Devolution in the Middle Ages*, edited by Lars Ivar Hansen, 133–65. Tromsø, 2000.

Grágás: Stykker, som findes i det Arnamagnæanske Haandskrift Nr. 351 fol. Skálholtsbók og en Række andre Haandskrifter. Edited by Vilhjálmur Finsen. Copenhagen, 1883.

Guerreau, Alain. *Lé féodalisme, un horizon théorique*. Paris, 1980.

Gurevich, Aaron. "Représentations et attitudes à l'égard de la propriété pendant le haut moyen âge." *Annales* 27 (1972): 523–47.

Haastrup, Ulla, and John H. Lind. "Dronning Margrete Fredkulla: Politisk magthaver og mæcen for byzantisk kunst i danske kirker i 1100-tallet begyndelse." In *Medeltidens genus: Kvinnors och mäns roller inom kultur, rätt och samhälle: Norden och Europa ca 300–1500*, edited by Lars Hermanson and Auður Magnúsdóttir, 29–71. Gothenburg, 2015.

Hansen, Lars Ivar. "Slektskap, eiendom og sosiale strategier i nordisk middelalder." *Collegium Medievale* 7 (1994): 103–54.

Hansen, Lars Ivar. "'Ætten' i de eldste landskapslovene – realitet, konstruksjon og strategi." In *Norm og praksis i middelaldersamfunnet*, edited by Else Mundal and Ingvild Øye, 23–55. Bergen, 1999.

Hansen, Lars Ivar. "Slektskap." In *Holmgang: Om førmoderne samfunn: Festskrift til Kåre Lunden*, edited by Anne Eidsfelt et al., 104–32. Oslo, 2000.

Hansen, Lars Ivar. "The Concept of Kinship According to the West Nordic Medieval Laws." In *How Nordic Are the Nordic Medieval Laws?* edited by Per Andersen, Ditlev Tamm, and Helle Vogt, 170–201. Copenhagen, 2011.

Hansen, Lars Ivar. "The Field of Property Devolution in Norway During the Late Middle Ages: Inheritance Settlements, Marriage Contracts and Legal Disputes." In *Disputing Strategies in Medieval Scandinavia*, edited by Kim Esmark, Lars Hermanson, Hans Jacob Orning, and Helle Vogt, 247–80. Leiden, 2013.

Herlihy, David. "Family." *The American Historical Review* 96 (1991): 116.

Hermanson, Lars. *Släkt, vänner och makt. En studie av elitens politiska kultur i 1100-talets Danmark*. Gothenburg, 2000.

Hermanson, Lars, and Auður Magnúsdóttir. "Inledning: Medeltidens genus." In *Medeltidens genus: Kvinnors och mäns roller inom kultur, rätt och samhälle – Norden och Europa ca 300–1500*, edited by Lars Hermanson and Auður Magnúsdóttir, 11–26. Gothenburg, 2016.

"Historia S. Kanvti Dvcis et Martyris." In *Vitae Sanctorum Danorum*, edited by Martin Clarentius Gertz, 189–204. Copenhagen, 1908–1912.

Johnsen, Arne Odd. *Fra ættesamfunn til statssamfunn*. Oslo, 1948.

Kræmmer, Michael. "Peder Torstensen af Borg." *Årbog for Historisk samfund for Sorø Amt* 88 (2001): 21–35.

Le Jan, Régine. *Famille et pouvoir dans le monde franc. VIIe-Xe siècles*. Paris, 1995.

Lind, John H. "De russiske ægteskaber: Dynasti- og alliancepolitiki 1130'ernes danske borgerkrig." *Historisk Tidsskrift* (D) 92 (1992): 225–63.

Livingstone, Amy. *Out of Love for My Kin: Aristocratic Family Life in the Lands of the Loire, 1000–1200*. New York, 2010.

Magnúsdóttir, Auður. "Förövare och offer: Kvinnor och våld i det medeltida Island." In *Medeltidens genus: Kvinnors och mäns roller inom kultur, rätt och samhälle – Norden och Europa ca 300–1500*, edited by Lars Hermanson and Auður Magnúsdóttir, 111–44. Gothenburg, 2016.

Merrill, Robert T. "Notes on Icelandic Kinship Terminology." *American Anthropologist* 66, no. 4 (1964): 868–71.

Miller, William I. *Bloodtaking and Peacemaking: Feud, Law and Society in Saga Iceland*. Chicago, 1990.

Moeslund, Søren Lau. "'Thet callum wi men alt fæthirnis iorth' – Slægt-individ relationer omkring jord." *Den jyske historiker* 42 (1987): 82–84.

Nors, Thyra. "Slægtsstrategier hos den danske kongeslægt i det 12. århundrede: svar til Helge Paludan." *Historie* 1 (2000): 55–66.

Paludan, Helge. *Familia og familie: To europæiske kulturelementers møde i højmiddelalderens Danmark*. Aarhus, 1995.

Sawyer, Birgit. "Women as Bridge Builders: The Role of Women in Viking Age Scandinavia." In *People and Places in Northern Europe 500–1600: Essays in Honour of Peter Hayes Sawyer*, edited by Ian Wood and Niels Lund, 211–25. Woodbridge, 1991.

Sawyer, Birgit. "The 'Civil Wars' revisited." *Historisk Tidsskrift* (N) 82, no. 1 (2003): 43–73.

Searle, Eleanor. *Predatory Kinship and the Creation of Norman Power, 840–1066*. Berkeley, 1988.

Sigurðsson, Jón Viðar. "Forholdet mellem frender, hushold og venner på Island i fristatstiden." *Historisk Tidsskrift* (N) 74 (1995): 311–30.

Sigurðsson, Jón Viðar, and Simon Teuscher. "Slektens rolle på Island og i Bern." In *Det europeiske mennesket*, edited by Sverre Bagge, 106–30. Oslo, 1998.

Sigurðsson, Jón Viðar. *Chieftains and Power in the Icelandic Commonwealth*. Translated by Jean Lundskær-Nielsen. Odense, 1999.

Sigurðsson, Jón Viðar. *Skandinavia i vikingtiden*. Oslo, 2017.

Sørensen, Preben M. *Saga og samfund: en indføring i oldislandsk litteratur*. Copenhagen, 1977.

Skyum-Nielsen, Niels. "Kvinde og slave: Danmarkshistorie uden retouche." *Historisk tidsskrift* (D) 13, no. 1 (1971): 398–405.

Tamm, Ditlev, and Helle Vogt. *The Danish Medieval Laws*. London, 2016.

Tönnies, Ferdinand. *Gemeinschaft und Gesellschaft: Grundbegriffe der reinen Soziologie*. Darmstadt, 1991 [1889].

Vestergaard, Torben A. "The System of Kinship in Early Norwegian Law." *Mediaeval Scandinavia* 12 (1988): 160–93.

Vogt, Helle. *The Function of Kinship in Medieval Nordic Legislation*. Leiden, 2010.

Vogt, Helle. "Protecting the Individual, the Kin and the Soul – Donation Regulations in Danish and Norwegian Medieval Legislation." In *Donations, Strategies and Relations in the Latin West/Nordic Countries from the Late Roman Period until Today*, edited by Ole-Albert Rønning, Helle Sigh, and Helle Vogt, 130–45. London and New York, 2017.

Vogt, Helle. "The Kin's Collective Responsibility for the Payment of Man's Compensation in Medieval Denmark." In *Wergild, Compensation and Penance: The Monetary Logic of Early Medieval Conflict Resolution*, edited by Stefan Esders, Han Nijdam, and Lukas Bothe. Boston and Leiden, forthcoming.

Ward, Jennifer. *Women of the English Nobility and Gentry, 1066–1500*. Manchester, 1995.

White, Stephen D. *Custom, Kinship, and Gifts to Saints: The Laudatio Parentum in Western France 1050–1150*. London, 1988.

White, Stephen D. *Re-Thinking Kinship and Feudalism in Early Medieval Europe*. Aldershot, 2005.

3 Lords and Followers
Patron-Client Relationships

Lars Hermanson and Hans Jacob Orning

Characteristics, Previous Research, and Sources

The terms "patron" and "client" originated in Roman society, and the idea of a patron-client relationship was first developed as an analytical term to describe that society.[1] However, it has proven to be a useful concept for classifying social bonds in other types of societies as well. Since the 1960s, sociologists and anthropologists have used the concept analytically to describe societies in universalist terms (patron-client relationships as a characteristic of all types of societies); to discuss a relationship which is present to differing degrees in given societies depending on other forms of social organization such as kinship, networks, feudalism, bureaucracies, markets, and others; and sometimes in the examination of a historical stage in the evolution of social organization from a kinship base, via patron-client relationships, to bureaucracies.[2]

In medieval scholarship, much of the discussion about patron-client relationships has been conducted within the framework of feudalism. Contrary to the broad term "feudalism," which has been described (most notably by Karl Marx) as a societal formation based on an exploitive relationship between landowners and unfree farmers, the feudal bond can be narrowly defined as a personal and hierarchical relationship within the elite between a lord and a vassal, including two elements: the ritual of homage, including the oath of fealty and sometimes a kiss, and the investiture of the fief.[3] At the root of this bond lies the personal and hierarchical relationship between patron and client (at a lower social level, the bond between landowners and their dependents entailed a similar relationship), but the combination of homage and enfeoffment has been considered a distinguishing mark of the feudal bond. In recent decades, the concept of feudalism has been severely criticized.[4] Scholars such as Frederic Cheyette, Stephen D. White, and Patrick Geary have emphasized the variability of the so-called feudal bond, underlining that homage, oaths, and the investment of fiefs occurred in all kinds of combinations, and maintaining that it is a mistake to assume that this bond can be subsumed under one heading with a precise legal definition.[5] What these scholars have done is to "de-reify" the idea of feudalism, making it broader and less unique, and thereby positioning it as a more cross-cultural concept that lends itself more easily to comparative approaches. Perhaps the most interesting analyses of the role of patron-client relationships in medieval politics have been undertaken by scholars who have avoided the F-word entirely, and who have abandoned the tradition of viewing formal institutions such as retinues, the legal apparatus, and the military levy as prefigurations of more full-blown state institutions. Here Gerd Althoff's book *Family, Friends and Followers: Political and Social Bonds in Medieval Europe* was crucial in analyzing the political culture in the Holy Roman Empire in terms of kinship, friendship, and lordship – bonds which were personal and informal, and hence at least partially "feudal," but still very powerful *social* institutions.[6]

In Nordic historiography, feudalism has typically been discussed in the context of whether Nordic countries were "feudal" or not, where "feudalism" has often been juxtaposed with the presence of fiefs and vassalage at the top level of society.[7] Combined with a widely held opinion that freeholders played a much larger role in Nordic societies than serfs, the answer to the question of Nordic feudalism has been predominantly negative, with the result that the region has a reputation of being different from the rest of Europe.[8] Broadening the concept of feudalism to include patron-client relationships allows for a more nuanced comparison of the role of personal dependencies in Scandinavia and Europe. In recent research there has been a move away from the notion that early Nordic societies were constituted of relatively equal freeholders (the Germanistic thesis) and towards the idea of a society dominated by local chieftains or magnates, with substantial numbers of freeholders. This shift is partly due to influence from anthropological models, partly to archaeological excavations of farmsteads, and partly to studies of dispersed property rights in societies with fragmented political authority.[9]

Definitions of patron-client relationships differ, but they usually include the following aspect: a relationship which is personal (as opposed to bureaucratic) and hierarchical (contrary to horizontal bonds), while remaining reciprocal (unlike relationships based on obedience).[10] Patronage delineates an asymmetrical relation between a client in need of protection and a patron who has the desire and the ability to take care of the client's concerns.[11]

The question of the nature of the inequality is open to dispute, and constitutes one of the most controversial aspects of patron-client relationships. On the one hand, patron-client relationships differ from horizontal friendships in that they are vertical, hierarchical, and uneven. On the other hand, inequality is also a contextual matter. Robert Paine states that these roles are not intrinsic to the relationship itself, but are determined by external interpretations: the patron is the one whose possessions or abilities are judged to be the more valuable.[12]

More fundamentally, the patron-client relationship is characterized by a mixture of voluntariness and coercion that can confuse a modern observer used to looking for antagonistic class relationships. Contrary to class relationships, where inequality is by no means camouflaged, patron-client relationships rely on the notion that they exist for mutual benefit, and they are therefore typically draped in the language of deference.[13] Some scholars take this benevolence more or less at face value, viewing the relationship as fundamentally positive; this point of view is most common among structural-functionalists intent on seeing the institution as serving an integrative purpose in society at large.[14] Others have been far more inclined to regard the deferential language as a legitimizing strategy primarily aimed at cementing power relationships and subduing the powerless.[15]

In Nordic medieval society power was to a large extent built from below. However, there are few Nordic studies with an explicit focus on patron-client relations, apart from those of Jón Viðar Sigurðsson on Free State Icelandic society and Viking Age and medieval Scandinavia.[16] One crucial reason for the limited Nordic research on patron-client relationships probably lies in the nature of the source material, since in many instances we simply do not have information about the relationship between elites and their followers on a local level. For instance, the narrative sources about Denmark and Norway mostly recount events taking place within the upper echelon of society, where specific information about the ability of elite individuals to raise troops and mobilize supporters is not recorded, apart from the intimation that those who were most successful in doing so were usually victorious in various struggles (in Sweden, we rarely even get this type of information). These sources are most valuable for investigating patron-client relationships at the top level of society, and, in combination with monastic sources, religious patronage. We shall return to both these issues later.

The one exception to this lack of sources is Iceland, where the sagas provide a fairly detailed description of how chieftains surrounded themselves with a network of supporters made up of friends/clients, household members, relatives, and neighbors. Yet it is problematic to suggest that the Icelandic case is representative of the entire Nordic region, since Free State Iceland is unique in many respects. Before the fall of the Free State in 1262/64, Iceland had no hierarchical royal apparatus based on prominent titles, offices, royal lands, and the like, and there are also considerable differences in its socio-agrarian structure (which was based on animal husbandry, little grain production, no towns, dependence upon imports), reflecting Iceland's minimal potential for agricultural activities – although to be sure, Icelandic society was nevertheless socially stratified. Hence, the Icelandic "bottom-up" perspective cannot be applied to Scandinavian conditions unreservedly, and interpretations of patron-client relationships in the rest of Scandinavia will therefore remain more hypothetical than in the Icelandic case. Yet narrative sources (kings' sagas and the *Gesta Danorum*), the laws, and a combination of archaeological and cameral sources contain glimpses of information on local patron-client relationships, and these images can be cautiously compared with the Icelandic material. Thus, in order to investigate the patron-client bond locally, we need to adopt a broad Nordic outlook, working with a variety of sources from different regions. This interweaving of material should take the Icelandic sources as a point of departure, which of course emphasizes the urgency of the issue of transferability. Bringing these various strands together can help us draw a picture in which at least some details can be discerned.

A Multifunctional Relationship

The obligations of patron-client relationships are both specific and diffuse.[17] They are all-encompassing in that they are non-specific, and this makes for very flexible relationships which are subject to differing interpretations. In line with this, in spite of friendship being associated with strong obligations in Old Norse society, such obligations were hardly ever specified. Even when it came to swearing oaths of allegiance, the level of specificity seldom went beyond demanding "loyalty" or that the oathtaker should not be friends with the patron's enemies. Hence, there is a contrast between the absolutely binding character of the relationship in principle, and the very loose content of its obligations when it came to actually interpreting them.[18]

A concomitant feature of the "loose" obligations inherent in patron-client bonds is that they were applied in a variety of settings, where different spheres of influence such as economics, politics, and religion were hardly separated. Working from archaeological evidence, a series of chieftain sites, often termed "central places," has been identified in Scandinavia. These are characterized by a multitude of functions – economic (agricultural production, markets), socio-political (assemblies, distribution of objects, cup marks), and cultic (burials, cultic activities) – concentrated within a restricted area. In places like Tissø and Lejre (in Denmark) and Borg (in Norway), large houses bear witness to chieftains' power.[19] Archaeologists have discovered a pattern in the concentrations of finds along the Norwegian coastline, which indicates a quite regular geographical dispersal of chieftain sites.[20]

There is every reason to believe that the economic, political, and religious aspects of chieftains' power were inextricably entwined. Archaeologist Frode Iversen has demonstrated that chieftain sites in western Norway usually had a big farm at their core, a surrounding circle of nameless farms – probably thrall farms – and an outer circle with named tenants' and freeholders' farms. This geographical pattern reflects the chieftains' dominance at a local level, and indicates that they governed the nearby farmers through all-encompassing patron-client relationships, where economic control over agricultural production went hand-in-hand with socio-political and religious dominance.[21] Their control varied from being almost total (thralls in the inner circle) to intermediate (tenants in the outer circle), and limited (freeholders), with substantial fluidity and variability between the different categories. Only later, probably during the twelfth century, did this diffuse and extensive dominance of chieftains yield to a more strictly economically based hegemony, manifested in the tenants' payment of land rent (*landskyld*), tithes, and taxes.[22]

Iceland provides the best example of this type of patron-client relationship. Jón Viðar Sigurðsson has argued that kinship bonds were much weaker than bonds based on friendship.[23] However, sometimes it can be difficult to separate the two, because friendship could incorporate fictive kinship-relations such as godparenthood and fosterage, which resemble what we would call patron-client relationships.[24] An important type of patron-client relationship is concubinage. Auður Magnúsdóttir has shown that concubinage was widely used by Icelandic chieftains in order to establish client relationships with families of lower status.[25]

Patronage also applies to the religious dimension both before the advent of Christianity and during the phase of private church-ownership (*Eigenkirchenwesen*), which characterized Church organization in Scandinavia until the twelfth century, and in Iceland until the late thirteenth century.[26] Even if the ecclesiastical organization was based on a formalized hierarchy, both bishops and monasteries were enmeshed in vertical secular relationships on local and regional levels. Nordic bishops were initially mainly recruited among foreigners, but during the twelfth century they usually descended from powerful aristocratic families and should therefore be considered as political players who drew on much the same resources as their lay counterparts. Indeed, some of the most prominent political actors in top-level politics from the mid-twelfth century on were bishops, such as archbishops Eskil and Absalon in Denmark, and Archbishop Oystein and Bishop Nikolas Arnesson in Norway.[27]

On the level below, the foundation of family monasteries, in particular in Denmark, offers a glimpse into how local patron-client relationships worked. Monks were dependent on military and juridical protection from local and regional lords; in some cases these patrons were also their local benefactors, who supplied them with material resources. Disputes between monasteries and local lords were common, and in these conflicts abbots often turned to patrons within the ecclesiastical hierarchy for aid, and sometimes to secular elites or royal families.[28] Donors to the Church established themselves in the role of patrons in specific exchanges which created relationships that often lasted for generations.[29] A subservient language imbued with the ideals of patron-client relationships was refined in the correspondence between dignitaries belonging to the episcopal Church and the monastic organizations.[30] However, we should always be aware of the difference between polite appeals and how the relations actually worked in practice, as stated by Sharon Kettering: "We must recognize that the language of patronage does not always provide reliable evidence of actual behavior, and that patrons and clients sometimes wrote one thing and did another."[31] Here it is important to bear in mind that the Nordic sources were predominantly written by men who were members of the top layers of society, and consequently it is their depictions of vertical relations – in which they were often patrons – that have been preserved for posterity.[32]

The Strength and Stability of Patron-Client Relationships

In Old Norse society, the term used in referring to both horizontal and vertical relationships was "friendship" (*vinátta*). If both horizontal and vertical relationships were described using the same term, what is the point in separating them analytically? One crucial reason is that even if the division between these relationships is not always clear-cut, they entailed very different obligations. According to Jón Viðar Sigurðsson, vertical friendship was by far the most important and solid social bond in Free State Iceland, more important than both kinship and horizontal friendship. Contrary to kinship, friendship delineated a bond which had to be actively formed and maintained. In effect, kinship often needed the additional confirmation of friendship in order to be able to function effectively as a social bond in concrete political situations. Vertical friendships were hedged by strong obligations, and it was risky to sever such a bond, because to do so would signal untrustworthiness. Horizontal friendships, in Jón Viðar Sigurðsson's opinion, were far easier to break, because the norms upholding them were much weaker.[33]

Were patron-client relationships as dominant in other Nordic areas as in Free State Iceland? We have no comparable sources concerning this type of relationship, but narrative and legal sources indicate that matters were not altogether different in Norway and Denmark. The kings' sagas dealing with Norway sometimes offer glimpses into the workings of local communities, where the dominant role of local chieftains emerges quite clearly.[34] *Heimskringla* (c. 1230) and *Morkinskinna* (c. 1220), the two most voluminous and elaborate sagas on these issues, were written by Icelanders, and one can therefore ask whether their authors projected onto Norway conditions which they were familiar with in Iceland. Nevertheless, these similarities in the depiction of patron-client relationships at a local level should be accorded some historical value, since this was not an ideologically charged theme which the sagas needed to embellish, and since conditions in Norway were not very dissimilar from Icelandic ones, at least not before the late twelfth century.[35] The Older Gulathing Law – the law for the western part of Norway before 1267 – opened by stating that "may he [the king] be our friend and we his friends, and may God be a friend to us all."[36]

Nordic medieval laws (though not Danish ones) attest to a hierarchical society at a local level, partly in the fines differentiated according to social status and partly in the detailed paragraphs on how the elite should handle the lower classes – thralls and, increasingly, tenants.[37] Finally, patronage is documented in Danish and Norwegian charters from the fourteenth century onwards, which depict local conditions in more detail.[38]

To what degree can we talk about patron-client relationships at the top level of society as a counterpart to the hierarchy of chivalry emerging in Europe in the High Middle Ages? Here we are certainly dealing with subordination in an honorable sense, but we also repeatedly encounter the blurred boundaries between horizontal and vertical bonds. The power balance between network members constantly shifted, so that the way horizontal and vertical bonds were interpreted was in permanent flux.

Different forms of debts of honor played a central role in these transformations. For instance, generous gifts and feasts could cause create an imbalance between former horizontal allies.[39] Scandinavian kings (and bishops) delegated power over royal lands in order to establish vertical bonds, and such landholdings were considered generous gifts.[40] Within royal and aristocratic families, patronage was often used to subdue or neutralize juvenile cognates in order to avoid future challenges.[41] Patronage was also intimately connected to various forms of fictive kinship relations, such as fosterage and godparenthood. In these latter cases the inferior parties should not be seen as "clients" in the real sense of the word, but rather as individuals who held positions associated with certain honor-based obligations linked to protection, kinship, and collective solidarity.

The Tension Between Honorable and Dishonorable Service

A distinction which is almost as important as the one between vertical and horizontal relationships is the one between honorable and dishonorable service. As mentioned, both the participants in vertical friendships were normally termed "friend" (ON *vinr*).

However, there was another term reserved for the inferior party in such a relationship, namely "servant" (ON *þjónustumaðr* or *þjónn*). This had a negative connotation in Old Norse, derived from its association with unfree servants.[42] Thus there were two idioms for characterizing clients: one honorable (friend) and one dishonorable (servant). One relationship was not necessarily any more "equal" than the other; the decisive difference was that in the first case the interaction between patrons and clients was cloaked in a language centered on equality and reciprocity, whereas the latter case acknowledged and even reinforced the inequality in the relationship.

From the twelfth century onwards, the Church tried to elevate the concept of service and free it from its humble (and humbling) origins: theoretically, by making humility a precondition for salvation, and practically, by hammering the message that service was honorable (for instance in the papal epithet *servus servorum Dei* – the servant of the servants of God). Soon these ideas were adopted by kings eager to promote the idea that subordination within the royal bureaucracy/retinue was equally elevated.[43] This process of a gradual disentanglement of certain modes of subordination from their pejorative roots can also be followed in other parts of Europe, where terms like *vassus/vassallus* and *miles* rose from their humble origins to acquire honorific meanings in the course of the High Middle Ages. Eventually these terms and their association with service came to define the elites, and were enmeshed in rituals intended to underline the honor of servitude, most succinctly expressed in the ideal of courtliness. The result was that vertical relations were split into honorable military vassalage on the one hand, and dishonorable manual labor on the other.[44]

On a local level Scandinavian kings used individuals with titles such as *ármenn, bryti/bryther, provisores* as their representatives. These were men of inferior or even unfree status who were often held in low esteem. The advantage of involving such men in royal service was that they were more loyal than "friends" in patron-client relationships, in which – though they could accommodate much inequality – both parties were regarded as honorable and considered to be on an equal footing. The problem was that their inferior status made them vulnerable as royal agents. Here, the elevation of service in the Church context was pivotal in enhancing their status. An alternative strategy of Scandinavian kings was to employ local elites as their representatives, with titles such as *stabularius, villicus, lendr maðr*, and *sýslumaðr*. Here the main problem was that the loyalty of such "officials" was variable at best; these men, being powerful in their own right, had less interest in serving kings unconditionally.[45] One could argue that in this relationship the transition between the horizontal and the vertical was blurred and changeable.

The predominant interpretation in older Nordic research was that the power in medieval Scandinavia emanated from the royal organization, and that kings introduced bureaucratic forms of government based on the delegation of duties to public officials.[46] However, in twelfth-century Scandinavia these "office-holders" could not be called officials in the true (modern) sense of the word, since it is not possible to connect their titles to specific functions, rights, or obligations, and the titles were not constant. Hence, a person addressed as *stabularius* in one charter could be mentioned as *villicus* in another. The implication here is that these titles should not be interpreted as fixed offices, since the men who held them filled diverse roles with multifaceted functions linked to, for instance, military, advisory, or administrative domains. Moreover, within the upper layers of society it is also difficult to separate office-holders' duties as servants of the royal household from their executorial functions. Office-holders such as *skenkjari/pincerna regis* (the king's cup-bearer) and *camerarius* (chamberlain) performed ministerial duties, but they were also linked to honorable service performed in the public arena of the royal hall or the king's chamber (*camera*).[47] Whereas many titles give the impression of a strictly vertical relationship of service (*þjónusta/servitium*), in practice they were often honorary posts linked to the transaction of favors symbolically performed at court and masked in the language of deference.[48] This indistinct separation between horizontal and vertical bonds, and between public and private functions, is in sharp contrast to the bureaucratic conditions within the Church organization, where the hierarchy was based on fixed offices with specified duties, meaning that clerical service was more or less unconditional.

Why were the divisions between horizontal and vertical bonds, between honorable and degrading service, and between public and private duties, so blurred in the case of the monarchy? From the king's perspective, the crucial issue was to integrate powerful local elites into the royal sphere, with the expectation that in exchange for their prominent titles the recipients would remain loyal to their lord. A prerequisite for being endowed with honorable titles was membership in an illustrious social network. Much like the king, these office-holders led itinerant lives, and in their capacity as counselors they had an active role in ruling the realm. Thus, their positions were only partly a result of delegated royal authority represented by a public office, since by virtue of their own material resources, together with their noble heritage and powerful networks, they were able to demand a high status among the political elites. This implies that government in high medieval Scandinavia had a collective character.[49] The king was *primus inter pares*, and his position was underpinned by a group of wealthy magnates whose landed properties were often symbolically transformed into royal fiefs in order to lubricate and manifest the reciprocal exchange according to the *quid pro quo* principle founded on power sharing.

Here it is also important to note that magnates, once integrated into the royal circle, could maintain their high positions when a new king ascended the throne. By acting as *seniores* with intimate bonds to the previous king, they could exert a great deal of political influence on the (often) young successor. It was also common for Scandinavian kings to entrust the upbringing of their intended heirs to loyal magnates.[50] Such fosterage can be interpreted as a double-edged type of patron-client relationship. The foster father had a strong obligation to support and protect the royal protégé. Simultaneously he acted as a patron for the king, and this role would usually continue even after the shift in power, although it took on a consultative function. The words of these *seniores* carried weight in both private rooms and public arenas.[51] Royal deputies can therefore not simply be interpreted as subordinate public officials used as tools in the royal administration, since they were in fact indispensable parts of a collective rule wherein royal and aristocratic lordship were closely intertwined. Sources mentioning persons as "being the king's men" thus cover a wide range of positions stretching from unfree "henchmen" (*kotkarl, þjónn*) whose subordination was strictly vertical, to members of the top layers of society ("the king's best men"), whose subservience was symbolic and linked to a high degree of reciprocity.

Formalization and Stratification

Formalization is a key concept in the development of this period.[52] It refers in part to society's tendency to become progressively more "compartmentalized" during the High Middle Ages; domains that previously had been closely intertwined with each other now attained a certain autonomy. We can see this process in a number of fields. The Church gained an independence from royal power which marked a new age of professional bureaucracy and created a sphere of learned culture (see more in volume III). In the economy, the gift-exchange that was deeply enmeshed in social relations gave way (in part) to market trade, in which transactions were undertaken without reference to the social relations involved. Evidence of this compartmentalization can also be found in agriculture, where all-inclusive patronage over tenants developed into a more purely economic relationship (*saklig-økonomiske forhold*).[53]

The process of formalization can also be related to the introduction and spread of writing, which gradually came to transform vague and all-encompassing obligations into far more precise and circumscribed duties.[54] The Church was a forerunner in the use of writing in administration, and its members also staffed the royal bureaucracy. The most visible expression of the latter trend is the royal chapels, which were liberated from episcopal control and placed directly under the authority of the kings, who drew on chapel clerics in their recruitment of loyal administrators.[55] In the royal administration, the Norwegian *Law of the Retinue* (*Hirðskrá*) from 1277 represents a watershed in that obligations towards the king were specified in oaths that members of each status group were to swear upon entering the retinue.[56] There is no doubt that the introduction of writing and the state development were conducive to the establishment of a more formalized culture, which turned previously poorly defined patron-client relationships into more precise and legally defined bonds. Nevertheless, this process was still underway, and there is no reason to suppose that the informal and "oral" character of social bonds vanished in a single stroke.

Stratification is closely related to formalization, in that these processes both reflected and drove the state formation in this period. Stratification occurred on several levels. On the ideological level, an important step towards a more hierarchical society was an increase in the prestige of clients in vertical relationships. We saw that in Old Norse society such inequalities were usually camouflaged as reciprocal "friendships," unless they involved people who were unfree or of low status, who could act as "servants." The Church initiated this new development by insisting that service should not be considered degrading, but as honorable, and even as a precondition for salvation. This message was communicated in all sorts of fora: to the common people (masses, prayers, homily books), to kings in royal ideology (*The King's Mirror*), and as a model for earthly society (Church laws, papal letters).[57]

Kings were quick to realize the advantages inherent in this ideology, even if it also contained the danger of making them subordinate to the Church. In *The King's Mirror* from c. 1250, service was upheld as the foundation of society, and for a retainer it constituted a core value. Not only should he be willing to serve the king, he also had to go a long way in learning the right modes of expressing his servitude, epitomized in the quality of *hæverska* (courtliness).[58] A similar ideology was expressed in the numerous chivalric sagas that were translated into Old Norse from 1226 onwards. Here the exclusivity of the elites, shorthand for the men frequenting the royal court, was emphasized.[59] In Iceland, a related phenomenon is visible in the *fornaldarsögur*, sagas about the mythical past involving a martial class of warriors who had little but contempt for ordinary farmers (in contrast to the far more "egalitarian" and non-martial ethos of the Icelandic family sagas), and who defined themselves as part of a Nordic and even European elite culture.[60]

On a practical level, it goes without saying that the image of society presented in the literary sources did not reflect actual conditions in twelfth-century Scandinavia. Nevertheless, the literary development can also be viewed as an expression of real historical changes. From the latter part of the twelfth century, the humble *ármenn* in Norway were replaced by *sýslumenn* as local royal bailiffs. *Sýslumenn* were drawn from the same social elites that *lendir menn* had been recruited from, but they performed more or less the same functions as *ármenn* (military, legal, and fiscal tasks). The rising status of monarchy went hand in hand with increased revenues (the late twelfth century also saw the introduction of regular taxes by both kings and prelates). A similar development is discernible in Denmark, where the title of *bryti* was replaced by *fogd*, which carried none of the degrading connotations of the former title.[61]

An important backdrop for the increasing stratification of the patron-client bond and the concomitant strengthening of monarchy must be sought in the Nordic political dynamic of the period. In areas and periods where power was distributed amongst several lords of roughly equal status and military strength, vertical bonds tended to be marked by voluntariness and reciprocity. Such a situation existed in Free State Iceland up to c. 1220, and one could argue that it also characterized the situation in Scandinavia for more than a century following the death of King Knud the Great in 1035, a period in which no Scandinavian king was able to obtain definite supremacy in the region. This meant that rival factions kept one another in check, and that there existed "exit options" for those who fell out with certain kings or elite factions (see Rønning's chapter in this volume). Interaction between pretenders and elites across the Scandinavian borders was at times very intense. In short, this type of situation can be described as a "buyer's market," since the opportunities for "shopping" loyalty were considerable.[62] However, it should be emphasized that hostilities between different groups were fairly limited, mostly operating within the confines of the feud.[63]

In regions dominated by one king or where conflicts between rival lords escalated towards plunder and war, the strain of coercion and constraint became stronger. A Scandinavian king who wanted to control large territories normally founded his power on a patchwork of small lordships. In turn, these local lords had clients depending on them for protection. Yet prolonged conflicts could lead to the strain and imbalance, maybe even the disintegration, of local patron-client systems, due to the fact that many local power holders had their material resources confiscated as spoils of war or feuds. The concept of a "protection racket" has been developed in order to account for patrons who create conditions in which the need for protection is steadily growing, meaning that the demand for their services grows accordingly, and what the client has to offer is devalued.[64] During the so-called civil wars in Denmark in 1131–57, in Norway and Sweden c. 1160–1240, and in Iceland c. 1220–64, local farmers were more or less forced to accept the "friendship" of the lord who was currently the most powerful in the area. Ravaging properties owned by farmers, or in some cases monasteries, was a widely used tactic on the European continent, and at times it was frequent in the Nordic countries as well. When local power was undermined and the atmosphere of mistrust intensified, patrons strengthened their hold on clients, since the urgency for protection was acute. Clients were more or less forced to do service that was more unilateral than they were used to as part of their more reciprocal friendship duties. Another factor diminishing the importance of "traditional" patron-client relationships was the Scandinavian kings' increasing use of "entrusted men" (*trúnaðarmenn*) bound to them through oaths of allegiance from the end of the twelfth century onwards. These relationships were also a type of patron-client bond, even if these clients were not usually seeking protection, but rather rewards in the form of money or personal property.[65] However, these relationships were more unilateral than earlier friendship bonds.

Hence, the increased formalization and stratification of patron-client relationships in the Nordic region during the High Middle Ages probably drove and reflected a centralization of authority which had both a "cultural" (read Christian) and "military" (coercive) aspect. In the long run, it weakened the "traditional" diffuse but all-encompassing patron-client relationships at the local level – although they did not perish.

Notes

1. See for instance Andrew Wallace-Hadrill, *Patronage in Ancient Society* (London, 1989); Richard P. Saller, *Personal Patronage Under the Early Empire* (Cambridge, 1982).
2. Ernest Gellner, "Patrons and Clients," in *Patrons and Clients in Mediterranean Societies*, ed. Ernest Gellner and John Waterbury (London, 1977), 1–6; Shmuel Noah Eisenstadt and Luis Roniger, "Personal Relations, Trust and Ambivalence in Relation to the Institutional Order," in *Patrons, Clients and Friends: Interpersonal Relations and the Structure of Trust in Society*, ed. Shmuel Noah Eisenstadt and Luis Roniger (Cambridge, 1984), 1–18; Anton Blok, "Variations in Patronage," *Sociologische Gids* 16 (1969): 365–78.
3. Classical analyses of feudalism include Marc Bloch, *Feudal Society*, vol. 2, trans. L. A. Manyon (London, 1975 [1939]); François-Louis Ganshof, *Feudalism*, trans. Philip Grierson (London, 1952 [1944]). Whereas Ganshof is legalistically oriented, Bloch is inspired by a more holistic, Durkhemian view of society.
4. For the most radical criticism, see Susan Reynolds, *Fiefs and Vassals: The Medieval Evidence Reinterpreted* (Oxford, 1994); Elizabeth A. R. Brown, "The Tyranny of a Construct: Feudalism and Historians of Medieval Europe," *The American Historical Review* 79, no. 4 (1974): 1063–88.
5. Fredric L. Cheyette, *Ermengard of Narbonne and the World of the Troubadours* (Ithaca, NY, 2001); Stephen D. White, "Feuding and Peace-Making in the Touraine Around the Year 1100," *Traditio* 42 (1986): 195–263; Patrick J. Geary, "Living with Conflicts in Stateless France: A Typology of Conflict Management Mechanisms," in *Living with the Dead in the Middle Ages*, ed. Patrick J. Geary (Ithaca, NY, 1994), 125–60.
6. Gerd Althoff, *Family, Friends and Followers: Political and Social Bonds in Medieval Europe* (Cambridge, 2004).
7. See, typically, scattered references to "feudal" in *The Cambridge History of Scandinavia*, vol. 1, ed. Knut Helle (Cambridge, 2008); See also Michael H. Gelting, "Europæisk feudalisme og dansk 1100–1200-tal," in *Kongemagt sog samfund i middelalderen: Festskrift til Erik Ulsig*, ed. Poul Enemark, Per Ingesman, and Jens Villiam Jensen (Copenhagen, 1988), 3–17.
8. For a recent classification upholding this divide, see Chris Wickham, *Medieval Europe* (New Haven, 2016), 89–98.
9. On anthropological influences, see Kåre Lunden, *Økonomi og samfunn* (Oslo, 1972); Sverre Bagge, "Borgerkrig og statsutvikling i Norge i middelalderen," *Historisk tidsskrift* (N) 65, no. 2 (1986): 145–97. On hierarchy going far back in time, see Dagfinn Skre, *Herredømmet: Bosetning og besittelse på Romerike 200–1350 e. Kr* (Oslo, 1996); Søren Michael Sindbæk and Bjørn Poulsen, ed., *Settlement and Lordship in Viking and Early Medieval Scandinavia* (Turnhout, 2011), 1–28. On property rights, see Tore Iversen, "Fremveksten av det norske leilendingesystemet i middelalderen – en forklaringsskisse," *Heimen* 2 (1995): 169–80.

10. See definitions in Alex Weinrod, "Patronage and Power," in *Patrons and Clients in Mediterranean Societies*, ed. Ernest Gellner and John Waterbury (London, 1977), 41–52 at 45; Saller, *Personal Patronage*, 126–27; Wallace-Hadrill, *Patronage*, 1–14.
11. Ronald Syme, *The Roman Revolution* (Oxford, 1939), 12.
12. Robert Paine, "A Theory of Patronage and Brokerage," in *Patrons and Brokers in the East Arctic*, ed. Robert Paine (Newfoundland, 1971), 8–21. See also Eric R. Wolf, "Kinship, Friendship, and Patron-Client Relations in Complex Societies," in *The Social Anthropology of Complex Societies*, ed. Michael Banton (London, 1966), 1–22. The contact between clients and patrons was often mediated through a third party, a so-called patronage broker. See e.g. Sean Gilsdorf, *The Favor of Friends: Intercession and Aristocratic Power in Carolingian and Ottonian Europe* (Leiden, 2014), 44–47.
13. Sharon Kettering, "Patronage in Early Modern France," in *Patronage in Sixteenth-and Seventeenth Century France* (Aldershot, 2002), 839–62 at 854–59.
14. Eisenstadt and Roniger, "Personal Relations," 19–28; Carl H. Landé, "Introduction," in *Friends, Followers and Factions: A Reader in Political Clientilism*, ed. Steffen W. Schmidt et al. (Berkeley, 1977), xiii–xxxvii; critique by Jeremy Boissevain, *Friends of Friends: Networks, Manipulators and Coalitions* (Oxford, 1978), 1–23; Fredrik Barth, *Political Leadership Among Swat Pathans* (London, 1965), 1–4.
15. Weinrod, "Patronage and Power," 41–45; Sydel Silverman, "Patronage as Myth," in *Patrons and Clients in Mediterranean Societies*, 7–20 at 17–20.
16. Jón Viðar Sigurðsson, *Chieftains and Power in the Icelandic Commonwealth* (Odense, 1999); Jón Viðar Sigurðsson, *Viking Friendship* (Ithaca, NY, 2017); Jón Viðar Sigurðsson, *Skandinavia i vikingtiden* (Oslo, 2017).
17. Eisenstadt and Roniger, "Personal Relations," 6–7.
18. Hans Jacob Orning, *Unpredictability and Presence: Norwegian Kingship in the High Middle Ages* (Leiden, 2008), 51; Bloch, *Feudal Society*, vol. 1, 231–36; Gerd Althoff, "The Variability of Rituals in the Middle Ages," in *Medieval Concepts of the Past: Ritual, Memory, Historiography*, ed. Gerd Althoff, Johannes Fried, and Patrick Geary (Washington, DC, 2002), 71–87.
19. For a discussion on "central place" see Dagfinn Skre, "Centrality, Landholding, and Trace in Scandinavia, c. AD 700–900," in Sindbæk and Poulsen, *Settlement and Lordship*, 197–212 at 199–200. For an example, see Gerd Stamsø Munch, Olav Sverre Johansen, and Else Roesdahl, *Borg in Lofoten: A Chieftain's Farm in North Norway* (Bøstad, 2003). See also Sigurðsson, *Skandinavia i vikingtiden*.
20. Bjørn Myhre, "Chieftain's Graves and Chiefdom Territories in South Norway in the Migration Period," *Studien zur Sachsenforschung* 6 (1987): 169–87; Inger Storli, *Hålogaland før rikssamlingen: politiske prosesser i perioden 200–900 e.Kr* (Oslo, 2006).
21. Frode Iversen, *Eiendom, makt og statsdannelse: Kongsgårder og gods i Hordaland i yngre jernalder og middelalder* (Bergen, 2004).
22. Iversen, "Fremveksten av det norske leilendingesystemet i middelalderen," 169–80.
23. Sigurðsson, *Chieftains and Power*.
24. John Boswell, *The Kindness of Strangers* (New York, 1988), 357–59; William Ian Miller, *Bloodtaking and Peacemaking: Feud, Law, and Society in Saga Iceland* (Chicago, 1990), 122, 171; Lars Hermanson, *Bärande band: Vänskap, kärlek och brödraskap i det medeltida Nordeuropa, ca 1000–1200* (Lund, 2009).

Lords and Followers 47

25. Auður Magnúsdóttir, "Frillor och fruar: Politik och samlevnad på Island 1120–1400" (PhD diss., Gothenburg University, 2001). Auður Magnusdóttir draws attention to "the strength of weak ties" by stating that concubine relationships could be stronger than relationships based on marriage, because of their more limited scope. Auður Magnusdóttir, "Älskas, giftas, stötta, slåss," in *Nätverk som social resurs: Historiska exempel*, ed. Einar Hreinsson and Tomas Nilson (Lund, 2003), 61–82.
26. On *Eigenkirchenwesen* in Iceland, see Magnús Stefánsson, "Islandsk egenkirkevesen," in *Møtet mellom hedendom og kristendom i Norge*, ed. Hans-Emil Lidén (Oslo, 1995), 234–54. In Norway, see Jan Brendalsmo, *Kirkebygg og kirkebyggere: byggherrer i Trøndelag Ca. 1000–1600* (Oslo, 2006). Internationally, see Susan Wood, *The Proprietary Church in the Medieval West* (Oxford, 2006).
27. See the contribution by Wojtek Jezierski and Kim Esmark in this volume, in chapters 9 "Angels in Scandinavia: Papal Legates and Networks of Nordic Elites, Twelfth–Thirteenth Centuries" and 15 "Social Power and Conversion of Capital: Sune Ebbesen of Zealand," respectivly.
28. See the contribution by Sveinung Kasin Boye in chapter 16. See also Kim Esmark, "Disputing Property in Zealand: The Records of Sorø Donation Book," in *Disputing Strategies in Medieval Scandinavia*, ed. Kim Esmark et al. (Leiden, 2013), 181–218; Christian Lovén, "Lordship Over Monasteries in Twelfth and Thirteenth Century Sweden and Denmark," in *Monastic Culture: The Long Thirteenth Century. Essays in Honour of Brian Patrick McGuire* (Odense, 2014), 119–47; Thomas Hill, *Könige, Fürsten und Klöster: Studien zu den dänischen Klostergründungen des 12. Jahrhunderts* (Frankfurt am Main, 1992).
29. Catharina Andersson, "Kloster och aristokrati: Nunnor, munkar och gåvor i det svenska samhället till 1300-talets mitt" (PhD diss., Gothenburg University, 2006). For the European context, see Barbara H. Rosenwein, *To Be the Neighbor of Saint Peter: The Social Meaning of Cluny's Property, 909–1049* (Ithaca, NY, 1989).
30. In Scandinavian letters abbots addressed bishops as their lords or patrons. See e.g. Abbot William's letters to Bishop/Archbishop Absalon in Lars Hermanson, "Discourses of Communion: Abbot William of Æbelholt and Saxo Grammaticus: Imagining the Christian Danish Community, Early Thirteenth Century," in *Imagined Communities on the Baltic Rim, from the Eleventh to Fifteenth Centuries*, ed. Wojtek Jezierski and Lars Hermanson (Amsterdam, 2016), 59–88 at 79–80.
31. Kettering, *Patronage*, 851.
32. Lars Hermanson has dealt with the problem partly from an ideological perspective by analyzing how hierarchical rhetoric was used by the Church, the kings, and feudal lords. Medieval scribes and authors were in most cases themselves clients of patrons who commissioned them to write literary works. For instance, Saxo Grammaticus was Archbishop Absalon's protégé: a patron-clientship that was later inherited by Absalon's successor, Archbishop Andreas Sunesen. Hermanson, *Bärande band*, 157–58.
33. Sigurðsson, *Chieftains and Power*, 135–40. Horizontal friendships are discussed further in the contribution by Lars Hermanson and Hans Jacob Orning in chapter 4 in this volume.
34. Magnates such as Sigurd Syr, Erling Skjalgsson, and Sveinke Gunnarsson are depicted in situations which reveal that they acted as great local patrons not dissimilar to Icelandic chieftains. See Sverre Bagge, *Society and Politics in Snorri Sturluson's Heimskringla* (Berkeley, 1991), 123–40.

35. Bagge, *Society and Politics*, 237–40; for a general approach to this topic see Sigurðsson, *Viking Friendship*.
36. Gulathing Law in NgL, vol. 1, 1; G 1. English translation in *The Earliest Norwegian Laws: Being the Gulathing Law and the Frostathing Law*, trans. Laurence M. Larson (New York, 1935), 35.
37. Tore Iversen, *Trelldommen: norsk slaveri i middelalderen* (Bergen, 1997); Michael H. Gelting, "Legal Reform and the Development of Peasant Dependence in Thirteenth-Century Denmark," in *Forms of Servitude in Northern and Central Europe: Decline, Resistance, and Expansion*, ed. Paul Freedman and Monique Bourin (Turnhout, 2005), 343–67.
38. Steinar Imsen, *Norsk bondekommunalisme: Fra Magnus Lagabøte til Kristian Kvart. 1: Middelalderen*, vol. 1 (Trondheim, 1990); Jeppe Büchert Netterstrøm, *At forsvare til rette: værnsforholdet og bøndernes retslige stilling i Danmarks senmiddelalder 1400–1513* (Kerteminde, 2003), 12–13.
39. Hans Jacob Orning, "Festive Governance: Feasts as Rituals of Power and Integration in Medieval Norway," in *Rituals, Performatives, and Political Order in Northern Europe, C. 650–1350*, ed. Wojtek Jezierski et al. (Turnout, 2015), 175–207.
40. Lars Hermanson, "How to Legitimate Rebellion and Condemn Usurpation of the Crown: Discourses of Fidelity and Treason in the *Gesta Danorum* of Saxo Grammaticus," in *Disputing Strategies in Medieval Scandinavia*, ed. Kim Esmark et al. (Leiden, 2013), 107–42 at 132–34; Sigurðsson, *Viking Friendship*, 47–71. For Europe see Stephen D. White, "The Politics of Exchange: Gifts, Fiefs, and Feudalism," in *Medieval Transformations: Texts, Power, and Gifts in Context*, ed. Esther Cohen and Mayke B. de Jong (Leiden, 2001), 167–88.
41. Hermanson, "How to Legitimate Rebellion," 122–23.
42. Iversen, *Trelldommen*, 149–53.
43. Orning, *Unpredictability and Presence*, 51–108.
44. Bloch, *Feudal Society*, vol. 1, 145–62.
45. See contributions by Poulsen and Orning in chapter 8 in volume I of this series.
46. For this interpretation, see Lars Hermanson, *Släkt, vänner och makt: En studie av elitens politiska kultur i 1100-talets Danmark* (Gothenburg, 2000), 61–63.
47. For parallels to the Anglo-Norman kingdom and the Holy Roman Empire, see John Horace Round, *The King's Serjeants and Officers of State with Their Coronation Services* (London, 1971 [1911]), 141–66.
48. Cf. Anglo-Norman England, where J. Horace Round points to the fact "that members of the mighty Norman houses of Bigod and of Giffard held, in succession, an Essex manor by the service of scalding the King's swine," Round, *King's Serjeants*, 9.
49. It was not only the king who surrounded himself with office-holders, but also the king's cousins and brothers, as well as the archbishop. On the distinction between delegated and shared authority see Hermanson, *Släkt, vänner och makt*, 61–79.
50. See contribution by Ian Peter Grohse in chapter 13 in this volume, with references to this practice in other parts of Europe.
51. This is a recurring theme, for instance in Saxo Grammaticus's *Gesta Danorum* and Snorri Sturluson's *Heimskringla*. See Hermanson, *Släkt, vänner och makt*. For the German context, see Althoff, *Family, Friends and Followers*. On fosterage and fictive kinship, see the contribution by Kim Esmark, Jón Viðar Sigurðsson, and Helle Vogt in chapter 2 in this volume. The institution of fosterage is an example wherein kinship, friendship, and patron-client relationships coalesce.

52. Charles West, *Reframing the Feudal Revolution: Political and Social Transformation Between Marne and Moselle, C.800–1000* (Cambridge, 2013), 1, 9; Wickham, *Medieval Europe*, 154–69 (using the terms "centralisation" and "institutionalisation").
53. Iversen, *Trelldommen*, 255–58.
54. Althoff, "The Variability of Rituals," 71–85.
55. Sverre Bagge, *Den kongelige kapellgeistlighet 1150–1319* (Bergen, 1976).
56. H, ch. 4, 5.
57. David Brégaint, *Vox Regis: Royal Communication in High Medieval Norway* (Leiden, 2016).
58. Hans Jacob Orning, "The *King's Mirror* and the Emergence of a New Elite in 13th Century Norway," in *Speculum Septentrionale*, ed. Karl Gunnar Johansson and Elise Kleivane (Oslo, 2017), 245–64.
59. Bjørn Bandlien, *Strategies of Passion: Love and Marriage in Medieval Iceland and Norway* (Turnhout, 2005); Jürg Glauser, "Romance (Translated *Riddarasögur*)," in *A Companion to Old Norse-Icelandic Literature and Culture*, ed. Rory McTurk (Malden, 2005), 372–87; Hans Jacob Orning, "The Reception and Adaption of Courtly Culture in Old Norse Society: Changing Conceptions of Hierarchy and Networks in Two Versions of Tristrams Saga," in *Friendship and Social Networks in Scandinavia, c. 1000–1800*, ed. Jón Viðar Sigurðsson and Thomas Småberg (Turnhout, 2013), 115–52.
60. Torfi H. Tulinius, *The Matter of the North: The Rise of Literary Fiction in Thirteenth-Century Iceland* (Odense, 2002); Hans Jacob Orning, *The Reality of the Fantastic: The Magical, Geopolitical and Social Universe of Late Medieval Saga Manuscripts* (Odense, 2017).
61. See the contribution by Hans Jacob Orning and Bjørn Poulsen in chapter 8 in volume I of this series.
62. On shopping loyalty, see Caroline Humfress, "Thinking Through Legal Pluralism: 'Forum Shopping' in the Later Roman Empire," in *Law and Empire*, ed. Jill Harries, Jeroen Duindam, Caroline Humfress, and Nimrod Hurvitz (Leiden, 2013), 161–84. On the situation of multiparty struggles (in modern Afghanistan), see Fotini Christia, *Alliance Formation in Civil Wars* (Cambridge, 2012).
63. Bagge, "Borgerkrig og statsutvikling i Norge i middelalderen," 145–97; Hans Jacob Orning, "Borgerkrig og statsutvikling i Norge i middelalderen – en revurdering," *Historisk tidsskrift* (N), no. 2 (2014): 193–216.
64. Charles Tilly, Gabriel Ardant, and Stein Rokkan, *The Formation of National States in Western Europe* (Princeton, 1975). Feudalism, apart from being more formal than patron-client relationships, can be classified as a condition in which patrons create a protection racket, thus increasing their own hegemony. See Gunner Lind, "Great Friends and Small Friends: Clientilism and the Power Elite," in *Power Elites and State Building*, ed. Wolfgang Reinhard (Oxford, 1996), 123–48.
65. Sigurðsson, *Chieftains and Power*, 76–79; Jón Viðar Sigurðsson, *Det norrøne samfunnet: Vikingen, kongen, erkebiskopen og bonden* (Oslo, 2008), 133–35; Hermanson, *Bärande band*, 147.

Dedicated Bibliography

Althoff, Gerd. "The Variability of Rituals in the Middle Ages." In *Medieval Concepts of the Past: Ritual, Memory, Historiography*, edited by Gerd Althoff, Johannes Fried, and Patrick J. Geary, 71–85. Washington, DC, 2002.

Althoff, Gerd. *Family, Friends and Followers: Political and Social Bonds in Medieval Europe* [*Verwandte, Freunde und Getreue: Zum politischen Stellenwert der Gruppenbindungen im früheren Mittelalter*]. Translated by Christopher Carroll. Cambridge, 2004.

Andersson, Catharina. "Kloster och aristokrati, Nunnor, munkar och gåvor i det svenska samhället till 1300-talets mitt." PhD diss., University of Gothenburg, 2006.

Bagge, Sverre. *Den Kongelige Kapellgeistlighet 1150–1319*. Bergen, 1976.

Bagge, Sverre. "Borgerkrig og statsutvikling i Norge i middelalderen." *Historisk tidsskrift* (N) 65, no. 2 (1986): 145–97.

Bagge, Sverre. *Society and Politics in Snorri Sturluson's Heimskringla*. Berkeley, 1991.

Bandlien, Bjørn. *Strategies of Passion: Love and Marriage in Medieval Iceland and Norway*. Turnhout, 2005.

Barth, Fredrik. *Political Leadership Among Swat Pathans*. London, 1965.

Bloch, Marc. *Feudal Society*, vol. 1. London, 1975.

Bloch, Marc. *Feudal Society*, vol. 2. Translated by L. A. Manyon. London, 1975 [1939].

Blok, Anton. "Variations in Patronage." *Sociologische Gids* 16 (1969): 365–78.

Boissevain, Jeremy. *Friends of Friends: Networks, Manipulators and Coalitions*. Oxford, 1978.

Boswell, John. *The Kindness of Strangers*. New York, 1988.

Brégaint, David. *Vox Regis: Royal Communication in High Medieval Norway*. Leiden, 2016.

Brendalsmo, Jan. *Kirkebygg og kirkebyggere: Byggherrer i Trøndelag ca. 1000–1600*. Oslo, 2006.

Brown, Elizabeth A. R. "The Tyranny of a Construct: Feudalism and Historians of Medieval Europe." *The American Historical Review* 79, no. 4 (1974): 1063–88.

Cheyette, Fredric L. *Ermengard of Narbonne and the World of the Troubadours*. Ithaca, NY, 2001.

Eisenstadt, Shmuel Noah, and Luis Roniger, "Personal Relations, Trust and Ambivalence in Relation to the Institutional Order." In *Patrons, Clients and Friends: Interpersonal Relations and the Structure of Trust in Society*, edited by Shmuel Noah Eisenstadt and Luis Roniger, 1–18. Cambridge, 1984.

Esmark, Kim. "Disputing Property in Zealand: The Records of Sorø Donation Book." In *Disputing Strategies in Medieval Scandinavia*, edited by Kim Esmark, Lars Hermanson, Hans Jacob Orning, and Helle Vogt, 181–218. Leiden, 2013.

Fotini, Christia. *Alliance Formation in Civil Wars*. Cambridge, 2012.

Ganshof, François L. *Feudalism*. Translated by Philip Grierson. London, 1952 [1944].

Geary, Patrick J. "Living with Conflicts in Stateless France: A Typology of Conflict Management Mechanisms." In *Living with the Dead in the Middle Ages*, edited by Patrick J. Geary, 125–60. Ithaca, NY, 1994.

Gellner, Ernest. "Patrons and Clients." In *Patrons and Clients in Mediterranean Societies*, edited by Ernest Geller and John Waterbury, 1–6. London, 1977.

Gelting, Michael H. "Europæisk feudalisme og dansk 1100–1200-tal." In *Kongemagt og samfund i middelalderen: Festskrift til Erik Ulsig*, edited by Poul Enemark, Per Ingesman, and Jens Villiam Jensen, 3–17. Copenhagen, 1988.

Gelting, Michael H. "Legal Reform and the Development of Peasant Dependence in Thirteenth-Century Denmark." In *Forms of Servitude in Northern and Central Europe: Decline, Resistance, and Expansion*, edited by Paul Freedman and Monique Bourin, 343–67. Turnhout, 2005.
Gilsdorf, Sean. *The Favor of Friends: Intercession and Aristocratic Power in Carolingian and Ottonian Europe*. Leiden, 2014.
Glauser, Jürg. "Romance (Translated *Riddarasögur*)." In *A Companion to Old Norse-Icelandic Literature and Culture*, edited by Rory McTurk, 372–87. Malden, 2005.
Helle, Knut, ed. *The Cambridge History of Scandinavia*, vol. 1. Cambridge, 2008.
Hermanson, Lars. *Släkt, vänner och makt: En studie av elitens politiska kultur i 1100-talets Danmark*. Gothenburg, 2000.
Hermanson, Lars. *Bärande band. Vänskap, kärlek och brödraskap i det medeltida Nordeuropa, ca 1000–1200*. Lund, 2009.
Hermanson, Lars. "How to Legitimate Rebellion and Condemn Usurpation of the Crown: Discourses of Fidelity and Treason in the *Gesta Danorum* of Saxo Grammaticus." In *Disputing Strategies in Medieval Scandinavia*, edited by Kim Esmark, Lars Hermanson, Hans Jacob Orning, and Helle Vogt, 107–40. Leiden, 2013.
Hermanson, Lars. "Discourses of Communion: Abbot William of Æbelholt and Saxo Grammaticus: Imagining the Christian Danish Community, Early Thirteenth Century." In *Imagined Communities on the Baltic Rim, from the Eleventh to Fifteenth Centuries*, edited by Wojtek Jezierski and Lars Hermanson, 59–87. Amsterdam, 2016.
Hill, Thomas. *Könige, Fürsten und Klöster. Studien zu den dänischen Klostergründungen des 12. Jahrhunderts*. Frankfurt, 1992.
Humfress, Caroline. "Thinking Through Legal Pluralism: 'Forum Shopping' in the Later Roman Empire." In *Law and Empire*, edited by Jill Harries Jeroen Duindam, Caroline Humfress, and Nimrod Hurvitz. Leiden, 2013.
Imsen, Steinar. *Norsk bondekommunalisme: Fra Magnus Lagabøte til Kristian Kvart: 1: Middelalderen*, vol. 1. Trondheim, 1990.
Iversen, Frode. *Eiendom, makt og statsdannelse: Kongsgårder og gods i Hordaland i yngre jernalder og middelalder*. Bergen, 2004.
Iversen, Tore. "Fremveksten av det norske leilendingesystemet i middelalderen – en forklaringsskisse." *Heimen* 2 (1995): 169–80.
Iversen, Tore. *Trelldommen: Norsk slaveri i middelalderen*. Bergen, 1997.
Kettering, Sharon. "Patronage in Early Modern France." In *Patronage in Sixteenth- and Seventeenth Century France*, edited by Sharon Kettering, 839–62. Aldershot, 2002.
Landé, Carl H. "Introduction." In *Friends, Followers and Factions: A Reader in Political Clientilism*, edited by Steffen W. Schmidt, Laura Guasti, Carl Landé, and James C. Scott, xiii–xxxvii. Berkeley, 1977.
Lind, Gunner. "Great Friends and Small Friends: Clientilism and the Power Elite." In *Power Elites and State Building*, edited by Wolfgang Reinhard, 123–48. Oxford, 1996.
Lovén, Christian. "Lordship Over Monasteries in Twelfth and Thirteenth Century Sweden and Denmark." In *Monastic Culture: The Long Thirteenth Century: Essays in Honour of Brian Patrick McGuire*, 119–47. Odense, 2014.
Lunden, Kåre. *Økonomi og samfunn*. Oslo, 1972.

Magnúsdóttir, Auður. "Frillor och fruar: politik och samlevnad på Island 1120–1400." PhD diss., University of Gothenburg, 2001.
Magnúsdóttir, Auður. "Älskas, giftas, stötta, slåss." In *Nätverk som social resurs: Historiska exempel*, edited by Einar Hreinsson and Tomas Nilson, 61–82. Lund, 2003.
Miller, William I. *Bloodtaking and Peacemaking: Feud, Law and Society in Saga Iceland*. Chicago, 1990.
Munch, Gerd Stamsø, Olav Sverre Johansen, and Else Roesdahl. *Borg in Lofoten: A Chieftain's Farm in North Norway*. Bøstad, 2003.
Myhre, Bjørn. "Chieftain's Graves and Chiefdom Territories in South Norway in the Migration Period." *Studien zur Sachsenforschung* 6 (1987): 169–87.
Netterstrøm, Jeppe Büchert. *At forsvare til rette: værnsforholdet og bøndernes retslige stilling i Danmarks senmiddelalder 1400–1513*. Kerteminde, 2003.
Orning, Hans Jacob. *Unpredictability and Presence: Norwegian Kingship in the High Middle Ages*. Translated by Alan Crozier. Leiden, 2008.
Orning, Hans Jacob. "The Reception and Adaption of Courtly Culture in Old Norse Society: Changing Conceptions of Hierarchy and Networks in Two Versions of *Tristrams Saga*." In *Friendship and Social Networks in Scandinavia, c. 1000–1800*, edited by Jón Viðar Sigurðsson and Thomas Småberg, 115–52. Turnhout, 2013.
Orning, Hans Jacob. "Borgerkrig og statsutvikling i Norge i middelalderen – en revurdering." *Historisk tidsskrift* (N) 93 (2014): 193–216.
Orning, Hans Jacob. "Festive Governance: Feasts as Rituals of Power and Integration in Medieval Norway." In *Rituals, Performatives, and Political Order in Northern Europe, C. 650–1350*, edited by Wojtek Jezierski et al., 175–208. Turnhout, 2015.
Orning, Hans Jacob. "The *King's Mirror* and the Emergence of a New Elite in 13th-Century Norway." In *Speculum Septentrionale*, edited by Karl Gunnar Johansson and Elise Kleivane, 245–64. Oslo, 2017.
Orning, Hans Jacob. *The Reality of the Fantastic: The Magical, Geopolitical and Social Universe of Late Medieval Saga Manuscripts*. Odense, 2017.
Paine, Robert. "A Theory of Patronage and Brokerage." In *Patrons and Brokers in the East Arctic*, edited by Robert Paine, 8–21. St John's, Newfoundland, 1971.
Reynolds, Susan. *Fiefs and Vassals: The Medieval Evidence Reinterpreted*. Oxford, 1994.
Rosenwein, Barbara H. *To Be the Neighbor of Saint Peter: The Social Meaning of Cluny's Property, 909–1049*. Ithaca, NY, 1989.
Round, John Horace. *The King's Serjeants and Officers of State with their Coronation Services*. London, 1971 [1911].
Saller, Richard P. *Personal Patronage Under the Early Empire*. Cambridge, 1982.
Sigurðsson, Jón Viðar. *Chieftains and Power in the Icelandic Commonwealth*. Translated by Jean Lundskær-Nielsen. Odense, 1999.
Sigurðsson, Jón Viðar. *Det norrøne samfunnet: Vikingen, kongen, erkebiskopen og bonden*. Oslo, 2008.
Sigurðsson, Jón Viðar. *Skandinavia i vikingtiden*. Oslo, 2017.
Sigurðsson, Jón Viðar. *Viking Friendship*. Ithaca, NY, 2017.
Silverman, Sydel. "Patronage as Myth." In *Patrons and Clients in Mediterranean Societies*, edited by Ernest Geller and John Waterbury, 7–20. London, 1977.

Sindbæk, Søren Michael, and Bjørn Poulsen, eds. *Settlement and Lordship in Viking and Early Medieval Scandinavia.* Turnhout, 2011.
Skre, Dagfinn. *Herredømmet: Bosetning og besittelse på Romerike 200–1350 e. Kr.* Oslo, 1996.
Skre, Dagfinn. "Centrality, Landholding, and Trace in Scandinavia, c. AD 700–900." In *Settlement and Lordship in Viking and Early Medieval Scandinavia*, edited by Bjørn Poulsen and Søren Michael Sindbæk, 197–212. Turnhout, 2011.
Stefánsson, Magnús. "Islandsk egenkirkevesen." In *Møtet mellom hedendom og kristendom i Norge*, edited by Hans-Emil Lidén, 138–56. Oslo, 1995.
Storli, Inger. *Hålogaland før rikssamlingen: Politiske prosesser i perioden 200–900 e. Kr.* Oslo, 2006.
Syme, Ronald. *The Roman Revolution.* Oxford, 1939.
Tilly, Charles, Gabriel Ardant, and Stein Rokkan. *The Formation of National States in Western Europe.* Princeton, 1975.
Torfi, H. Tulinius. *The Matter of the North: The Rise of Literary Fiction in Thirteenth-Century Iceland.* Odense, 2002.
Wallace-Hadrill, Andrew, ed. *Patronage in Ancient Society.* London, 1989.
Weinrod, Alex. "Patronage and Power." In *Patrons and Clients in Mediterranean Societies*, edited by Ernest Gellner and John Waterbury, 41–52. London, 1977.
West, Charles. *Reframing the Feudal Revolution: Political and Social Transformation Between Marne and Moselle, c. 800–1000.* Cambridge, 2013.
White, Stephen D. "Feuding and Peace-Making in the Touraine Around the Year 1100." *Traditio* 42 (1986): 195–263.
White, Stephen D. "The Politics of Exchange: Gifts, Fiefs, and Feudalism." In *Medieval Transformations: Texts, Power, and Gifts in Context*, edited by Esther Cohen and Mayke B. de Jong, 167–88. Leiden, 2001.
Wickham, Chris. *Medieval Europe.* New Haven, 2016.
Wolf, Eric R. "Kinship, Friendship, and Patron-Client Relations in Complex Societies." In *The Social Anthropology of Complex Societies*, edited by Michael Banton, 1–22. London, 1966.
Wood, Susan. *The Proprietary Church in the Medieval West.* Oxford, 2006.

4 Friends and Allies
Networks of Horizontal Bonds

Lars Hermanson and Hans Jacob Orning

Characteristics, Previous Research, and Sources

The concept of a horizontal bond is here defined as a symmetrical relationship based on voluntariness and consensus. It is established between individuals or groups of individuals with common interests. Horizontal bonds are primarily formed between parties of equal status. The reciprocal exchange of favors serves the purpose of creating trust, predictability, loyalty, and confidence. Horizontal relationships are constituted of bonds such as kinship, fictive kinship, friendship, and various forms of companionship. Anthropologists have made a distinction between relationships based on friendship vis-à-vis relations founded on kinship by emphasizing the dichotomy between "achievement/voluntarism versus ascription/constraint."[1] Political goal-oriented concepts like alliances, pacts, or action-sets could also be classified as horizontal bonds. Thus, these liaisons serve both long-term and short-term interests, implying that the durability and stability of horizontal bonds varies depending on their purpose and context. Though personal and based on a face-to-face relationship, the horizontal bond forms a significant constituent part of extensive socio-political systems, which scholars during the latest decades have sometimes preferred to designate as "networks." In this chapter, the terms "network" and "horizontal" bond will be used interchangeably.

A network is an analytical concept that has attracted much attention following the publication of the article "Neither Market nor Hierarchy: Network Forms of Organization" by Walter W. Powell in 1991.[2] Powell argues that networks can be defined as a system opposed to *markets* (by building on trust), and *hierarchies* (by being non-hierarchical). The advantage of basing social relationships on networks is that it ensures a more flexible and dynamic function, since they are founded on mutual trust and knowledge, and operate with implicit rather than explicitly defined legal rules, which create patterns of interaction between groups and individuals. The idea of the crucial importance of trust and predictability is inspired by Niklas Luhmann's research, and Powell uses Marcel Mauss's gift-theory to explain how the exchange within social networks functions.[3] However, networks also have their disadvantages, namely that it requires a continual effort to maintain these bonds, and they can easily develop into more coercive and hierarchical relationships.

Network analysis focuses on individuals and their political strategies and has often been proposed as an alternative to structuralist approaches in anthropology and sociology. One of the most ardent proponents of networks as a countermeasure to structuralist fallacies was the anthropologist Jeremy Boissevain, who maintained that strategy and transactions, not the quest for integrative and coercive mechanisms in society, should form the core of social analysis.[4] A useful concept here is Pierre Bourdieu's concept of field, which can be defined as a system of relations involving people competing for values and assets they consider to be vital.[5] These approaches focus on patterns rather than on structures. Scholars dealing with network analysis have used Bourdieu's categorization of different capital formations, i.e., economic capital, social capital, cultural capital, and symbolic capital, in order to explain the exchanges within a network. They interpret the network as a forum for interaction with the purpose of shaping, reproducing, and converting capital formations in accordance with the network's internal criteria.[6]

Powell's followers have defined social networks as relationships that are enduring, voluntary, informal, and non-hierarchical.[7] However, this definition does not stand alone. Some scholars have criticized the sharp distinction made between networks and hierarchies, claiming that there is a certain degree of verticality within every network, even if it is not formalized or predetermined.[8] Other scholars have criticized Powell's network analysis for being elite-centered and solely based on qualitative methods. They assert that this approach has been too concerned with the problem of how networks are maintained and reproduced, and not with how they are originally formed.[9] There are also many scholars who have chosen to advocate for quantitative methods instead in order to study wider social strata and thereby reach beyond the top layers of society.[10]

Powell's network theory has been applied to modern social organizations in order to analyze how economic or political interchanges work in private channels of power, i.e., through informal relationships. In medieval society, however, horizontal bonds were usually not informal in the sense of being private – often quite the opposite. For instance, it was common for pacts of friendship to be sealed in solemn public rituals, and political alliances were confirmed through ceremonial oaths taken in front of large audiences. Thus, we must bear in mind that Powell's network theory is most relevant in societies where it is possible to draw a dividing line between the public and the private sphere, something which is not always easy to do when it comes to medieval society.

The advantage of a network approach is that it offers an alternative to studying medieval politics in terms of *state formation* and the development of formal institutions. As such, it implies that broader strata of society beyond kings/states and their officials are included in the analysis of socio-political power. The sociologist Michael Mann has analyzed the long-term development of Western societies from the Middle Ages until today by studying different types of networks: economic (production), military, political, and ideological (mainly the Church).[11] By analyzing politics as the intersection of different types of networks, this approach avoids a state bias and the problematic notion of sovereignty, and allows for sudden historical changes to be addressed while maintaining the focus on a long-term process. Inspired by Mann's analysis, the medieval historian Arnoud-Jan Bijsterveld has proposed that what is missing is a *social network*.[12] This omission is precisely what this project seeks to address.

Studying medieval politics as the actions of elite networks has been advocated by Gerd Althoff.[13] Here the focus on networks serves to highlight the issue of trust and the significance of implicit norms, what Althoff calls *Spielregeln* ("rules of the game") in medieval politics.[14] These are necessary ingredients for creating an atmosphere of mutual confidence among equal parties at the top level of society, which is a precondition for solving delicate political controversies in a way that allows all parties to save face and avoid dishonor. Althoff can to some extent be seen as a part of a German tradition called *Gruppenforschung* founded by scholars such as Gerd Tellenbach and Karl Schmid.[15] In this context one should also mention British scholars such as Susan Reynolds, who has interpreted medieval society as constituted of a myriad of "communities" based on horizontal bonds.[16] Reynolds's approach covers a wide social spectrum and offers an explanation of how the interaction between horizontal and vertical structures worked.

The concept of networks has received very little attention in Nordic medieval research, apart from a few notable exceptions: In *Kinship, Friends, and Power: A Study of the Elite's Political Culture in Twelfth-Century Denmark*, Lars Hermanson focused on elite groups in his analysis of twelfth-century Danish politics.[17] Moreover, Jón Viðar Sigurðsson has studied politics in Free State Iceland and high medieval Norway through the lens of friendship, which includes both horizontal and vertical relationships, of which he considers the latter to be the strongest and most important social bond.[18] And although network relations have often been contrasted with kinship, by highlighting the bilateral character of Nordic kinship, Lars Ivar Hansen has shown how strategic marriages could be used to create horizontal alliances.[19]

Compared to the case of patron-client relationships, the sources for studying Nordic networks are somewhat better, because networks operate more clearly on the top level of society.[20] This means that not only Icelandic sources are relevant for this topic, but also kings' sagas and chronicles which go into some detail about politics, such as Saxo Grammaticus's *Gesta Danorum* (c. 1208–16), Snorri Sturluson's *Heimskringla* (c. 1230), the anonymous *Morkinskinna* (c. 1220), and the contemporary kings' sagas *Sverris saga* (c. 1185–1200) and *Hákonar saga Hákonarsonar* (c. 1265).

A Multifunctional Relationship

In medieval Nordic societies, alliances were crucial. The Eddic poem *Hávamál* emphasized the importance of horizontal friendship. Forming a bond of friendship was as important as it was complicated, since it implied the creation of trust between parties that had no prior obligations towards one another.[21] As soon as a relationship had been established, complete trust and confidence were required and expected – although breaches of horizontal friendship bonds were far more common than *Hávamál* suggests. The establishment of horizontal bonds can be considered an alternative strategy to forming vertical bonds, since the focus was on equality and not hierarchy. However, both strategies served the same purpose – to protect and strengthen the position of those involved – and they also drew on the same vocabulary of friendship. Moreover, in practice the two bonds are often difficult to separate from one another, a theme we shall return to.

Horizontal bonds could fulfill many functions that we would normally consider to be separate fields. Economically, gift exchange was a prime mover of wealth in a society basically oriented towards self-sufficiency. The giving of gifts signaled reciprocity and equality, but it could also create a vertical relationship if the recipient did not reciprocate in kind. However, such a shift was undertaken with great caution, as it required the recipient to acknowledge his inferiority by transforming his debt into loyalty and service.[22] Network relations were also activated in primitive market trade. The earliest form of Nordic trade organization was the so-called *félag*, an enterprise in which equal parties shared both risk and profit.[23] Guilds played on the same sense of reciprocity, and fulfilled a number of functions in addition to their economic one, which included protecting their members, organizing feasts and religious rituals, and commemorating their deceased brothers.[24]

The notion of networks also transcended the earthly zone. Before Christianization, people's relationship to the gods was a bond of friendship, which was based on trust and its concrete manifestation in gifts and counter-gifts. Christianity reshaped the gift–counter-gift relationship with the divine powers, although vital aspects of reciprocity continued on in the new religion, particularly in the cult of saints.[25] Reciprocal agreements to pray for each other's souls were made not only between clerical communities, but also between, for instance, monastic brotherhoods and secular groups. This type of gift exchange served spiritual as well as pragmatic purposes, since a monastery's survival depended on its network. Material wealth was secured through alliances with patrons belonging to the local or regional elites who donated land and vowed to protect the monks or nuns in return for prayers and the promise of salvation.[26] In conflicts, monastic brother- or sisterhoods could utilize networks on the macro-level by seeking support from kings, bishops, or the Roman curia. Thus, these networks were both vertical and horizontal, and their spiritual, economic, and socio-political aspects overlapped.

Networks were variable in their outreach. For analytical purposes, it is possible to distinguish among elite networks operating on three different regional levels: local, "national" (inside the confines of the kingdom), and international. As a rule, members of the elite were leaders of localities or regions, where they collected material resources, were engaged as patrons (see previous chapter), and formed networks with other magnates. These were the persons whom the king or prince would have to placate in order to secure support beyond his own small demesne of direct control. He did this by granting them favors and promising them assistance and friendship in exchange for their support.

Elites engaged in networks on a "national" level within the kingdom. The retinue was decisive in creating networks on this level. In Norway, the *Law of the Retinue* (*Hirðskrá*) was written down in 1277, with oral precedents dating back to at least the time of King Sverre (r. 1179/84–1202).[27] Formally, membership within the monarchical organization granted access to a network which was defined through both a vertical relationship to the king and a horizontal community of the king's men who were subject to a common set of rules and norms. In royal ideology, as formulated in the Norwegian *King's Mirror* (*Konungs skuggsiá*) from c. 1250, the courtly culture nurtured a crude form of nationalism that was firmly tied to the royal retinue, with a negative attitude towards unattached magnates.[28] Yet in practice the crisscrossing obligations of bonds to the king and to fellow elites could be extremely complicated, as attested in the Sturlung Age in Iceland (c. 1220–64).

However, the "national" character of networks can easily be exaggerated, as elite networks tended to extend beyond national barriers. The obvious example of an international elite culture is of course the clerical culture, but it was also represented among the secular elites, in particular after the introduction of the concept of chivalry to the North. Although it was cultivated in close connection to the royal courts, this culture propagated a truly European elite ideal.[29] Another example is the widespread inter-Nordic marriages, which undermine any attempt to draw a firm internal/external divide during the so-called civil wars in Scandinavia.[30] Not only marriage alliances, but also political pacts and more general networks transcended these national borders. These intersecting elite networks made northern Europe into a tightly integrated area, where conflicts seem to "travel" between different regions in the period c. 1130–1260, often producing a pattern of strong realms with weak neighbors (with internal strife) whose roles were periodically reversed.[31] Elite networks beyond the borders of a kingdom were successfully activated in situations where sudden defeats were combined with mighty neighbors.

The Strength and Stability of Horizontal Bonds

How strong and stable were horizontal bonds in Nordic medieval societies? The establishment, maintenance, and dissolution of networks constituted the core of high medieval politics, both in Scandinavia and on the European continent. It should be emphasized that elite networks are of primary interest, not only because sources rarely allow us to venture beyond this level of medieval society, but also – and mainly – because a distinguishing mark of the upper classes is that they had the opportunity to engage in the formation and cultivation of horizontal relationships, which were formed (relatively) voluntarily.

The construction of horizontal bonds was based on long-term strategic planning; they took multiple possible outcomes into consideration and sometimes stretched over generations. These liaisons were often aimed at avoiding violent conflicts. Thus, networks functioned as "socio-political assurances," since their members could rely on support and protection in the event of a conflict breaking out. Networks contributed to predictability, making it possible to estimate one's own and one's opponent's resources, and to anticipate the actions of an enemy. Members of extensive networks had the advantage of choosing from among several allies – the choice of partner varying with the context of each situation.[32]

This implies that social networks were always ego-centered. Each individual had their own unique network which provided them with a variety of options. Overlapping bonds occasionally gave rise to conflicts of loyalty where temporary factions were framed within or between extensive networks. At other times, such overlapping could assist in reconciliation by putting a large number of people in an intermediate position favorable for seeking flexible compromises.[33]

There are some interesting divergences in the historiography as to how stable and enduring the networks at the top level of society in the Nordic area are assumed to be. Lars Hermanson's previously mentioned study on the elites' political culture in twelfth-century Denmark focused on collectives based on a mixture of kinship, marriage, friendship, and lordship, and held together by common interests. Yet once these networks were established, Hermanson believes, the expectation to support one's allies was strong. The groups were united and unified through rituals, such as gift-giving, oath-taking, feasting, and other ceremonies. In *Chieftains and Power in the Icelandic Commonwealth*, Jón Viðar Sigurðsson draws attention to networks operating at the top level of Icelandic Free State society, but unlike Hermanson, he does not see them as particularly stable. He underlines the fragile character of such bonds, stating that they could easily dissolve if the interests of the various parties began to diverge.[34]

How are we to interpret these different views on the stability of network relationships? One answer may be found in regional variations. Icelandic networks may have been less stable than Danish ones, and their politics accordingly more "open" and less susceptible to binding norms tying members of a group together. It could be that in a society without a king, politics were less restricted by formal or institutionalized norms, leaving larger scope for individual choices and interests than under the established monarchy in Denmark.

Another explanation for the difference in stability and durability of horizontal bonds might be that the scholars direct their arguments against different historiographical traditions. Lars Hermanson opposes the view that Danish politics should be analyzed in terms of formal institutions emanating from the kingdom and the Church. Hence, he highlights the importance and durability of networks as a counterweight to formal institutions.[35] Jón Viðar Sigurðsson, on the other hand, argues against the view that Free State Iceland was a "kinship society" in which familial relationships determined political actions. His emphasis on the strength of vertical friendship (and the weakness of horizontal social bonds) serves to counter this view (cf. patron-client relationships).[36]

Yet another answer relates to the diversity of various types of sources from different countries. Iceland and Denmark have very different sources. The most important Icelandic source referring to the period, the saga compilation called *Sturlunga saga*, was probably written by secular writers, in contrast to the main Danish source, Saxo Grammaticus's *Gesta Danorum*. The Icelandic material therefore contains fewer moral overtones than the Danish one. Icelandic sources also describe an earlier stage of society. For instance, in *Heimskringla* Snorri Sturluson wrote about Norwegian politics before the reign of King Sverre, whereas Saxo's work is clearly influenced by the strength of the Danish Valdemarine kingship and the clerical milieu linked to his patron Archbishop Absalon. These tendencies are of course not consistent, and may be not even relevant as an explanatory factor of the differences between Iceland and Denmark (Norway occupying a position towards the middle of these two extremes). However, the issue of source divergence cannot be ruled out as a factor contributing to the different images of elite networks in the North.

It is interesting to bring these various Nordic traditions together, since it can counter some of the biases that may arise when working within a single national tradition. These divergences underline the importance of differentiating between levels of analysis, as the fragility of individual networks should not divert attention from the fundamental issue that politics during the High Middle Ages, including the mobilization of armed forces, was totally dependent on social networks. While this created significant rivalry, it also served to stabilize monarchy in that it functioned as an umbrella accommodating differing factions and balancing them against one another. The rivalry between competing kings and their networks could be controlled as long as there was enough overlap between these networks and no king acted too aggressively against his opponents.[37]

Moreover, Hermanson and Sigurðsson agree on the large scope of opportunities available to persons operating in a number of networks, since the party "in the middle" took on a very powerful position as a potential mediator. The widespread occurrence of crisscrossing networks explains the flexibility with which conflicts could be resolved in these societies: There was always a substantial group interested in working out a compromise.

However, these properties also attest to the vulnerability of networks. If a network's key figure died, the network might collapse if the majority of the members had strong personal links to this key figure, but not to each other.[38] This is what happened when Margret Fredkulla, the queen of Denmark, died in the end of the 1120s. Margret was the daughter of the Swedish king Inge the Elder, and her siblings and nieces were married to Danish princes and princesses belonging to different branches of the royal family. It was probably thanks to this arrangement that King Niels (r. 1104–34) was able to rule Denmark for nearly thirty years. After Margret died a fierce feud erupted, which soon escalated into a civil war wherein different elite networks supported the various royal factions. The first phase of the internal conflicts ended with the death of King Niels and his son in 1134; the top governing layer of society had been removed and replaced by a new network of princes, bishops, and magnates led by King Erik Emune ("the Memorable," r. 1134–1137).[39] A similar large-scale shift in networks occurred when King Sverre conquered his royal opponent Magnus Erlingsson in 1184, whereupon a new network of magnates rose to power, although they created continuity by marrying the widows of their slain enemies. However, such radical shifts in networks were probably quite uncommon.

The stability of elite networks in high medieval Scandinavia was extremely variable. Some networks, such as the Hvide clan in Denmark and the Bjälbo clan in Sweden, were quite stable for many decades, and members of these networks held the most prominent offices in their respective regions. Other networks, such as the powerful Danish Trund clan, rapidly fell apart when their key figure, here Archbishop Eskil (b. 1134–77), was politically outmaneuvered, giving his opponents free rein to weed out the remaining members of his network.[40] A similar dynamic is discernible in thirteenth-century Iceland, where groups emanating from the kin-groups of the Sturlungar, Haukdælir, Ásbirningar, and Oddaverjar held prominent positions, even though alliances were often formed across kin-groups, and rivalries could follow along intra-familial lines.[41] In Norway, different factions competed for influence with juvenile kings during much of the twelfth century, in particular during the period 1130–60.[42] Accordingly, extensive networks dependent on key figures could be very unstable, whereas other types of networks show more durability. Is this a matter of coincidence, different network patterns, regional/"national" differences, or of various historiographical positions? These questions will form an important backdrop for the analyses in the present book.

The Tension Between Horizontal and Vertical Bonds

Tension is an undeniable aspect within all horizontal and vertical bonds. The perfect "egalitarian" relationship is an ideal rather than a reality, and the significance of "debt," which serves such an important role in holding patron-client relationships together, will always be present in networks, threatening to expose their inequality.[43] For instance, feasts were the perfect occasions for defining and redefining relationships of debt through symbolic means and gestures.[44]

The growth of royal power and the introduction of institutional forms of government, both supported by the Church, inevitably sharpened the tensions between horizontal and vertical bonds. The Scandinavian civil wars led to an increased need for securing trust and loyalty. For kings and claimants to the throne, horizontal bonds were as indispensable as they were costly. Kings therefore strove to free themselves from horizontal obligations, or to weaken them by transforming them into vertical relationships, and to position themselves in the center of the distribution of gifts and honors.[45] In order to achieve this, they used the same strategies as their counterparts elsewhere in Europe. One method was to transform the royal court into a more hierarchical organization by granting desirable offices to men of humble origins or foreigners with limited networks in order to create debts of gratitude.[46] Similarly, kings tried to infiltrate horizontal groups based on economic cooperation, such as the guilds, by giving them royal patronage. Furthermore, kings built on the Church organization and its officials for a variety of reasons. First, entrusting important commissions to clerics provided the monarchy with personal scribes who were skilled in writing, a medium which was used to enhance the prestige of royalty. Second, the Church dogma of service and obedience could be utilized to increase the appeal of service in the royal retinue by depicting it as honorable and exclusive. Third, clerics were involved in building up the cult of royal saints that lent the reigning royal family a uniquely sacral charisma. Finally, by emphasizing the legal aspect of kingship, the juridical apparatus could be activated in order to condemn opponents as traitors to the royal majesty or the kingdom (*lese-majesty*).[47]

All these strategies posed a threat not only to the secular elites, but also to princes who belonged to other branches of the royal family. In sources such as Saxo Grammaticus's *Gesta Danorum* and Snorri Sturluson's *Heimskringla*, tensions between the horizontal and vertical bonds within royal government are clearly visible. Both Saxo and Snorri believed that royal rule ought to be founded on consensus, implying that kings should rule in close cooperation with the elites. According to this view, kings who did not live up to the ideal of generosity were rightfully abandoned by their allies and condemned as greedy, self-serving tyrants. Saxo and Snorri also give a negative portrayal of kings who use lowborn men or foreigners at court or in the royal administrative organization. In their narratives, elite councilors live in constant fear of being replaced by members of other networks.[48]

The elites made use of multiple strategies in order to counteract the kings' attempts to liberate themselves from obligations linked to horizontal bonds. During the latter part of the twelfth century, elite networks were stabilized and consolidated through the monopolization of access to prominent offices and titles. In Sweden, the Bjälbo clan controlled important offices such as *jarl* (earl), bishop, and *lagman* (lawman) for several generations. While two Swedish royal families continuously struggled for the throne, the Bjälbo clan was more or less stable for nearly a century.[49] In Denmark, the Hvide clan gained a virtual monopoly on the most important offices in the realm, making their network more formal and public and associating themselves with a specific status in the royal organization and the Church hierarchy. Some members of the Hvide clan were connected to the Valdemarine family through patron-client relationships, such as fosterage and patronage.[50] These kinds of relationships were also common in Norway, where powerful magnates backed and invented successors to the throne in order to strengthen their own networks by making the royal candidates totally dependent on their support.[51] On a smaller scale, Scandinavian magnates used similar strategies as the members of royal families to enhance their network's reputation and exclusivity, for instance by establishing family monasteries (*Hausklöster*), erecting imposing churches, or giving generous donations to the Church.[52]

The Church played an ambiguous role in the relationship between kings and magnates. On the one hand, as seen previously, kings used the Church's personnel and its ideology to elevate the monarchy above elite networks. On the other hand, members of the secular elite almost exclusively filled the offices of bishops from the twelfth century onwards, and their double-edged loyalty gave them substantial opportunities for maneuvering. On an international level, they represented the papal Church. On the national level, they represented both their archbishopric and the Christian kingdom. On a local level, they acted as patrons for churches and monasteries. This meant that bishops did not solely represent the interests of the Church, but were also deeply concerned with maintaining their own networks. Thus, many bishops chose to work with the reigning kings when cooperation could benefit their own network; but in situations where kings threatened their interests, bishops possessed the power to oppose them.[53]

In older research such conflicts were often placed within a classical *regnum contra sacerdotium* framework, but recent research suggests that bishops acted as heads of networks in a way not dissimilar to secular elites or kings. Clerical dynasties were often created through "practical" ties of kinship (such as those with siblings, nephews, and second cousins), supplemented by bonds of friendship. These networks also had strong vertical components, partly due to the bishops' formal role as Church pastors, and partly to their more informal paternal role as "head of the clan." Thus, kings and bishops were similar in that both had informal networks and a hierarchical organization (based on officials) at their disposal. This meant that they shared a community of interests, but, equally, it could be a cause of conflict. For instance, in twelfth-century Denmark Bishop (later Archbishop) Absalon's network was closely intertwined with the royal family, reinforced by the fact that King Valdemar was Absalon's foster brother.[54]

Bishops can serve as an example of how problematic it is to distinguish between horizontal and vertical bonds, and between clerical and secular matters. In political matters, bishops seldom acted together as representatives of the Church, and conflicts among bishops were not unusual. For example, disputes between abbots and bishops were often complicated, and in some of these conflicts bishops were supported by the king, while abbots were backed up by bishops (or archbishops) reinforced by Rome.[55]

Formalization

In the previous chapter, changes in patron-client relationships were linked to the increased stratification of society ("compartmentalization") and to the increased use of writing within the administration ("explicitly defined legal rules"). Both these processes were related to the centralization of society in the High Middle Ages, and they had a similar impact on horizontal bonds, which tended to become more goal-oriented, as well as more specific in their scope and outreach. These two interrelated tendencies will be discussed in the following section, before we conclude with a discussion of the relationship between formalization and power in the Nordic area.

Generally, networks span the entire spectrum from informal, loose, and extensive connections to formalized, goal-oriented, and clearly defined relationships/pacts, but there was a tendency for the latter type to grow in importance during the period of study. More narrowly defined networks were often established with a particular objective and disintegrated or actively dissolved as soon as their goals had been achieved.

They could create bonds of trust that were stronger and less likely to overlap than extensive networks. Such groups can be labeled as factions, defined as "political action groups characterized as non-corporate and leadership-oriented."[56] Factions were created as the result of a community of interest, sometimes between partners who had no previous history of personal connections, and these alliances were more specifically goal-oriented than extensive networks. Factions could be formed as aggressive pacts designed for attack or as non-aggressive settlements where the main purpose was to obtain recognition from another party. They were often sealed by the creation of social bonds, such as pacts of friendship or marriage alliances. For instance, the Danish king Niels Svendsen established an aggressive pact with the Polish duke Boleslaw in opposition to their shared enemy, the Pomeranian prince Vartislaw. The pact was confirmed through a marriage between Boleslaw's daughter Rikissa and Niels's son Magnus.

Not all factions were public. Secret pacts involving a small number of sworn members are a recurring theme in both Nordic and west European sources. Secret pacts were often established in order to avoid accusations of disloyalty and thereby the risk of losing one's honor.[57] However, they operated on the margins of accepted behavior, since they evaded the principle of public declarations of intent that, for instance, separated openly committed homicide from secretly committed murder, and robbery from theft.[58] Accomplices in secret pacts could suffer severe consequences, especially if the strategy failed, but the great asset of such pacts was that they could alter the political landscape substantially when they succeeded. *The Legend of Knud Lavard* (c. 1170) and Saxo Grammaticus's *Gesta Danorum* reveal how a group of conspirators created a pact with the aim of murdering Duke Knud Lavard. The assassination succeeded, but the long-term result was the outbreak of an intense civil war in which the plotters lost their lives.[59] In Norway, the Island Beard rebellion of 1193–94 was initiated by some of King Sverre's closest followers. *Sverris saga* recounts the king's suspicion of their covert arrangements, but the rebels nevertheless succeeded in gathering a navy. When King Sverre defeated it, he showed no mercy to the rebel leaders, probably in retaliation for the secrecy surrounding the rebellion.[60] The largest battle in Icelandic history, at Örlygsstaðir in 1238, was fueled by a clandestine alliance between the enemies of Sturla Sighvatsson. Their legitimation for attacking Sturla in secret was that he had forced them to swear oaths of allegiance to him, something that was clearly considered inappropriate to ask of one's fellow chieftains.[61]

As we have observed, medieval society was not strictly divided into separate spheres, such as economics, politics, and religion. However, with the increasing differentiation/compartmentalization that took place during this period, networks were increasingly formed in order to serve more specific purposes. The main purpose of economic networks was to provide their members with material resources – an issue that is mainly treated in volume I of this series. As towns and market economies developed in the Scandinavian countries, a more specific economic sphere evolved. Commercial treaties were made between kings and towns, and guilds were established with the explicit purpose of regulating production and trade.[62]

However, even in these instances, economic functions did not provide the sole legitimation of such networks. For example, gift-giving, religious processions and rituals, as well as political issues, were all part of the guilds' tasks and duties. These horizontal fraternities were based on both fictive kinship relations and bonds of friendship, and their members were obliged to swear an oath in the name of the guild's patron saint in which they vowed to follow the rules of the brotherhood. Like other associations, such as the Scandinavian retinues (*hird*; see later in the chapter), the guilds had their own laws (sometimes called "the laws of friendship") which stipulated how members were to behave towards each other and towards non-members. These strict rules undoubtedly lent the guilds a level of stability that set them apart from other horizontal groups.[63]

Religious networks also became progressively more specialized in the period. The international networks of the Church and the monastic establishment were to a large extent based on correspondence, for instance between (or within) monastic orders, or between Scandinavian dignitaries and the Roman curia.[64] These intellectual networks were grounded in a common culture, based on the spirit of a learned and exclusive community. Latin was considered a sacred language, and a complete mastery of this tongue was a prerequisite for entrance into these communities.[65] Although these networks were held together by the written word, they utilized mechanisms of exchange that were similar to those of networks marked by face-to-face relationships. Trust/*fides* was a prerequisite for a harmonious and stable community, and in both kinds of networks the exchange of gifts and favors played an important role in generating trust. However, the items of exchange in religious networks were different. Letters were considered to be exclusive gifts serving the purpose of maintaining relationships. Another much-coveted gift among clerical groups were reciprocal agreements to pray for each other's souls. Such agreements were also made with secular groups, who were no less eager to participate in gift-exchanges relating to their salvation.[66]

In the political sphere, the most succinct expression of the increased formalization can be seen in the development of the royal retinue. In the Norwegian *Law of the Retinue* from 1277, the retinue was divided into various groups, from earl and duke through *lendir menn* and other hird leaders (*hirðstjóri*) down to ordinary retainers (*hirðmenn*), and the guests (*gestir*).[67] This hierarchy of offices required every member to swear separate oaths, and take on unique duties attached to their specific roles. Even though the degree of specification was still very rudimentary, the attention to specification is in itself a clear sign that a process of formalization was underway. The retainers had a hierarchical relationship to the king (see chapter 3 on patron-client relationships), but together they formed a community of equal members, and they had specific obligations towards one another. If they broke with these rules, they would be put on trial, and the case was to be investigated through designated procedures.[68]

How did power relations in the Nordic region affect the formation of elite networks in the High Middle Ages? The disintegration of the Danish empire of King Knud the Great in 1035 was followed by more than a century in which there existed a rough balance of power between the Norwegian, Danish, and Swedish kings. This gave the elites an "exit option" should they disagree with their lords, and maintaining relationships with various kings could also place them in a strong bargaining position. When the Hebridean king Jon Dungadsson was told that, according to the Bible, serving two masters was a sin, he responded that serving two masters was not a problem unless they were in conflict with one another.[69] This dynamic can be seen in numerous conflicts in *Morkinskinna*, where magnates seek out allies across the border when their own king acts too harshly.[70]

After Valdemar the Great managed to become sole king of Denmark in 1157, he gained a more secure grip on his territory, putting the remaining Scandinavian kingdoms under pressure. In Norway, the reigning earl and kingmaker, Erling Skakke, survived only by submitting to King Valdemar (Valdemar himself experienced similar pressure from Emperor Frederick Barbarossa).[71] The dominance of one power in Scandinavian politics reduced the opportunities for magnates to seek alternative patrons or networks should their current situation become unsatisfactory. As for patron-client relationships, the "shopping" of loyalty was no longer an option. Moreover, the increased level of hostility significantly contributed to the transformation of elite networks. This is most visible in Norway, where until c. 1160 factions were quite loosely put together, switching sides was frequent, and these groups had no particular territorial basis.[72] This reflected the fact that hostilities were rather low-scale. Families often had divided loyalties, and it was possible to occupy a position "in the middle" with connections to more than one faction.[73] After c. 1160 struggles intensified, resulting in more tightly knit groups with clearer territorial bases. This implied that people living in a particular region had little choice but to support the hegemonic faction residing there (see the concept of a "protection racket" in chapter 3 of this volume). For the elites, switching sides grew more difficult, and the position of mediator was almost exclusively reserved for the high clergy. For elite members, the question was increasingly "are you with us or against us?" – a middle ground no longer existed.[74]

Previous research has often summarized the political development of the High Middle Ages as a process of state formation. This is true insofar as that kings grew stronger in the period, and an increased formalization took place. However, this argument easily develops into a one-sided account that ignores the tensions between horizontal and vertical relationships that persisted throughout the Middle Ages; the main development being that the power sharing between king and aristocracy became more formalized through institutions such as the Council of the Realm. Moreover, the networks of the elites continued to extend beyond national borders, and increasingly so, strengthening a Nordic and, indeed, "European" elite identity.[75] Finally, state formation can be seen as one aspect of a broader process of formalization, which included a development towards specifying the terms of social obligations through the use of written agreements.[76]

Notes

1. Sandra Bell and Simon Coleman, "The Anthropology of Friendship: Enduring Themes and Future Possibilities," in *The Anthropology of Friendship*, ed. Sandra Bell and Simon Coleman (Oxford, 1999), 1–21 at 3–5; See also Julian A. Pitt-Rivers's way of classifying social relationships into "amiable relations vs. non-amiable social relationships." Julian A. Pitt-Rivers, "The Kith and the Kin," in *The Character of Kinship*, ed. Jack Goody (Cambridge, 1973), 89–106 at 96.
2. Walter W. Powell, "Neither Market nor Hierarchy: Network Forms of Organization," in *The Sociology of Organization: Classic, Contemporary and Critical Readings*, ed. Michael J. Handel (Madison, 2003), 315–30.
3. Niklas Luhman, *Trust and Power: Two Works* (Chichester, 1979); Marcel Mauss, *The Gift: The Form and Reason for Exchange in Archaic Societies* (London, 2002 [1925]).
4. Jeremy Boissevain, *Friends of Friends: Networks, Manipulators and Coalitions* (Oxford, 1978); Similarly, Fredrik Barth, *Political Leadership Among Swat Pathans* (London, 1965).
5. Donald Broady, "Nätverk och fält," in *Sociala nätverk och fält*, ed. Håkan Gunneriusson (Uppsala, 2002), 49–72; Einar Hreinsson and Tomas Nilson, "Nätverk Som Social Resurs," in *Nätverk Som Social Resurs: Historiska Exempel*, ed. Einar Hreinsson and Tomas Nilson (Lund, 2003), 7–30.
6. Bourdieu himself rejected social network analysis as a method for analyzing fields. Instead he recommended correspondence analysis. Wouter de Nooy, "Fields and Networks: Correspondence Analysis and Social Network Analysis in the Framework of Field Theory," *Poetics* 31 (2003): 305–27.
7. Hreinsson and Nilson, "Nätverk Som Social Resurs," 21. Regarding the development of network analysis see e.g. Stephen D. Berkowitz, *An Introduction to Structural Analysis: The Network Approach to Social Research* (Toronto, 1982); John Scott, *Social Network Analysis: A Handbook* (London, 1991).
8. Hreinsson and Nilson, "Nätverk Som Social Resurs," 23–28.
9. Ibid.
10. See e.g. Leos Müller, *The Merchant Houses of Stockholm, c. 1640–1800: A Comparative Study of Early-Modern Entrepreneurial Behaviour* (Uppsala, 1997).

11. Michael Mann, *The Sources of Social Power, Vol I: A History of Power from the Beginning to A.D. 1760* (Cambridge, 1986).
12. Arnoud-Jan Bijsterveld, "Aristocratic Identities and Power Strategies in Lower Lotharingia: The Case of the Rode Lineage (Eleventh and Twelfth Centuries)," in *La Lotharingie en question: identités, oppositions, intégration, Lotharingische Identitäten Im Spannungsfeld Zwischen Integrativen Und Partikularen Kräften. Actes Des 14es Journées Lotharingiennes. 10–13 Octobre 2006*, ed. Michel Margue and Hérold Pettiau (Luxembourg, 2006), 167–207.
13. Gerd Althoff, *Family, Friends and Followers: Political and Social Bonds in Medieval Europe* [*Verwandte, Freunde und Getreue: Zum politischen Stellenwert der Gruppenbindungen im früheren Mittelalter*], trans. Christopher Carroll (Cambridge, 2004).
14. Gerd Althoff, *Spielregeln der Politik im Mittelalter: Kommunikation in Frieden und Fehde* (Darmstadt, 1997).
15. Historians such as Hagen Keller and Otto Gerhard Oexle could also be seen as modern representatives of the German *Gruppenforschung*.
16. Susan Reynolds, *Kingdoms and Communities in Western Europe, 900–1300* (Oxford, 1984).
17. Lars Hermanson, *Släkt, vänner och makt: en studie av elitens politiska kultur i 1100-talets Danmark* (Gothenburg, 2000).
18. Jón Viðar Sigurðsson, *Viking Friendship: The Social Bond in Iceland and Norway, c. 900–1300* (Ithaca, NY, 2017); Jón Viðar Sigurðsson, *Chieftains and Power in the Icelandic Commonwealth* (Odense, 1999). Sverre Bagge and Hans Jacob Orning have also drawn attention to the importance of elite networks in understanding medieval politics. Sverre Bagge, *From Viking Stronghold to Christian Kingdom: State Formation in Norway, c. 900–1350* (Copenhagen, 2010); Hans Jacob Orning, *Unpredictability and Presence: Norwegian Kingship in the High Middle Ages* (Leiden, 2008).
19. Lars Ivar Hansen, "The Concept of Kinship According to the West Nordic Medieval Laws," in *How Nordic Are the Nordic Medieval Laws?* ed. Per Andersen, Ditlev Tamm, and Helle Vogt (Copenhagen, 2011), 177–206.
20. The Sagas of Icelanders provide so much information that it is possible to establish schemes and figures on the basis of the total number of persons and their interactions mentioned in the sagas. See contribution by Ralph Kenna and Pàdraig MacCarron in chapter 8 in this volume.
21. Jón Viðar Sigurðsson, "The Changing Role of Friendship in Iceland, c. 900–1300," in *Friendship and Social Networks in Scandinavia, c. 1000–1800*, ed. Jón Viðar Sigurðsson and Thomas Småberg (Turnhout, 2013), 43–64.
22. See Aaron Gurevich, "Wealth and Gift-Bestowal Among the Ancient Scandinavians," *Scandinavica* 7 (1968): 126–38; William I. Miller, "Gift, Sale, Payment, Raid: Case Studies in the Negotiation and Classification of Exchange in Medieval Iceland," *Speculum* 61 (1986): 18–50.
23. "Félag," KLNM, vol. 4, cols. 212–13.
24. Håkon Haugland, "Guilds as a Political Playground: The Ritual of the *Gildedrikk* in High and Late Medieval Scandinavia," in *Rituals, Performatives, and Political Order in Northern Europe, c. 650–1350*, ed. Wojtek Jezierski et al. (Turnhout, 2015), 321–57.
25. Lars Hermanson, *Bärande band: Vänskap, kärlek och brödraskap i det medeltida Nordeuropa, ca 1000–1200* (Lund, 2009), 206–24. See also articles in Ildar H. Garipzanov and Rosalind Bonté, *Conversion and Identity in the Viking Age* (Turnhout, 2014).
26. Arnoud-Jan A. Bijsterveld, *Do Ut Des: Gift Giving, Memoria, and Conflict Management in the Medieval Low Countries* (Hilversum, 2007); Barbara

H. Rosenwein, *To Be the Neighbor of Saint Peter: The Social Meaning of Cluny's Property,* 909–1049 (Ithaca, NY, 1989); Stephen D. White, *Custom, Kinship, and Gifts to Saints: The Laudatio Parentum in Western France, 1050–1150* (Chapel Hill, 1988).
27. H (see abbreviations).
28. Sverre Bagge, *The Political Thought of the King's Mirror* (Odense, 1987), 26–31, 174–85.
29. Joachim Bumke, *Courtly Culture: Literature and Society in the High Middle Ages* (Berkeley, 1991). On courtly influences in the Nordic area, see references in the previous chapter.
30. Hermanson, *Släkt, vänner och makt,* 92–176; Birgit Sawyer, "The 'Civil Wars' Revisited," *Historisk Tidsskrift* (N) 82, no. 1 (2003): 43–73.
31. Ole-Albert Rønning, "Beyond Borders: Material Support From Abroad in the Scandinavian Civil Wars, 1130–1180" (MA thesis, University of Oslo, 2015); Sören Döpker, "Forholdet mellom Det tysk-romerske riket og Danmark mellom 1125 og 1185" (MA thesis, University of Oslo, 2016).
32. Hermanson, *Släkt, vänner och makt,* 60, 105.
33. Ibid., 172–76; Sigurðsson, "The Changing Role of Friendship," 43–64.
34. Sigurðsson, *Chieftains and Power.*
35. Hermanson, *Släkt, vänner och makt,* 1–13.
36. Sigurðsson, "The Changing Role of Friendship," 43–64.
37. Hans Jacob Orning, "Borgerkrig og statsutvikling i Norge i middelalderen – en revurdering," *Historisk tidsskrift* (N) 93 (2014): 193–216; countered by Sverre Bagge, "Borgerkrig og statsutvikling – svar til Hans Jacob Orning," *Historisk tidsskrift* (N) 94 (2015): 91–110.
38. Cf. the different types of networks by Ralph Kenna and Pàdraig MacCarron in chapter 8.
39. Hermanson, *Släkt, vänner och makt,* 92–137.
40. Ibid., 233–41.
41. Jón Viðar Sigurðsson, *Frá goðorðum til ríkja: þróun goðavalds á 12. og 13. öld* (Reykjavík, 1989).
42. See the contribution by Ian Peter Grohse in chapter 13 in this volume.
43. Many of Powell's followers have dismissed the idea of any form of hierarchy within networks. However, Powell himself never denies the existence of internal, informal hierarchies within networks. On this debate se e.g. Hreinsson and Nilson, "Nätverk Som Social Resurs," 26–28.
44. See, for instance, contributions in part III in Jezierski et al., *Rituals, Performatives.*
45. Gerd Althoff, "Friendship and Political Order," in *Friendship in Medieval Europe,* ed. Julian Haseldine (Stroud, 1999), 91–105; Orning, *Unpredictability and Presence,* 69–108; Hermanson, *Bärande band,* 172.
46. Raphaëlle Schott, *Les conseillers au service de la reine Marguerite: étude prosopographique des Riksråd Nordiques (1375–1397)* (Paris, 2014); Herman Schück, "The Political System," in *The Cambridge History of Scandinavia, vol 1. Prehistory to 1520,* ed. Knut Helle (Cambridge, 2003), 679–709.
47. Lars Hermanson, "How to Legitimate Rebellion and Condemn Usurpation of the Crown: Discourses of Fidelity and Treason in the *Gesta Danorum* of Saxo Grammaticus," in *Disputing Strategies in Medieval Scandinavia,* ed. Kim Esmark et al. (Leiden, 2013), 107–42 at 127–32.
48. Hermanson, *Bärande band,* 69, 77. Cf. the importance of concepts such as *huld* (favor) in Althoff, *Spielregeln der politik,* 199–228, and *königsnähe* in Gerd Tellenbach, "From Carolingian Imperial Nobility to the German Estate of Imperial Princes," in *The Medieval Nobility: Studies of the Ruling Classes of France and Germany from the Sixth to the Twelfth Century,* ed. and trans. Timothy Reuter (Amsterdam, 1979), 203–31.

49. Sten Carlsson, "Folkungarna – en släktkonfederation," *Personhistorisk tidsskrift* 51 (1953): 73–105.
50. See the contribution by Kim Esmark in chapter 15 in this volume.
51. Jón Viðar Sigurðsson and Anne Irene Riisøy, *Norsk historie 800–1536. Frå krigerske bønder til lydige undersåttar* (Oslo, 2011), 99.
52. See the contribution by Kim Esmark in chapter 15 in this volume.
53. See the contribution by Sveinung Kasin Boye in chapter 16 in this volume.
54. Hermanson, *Släkt, vänner och makt*, 190–208. Absalon was the most prominent member of the Hvide-clan.
55. See the contribution by Sveinung Kasin Boye in chapter 16 in this volume.
56. Thomas J. Barfield, *The Dictionary of Anthropology* (Oxford, 1997), 110.
57. Lars Hermanson, "Holy Unbreakable Bonds: Oaths and Friendship in Western and Nordic European Societies, c. 900–1200," in Sigurðsson and Småberg, *Friendship and Social Networks*, 15–42; Robert Bartlett, *England Under the Norman and Angevin Kings, 1075–1225* (Oxford, 2000), 60–61.
58. William Ian Miller, *Bloodtaking and Peacemaking: Feud, Law and Society in Saga Iceland* (Chicago, 1990), 89.
59. Hermanson, *Släkt, vänner och makt*, 92–137; Kim Esmark, "Just Rituals: Masquerade, Manipulation, and Officializing Strategies in Saxo's *Gesta Danorum*," in *Rituals, Performatives*, 237–68 at 247–50.
60. Hans Jacob Orning, "Royal Anger Between Christian Doctrine and Practical Exigencies," *Collegium Medievale* 22 (2009): 35–54.
61. Sverrir Jakobsson, "The Process of State-Formation in Medieval Iceland," *Viator* 40, no. 2 (2009): 151–70.
62. See Christoph Anz, *Gilden im mittelalterlichen Skandinavien* (Göttingen, 1998); Lars Bisgaard, *De glemte alter: Gildernes religiøse rolle i senmiddelalderens Danmark* (Odense, 2001); Håkon Haugland, *Felleskap og brorskap: En komparativ undersøkelse av gildenes sociale, religiøse og rettslige rolle i et utvalg nordiske byer fra midten av 1200-tallet til reformasjonen* (Bergen, 2012).
63. Hermanson, *Bärande band*, 204.
64. Mia Münster-Swendsen, *Masters and Paragons: Learning, Power and the Formation of a European Academic Culture* (Copenhagen, 2004); Hermanson, *Bärande band*, 52–53, 58–60.
65. The role of the Church as a producer of an ideology which legitimated the positions of the elite will be treated in volume III of this series.
66. Hermanson, *Bärande band*, 65–67; Kim Esmark, "De hellige døde og den sociale orden. Relikviekult, ritualisering og symbolsk magt" (PhD diss., University of Roskilde, 2002); Patrick J. Geary, *Living with the Dead in the Middle Ages* (Ithaca, NY, 1994).
67. H (see abbreviations).
68. Hans Jacob Orning, "Det rettsantropologiske perspektivet og staten: konfliktløsning og byråkratisering i høymiddelalderen," in *Gaver, ritualer, konflikter: Et retsantropologisk perspektiv på nordisk middelalderhistorie*, ed. Hans Jacob Orning et al. (Oslo, 2010), 251–90; Bagge, *Viking Stronghold*, 233–43.
69. Orning, *Unpredictability and Presence*, 179–80.
70. Hans Jacob Orning, "Conflict and Social (Dis)order in Norway, c. 1030–1160," in *Disputing Strategies*, 45–82.
71. Orning, "Conflict and Social (Dis)order," 77–79.
72. Sverre Bagge, "The Structure of the Political Factions in the Internal Struggles of the Scandinavian Countries During the High Middle Ages," *Scandinavian Journal of History* 24 (1999): 299–320.
73. On mediators and arbitrators, see Jón Viðar Sigurðsson, "The Role of Arbitration in the Settlement of Disputes in Iceland *c.* 1000–1300," in *Law and*

Disputing in the Middle Ages, ed. Per Andersen et al. (Copenhagen, 2013), 123-35.
74. Bagge, "The Structure of the Political," 316-20; Orning, "Conflict and Social (Dis)order," 66-79.
75. On the effect of immigration on elite networks particularly in the late Middle Ages, see Erik Opsahl and Sølvi Sogner, *I kongenes tid, 900-1814* (Oslo, 2003); On a Nordic elite identity in the late Middle Ages, see Hans Jacob Orning, *The Reality of the Fantastic: The Magical, Geopolitical and Social Universe of Late Medieval Saga Manuscripts* (Odense, 2017).
76. Parallels could be drawn to the Holy Roman Empire during the twelfth century. See Althoff, "Friendship and Political Order," 100.

Dedicated Bibliography

Althoff, Gerd. *Spielregeln der Politik im Mittelalter: Kommunikation in Frieden und Fehde*. Darmstadt, 1997.
Althoff, Gerd. "Friendship and Political Order." In *Friendship in Medieval Europe*, edited by Julian Haseldine, 91-105. Stroud, 1999.
Althoff, Gerd. *Family, Friends and Followers: Political and Social Bonds in Medieval Europe* [*Verwandte, Freunde und Getreue: Zum politischen Stellenwert der Gruppenbindungen im früheren Mittelalter*]. Translated by Christopher Carroll. Cambridge, 2004.
Anz, Christoph. *Gilden im mittelalterlichen Skandinavien*. Göttingen, 1998.
Bagge, Sverre. *The Political Thought of the King's Mirror*. Odense, 1987.
Bagge, Sverre. "The Structure of the Political Factions in the Internal Struggles of the Scandinavian Countries During the High Middle Ages." *Scandinavian Journal of History* 24 (1999): 299-320.
Bagge, Sverre. *From Viking Stronghold to Christian Kingdom: State Formation in Norway, c. 900-1350*. Copenhagen, 2010.
Bagge, Sverre. "Borgerkrig og statsutvikling – svar til Hans Jacob Orning." *Historisk tidsskrift* (N) 94 (2015): 91-110.
Barfield, Thomas J. *The Dictionary of Anthropology*. Oxford, 1997.
Barth, Fredrik. *Political Leadership Among Swat Pathans*. London, 1965.
Bartlett, Robert. *England Under the Norman and Angevin Kings, 1075-1225*. Oxford, 2000.
Bell, Sandra, and Simon Coleman. "The Anthropology of Friendship: Enduring Themes and Future Possibilities." In *The Anthropology of Friendship*, edited by Sandra Bell and Simon Coleman, 1-21. Oxford, 1999.
Berkowitz, Stephen D. *An Introduction to Structural Analysis: The Network Approach to Social Research*. Toronto, 1982.
Bijsterveld, Arnoud-Jan A. "Aristocratic Identities and Power Strategies in Lower Lotharingia: The Case of the Rode Lineage (Eleventh and Twelfth Centuries)." In *La Lotharingie en question: identités, oppositions, intégration. Lotharingische Identitäten Im Spannungsfeld Zwischen Integrativen Und Partikularen Kräften. Actes Des 14es Journées Lotharingiennes. 10-13 Octobre 2006*, edited by M. Margue and H. Pettiau, 167-207. Luxembourg, 2006.
Bijsterveld, Arnoud-Jan A. *Do Ut Des: Gift Giving, Memoria, and Conflict Management in the Medieval Low Countries*. Hilversum, 2007.

Bisgaard, Lars. *De glemte altre: Gildernes religiøse rolle i senmiddelalderens Danmark*. Odense, 2001.

Boissevain, Jeremy. *Friends of Friends. Networks, Manipulators and Coalitions*. Oxford, 1978.

Broady, Donald. "Nätverk och fält." In *Sociala nätverk och fält*, edited by Håkan Gunneriusson, 49–72. Uppsala, 2002.

Bumke, Joachim. *Courtly Culture: Literature and Society in the High Middle Ages*. Berkeley, 1991.

Carlsson, Sten. "Folkungarna – en släktkonfederation." *Personhistorisk tidsskrift* 51 (1953): 73–105.

de Nooy, Wouter. "Fields and Networks: Correspondence Analysis and Social Network Analysis in the Framework of Field Theory." *Poetics* 31 (2003): 305–27.

Döpker, Sören. "Forholdet mellom Det tysk-romerske riket og Danmark mellom 1125 og 1185." MA thesis, University of Oslo, 2016.

Esmark, Kim. "De hellige døde og den sociale orden. Relikviekult, ritualisering og symbolsk magt: Anjou, 10.-12. Århundrede." PhD diss., University of Roskilde, 2002.

Esmark, Kim. "Just Rituals: Masquerade, Manipulation, and Officializing Strategies in Saxo's *Gesta Danorum*." In *Rituals, Performatives, and Political Order in Northern Europe, c. 650–1350*, edited by Wojtek Jezierski, Lars Hermanson, Hans Jacob Orning, and Thomas Småberg, 237–68. Turnhout, 2015.

Garipzanov, Ildar H., and Rosalind Bonté, eds. *Conversion and Identity in the Viking Age*. Turnhout, 2014.

Geary, Patrick J., ed. *Living with the Dead in the Middle Ages*. Ithaca, NY, 1994.

Gurevich, Aaron. "Wealth and Gift-Bestowal Among the Ancient Scandinavians." *Scandinavica* 7 (1968): 126–38.

Hansen, Lars Ivar. "The Concept of Kinship According to the West Nordic Medieval Laws." In *How Nordic Are the Nordic Medieval Laws?* edited by Per Andersen, Ditlev Tamm, and Helle Vogt, 177–206. Copenhagen, 2011.

Haugland, Håkon. *Felleskap og brorskap: En komparativ undersøkelse av gildenes sociale, religiøse og rettslige rolle i et utvalg nordiske byer fra midten av 1200-tallet til reformasjonen*. Bergen, 2012.

Haugland, Håkon. "Guilds as a Political Playground: The Ritual of the *Gildedrikk* in High and Late Medieval Scandinavia." In *Rituals, Performatives, and Political Order in Northern Europe, c. 650–1350*, edited by Wojtek Jezierski, 321–57. Turnhout, 2015.

Hermanson, Lars. *Släkt, vänner och makt: En studie av elitens politiska kultur i 1100-talets Danmark*. Gothenburg, 2000.

Hermanson, Lars. *Bärande band: Vänskap, kärlek och brödraskap i det medeltida Nordeuropa, ca 1000–1200*. Lund, 2009.

Hermanson, Lars. "Holy Unbreakable Bonds: Oaths and Friendship in Western and Nordic European Societies, c. 900–1200." In *Friendship and Social Networks in Scandinavia, c. 1000–1800*, edited by Jón Viðar Sigurðsson and Thomas Småberg, 15–42. Turnhout, 2013.

Hermanson, Lars. "How to Legitimate Rebellion and Condemn Usurpation of the Crown: Discourses of Fidelity and Treason in the *Gesta Danorum* of Saxo Grammaticus." In *Disputing Strategies in Medieval Scandinavia*, edited by

Kim Esmark, Lars Hermanson, Hans Jacob Orning, and Helle Vogt, 107–40. Leiden, 2013.
Hreinsson, Einar, and Tomas Nilson. "Nätverk Som Social Resurs." In *Nätverk Som Social Resurs: Historiska Exempel*, edited by Einar Hreinsson and Tomas Nilson, 7–30. Lund, 2003.
Jakobsson, Sverrir. "The Process of State-Formation in Medieval Iceland." *Viator* 40, no. 2 (2009): 151–70.
Luhman, Niklas. *Trust and Power: Two Works*. Chichester, 1979.
Mann, Michael. *The Sources of Social Power, Vol I: A History of Power from the Beginning to A.D. 1760*. Cambridge, 1986.
Mauss, Marcel. *The Gift: The Form and Reason for Exchange in Archaic Societies*. London, 2002 [1923].
Miller, William I. "Gift, Sale, Payment, Raid: Case Studies in the Negotiation and Classification of Exchange in Medieval Iceland." *Speculum* 61 (1986): 18–50.
Miller, William I. *Bloodtaking and Peacemaking: Feud, Law and Society in Saga Iceland*. Chicago, 1990.
Müller, Leos. *The Merchant Houses of Stockholm, c. 1640–1800: A Comparative Study of Early-Modern Entrepreneurial Behaviour*. Uppsala, 1997.
Münster-Swendsen, Mia. *Masters and Paragons: Learning, Power and the Formation of a European Academic Culture*. Copenhagen, 2004.
Opsahl, Erik, and Sølvi Sogner. *I kongenes tid, 900–1814. Norsk innvandringshistorie*, vol. B. 1. Oslo, 2003.
Orning, Hans Jacob. *Unpredictability and Presence: Norwegian Kingship in the High Middle Ages*. Translated by Alan Crozier. Leiden, 2008.
Orning, Hans Jacob. "Royal Anger Between Christian Doctrine and Practical Exigencies." *Collegium Medievale: Interdisciplinary Journal of Medieval Research* 22 (2009): 34–54.
Orning, Hans Jacob. "Det rettsantropologiske perspektivet og staten: Konfliktløsning og byråkratisering i høymiddelalderen." In *Gaver, ritualer og konflikter: Et rettsantropologisk perspektiv på nordisk middelalderhistorie*, edited by Hans Jacob Orning, Kim Esmark, and Lars Hermanson, 251–90. Oslo, 2010.
Orning, Hans Jacob. "Conflict and Social (Dis)order in Norway c. 1030–1160." In *Disputing Strategies in Medieval Scandinavia*, edited by Kim Esmark, Lars Hermanson, Hans Jacob Orning, and Helle Vogt, 45–82. Leiden, 2013.
Orning, Hans Jacob. "Borgerkrig og statsutvikling i Norge i middelalderen – en revurdering." *Historisk tidsskrift* (N) 93 (2014): 193–216.
Orning, Hans Jacob. *The Reality of the Fantastic: The Magical, Geopolitical and Social Universe of Late Medieval Saga Manuscripts*. Odense, 2017.
Pitt-Rivers, Julian A. "The Kith and the Kin." In *The Character of Kinship*, edited by Jack Goody, 89–106. Cambridge, 1973.
Powell, Walter W. "Neither Market nor Hierarchy: Network Forms of Organization." In *The Sociology of Organization: Classic, Contemporary and Critical Readings*, edited by Michael J. Handel, 315–30. Madison, 2003.
Reynolds, Susan. *Kingdoms and Communities in Western Europe, 900–1300*. Oxford, 1984.
Rønning, Ole-Albert. "Beyond Borders: Material Support from Abroad in the Scandinavian Civil Wars, 1130–1180." MA thesis, University of Oslo, 2015.
Rosenwein, Barbara H. *To Be the Neighbor of Saint Peter: The Social Meaning of Cluny's Property, 909–1049*. Ithaca, NY, 1989.

Sawyer, Birgit. "The 'Civil Wars' Revisited." *Historisk Tidsskrift* (N) 82, no. 1 (2003): 43–73.
Schott, Raphaëlle. "Les conseillers au service de la reine Marguerite: étude prosopographique des Riksråd Nordiques." PhD diss., University of Paris, 2014.
Schück, Herman. "The Political System." In *The Cambridge History of Scandinavia, Vol 1: Prehistory to 1520*, edited by Knut Helle, 679–709. Cambridge, 2003.
Scott, John. *Social Network Analysis: A Handbook*. London, 1991.
Sigurðsson, Jón Viðar. *Frá goðorðum til ríkja: Þróun goðavalds á 12. og 13. öld*. Reykjavík, 1989.
Sigurðsson, Jón Viðar. *Chieftains and Power in the Icelandic Commonwealth*. Translated by Jean Lundskær-Nielsen. Odense, 1999.
Sigurðsson, Jón Viðar, and Anne Irene Riisøy. *Norsk historie 800–1536: Frå krigerske bønder til lydige undersåttar*. Oslo, 2011.
Sigurðsson, Jón Viðar. "The Changing Role of Friendship in Iceland, c. 900–1300." In *Friendship and Social Networks in Scandinavia, c. 1000–1800*, edited by Jón Viðar Sigurðsson and Thomas Småberg, 43–64. Turnhout, 2013.
Sigurðsson, Jón Viðar. "The Role of Arbitration in the Settlement of Disputes in Iceland c. 1000–1300." In *Law and Disputing in the Middle Ages*, edited by Per Andersen, Kirsi Salonen, Helle Møller Sigh, and Helle Vogt, 123–35. Copenhagen, 2013.
Sigurðsson, Jón Viðar. *Viking Friendship: The Social Bond in Iceland and Norway, c. 900–1300*. Ithaca, NY, 2017.
Tellenbach, Gerd. "From Carolingian Imperial Nobility to the German Estate of Imperial Princes." In *The Medieval Nobility: Studies of the Ruling Classes of France and Germany from the Sixth to the Twelfth Century*, edited and translated by Timothy Reuter, 203–31. Amsterdam, 1979.
White, Stephen D. *Custom, Kinship, and Gifts to Saints: The Laudatio Parentum in Western France 1050–1150*. Chapel Hill, 1988.

Section II
Patterns of Networks

5 Aristocratic Networks During the Late Viking Age in the Light of Runic Inscriptions

Magnus Källström

"*These brothers were among the best men in the country and out in the host.*"

The quotation is taken from a runestone at Turinge church in Södermanland (Sö 338, Figure 5.1), which consists of a large block of sandstone that was built into the parish church during the Middle Ages. The stone commemorates a man called Torsten, and the inscription as well as the size of the stone show that we are dealing with a family from one of the highest levels in Viking Age society.

Except for runic inscriptions, there are not many written sources concerning Sweden in this period. In fact, our knowledge is restricted to two major works: Rimbert's biography of the missionary bishop Ansgar (*Vita Ansgarii*) from 865–76 and Adam of Bremen's chronicle about the history of the Hamburg-Bremen diocese (*Gesta Hammaburgensis ecclesiae pontificum*), written between 1073 and 1076.[1] All other historical records of Swedish conditions date from later periods. This can be compared with the number of runic inscriptions from the same period, which in Sweden amount to about 3,000, most of them carved in stone.

The inscriptions on Viking Age runestones are very homogeneous. The majority consist of memorial texts constructed using fixed, and rather simple, formulas, and they are normally quite brief. There are, however, two major benefits to this source material: The inscriptions are always more or less contemporary with the events and matters described in the texts, and since the material consists of stone monuments they have rarely been removed any great distance from the place where they were created.

In a discussion of bonds and social networks in the Viking Age, the runic evidence should not be excluded, though there are pitfalls and dangers hidden in the use of these sources.[2] The principal goal of this study is to examine the kinds of relations represented in the material and to determine how we can use this information to reach further conclusions. This will be done mainly with examples taken from the Swedish runic corpus.[3]

Figure 5.1 The runestone Sö 338 from Turinge church in Södermanland.
Photo: Harald Faith-Ell/ATA.

The Runestone Custom

The act of putting up a stone inscribed with runes is a uniquely Scandinavian phenomenon. With a few exceptions, such as in the British Isles, runestones are found only in Scandinavia – in Denmark, Sweden, and Norway. The earliest examples probably date back to the fifth century and the Roman Iron Age, but the majority belong to the transitional period between the Viking Age and the Middle Ages, from the end of the tenth century to the beginning of the twelfth century. From this short period, we know of 2,700 runic inscriptions in stone. These runestones are unevenly distributed across Scandinavia. About 270 are considered to be Danish (but about fifty of these are found in present-day Sweden and Germany), about seventy are Norwegian, and the remainder belong to Sweden. In the latter country runestones are found as far north as Jämtland, but the majority (about 1,500 inscriptions) are concentrated in central Sweden in the provinces of Södermanland and Uppland, situated on either side of Lake Mälar.

Most runestone texts relate to personal matters – usually the commemoration of a lost family member – but at the same time they are public monuments that were intended to be read by the people who passed by. Some runestones were placed at burial grounds, but in most cases they are found along the communication routes, close to roads and watercourses and often in places where these two elements met: at bridges and fords. These locations are usually not far from the hamlet where the person commemorated once resided.

There is no single accepted explanation for the dramatic increase in the production of commemorative runestones in the late tenth century. Some researchers have linked it to Viking activities abroad, whereas others believe that it is closely connected to Christianization and conversion. There is probably some truth in both theories. The Viking forays – the ferocious raids as well as the trading expeditions – must have resulted in a surplus of wealth that could be used for this kind of monument.[4] Moreover the late Viking Age runestones are often explicitly Christian, with Christian crosses and in some cases even Christian prayers, demonstrating a close connection with the conversion of Scandinavia.

It has also been suggested that the inscriptions are declarations of inheritance, which would explain why the relationships between the sponsors and the deceased are described in such detail. This approach has its main proponent in Birgit Sawyer, who also describes the runestone custom as a "symptom of crisis" in a period of both conversion and state formation.[5]

Not everyone had the capacity or the economic resources to produce a runic inscription in stone, and therefore the runestones must have been a way to show – or at least claim – importance and status in Viking Age society. Wooden monuments may have served the same purpose, and it is possible that some existed, but the medium of stone was clearly chosen for its durability and with the intention of preserving the written message.

The People Behind the Runic Texts

The runestone custom was probably originally restricted to the upper levels of society, the elites. In Denmark there are even several runic monuments commissioned by members of the royal families. These include the two Haddeby stones (DR 2, DR 4)[6] commemorating a King Sigtrygg in the 930s, as well as the two famous runestones in Jelling from the midtenth century, one raised by King Gorm (DR 41) and the other by his son Harald Bluetooth (DR 42).[7]

In Sweden this kind of royal involvement in the runestone tradition is almost unknown. The only exception is a rune-inscribed boulder at Hovgården on Adelsö (U 11, Figure 5.2), which according to the traditional interpretation was commissioned by a king's servant (ON *bryti*) in memory of himself and his wife and carved at the request of a man called Haakon. The latter is usually identified as the Swedish king Haakon Röde ("Håkon the Red"), who reigned for a short period in the 1070s.[8]

Figure 5.2 The rune-inscribed boulder U 11 at Hovgården in Adelsö parish, Uppland.

Photo: Magnus Källström.

Apart from this specific stone there is no clear evidence of Swedish royals being involved in the late runestone tradition, but there are several examples of the participation of families that must have belonged to the social level just below the king. A runestone from Bro church (U 617), for example, commemorates a man called Assur, who is said to have been the son of Haakon *jarl*. It is impossible to say whether this Haakon could be identified as one of the famous Norwegian earls with this name or an otherwise unknown Swedish earl,[9] although the latter is probably more likely.

Another possible example can be found on a couple of runestones (U 513, U 540) in the vicinity of Norrtälje in Uppland, which were commissioned by a family with a very special set of personal names. The brothers are called Anund, Erik, Haakon, Ingvar, and Ragnar, which in this combination express a special "royal" taste in naming. Some attempts have been made to connect them with members of the Swedish royal dynasty in the late Viking Age,[10] but it seems more likely that they were only related to them in some way or represented a family with royal ambitions (see later in the chapter).

The runestone custom was soon adopted by a broader class in the Viking Age society. About ten percent of the material mentions persons who have traveled abroad, but the majority of the inscriptions lack this kind of information, and must have been made in honor of those who stayed at home. The overall impression is that most of the "runestone families" in the eleventh century belonged to a class of settled yeomen who owned their own hamlets or villages and acted on a local level.

Vertical Relations: From the Chieftain to the Thrall

Vertical relations of the patron-client type are not so easy to discern in the runic corpus, but there are some examples connected to Viking raids or larger campaigns in foreign countries. A typical example is provided by the runestone Vs 18 from Berga in Skultuna parish in the province of Västmanland, with the following text:

Gunnaldr lēt rǣisa stǣin þennsa ǣftiʀ Gǣiʀfast, sun sinn, drǣng gōðan, ok vas farinn til Ænglands. Hialpi Guð sālu hans.

Gunnald had this stone raised in memory of Gerfast, his son, a good (young) man, and he had traveled to England. May God help his soul.

Gunnald also put up a second runestone (Vs 19) at the same spot as a memorial for his stepson Orm, who went eastwards with a chieftain named Ingvar and never returned. Even if the information given is very brief, it offers a glimpse of Swedish society in the first half of the eleventh century. The two sons traveled in different directions on Viking raids, and both lost their lives. No other relatives are mentioned in the texts. Naturally, there must have been a mother, although she might have been dead by this time, but probably no other siblings. From the texts we also learn that Gunnald was a Christian, since he invokes God to help the souls of his sons.

In isolation these memorial texts might not seem very informative, but the multitude of runic monuments from the period make it possible to put them in a wider context. The Viking raids on England as well as the campaign led by Ingvar are named on other runestones in Sweden, which enables us to map networks of individuals and identify groups with mutual interests in a certain region and sometimes over a wider area.

The reference to England is in this case too vague to be linked to a particular event, whereas Ingvar's campaign is well known. About twenty-five Swedish runestones commemorate men who traveled eastwards with him, and these stones are found in no fewer than four provinces in central Sweden.[11] Such a large number of memorials recording a single event is unparalleled in the whole runic corpus, which stresses the importance of Ingvar's campaign. In addition, Ingvar is one of the few local chieftains known from the runic inscriptions who can be identified in other sources. He has long been recognized as Yngvarr inn víðfǫrli, "Ingvarr the Far-traveled," who is the main character and hero of an Icelandic saga preserved in a manuscript from the fourteenth century.[12] Even though this fantastic saga does not convey much information of historical value, there is no doubt that it refers to the event recorded on Swedish runestones.

Other local chieftains were probably important in their time, but are now long forgotten. For instance, on a great erratic boulder at Kyrkstigen in Ed parish in Uppland (U 112), we can read about Ragnvald, who had been in Greece as a *liðs forungi* "leader of the host." It has been suggested that Ragnvald was engaged by the Byzantine emperor in Constantinople and that he probably held some prominent position in the famous Varangian Guard. Ragnvald commissioned this memorial himself, but the deeds of other local chieftains are mainly recorded by the people who followed them. About a man from Södermanland it is said that "He was westwards with Ulv, Haakon's son" (Sö 260). This Ulv was probably another famous chieftain at that time, but we have no further information about him.

A special issue concerns the words *drængʀ* and *þegn*, which often occur in laudatory epithets where the deceased is called *dræng gōðan, harða gōðan þegn* and the like. It is much debated whether these words in this connection are used as titles referring to men in royal service (comparable with the *þegnas* and *drengas* known from Old English) or if they just denote men of different ages and occupations, where a *drengr* is a young unmarried man seeking his fortune and *þegn* the designation for the mature farmer and yeoman.[13] The runic and skaldic evidence as presented and analyzed by Judith Jesch speaks for the latter explanation.[14] In the runic inscriptions the word *drængʀ* is often connected to warfare and travels abroad, which is not the case with *þegn*. Only two inscriptions in Södermanland that use this word (Sö 34, Sö 170) mention such voyages. On the other hand there exist place names in Sweden of the type *Tägneby* (ON **Þegnabýʀ* "village of the thegns") that indicate that *þegn* originally was a military term in Scandinavia. It is possible, however, that it had lost much of this meaning in the Viking Age and just denoted a free man in general.[15]

Other vertical relations are rarely visible in the runic texts, and servants and the like occur very seldom. One example is the *bryti* on the stone from Hovgården mentioned earlier. In this case the word is possibly used as a byname[16] – *Tōliʀ Bryti* – and can be translated as "bailiff" or "understeward." Since *Tōliʀ* was in the service of a king, he was probably a steward at a royal estate. The *bryti* was originally a foreman for the thralls, and it is known from later provincial laws that, despite his position on the farm or the estate, he could nevertheless be unfree.[17] The designation for "thrall" or the like does not occur on any Swedish runestone, but there are two instances (U 168, U 696) of someone commemorating his *løysi*, which must have been a counterpart to the Old West-Nordic *leysingi*, m. "freedman."[18]

A special problem is presented by the designations *fōstri* m. and *fōstra* f., which in Old West-Nordic had the respective meanings of "foster son, foster brother, foster father" and "foster daughter, foster mother." When these words occur on Swedish runestones they probably had the same meaning, but it is not impossible that they could mean something similar to Old Swedish *fostre*, which in the medieval provincial laws was also used to describe a "thrall that is born and brought up at home."[19]

Kinship and Other Horizontal Bonds: The Jarlabanke Family and Others

The horizontal bonds that might be identified in the runic corpus consist mainly of family relationships, and they normally concern the members of the nuclear family, although more distant relatives like grandfathers, uncles, and nephews may also be referred to. The most interesting relationships are probably those which involve marriage, since these are examples of connections between different families. It is reasonable to see these relationships as founded on a more or less equal basis, even though the real circumstances behind marriages may have varied significantly. The relationship between male members of different families is often expressed in the inscriptions by the word *māgʀ*, which is the same word as the modern Swedish *måg* "son-in-law." In the Viking Age this word had the wider denotation of "male relative by marriage" and could also mean "father-in-law" and "brother-in-law."

In a few inscriptions there are examples of horizontal relationships which are not based on kin, but on a mutual interest, such as *fēlagi*,[20] "partner, shareholder of any kind" and *gildi*,[21] "guild-brother." An interesting example of the former word is found on the runestone Sö 292, which reads: "Vigmar had this stone raised in memory of Järund, his relative by marriage and partner (*māg ok fēlaga sinn*) and the brother of." This Vigmar was not only related to Järund by one of their marriages but also through some kind of partnership. The concept of *vinr*, "friend," on the other hand is foreign to the vocabulary of the Viking Age memorial inscriptions. There is only one possible instance of this word, from the runestone U 620, and the context is unfortunately incomplete and unclear: "*dauðan vin*," "a dead friend."

Most people recorded in the runic material are known only from a single stone, but there are some individuals who reappear in different roles on different runestones, which enables us to map larger family networks. One such network is the Jarlabanke family from Uppland. About twenty monuments are linked to this family, which can be followed through at least four generations. The family tree is normally depicted as in Figure 5.3.

The earliest inscription connected to this family can be dated to the second quarter of the eleventh century, and the latest stones were raised

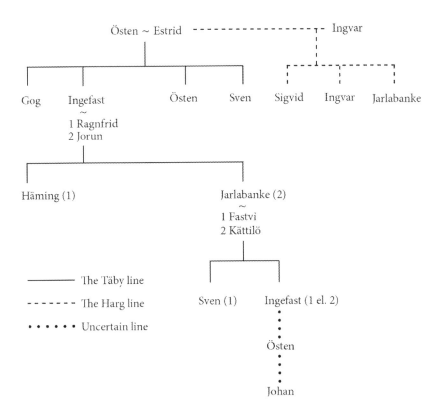

Figure 5.3 The family tree of the Jarlabanke family in Täby, Uppland, based on Gustavson and Selinge, 1988.

Aristocratic Networks in the Late Viking Age 87

towards the end of the same century. The leading figure (at least from our late perspective) is Jarlabanke Ingefastsson, who belongs to the third known generation. He is famous for raising runestones in memory of himself; no fewer than six such stones are known, and on five of them he also declares that he "alone owned the whole of Täby" (*æinn átti allan Tæby*). At the time Täby was only the name of a hamlet or village, but subsequently came to denote the entire medieval parish. From Jarlabanke's own stones we know that he built a lavish bridge "for his soul" close to his farm and that he also established an assembly place in the nearby parish of Vallentuna. The assembly place is mentioned on a large runestone found in Vallentuna church (U 212). The stone is inscribed on two faces, and on the reverse Jarlabanke also claims that he "owned alone the whole of this hundred" (*æinn átti allt hundari þetta*). The meaning of the last statement is much disputed and, unlike the proclamation on the front side that he "alone owned the whole of Täby," this can hardly mean that the whole hundred was in his private possession.[22]

Jarlabanke was married twice, first to Fastvi, who gave birth to his elder son, Sven, then to Kättilö, who was the mother of his second son, Ingefast, and who also outlived him. The family tree of the Jarlabanke clan shows that it was not uncommon for a family member to remarry when their husband or wife passed away. Jarlabanke's grandmother Estrid was married twice, and so too was his father Ingefast. This was probably the normal procedure in the late Viking Age, but it is rather unusual to be able to follow a family in the runestone material for more than two generations.

It has been stressed that there are very few women represented in this family and that they are only mentioned as mothers and wives, and never as daughters. Some have suggested that infanticide was practiced in this family,[23] but this seems unlikely. Parallels with other families reconstructed from the runic inscriptions show that the whole family is not always (or maybe never) represented in these texts. If the information about family relations in, for example, a couple of runic inscriptions from Bromma (U 57, U 58) in Uppland is taken literally, we get a family of three generations consisting of only men!

There must have been several daughters in the Jarlabanke family in the four generations documented in the runic inscriptions, and they were probably married to men from other prominent families in the area. Since daughters are not mentioned on the family's own runestones, these connections are now impossible to trace. At the same time, we know of other family networks where daughters played an important role, for example in the family known from a long inscription on a rock at Hillersjö in Hilleshög parish (U 29, Figure 5.4). This unique inscription enables us to follow the relationships between several families and observe how property and estates were transferred from one family to another through marriage and inheritance.

In the inscription we are told that a man named Germund married Gerlög when she was a maiden and that they had a son who later died.

88 *Magnus Källström*

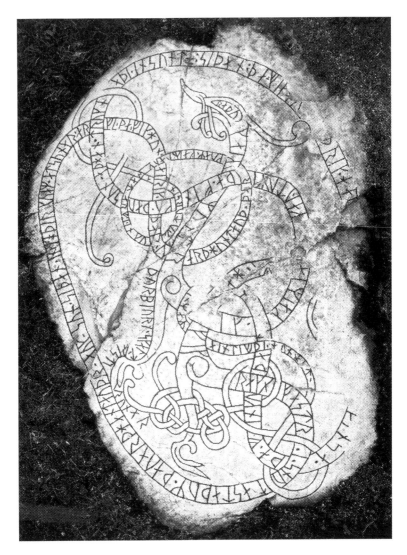

Figure 5.4 The rock-inscription U 29 at Hillersjö in Hilleshög parish, Uppland.
Photo: Harald Faith-Ell/ATA.

Unfortunately, Germund drowned and Gerlög then married a man called Gudrik, who may have owned the hamlet where the carving is situated. Gudrik and Gerlög had several children, but only a daughter named Inga survived. She was married to Ragnfast, who lived in Snottsta in Markim, about thirty kilometers north-east of Hilleshög. They had a son together, but then Ragnfast died and their son inherited his father's property. When this (probably underage) son passed away, Inga inherited from her child.

Inga married a man called Erik before her own death. Then Gerlög inherited her daughter's property, which meant that she was now in possession of three different estates that had originally belonged to three different families. The reason why this long story was hewn into the rock is probably that it was unusual and remarkable, but it is also a good illustration of how networks were established through marriage between leading families.

Detecting Networks Through Rune Carvers

Another way of mapping networks is by analyzing those who made the stones, namely the rune carvers. Unfortunately, we are seldom able to determine the relationship between the rune carver and the sponsor of the stone. In a few cases there is direct evidence that the rune carver belonged to the same class or even the same family as the sponsor. An example is Ulv in Borresta, one of the few carvers for which enough information is available in the runic inscriptions to write something like a biography.[24] We know not only where he lived, but also that he probably inherited this hamlet from his uncle Onäm; that he went to England on three occasions; and that he had a share in three Danegelds under three different chieftains. Ulv signed only one surviving runestone (U 161), at Risbyle in Täby parish, which reads: "Ulv in Borresta cut in memory of Ulv in Skålhamra, his good *māgR*. Ulvkell had the stone cut." The word *māgR* "relative through marriage" shows that Ulv in Borresta was from the same family as the wife of Ulv in Skålhamra. She was named Gyrid and probably was the daughter of his uncle Onäm. Gyrid is also known from two other runestones commissioned by the same family, U 100 and U 226.

Ulv's carvings number less than ten, and they are restricted to a very limited area in south-east Uppland that measures about twenty square kilometers (see Map 5.1). Three of his stones were put up in memory of Ulv in Skålhamra (U 160, U 225, U 226), but the alleged family connection on a fourth stone (U 328) should probably be dismissed.[25] In the rest of his inscriptions there are no obvious links between the carver and the sponsors of the runestones, but it should be noted that all the stones are located in the area between the hamlets owned by Ulv in Borresta and his kinsman Ulv in Skålhamra.

Occasionally, the distribution of the runic inscriptions by a certain rune carver might be used to trace relations between different groups of sponsors. This is the case, for example, with Torbjörn Skald ("Torbjörn the Poet"), who is responsible for twelve known runic monuments in the Mälar region.[26] His carvings show a very specific distribution and are found in two rather widely separated areas: one with its center on some of the larger islands in Lake Mälar and one in the vicinity of Norrtälje in the eastern part of the Upplandic mainland close to an inlet of the Baltic Sea (see Map 5.2).

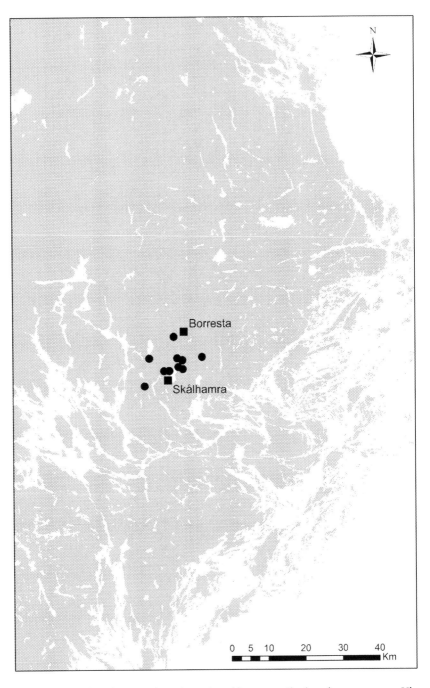

Map 5.1 The distribution of carvings signed by or ascribed to the rune carver Ulv in Borresta. The positions of the two hamlets, Borresta and Skålhamra, are also marked on the map.

Source: Map by Laila Kitzler Åhfeldt

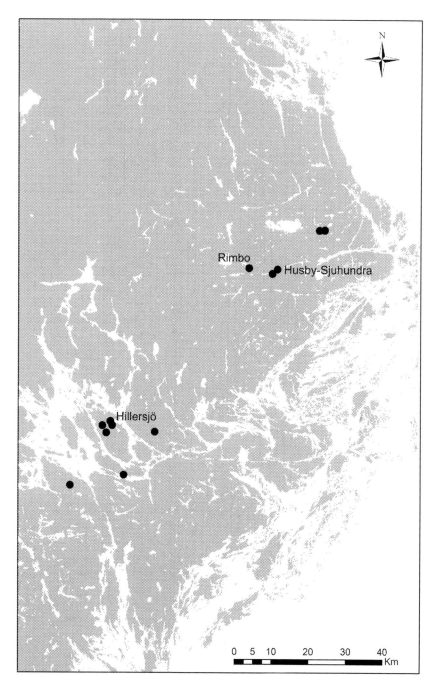

Map 5.2 The distribution of rune carvings by the rune carver Torbjörn Skald.
Source: Map by Laila Kitzler Åhfeldt.

Two of Torbjörn Skald's carvings have already been touched upon in this chapter. One is found in Rimbo church (U 513) and was raised by the four brothers Anund, Erik, Haakon, and Ingvar in memory of their brother Ragnar. The second is a long inscription on a rock at Hillersjö in Hilleshög parish (U 29) that tells the story of Gerlög and Inga. Both these inscriptions seem to have had a connection with the highest social strata in the area at the time. The family from Rimbo is also documented on a second runestone at Husby-Sjuhundra (formerly Husby-Lyhundra) church (U 540), which was set up by Erik, Haakon, Ingvar, and a woman, Ragnhild, in memory of a man who lost his life in Greece. The name of the deceased has broken away, but since Anund from the Rimbo inscription is missing, the stone is probably dedicated to him.

It is very unusual to find the works of a single rune carver distributed in two different areas, as is the case with Torbjörn Skald, and probably the explanation can be found among his sponsors. Inga's last husband was named Erik, and it is not unlikely that he was the second eldest brother in the Rimbo-Husby family. The name *Erik* is very rare in the Viking Age runic inscriptions, and the highest number of possible name-bearers known from this material in Uppland is only four, which lends support to the idea that it might be the same Erik.

The Turinge Stone: Landowners and East-Travelers

With this background, it is time to return to the runestone from Turinge church (Sö 338), situated seven kilometers west of the town of Södertälje in Södermanland. The stone consists of a large rectangular block of sandstone, two meters high and 1.2 meters wide, and bears a long inscription with more than 200 runes. The stone has been known since the seventeenth century and was built into the east wall of a church. When the stone was removed from the wall in the eighteenth century it was discovered that there were also a couple of lines of runes along the narrow right side. On the front face of the stone there is a large, elaborate cross (Figure 5.1). This is unquestionably a high-status monument, and many of the phenomena discussed earlier in this chapter are also present here.

The first part of the inscription consists of a memorial formula and runs (mainly following the interpretation by Elias Wessén in SRI 3, 325):

Kætill ok Biorn þæiR ræistu stæin þenna at Þorstæin, faður sinn, Anundr at broður sinn ok huskarlaR æftiR(?) iafna, Kætiløy at boanda sinn.

Kättil and Björn they raised this stone in memory of Torsten, their father, Anund in memory of his brother and the retainers in memory(?) of the just one(?), Kättilö in memory of her husband.[27]

The impressive stone was thus raised in memory of a man called Torsten, not only by his sons, but also by his brother, his retainers, and his wife. In the last part of the inscription there is a long section composed in verse, where we get a great deal of valuable information about his deeds. This part of the inscription also concerns his brother Anund:

Brø̄ðr vaʀu þæiʀ	bæztra manna,
ā landi	ok ī liði uti,
heldu sina	huskarla vel.
Hann fioll ī orrustu	austr ī Garðum,
liðs forungi,	landmanna bæztr.

The brothers were	among the best men
in the country	and out in the host
treated their	retainers well.
He fell in action	east in Garðariki,
The host's captain,	of "land-men" the best.

Here we are told that the brothers were among the best men *ā landi* (which can mean "in the country" as well as "on land") and when they were out in the host (*ī liði ūti*). It has been argued that the use of past tense in this clause excludes Anund from the statement and that it must refer to a second, otherwise unknown brother. This seems like an unnecessary assumption, since the clause might allude to a previous situation when the brothers acted together as a pair.

The word *lið* means "host, folk, people." In this case, when it is combined with the adverb *ūti* and opposed to the preceding *ā landi*, it has been suggested that it probably refers to a ship-borne troop.[28] In many runic inscriptions the word *lið* occurs in combination with a personal name in the genitive, such as *ī Ingvars lið* "Ingvar's host."

In the third pair of lines it is said that they treated their retainers well (*heldu sina huskarla vel*). The word *huskarl* occurs in two inscriptions from Uppland.[29] In U 330 – one of the stones that Inga put up in memory of her husband Ragnfast in Snottsta – it is mentioned that "Assur was his *huskarl*." Not far from this stone in Orkesta church is a runestone (U 335) dedicated to a man named Hära, who was the *huskarl* of Sigröd. From the stone at Snottsta it is evident that Ragnfast had only one *huskarl* in his household. Probably he was something like a bailiff, which might be the reason Inga included him on one of her husband's memorial stones. In the inscription on the Turinge stone the word *huskarl* appears twice in the plural, and this is the only known runic inscription where the plural form of this word is used. These men were probably not only part of the household but also members of the host mentioned later in the inscription. This indicates that the persons on the Turinge stone belonged to a social setting that might have been rather different from the one we encounter in the majority of runic inscriptions from the Mälar area.

In the last part of the inscription it is said that Torsten fell in action eastwards in *Garðar*, which corresponds to *Garðaríki*, "Russia" in West-Norse sources.[30] References to this area occur in at least four Swedish runic inscriptions, of which two are a little more informative than simply telling us that someone lost his life there.[31] On the Gårdby stone (Öl 28) from Öland is said about the deceased that *Halfborinn, brōðiʀ hans, sitr Garðum* "Halvboren, his brother, resides in Garðariki," whereas a rock inscription at Veda in Angarn parish (U 209) in Uppland proclaims that a man named Torsten (or his son Ärinmund) *køypti þennsa bȳ ok aflaði austr ī Garðum* "bought this hamlet and raised money [to buy it] eastwards in Garðariki." It seems reasonable to assume that both Halvboren and Torsten (or Ärinmund) were some kind of mercenary soldiers, probably in the service of the grand prince of Rus.

In the last line on the Turinge stone, Torsten is given the epithet *liðs forungi*, "the leader of the host." This is exactly the same phrase as is recorded on the large rune-inscribed boulder at Kyrkstigen (U 112) mentioned earlier. In this case it denotes a man who probably held a position in the guard of the Byzantine emperor. Nothing prevents us from assuming that Torsten might have been connected to the grand prince of Rus in a similar way, but it must be stressed that this suggestion is only based on circumstantial evidence.

The final line also includes an expression in which Torsten is praised as *landmanna bæztr* "the best of *landmænnr*." The same word is also attested on two other runestones. On the Skivum stone (DR 133) from North Jutland, where it is said about the deceased that "he was the best of 'land-men' in Denmark and first" (*Hann vas landmanna bæztr i Danmarku ok fyrstr*). The second example is found on the nearly four-meter-high runestone from All Saint's Church in Lund (DR 314) in Scania, where the two deceased brothers are called "good land-men" (acc. *landmænnr gōða*).

The exact meaning of the word *landmaðr* is disputed. The word is known from Old West-Nordic sources, where it is synonymous with the word *landsmaðr* and means "inhabitant in the country." Elias Wessén suggests that the phrase *liðs forungi, landmanna bæztr* on the Turinge stone has roughly the same meaning as *bæztra manna, ā landi ok ī liði uti* earlier in the inscription and that *landmanna bæztr* means "the best of men in the country."[32] This view is challenged by K. G. Ljunggren, who asserts a meaning closer to Old West-Nordic *lendr maðr*, "a 'landed man,' someone who holds land or emoluments from the king."[33] His main argument is that the stones where this expression occurs are all high-status monuments, and therefore *landmaðr* must have a wider meaning than just "inhabitant in the country." On the Turinge stone it is not necessary that the phrase *landmanna bæztr* have the same sense as *bæztra manna, ā landi* as Wessén suggested, and due to variation one would here expect a different meaning. It does not follow that a *landmaðr* must be the same as a *lendr maðr*, which is a different formation with an adjective, not a noun as the first element.

The best parallel to *landmænnr* is probably the phrase *landburniʀ mænnr* found on another runestone in Södermanland (Sö 54 Bjudby, Blacksta parish). This stone is also a high-status monument, three meters high, and possibly erected close to an old assembly place. Three brothers have commemorated two of their other brothers and claim that they "were all Vikings' sons." Then follows the clause *Landburniʀ mænnr lētu rētta stæin* " 'Land-born' men had the stone set up." In the glossary to *Södermanlands runinskrifter*, two different translations are given: "born to an estate" and "born of a family of liegemen = Icelandic *lendrborinn*."[34] It has also been suggested that *landborinn* simply meant "born in the country," but this seems rather unlikely in this context. The closest translation is "born to land," which means that the brothers had a right to land by birth and that this "land" referred to something more extensive than just the territory of a hamlet or a village. It is tempting to assume that *landmaðr* had a similar meaning. According to Judith Jesch the translation of "landholders" seems most appropriate for the Turinge stone.[35]

The runestone has been part of the church in Turinge since the Middle Ages, and we have no knowledge of its original position or where the associated family lived. Considering the size of the stone, it was probably not moved any great distance. Maybe it was originally placed on the same site as the later church, which might have been some kind of meeting place for the district, while the family could have resided some distance away. Recently Sten Tesch has suggested a possible connection between the runestone and a rich and spectacular boat grave from the middle of the eleventh century excavated at the hamlet of Årby about two kilometers east of the church.[36] His main argument is that the boat grave and the Turinge stone are the only phenomena in the vicinity that point to residents of higher status, whereas large mounds or larger cemeteries are missing.

Tightening the Net: The Turinge Family in the Local Context

The personal names that occur on the Turinge stone are all common and therefore cannot be linked to other runestones with any confidence. By identifying the carver behind the stone, however, it is possible to place this family in a wider context. The stone is not signed, but the characteristic ornamentation shows that it must be the work of Östen, an often-overlooked rune carver.[37] He is mainly known from three carvings in the town of Södertälje cut into a cliff face adjacent to the old main road to Turinge (Sö 311–313). In the inscriptions, a certain Holmfast commemorates his father and mother not only by naming them with the rune carvings, but also by noting that he built bridges and cleared roads in their memory.

Östen is responsible for at least three other carvings in the vicinity. Two of these are cut into steep cliffs and are situated on each side of an inlet of Lake Mälar north of Södertälje, at Kiholm (Sö 344) and Vitsand (discovered in 2007).[38] Both face the water and are definitely intended to be seen from out on the lake. A third rune carving by Östen was recently identified at Björkö village on Björkö (the site of the former town of Birka), when ten sandstone fragments that were thought to be the remains of at least three different runestones (U 6–8) were shown to be parts of a single runestone.[39] The original position of this stone is unknown, but it is not impossible that it once faced the water and functioned as some kind of landmark for the village's harbor.

Östen had several different clients, but, as with the rune carver Torbjörn Skald, it is likely that they were connected to each other. It is not impossible, for example, that the carving at Vitsand was commissioned by the same Holmfast who sponsored the inscriptions in Södertälje (the name is partly damaged). In this inscription there is also the male name *Iafna* (nom.) that might have something to do with the slightly mysterious designation *iafna* (acc.) "the just one(?)" on the Turinge stone, though the words cannot be identical for grammatical reasons.[40] The carving at Kiholm (Sö 344) is dedicated to a man named Björn, and one of the sponsors on the Björkö stone (U 6) is called Torbjörn. Both these names occur on the Turinge stone, but since they are among the most common names in Viking Age runic inscriptions, it is impossible to tell whether they refer to the same individuals.

From one of the carvings in Södertälje (Sö 312) we learn that Holmfast's father lived in a hamlet called Näsby, which was situated west of Södertälje. It is possible that Holmfast also had interests in another hamlet from which there are accounts of a now-lost runestone (Sö 310) with an inscription including this name. Both these settlements are situated close to the old main road from Södertälje to Turinge.

The spatial distribution of Östen's carvings creates a very interesting picture (see Map 5.3). They are all found along two important communication routes: the north-east watercourse from Björkö to the Baltic Sea and the land route from today's Stockholm westwards towards the southern provinces. This connects Björkö hamlet, as well as Turinge, with the place that later became the medieval town of Tälje (Södertälje). It looks as if Holmfast had a special interest in this place, and possibly his efforts to build bridges and clear roads were a part of a larger campaign to establish Tälje as a trans-shipment point or a trading center. Maybe there were even ideas of creating some kind of successor to the long-abandoned town of Birka on Björkö.

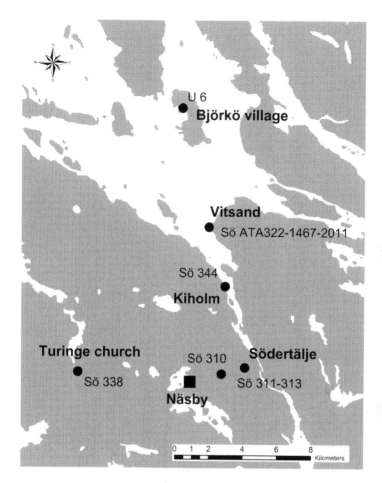

Map 5.3 The distribution of rune carvings by the rune master Östen. Näsby is the hamlet owned by Holmfast, one of his main sponsors.
Source: Map by Laila Kitzler Åhfeldt.

The persons known from the Turinge stone are not overtly visible in this process, but it is not unlikely that they were a part of it. By analyzing the ornamentation of Östen's carvings it is also possible to estimate the time of these events as the decades around 1070.[41] This date happens to correspond to the famous description of the land route from Scania to Sigtuna found in chapter 29 in the fourth book of Adam of Bremen. Maybe it is more than a coincidence that Tälje and Birka are among the few place names along this route explicitly mentioned in this text.

Closing Remarks and a Possible Link to "Written History"

The inscriptions discussed earlier offer us an interesting insight into relations and connections between different families and individuals in central Sweden in the second half of the eleventh century. Using the small pieces of information in the inscriptions, combined with the distribution of the monuments and their design, it is possible to get a glimpse of some of the most important actors in this society. What have been preserved are, unsurprisingly, only small fragments of relations and events in this area in the late Viking Age, but they can be used as good examples of how the society was organized on different levels. As pointed out earlier, the runic evidence has the virtue of being more or less contemporary with the conditions described in the texts. At the same time, it is very difficult to link this material to other historical sources, since those concerning this part of Scandinavia in the period are very rare.

There are, however, a few paragraphs in the writings of Adam of Bremen that might be of interest in this context. In his third book (chapter 53) Adam describes the situation after the death of King Stenkil (around 1066) when two kings named Erik struggled for royal power; he says that in this battle both kings and all of the Swedish nobility were killed. A scholium to this passage (scholium 84) adds that after the deaths of the two kings, Stenkil's son Halsten was made king, but was soon expelled. Then they called for "Anund from Russia" to become their ruler. After he had been deposed, the Swedes elected a man named "Hakon" as their king.[42]

We recognize some of the personal names in these passages from the runic inscriptions discussed earlier: *Erik*, *Anund*, and *Haakon*. There have been attempts to link these persons to the runic material, but with unconvincing results.[43] That the "Hakon" who was elected as king after Halsten's death is the Haakon on the rune-inscribed boulder U 11 at Hovgården is, however, accepted by most scholars.[44]

In light of the material presented in this chapter it might also be interesting to discuss the two kings called Erik as well as "Anund from Russia," who was called in to replace King Halsten. As we saw earlier, *Erik* is not a very common name in the Viking Age runic inscriptions from the Mälar area in the eleventh century. If I am correct in the identification of Erik on U 513 and U 540 as Inga's second husband, the number of individuals recorded in this material can be reduced to three. One was a rune carver active in the western part of Uppland in the first half of the eleventh century;[45] the second, a person named on a runestone at Vaksala church (U 960),[46] who, to judge from the ornamentation of the stone, must have died before the mid-eleventh century. We are then left with only one candidate – Erik from Rimbo/Husby, who probably married Inga from Hillersjö. This Erik must have been a very prominent man, though we know nothing of his deeds. From a chronological point of view, it is quite reasonable to assume that he was in fact one of the "kings" with the name Erik who struggled for the Swedish crown in the 1070s. Who the other was is impossible to say.

Unlike the name *Erik*, *Anund* was a very common name in the eleventh century. In the Mälar area it is recorded in about fifty runic inscriptions, although this name is rather rare in other Swedish provinces except for Östergötland. It is therefore likely that "Anund from Russia" had his roots in central Sweden. To choose one Anund out of fifty candidates is impossible, but at least one can be excluded, namely the Anund who was the brother of Erik in Rimbo/Husby. From the runestone in Husby-Sjuhundra church (U 540) – if the reconstruction of the inscription is correct – we learn that he lost his life in Greece at an earlier point.[47]

In this case it might be fruitful to look at the Turinge stone once again. Torsten, who fell in battle eastwards in Garðariki, had a brother named Anund. He is one of the sponsors behind the stone and, as claimed previously, is probably included in the clause that states that "these brothers were the best men in the land and out in the host." Certainly he took part in the same battles in the east as his brother, but returned home safely. If the classification of the ornamentation of the Turinge stone is correct, this would have taken place sometime around 1070. It is therefore not unlikely that the Anund on the Turinge stone might be Adam's "Anund from Russia." With the information about the social setting found in this inscription, he is in fact the best candidate.

Notes

1. *Quellen des 9. und 11. Jahrhunderts zur Geschichte des Hamburgischen Kirche und des Reiches*, ed. Werner Trillmich, Rudolf Buchner, and Volker Scior (Darmstadt, 2000).
2. Concerning runestones as sources for social history, cf. also Henrik Williams, "Runstenarnas sociala dimension," *Futhark: International Journal of Runic Studies* 4 (2013): 61–76.
3. The runic inscriptions from Sweden are published in SRI (see abbreviations). The texts are here given in "runic Swedish" and are mainly based on the transcriptions in the corpus editions, but I have added designations for vowel length.
4. Sven B. F. Jansson, *Runes in Sweden* (Stockholm, 1987), 38; cf. Birgit Sawyer, *The Viking-Age Rune-Stones: Custom and Commemoration in Early Medieval Scandinavia* (Oxford, 2000), 16–20.
5. The theories are summarized in Sawyer, *Viking-Age Rune-Stones*.
6. See abbreviations.
7. Concerning the dating of these stones, see Marie Stoklund, "Chronology and Typology of Danish Runic Inscriptions," in *Runes and their Secrets: Studies in Runology*, ed. Marie Stoklund, Michael Lerche Nielsen, Bente Holmberg, and Gillian Fellows-Jensen (Copenhagen, 2006), 368–70.
8. See Magnus Källström, "Kungen, bryten och market: Till tolkningen av runblocket U 11 vid Hovgården på Adelsö och något om runstenarnas placering,"

Saga och Sed (2015): 67–86; cf. Staffan Fridell and Mats G. Larsson, "Runristningen på Hovgårdsstenen," Saga och Sed (2013): 95–109; Staffan Fridell and Mats G. Larsson, "Märkligt märke," Saga och Sed (2015): 87–89.
9. See Wessén in SRI 7, 36–39.
10. Fedir Braun, "Hvem var Yngvarr enn Viðfǫrli? Ett bidrag till Sveriges historia under XI århundradets första hälft," Fornvännen 5 (1910): 99–118.
11. Elias Wessén, Historiska runinskrifter (Stockholm, 1960), 30–46; Jansson, Runes in Sweden, 63–70; Mats G. Larsson, "Ingvarstågets arkeologiska bakgrund," Fornvännen 81 (1986): 98–113; Mats G. Larsson, Runstenar och utlandsfärder: Aspekter på det senvikingatida samhället med utgångspunkt i de fasta fornlämningarna (Lund, 1990), 106–14.
12. Yngvars saga víðfǫrla jämte ett bihang om Ingvarsinskrifterna, ed. Emil Olson (Copenhagen, 1912). In English translation: Hermann Pálsson and Paul Edwards, ed. and trans., Vikings in Russia: Yngvar's Saga and Eymund's Saga (Edinburgh, 1989), 44–68.
13. Sawyer, Viking-Age Rune-Stones, 103–7.
14. Judith Jesch, Ships and Men in the Late Viking Age: The Vocabulary of Runic Inscriptions and Skaldic Verse (Woodbridge, 2001), 216–32.
15. Cf. Jan Paul Strid, "Runic Swedish thegns and drengs," in Runor och runinskrifter: Föredrag vid Riksantikvarieämbetets och Vitterhetsakademiens symposium 8–11 september 1985 (Stockholm, 1987), 301–16 at 303–06.
16. See Källström, "Kungen, bryten och märket," 82.
17. Stefan Brink, "ambátt, seta, deigja – þræll, þjónn, bryti: Termer för trälar belyser träldomens äldre historia," in Trälar: Ofria i agrarsamhället från vikingatid till medeltid, ed. Thomas Lindkvist and Janken Myrdal (Stockholm, 2003), 105–8; Stefan Brink, Vikingarnas slavar: Den nordiska träldomen under yngre järnålder och äldsta medeltid (Stockholm, 2012), 114–16, 139–49.
18. Wessén in SRI 6, 256–57; Brink, Vikingarnas slavar, 118–19.
19. See Brink, "ambátt, seta, deigja," 108; Brink, Vikingarnas slavar, 149–50.
20. See Jesch, Ships and Men, 232–35.
21. Ibid., 239–42.
22. See discussion in Thorsten Andersson, "Iarlabanki atti alt hundari þetta: Till tolkningen av Jarlabanke-ristningen i Vallentuna," in Svenska studier från runtid till nutid tillägnade Carl Ivar Ståhle (Stockholm, 1973), 16–29; Helmer Gustavson and Klas-Göran Selinge, "Jarlabanke och hundaret: Ett arkeologiskt/ runologiskt bidrag till lösningen av ett historiskt tolkningsproblem," Namn och bygd 76 (1988): 62–67.
23. Anne-Sofie Gräslund, " 'Gud hjälpe nu väl hennes själ': Om runstenskvinnorna, deras roll vid kristnandet och deras plats i familj och samhälle," Tor 22 (1989): 235–40.
24. See Magnus Källström, Mästare och minnesmärken: Studier kring vikingatida runristare och skriftmiljöer i Norden (Stockholm, 2007), 262–67.
25. See Ibid., 266.
26. Magnus Källström, Torbjörn skald och Torbjörn: Studier kring två mellansvenska runristare (Stockholm, 1999), 53–72.
27. The translation of the poetical part of the inscription is adapted from Peter Foote (in Jansson, Runes in Sweden, 58–60).
28. Jesch, Ships and Men, 187.
29. Ibid., 237–39.
30. Jesch, Ships and Men, 95–99.
31. Öl 28, Sö 148, U 209, U 636. It has been proposed that Garðar is also mentioned on the rune stones Sö 130 and Vs 1, but this suggestion should probably be dismissed.

32. In SRI 3, 329.
33. K. G. Ljunggren, "*Landman* och *boman* i vikingatida källor," *Arkiv för nordisk filologi* 74 (1959): 115–35.
34. SRI 3, 414.
35. Judith Jesch, "Runic Inscriptions and the Vocabulary of Land, Lordship, and Social Power in the Late Viking Age," in *Settlement and Lordship in Viking and Early Medieval Scandinavia*, ed. Bjørn Poulsen and Søren Michael Sindbæk (Turnhout, 2011), 40.
36. Sten Tesch, "A Lost World? Religious Identity and Burial Practices During the Introduction of Christianity in the Mälaren Region, Sweden," in *Dying Gods: Religious Beliefs in Northern and Eastern Europe in the Time of Christianisation*, ed. Christiane Ruhmann and Vera Brieske (Hannover, 2015), 191–210 at 206–7.
37. See Wessén in SRI 3, xxviii; Gunnar Andersson, Magnus Källström, and Kerstin O. Näversköld, "Runstensfyndet från Björkö by," *Fornvännen* 111 (2016): 102–17 at 107.
38. Concerning the latter, see Thorgunn Snædal, "Angående en nyfunnen runristning [from Vitsand, Salem parish]," unpublished report from 2011 in Antikvarisk-topografiska arkivet, Riksantikvarieämbetet, Stockholm (dnr 322-1467-2011), www.raa.se/app/uploads/2013/11/rapp2011_12-Vitsand-Salem.pdf.
39. Andersson et al., "Runstensfyndet från Björkö by."
40. Ibid., 114.
41. Ibid., 110.
42. See e.g. Peter Sawyer, *När Sverige blev Sverige* (Alingsås, 1991), 36–37.
43. e.g. Braun, "Hvem var Yngvarr enn Viðfǫrli?"; cf. Otto von Friesen, "Hvem var Yngvarr enn Viðfǫrli?" *Fornvännen* 5 (1910): 199–209.
44. See e.g. Elias Wessén SRI 6, 18–19; Erland Hjärne, *Rod och runor* (Uppsala, 1947); Källström, "Kungen, bryten och märket," 67–72.
45. Magnus Källström, "Från Forneby till Gamla Uppsala – några nyheter om runristaren Erik," *Festskrift till Per Stille*, Humanetten 32 (2014): 33–41.
46. Concerning the interpretation of U 960, see Henrik Williams, "Runsvenska namnproblem 1. Om Erik på Vaksalastenen (U 960)," *Studia Anthroponymica Scandinavica* 9 (1991): 13–19.
47. See Wessén in SRI 7, 427.

Dedicated Bibliography

Andersson, Gunnar, Magnus Källström, and Kerstin O. Näversköld. "Runstensfyndet från Björkö by." *Fornvännen* 111 (2016): 102–17.

Andersson, Thorsten. "Iarlabanki atti alt hundari þetta: Till tolkningen av Jarlabanke-ristningen i Vallentuna." In *Svenska studier från runtid till nutid tillägnade Carl Ivar Ståhle*, 16–29. Stockholm, 1973.

Braun, Fedir. "Hvem var Yngvarr enn Viðfǫrli? Ett bidrag till Sveriges historia under XI århundradets första hälft." *Fornvännen* 5 (1910): 99–118.

Brink, Stefan. "*Ambátt, seta, deigja – þræll, þjónn, bryti*: Termer för trälar belyser träldomens äldre historia." In *Trälar: Ofria i agrarsamhället från vikingatid till medeltid*, edited by Thomas Lindkvist and Janken Myrdal, 105–8. Stockholm, 2003.

Brink, Stefan. *Vikingarnas slavar: Den nordiska träldomen under yngre järnålder och äldsta medeltid*. Stockholm, 2012.

Fridell, Staffan. "Runristningen på Hovgårdsstenen." *Saga och Sed* (2013): 95–109.
Fridell, Staffan, and Mats G. Larsson. "Märkligt märke." *Saga och Sed* (2015): 87–89.
Friesen, Otto von. "Hvem var Yngvarr enn Viðforli?" *Fornvännen* 5 (1910): 199–209.
Gräslund, Anne-Sofie. "'Gud hjälpe nu väl hennes själ': Om runstenskvinnorna, deras roll vid kristnandet och deras plats i familj och samhälle." *Tor* 22 (1989): 235–40.
Gustavson, Helmer, and Klas-Göran Selinge. "Jarlabanke och hundaret: Ett arkeologiskt/runologiskt bidrag till lösningen av ett historiskt tolkningsproblem." *Namn och bygd* 76 (1988): 62–67.
Hjärne, Erland. *Rod Och Runor*. Uppsala, 1947.
Jansson, Sven B. F. *Runes in Sweden*. Stockholm, 1987.
Jesch, Judith. *Ships and Men in the Late Viking Age: The Vocabulary of Runic Inscriptions and Skaldic Verse*. Woodbridge, 2001.
Jesch, Judith. "Runic Inscriptions and the Vocabulary of Land, Lordship, and Social Power in the Late Viking Age." In *Settlement and Lordship in Viking and Early Medieval Scandinavia*, edited by Bjørn Poulsen and Søren Michael Sindbæk, 31–44. Turnhout, 2011.
Källström, Magnus. *Torbjörn skald och Torbjörn: Studier kring två mellansvenska runristare*. Stockholm, 1999.
Källström, Magnus. *Mästare och minnesmärken: Studier kring vikingatida runristare och skriftmiljöer i Norden*. Stockholm, 2007.
Källström, Magnus. "Från Forneby till Gamla Uppsala – några nyheter om runristaren Erik." *Festskrift till Per Stille, HumaNetten* 32 (2014): 33–41.
Källström, Magnus. "Kungen, bryten och märket: Till tolkningen av runblocket U 11 vid Hovgården på Adelsö och något om runstenarnas placering." *Saga Och Sed* (2015): 67–86.
Larsson, Mats G. "Ingvarstågets arkeologiska bakgrund." *Fornvännen* 81 (1986): 98–113.
Larsson, Mats G. *Runstenar och utlandsfärder: Aspekter på det senvikingatida samhället med utgångspunkt i de fasta fornlämningarna*. Lund, 1990.
Ljunggren, Karl Gustav. "*Landman* och *boman* i vikingatida källor." *Arkiv för nordisk filologi* 74 (1959): 115–35.
Quellen des 9. und 11. Jahrhunderts zur Geschichte des Hamburgischen Kirche und des Reiches. Edited by Werner Trillmich, Rudolf Buchner, and Volker Scior. Darmstadt, 2000.
Sawyer, Birgit. *The Viking-Age Rune-Stones: Custom and Commemoration in Early Medieval Scandinavia*. Oxford, 2000.
Sawyer, Peter Hayes. *När Sverige blev Sverige*. Alingsås, 1991.
Snædal, Thorgunn. "Angående en nyfunnen runristning [from Vitsand, Salem parish, Södermanland]." Unpublished report from 2011 in Antikvarisk-topografiska arkivet, Riksantikvarieämbetet, Stockholm (dnr 322–1467–2011). www.raa.se/app/uploads/2013/11/rapp2011_12-Vitsand-Salem.pdf.
Stoklund, Marie. "Chronology and Typology of Danish Runic Inscriptions." In *Runes and Their Secrets: Studies in Runology*, edited by Marie Stoklund, Michael Lerche Nielsen, Bente Holmberg, and Gillian Fellows-Jensen, 355–83. Copenhagen, 2006.

Strid, Jan Paul. "Runic Swedish Thegns and Drengs." In *Runor och runinskrifter: Föredrag vid Riksantikvarieämbetets och Vitterhetsakademiens symposium 8–11. september 1985*, 301–16. Stockholm, 1987.

Tesch, Sten. "A Lost World? Religious Identity and Burial Practices During the Introduction of Christianity in the Mälaren Region, Sweden." In *Dying Gods: Religious Beliefs in Northern and Eastern Europe in the Time of Christianisation*, edited by Christiane Ruhmann and Vera Brieske, 191–210. Hannover, 2015.

Vikings in Russia: Yngvar's Saga and Eymund's Saga. Edited and translated by Hermann Pálsson and Paul Edwards. Edinburgh, 1989.

Wessén, Elias. *Historiska runinskrifter*. Stockholm, 1960.

Williams, Henrik. "Runsvenska Namnproblem 1: Om *Erik* på Vaksalastenen (U 960)." *Studia Anthroponymica Scandinavica* 9 (1991): 13–19.

Williams, Henrik. "Runstenarnas Sociala Dimension." *Futhark: International Journal of Runic Studies* 4 (2013): 61–76.

Yngvars saga víðforla jämte ett bihang om Ingvarsinskrifterna. Edited by Emil Olson. Copenhagen, 1912.

6 Nordic and Eastern Elites. Contacts Across the Baltic Sea
An Exiled Clan

John H. Lind

Using one of the most important, but also the most complex, sources on early Rus' history and spirituality,[1] the *Paterikon of the Kievan Caves Monastery*,[2] we shall explore aspects of networking between the Scandinavian motherland and Scandinavian Rus', and the formation of social capital that followed.

The first three of the *Paterikon's* thirty-eight tales reveal the role played by Shimon (Sigmund), a magnate of Scandinavian origin, when this famous monastery was established in the 1070s. We learn how he contributed to the way early Christianity was practiced in the monastery, and subsequently in Rus', as a blend of influences from both Constantinople and the Latin West in what could be characterized as Varangian Christianity.[3] Of the three tales it is only in the first that we receive detailed personal information about Sigmund. Here we are told that his father was Afrikan (Alfrik), brother of Jakun (Haakon) the Blind who lost his golden coat fighting with Prince Jaroslav Vladimirovich (d. 1054) of Kiev against Prince Mstislav Vladimirovich (d. 1036) of Tmutarakan' (later also of Chernigov). This episode refers to Haakon's participation as head of a Varangian force in the Battle at Listven' in 1024 (see map and later in the chapter).[4] Alfrik had two sons, Friand and Sigmund. When Alfrik died, Haakon expelled his two nephews from their lands and Sigmund sought refuge in Rus'. He was well received by Prince Jaroslav, who instated him as mentor to his favorite son, Vsevolod (d. 1093). In Vsevolod's service Sigmund became a powerful man.[5]

In 1068 Sigmund is said to have joined the three ruling princes in a visit to the Hermit Antonii in one of the caves of the future monastery prior to their attempt to fend off an attack from one of the nomadic peoples from the steppes, the Turkic Polovtsians (also known as Cumans).[6] Sigmund is told that they face defeat but that he will survive and be the first to be buried in a church yet to be built. After returning from the battle alive, Sigmund finances the building of the church and also introduces some Latin rituals.[7]

In a later addition to the first tale, which includes a further description of the fate of Sigmund and his son Georgii, we are told that Sigmund, now with the baptismal name Simon, converted to Orthodoxy together with his entire household of 3,000 persons, including priests, and that he was the first to be buried in the church he had built. This part of the first tale ends by stating that Georgii inherited his father's great love for the monastery and that he was sent by Grand Prince Vsevolod's son, Vladimir Monomakh (d. 1125), to the principality of Suzdal' in the service of Vladimir's son Jurii Vladimirovich (Dolgorukii, d. 1157). Later, when Jurii Dolgorukii came to reside as grand prince in Kiev (1149–51, 1155–57), he is said to have considered Georgii as a father, putting him in charge of Suzdal' as *tysiatskii*, one of the highest offices in the princely administration.[8]

The *Paterikon* returns to Georgii in its tenth tale. Here, Bishop Simon of Suzdal' (d. 1226), one of the work's two compilers and initiators, relates how Georgii donated silver and gold with which to embellish the shrine of St Feodosii (d. 1074). He charged one of his boiars from Suzdal' with organizing the gift. The unwilling boiar wondered why the "prince" (*kniaz'*) wished to squander so much money.[9] Georgii's embellishment of the shrine is also mentioned s.a. 1130 in the *Ipat'evskaia letopis'*, where he is referred to as "*Rostov'skyi tysiachkoi.*"[10] The tenth tale ends by affirming that when it was recorded, i.e., prior to 1226, his (Sigmund's or Georgii's) great-grandsons still continued to show the monastery their affection. Obviously, the clan saw the Kievan Caves Monastery as a kind of *Hauskloster*.[11]

It is obvious from the *Paterikon* as well as their mention in the *Ipat'evskaia Chronicle* that this wealthy and powerful clan belonged to the highest aristocracy, almost on par with the princely family of Riurikids. This is evident from the role Sigmund played in the foundation of the Caves Monastery, the size of his household when he converted from the Latin to the Orthodox Church, and the high positions which his son Georgii held in the princely administration. Their importance is underlined by the fact that both father and son were instated as the mentors of ruling Riurikid grand princes' young sons, boys who were themselves to become grand princes of Kiev. Furthermore we saw that Georgii had his own service nobility in the shape of boiars and, last but not least, that he is given the title of *kniaz'*, otherwise a prerogative of the Riurikids.[12]

Before attempting to trace our clan to Scandinavia, we shall give an overview of the Scandinavian impact on the formation of the Rus' polity and the interaction between Scandinavia and Rus' up to 1024, which is the first date that can be linked to the clan.

Early Scandinavian Power Centers in the East: A Brief Prosopographic Outline of the Formation of Scandinavian Rus'

Most archaeologists agree that Scandinavians began to enter the east-European system of rivers by the mid-eighth century at the latest.

106 *John H. Lind*

Nevertheless, it takes more than a century before we can name any individuals active in this region, and then only on the level of the ruling magnates. These represented several Scandinavian power centers, which through a process of conquests and alliances combined to form the Rus' polity.[13] By listing these centers in the order they were established we also get an impression of how this process worked:

1. Kiev. The earliest power center to be mentioned in this region is also the most distant. Here we find Askold (Hoskuld) and Dir (Dyri) as joint leaders. From Kiev they controlled the Dnepr route to the Black Sea, and from there they orchestrated an attack on Byzantium in 860.[14]
2. Staraia Ladoga. Later in the ninth century an important power center arose in the north, close to the future town of Novgorod, with Riurik (Hrorek) and Oleg (Helgi) as its rulers.[15] From there they had access to both the Volga route towards the Caliphate and the Dnepr route. Towards the end of the ninth century, Oleg moved south with the infant Igor (Ingvor), reputed to be Riurik's son. There he defeated Askold and Dir, and established himself in Kiev.[16] This merger of the southern and northern centers essentially constituted the creation of the Rus' polity, evidenced by a number of treaties contracted with the Byzantine emperors, first by Oleg in 907/911 and later by Igor' in 944.[17]
3. Pskov. This power center is known from the reported marriage between Igor and Olga (Helga) from Pskov in 903. Olga is mentioned so prominently that Pskov must have been a separate power center.[18] From Pskov another river route could be controlled, originating in the Gulf of Finland and linking up with the Dnepr route via the river Narova, Lake Peipus, and the river Velikaia.
4. Polotsk. In order to set himself up as sole ruler of Rus' during a fratricidal war for power in the 970s, Vladimir Sviatoslavich (St Vladimir, d. 1015) launched an attack from his residence in Novgorod against his brother Jaropolk in Kiev. However, on his way south Vladimir first defeated and killed a man named Rogvolod (Rognvald). Rogvolod had himself arrived from Scandinavia (*"iz zamor'ia,"* lit. "from beyond the sea") and established his power base at Polotsk on the river Dvina/Daugava, from which he controlled the entrance from the Baltic Sea to the Dnepr route along this river.[19]

No Known Links to the Scandinavian Motherland

In the early period of its existence and well into the tenth century, Rus' was politically a Scandinavian-dominated polity. This is demonstrated by the previously mentioned treaties contracted with the Byzantine emperors. These treaties mention close to eighty persons who either negotiated

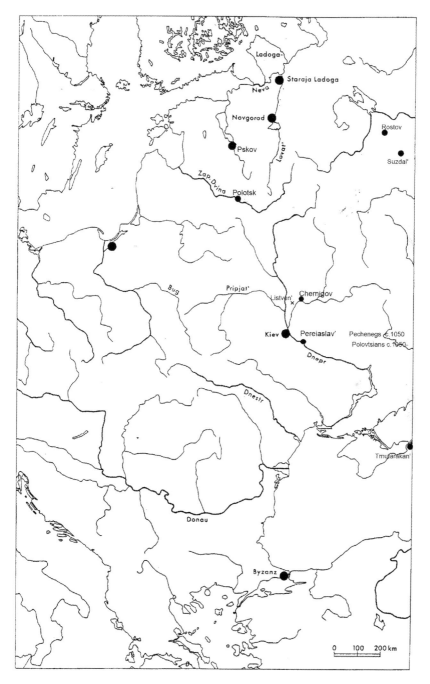

Map 6.1 Kievan-Rus Map

the treaties or on whose behalf the treaties were contracted, the overwhelming majority of whom have names of pure Scandinavian origin.[20] The same is true for the large number of followers who accompanied Princess Olga when, in 946 or 957, she visited the Byzantine emperor Constantine Porphyrogennetos and was baptized.[21]

Bearing in mind the significance of the formation of this Scandinavian-dominated Rus' polity to European history, it is remarkable that none of the founders of these power centers can be linked to known rulers or magnates in Scandinavia. The only possible exception is Riurik (Hrorek), whom some scholars have identified as Rorik, the Danish princeling who became a vassal of the Franks as defender of Frisia and who died around 880. It is, however, an assumption that is difficult to verify.[22] The reason is of course the general lack of Scandinavian sources from this period.

Trade and control of trade appear to have been the main sources of power and wealth for these Scandinavian magnates in the East; in order to make the trade system work, they must have retained contacts, including those on a personal level, with their countries of origin and other participating regions of the Scandinavian motherland. Therefore the first generations of these rulers, if not accompanied by wives, may have imported them from Scandinavia. There is no evidence of this practice during the early period, and the first marital link we know of was local: the marriage between Igor' and Olga. The next example occurred two generations later when Vladimir Sviatoslavich, after slaying Rogvolod of Polotsk, took his daughter Rogneda (Ragnheid) by force.

This coupling was particularly important for future links to Scandinavia; Rogneda was Vladimir's only wife or concubine of Scandinavian origin. Apart from the Byzantine princess Anna, whom Vladimir married when he adopted Christianity in 988 or 989, she is his only wife to be mentioned by name; and, apart from Anna, she is the only one whose death is mentioned in the chronicles (d. 1000).[23] Finally, Rogneda was probably Vladimir's favorite; she is reported to have borne him more children than any of his other women.

Among Rogneda's children, four sons are listed in the chronicles.[24] Of these at least two are important for us with regard to dynastic links with Scandinavia. The oldest was probably Iziaslav, whom Vladimir installed in Polotsk, where he became the founder of a new Polotsk dynasty. In contrast to other nominal principalities under the grand prince of Kiev, the Polotsk dynasty obtained a semi-independent status, preserving the name "Rogvolod" in the princely family. With its location on the Dvina/Daugava, Polotsk must have upheld many links with Scandinavia. Although it is believed that a chronicle from Polotsk once existed, it is now lost. Therefore we get detailed information about the Polotsk principality only from the beginning of the thirteenth century, when Western crusaders targeted the region and also introduced local chronicle writing. Thus, from Henry of Livonia, writing in the 1220s, we know that the Polotsk prince at that time had installed princelings in fortified outposts along the Dvina/Daugava, thereby securing full control of the river until he fell out with the crusaders.[25] Even though we have hardly any information concerning the intervening period, we know from a variety of Western sources that a Danish queen, Sophia Volodarevna (queen of Denmark 1157–82, d. 1198), Valdemar the Great's wife, was a scion of the Polotsk dynasty.[26]

The most important of Vladimir's sons by Rogneda, with regard to both future Russian history and the links between Rus' and Scandinavia, was Jaroslav Vladimirovich (the Wise). Apart from Valdemar the Great's marriage with Sophia, most dynastic links between Rus' and Scandinavia involve Jaroslav or his direct descendants.

Vladimir Sviatoslavich and Olav Tryggvason: The First Known Direct Links Between Rulers in Rus' and Scandinavia

From the late tenth century, more or less indigenous sources began to cover events in Rus' and Scandinavia, showing, as we would expect, that a mutual awareness existed. This applies both to the Russian chronicles that began to be compiled during the eleventh century and to the Norse saga literature from the twelfth century onwards, especially the kings' sagas. A significant difference between these two types of sources is that the Russian chronicles place events within a partly constructed, superimposed, annalistic chronological framework,[27] whereas the sagas apply a relative chronology. Therefore we cannot be sure of their mutual chronology at this early stage.

The two types of sources differ in another interesting and important respect. The Russian chronicles, apart from a few prominent females, usually only name male members of the Riurikids and a few magnates and members of the highest ecclesiastical hierarchy. Accordingly, we are hardly ever given the names of visiting Scandinavians except as members of Varangian troops. By contrast, naming people from every social stratum came naturally to the saga writers.

Against this background the two types of sources more or less agree on the timing of the first two interactions between ruling houses of Scandinavia and Rus'. Both cases involved activating what we can call the "exit option," one of the advantages of having accumulated social capital through established networks, in order to seek asylum and, if possible, military support for a comeback. It is, however, uncertain who was first to flee his country. What is certain is that Vladimir Sviatoslavich is mentioned in both cases and that he was the first Riurikid to be mentioned in a Norse source. He was also the first to seek asylum in Scandinavia.

As the youngest son of Sviatoslav Igorevich (d. 972), Vladimir had been placed as auxiliary prince in the still-insignificant Novgorod, subject to his father in Kiev. However, when Sviatoslav died Vladimir was forced into exile in 977 during the battle for the succession between his older brothers. The location of the exile is described as somewhere in Scandinavia ("*za more*," i.e., "beyond the sea"). In 980 Vladimir was able to return with an army of Varangians, with which he first conquered Novgorod and later Kiev.[28]

Vladimir's exile almost coincides with young Olav Tryggvason's visit to Rus'. According to *Odd Snorrason's saga* and *Heimskringla*, Astrid, Olav's mother, hoped to ensure their safety by traveling via Sweden to join her brother Sigurd Eiriksson, who is said to have served in Rus' with Vladimir (Valdimar/Valdamarr, etc. in Norse sources). Judging by the presumed chronology of Olav's life this must have happened before Vladimir went into exile. At the outset of the journey Olav is said to be no more than three years old. Before reaching Rus', Olav's ship was captured by Estonian Vikings, and he was held in captivity for six years before being freed by Sigurd.[29] Apart from his name, the Norse sources provide no information about Vladimir except that he ruled Rus' (Gardariki) or Novgorod (Holmgard) and fathered Jaroslav, whose description in the sagas is much more detailed. For instance, the sagas reveal nothing about Vladimir's exile in Scandinavia. Of course, if it was in Denmark, it may easily have been forgotten long before it could have become known to the Norse saga writers.[30]

According to both *Odd's saga* and *Heimskringla*, Olav spent the remainder of his youth in Rus', but the two sources differ in their accounts of his adult life. According to *Odd*, after a short sojourn among the Wends, Olav returned to Rus'. He then visited Greece, where he was prime-signed before he continued to the British Isles, and from there to Norway, where he replaced Haakon Jarl Sigurdsson as ruler.[31] *Heimskringla* and other Norse sources, however, omit Olav's second stay in Rus' and have him travel directly from the Wends to Britain. Perhaps they wished to avoid the impression that Olav had adopted Christianity in the East.[32]

Scandinavians Active in Both East and West

In any case, Olav Tryggvason was the first known Scandinavian royal to have been active both east and west of the Scandinavian motherland. At the time, members of the royal family descended from Harald Fairhair were in fierce competition with the clan of the Hlaðir (Lade) earls in Norway.

Later, two more Norwegian kings also became active in both the East and the West, Olav Haraldsson and his half-brother Harald Sigurdsson. However, we have evidence of Scandinavians from a lower level of society who were active in both spheres as well. This applies both to members of the clan of the Hlaðir earls and others further down the social ladder. Evidence of the latter's movement is found on two runestones from Swedish territory, while a third mentions two brothers – one who died in the West, the other in the East.[33] No doubt the persons mentioned belonged to the group of local magnates who in the East may well have been members of the famed Varangians, perhaps even the imperial Varangian Guard in Byzantium, while in the West they most likely took part in the Danish conquest of England for which Scandinavian warriors received payment (*giald*) from King Knud.[34]

The Fratricidal War for the Succession in Rus' 1015–19 and Links to Scandinavia

The story of the exit option was about to repeat itself in the next generation of rulers and pretenders, both as an opportunity and as a last resort. In various corners of the Scandinavian commonwealth this period was characterized by ever more brutal struggles for the succession, and it also saw several attempts to topple rulers – as was about to happen to the aging Vladimir Sviatoslavich in 1014. With close links to Scandinavia and using his position as auxiliary prince in Novgorod, Vladimir's second son by Rogneda, Jaroslav, prepared an uprising against his father in order to separate Novgorod from Kiev. In response, Vladimir got ready to attack Jaroslav. Faced with this threat, which might well have led to his exile in Scandinavia, just as it had for Vladimir a generation earlier, Jaroslav requested and received Varangian forces from Scandinavia. However, before Vladimir had completed his preparations he fell ill and died in 1015.[35]

Vladimir's death unleashed a violent fratricidal war for the succession between his many sons, involving different ethnic groups and foreign powers in a reflection of the various networks of each contender. Even though we do not have the full picture, these networks seem to have been linked to both the maternal origins and matrimonial links of each son.

We have two sources with fairly detailed information on this conflict. The most detailed account is found in *Povest' vremennykh let* (*PVL*, lit. "The Tale of Bygone Years"), where traditional chronicle accounts are interwoven with hagiographical texts concerning two of the sons slain at the outset of the conflict, Boris and Gleb. The other source is a contemporary account in Thietmar of Merseburg's chronicle. Before his death in 1018, Thietmar managed to record the latest news from Kiev, which he received from an observer who accompanied the Polish troops with auxiliaries from Hungary and Germany. These forces supported Vladimir's oldest son, Sviatopolk, who was married to a daughter of Duke Bolesław the Brave of Poland.

When Vladimir died, Sviatopolk was present in Kiev. With the help of his Pecheneg allies from the steppes, predecessors of the Polovtsians, he managed to kill three of his brothers, Boris, Gleb, and Sviatoslav. News of the murders reached Jaroslav in Novgorod, and with his Varangians he was able to defeat Sviatopolk in 1016 and take Kiev. Sviatopolk sought refuge with his father-in-law, who saw this as an opportunity to extend his power base into Rus'. With the Sviatopolk's Pechenegs, Bolesław managed to defeat Jaroslav in 1018 at the river Bug and retake Kiev.[36]

By and large the accounts in the Russian chronicles agree with those of Thietmar. However, Thietmar's account ends with Sviatopolk and Bolesław still in control of Kiev.[37] Soon after Thietmar stopped writing, Jaroslav managed to advance on Kiev with freshly imported Varangians, once more forcing Sviatopolk to flee to Poland, where he died.[38]

The First Known Direct Matrimonial Links Across the Scandinavian Commonwealth

The Russian chronicles never inform us of the origin of the Varangians who were called in by the Riurikids. However, among the last news Thietmar received from his observer in Kiev is a note on the presence of a potent force of "fast-moving Danes" who had been able to resist the many Pecheneg attacks and also defeat other enemies.[39] In his chronicle, Thietmar distinguished between "Northmans," the general term for Scandinavians, and Danes, with whom he was well acquainted. Therefore there is no reason to doubt that these Varangians were indeed Danes. The Varangians mentioned here must represent those called in by either Jaroslav or his father, Vladimir. Their Danish origin probably reflects the military power of the Danish kings at that time.[40] In any case, these "fast-moving Danes" may well be linked to one of the two earliest known direct dynastic links between Rus' and Scandinavia.

In book II, chapter 54 (52) of his *Chronicle of the Hamburg Bishops*, Adam of Bremen entered a short account of Knud the Great's seizure of the English crown. Here, Adam lists a number of matrimonial contracts that were part of the kinship web Knud formed in order to secure the loyalty of the English and Normans. Knud himself married his predecessor's widow, Emma, a sister of Duke Richard of Normandy, to whom Knud then offered his sister, Margaret[-Estrid]. When Richard repudiated her, Knud gave her to Duke Ulf "of England" instead. Ulf's sister Gytha was married to Earl Godwin of Wessex. Adam recorded some of the children from these marriages – those who had risen to prominence by the time of his writing c. 1070. Thus, Ulf and Margaret had sons Svend and Bjørn, while Godwin and Gytha had Sweyn, Tostig, and Harold. This demonstrates that Knud the Great used matrimonial links to stabilize the rule of his widespread empire, both horizontally by creating bonds with other princely houses and vertically by forming links between his relatives and local aristocracies in his various polities.

To this account, Adam added the particularly interesting scholion 39, in which he tells us that "Knud gave his sister Estrid in marriage to the son of the king of Russia."[41] Considering Adam's claim to have received information directly from Estrid's son, King Svend Estridsen, we cannot disregard this statement. However, the point in Estrid's marital career at which this Russian union occurred remains unclear. It is unlikely to have been a third marriage, taking place after King Knud had Ulf the Earl killed in 1026,[42] a time when it would have been difficult to find Estrid a suitable Rus' husband. More importantly, with her large donation to the cathedral of Roskilde after Ulf's death, Estrid became such an important person in Denmark that it is hardly feasible that such a late marriage would have gone unmentioned in Norse sources, and we would expect Svend Estridsen to have been better informed. Therefore, the Russian union is more likely to have been her first marriage, and her husband could have been one of Vladimir Sviatoslavich's many sons killed during the war of succession, leaving her free to be part of the Norman deal. It could also have been Jaroslav Vladimirovich's son from an early marriage, Ilia, who soon disappeared from the sources.[43] Either way, this union could also explain the presence of Danish Varangians in Kiev in 1018.

It would also be contemporaneous with the marriage, his second at least, that Jaroslav contracted with Ingegerd, the daughter of the Swedish king Olof Skötkonung. This is mentioned both by Adam of Bremen[44] and Snorri. By then another of Olof's daughters, Holmfrid, had already married Svein, a son of the old Hlaðir earl Haakon Sigurdsson, as part of an alliance that became apparent at the Battle at Svoldr in 1000, where Olav Tryggvason lost his life.[45] Through his marriage, Jaroslav therefore formed a kinship link to the Hlaðir earls. However, before Ingegerd married Jaroslav she had already been wooed by Olav Haraldsson, who in 1015 had replaced the Hlaðir earls as ruler of Norway. With Ingegerd gone to Rus', Olav had to settle for her half-sister Astrid. Accordingly, within a few years a kinship web was formed which comprised rulers of all three Scandinavian kingdoms, including Knud the Great's England and Jaroslav's Rus'. With regard to the dynastic link between Olof and Olav, this can perhaps be seen as at least a temporary nullification of the alliance Olof had had with the Hlaðir earls. However, even if the formation of this kinship web represented a change of allegiance, awareness of the earlier links, and the alliances that had brought them about, lingered on and could be reactivated if the need arose.

The kinship web that was now formed is perhaps best known for its role as the escape route used by the Norwegians when they had to activate their exit option. This applies to the three successive kings, Olav Haraldsson, Magnus Olavsson, and Harald Sigurdsson, as well as members of the clan of the Hlaðir earls, their competitors for power in Norway. This movement was partly dependent on the fluctuating strength of Knud the Great's North Sea empire and his ability to exercise influence in Norway. Accordingly, we no longer hear of princelings from Rus' seeking refuge in Scandinavia; it was now Scandinavians who found a safe haven in Rus' when circumstances at home forced them to flee.

In some cases, a Scandinavian ruler forced an exit option upon a rival as a humane alternative to killing them! We find two examples of this merciful approach, both linked to Knud the Great's conquest of England. According to Adam of Bremen, King Knud sent the two sons of his immediate predecessor, Edmund Ironside, into exile in Rus'.[46] The second case is, however, more relevant here. Olav Haraldsson, who had originally sided with Knud before they fell out in 1015, decided to go to Norway and claim the crown. Upon his arrival in Norway, Olav managed to capture Earl Haakon Eiriksson, who at that time ruled the country on behalf of the Danes. Promising not to oppose Olav, Haakon was allowed to go into exile with Knud in England, an act of mercy Olav must later have come to regret.[47]

The Battle at Listven' – Haakon the Blind, or the Handsome?

By the early 1020s most of Vladimir Sviatoslavich's sons had been lost to the fratricidal war for the succession. Jaroslav Vladimirovich had gained control over Kiev and most of Rus' to the north including Novgorod. To the south, however, one of Vladimir's two sons by the name of Mstislav had a strong position as prince of Tmutarakan', a principality on the shores of the Sea of Azov, separated from the rest of Rus' by steppes. He had not been part of the struggle for the succession in 1015–19 but had strengthened his position in the early 1020s by defeating neighboring tribes. In 1023, with Jaroslav in distant Novgorod, Mstislav decided to move northwards into Rus' proper with Khazar auxiliaries.[48] In 1024 he arrived at Kiev but was not admitted into the city. Instead he established himself in nearby Chernigov.

Faced with this treat, Jaroslav once again sent overseas for Varangian troops. The request was answered with the arrival of Haakon the Blind at the head of a Varangian force; the same Haakon who expelled his nephew Sigmund in the first tale of the *Paterikon of the Kievan Caves Monastery*. The battle ended in defeat for Jaroslav and Haakon. While Haakon immediately went back home, Jaroslav decided to retain Novgorod as his residence, only moving to Kiev after Mstislav died in 1036.[49]

The description of Haakon in the chronicle is unusual in both mentioning his name and including a number of his characteristics. Most remarkable is, of course, his alleged but dubious blindness. This trait may actually be the result of a mistake in the transmission of the chronicle text, as pointed out in the nineteenth century. It seems that the term *slepъ* ("blind") in a manuscript, customarily written without word division, had been mistaken for *sьlepъ*, which with modern word division would be *sь* (the) *lepъ* (handsome), turning Haakon's blindness into beauty.

Another unusual feature is that Haakon is given the title "prince" (*kniaz'*), otherwise a prerogative of the Riurikids, as mentioned previously with regard to the same title being assigned to Georgii Simonovich, the son of Haakon's nephew. This places Haakon on par with Jaroslav himself among the highest aristocratic stratum of rulers with close links to royalty. Among the contemporary Haakons who are known to us, one in particular stands out: Haakon Eiriksson of the clan of the Hlaðir earls.[50] We met him in 1015 when, as joint ruler of Norway on behalf of Knud the Great, he was captured by Olav Haraldsson and sent into exile in England. With Svend Forkbeard as his grandfather – his mother was Gytha Svendsdaughter – Earl Haakon Eiriksson was closely linked to the Danish royal family. While in England Haakon had been in Knud's service and appears in various capacities with the title *dux* or earl, depending on the language.[51] When Olav Haraldsson was expelled from Norway in 1028, Haakon was once more installed as ruler, and he continued to have good relations with King Knud, whose niece he married just before he drowned on his way back to Norway in 1029 or 1030, a disaster for King Knud's hold on Norway.[52]

By 1024 Knud's hold on his empire had probably become sufficiently stable for him to allow Earl Haakon to absent himself on an expedition in Rus' as head of a detachment of Varangians recruited by their kinsman Jaroslav Vladimirovich in order to help him in the struggle for supremacy in Rus'. Here his appearance had clearly caught the imagination of the author or compiler of the *PVL*.[53]

If we identify Haakon Eiriksson as Sigmund's uncle, and attempt to understand this course of events in a feasible contemporary situation, Alfrik was probably Haakon's half-brother with a life in Norway, where he may have sided with Olav Haraldson and gone into exile with him when Haakon returned as Norwegian ruler in 1028.

The Clan, Links to Scandinavia, and the Fragmentation of Rus'

In Rus' our clan was linked to four generations of Riurikid rulers. Sigmund was received by Prince Jaroslav and instated as mentor for his favorite son Vsevolod (c. 1030–1093). Later Vsevolod's son Vladimir Monomakh (1053–1125) instated Sigmund's son Georgii in a similar capacity for his son Jurii Dolgorukii (c. 1099–1157).

Even though Vsevolod was only Jaroslav and Ingegerd's fourth son, it was for him that Jaroslav secured the most prominent wife, a daughter or close relative of the reigning Byzantine emperor, Constantine IX

116 *John H. Lind*

Monomachos. It was from this marriage that the most powerful branch of the Riurikids originated, and it was their children, grandchildren, and great-grandchildren who upheld the closest relations with the Scandinavian world and also linked the Scandinavian royal houses with Byzantium.

To avoid another violent fratricidal war of succession among his sons, Jaroslav instituted a system of succession by seniority, so that his three oldest surviving sons by Ingegerd, with Vsevolod as the youngest, acted as a triumvirate. We meet this triumvirate, along with Sigmund, in 1068. The oldest son resided as grand prince in Kiev, the next in Chernigov, and the third in Pereiaslavl'-Russkii. When a member of the triumvirate died, a younger brother would succeed him, a custom which was carried on by the next generation.[54]

By 1078 both of Vsevolod's two older brothers had died and as grand prince of Kiev he was now able to concentrate power into the hands of himself and his son, Vladimir Monomakh. They consolidated their power by managing to install Vladimir's twelve-year-old son, Mstislav-Harald, as prince in Novgorod in 1088. The family thereby secured their portion of the wealth Novgorod's growing trade with western Europe brought to both the city and its prince.

It was Vsevolod who renewed the tradition of forming matrimonial links with the Scandinavian world. With Svend Estridsen as go-between, he married his oldest son, Vladimir Monomakh, to Gytha, daughter of the last Anglo-Saxon king, Harold Godwinson. Gytha was a granddaughter of King Svend's aunt, and both she and her brothers had fled to Svend after their father's death at Hastings in 1066.[55]

In turn, Vladimir Monomakh married his first son, Mstislav (1076–1132, called "Harald" in Norse sources after his grandfather), to Kristina, daughter of the Swedish king Inge Stenkilsson. Another of King Inge's daughters, Margrete Fredkulla, first married the Norwegian king Magnus Barefoot and, after his death in 1103, the Danish king Niels. Thus we have a very closely knit kinship web comprising the leading princely family among the Riurikids and all the Scandinavian kingdoms. This web was extended in the next generation, when, among the daughters of Mstislav and Kristina, Ingeborg married Knud Lavard, Malmfrid first married the Norwegian king Sigurd Jorsalfar and later the Danish king Erik Emune, while a third daughter in 1122 married a son of the Byzantine emperor.[56] So even though we have no knowledge of links between our clan and Scandinavia after its exile – which we could not really expect considering the nature of the sources – it is likely that both Sigmund and his son Georgii were involved in facilitating these links.

However, with the death of Mstislav-Harald in 1132 the fragmentation of Rus' as a political entity accelerated. Novgorod severed its links with Kiev and began to elect its princes from among the many branches of the Riurikid family. At the same time, the political center in Rus' moved from Kiev to the northeast, where Vladimir-Suzdal' became the new center: a process spearheaded by Vladimir Monomakh's younger son, Jurii Dolgorukii, in which Sigmund's son Georgii, as Jurii's mentor, may have played a part as *tysiatskii* in Suzdal' and Rostov.[57]

These political changes in Rus' more or less ended the tradition of forming dynastic links between Scandinavia and Rus'. Scandinavian interests in Rus' were now focused on Novgorod as a trading center. With the Novgorodian princes being rapidly elected and expelled, making matrimonial agreements with them made no political sense. The fact that Valdemar the Great nevertheless married a Russian princess in 1157 was the result of internal Scandinavian politics.[58]

Final Reflections

Our clan seems to be unique, which is surprising considering the massive presence of Scandinavians or people of Scandinavian descent involved in the formation of the Rus' polity in the tenth century. Although many of these individuals probably upheld links to the Scandinavian motherland, they are difficult to identify in Russian sources. With the advent of Christianity, a system of Christian name-giving based on the use of Church Slavonic as lingua franca became dominant. Individuals are seldom

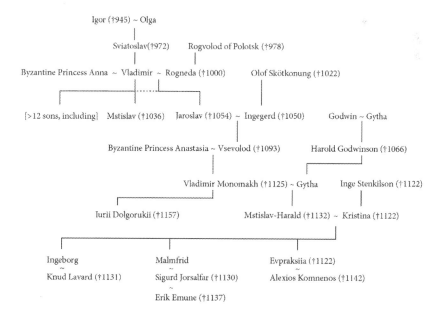

Figure 6.1 Lineage of the Riurikid dynasty

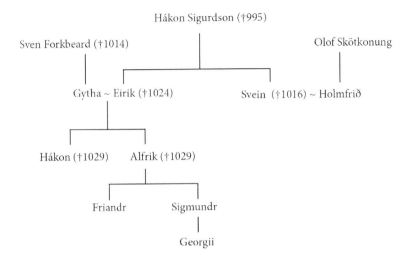

Figure 6.2 Lineage of the Hlaðir earls

Figure 6.3 Olof Skötkonung in the kinship web

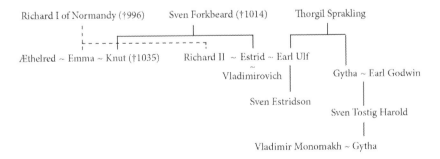

Figure 6.4 Knut the Great's kinship web

mentioned by names other than their (Orthodox) Christian ones – as in the case of our Georgii Simonovich. Therefore it becomes difficult to distinguish persons of Scandinavian origin from those of Finnic, Baltic, or East Slavic origin, who together combined to form the Rus' polity.[59]

Notes

1. The best introduction in English to early Russian history is still Simon Franklin and Jonathan Shepard, *The Emergence of Rus, 750–1200* (London and New York, 1996).
2. For the *Paterikon* in general see the introduction in the English translation of the *Paterikon*, the *Paterik of the Kievan Caves Monastery*, trans. Muriel Heppell (Cambridge, MA, 1989), xvi–lii. For the *Paterikon*, the monastery, and the role the Latinity of Sigmund came to play in the formation of early Christianity in Rus', see John H. Lind, "Christianity on the Move: The Role of the Varangians in Rus' and Scandinavia," in *Byzantium and the Viking World*, ed. Fedir Androshchuk, Jonathan Shepard, and Monica White (Uppsala, 2016), 409–40 at 421–29.
3. Varangians (from Old Norse *væringjar*) were groups of (mainly) Scandinavians joined by oath for military or commercial purposes, active in Eastern Europe and Byzantium, where they, amongst others, formed the Varangian Guard (c. 980–1204). John H. Lind, " 'Varangian Christianity' and the Veneration of Anglo-Saxon and Scandinavian Saints in Early Rus'," in *Identity Formation and Diversity in the Early Medieval Baltic and Beyond*, ed. Johan Callmer, Ingrid Gustin, and Mats Roslund (Leiden, 2017), 106–35.
4. The battle is mentioned under the year 1024 in the main Russian chronicle for the period up to 1110/1116, the *PVL* (Lit. "The Tale of Bygone Years"). The *PVL* is best reflected in "Lavrent'evskaia letopis'," in *Polnoe sobranie russkikh letopisei*, vol. 1, ed. Afanasij F. Bychkov (Leningrad, 1926) or "Ipat'evskaia letopis'," in *Polnoe sobranie russkikh letopisei*, vol. 2, ed. Aleksei A. Shakhmatov (St Petersburg, 1908). English translation, Samuel H. Cross and Olgerd P. Sherbowitz-Wetzor, ed., *The Russian Primary Chronicle, Laurentian Text* (Cambridge, MA, 1953). In addition to the *PVL* we have a fairly short compilation from c. 1095, *Nachal'nyi svod*, partly preserved in the *First Novgorod Chronicle Younger Version*; see *Novgorodskaia pervaia letopis' starshego i mladshego izvodov*, ed. Arsenii N. Nasonov (Moscow, 1950). This short compilation was used by the compiler of the *PVL*, who often deliberately contradicted his source.
5. "Kievo-Pecherskii paterik," in *Biblioteka literatury drevnei Rusi*, vol. 4, ed. L. A. Ol'shevskaia (St. Petersburg, 1997), 296.
6. The defeat is mentioned under the year 1068 in the *PVL*; see Bychkov, "Lavrent'evskaia letopis'," 167.
7. Lind, "Christianity on the Move," 421–29.
8. On the chronological overlay in the first tale see Lind, "Christianity on the Move," 424–28.
9. Ol'shevskaia, "Kievo-Pecherskii paterik," 330–32.
10. Shakhmatov, "Ipat'evskaia letopis'," 293.
11. Ol'shevskaia, "Kievo-Pecherskii paterik," 330–36.
12. In the sources all Riurikids, if mentioned with a title, are given the title *kniaz'*. Even though *kniaz'* has the same etymology as "king" in English, it is habitually rendered as "prince" or, more seldom, as "duke." The ruling prince in Kiev was often referred to as *velikii kniaz'* (grand prince).

13. John H. Lind, "Tissø – Kiev – Konstantinopel: Danske netværk i øst?" in *Vikingetidens aristokratiske miljøer*, ed. Henriette Lyngstrøm and Lasse C. A. Sonne (Copenhagen, 2014), 69–76.
14. Nasonov, *Novgorodskaia pervaia letopis'*, 106. The date 860 is known from Byzantine sources.
15. Shakhmatov, "Ipat'evskaia letopis'," 14. As an archaeological site, Staraia Ladoga is known from the mid-eighth century.
16. Nasonov, *Novgorodskaia pervaia letopis'*, 107.
17. Bychkov, "Lavrent'evskaia letopis'," 30–37, 46–54.
18. Ibid., 29.
19. Ibid., 76.
20. Elena A. Mel'nikova, "The Lists of Old Norse Personal Names in the Russian Byzantine Treaties of the Tenth Century," in *Studia Anthroponymica Scandinavica* 22 (2004): 5–27.
21. James Howard-Johnston, "The De Administrando Imperio: A Re-examination of the Text and a Re-evaluation of Its Evidence About the Rus'," in *Les centres proto-urbains russes entre Scandinavie, Byzance et Orient*, ed. Michelle Kazanski, Anne Nercessian, and Constantin Zuckerman (Paris, 2000), 301–36 at 302.
22. John Lind, "De russiske ægteskaber. Dynasti- og alliancepolitik i 1130'ernes danske borgerkrig," *Historisk Tidsskrift* (D) 92 (1992): 225–63 at 226, n. 3.
23. Bychkov, "Lavrent'evskaia letopis'," 129.
24. Ibid., 79–80.
25. Anne Bysted, Carsten S. Jensen, Kurt V. Jensen, and John H. Lind, *Jerusalem in the North: Denmark and the Baltic Crusades 1100–1522* (Turnhout, 2012), 157–60, 185–88.
26. Lind, "De russiske ægteskaber," 225–63.
27. The genealogy and chronology for the early Riurikids in the *PVL* is suspect. Based on the few fixed chronological fix-points in the treaties between Rus' and the Byzantine emperors (907, 911, 944, and 971), the compiler superimposed a constructed chronological framework, where he allotted thirty-three years for each generation of rulers and seventeen for the newcomer Riurik. Thus Riurik fathered Igor before dying in 879 and Igor married Olga in 903 but only fathered Sviatoslav c. 940, a date that is confirmed by Constantine Porphyrogennetos.
28. Bychkov, "Lavrent'evskaia letopis'," 75–79.
29. This is not the place to delve into the chronology of Olav's life. However, in his *Olav's saga*, Oddr Snorrason (*The saga of Olaf Tryggvason by Oddr Snorrason*, ed. Theodore M. Andersson (Ithaca, NY, 2003), 73) refers to two different views in his sources on Olav's age when he assumed rule in Norway, c. 995. Thus, according to Ari fróði, Olav was then only twenty-two, while according to others he was thirty-two. It seems the latter view is most commonly upheld but is difficult to reconcile with the chronology of the Russian chronicles.
30. Even though we tend to think that most Scandinavians active in Rus' came from Swedish territory, judging by persons actually mentioned in sources as active in Rus' and Byzantium, we would suspect that the majority came from Norway and Iceland.
31. Andersson, *The saga of Olaf Tryggvason*, 44–49, 52–55; "Óláfs saga Tryggvasonar," Hkr 1, 254–300; Jan Ragnar Hagland, "State Formation and Early Christianization in Norway: The Problem of Possible Eastern Influences," *Motskrift* (2007): 48–52 at 50.
32. "Óláfs saga Tryggvasonar," Hkr 1, 263–67. Being "prime-signed" was a preliminary step towards baptism.

33. Samnordisk runtextdatabas (Scandinavian Runic-text Data Base) under the signa Sö 173, U 504 and Vg 197.
34. This can be supplemented with a number of persons mentioned in several sagas, even some of the legendary sagas. This reflects a continuous awareness over the centuries in Iceland of visits to the East. Information on this is provided in Roland Scheel, *Skandinavien und Byzanz: Bedingungen und Konsequenzen mittelalterlicher Kulturbeziehungen*, 2 vols. (Göttingen, 2015).
35. Bychkov, "Lavrent'evskaia letopis'," 130.
36. Ibid., 130–45.
37. Thietmar von Merseburg, *Chronik*, ed. Werner Trillmich (Darmstadt, 1974), 472–76.
38. Bychkov, "Lavrent'evskaia letopis'," 130–45.
39. "et maxime ex velocibus Danis, multum se nocentibus Pecinegis hactenus resistebat et alios vincebat": Thietmar von Merseburg, *Chronik*, 474.
40. Archaeologists, including those from Ukraine and Russia, increasingly take the view that the Varangians imported by Vladimir and Jaroslav most likely came from Denmark. See Volodymyr Kovalenko, "Scandinavians in the East of Europe: In Search of Glory or a New Motherland?" in *From Goths to Varangians: Communication and Cultural Exchange Between the Baltic and the Black Sea*, ed. Line Bjerg, John H. Lind, and Søren Sindbæk (Aarhus, 2013), 257–94 at 287–89.
41. "Chnut sororem suam Estred filio regis de Ruzzia dedit in matrimonium," GH, 292–94.
42. See Jarl Gallén, "Vem var Ulf jarl, Sven Estridsens far?" *Scandia* 58 (1992): 13–30 at 15.
43. Lind, "De russiske ægteskaber," 227; Aleksandr V. Nazarenko, *Drevniaia Rus' na mezhdunarodnykh putiakh: Mezhdistsiplinarnye ocherki kul'turnykh, torgovykh, politicheskikh sviazei IX – XII vekov* (Moscow, 2001), 476–78, 484–89.
44. GH, 274.
45. "Óláfs saga Tryggvasonar," Hkr 1, 370–72.
46. GH, 292.
47. "Óláfs saga helga," Hkr 2, 36–39.
48. A Turkic people from the former Jewish state of Khazaria to the east of Tmutarakan' towards the Caspian Sea and Caucasus.
49. Bychkov, "Lavrent'evskaia letopis'," 147–49.
50. Other Haakons have been mentioned in this context. A Norwegian Earl Haakon Ivarsson is mentioned in the kings' sagas, exiled to both Sweden and Denmark and active in the Baltic Sea ("Haralds saga Sigurðarsonar," Hkr 3, 121–32, 150–65). He is too young to be our Haakon, but may be one or both of the earls mentioned in Swedish runic inscriptions, U 617 and Sm 76. U 16 mentions a prominent but titleless Haakon as head of a flotilla (*róði Hákonar*). Finally, a seemingly less prominent Haakon is mentioned on two runic stones, Ög 162 and Ög Fv1970; 310 (see abbreviations). It is a problem that runic inscriptions are difficult to date, and the datings of runologists are seldom sufficiently convincing for us to establish identifications with persons in other types of sources. Furthermore, we must ask whether any of these Haakons was sufficiently prominent to earn the title of *kniaz'* in a Rus' context.
51. For his English career see Timothy Bolton, *The Empire of Cnut the Great* (Leiden, 2009).
52. Bolton, *Empire*, 267, n. 89.
53. The chronicle account of "Prince" Haakon's role in the Battle at Listven' contains a number of literary motifs which also caused recent scholars to

link Haakon to the clan of Hlaðir earls: his alleged handsomeness and the gold-woven mantle which he abandons while fleeing from the defeat in the battle. See Anna F. Litvina and Fjodor B. Uspenskii, "Pochemu variag Iakun "otbezhe ludy zlatoe"? Stseny listvenskoi bitvy 1024 g," in *Drevniaia Rus'*: *Voprosy medievistiki 1* (2016): 27–40; A. A. Gippius, "Begstvo ot plashcha: Zametki o 'zolotoi lude' Jakuna 'Slepogo'," *Terra Slavica/Terra Balcanica. K jubileiu T.V. Tsiv'ian* (Moscow, 2007), 52–58; S. M. Mikheev, "Variazhskie kniaz'ia Jakun, Afrikan i Shimon: Liteteraturnye siuzhety, transformatitsia imen i istoricheskii kontekst," *Drevniaia Rus'*. *Voprosy medievistiki 2* (2008): 27–32.
54. The system, as described in the *PVL*, may be a reconstruction based on observed facts, just like Saxo's description of a comparable system in Denmark after the death of Svend Estridsen. See John H. Lind, "Knes Kanutus: Knud Lavard's Political Project," in *Of Chronicles and Kings: National Saints and the Emergence of Nation States in the Early Middle Ages*, ed. John Bergsagel, Thomas Riis, and David Hiley (Copenhagen, 2015), 113–38 at 113–15.
55. Saxo, 16.
56. Ulla Haastrup and John H. Lind, "Dronning Margrete Fredkulla: Politisk magthaver og mæcen for byzantisk kunst i danske kirker i 1100-tallet begyndelse," in *Medeltidens genus. Kvinnors och mäns roller inom kultur, rätt och samhälle: Norden och Europa ca 300–1500*, ed. Lars Hermanson and Auður Magnúsdóttir (Göteborg, 2015), 29–71.
57. John H. Lind, "The 'Brotherhood' of Rus': A Pseudo-Problem Concerning the Origin of Rus'," *Slavica Othiniensia* 5 (1982): 66–81.
58. Lind, "De russiske ægteskaber," 251–53.
59. Scholars have pointed to the possible Scandinavian origin of a clan of *posadniks* (the highest civil office in Novgorod from the eleventh century onwards), because the name "Jakun" and a presumed "Rogvolod" occur in the family. A. A. Gippius, "Skandinavskij sled v istorii novgorodskogo boiarstva (v razvitie gipotezy A.A. Molchanova o proiskhozhdenii posadnich'ego roda Giuriatinovichei-Rogovichei)," *Slavica Helsingiensia* 27 (2006): 94–108.

Dedicated Bibliography

Bolton, Timothy. *The Empire of Cnut the Great*. Leiden, 2009.

Bysted, Ane L., Carsten Selch Jensen, Kurt Villads Jensen, and John H. Lind. *Jerusalem in the North: Denmark and the Baltic Crusades, 1100–1552*. Translated by Sarah Pedersen and Fredrik Pedersen. Turnhout, 2012.

Cross, Samuel H., and Olgerd P. Sherbowitz-Wetzor, eds. *The Russian Primary Chronicle, Laurentian Text*. Cambridge, MA, 1953.

Franklin, Simon, and Jonathan Shepard. *The Emergence of Rus, 750–1200*. London and New York, 1996.

Gallén, Jarl. "Vem var Ulf Jarl, Sven Estridsens far?" *Scandia: Tidskrift för Historisk Forskning* 58 (1992): 13–30.

Gippius, A. A. "Skandinavskij sled v istorii novgorodskogo boiarstva (v razvitie gipotezy A. A. Molchanova o proiskhozhdenii posadnich'ego roda Giuriatinovichei-Rogovichei)." *Slavica Helsingiensia* 27 (2006): 94–108.

Gippius, A. A. "Begstvo ot plashcha: Zametki o 'zolotoi lude' Jakuna 'Slepogo'." In *Terra Slavica/Terra Balcanica. K jubileiu T.V. Tsiv'ian*, 52–58. Moscow, 2007.

Haastrup, Ulla, and John H. Lind. "Dronning Margrete Fredkulla: Politisk magthaver og mæcen for byzantisk kunst i danske kirker i 1100-tallet begyndelse." In *Medeltidens genus: Kvinnors och mäns roller inom kultur, rätt och samhälle: Norden och Europa ca 300–1500*, edited by Lars Hermanson and Auður Magnúsdóttir, 29–71. Gothenburg, 2015.

Hagland, Jan Ragnar. "State Formation and Early Christianization in Norway – The Problem of Possible Eastern Influences." *Motskrift* (2007): 48–52.

Howard-Johnston, James. "The De Administrando Imperio: A Re-examination of the Text and a Re-evaluation of Its Evidence About the Rus'." In *Les centres proto-urbains russes entre Scandinavie, Byzance et Orient*, edited by Michel Kazanski, Anne Nercessian, and Constantin Zuckerman, 301–36. Paris, 2000.

"Ipat'evskaia letopis'." In *Polnoe sobranie russkikh letopisei*, vol. 2, edited by Aleksei A. Shakhmatov. St Petersburg, 1908.

John H. Lind. "De russiske ægteskaber: Dynasti- og alliancepolitiki 1130'ernes danske borgerkrig." *Historisk Tidsskrift* (D) 92 (1992): 225–63.

John H. Lind. "Knes Kanutus: Knud Lavard's Political Project." In *Of Chronicles and Kings: National Saints and the Emergence of Nation States in the Early Middle Ages*, edited by John Bergsagel, Thomas Riis, and David Hiley, 113–38. Copenhagen, 2015.

John H. Lind. "Christianity on the Move: The Role of the Varangians in Rus' and Scandinavia." In *Byzantium and the Viking World*, edited by Fedir Androshchuk, Jonathan Shepard, and Monica White, 409–40. Uppsala, 2016.

"Kievo-Pecherskii paterik." In *Biblioteka literatury drevnei Rusi*, vol. 4, edited by L. A. Ol'shevskaia, 296–488. St Petersburg, 1997.

Kovalenko, Volodymyr. "Scandinavians in the East of Europe: In search of Glory or a New Motherland?" In *From Goths to Varangians from the Baltic to the Black Sea*, edited by Line Bjerg, John H. Lind, and Søren Sindbæk, 257–94. Aarhus, 2013.

"Lavrent'evskaia letopis'." In *Polnoe sobranie russkikh letopisei*, vol. 1, edited by Afanasij F. Bychkov. Leningrad (St. Petersburg), 1926.

Lind, John. "The 'Brotherhood' of Rus: A Pseudo-Problem Concerning the Origin of Rus'." *Slavica Othiniensia* 5 (1982): 66–81.

Lind, John. "Tissø – Kiev – Konstantinopel: Danske netværk i øst?" In *Vikingetidens aristokratiske miljøer*, edited by Henriette Lyngstrøm and Lasse Christian Arboe Sonne, 69–76. Copenhagen, 2014.

Lind, John. "'Varangian Christianity' and the Veneration of Anglo-Saxon and Scandinavian Saints in Early Rus'." In *Identity Formation and Diversity in the Early Medieval Baltic and Beyond*, edited by Johan Callmer, Ingrid Gustin, and Mats Roslund, 106–35. Leiden, 2017.

Litvina, Anna F., and Fjodor B. Uspenskii. "Pochemu variag Iakun 'otbezhe ludy zlatoe?' Stseny listvenskoi bitvy 1024 g." *Drevniaia Rus': Voprosy medievistiki* 1 (2016): 27–24.

Mel'nikova, Elena A. "The Lists of Old Norse Personal Names in the Russian Byzantine Treaties of the Tenth Century." *Studia Anthroponymica Scandinavica*, no. 22 (2004): 5–27.

Mikheev, S. M. "Variazhskie kniaz'ia Iakun, Afrikan i Shimon: Literaturnye siuzhety, transformatitsia imen i istoricheskii kontekst." *Drevniaia Rus': Voprosy medievistiki* 2 (2008): 27–32.

Nazarenko, Aleksandr V. *Drevniaia Rus' na mezhdunarodnykh putiakh: Mezhdistsiplinarnye ocherki kul'turnykh, torgovykh, politicheskie sviazei IX – XII vekov*. Moscow, 2001.
Novgorodskaia pervaia letopis' starshego i mladshego izvodov. Edited by Arsenii N Nasonov. Moscow, 1950.
The Paterik of the Kievan Caves Monastery. Translated by Muriel Heppell. Cambridge, MA, 1989.
The saga of Olaf Tryggvason by Oddr Snorrason. Edited by Theodore M. Andersson. Ithaca, NY, 2003.
Samnordisk runtextdatabas (Scandinavian Runic-text Data Base). www.runforum.nordiska.uu.se/srd/.
Scheel, Roland. *Skandinavien und Byzanz: Bedingungen und Konsequenzen mittelalterlicher Kulturbeziehungen*, 2 vols. Göttingen, 2015.
Thietmar von Merseburg. *Chronik*. Edited by Werner Trillmich. Darmstadt, 1974.

7 Contact and Continuity
England and the Scandinavian Elites in the Early Middle Ages

Marie Bønløkke Missuno

Scandinavian activities in England are well documented. From the Viking raids of the ninth century to the Scandinavian settlement that followed, the early medieval period witnessed the formation of significant links across the North Sea.[1] These connections were actively created, maintained, and utilized by groups and individuals engaged in processes of political, economic, and cultural exchange. In the early eleventh century, with the 1016 conquest of England by Knud II the Great, the kingdoms of England and Denmark – and later Norway and Sweden – were united under one ruler, and links across the North Sea multiplied and intensified to the point where it is possible to contemplate the existence of an Anglo-Scandinavian (or Anglo-Danish) elite with a shared identity and activities on both sides of the North Sea.[2]

The close bonds created during the reign of Knud are rarely explored beyond the death of his son and successor, Hardeknud – and with it the final collapse of a joint North Sea realm in 1042. Close to three decades later, the events of the year 1066 are traditionally credited as the end of the Anglo-Scandinavian connections that had originated in the Viking period. The Battle of Stamford Bridge, in which the Norwegian King Harald Hardrada was defeated by the English king Harold II Godwinson, is often considered to be the end of the Viking Age; this is a truth with moderations. Scandinavian expeditions to England were mounted from Denmark in 1069–70, 1075, and 1085, although this final campaign never left the Danish shores. Nevertheless, the strict periodization of 1066 is often encountered in textbooks dealing with the world of the Vikings.[3]

In English historiography the Battle of Hastings in 1066 and the Norman Conquest that followed are similarly argued to constitute a breaking point in history, and though there is no disputing the fact that the Norman invasion did have a significant impact on English society, various projects have also highlighted areas of continuity.[4] However, it remains clear that the cultural distance between England and Scandinavia – once closely linked on multiple levels – gradually widened as Norman settlement and power was consolidated and the Anglo-Saxon elite submitted and were integrated into the new order. The Icelandic author of the late thirteenth-century *Gunnlaugs saga Ormstungu* put this sense of loss of a shared identity into words when he wrote that the same tongue was once spoken in England, Norway, and Denmark, but the English tongue changed when William the Bastard won the country and thereafter *valska* ("Welsh," i.e., foreign, but especially used for the French language) was spoken there.[5]

This chapter explores the continuity and transformation of relations between the upper elite strata of England and Scandinavia across the divide of 1066. While some contacts may be seen as an extension and continuation of the networks forged during the Viking period and the North Sea empire under Knud the Great, others were the result of new opportunities and developments in England as well as in Scandinavia.

The Godwinson Dynasty

The bonds between the Scandinavian and English elites that characterized the eleventh century, and the ways in which they were utilized, are most clearly demonstrated by the connections of the Anglo-Danish family of the Godwinsons. Through the contracting of two marriages during the early years of the reign of Knud the Great, the English earl Godwine became intimately linked to the Danish royal house (Figure 7.1). Adam

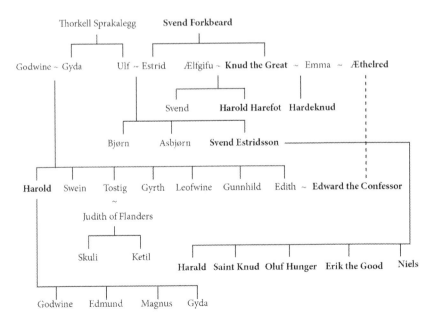

Figure 7.1 Dynastic links between the Godwinsons and the Danish royal house. Kings in bold.

of Bremen's *Gesta Hammaburgensis Ecclesiae Pontificum*, written in the 1070s, reports how Knud, king of the Danes, gave his sister Estrid in marriage to Ulf. Although Adam describes Ulf as *dux Angliae*, it is unlikely (when the Scandinavian tradition is taken into account)[6] that this is a reference to English descent.[7] Rather, it alludes to Adam's belief that Ulf held some form of office in England under Knud, although his area of responsibility remains unknown.[8] In the English documentary evidence, the signature of *Ulf dux* first occurs in a charter dated 1022,[9] but his background and early career is difficult to establish until he emerges as one of the most powerful Danish earls in the late 1020s, when he became regent of Denmark in the absence of Knud the Great.

Following the marriage of Estrid and Ulf, Adam informs us that Knud then proceeded to marry Ulf's sister, Gyda, to the English earl Godwine.[10] The origins of Earl Godwine himself are unknown, but he appears to have been of relatively modest descent, though he may have held some position at the court of the English king Æthelred the Unready.[11] In any case, Godwine seems to have been well placed to take advantage of the Danish takeover, and he soon rose to prominence under Knud. He first witnessed a charter as an earl in 1018, and from 1023 he took the position of first attestor after the king.[12] From this point onwards he was the most prominent earl in England.[13]

The *Vita Ædwardi Regis*, written in the late 1060s by a monk of presumably Flemish origin, tells us that Godwine's position with the new king was due to his being "the most cautious in counsel and the most active . . . in war" (cum consilio cautissimus, tum bellicis [. . .] strenuissimus).[14] The *Vita Ædwardi*, contrary to its title, reads more like a panegyric for Earl Godwine than a hagiography of King Edward. The text was commissioned by the widowed Queen Edith, Godwine's daughter, shortly after the death of the king in 1066.[15] Amid much laud and exoneration, the anonymous author provides us with valuable information on the parts Godwine played, not only in Knud's English kingdom, but in Denmark as well. The earl had a central position in the Anglo-Scandinavian network and appears to have fully integrated himself into the Scandinavian elite, although he may also have acted as a mediator between Scandinavian and Anglo-Saxon factions. Of a journey to Denmark on which Godwine accompanied Knud, the hagiographer writes:

> Here the king tested more closely his wisdom, here his perseverance, here his courage in war, and here the strength of this nobleman. He also found out how profound he was in eloquence, and what advantage it would be to him in his newly acquired kingdom if he were to bind him more closely to him by means of some fitting reward. Consequently he admitted the man, whom he had tested in this way for so long, to his council and gave him his sister as wife. And when

Godwin returned home, having performed all things well, he was appointed by him earl and office-bearer of almost all the kingdom.[16]

The marriage between Gyda and Godwine created the most prominent Anglo-Scandinavian family of the eleventh century. Together the couple had at least six sons and three daughters. It is noteworthy that of Godwine's nine children, five – Swein, Harold, Tostig, Gyrth, and Gunnhild – were given Scandinavian names, highlighting the importance of the Danish connection in Godwine's life and career. Pursuing the evidence of the personal names further, it is interesting to note that the preference for Danish names continues on in the generation of Godwine's grandchildren – among the children of Harold Godwinson we find the names Magnus, Gyda, and Gunnhild.[17] Early medieval naming practices were highly conservative and bound up in social and cultural networks and affiliations. Most often children were named after relations, be they familial, religious, or of a patron-client type.[18] There is reason, therefore, to take notice when entirely new names enter into a family, as this suggests a break of some sort. In the case of the Godwine dynasty, the names Swein, Harold, Gyrth, and Gunnhild honor a particular link with the most prominent Scandinavian families, including the royal house; as the names are carried down through several generations we must assume that this was an association that Godwine and his descendants wished to uphold and express. It is important to note that Godwine's connections with Denmark were not unilateral but also created opportunities in England for members of the Danish elite. At least one of the children of Ulf and Estrid, Bjorn, gained a position in England through Godwine.[19]

Connections in Use

The sources attesting to the bonds between Scandinavian and English families in the mid-eleventh century are predominantly of English origin and it is consequently difficult to assess how these connections worked and were utilized in a Scandinavian context. Some members of the Scandinavian elite may have used their English contacts to go abroad and gain high position, wealth, and experience. Bjorn Estridsen provides an example. Around 1045 he was awarded an earldom in the East Midlands under Edward the Confessor, and the same year he attested three royal charters as *Beorn dux*. His name immediately follows the names of the Godwinsons.[20]

Their English connections brought the Scandinavian elites into contact with a culture and society in which supranational institutions were firmly established in a way that was not present in Scandinavia, and this provided an opportunity for the transfer of new ideas, models, and technologies. Clear examples of how the Scandinavian elites used this social resource are few and far between, but a possible case is found in

Roskilde, Denmark. On a hill overlooking what was once the central Viking Age harbor and the boundaries of the medieval town, the church of St Clement (now Skt. Jørgensbjerg) hides the remnants of a previous church dated to the period 1029–35.[21] This early building exhibits clear architectural links to Anglo-Saxon England and, as the technique of building in stone was not yet known in Denmark, it is generally accepted that the church was built by English masons.[22] The main agent in bringing these masons to Denmark is most likely to have been Estrid, sister of Knud the Great, Ulf's wife, and mother of King Svend Estridsen.

According to the *Anglo-Saxon Chronicle*, in the year 1026, Ulf, who had been awarded the rule of Denmark in Knud's absence, joined a campaign against the Anglo-Danish king alongside kings Olav Haraldsson of Norway and Anund Jakob of Sweden.[23] The outcome of the ensuing Battle of the Holy River is disputed, but accounts generally agree that Ulf survived the battle only to be killed by Knud in Roskilde shortly after. The *Chronicon Roskildense*, written in 1137–38, relates how the murder took place in church as Ulf was attending matins. The anonymous author adds that the widowed Estrid gave her husband an honorable funeral and that she had the old wooden church replaced by a new one built in stone.[24] It seems reasonable to argue that Estrid would have engaged English masons for the erection of this church. Estrid's church, however, is unlikely to be the church of St Clement, which is located outside the center of medieval Roskilde. Instead, it was probably erected on the royal estate in the area surrounding the present-day cathedral, although no clear evidence has been found. Olsen has hypothesized that the masons, when they had finished their work on Estrid's church, moved to the hill near the harbor to build the church of St Clement.[25]

The Anglo-Scandinavian Network c. 1066

The personal relationships created between the English and Danish elites, and exemplified here by the Godwinsons, were part of a larger network of Anglo-Scandinavian connections in which one set of bonds could lead to further connections. This becomes especially evident in the events leading up to the Norman Conquest of 1066. The Battle of Stamford Bridge, which took place only weeks before the decisive battle at Hastings between the English and an invading army led by William of Normandy, brought the English king Harold against a Norwegian army led by Harald Hardrada. Harold, son of Godwine, had assumed the English throne upon the death of Edward the Confessor, but his legitimacy was contested on several fronts.

Harald Hardrada's perceived claim to the English throne ran through Denmark. According to the *Chronicon Roskildense* and the twelfth-century *Ágrip af Nóregskonungasögum*, Hardeknud, son of Knud the Great, and Magnus, son of Olav Haraldsson, had reached an agreement whereby the one who lived longer was to inherit the kingdom from the other, but each would rule his own kingdom while they both lived.[26] As the successor to the throne of Magnus in Norway, Harald extended his claim to the throne of Denmark but was held back by Svend Estridsen (r. 1047–76). In this conflict, the Danish king looked to his English connections for assistance. *The Chronicle of John of Worcester* relates:

> Swein, king of the Danes, sent envoys to Edward, asking him to send naval assistance, but although Earl Godwine was willing for at least fifty ships to be sent, Earl Leofric and the people with one voice opposed it.[27]

Despite the refusal of help from England, Svend managed to defend his kingdom against repeated attacks from Norway, and in 1064 he and Harald entered peace negotiations. Harald then turned his attention towards England, where he claimed that as the successor of Magnus, who had been the rightful heir of Hardeknud, he also had a legitimate right to the English throne.[28] The events of 1066 are inextricably linked to the Godwinson dynasty and their connections to Scandinavia. For the attack on England in 1066 Harald had entered into an alliance with Tostig Godwinson, a brother of Harold. The movements of Tostig in the years leading up to Stamford Bridge exemplify how links between the English and Scandinavian elites went beyond those created through marriage or blood.

In 1055 Tostig had been made earl of Northumbria.[29] His rule north of the Humber is commented favorably in the *Vita Ædwardi*, and he and his Flemish wife, Judith, are remembered as generous patrons in Simeon of Durham's history of the Church in Durham, written between 1104 and 1107.[30] In 1065, however, the Northumbrians rose up against Tostig and the earl went into exile.[31] The *Vita Ædwardi* describes how the deposed earl went to his mother to say his farewells and then proceeded to Flanders with his wife, children, and a company of thegns.[32] Snorri Sturluson, in his saga of Harald Sigurdson (i.e., Harald Hardrada), maintained that Tostig then traveled to Denmark and later to Norway in order to secure the support of his cousin, the Danish king Svend, against his brother Harold – who by then had been made king of the English following the death of Edward the Confessor.[33] According to Snorri, the Danish king offered Tostig an earldom but did not extend his help to an attack on England.[34] Snorri may have constructed the exchange between Tostig and Svend to suit his narrative purposes, but we should not wholly dismiss the possibility that such an offer, or something similar, could or did take place. The story of Tostig's visit to Denmark is omitted in an account of the earl's movements given by the twelfth-century Anglo-Norman chronicler Orderic Vitalis, who instead asserts that Tostig went to see Duke William of Normandy to enlist his help in disputing his brother's claim to the throne.[35] All accounts agree, however, that Tostig proceeded to Norway, where he entered into an alliance with Harald Hardrada.[36] What followed is well known. The Norwegian forces were defeated at Stamford Bridge on 25 September, but only days later King Harold Godwinson was faced with a Norman invasion led by William the Bastard, soon to be known as the Conqueror, and at the Battle of Hastings on 14 October the Normans were victorious.

English Exiles in Scandinavia

In the aftermath of the Norman Conquest a significant number of Englishmen sought refuge in Scandinavia. They were survivors fleeing the Battle of Hastings, retreating to regroup, seek support, and gather the strength to return. According to William of Malmesbury, members of the English elite left England for Ireland and Denmark, where they assembled armies.[37] William of Jumièges, biographer of the Norman dukes and a contemporary of William the Conqueror, writes that the Anglo-Saxons sent messengers to Denmark and that some went into exile after 1066.[38] Although this early wave of exiles may have included women and children, it is unlikely that anyone regarded their status as being anything but temporary. It is also possible that the exiles did not stay in Denmark throughout this initial period of expatriation but remained mobile in their efforts to gather forces to return to England.[39]

The sons of the defeated Harold Godwinson, along with the rest of the remaining members of the Godwinson dynasty, are some of the most prominent and best documented exiles of the period. Their different paths provide illuminating examples of the role of North Sea connections in the struggles of the Anglo-Saxon nobility in the wake of the Norman Conquest. Judith of Flanders, the wife of Harold's brother, Earl Tostig, presumably left the country before the turmoil of 1066. The year before, as a result of the rebellion against Tostig's rule of Northumbria, the family had fled to St Omer, where they were welcomed by Judith's half-brother, Count Baldwin of Flanders.[40] E. A. Freeman and later Frank Barlow have argued that Tostig's sons can be identified as Skuli and Ketil, the two brothers of noble English kin who, according to Snorri's saga of Harald Sigurdson, were taken to Norway by Olav Kyrre after their father's defeat at Stamford Bridge.[41] Considering Tostig's alliance with Harald Hardrada it is not entirely impossible that his sons (if they were of age) would have sought refuge there.[42]

The remaining members of the Godwinson family had remained loyal to Harold throughout the troubles of 1066. His brothers Gyrth and Leofwine died alongside him in the Battle of Hastings.[43] The surviving Godwinsons and their descendants were left in a difficult situation after the Norman invasion. Harold's sons, Godwine, Edmund, and Magnus, fled to Ireland, where they gathered their forces to return to England

132 *Marie Bønløkke Missuno*

in the following years. In 1068 they arrived with a fleet in Somerset, but after a few battles they returned to Ireland.[44] The same pattern was repeated the following year.[45] At this point the sons of Harold Godwinson are lost from the insular annals, but they reappear in Denmark in Saxo's history of the Danes:

> His [Harold's] two sons departed with all speed for Denmark accompanied by their sister. Sven, overlooking their father's true deserts, received them with the kind of affection that befits relatives and gave the girl in marriage to the Russian king, Valdemar, who was also known as Yaroslav by his people.[46]

It is puzzling how Saxo, who is otherwise rarely well informed on either the eleventh century or English history, should have acquired this knowledge. Conceivably, the story could have been maintained in the tradition of the Danish royal house, which would thus indicate the English past as something worth upholding. Saxo's story may also be connected to the arrival of another prominent Anglo-Danish figure in Denmark.

After the Norman invasion, Gyda, the widow of Earl Godwine and mother of the defeated King Harold, initially retired to the family estate in Exeter. However, during the spring of 1068 William the Conqueror went into Devonshire and besieged Exeter, so she was forced to flee to the island of Flat Holm in the Severn. According to the *Anglo-Saxon Chronicle*, Gyda was accompanied by many distinguished men's wives, and Orderic Vitalis adds that she had collected (and brought with her) a great store of treasure.[47] It is highly likely that her daughter Gunnhild and granddaughter Gyda (the daughter of Harold Godwinson, who is mentioned by Saxo) were among the ladies in the company.[48] From Flat Holm they moved on to St Omer in Flanders, but from there their movements are more difficult to follow. Timothy Bolton has brought attention to a small lead plaque dedicated to Gunnhild, found in 1786 in the now-destroyed cathedral church of St Donatian in Bruges.[49] Part of the inscription reads:

> Gunnhild, born of noble parents of English descent: her father, Earl Godwine, under which lord the greatest part of England served, her mother, Gyda, sprung from a famous Danish family. . . . And now when she had reached a marriageable age, since England had been conquered by William, count of the Normans, and her brother Harold, king of the English, had been slain by the same, she abandoned her native land and was exiled for some years at Saint-Omer in Flanders. . . . From there she went over to Bruges, and stayed here for several years, and thence crossed into Denmark. When she returned to this place, the virgin took up residence with the Lord, in the year of the incarnation of the Lord 1087.[50]

That Gunnhild continued from Flanders to Denmark, and the fact that the three children of Harold Godwinson made their way there as well, increases the possibility that this was also the destination of the older Gyda.[51]

No written records exist to tell us what happened to the members of the Godwinson family and their followers who went to Denmark in the aftermath of the Norman Conquest, but a model for land acquisition by English exiles elsewhere in Scandinavia could provide hints. The earliest Icelandic chronicle of the medieval kings of Norway, *Morkinskinna*, reports how the Norwegian king Olav Kyrre (who also housed an English cleric by the name of Turgot who had fled the captivity of William the Conqueror) offered an earldom to Skuli, son of Tostig Godwinson. Skuli refused the offer in favor of a grant of land.[52] Both opportunities – land and position – appear to have been available to at least the most prominent of the Anglo-Saxon exiles in Scandinavia, but the effect of the arrival of people of English origin or with strong English connections in Scandinavia is difficult to ascertain. It may be argued that the number of links between England and Scandinavia increased on a strictly personal level, but how they could be converted into an active resource remains unknown.

Those who had left England permanently are likely to have been those whose opportunities in England under Norman rule were exhausted. The nature of the bonds consequently changed. The dynastic links between England and Scandinavia exemplified by the Godwinson dynasty appear to have lost their significance, and in some cases to have come to an end, when Anglo-Saxon rebellions against Norman rule subsided and no further campaigns of re-conquest were mounted from Scandinavia. In place of the very personal and familial ties which had dominated the Anglo-Scandinavian elite network since the reign of Knud the Great, a range of more formal and institutional bonds emerged. Some of these had existed before, and nearly all were founded on the basis of the closer connections of the preceding decades.

Ecclesiastical Connections

The ecclesiastical links are the ones most clearly documented in the extant sources. The role of English missionaries in the earliest phases of the Christianization of Scandinavia is well documented.[53] Connections between England and the Norwegian Church extended well into the High Middle Ages. Rainald, the first bishop of Stavanger, consecrated sometime in the 1120s, is likely to have been of English origin.[54] He is mentioned briefly in the collections of kings' sagas *Fagrskinna* and *Morkinskinna*, as well as in Snorri Sturluson's *Heimskringla*, though only the latter identifies him as English.[55] The connection between England and the Church in Stavanger is supported by the architecture of the cathedral – which shows strong English influence – and by the dedication of the cathedral to the English St Swithun; the cathedral is known to have possessed a relic of the saint.[56] Similarly, a number of architectural features on fragments from the Nidaros Cathedral testify to a connection with the masons of the York Minster workshop in the 1170s.[57] Furthermore, in the years 1181–82 Oystein, the archbishop of Nidaros, was in exile at the monastery of Bury St Edmunds in England.[58] The Church in Sweden appears to have had similar links – some of which may have extended through Norway or Denmark – though these are often more difficult to date.[59]

In Denmark, the appointment of English bishops also continued after the Norman Conquest, and English influence is well attested, especially in Odense.[60] The main sources for these connections are a number of literary pieces written in Denmark in the period c. 1095–1113 and collectively known as the Odense literature. The works all relate to the sanctification of Knud IV the holy (r. 1080–86) and bear witness to links to England on several levels.

Knud himself had been in England on multiple occasions. The first attested journey took place in 1069, when the future king crossed the North Sea as part of a fleet under the leadership of his uncle Asbjorn.[61] The force ravaged York in support of an English rebellion against the Normans and then spent the winter between the Ouse and the Trent.[62] When spring arrived they went south into the Fenlands, where they again supported the local resistance before they returned home.[63] In 1075 Knud himself led a fleet to England, presumably in response to a call for assistance from a group of English earls who were plotting a rebellion against their king. But by the time the Danes arrived in England the planned rebellion had been dissolved and the ringleaders captured. The fleet then proceeded to York, where they broke into the Minster and seized a large amount of treasure, then sailed overseas to Flanders before continuing home.[64] Ten years later, when Knud had ascended to the Danish throne, he planned a final attack on England, but this time his fleet never left the Danish shores; the fleet had assembled in the Limfjord but the king was detained by trouble on the southern border and was unable to join the expedition. As autumn drew closer, members of the fleet began returning home. Knud responded by fining the men who had abandoned the fleet, leading to a revolt in the north of Jutland which spread across the peninsula. The king fled to Odense, where he was killed in the church dedicated to St Alban on 10 July 1086.[65] Less than ten years later he was venerated as a royal martyr.

The earliest text to relate the story of Knud's death is the *Tabula Othiniensis* – a copper plate that was placed in the king's shrine during his elevation in 1095. The inscription informs us that it was Knud himself who had brought the relics of St Alban to Odense from England.[66] The context of the relics' removal from England is unknown, but Knud's

English connections and his travels there would have provided ample opportunity. According to the *Anglo-Saxon Chronicle*, in 1070 the fleet of Asbjorn had assembled at Ely, where the local monastery claimed to have Alban's bones.[67] Knud is also regularly credited with the donation of the relics of St Oswald to Odense, which he could have acquired in York or Peterborough. However, as Haki Antonsson has pointed out, English kings in the eleventh century were known for presenting relics of St Oswald to foreign kings as a gift when establishing alliances, and any of the English relics in Odense could have arrived through legitimate channels.[68] Furthermore, the *Tabula* lists the names of Knud's companions, and though the names are of Danish origin, some are spelled according to Anglo-Saxon sound laws, suggesting that the scribe is likely to have been of English origin.[69]

Following the elevation of Knud in 1095, the need arose for a hagiographic-liturgical text to be read on the saint's feast day. The anonymous *Passio sancti Kanuti regis et martiris*, written sometime between 1095 and 1101, is the earliest work of hagiography from Scandinavia.[70] Again, the author appears to be of English origin. This identification is based mainly on the author's thinly disguised animosity towards the Normans in England as well as his reflections on Knud's failed expedition to England.[71] The text recounts the elevation of Knud on 31 March 1095, at which the author himself was present, and the ceremony surrounding it, which included testing the bones by fire. Kim Esmark has convincingly argued that this particular ritual was introduced to Odense from England.[72]

The most famous piece of the Odense literature is Ailnoth's *Vita et Passio Sancti Canuti*, dated to the period 1110–13, most likely 1111–12.[73] In Ailnoth's text, the English element is easily identified. In his preface, he himself informs us that he was born in Canterbury but at the time of writing had spent twenty-four years in Denmark; and he appears to have been influenced by a range of English sources.[74] Although there is a clear connection between Ailnoth's text and Odense there is no solid evidence that he was permanently established there, and he might instead have been attached to the royal court.[75]

From documentary sources we do know of twelve Benedictine monks who came to Odense from the English monastery of Evesham sometime between 1095 and 1100, though an early date of 1095/6 for their arrival is generally favored.[76] They were invited by Erik I the Good (r. 1095–1103) to establish a cathedral chapter after the English model, but it is evident that English clerics were present at St Alban's in Odense prior to Erik's ascension to the Danish throne, which only took place after the elevation of Knud on 31 March 1095.[77] We do not know where these early English monks came from but, as shown previously, they were actively engaged in the cult of St Knud through literature and liturgy. Esmark has suggested that they had links to Evesham, which also held relics of St Oswald and where a fire trial similar to the one performed in Odense had taken place in 1080.[78] Knud the Great had been among the benefactors of the abbey, and Aelfweard, its abbot in the period 1014–40, is reported to have been a relative of Knud's.[79] It is also relevant to note that Erik the Good is likely to have visited England, perhaps as early as 1095, and that his itinerary included the monastic community at Durham which had been refounded in 1083 by monks from Wearmouth and Jarrow, which in turn had been refounded by monks from Evesham in the 1070s.[80] It is also possible that the early Odense monks had brought the relics of Alban (and Oswald) to Denmark. And, finally, the exiles who had left England following the Norman Conquest also included ecclesiastics – Ailnoth may perhaps be counted among them.[81]

Irrespective of the exact earlier connections, the arrival of the Evesham monks in Odense exemplifies the intersection of elite ambitions – sacred and secular – and the exploitation of international networks and resources to fulfill them. The Danish king and the monastic community of St Alban in Odense had a common interest in the cult of Knud. The establishment of a monastic community staffed by English monks – well-versed in the promotion of royal saints – was an effective way to achieve their goals.

Conclusion

In order to fully understand the nature of the links between English religious communities and Scandinavian elites, they must be seen as part of a multi-faceted network that included a variety of different bonds – ecclesiastical, secular, dynastic, and political. This had been the case since the Viking period, and different bonds and types of bonds would often overlap. In this respect, the later medieval links between England and Scandinavia do not differ significantly from those of the earlier period, though it is possible to identify some transformations throughout the eleventh century and into the twelfth. Whereas the earlier networks were characterized by bonds of family and kinship (here exemplified by the Godwinsons), the later links appear to have been more formalized. The Benedictine cathedral chapter at Odense, for example, was incorporated into the monastic organization of mother- and daughter-houses. This facilitated regular and long-term contact and exchanges, as witnessed by the renewals of confraternity between Odense and Evesham (and later also Malmesbury and York) several times throughout the twelfth century.[82] At the same time, the apparent decline in direct personal bonds (through, for example, kinship) makes the Anglo-Danish network less clearly defined in this period.

Notes

1. See for example *Cultures in Contact: Scandinavian Settlement in England in the Ninth and Tenth Centuries*, ed. Dawn M. Hadley and Julian D. Richards (Turnhout, 2000); Jonathan Adams and Katherine Holman, *Scandinavia and Europe 800–1350: Contact, Conflict, and Coexistence* (Turnhout, 2004).

2. See for example Anne Pedersen, "Anglo-Danish Contact Across the North Sea in the Eleventh Century: A Survey of the Danish Archaeological Evidence," in *Scandinavia and Europe 800–1350*, 43–67; Else Roesdahl, "Denmark-England in the Eleventh Century: The Growing Archaeological Evidence for Contacts Across the North Sea," in *Beretning fra Seksogtyvende Tværfaglige Vikingesymposium*, ed. Niels Lund (Højbjerg, 2007), 7–31; Marie Bønløkke Spejlborg, "There and Back Again: English Connections in Early Medieval Denmark, c. 991–1086" (PhD diss., University of Aarhus, 2016).
3. Stefan Brink, "Who Were the Vikings?" in *The Viking World*, ed. Stefan Brink and Neil Price (London, 2012), 4–7.
4. See for example Orietta Da Rold, "English Manuscripts 1060 to 1220 and the Making of a Re-Source," *Literature Compass* 3, no. 4 (2006): 750–66 at 752.
5. "Gunnlaugs saga Ormstungu," in *Borgfirðinga Sǫgur*, ed. Sigurður Nordal and Guðni Jónsson (Reykjavík, 1938), ch. 7.
6. Jarl Gallén, "Vem var Ulf Jarl, Sven Estridsens far?" *Scandia: Tidskrift för Historisk Forskning* 58 (1992): 13–30.
7. Adam of Bremen, *Gesta Hammaburgensis Ecclesiae Pontificum*, ed. Bernhard Schmeidler (Hannover, 1917), 2.54.
8. John of Worcester, *The Chronicle of John of Worcester*, vol. 2, ed. R. R. Darlington and Patrick McGurk, trans. Jennifer Bray and Patrick McGurk (Oxford, 1995), s.a. 1049.
9. Peter H. Sawyer (=S), ed., *Anglo-Saxon Charters: An Annotated List and Bibliography* (London, 1968), 984. He is likewise listed among the attestations of S 980 (dated 1021–3) and S 981 (no date) but both of these are of questionable authenticity. Indeed S 980 may have been modeled on S 984.
10. Adam of Bremen, *Gesta*, 2.54.
11. Frank Barlow, *The Godwins: The Rise and Fall of a Noble Dynasty* (Harlow, 2001), 23–36.
12. S 951 and 977.
13. Simon Keynes, *An Atlas of Attestations in Anglo-Saxon Charters c. 670–1066* (Cambridge, 2002), table LXIX.
14. *Vita Ædwardi Regis: The Life of King Edward Who Rests at Westminster*, ed. and trans. Frank Barlow (London, 1962), 1.1.
15. Frank Barlow, *Edward the Confessor* (London, 1970), 291–300.
16. "Hic eius prudentiam, hic laborum constantiam, hic uirtu[ti]s militiam, hic attentius expertus est idem rex tanti principis ualentiam, quam profundus eloquio, et si eum sibi artius asstringeret quouis decenti beneficio, quante commoditatis sibi foret in nouiter acquisito Anglorum regno. Taliter ergo diutius probatum, ponit eum sibi a secretis, dans illi in coniugem sororem suam. Vnde cum repatriaret in Angliam, feliciter actis omnibus, totius pene regni ab ipso constituitur dux et baiulus." *Vita Ædwardi Regis*, 1.1. The author mistakenly identifies Gyda as the sister of Knud.
17. Alfred Anscombe, "The Pedigree of Earl Godwin," *Transactions of the Royal Historical Society* 7 (1924): 129–50.
18. Matthew Townend, *Scandinavian Culture in Eleventh-Century Yorkshire* (Kirkdale, 2007), 7–10.
19. See below.
20. S 1008, S 1009, S 1010.
21. Barbara E. Crawford, "The Cult of Clement in Denmark," *Historie* 2 (2006): 235–81 at 246–47; Jørgen Steen Jensen, ed., *Tusindtallets Danske Mønter fra Den kongelige Mønt- og Medaillesamling* (Copenhagen, 1995), 38.
22. Olaf Olsen, *St. Jørgensbjærg Kirke: Arkæologiske Undersøgelser i Murværk og Gulv* (Copenhagen, 1960), 34.

23. ASC E, s.a.1025 (1026).
24. *Chronicon Roskildense*, in SM, vol. 1, ch. 7.
25. Olsen, *St. Jørgensbjærg Kirke*, 30.
26. *Ágrip af Nóregskonungasǫgum: A Twelfth-Century Synoptic History of the Kings of Norway*, ed. and trans. Matthew James Driscoll, 2nd rev. ed. (London, 2008), ch. 36; *Chronicon Roskildense*, ch. 9.
27. "Ad quem etiam rex Danorum Suanos legatos mittens, rogauit ut ei nauale mitteret adiutorium, sed licet comes Goduuinus uoluisset ut saltem. l. naues illi mitterentur, Leofricus comes omnisque populus uno ore contradixerunt." John of Worcester, *Chronicle*, vol. 2, s.a. 1048. See also ASC D, s.a. 1048 (1047–1048).
28. Claus Krag, "Harald Hardrada (1015–1066)," in *Oxford Dictionary of National Biography* (Oxford, 2004), www.oxforddnb.com/view/article/49272.
29. ASC E, s.a. 1055.
30. *Vita Ædwardi Regis*, 1.5; Simeon of Durham, *Libellus de exordio atque procursu istius hoc est dunhelmensis ecclesie*, ed. David W. Rollason (Oxford, 2000), 3.11.
31. ASC E, s.a. 1065. See the contribution by Ole-Albert Rønning in chapter 14 in this volume.
32. *Vita Ædwardi Regis*, 1.6.
33. "Haralds saga Sigurðarsonar," Hkr 3, 170–75.
34. Ibid., 172–73.
35. *The Ecclesiastical History of Orderic Vitalis*, vol. 1, ed. and trans. Marjorie Chibnall (Oxford, 1968), 3.2.120.
36. "Haralds saga Sigurðarsonar," Hkr 3, 172–75; *Ágrip*, ch. 42; Chibnall, *Orderic Vitalis*, 3.2.123.
37. William of Malmesbury, *Gesta Regum Anglorum*, vol. 1, ed. and trans. R. A. B. Mynors, Rodney M. Thomson, and Michael Winterbottom (New York, 1998), 3.254.2.
38. *The Gesta Normannorum Ducum of William of Jumièges, Orderic Vitalis, and Robert of Torigni*, vol. 2, ed. and trans. Elisabeth van Houts (Oxford, 1995), 7.19.
39. On exiles in medieval Scandinavia see the contribution by Ole-Albert Rønning in chapter 14 in this volume.
40. *Vita Ædwardi Regis*, ch. 7.
41. "Haralds saga Sigurðarsonar," Hkr 3, 197–98; Barlow, *Godwins*, 138, 168.
42. *Ágrip*, ch. 42.
43. David Mackenzie Wilson, *The Bayeux Tapestry: The Complete Tapestry in Colour* (London, 2004), 63–65.
44. ASC D, s.a. 1067 (1068); John of Worcester, *The Chronicle of John of Worcester*, vol. 3, ed. and trans. Patrick McGurk (Oxford, 1998), s.a. 1068.
45. John of Worcester, *Chronicle*, vol. 3, s.a. 1069; ASC D, s.a. 1069.
46. "Cuius filii duo confestim in Daniam cum sorore migrarunt. Quos Sueno paterni eorum meriti oblitus consanguinee pietatis more excepit puellamque Rutenorum regi Waldemaro, qui et ipse Iarizlauus a suis est appellatus, nuptum dedit." Saxo, 11.6.3.
47. ASC D, s.a. 1067 (1068).
48. Timothy Bolton, "English Political Refugees at the Court of King Sveinn Ástríðarson," *Mediaeval Scandinavia* 15 (2005): 17–36 at 19–20.
49. Barlow, *Godwins*, 167–68; Bolton, "English Political Refugees," 19.
50. "Gunildis nobilissimis orta parentibus, genere Anglia, patre Godwino comite, sub cujus domini maxima pars militabat Angliæ, matre Githa, illustri prosapia Dacorum oriunda . . . Hæcque dum jam ad nubilem ætatem

pervenisset, Anglia devicta a Willelmo Normannorum comite et ab eodem interfecto frater suo Rege Anglorum Haroldo, relicta patria, apud sanctum Audomarum aliquot annos exulans in Flandria . . . Dehinc transiens Bruggas, et ibi transvolutis quibusdam annis et inde pertransiens in Dacia, huc reversa, virgo transmigravit in Domino, Anno incarnationis domini millesimo LXXXVII." Edward A. Freeman, *The History of the Norman Conquest of England*, vol. 4 (Oxford, 1876), 754–55. My translation.
51. Bolton, "English Political Refugees," 20.
52. Msk, ch. 55.
53. Lesley Abrams, "The Anglo-Saxons and the Christianization of Scandinavia," *Anglo-Saxon England* 24 (1995): 213–49; Lesley Abrams, "Eleventh-Century Missions and the Early Stages of Ecclesiastical Organisation in Scandinavia," *Anglo-Norman Studies* 17 (1995): 21–40; Susan Edgington, "Siward – Sigurd – Sigfrid? The Career of an English Missionary in Scandinavia," *Northern Studies* 26 (1989): 56–59; Arne Odd Johnsen, "Om Misjonsbiskopen Grimkellus," *Historisk Tidsskrift* (N) 54 (1975): 22–34; Toni Schmid, *Den Helige Sigfrid* (Lund, 1931).
54. See for example, Henry Goddard Leach, "The Relations of the Norwegian with the English Church, 1066–1399, and Their Importance to Comparative Literature," *Proceedings of the American Academy of Arts and Sciences* 44, no. 20 (1909): 531–60 at 534.
55. "Magnús saga blinda," Hkr 3, 287–88.
56. Christopher Hohler, *The Cathedral of St. Swithun at Stavanger in the Twelfth Century* (London, 1964), 93.
57. Margrete H. Syrstad, "Smekre vannliljekapiteler og rike chevroner: Spor av Yorkbygghyttens folk i Trondheims- og Bergensområdet 1160–80," *Årbok: Foreningen til Norske Fortidsminnesmerkers Bevaring* 155 (2001): 75–89.
58. Jocelin of Brakelond, *The Chronicle of Jocelin of Brakelond, Monk of St. Edmundsbury*, ed. and trans. L. C. Jane (London, 1907), s.a. 1181.
59. See for example Jarl Gallén, "De engelska munkarna i Uppsala – ett katedralkloster på 1100-talet," *Historisk Tidsskrift* (F) 61 (1976): 1–21.
60. Peter King, "English Influence on the Church at Odense in the Early Middle Ages," *Journal of Ecclesiastical History* 13 (1962): 144–55; Peter King, "The Cathedral Priory of Odense in the Middle Ages," *Kirkehistoriske Samlinger* 7 (1966): 1–20.
61. ASC D, s.a. 1068 (1069).
62. John of Worcester, *Chronicle*, vol. 3, s.a. 1069; ASC E, s.a. 1069; ASC D, s.a. 1068 (1069).
63. ASC E, s.a. 1070.
64. Henry of Huntingdon, *Historia Anglorum: The History of the English People*, ed. and trans. Diana Greenway (Oxford, 1996), 6.34; ASC D, s.a. 1076 (1075) and E, s.a. 1075.
65. ASC E, s.a. 1085; Ailnoth, *Gesta Swenomagni Regis et filiorum eius et passio gloriosissimi Canuti Regis et martyris*, in VSD, chs. 11–13; Ole Fenger, *Gyldendal og Politikens Danmarkshistorie*, vol. 4, ed. Olaf Olsen (Copenhagen, 1989), 65–69.
66. *Tabula Othiniensis*, VSD, 60–62.
67. ASC E, s.a. 1070; Abrams, "The Anglo-Saxons and the Christianization of Scandinavia," 240.
68. Haki Antonsson, "Saints and Relics in Early Christian Scandinavia," *Mediaeval Scandinavia* 15 (2005): 51–80 at 61–62.
69. Henry Goddard Leach, *Angevin Britain and Scandinavia* (Cambridge, 1921), 78.
70. *Passio sancti Kanuti regis et martiris*, in VSD, 62–76.

71. Haki Antonsson, "Sanctus Kanutus Rex," in *Medieval Nordic Literature in Latin: A Website of Authors and Anonymous Works c. 1100–1530*, ed. Stephan Borgehammar, Karsten Friis-Jensen, Lars Boje Mortensen, and Åslaug Ommundsen (Bergen, 2012), https://wikihost.uib.no/medieval/index.php/Sanctus_Kanutus_rex.
72. Kim Esmark, "Hellige ben i indviet ild: Den rituelle sanktifikation af Kong Knud IV, 1095," in *Gaver, ritualer, konflikter: et rettsantropologisk perspektiv på nordisk middelalderhistorie*, ed. Hans Jacob Orning, Kim Esmark, and Lars Hermanson (Oslo, 2010), 161–210.
73. Michael H. Gelting, "Two Early Twelfth-Century Views of Denmark's Christian Past: Ailnoth and the Anonymous of Roskilde," in *Historical Narratives and Christian Identity on a European Periphery: Early History Writing in Northern, East-Central, and Eastern Europe (c. 1070–1200)*, ed. Ildar H. Garipzanov (Turnhout, 2011), 33–55 at 38–39.
74. Ailnoth, *Gesta*, ch. 1; Jacob Isager and Aidan Conti, "Ailnothus," in *Medieval Nordic Literature in Latin: A Website of Authors and Anonymous Works c. 1100–1530*.
75. Gelting, "Early Twelfth-Century Views," 40.
76. DD 1.2.24. For a discussion see Gelting, "Early Twelfth-Century Views," 36, n. 7.
77. The death of Erik's predecessor, Oluf, is recorded as 18 August in the *Necrologium Lundense*. It is possible, however, that this is a scribal error and that he in fact died before 19 April. VSD, 30, n. 1.
78. Esmark, "Hellige ben i indviet ild," 195–200.
79. Thomas of Marlborough, *History of the Abbey of Evesham*, ed. and trans. Jane E. Sayers and Leslie Watkiss (Oxford, 2003), 3.146.
80. Paul Gazzoli, "Anglo-Danish Connections and the Origins of the Cult of Knud," *Journal of the North Atlantic* 4 (2013): 69–76 at 72.
81. Bolton, "English Political Refugees."
82. DD, 1.2.66–77; DD, 1.3.48 and 171.

Dedicated Bibliography

Abrams, Lesley. "The Anglo-Saxons and the Christianization of Scandinavia." *Anglo-Saxon England* 24 (1995): 213–49.

Abrams, Lesley. "Eleventh-Century Missions and the Early Stages of Ecclesiastical Organisation in Scandinavia." *Anglo-Norman Studies* 17 (1995): 21–40.

Adam von Bremen. *Gesta Hammaburgensis Ecclesiae Pontificum*. Edited by Bernhard Schmeidler. Hannover, 1917.

Adams, Jonathan, and Katherine Holman, eds. *Scandinavia and Europe 800–1350: Contact, Conflict, and Coexistence*. Turnhout, 2004.

Ágrip af Nóregskonungasǫgum: A Twelfth-Century Synoptic History of the Kings of Norway. Edited and translated by Matthew James Driscoll. 2nd rev. ed. London, 2008.

Ailnoth. *Gesta Swenomagni Regis et filiorum eius et passio gloriosissimi Canuti Regis et martyris*. VSD, 77–136.

Anscombe, Alfred. "The Pedigree of Earl Godwin." *Transactions of the Royal Historical Society* 7 (1924): 129–50.

Antonsson, Haki. "Saints and Relics in Early Christian Scandinavia." *Mediaeval Scandinavia* 15 (2005): 51–80.

Antonsson, Haki. "Sanctus Kanutus Rex." In *Medieval Nordic Literature in Latin: A Website of Authors and Anonymous Works c. 1100–1530*, edited

by Stephan Borgehammar, Karsten Friis-Jensen, Lars Boje Mortensen, and Åslaug Ommundsen. Bergen, 2012. https://wikihost.uib.no/medieval/index.php/Sanctus_Kanutus_rex>
Barlow, Frank. *Edward the Confessor*. London, 1970.
Barlow, Frank. *The Godwins: The Rise and Fall of a Noble Dynasty*. Harlow, 2001.
Bolton, Timothy. "English Political Refugees at the Court of King Sveinn Ástríðarson." *Mediaeval Scandinavia* 15 (2005): 17–36.
Brink, Stefan. "Who Were the Vikings?" In *The Viking World*, edited by Stefan Brink and Neil Price, 4–7. London, 2012.
Crawford, Barbara E. "The Cult of Clement in Denmark." *Historie* 2 (2006): 235–81.
Da Rold, Orietta. "English Manuscripts 1060 to 1220 and the Making of a Re-Source." *Literature Compass* 3, no. 4 (2006): 750–66.
Edgington, Susan. "Siward – Sigurd – Sigfrid? The Career of an English Missionary in Scandinavia." *Northern Studies* 26 (1989): 56–59.
Esmark, Kim. "Hellige ben i indviet ild: Den rituelle sanktifikation af Kong Knud IV, 1095." In *Gaver, Ritualer, Konflikter: et rettsantropologisk perspektiv på nordisk middelalderhistorie*, edited by Hans Jacob Orning, Kim Esmark, and Lars Hermanson, 161–210. Oslo, 2010.
Fenger, Ole. *Gyldendal og Politikens Danmarkshistorie*, vol. 4. Edited by Olaf Olsen. Copenhagen, 1989.
Freeman, Edward A. *The History of the Norman Conquest of England*, vol. 4. Oxford, 1876.
Gallén, Jarl. "De engelska munkarna i Uppsala – ett katedralkloster på 1100-talet." *Historisk Tidsskrift* (N) 61 (1976): 1–21.
Gallén, Jarl. "Vem var Ulf Jarl, Sven Estridsens far?" *Scandia: Tidskrift för Historisk Forskning* 58 (1992): 13–30.
Gazzoli, Paul. "Anglo-Danish Connections and the Origins of the Cult of Knud." *Journal of the North Atlantic* 4 (2013): 69–76.
Gelting, Michael H. "Two Early Twelfth-Century Views of Denmark's Christian Past: Ailnoth and the Anonymous of Roskilde." In *Historical Narratives and Christian Identity on a European Periphery: Early History Writing in Northern, East-Central, and Eastern Europe (c. 1070–1200)*, edited by Ildar H. Garipzanov, 33–55. Turnhout, 2011.
"Gunnlaugs saga Ormstungu." In *Borgfirðinga Sǫgur*, edited by Sigurður Nordal and Guðni Jónsson, Íslenzkfornrit 3, ch. 7. Reykjavík, 1938.
Hadley, Dawn M., and Julian D. Richards, eds. *Cultures in Contact: Scandinavian Settlement in England in the Ninth and Tenth Centuries*. Turnhout, 2000.
Henry of Huntingdon. *Historia Anglorum: The History of the English People*. Edited and translated by Diana Greenway. Oxford, 1996.
Hohler, Christopher. *The Cathedral of St. Swithun at Stavanger in the Twelfth Century*. London, 1964.
Isager, Jacob, and Aidan Conti. "Ailnothus." In *Medieval Nordic Literature in Latin: A Website of Authors and Anonymous Works c. 1100–1530*, edited by Stephan Borgehammar, Karsten Friis-Jensen, Lars Boje Mortensen, and Åslaug Ommundsen. Bergen, 2012. https://wikihost.uib.no/medieval/index.php/Ailnothus>
Jensen, Jørgen Steen, ed. *Tusindtallets Danske Mønter fra Den kongelige Mønt- og Medaillesamling*. Copenhagen, 1995.

Jocelin of Brakelond. *The Chronicle of Jocelin of Brakelond, Monk of St. Edmundsbury*. Edited and translated by Lionel Cecil Jane. London, 1907.

John of Worcester. *The Chronicle of John of Worcester*, vol. 2. Edited by Reginald R. Darlington and Patrick McGurk, translated by Jennifer Bray and Patrick McGurk. Oxford, 1995.

John of Worcester. *The Chronicle of John of Worcester*, vol. 3. Edited and translated by Patrick McGurk. Oxford, 1998.

Johnsen, Arne Odd. "Om Misjonsbiskopen Grimkellus." *Historisk Tidsskrift* (N) 54 (1975): 22–34.

Keynes, Simon. *An Atlas of Attestations in Anglo-Saxon Charters c. 670–1066*. Cambridge, 2002.

King, Peter. "English Influence on the Church at Odense in the Early Middle Ages." *Journal of Ecclesiastical History* 13 (1962): 144–55.

King, Peter. "The Cathedral Priory of Odense in the Middle Ages." *Kirkehistoriske Samlinger* 7 (1966): 1–20.

Krag, Claus. "Harald Hardrada (1015–1066)." In *Oxford Dictionary of National Biography*. Oxford, 2004. www.oxforddnb.com/view/article/49272.

Leach, Henry Goddard. "The Relations of the Norwegian with the English Church, 1066–1399, and Their Importance to Comparative Literature." *Proceedings of the American Academy of Arts and Sciences* 44, no. 20 (1909): 531–60.

Olsen, Olaf. *St. Jørgensbjærg Kirke: Arkæologiske Undersøgelser i Murværk og Gulv*. Copenhagen, 1960.

Orderic Vitalis. *The Ecclesiastical History of Orderic Vitalis*, vol. 2, edited and translated by Marjorie Chibnall. Oxford, 1968.

Pedersen, Anne. "Anglo-Danish Contact Across the North Sea in the Eleventh Century: A Survey of the Danish Archaeological Evidence." In *Scandinavia and Europe 800–1350: Contact, Conflict, and Coexistence*, edited by Jonathan Adams and Katherine Holman, 43–67. Turnhout, 2004.

Roesdahl, Else. "Denmark-England in the Eleventh Century: The Growing Archaeological Evidence for Contacts Across the North Sea." In *Beretning fra Seksogtyvende Tværfaglige Vikingesymposium*, edited by Niels Lund, 7–31. Højbjerg, 2007.

Sawyer, Peter H., ed. *Anglo-Saxon Charters: An Annotated List and Bibliography*. London, 1968.

Schmid, Toni. *Den Helige Sigfrid*. Lund, 1931.

Simeon of Durham. *Libellus de exordio atque procursu istius hoc est dunhelmensis ecclesie*. Edited by David W. Rollason. Oxford, 2000.

Spejlborg, Marie Bønløkke. "There and Back Again: English Connections in Early Medieval Denmark, c. 991–1086." PhD diss., University of Aarhus, 2016.

Syrstad, Margrete H. "Smekre vannliljekapiteler og rike chevroner: Spor av Yorkbygghyttens folk i Trondheims-og Bergensområdet 1160–80." *Årbok: Foreningen til Norske Fortidsminnesmerkers Bevaring* 155 (2001): 75–89.

Thomas of Marlborough. *History of the Abbey of Evesham*. Edited and translated by Jane E. Sayers and Leslie Watkiss. Oxford, 2003.

Townend, Matthew. *Scandinavian Culture in Eleventh-Century Yorkshire*. Kirkdale, 2007.

Vita Ædwardi Regis: The Life of King Edward Who Rests at Westminster. Edited and translated by Frank Barlow. London, 1962.

William of Jumièges. *The Gesta Normannorum Ducum of William of Jumièges, Orderic Vitalis, and Robert of Torigni*, vol. 2. Edited and translated by Elisabeth van Houts. Oxford, 1995.

William of Malmesbury. *Gesta Regum Anglorum*, vol. 1. Edited and translated by Roger Aubrey Baskerville Mynors, Rodney M. Thomson, and Michael Winterbottom. New York, 1998.

Wilson, David Mackenzie. *The Bayeux Tapestry: The Complete Tapestry in Colour*. London, 2004.

8 Character Networks of the *Íslendinga Sögur* and *Þættir*

Ralph Kenna and Pádraig MacCarron

Introduction

In the past two decades the study of networks has gone from a relatively small branch of mathematics to the development of powerful and wide-ranging tools applicable to a plethora of disciplines.[1] Although network science or graph theory has been applied to social systems since the 1930s, recent availability of online resources and modern computing facilities allow us to harvest data and investigate social structures on a much larger scale than ever before. Such studies reveal that social networks have properties distinct from other types of complex systems.[2] This is in part due to what is known as *homophily*, the propensity for people to associate with those like themselves.

The vast majority of social networks thus far analyzed have been of modern societies and often are derived from online mediums. We suggest that literature can also provide us with information on social structures – in particular ones from bygone eras. This allows us to investigate past cultures in a very modern way. For example, we can investigate whether the established core properties of social complex networks are unique to our current society or whether they are also to be found in ancient descriptions of past societies.

Complex network analysis is essentially statistical. As with any investigation which is based on statistics, the larger the data set the better. This is connected to the notion of statistical power. The power of any statistical study is related to its capacity to distinguish a real effect or result from a misleading one, arising by chance.

The *Íslendinga sögur* ("Sagas of Icelanders") and *þættir* ("short tales") provide us with a particularly good corpus of texts describing culture from a different time. The narratives contain vast amounts of information on families and relationships between them. Although they are set in the settlement period of Iceland (and some partly in Norway) from the late ninth to the early eleventh centuries, it is believed that they were committed to writing in the thirteenth and fourteenth centuries by unknown or uncertain authors.[3] The tales themselves give details of events, struggles,

Character Networks 145

and conflicts in a plausible manner. A notable feature of the *Íslendinga sögur* and *þættir* is their consistency and their presentation as chronicles; main characters in one text often appear as minor ones in another. The narratives are interwoven in such a way that the plots in different texts overlap. Together the sagas and *þættir* involve thousands of characters and interactions between them. The huge network obtained by combining *Íslendinga sögur* and *þættir* delivers an ideal subject for statistical analysis.

The uniqueness of the texts and their restrained, dispassionate, and apparently objective narrative style make them an important element of world literature. As with other ancient narratives, the historicity of the *Íslendinga sögur* has long been the subject of scholarly investigations.[4] The widely accepted consensus since the late 1980s is that when read in an anthropological or sociological manner, the sagas say more about the societies in which they were written than about the societies they depict.[5] Thus, they better reflect the time-frame of this volume than the Viking Age. One of our objectives here is to expand the argument on the societal veracity and trustworthiness of Icelandic sagas and *þættir* through a character-networks investigation of the societal structures they depict.

To this end, we report here on such an investigation into eighteen overlapping texts of *Íslendinga sögur* and *þættir* with a combined cast of 1,549 individuals. Five of these are sagas containing networks which are extensive in their own right, comprising more than one hundred characters each. This allows us to also investigate each of these five individually. We can then compare these to each other, to their amalgamation, to a larger set of eighteen that also includes thirteen *þættir*, and to other complex networks from modern society and from other ancient narratives.

Besides being the best known of the sagas, *Njáls saga* is widely regarded as the greatest prose literature of the Viking era. It also has the most surviving vellum manuscripts.[6] It recounts feuds and the escalation of minor incidents into major bloodshed (but also positive interconnections such as marriages, lawsuits, and alliances). More than five hundred named characters appear in the narrative. The second-highest number of medieval saga manuscripts to survive contain *Laxdæla saga*, the saga of the people of Laxárdalur. This also includes the second-largest number of characters. It is believed that the author of *Njáls saga* may have used *Laxdæla saga* as a source.[9] One of the storylines of this richly detailed and complex saga includes a love triangle which eventually leads to enmity and death. The third major saga on our list is *Vatnsdæla saga*, the story of the people of Vatnsdalur. This tracks the family of the grandson of a Norwegian chieftain from his arrival in Iceland until the coming of Christianity in the late tenth century. *Egils saga* also starts off in Norway: after a dispute with the king, a man named Skallagrímr and his family leave for Iceland, where Skallgrimr's son Egil is born. *Gísla saga* is different from the previous four in that it is an outlaw narrative, in which the eponymous character is on the run for a number of years before finally being killed. Thus, these five major sagas demonstrate that the tales come in different types – ranging from narratives that cover generations to an outlaw saga mostly centered on one character. Our objective here is to gather statistical information on interrelationships between characters in various sagas to enable quantitative comparison of the societies depicted in the narratives. We refer to these as saga social networks and compare both to each other and to other social networks.

Over the years, different types of networks have been studied, documented, and classified according to their statistical properties.[7] Researchers have shown that the social networks that bind real people tend to have particular distinguishing features. Technically, they usually are *small world* with broad-tailed degree distributions distinguishing them from simpler random and regular networks.[8] They tend to be *assortatively mixed* and to exhibit *community structures* with high *modularity*. (See the non-technical explanation of these terms later on.) While none of these features is unique to social networks, they all are commonly found in them and are therefore characteristic of them. We have therefore investigated whether the same properties are detectable in the character networks embedded in Icelandic sagas and *þættir*. We have found that they are, to varying degrees. In this chapter we show that although the narratives have many common features, the statistical approach is capable of picking up differences in detail between them. We also interpret results – identifying reasons behind the similarities and differences among the narratives and between saga social networks and the modern world ones.

The Complex Networks of the *Íslendinga Sögur* and *Þættir*

A network is a collection of nodes which are connected by links. A collection of interacting people is an example of such a network, and we refer to such structures as *social networks*. Thus, in social networks the nodes represent people and the links interactions between them. Other types of real-world networks include computer networks, transport networks, communications networks, and brain networks (to name but a few). Social networks tend to have measurably different structures from other complex networks, and we will discuss some of these differences in the following text.

In the case of literature, we are interested in networks of characters interacting with each other. We refer to the corresponding structures as *character networks*. One of our primary interests here is whether the character networks of the *Íslendinga Sögur* and *þættir* resemble more closely the social networks of real society, or whether they look like some other forms of networks. In the specific case of the *Íslendinga Sögur* and *þættir*, we sometimes refer to character networks as *saga networks*.

To construct the saga networks we carefully read English translations of the narratives and recorded all interactions between characters.[9] We identify two types of links, social (or positive) links where two characters clearly know each other and hostile (negative) links. The latter is useful in the case where we do not know if two characters are acquainted but then they have a physical conflict so there is a definite interaction between them in the narrative. In other cases positive links are identified: for example if two characters are related, speak directly to one another, speak about one another, or are present together, and it is clear that they know each other (even if they are enemies). Two given characters can be connected by both positive and negative links (for example, if one of them changes sides during the narrative). One can introduce a greater level of nuance by weighting the links according to how many times they interact in the narrative or by some other measure of the intensity of their interactions. However, experience in statistical physics shows that there is a lot to be gained already by the minimalist approach; the statistical averaging process washes out much of the nuanced details. Here we report on such non-weighted analysis, leaving the more nuanced approach to the future.

In Figure 8.1 we present a small network for illustration purposes. Positive and negative interactions are represented by the solid lines and dashed ones, respectively. Such a partitioning is frequently found in social networks of humans. In such a real-world society it is difficult to maintain friendships between two acquaintances that are mutually hostile; there is a propensity to take sides. Similarly, three negative links in a triangle are rare, as one may frequently take the view that "the enemy of an enemy is a friend." These social phenomena, which are related to a notion called *structural balance*, mean that in human networks odd numbers of negative links in a triangle are rare.[10] In Figure 8.1 nodes A, G, and H form a mutually connected arrangement called a *triad*. This triad has two positive links (AG and AH) and one negative one (GH). Such an arrangement – with an odd number of negative links – would be hard to maintain in a real-life social network; the enmity between G and H endangers A's friendship with both of them; ultimately he or she may have to take sides in the conflict. Indeed, E is also connected to G and H. In this case it has proven too difficult for E to remain on good terms with both of them and E has chosen to form an alliance with G. Such a triad, with an even number of negative links, is more realistic in human society. Thus a characteristic feature of social networks is that the proportion of closed triads containing odd numbers of negative links is small. When we examined the various networks corresponding to the *Íslendinga sögur* and *þættir*, whether the five major stories individually or all eighteen combined, we found that no more than 10% of closed triads contain odd numbers of negative links. This means that the saga networks are structurally balanced, just as modern social networks are.

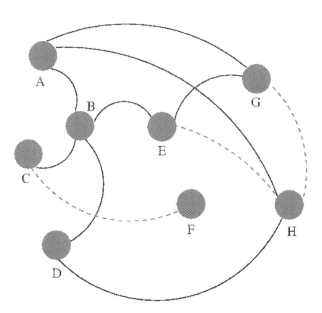

Figure 8.1 Networks are collections of nodes and links which connect them. The nodes may represent, for example, people in real life or characters in a text; and the links between them denote interactions or relationships. Network science captures the statistics relating to how these links are distributed. Here, the solid links and the dashed ones represent positive (friendly) and negative (hostile) interactions, respectively.

Besides structural balance, there are other statistical measures which capture important features of networks and thereby enable quantitative comparisons of them. One such statistic, which gauges the extent to which a network is connected, is called the *mean path length*. It is the average number of steps needed to connect any two individuals in the network. For example, in Figure 8.1 the shortest path between nodes G and D has only two steps (namely G → H → D). Nodes F and D, on the other hand, need at least three steps to link them (F → C → B → D). The average length of all of the shortest paths in the entire network is its *mean path length*. A famous instance of this notion is found in sociology in the concept of *six degrees of separation*: Although the world's population exceeds seven billion people, it is claimed that the average number of steps required to link everyone to everyone else is only about six.[11] We measured that the corresponding numbers for the five major sagas range from 3.4 to 5.1. For the eighteen sagas and *þættir* amalgamated it is 5.7, remarkably close to the real-world figure. These and other essential network statistics are recorded in Table 8.1.

Table 8.1 Some network statistics for the five major sagas and for the amalgamation of eighteen narratives. Here, "# nodes" and "# links" stand for number of nodes and links, respectively.

Saga	# nodes	# links	Mean degree	Mean path length	Clustering coefficient	Assortativity
Gísla	103	254	4.9	3.4	0.6	−0.15(5)
Vatnsdæla	132	290	4.4	3.9	0.5	0.00(6)
Egils	293	769	5.3	4.2	0.6	−0.07(3)
Laxdæla	332	894	5.4	5.0	0.5	0.19(4)
Njáls	575	1,612	5.6	5.1	0.4	0.01(2)
All 18 narratives combined	1,549	4,266	5.5	5.7	0.5	0.07(2)

The networks for the five major sagas are depicted in Figures 8.2–8.6. In the figures, the sizes of the nodes are proportional to the degrees of the corresponding characters. Light and dark links represent positive and negative interactions, respectively.

In real-world social networks, if an individual is acquainted with two others, there is a high probability that the two neighbors of a node are themselves acquainted.[12] The extent to which this is true is measured by the *clustering coefficient*. In Figure 8.1, for example, node A has 3 neighbors (namely B, G, and H). We saw earlier that the set AGH forms a triad. If B were directly connected to G, the set ABG would also form a triad. The same holds for ABH. So, of the three potential triads involving node A (namely ABG, ABH, and AGH), only one (AGH) is actualized. Therefore the clustering coefficient for node A is one out of three (1/3). If we perform similar calculations for each node of the network and then take an average, we obtain the mean *clustering coefficient* for the entire network. For the *Íslendinga sögur*, we measure clustering coefficients ranging from 0.4 in *Njáls saga* to 0.6 in *Gísla saga* and *Egils saga*. The average clustering of the amalgamation of all eighteen narratives is between these two values, with a clustering coefficient of 0.5. These statistics are also recorded in Table 8.1.

It is often useful (and, indeed, is standard practice in network science) to compare complex networks to other, more simple networks, to get an idea of how they differ. To do this in a meaningful manner, we compare to a network with the same number of nodes and the same number of links, but with the links distributed randomly between the nodes. These random networks lack the more sophisticated structure of complex networks, but their properties are mathematically more tractable.

A network which has a small path length and a high clustering coefficient is called *small world*.[13] To determine how small is "small" and how high is "high" we compare to the path length and clustering coefficient of

Figure 8.2 The character network for *Njáls saga*. As with Figures 8.3–8.6, the sizes of the nodes are proportional to the degrees of the corresponding characters. Light and dark links represent positive and negative interactions, respectively. *Njáls saga* is the only one in which 100% of characters are connected to at least one other. Of the five major sagas, it is the least structurally balanced, as 10% of closed triads contain an odd number of negative links. On average, characters in *Njála* are directly linked to 5.6

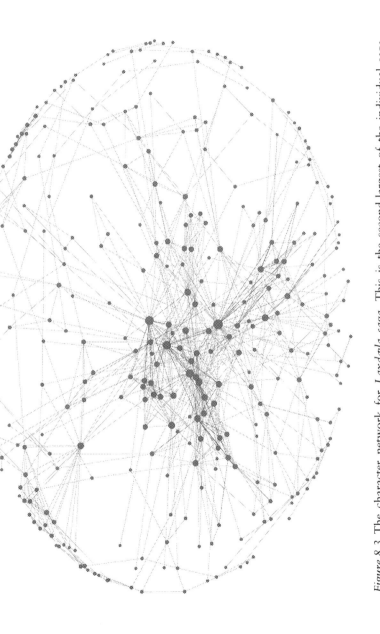

Figure 8.3 The character network for *Laxdæla saga*. This is the second-largest of the individual saga societies and the second most connected, with 99% of characters having at least one link. It also has the second-highest values of the mean degree (5.4) and path length (5.0). It is structurally balanced, with only 6% of closed triads containing odd numbers of hostile links. It contains far fewer hostile links than *Njáls saga*. This is the only strongly assortative saga.

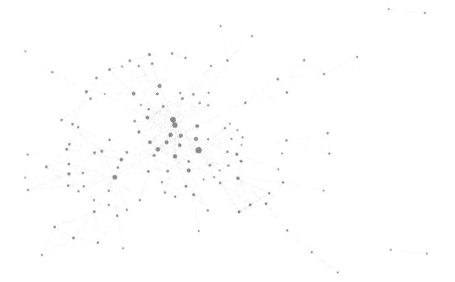

Figure 8.4 The saga of the people of *Vatnsdal* is the third of the five sagas we studied in depth. It is the most structurally balanced of the five, with only 2% of triads having an odd number of negative links; 97% of characters are connected to the giant component (i.e., have a least one link). On average, characters have 4.4 links and are connected to each other via 3.9 steps. The network is borderline assortative.

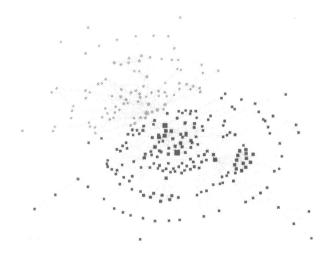

Figure 8.5 The character network for the giant component of *Egils saga*. Part of the narrative is set in Norway and part in Iceland. Here, light nodes represent individuals that appear in the first part of the tale, which is set in Norway. Dark nodes are characters that appear later, during Egil's time in Iceland. Only 5% of triads have odd numbers of hostile links and the giant component contains 97% of the nodes. The mean degree is 5.3 and the mean path length is 4.2. The network is marginally disassortative.

Figure 8.6 The character network for *Gísla saga*. This is the second-least structurally balanced of the five major sagas, with 9% of closed triads having odd numbers of negative links. The giant component contains 98% of network nodes. On average, characters in *Gísla saga* are directly connected to 4.9 others. They are connected to all others by a mean path length of 3.4. Of those analyzed, this is the only strongly disassortative saga. This is explained by the fact that it is an outlaw saga; the protagonist interacts with many minor characters.

a random network which has the same number of nodes and links as our network. If the path length of the network to hand is about the same as that of the random network, and if the clustering is significantly greater, we may consider our network as small world. In such societies, everyone can be considered to be closely connected to everyone else. Real social networks are small worlds.

We said earlier that the character networks of the five sagas have mean path lengths ranging from 3.4 to 5.1 (Table 8.1). It turns out that the path lengths for random networks of the same sizes have similar path lengths, albeit a little shorter. They are 2.9 for a random network of the same size as *Gísla saga*; 3.3 for one like *Vatnsdæla saga*; 3.4 for *Egils saga*; 3.5 for *Laxdæla saga*; and 3.7 for the random equivalent to *Njáls saga*. Although these are not identical to the path lengths of the actual saga societies, they are of the same order of magnitude. The clustering coefficients for the random networks are, however, far smaller – of a lower order of magnitude. They range from 0.01 (for a random network of the size of *Njáls saga*) to 0.05 (for one like *Gísla saga*). These are of a lower order of magnitude. Therefore each of the five major sagas is a small world in its own right, a property consistent with real world social networks.

The same applies to the combination of all eighteen narratives. The path length and clustering coefficient for the saga social networks are 5.7 and 0.5, respectively. The corresponding numbers for the counterpart random network are 3.5 and 0.02. Because the path lengths are of the same order of magnitude but the clustering coefficient for the random network is so much smaller than that for the actual saga network, we can say that this combined saga society is also a small world.

We found that the giant components of each of the five major sagas contain over 97% of nodes in each case. In other words, very few characters are disconnected from the main component. Typically, the few who are disconnected have only one or two links. Similarly, when we combine all eighteen networks into a single social network, the corresponding network is structurally very intact; 99% of its nodes belong to the giant component, with only 1% adrift or disconnected.

Degree Distributions

The previous examples are of global network statistics; they describe properties which are averaged over entire societies. At a more fundamental level we are also interested in how properties are spread from node to node (from character to character in the present instance). One of the most basic of such quantities in a network is the *degree* of each node. This is the number of links associated with that node. For example, in Figure 8.1, character A is linked to three other nodes (B, G, and H). Therefore the degree of node A is three. Different nodes have different degrees. We are interested in the distribution of degrees across all the nodes of the network. We regard the probability that nodes have specific degree values as given by the *degree distribution*. If our network were a simple, regular lattice in which the links form a series of squares or rectangles, every (interior) node would have the same degree. But, like random networks, such simple structures are unable to sustain the complex set of interactions typical of social or character networks. In a sense, the random network sits at the opposite end of the spectrum to the lattice structure of a regular grid. However, complex networks are far from both – they are neither random nor regular. In the more realistic settings to which they pertain, many nodes have a small number of links, but a few are highly connected and have many links. Complex networks like these are found to mostly come in three different classes of degree distributions. These are (i) power laws, (ii) the exponential family, and (iii) truncated power laws. Because we encounter all three in our Icelandic narratives, we describe them in turn.

Type (i) – **Power-law networks**: In a network with a power law degree distribution, a small number of nodes have a disproportionally high degree. For example, of the 103 characters in *Gísla saga*, only two interact with more than twenty characters. By contrast, sixty-five characters have degree under 5. The eponymous protagonist himself interacts with almost half the characters in the saga! His degree is therefore far greater than the average degree of the other characters in the narrative. Power-law distributed networks tend to rely heavily on a small number of vertices. In this type of network, if the highest degree nodes are removed, the network may no longer be fully connected.

When two quantities are related by a power law, a relative change in one instigates a relative change in the other, independent of their initial values. We say one quantity is a *power* of another. When complex networks have degree distributions of this type, the power is usually between 2 and 3. For instance, for *Njáls saga*, we measured that the probability that a node has a certain degree is (approximately) inversely proportional to the value of that degree to the power of 2.6. This means that if the probability for a node to have a certain degree is p, its probability to be twice as strongly connected is (approximately) $p/2^{2.6} \approx p \times 0.16$. In other words, doubling the degree corresponds to multiplying the probability by 0.16. If such a relationship holds for all nodes, we say the distribution is *scale free*.

For *Njáls saga*, the power in question is 2.6. By comparing such numbers between different networks, we can quantitatively compare different societies to each other. For example, it turns out that the power that describes *Gísla saga* is also 2.6. This tells us that the distributions of interactions across *Njáls saga* and *Gísla saga* are similar. This is further witnessed in the top panel of Figure 8.7, where the degree distributions of the two networks are plotted in such a way as to draw out the power; here it is manifest as the slope of the graph. The overlap between the data for *Njáls saga* and *Gísla saga* signals that they have similar degree distributions. The degree distributions of *Vatnsdæla saga* and *Egils saga* are also well fitted by power laws (middle panel of Figure 8.7). The powers in these cases are 2.8 and 2.7, respectively. However, a power law does not fit *Laxdæla saga* well, as evidenced by the curvature of the data in the bottom panel of Figure 8.7.

Type (ii) – Exponential networks: Networks described by the exponential family (ii) are more homogeneous than power-law networks. In fact, *Laxdæla saga* is better described by an exponential degree distribution than by a power law. Here there is no character that interacts with almost half the network; instead the highest-degree character interacts with about one-eighth of the network. This network is considered to be more robust, as there is no single node that is holding the entire structure together.

We refer to the high-degree, low-probability region of the degree distribution as its *tail*. To explore what happens in the tail, we can successively

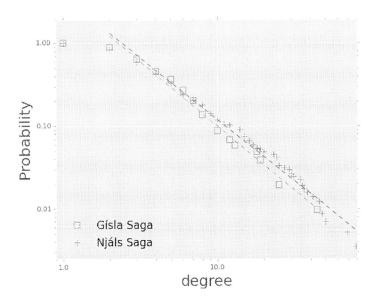

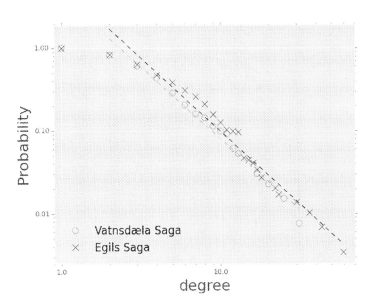

Figure 8.7 The degree distributions of *Njáls saga* and *Gísla saga* (top panel) are very similar – they are both well described by power laws (manifest in these plots by straight lines). *Vatnsdæla saga* and *Egils saga* (middle panel) are best fitted by similar power laws. A power law is not appropriate for *Laxdæla saga*, a circumstance indicated by the curvature of the corresponding plot (bottom panel). This network is better fitted by an exponential distribution.

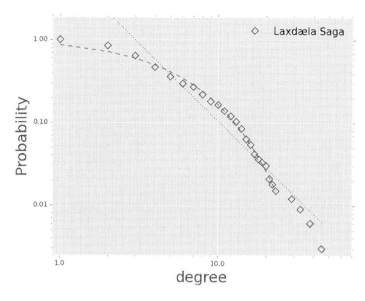

Figure 8.7 (Continued)

double up on the degree of the nodes. In the power-law case, we saw that the mathematical consequence of this corresponds to multiplying the probability of its existence by a fixed number (0.16 in the examples of *Njáls saga* and *Gísla saga* earlier). Doubling the degree of a node in an exponential distribution requires a different functional change to the probability p. Instead of multiplying p by a constant value like 0.16, we have to multiply p by itself. This is a much stronger effect, when p is very small (smaller than 0.16). Remember, p is small when the degree is high. Therefore distribution described by the exponential family decays even quicker, so there tend not to be many characters with very large degrees. This reflects the fact that they tend to have less prominent central characters. We refer to the tails in the power-law degree distributions as *fat* and those in the exponential distributions as *thin*.

Type (iii) – Truncated power laws: Networks of the third type have structures somewhere between (i) and (ii). They are formed by multiplying functions of type (i) and type (ii) together. This has the effect of looking like a power law when the degree is relatively low. But when the degree is high, this power law is overwhelmed by the exponential, which then dominates into the tail. The outcome is a hybrid beginning with a power law but a fast decaying tail.[14]

Such networks tend to have a larger number of core characters holding the structure together than in the pure power-law case, but the network tends to be dependent on these characters, unlike in the pure exponential case. There tend to be multiple important characters instead of just one or two. A truncated power-law degree distribution results from amalgamating the societies of various sagas into a single network (discussed later on).

To conclude, the degree distributions of *Njáls saga*, *Gísla saga*, *Vatnsdæla saga*, and *Egils saga* are all very similar; they are each of type (i) – scale-free power laws. The degree distribution of *Laxdæla saga* is of type (ii). Of the five major networks studied here, it is the only one best described by an exponential distribution. We will see next that an amalgamation of sagas and *þættir* is well described by a degree distribution of type (iii) – a truncated power law. Although the previous analysis of degree distributions captures important features of the various networks, it would be a mistake to consider it as the primary discriminator between different types. *Gísla saga* is an outlaw saga and, as such, is very different to *Njáls saga*, even though they have very similar degree distributions. We claim that homophily (assortativity) plays that role. Indeed we will now see that a careful study of assortativity is capable of separating the outlaw-saga network from those of the other four narratives.

Assortativity

In social networks, people tend to form friendships with people who are similar to themselves.[15] This is the property of *homophily* alluded to in the introduction. In human society, people of similar culture, ethnicity, status, wealth, and so on tend to associate with each other. Popular or influential people also tend to mingle with other popular people (e.g., celebrities tend to form personal relationships with one another in modern society). In networks science we are especially interested in the latter type of homophily – the one related to popularity. This is because, in networks, popularity is measured very simply – it is just the degree of the various nodes, which are easily counted. Networks which have links between nodes of similar degrees are termed *assortative*. For such networks, high-degree nodes associate with (i.e., are linked with) other high-degree nodes. Similarly, the links of low-degree nodes tend also to be to nodes of low degree. The opposite feature, in which high-degree nodes tend to link to low-degree ones, is called *disassortativity*.[16] See Figure 8.8 for examples of these two types of network.

We can measure assortativity as a quantity between −1 and 1. A positive value indicates that the network is assortative; the more assortative it is, the higher the value comes out to be. Similarly, a negative value indicates the network is disassortative. A value close to zero means that nodes (people or characters) mix indiscriminately. This is a particularly important concept in the present instance because assortativity helps distinguish social networks from other types of network; i.e., it helps us to identify the social nature of networks. Most non-social networks

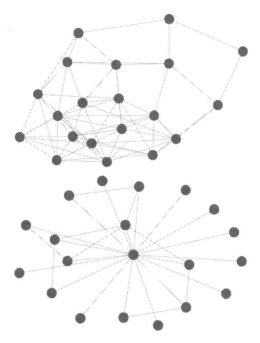

Figure 8.8 The upper network is assortative because nodes of high degree tend to be linked to other nodes of high degree and because nodes of low degree tend to connect to other low-degree nodes. The network on the bottom has the opposite tendency – the high-degree node in the center has many low-degree neighbors. It is therefore disassortative.

are disassortative. Examples include transport networks and networks of computers linked together. Thus, assortativity is a particularly human feature. In the context of narratives, an assortative network strongly resembles real human social networks. This does not mean that a disassortative character network is not based on reality – disassortativity could indicate that the focus of a story is upon a few individuals rather than on an entire society. So interpretations have to be made with great care and in a holistic manner, taking into account the knowledge base established using more traditional approaches.

We found that some of the sagas we studied in depth are assortative, and only *Gísla saga* is strongly disassortative. This reflects the fact that Gisli the outlaw interacts with many minor characters in the tale. We interpret this as meaning that the story is rather more centered on this single protagonist's exploits than it is on a larger society. *Egils saga* has assortativity close to 0, in particular when we just consider the positive network. This implies that there is a lot of emphasis on the central character but there is still much information about the relationships of less important characters. This is similar for *Vatnsdæla saga* and *Njals saga*.

The Community-Structure of the *Íslendinga sögur* and *Þættir*

Previously we considered triads in which every node is linked to every other node. We can extend this idea to larger collections of nodes; if they are all mutually linked, they form a *clique*. A looser collection of nodes, wherein they are not all linked to each other yet form an identifiably cohesive collection, may form a *community*. The upper graph of Figure 8.9 gives an example of a network comprising two communities (identifiable by eye in this instance). Social networks often have community structures, and one way to identify them is through measuring the *modularity*.[17] The modularity of a given network is determined by a community-detection algorithm which seeks to split up densely connected clusters into fragments;[18] in Figure 8.9, this is achieved by elimination

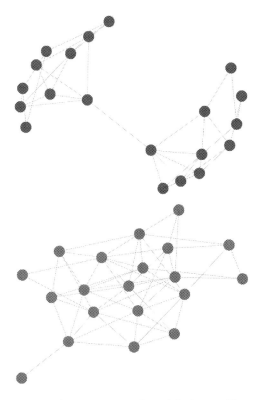

Figure 8.9 The notions of community and modularity are illustrated by the network on the top – a community-detection algorithm can easily break the network into two fragments. Its modularity is measured to be approximately 0.5. The network on the bottom is entirely random. It has no community structure and the algorithm is unable to identify communities. Its modularity is –0.1.

of a single link. If the network is evenly partitioned into a number of sparsely inter-connected communities, the value for the modularity comes out close to 1. If the network lacks community substructure, the modularity comes out closer to 0. Values of the modularity in between indicate intermediate, more complex community substructures.

We mentioned earlier that a notable feature of the *Íslendinga sögur* is their interconnectivity, as characters appear in multiple tales. To investigate this, we merged the five large networks into one super-network. We are interested to know whether the result looks like one homogeneous super-network or if it looks like five weakly inter-connected communities. The result is depicted in Figure 8.10, where different shades represent the original sagas. To see if we could break this back down into its five original components, we next applied the community-detection algorithm. The process failed to separate *Njáls saga* and *Laxdæla saga*. We interpret this as signaling a strong degree of overlap between these two tales. This in turn may be explained by the hypothesis mentioned previously that one saga may have been used as a source for the other.

We then merged the entire corpus of all eighteen sagas and *þættir* into one huge network (Figure 8.11). The resulting saga social network is also a structurally balanced, assortative, small world, the giant component of which contains nearly 99% of the unique characters. The average path length is 5.7, which is remarkably close to the six degrees of separation of modern society. Instead of a simple power law, the degree distribution for the entire saga social network is best described by a truncated power law with an exponentially fast cut-off. As explained previously, this extra function, overlaid upon the power law, forces the high-degree tail of the distribution to decay rapidly. In these networks the highest connected nodes are not as dominant as in the pure power law. We believe the truncation brought about by the amalgamation is because no single protagonist appears as a major player in all of the sagas; if characters have a high degree in one tale they only play a minor role in another. This is why the associated degree does not grow indefinitely as the network size increases.

We then used several iterations of the community-detection algorithm in an attempt to break the amalgamated network back down into its components. Along the way, we monitored the modularity at each stage. This measures the number of sparsely interconnected communities. It reaches a plateau at over 0.7 when there are nine (not eighteen) communities. This indicates that the super-network is not easily split into the eighteen separate narratives, again demonstrating their interconnectedness.

It is also interesting to compare the *Íslendinga sögur* and *þættir* to the epics we analyzed in earlier publications, as well as to works of literature.[19] A notable difference between the Icelandic texts and Homer's *Iliad*, for example, is that, in contrast to the full saga network the *Iliad* is not assortative. However, when only positive links are used in the case

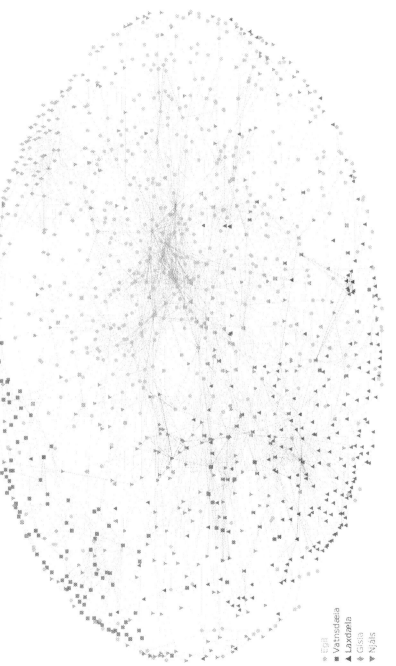

Figure 8.10 The five networks amalgamated into one network. There is a large overlap of characters from *Laxdæla saga* (triangle) and *Njáls saga* (face-down triangle).

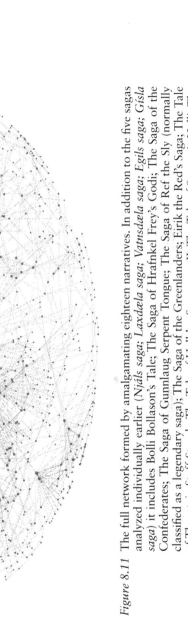

Figure 8.11 The full network formed by amalgamating eighteen narratives. In addition to the five sagas analyzed individually earlier (*Njáls saga*; *Laxdæla saga*; *Egils saga*; *Gísla saga*) it includes Bolli Bollason's Tale; The Saga of Hrafnkel Frey's Godi; The Saga of the Confederates; The Saga of Gunnlaug Serpent Tongue; The Saga of Ref the Sly (normally classified as a legendary saga); The Saga of the Greenlanders; Eirik the Red's Saga; The Tale of Thorstein Staff-Struck; The Tale of Halldor Snorrason II; The Tale of Sarcastic Halli; The Tale of Thorstein Shiver; The Tale of Audun from the West Fjords; The Tale of the Story-wise Icelander (the five last narratives are *þættir* in the kings' saga Morkinskinna).

of the *Iliad*, the two networks become more similar (the *Iliad* is then assortative). This means that the *Íslendinga sögur* and *þættir* have similar network properties to the *Iliad* only when hostility is removed from the latter. The similarity between the network structures of *Njáls saga* and the *Iliad* is boosted by looking at the detail of their degree distributions allowing for a cut-off; they are described by very similar truncated power laws.[20] However, the community detection algorithm separates the two main factions clearly in the *Iliad*, whereas there are no such clear-cut clusters in the sagas.

Summary

The *Íslendinga sögur* and *þættir* have fascinated researchers and scholars of the humanities for generations. We hope we have brought a new and unique statistical perspective to the study of the texts. It is an example of how quantitative techniques applied to the humanities can help open new ways to investigate old questions and inspire new ones.[21]

By analyzing the combined interconnectivity of the social structures in the narratives rather than the characters themselves, we were able to statistically compare the tales in a variety of ways. Of the various statistical indicators, we have demonstrated that assortativity is the most powerful; it helps to categorize the tales into different types. We found that the outlaw saga (*Gísla saga*) is distinct from the others in that it is the only one whose network is strongly disassortative. *Laxdæla saga* also has properties distinct to the others in that it is strongly assortative and has a different degree distribution. This implies that the narrative is much more centered on a group than on an individual. The degree distributions and assortativities of *Njáls saga*, *Vatnsdæla saga*, and *Egils saga* are similar to each other, implying that their character networks are more alike. We hope that our approach will inspire similar studies by other researchers so that we can build a catalogue of networks appearing in ancient and not-so-ancient literature. This may assist in making broader comparisons of epic and mythological literature and in identifying similarities and differences between them.

The work initiated here can be extended in a number of ways. For example, here we have chosen to use unweighted and undirected networks. A greater degree of nuance could be achieved by weighting the links according to how many times characters meet or interact in the narrative, or by some other method. Adding a direction or orientation to the links would account for interactions which are not reciprocated. Additionally one could consider temporal networks instead of the static ones presented here.[22]

As students of the sagas have shown, an important aspect of the social connectivity on Iceland is the tension between so-called horizontal and vertical bonds. The first of these represents interactions between characters of the same social status. The second represents interactions between

Character Networks 165

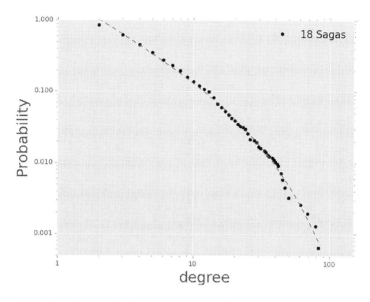

Figure 8.12 The degree distribution of the amalgamation of eighteen narratives is of type (iii) – a truncated power law. Because main protagonists of any particular saga tend to play only a minor role in other sagas, their degrees do not increase by any great extent when the sagas are combined. On the other hand, the degrees of characters that have only minor roles in a number of sagas can accumulate as the sagas are combined. An example of such a character is Olafr Feilan. The effect of these phenomena is that the distribution starts off as a power law for low-degree values but decreases rapidly as the core characters become less important to the overall network.

individuals of different status. Furthermore, Jón Viðar Sigurðsson has suggested that the vertical bonds connecting a large number of people of varying social status to some central chieftains and their families tend to be more stable than horizontal networks consisting of people of similar social standing but of peripheral importance. Although our current study was not designed to test Jón Viðar Sigurðsson's suggestion, a hypothesis could be put forward that asymmetric clusters with many characters connected to a central figure or a similar number of central figures reflect the previously mentioned tendency. It would be a relatively straightforward matter to quantitatively investigate the hypothesis that the stability of the network has different functional dependencies on vertical as opposed to horizontal bonds by testing the robustness of the network as they are removed.

Obviously the comparisons and conclusions drawn on the basis of the work described here are from a statistical, network-theoretic point of view. It goes without saying that, for a more complete and thorough view, our work must be combined with that from other fields – e.g., archaeology, history, literature, and comparative mythology. Nonetheless, our analysis indicates that whether the sagas are historically accurate or not, and whether they describe the Viking Age, the period 1050–1250, or similar, the properties of the social worlds they record are strikingly similar to those of real social networks. Although one cannot conclusively determine whether the societies described in the sagas of Iceland are real, on the basis of network theory we can conclude that they are remarkably realistic.

Notes

1. Luciano D. F. Costa et al., "Analyzing and Modeling Real-World Phenomena with Complex Networks: A Survey of Applications," *Advances in Physics* 60 (2011): 329–412. This project was supported by the Leverhulme Trust and European Union Marie Curie IRSES grants. We are grateful to Joseph Yose for help in gathering the data. We are also grateful to Wojtek Jezierski and Hans Jacob Orning for encouraging our contribution to this volume and for help in tailoring the material for the appropriate audience.
2. Mark E. J. Newman and Juyong Park, "Why Social Networks Are Different from Other Types of Networks," *Physical Review E* 68 (2003): 036122.
3. Jónas Kristjánsson, *Eddas and Sagas: Iceland's Medieval Literature*, trans. Peter Foote (Reykjavik, 1997).
4. For a short introduction to the topic, accessible to non-experts, see H. O'Donoghue, *Old Norse-Icelandic Literature: A Short Introduction* (Oxford, 1997); H. O'Donoghue, *A Companion to Old Norse-Icelandic Literature and Culture*, ed. Rory McTurk, Blackwell Companions to Literature and Culture (Malden, 2005), 190–204.
5. Jesse L. Byock, *Medieval Iceland: Society, Sagas, and Power* (Berkeley, 1990); William Ian Miller, *Bloodtaking and Peacemaking: Feud, Law, and Society in Saga Iceland* (Chicago, 1990); Jón Viðar Sigurðsson, *Chieftains and Power in the Icelandic Commonwealth* (Odense, 1999).
6. *Njal's Saga*, trans. Magnus Magnusson and Hermann Pálsson (Middlesex, 1960); Andrew J. Hamer, *Njáls Saga and Its Christian Background: A Study of Narrative Method* (Groningen, 2008).
7. Mark E. J. Newman, *Networks: An Introduction* (Oxford, 2010).
8. Réka Albert and Albert-László Barabási, "Statistical Mechanics of Complex Networks," *Reviews of Modern Physics* 74, no. 1 (2002): 47–97.
9. Jane Smiley and Robert J. Kellogg, *The Sagas of the Icelanders: A Selection* (Middlesex, 2001).
10. Tibor Antal, Paul L. Krapivsky, and Sidney Redner, "Social Balance on Networks: The Dynamics of Friendship and Enmity," *Physica D* 224 (2006): 13036; Dorwin Cartwright and Frank Harary, "Structural Balance: A Generalization of Heider's Theory," *Psychological Review* 63 (1956): 277–93.
11. Stanley Milgram, "The Small World Problem," *Psychology Today* 2 (1967): 60–67.
12. Stanely Wasserman and Katherine Faust, *Social Network Analysis: Methods and Applications* (Cambridge, 1994).
13. Duncan James Watts and Steven Henry Strogatz, "Collective Dynamics of 'Small-World' Networks," *Nature* 393 (1998): 440–42.

14. Luis A. Nunes Amaral, Antonio Scala, Marc Barthelemy, and Henry Eugene Stanley, "Classes of Small-World Networks," *Proceedings of the National Academy of Sciences of the United States of America* 97, no. 21 (2000): 11149–52.
15. Miller McPherson, Lynn Smith-Lovin, and James M. Cook, "Birds of a Feather: Homophily in Social Networks," *Annual Review of Sociology* 27 (2001): 415–44.
16. Mark E. J. Newman, "Assortative Mixing in Networks," *Physical Review Letters* 89 (2002): 208701.
17. Mark E. J. Newman and Michelle Girvan, "Finding and Evaluating Community Structure in Networks," *Physical Review E* 69 (2004): 026113.
18. Michelle Girvan and Mark E. J. Newman, "Community Structure in Social and Biological Networks," *Proceedings of the National Academy of Sciences of the United States of America* 99 (2002): 7821–26.
19. Pádraig MacCarron and Ralph Kenna, "Universal Properties of Mythological Networks," *Europhysics Letters* 99 (2012): 28002; Pádraig MacCarron and Ralph Kenna, "Network Analysis of the Íslendinga sögur – The Sagas of Icelanders," *European Physical Journal B* 86 (2013): 407.
20. Pádraig MacCarron, *A Network Theoretic Approach to Comparative Mythology* (Coventry, 2014).
21. Ralph Kenna, Máirín MacCarron, and Pádraig MacCarron, ed., *Maths Meets Myths: Quantitative Approaches to Ancient Narratives* (Berlin, 2016).
22. Sandra D. Prado et al., "Temporal Network Analysis of Literary Texts," *Advances in Complex Systems* 19 (2016): 1650005.

Dedicated Bibliography

Albert, Réka, and Albert-László Barabási. "Statistical Mechanics of Complex Networks." *Reviews of Modern Physics* 74, no. 1 (2002): 47–97.
Amaral, Luis A. Nunes, Antonio Scala, Marc Barthelemy, and Harry Eugene Stanley. "Classes of Small-World Networks." *Proceedings of the National Academy of Sciences of the United States of America* 97, no. 21 (2000): 11149–52.
Antal, Tibor, Paul L. Krapivsky, and Sidney Redner. "Social Balance on Networks: The Dynamics of Friendship and Enmity." *Physica D* 224 (2006): 130–36.
Byock, Jesse L. *Medieval Iceland: Society, Sagas, and Power*. Berkeley, 1990.
Cartwright, Dorwin, and Frank Harary. "Structural Balance: A Generalization of Heider's Theory." *Psychological Review* 63 (1956): 277–93.
Costa, Luciano da F., Osvaldo N. Oliveira Jr., Gonzalo Travieso, Francisco A. Rodrigues, Paulino R. Villas Boas, Lucas Antiqueira, Matheus P. Viana, and Luis E. C. da Rocha. "Analyzing and Modeling Real-World Phenomena with Complex Networks: A Survey of Applications." *Advances in Physics* 60 (2011): 329–412.
Girvan, Michelle, and Mark E. J. Newman. "Community Structure in Social and Biological Networks." *Proceedings of the National Academy of Sciences of the United States of America* 99 (2002): 7821–26.
Hamer, Andrew J. *Njáls Saga and Its Christian Background: A Study of Narrative Method*. Groningen, 2008.
Kenna, Ralph, Máirín MacCarron, and Pádraig MacCarron, eds. *Maths Meets Myths: Quantitative Approaches to Ancient Narratives*. Berlin, 2016.

Kristjánsson, Jónas. *Eddas and Sagas: Iceland's Medieval Literature*. Translated by Peter Foote. Reykjavik, 1997.

MacCarron, Pádraig, and Ralph Kenna. "Universal Properties of Mythological Networks." *Europhysics Letters* 99 (2012): 28002.

MacCarron, Pádraig, and Ralph Kenna. "Network Analysis of the Íslendinga sögur – The Sagas of Icelanders." *European Physical Journal B* 86 (2013): 407.

MacCarron, Pádraig. *A Network Theoretic Approach to Comparative Mythology*. Coventry, 2014.

McPherson, Miller, Lynn Smith-Lovin, and James M. Cook. "Birds of a Feather: Homophily in Social Networks." *Annual Review of Sociology* 27 (2001): 415–44.

Milgram, Stanley. "The Small World Problem." *Psychology Today* 2 (1967): 60–67.

Miller, William Ian. *Bloodtaking and Peacemaking: Feud, Law and Society in Saga Iceland*. Chicago, 1990.

Newman, Mark E. J. "Assortative Mixing in Networks." *Physical Review Letters* 89 (2002): 208701.

Newman, Mark E. J. *Networks: An Introduction*. Oxford, 2010.

Newman, Mark E. J., and Michelle Girvan. "Finding and Evaluating Community Structure in Networks." *Physical Review E* 69 (2004): 026113.

Newman, Mark E. J., and Juyong Park. "Why Social Networks Are Different from Other Types of Networks." *Physical Review E* 68 (2003): 036122.

Njal's Saga. Translated by Magnus Magnusson and Hermann Pálsson. Middlesex, 1960.

O'Donoghue, Heather. *Old Norse-Icelandic Literature: A Short Introduction*. Oxford, 1997.

Prado, Sandra D. et al. "Temporal Network Analysis of Literary Texts." *Advances in Complex Systems* 19 (2016): 1650005.

Rory McTurk, ed. *A Companion to Old Norse-Icelandic Literature and Culture*. Blackwell Companions to Literature and Culture, 190–204. Malden, 2005.

Sigurðsson, Jón Viðar. *Chieftains and Power in the Icelandic Commonwealth*. Translated by Jean Lundskær-Nielsen. Odense, 1999.

Smiley, Jane, and Robert L. Kellogg. *The Sagas of the Icelanders: A Selection*. Middlesex, 2001.

Wasserman, Stanely, and Katherine Faust. *Social Network Analysis: Methods and Applications*. Cambridge, 1994.

Watts, Duncan James, and Steven Henry Strogatz. "Collective Dynamics of 'Small-World' Networks." *Nature* 393 (1998): 440–42.

9 Angels in Scandinavia
Papal Legates and Networks of Nordic Elites, Twelfth–Thirteenth Centuries

Wojtek Jezierski

"If angels were to govern men, neither external nor internal controls on government would be necessary."
– James Madison, *The Federalist Papers no. 51* (1788)

On 31 December 1224, Pope Honorius III (r. 1216–27) appointed Bishop William of Modena (1184–1251) as his legate to Livonia and Prussia, the north-eastern frontiers of Christianity. In his letter of commendation, the pope expressed his regret that he could not be everywhere at once, but that some form of mediation was necessary. Honorius also instructed all those who were to receive William to treat his angel-like envoy ("faciat spiritus suos angelos et ministros") with due humility and to assist him in fulfilling his spiritual as well as worldly tasks ("spiritualia seminanti temporalia ministrando").[1] During the next two years William followed an impressive itinerary in Livonia and Estonia, where he extensively preached the crusade against the pagans and "diligently ministered [*ministravit*] the word of God and gave many indulgences" to the emerging German and Danish elites of the new colony.[2] William also made a failed attempt to secure considerable parts of Danish Estonia for the Apostolic See by bringing them under the wing of the pope, but an annexation of the region by the order of the Sword Brethren in 1227 brought these plans to naught.[3]

Papal legates were rare but unusually mighty creatures and comparing them to angels,[4] as Honorius III did, was not far off the mark.[5] They represented the top echelon of the ecclesiastical hierarchy and were appointed as the pope's plenipotentiaries according to the emerging idea of *plenitudo potestatis*, a prerogative which allowed them to directly intervene in decision making and appointments at every level of ecclesiastical authority.[6] Given their extensive discretionary power, they were not just the pope's assistants or mere messengers between the Lateran palace and the local churches; they were executives acting as the pope's ministers.[7] As they journeyed from one place to another they brought with them a mini Roman Curia able to make decisions in a broad range of situations: regulating clerical discipline, resolving doctrinal disputes, planting and abolishing ecclesiastical bodies, presiding over secular legal disputes, and so forth. What must have been particularly difficult to comprehend for those who met them was that these men – regardless of their formal position in the ecclesiastical hierarchy – were, in their legatine capacity, veritable incarnations of the pope's authority acting as essential doubles of the Roman pontiff, capable of deposing bishops or archbishops.[8] Through this type of activity they had a direct impact on the networks of power spun by the local elites. For that reason, the Nordic elites sought proximity to the popes' proxies whenever they landed in the North.

This chapter takes a closer look at the activities and itineraries of several papal legates in order to demonstrate how the Nordic elites were able to transform their own networks and power bases through contact with Rome's deputies. Using a handful of specific examples, I would also like to show how, in the course of the twelfth and thirteenth centuries, the transformation of the clerical and educational networks in which the Nordic ecclesiastical elites participated made the members of the Nordic elite eligible to be papal legates. In other words, the purpose of this chapter is to explore the activity of papal legates as nodes, constricting or enabling interaction between an array of networks, and as mediators providing occasions for conversion between different types of capital – social, dynastic, educational, and symbolic – which the Nordic elites had at their disposal.[9]

Case I: The "Romans" in the North

William of Modena was not the first papal emissary to draw the Scandinavian elite into contact with the Roman Curia. As early as 1152–54, the papal legate Nicholas Breakspear visited Scandinavia. During his itinerary he established the archiepiscopal see at Trondheim and paved the way for a similar arrangement at Uppsala as the archbishopric of Sweden, although it was not in place before 1164 and for a long period was subjected to the primacy of the archbishops of Lund.[10] Nicholas, who was soon elected pope as Hadrian IV (r. 1154–59), was an Englishman educated at St Albans and can be seen as yet another link in the extended English connection which dominated the educational and ecclesiastical development of Scandinavia, particularly Denmark, from the turn of the millennium, as is more thoroughly explored in Marie Bønløkke Missuno's chapter in this volume.[11]

One of the people in Nicholas's retinue on his journey through the North was an English cleric by the name of Henry (d. 1156). He was to become responsible for the Swedish Christianization of southwest Finland (Finland Proper) in the so-called First Finnish Crusade, which he allegedly led together with the Swedish king Erik IX den helige ("the

Saint," r. 1155–60) in the mid-1150s. Henry was supposedly also the first bishop of Turku/Åbo and subsequently called a saint after his martyrdom in 1156. Even if the historicity of the events surrounding both Erik's and Henry's actions has been seriously questioned, neither the important influence of the missionary and papal networks they partook in nor the strong ideational impact of their memory on the Swedish missionary activity in Finland can be denied.[12]

After Breakspear, we know that Rome continued to send its plenipotentiaries to the North, although the information about the nature of their errands, especially if they did not concern Denmark, is often fragmentary.[13] For instance, *Sverris saga* tells of an anonymous papal legate, whom King Sverre of Norway (r. 1184–1202) wanted to crown him at Konghelle (north of Gothenburg in today's Sweden) on Easter of 1194. Apparently unaware that the king was under a papally approved ban issued by Archbishop Eirik Ivarsson (r. 1188–1205, at that time in exile at Archbishop Absalon's cathedral in Lund), the legate was stopped at the last moment before consecrating the king. Sverre, reluctant to submit to the legate's appeal to make peace with Eirik and the estranged Norwegian episcopate, found his meddling useless and sent him back to Rome.[14]

Even during times when Danish prelates were eligible as papal legates (see later on), the Roman Curia continued to send the pope's plenipotentiaries to Denmark. One of them was Gregorius de Crescentio (d. 1227), whom his Nordic recipients were instructed to honor as Honorius III's actual avatar by the pope's own unequivocal command.[15] Anthony Perron, who traced Gregorius's mission of 1222, suggested that his visit might have been prompted by an internal Danish request for help in enforcing clerical celibacy or by the dynastic struggles in Sweden at the time. Yet another explanation for the dispatch concerns the ecclesiastical competition in Estonia between the Danish Church on one side, and the Sword Brethren as well as the Bishop of Riga, Albert of Buxhoeveden (r. 1199–1229), on the other, in which Gregorius was to act as an arbitrator. After the Estonian relapse and revolt in 1222/3 the entire missionary effort in Estonia was called into question, although this does not mean that Gregorius remained idle. On the contrary, during his visit to Denmark the legate took the chance to renew his friendship with a study companion from Paris, Abbot Gunner of Øm Abbey (r. 1216–22).[16] In a clear case of a papal intermediary converting a personal bond and educational capital into institutionalized recognition, Gregorius took the opportunity presented by the vacant episcopal see of Viborg to persuade the canons there to appoint his competent and eloquent friend Gunner as bishop (r. 1222–51). The canons unanimously agreed.[17] During his visit Gregorius also managed to reinforce the connection between the envoys of Dominic de Guzmán (St Dominic) and Archbishop Anders Sunesen, which led to the introduction of Dominican friars first to Lund (1222/3) and then across Denmark, and their employment in missions to Estonia.[18]

Case II: Absalon of Lund

A papal legate's task always entailed a delicate balance. On the one hand, he represented the universal Church as the pope's direct plenipotentiary. It is important to remember that papal legates and the idea of the papal *plenitudo potestatis* emerged in the wake of the Gregorian Reform as a response to the development of the Papal States, which effectively became what Maureen C. Miller dubbed a "radically disarticulated composite state."[19] This archipelago of isolated holdings scattered across the Apennine Peninsula could be held together only through the networks and constant movement of people invested with the full power of their lord. As well, the new definition of papal authority initiated by Gregory VII, developed by Alexander III, and radically advanced by Innocent III (r. 1198–1216) necessitated a strong connection with the local members of the universal Church so that the ever-growing scope of papal regulations could be executed exhaustively.[20] On the other hand, this universal and unifying force had to be counterbalanced by a bottom-up movement in the European peripheries. Popes' centrally appointed emissaries did not always possess sufficient local knowledge and connections. In order to remain effective in solving the problems on the ground, the popes quite commonly appointed high-ranking locals with social and political clout. It also took less time to send a *plenitudo potentatis* to a powerful local bishop, who would act without delay, than to wait for a dispatch from Rome. For instance, six months stretched between William of Modena's appointment on New Year's Eve and his arrival in Livonia in the summer of 1225. Finally, the legatine tasks on the Nordic periphery were not always considered vital enough to require a journey all the way from Italy.

In order for a local appointment to be deemed viable, however, the high-ranking local clerics needed to be both sufficiently competent and familiar to the Roman Curia. It seems that by the late twelfth century the time was ripe to appoint members of the Nordic ecclesiastical elite – at least those in Denmark – as papal legates.[21] Fortunately, we have at our disposal the opinion about members of this group which circulated in northern European ecclesiastical circles at that time. As the well-informed Abbot Arnold (r. 1177–1211/1214) of the Benedictine monastery of St John in Lübeck wrote:

> The Danes have made no insignificant progress also in science and education. The magnates in the country send their sons to Paris not only to an ecclesiastical career, but also to acquire secular knowledge. They learn literature and the language of the country, and they have become advanced not only in the liberal arts, but also in theology. Because of the natural speediness of the Danish language, they are subtle not only in dialectics, but also in all matters pertaining to church affairs, and they become good ecclesiastical or secular lawyers and judges.[22]

Arnold clearly appreciated the ruling Danish elite's investment in their sons' acquisition of educational capital, which turned them into reliable men of the Church. Furthermore, as we shall see later on in the examples of two locally appointed papal legates, Absalon of Lund and Anders Sunesen (who seem to have taken the initiative for receiving legatine distinctions), their educational and symbolic capital was directly proportional to their social capital both at home and abroad.

Although Archbishop Absalon of Lund (r. 1178–1201) was not the first Danish church official to be appointed as papal legate (his predecessor and direct sponsor to the archiepiscopal see, Eskil of Lund, enjoyed this privilege before him),[23] he can serve as a good example of how the Nordic elites used their economic and social positions in interactions with European elites and the papacy in order to strengthen and transform their local status and power base. Absalon's well-researched, singular importance in the development of the ecclesiastical organization in Scandinavia, his role in Danish politics, and the territorial expansion of the Lund archbishopric in the second half of the twelfth century can hardly be overstated.[24] Here I would like to point to a handful of social networks of which Absalon was a member, which either made him eligible as papal legate in the eyes of the Roman Curia or directly benefitted from his legatine appointment.

Absalon was a scion of the Skjalm clan (sometimes referred to as the "Hvide family"), arguably one of the two most powerful aristocratic families in Denmark at the time. During Absalon's career the family's power base was centered at Fjenneslev in western Zealand and the nearby Sorø Abbey, which Absalon's father, Asser Rig (c. 1080–1151), founded together with his brother Ebbe Skjalmsen Hvide (c. 1085–1150/1) in the 1140s. When Absalon succeeded Eskil to the see of Lund in 1177/8, a substantial shift occurred in Denmark's landscape of power. The hegemony of the aristocratic clan of Trund (Eskil's kin) and its conflict-ridden relationship with King Valdemar the Great (r. 1157–82), was replaced by the king's close alliance with the Skjalm clan. Absalon was Valdemar's foster-brother and their lifelong friendship – a relationship later successfully transferred to Valdemar's heir, Knud VI (r. 1182–1202) – benefitted both the *regnum* and the *sacerdotium*.[25]

Importantly, Absalon's career attests to a growing tendency among Nordic aristocratic elites to seek novel forms of symbolic and cultural capital which would demonstrate their social and political standing. In the late 1140s and early 1150s, Absalon became one of the first Danes to be sent to study abroad (Archbishop Eskil was trained at Hildesheim) when he went to be educated at Ste Geneviève Abbey in Paris – thus avoiding involvement in yet another bloodstained period of the so-called civil wars in Denmark. During his stay, Absalon befriended a certain Canon Regular by the name of Guillaume (c. 1127–1203). Guillaume served as sub-prior at Ste Geneviève and was in close contact with Pope

Eugene III (r. 1145–53), who in turn was a former pupil of Bernard of Clairvaux (incidentally, Archbishop Eskil's close friend) and the first Cistercian to be elected pope. William of Æbelholt, as Guillaume is now commonly known, was invited to Denmark by Absalon in 1165 in order to introduce the order of Canons Regular to the monastery of Eskilsø, which he subsequently transferred to Æbelholt in 1176.[26] The weight of the educational and ecclesiastical connections which William offered to the local clerical elites was decisive for pulling them into the wider European and papal gravitational sphere in both Absalon's and his successors' generations (see later on). Little wonder that the leaders of the Danish Church wanted to capitalize on William even *post mortem*, by converting this former node of social and cultural resources into an officially recognized symbolic asset and object of veneration.[27] In response to the Archbishop of Lund's request, in 1218 the pope set up a Danish committee to prove William's sanctity. Honorius III's final approval was withheld until the previously mentioned papal legate, Gregorius de Crescentio, returned to Rome in 1223 and provided the decisive confirmation of the miracles presented in the suitably produced *Sancti Willelmi Abbatis vita et miracula*. William was canonized and enshrined in 1224, which allowed his remains to exert a new type of influence and render further services to the Danish elites in his freshly formalized and fossilized state.[28]

The Cistercian connection, mediated through both Eskil and Parisian contacts, proved to be a lasting element in Absalon's activity. His family's *Hauskloster*, Sorø Abbey in Zealand, was reformed from Benedictine to Cistercian in 1161/2 by translating monks from Esrum (a daughter house of Clairvaux). The monastic establishments following Absalon and Valdemar's conquest of Rügen in 1168/9 were also almost exclusively Cistercian.[29]

In the 1180s and 1190s Absalon seems to have devoted his legatine authority and attention mainly to achieving temporal rather than spiritual objectives. Most of the diplomas he issued at this time regulated the internal and administrative matters of the Danish Church, issuing protection to various monasteries' possessions or confirming donations and wills of both church officials and secular persons. It is significant that in the diplomas Absalon's legatine capacity is referred to in the same breath as his archiepiscopal or episcopal functions. This suggests that he did not make a special distinction with respect to this function, but rather added this official symbolic resource, and the Roman connection behind it, to his previous ones to boost his aggregated authority, with his titles typically running like this: "Absalon, dei gratia Lundensis archiepiscopus, apostolice sedis legatus, primas Danie atque Suethie" (Absalon, by the grace of God Archbishop of Lund, legate of the apostolic See, primate of Denmark and Sweden).[30] Particularly conspicuous in his issuing of diplomas and letters at that time – although not at all surprising – are his efforts to secure the best possible protection and a virtual legal asylum for Sorø Abbey.[31] Absalon also used his connection to the Roman Curia to assure Sorø's protection and to grant privileges to the Cistercian monks as well as their patrons and donors – Absalon himself, his brother Esbern Snare, and cousin Sune Ebbesen – by exempting the monks from paying the tithe.[32] Sorø, as a node in the Skjalm clan's web of possessions, *memoria*, and power, was now enjoying papal sanction, friendship, and defense. For his friend's abbey in Æbelholt, Absalon achieved nothing less.[33]

The final clauses of a vast bulk of Absalon's diplomas issued in his legatine capacity, both for Sorø and on other occasions, are equipped with divine and saintly maledictions as well as threats of excommunication.[34] This discourse largely imitates the papal diplomas that Absalon was receiving from Rome at the time, which included very similar threats.[35] In a sense, the archbishop was not only using the Roman Curia to sanction protection for his own, his friends', and his family's foundations, but he was effectively appropriating the papal symbolic capital and converting it into economic and symbolic exemptions at home. Even though threats of excommunication, anathema, and saintly wrath are commonplace in the final clauses of episcopal diplomas of that period, and even if those included in Absalon's diplomas and the papal bulls listed here for the most part sound repetitive and formulaic, these threats were not always empty.[36] After all, at its core the episcopal ban cut off the perpetrators from all their social attachments and excluded them not only from the glory of partaking in the life of the *ecclesia*, but above all from receiving its protection.[37] On at least one occasion, Pope Celestine III (r. 1191–98) had to remind Absalon what his legatine responsibilities were in this regard – even when angels governed men, some external control was necessary.

In 1193 Celestine III urged his legate in Denmark to consider using his power of excommunication in order to intervene in the well-known case of Bishop Valdemar of Schleswig (r. 1188–1208), who had been held captive by King Knud VI for thirteen years (1193–1206) after his attempt to take the Danish throne. In the initial stage of the conflict, the pope – taking the side of Bishop Valdemar – sent a letter to his legate harshly reproving him for inaction with regard to the conflict, for ignoring his previous letters, and for not putting a stop to the violence and outrageous infringements on ecclesiastical freedom. Absalon was to promptly investigate the case and verify the pope's information. If the perpetrators – particularly Duke Valdemar (the future King Valdemar Sejr, "the Victorious," r. 1202–41) and bishops Omer of Ribe, Peder of Zealand, and Asser of Viborg – did not reprove and release the bishop, Absalon was to put all of Denmark under interdict, excommunicate the duke and his helpers, and immediately suspend the bishops. Next, the pope sent letters to all Danish bishops, abbots, provosts, and priests, thus mobilizing the entire ecclesiastical organization to aid Absalon in this task.[38] Even though Celestine III soon switched sides and started supporting the king and the archbishop against Valdemar, these three letters from 23 December 1193 bear witness to the enormous legatine potential (especially if combined with archiepiscopal might) when mustering ecclesiastical networks to threaten and disrupt those of the secular elites.

Case III: Anders Sunesen

Anders Sunesen (r. 1202–24), successor to Archbishop Absalon in the see of Lund, was also appointed as papal legate and enjoyed the trust and delegated authority of two subsequent popes. Again, it is important to briefly sketch Anders's background, indicative of his kin's reproduction strategies, in order to better understand how his connections and networks made him eligible for the office. Anders was a nephew of Absalon and was thus also a scion of the Skjalm clan. His brother Peder Sunesen – a pupil of William at Æbelholt – was Absalon's successor as bishop of Roskilde (r. 1191–1214), where Anders served as provost in the 1190s. From the Roman Curia's point of view, however, it must have been his family's international, and Anders's personal, connections preceding his ascension to the archiepiscopal honors that made his name renowned in the wider ecclesiastical circles of Europe. Just like Absalon, Anders began his career by being dispatched together with his brother to study in Paris in the early 1180s. However, such an investment required nurturing along the way. When Peder fell seriously ill during his studies at Ste Geneviève monastery, Archbishop Absalon used his connections and wrote directly to Abbot Stephen, who presided over his *alma mater*, to take good care of Peder's physical and spiritual condition.[39]

After Paris, Peder returned to Denmark, whereas Anders continued his education at the universities of Bologna and possibly Oxford, traveling widely in Europe as a teacher and preacher until the early 1190s.[40] In 1194, as chancellor to King Knud VI, Anders toured from Denmark to Rome, together with none other than William of Æbelholt, to plead with Pope Celestine III to support Ingeborg of Denmark (1175–1236) in her marital dispute against King Philip Augustus of France (r. 1180–1223). It was either during his studies in Paris or during the negotiations in Rome in 1194 that Anders encountered Lotario dei Conti di Segni, the future pope Innocent III. Lotario, at the time papal chancellor, proved to be a vital influence in Anders's stellar career and particularly in his future legatine appointments.[41] Anders's theological training, skillful preaching, and devotion to the missionary cause did not go unnoticed, as we know from Arnold of Lübeck's testimony penned in the 1200s.

It is clear from this brief survey that during his star-spangled trajectory Anders constantly converted different forms of capital into new ones, reaping profits at every turn. His family connections and economic base were converted into his personal educational capital, which in turn yielded social connections in both the Western educational centers and ecclesiastical circles. Anders converted his educational capital into its symbolic and cultural forms through his preaching – most notably demonstrated in the invitation from Bishop Albert of Buxhöveden to educate the clerics in the Rigan cathedral chapter, which he visited in 1206/7[42] – and his theological poetry such as *Hexaëmeron*, as well as sponsorship of historiographical works such as the *Gesta Danorum*.[43] Recognition in these fields could be converted into more objectified forms of capital such as institutional appointments like the chancellorship and episcopal titles, which in turn broadened his network to an even greater degree.[44] After his appointment to the archbishopric of Lund and after he had ensured direct access to the pope, Anders's advancement into the angelic bureaucracy in the form of legatine honors was a natural next step. "For whosoever hath, to him shall be given, and he shall have more abundance," as the Evangelist put it (Matt. 13:12).

Anders's legatine appointments seem to have had a sharper focus and were briefer than Absalon's, whose legatine capacity was somewhat panoramic and undefined. Anders was appointed as papal legate to Denmark and Sweden for the first time in 1204, a title he held until 1206. As mentioned earlier, in his new legatine role the archbishop acquired immense powers to redraw the diocesan map in Scandinavia as he saw fit.[45] Among his rather extraordinary prerogatives as legate was permission to give or refuse dispensation in the not uncommon instances of *defectus natalium*, that is, appointing to episcopal offices candidates born out of Christian wedlock. It means that Anders effectively controlled the ecclesiastical elites' access to the episcopal nominations in Denmark, Sweden, and Finland, which in a new, papally sanctioned manner reproduced the brokerage position his predecessors in Lund had enjoyed. The issue of episcopal appointments was particularly pressing in the case of Finland, where few bishops dared to go in the early thirteenth century, meaning even such canonically defective candidates had to be taken into consideration.[46]

The second time Innocent III appointed Anders as his legate was in 1212, an assignment we unfortunately know little about. Nonetheless, the wording of the papal bull bears detectable traces of the Roman Curia's appreciation for Anders's symbolic and cultural capital in the form of his personal reputation and his unique devotion to preaching and crusading.[47] The focus on missioning and evangelization is hardly surprising, given Anders's dedication to these tasks ever since he first launched a crusade against the Öselians in 1206 and the broader involvement of the Danish kingdom in crusading on the Baltic Rim at the time.[48] Admittedly, as argued by Iben Fonnesberg-Schmidt, the appointment of Anders as papal legate in 1212 could be a sign that the pope did not yet attach great importance to crusading on this edge of the world, but relied on local initiatives rather than diverting his attention from the crusades to the Holy Land and Constantinople. Perhaps even the legatine appointment itself was something of a consolation prize for the archbishop, as Lund's primacy over Sweden was slipping out of his hands.[49] Nevertheless, it is telling that the web of connections intersecting in Anders Sunesen's persona was considered by Rome to be dependable enough to leave the North to his control.

Finally, a good example of how attractive the connectedness and symbolic clout of the legatine office could appear to the local ecclesiastical elites can be found in the curious case of a counterfeit legate that appeared during the Danish crusade to Prussia in the 1200s and 1210s. The crusade was a partially competitive, partially cooperative effort of the archbishoprics of Lund and Gniezno, represented in the region by the Cistercian monasteries in Colbatz (Polish: Kołbacz) and Łekno, respectively. It seems that the initiative for the crusade in the region originated in the mind of Abbot Godefrid of Łekno. His enterprise was soon highjacked, however, by Christian (future Bishop of Prussia, r. 1215/16–1245), a monk from Colbaz, which was a Danish foundation from Esrum. Christian not only bypassed Godefrid in receiving support for the crusade from Rome but also received backing from Gniezno and its Archbishop Henryk Kietlicz (r. 1199–1219). As an effect of the crusading bull from 1210, Valdemar the Victorious's troops entered Prussia, and the king vowed to fight against the pagans and assist in their conversion. What was originally a local crusade in Pomerelia directed mainly from Greater Poland was becoming an international affair dominated by the Danish elites.[50]

In the midst of the crusade, in March 1213, Anders Sunesen received a bull from the pope regarding an imposter passing as bishop and papal legate who, after his capture, was in Anders's custody.[51] According to the scholars who have studied this unusual case, the exchange between Innocent III and Anders – the actual papal legate at the time – concerning the spurious emissary most likely referred to the previously mentioned Godefrid from Łekno acting in the missionary region.[52] Thanks to the pope's intervention, the false legatine and episcopal decisions were to be annulled, and the archbishop of Lund received permission to imprison the impersonator for life. Setting aside the fact that the papal bull of 1213 in all probability meant a decisive blow for the Gniezno archbishopric's crusading efforts, the document is a testament to how much symbolic clout and institutional influence the legatine title offered – so much so that one was tempted to counterfeit it.

Case IV: Meeting in Skänninge, 1248

William of Modena returned to the North again in the 1230s, and for the last time in the 1240s, this time as Cardinal of Sabina. William's first important stopover was Bergen in Norway, where he crowned King Haakon Haakonson (r. 1217–63) in 1247. From there he headed southeast. During his visit to Sweden, on 1 March 1248, together with Birger Magnusson (r. 1248–66 as Birger Jarl, i.e., earl of Sweden), William issued a document at the synod in Skänninge which was a ripple of the Gregorian Reform as well as the First (1123), Second (1139), and Fourth (1215) Lateran Councils and as such had an essential bearing on the definition of the status of priests and bishops in Sweden. As he stated, upon his visit William found the Swedish priesthood in utter moral disarray, something he attributed to the raging civil war in which King Erik Eriksson (r. 1222–29, 1234–50) fought against a part of the aristocracy. This chaos, which enabled many clergymen to take wives or concubines, led to endemic nepotism when priestly sons inherited their fathers' offices – a concern which the Danish episcopate had already dealt with half a century earlier. In effect, Church property in Sweden was being alienated, and William's intervention was intended to end these practices.[53] The decrees of Skänninge thus had a direct impact on the relationship between the powerful families and their members entering the Church's service. From that point, these groups were to be more clearly separated and the uncircumscribed flow of property between the secular and ecclesiastical elites was to be frozen or slowed down at the very least. As well, in light of regulations introduced by the pope's legates at the time, the episcopal appointments could no longer consider men born out of properly sanctioned wedlock as they had before, at least not without a dispensation.[54] In other words, Swedish priests and bishops should be more angel-like, William insisted.

It is important to take a closer look at the power position from which William was issuing his decree and the occasional node which made this position possible. During his visit the papal legate was effectively the earl's guest, considering that Skänninge, where the meeting took place, lies just five kilometers from Birger Magnusson's family's power base in Bjälbo (Östergötland), crowned by a monumental forty-meter-high church tower raised only a decade or two earlier.[55] Aligning himself with Birger Jarl – the most serious contender for the position of acting ruler of Sweden at that point – and receiving his backing for the new regulations was a way for the legate to see that the papal provisions were implemented. Most likely William had also heard about, and approved of, the so-called Second Swedish Crusade conquering southwestern Finland, which Birger organized a decade earlier, in 1236/7.[56] The political attraction between these two men must have been mutual, since the powerful magnate also greatly benefitted from a papal plenipotentiary's recognition. The document secured the ecclesiastical support of William's normative transformation in no uncertain terms. The current Archbishop of Uppsala, Jarler (r. 1236–55), and his suffragan bishops were made responsible for taking control of their subjects' morality and giving back to the pope what was duly his. The absence of the current king of Sweden from the document is conspicuous to say the least.

180 Wojtek Jezierski

If we view the synodic decree of 1248 as a node in which different networks interacted and from which others were excluded, we should conclude that the Skänninge provision was as much documenting the papal recognition of the alignment between Birger Jarl and the Swedish Church, vis-à-vis the king and other groups of the aristocracy, as it was bringing this new coalition into existence. It is of little wonder that in the very same year, King Erik recognized Birger's position and gave him the title of *jarl*, which made him the *de facto* ruler of Sweden. The far-reaching consequences of the coalition materialized in William's document soon became tangible. Within three years of the Skänninge synod, Birger Jarl managed to marry off his daughter Rikissa to the future heir of Norway, decisively defeated the magnates opposing his hegemony at the Battle of Herrevadsbro (1251), and had his son Valdemar enthroned (r. 1250–75).

William of Modena's/Sabina's decree of 1248 also introduced new formalizations of the episcopal power and the influence bishops could exert on the Swedish elites' social capital. Similarly to the involvement of papal legate Guido in Øm Abbey's dispute with its bishop, studied by Sveinung K. Boye in this volume, William's decree regulated the provisions of hospitality that visiting bishops could expect from their subjects. For instance, episcopal visitations in a diocese were to become more formalized, limited only to the bishop's closest retinue. Their length was limited to a maximum of four days, and payment for their accommodation became clearly defined.[57] Previous ambiguities about how many guests could be invited, and by whom, were being cleared up. In other words, the means and the character of their reception were less susceptible to negotiation and were no longer understood as a type of voluntary gift or an expression of friendship. From now on hospitality towards bishops constituted a service and an obligation, from which their subjects could simply buy themselves out.[58] In other words, the legate was durably transforming the material and formal means through which the Swedish elites were able to reproduce their positions.

In the same way, William arranged for the power of the bishops to destroy the social networks of those violating the Church's regulations as well as its declared enemies. The preiously mentioned separation between priests and their unlawful families was enforced under the ban of excommunication, if with some tolerance for the elderly priests permitted to keep their wives under the provision of chastity. Bishops demanding undue hospitality from their clerical subjects also risked being excommunicated. Besides these general regulations, the potential violators of the Dominican monasteries in Sigtuna and Skänninge ran an exceptional risk of excommunication, even if the king and the jarl were explicitly excluded from this threat.[59]

Such specific protection provided for the Dominicans in Sweden was not a coincidence. The preaching friars were very close to William of

Modena's/Sabina's heart. He considered them to be an important element in a wider network aimed at full conversion of the Scandinavian and Baltic peripheries. Already in the 1220s William had installed Dominican priests throughout Livonia explicitly for missionary purposes, a process initiated by Anders Sunesen. Moreover, the Dominicans from Sigtuna, supported by a great many letters of indulgence from William of Modena/Sabina during the winter of 1247/48,[60] subsequently became engaged in the promotion of the cult of Swedish missionary martyrs such as the saints Erik and Henry, in whose footsteps Birger Jarl had organized the crusade to Finland. Just two weeks before the meeting in Skänninge, William of Modena/Sabina confirmed the donation of a pious book from Bishop Thomas of Åbo (124?–1245) to Sigtuna monastery.[61] The Sigtuna Dominicans' special connection to the bishopric of Åbo continued to develop and flourish afterwards and eventually their prior, Johannes, ascended to the episcopal office there in 1286.[62]

Conclusions

The pontificate of Innocent III bridging the twelfth and thirteenth centuries and his extension of the papal *plenitudo potestatis* constituted a watershed in the Lateran's attitude towards the independence of local churches in Europe. As Perron states, the archiepiscopate of Anders Sunesen marked both the apex and decline of the Danish prelates' widely defined papal authority in Scandinavia. After Anders's death the Roman Curia tended to micromanage local churches more and more through men like William of Modena – that is, by appointing a *legatus missus* or *a latere* sent directly from Rome, rather than an influential local *legatus natus* like Anders or Absalon.[63] The extraordinary impact of these two men thus reflects a transformation during which the Nordic ecclesiastical elites made remarkable use of their informal networks and different sorts of capital before the arrival of new formalizations of church offices molded in Rome and supervised from there.

Although the examples discussed earlier do not exhaust the range of papal interventions in Nordic ecclesiastical politics or cover the full scope of legatine appointments during the period at hand, it is important to appreciate how such momentary and momentous visits from papal legates connected many different types of networks by pulling together elites from the entire region and the rest of Europe. During these visits matters of ecclesiastical discipline or of granting access (or required dispensation) to church offices were interwoven and interlaid with more topical issues of missioning and crusading in the region, reforming monastic houses, establishing entirely new monastic orders and episcopal sees, and building or breaking dynastic alliances. The *spiritualia* flowed seamlessly into the *temporalia*.

The papal concerns of clerical purity, indulgences, and bringing salvation to the pagans represented in the cases discussed here – especially during the period leading up to the Fourth Lateran Council and directly afterwards – may have been universal and stated in sophisticated theological language. But in their practical application by the papal emissaries these issues often hinged on factors that turned out to be personal and often quite mundane, and in order to achieve their goals the angels had to play all the angles. In the legatine appointments, rather than sending its plenipotentiaries into the unknown, the Roman Curia relied on pre-established contacts. It was because of friendships, common acquaintances, and intercessions – especially those forged in the European educational centers – that the popes and their advisors could be confident that their emissaries' policies would not fall on barren ground. Through these channels the Roman Curia could also become acquainted with the members of the local Nordic elites either through intermediaries, or personally when they came across the Tiber on particularly pressing ecclesiastical and dynastical errands. Similarly, from the local elites' point of view, papal legates dispatched from Rome could be considered an asset only if they already had a social reputation anchored in their local connections. As a result, the members of the local elites were prone to using the legates as leverage in their own politics by persuading them to side with some factions against others.

As we saw in the examples of Absalon and Anders Sunesen, the locally appointed papal legates functioned as virtual exchange bureaus. They converted and transubstantiated papal authority and protection, recognition in international educational circles, or crusading appeals into local currencies and forms of social and political capital, which tied together powerful families, their local monastic foundations, and political ambitions both at home and abroad. In other words, the local legates aligned the concerns of the universal Church with their own interests and agendas. By appropriating the symbolic power and discourse of malediction from the Roman pontiffs in the form of a holy, inseparable fusion of the priestly *ministerium* and governmental *mysterium* invested in legatine office, they made the "generals' ideas appear in the local context as general ideas."[64] Finally, for the Nordic elites the papal legates – both Roman and local – constituted very appealing, incarnated annunciations of what a sacralized 'political technology of delegation' looked like. In this sense, the legates transformed these elites' ideas about the future potential for efficiency and representative glory created by their own institutionalized governance and bureaucratic hierarchy.[65] It is of little wonder that popes began to consider them their angels.

Notes

1. *Liv- Esth- und Curlandisches Urkundenbuch nebst Regesten: 1093–1300*, vol. 1, ed. Friedrich Georg von Bunge and Hermann Hildebrand (Reval, 1853), no. 69, cols. 73–75 at cols. 74–75: "Ideoque universitatem vestram rogamus, monemus, ac hortamur, ac per apostolica vobis scripta firmiter praecipiendo mandantes, quatinus eumdem apostolicae sedis legatum

Angels in Scandinavia 183

recipientes humiliter, et devote ipsius salubribus mandatis et monitis efficaciter pareatis, et spiritualia seminanti temporalia ministrando, ita quod exinde divinam et nostrum gratiam possitis uberius promereri."
2. Heinrich von Lettland, *Chronicon Livoniae/Livländische Chronik*, ed. and trans. Albert Bauer (Darmstadt, 1959), ch. XXIX.3.316–17: "verbum Dei sedulo ministravit et indulgentias multas cum gaudio donavit," translation by James A. Brundage in Henricus Lettus, *The Chronicle of Henry of Livonia* (New York, 2003), 230.
3. Ane L. Bysted, Carsten Selch Jensen, Kurt Villads Jensen, and John H. Lind, *Jerusalem in the North: Denmark and the Baltic Crusades, 1100–1552*, trans. Sarah Pedersen and Fredrik Pedersen (Turnhout, 2012), 221; Mihkel Mäesalu, "Päpstliche und kaiserliche Machtansprüche im livländischen Kreuzzugsgebiet im 13. Jahrhundert," *Zeitschrift für Ostmitteleuropa-Forschung* 62 (2013): 472–89.
4. Cf. also the letter of Archbishop Thomas Becket to Papal Legate Otto of Brescia, Cardinal deacon of San Nicola in Carcere Tulliano (r. 1153–75), from September–October 1167: Thomas Becket, *The Correspondence of Thomas Becket, Archbishop of Canterbury, 1162–1170*, vol. 1, ed. and trans. Anne Duggan (Oxford, 2000), no. 134, 624–27: "Audito aduentu magnitudinis uestre, proscriptorum Christi coexulantium nobis exhilaratus est cetus, et, quasi ad consolationem ecclesie et cleri liberationem de celo missus sit angelus, exultauit, et gratias egit omnis ecclesia sanctorum."
5. Giorgio Agamben, *The Kingdom and the Glory: For a Theological Genealogy of Economy and Government*, trans. Lorenzo Chiesa and Matteo Mandarini (Stanford, 2011), 144–66. Although the early medieval idea of angelic bureaucracy and angelology had to wait for Thomas of Aquinas to receive a proper treatment, the papal letter for William bears evident traces of this idea. To briefly explain: Agamben shows how the theological parallels between the ecclesiastical and political hierarchies have been modeled on the angelic choirs and celestial hierarchies and the irreducibly mediated economy of salvation. In this sense, in the thirteenth century the majestic and delegated (and thus perfectible) panoply of administrative angels (or ministers) appeared as preferable to the unimpressive immediacy of divine (papal/royal) government over men, which would ignore the too distant and thus incompatible difference in nature between God (pope/king) and people.
6. Torben K. Nielsen, "*Vicarius Christi, Plenitudo Potestatis* og *Causae Maiores*. Teologi og jura hos Pave Innocens III (1198–1216) og Ærkebiskop Anders Sunesen (1201–1223)," *Historisk tidsskrift* (D) 94 (1994): 1–29 at 3–5, 10–12; Colin Morris, *The Papal Monarchy: The Western Church from 1050 to 1250* (Oxford, 1989), 205–10, 432.
7. *Liv- Esth- und Curlandisches Urkundenbuch*, vol. 1, no. 69, cols. 73–75: "Cum is, qui secundum suae omnipotentiam maiestatis, nec loco potest nec tempore comprehendi, utpote incircumscriptibilis, et immensus et stabilis manens, dat cuncta moveri, *faciat spiritus suos angelos et ministros, coelorumque altitudine inclinata carnem assumens humanam pro eo*, qui deliciae suae se esse cum filiis hominis, discipulos, quos elegerat, in mundum destinaverit universum, ut omni praedicarent evangelium creaturae, suo nos instruxit exemplo, ut eius sequentes vestigia cum assumpti simus in *plenitudinem potestatis*, nec per nos ipsos possimus singulis negotiis imminere, inter eos, quos in partem sollicitudinis evocavimus, onera, quasi Gethro usi consilio, dividamus unicuique secundum virtutem propriam, quam variis temporibus immitent committendo." [emphasis mine]; the *arenga* of Honorius III's letter for William of Modena quoting Ps. 104:4 and Heb. 1:7 in regard to the ministry of angels was not unique, but rather programmatic of the pope's policies. He had used it in similar, crusade-related legatine

appointments in March of the same year, in 1221, and in 1217: Thomas William Smith, "Pope Honorius III and the Holy Land Crusades, 1216–1227: A Study in Responsive Papal Government" (PhD diss., University of London, 2013), 212–15.
8. Harald Müller, "The Omnipresent Pope: Legates and Judges Delegate," in *A Companion to the Medieval Papacy: Growth of an Ideology and Institution*, ed. Keith Sisson and Atria A. Larson (Boston, 2016), 199–221 at 207–8; Ernst H. Kantorowicz, *The King's Two Bodies: A Study in Mediaeval Political Theology* (Princeton, 1997), 90–92, 282–83; Pierre Bourdieu, *Language and Symbolic Power*, ed. John B. Thompson (Cambridge, MA, 1991), 203–19.
9. Bruno Latour, *Reassembling the Social: An Introduction to Actor-Network-Theory* (Oxford, 2005), 43–62.
10. DD 1.2.115; Nils Blomkvist, Stefan Brink, and Thomas Lindkvist, "The Kingdom of Sweden," in *Christianization and the Rise of Christian Monarchy: Scandinavia, Central Europe and Rus' c. 900–1200*, ed. Nora Berend (Cambridge, 2007), 167–213 at 200.
11. Mia Münster-Swendsen, "Educating the Danes: Anglo-Danish Connections in the Formative Period of the Danish Church, c. 1000–1150," in *Friendship and Social Networks in Scandinavia c.1000–1800*, ed. Jón Viðar Sigurðsson and Thomas Småberg (Turnhout, 2013), 153–73; Marie Bønløkke Spejlborg, "Anglo-Danish Connections and the Organisation of the Early Danish Church: Contribution to a Debate," *Networks and Neighbours* 2 (2014): 71–86.
12. Tuomas Heikkilä, *Sankt Henrikslegenden*, trans. Rainer Knapas (Helsinki, 2009), 48–52, 140; Tuomas Heikkilä, "An Imaginary Saint for an Imagined Community: St. Henry and the Creation of Christian Identity in Finland, Thirteenth–Fifteenth Centuries," in *Imagined Communities on the Baltic Rim, from the Eleventh to Fifteenth Centuries*, ed. Wojtek Jezierski and Lars Hermanson (Amsterdam, 2016), 223–52; Philip Line, "Sweden's Conquest of Finland: A Clash of Cultures?" in *The North-Eastern Frontiers of Medieval Europe: The Expansion of Latin Christendom in the Baltic Lands*, ed. Alan V. Murray (Farnham, 2014), 57–99; Jens E. Olesen, "The Swedish Expeditions ('Crusades') Towards Finland Reconsidered," in *Church and Belief in the Middle Ages: Popes, Saints, and Crusaders*, ed. Kirsi Salonen and Sari Katajala-Peltomaa (Amsterdam, 2016), 251–67 at 255–59.
13. Michael Gelting, "The Kingdom of Denmark," in *Christianization and the Rise of Christian Monarchy*, 73–120 at 95–96.
14. Karl Jónsson, *Sverris saga etter AM 327, 4to*, ed. Gustav Storm (Oslo, 1981 [1920]), ch. 122, 130; David Brégaint, *Vox regis: Royal Communication in High Medieval Norway* (Leiden, 2016), 124–25.
15. DD 1.5.177: "Ipsum [Gregorium] sicut personam nostrum curabis cum honorificentia te et ipso digna recipere. et in eo deuotionem quam ad Romanam habes ecclesiam exhibere."
16. *Vita Gunneri episcopi vibergensis*, SM II, ch. I, 266: "Verum quia ipse cardinalis et *abbas memoratus college fuerunt aliquando Parisius et socij*, eum per omnia nouit, quod de septem liberalibus aliquam partem haberet et noticiam atque competentem ad hec prudentiam et discrecionem." [emphasis mine]; Anthony Perron, "Metropolitan Might and Papal Power on the Latin-Christian Frontier: Transforming the Danish Church Around the Time of the Fourth Lateran Council," *The Catholic Historical Review* 89 (2003): 182–212 at 204–5, esp. n. 101.
17. *Vita Gunneri*, ch. I, 266: "Cardinalis vero ad sedem Wibergensem veniens, cum de eligendo aliquo in episcopum canonici ipsius sedis non sane [de

Angels in Scandinavia 185

aliquo] potuerunt conuenire, dixit se cardinalis scire quemlibet virum tante sedi et honori competentem et vtilem, si vellent sibi consentire. Quod se facturos vnanimiter spoponderunt"; see also DD 1.5.201.

18. Perron, "Metropolitan Might," 205–6; Johnny Grandjean Gøgsig Jakobsen, "Friars Preachers in Frontier Provinces of Medieval Europe," in *Medieval East Central Europe in a Comparative Perspective: From Frontier Zones to Lands in Focus*, ed. Gerhard Jaritz and Katalin Szende (London, 2016), 123–36; see also the contribution by Johnny Grandjean Gøgsig Jakobsen in chapter 10 in this volume.

19. Maureen C. Miller, "Beyond National Narratives: Culture, States, and Reframing 'Gregorian' Reform," Keynote Lecture, *International Medieval Congress* (Leeds, UK, July 6, 2015); see also J. H. Elliott, "A Europe of Composite Monarchies," *Past & Present* 137 (1992): 48–71 at 50–52. I would like to thank Professor Miller for generously sharing her materials which allowed me to develop this part of the argument.

20. Sandro Carocci, "Popes as Princes? The Papal States (1000–1300)," in *Companion to the Medieval Papacy*, 66–84; Müller, "Omnipresent Pope," 199–221; Krzysztof Skwierczyński, *Recepcja idei gregoriańskich w Polsce do początku XIII wieku* (Wrocław, 2005), 271–78; Antonín Kalous, "Biskupské a legatské rituály a ceremonie," in *Slavnosti, ceremonie a rituály v pozdním středověku*, ed. Martin Nodl and František Šmahel (Prague, 2014), 315–67 at 347–55.

21. Perron, "Metropolitan Might," 190–92.

22. Arnold von Lübeck, *Chronica Slavorum*, ed. Johann M. Lappenberg, MGH *Scriptores in folio* 38 (Hannover, 1868), bk. III, ch. 5, 77: "Scientia quoque litterali non parum profecerunt, quia nobiliores terre filios suos non solum ad clerum promovendum, verum etiam secularibus rebus instituendos Parisius mittunt. Ubi litteratura simul et idiomate lingue terre illius imbuti, non solum in artibus, sed etiam in theologia multum invaluerunt. Siquidem propter naturalem lingue celeritatem non solum in argumentis dialecticis subtiles inveniuntur, sed etiam in negotiis ecclesiasticis tractandis boni decretiste sive legiste comprobantur." English translation by Kurt Villads Jensen, "Martyrs, Total War, and Heavenly Horses: Scandinavia as Centre and Periphery in the Expansion of Medieval Christendom," in *Medieval Christianity in the North: New Studies*, ed. Kirsi Salonen, Kurt Villads Jensen, and Torstein Jørgensen (Turnhout, 2013), 89–120 at 113.

23. Perron, "Metropolitan Might," 185–87.

24. Cf. *Absalon: fædrelandets fader*, ed. Tom Christensen, Inge Skovgaard-Petersen, and Frank A. Birkebæk (Roskilde, 1996).

25. Lars Hermanson, *Släkt, vänner och makt: en studie av elitens politiska kultur i 1100-talets Danmark* (Gothenburg, 2000), 149–54, 191–201, 229–36; Lars Hermanson, "How to Legitimate a Rebellion and Condemn Usurpation of the Crown: Discourses of Fidelity and Treason in the *Gesta Danorum* of Saxo Grammaticus," in *Disputing Strategies in Medieval Scandinavia*, ed. Kim Esmark et al. (Leiden, 2013), 107–40 at 108–10; see also the contribution by Kim Esmark in chapter 15 in this volume.

26. *Sancti Willelmi Abbatis vita et miracula*, in VSD, 300–77 at ch. X, 320: "Reminiscitur [Absalon] tandem familiaritatis et amicicie, quam cum Willelmo, uiro religioso, olim pepigerat, cum Parisius studendi gracia moraretur; attendensque eum uirum honestum, uirum utique prouidum et discretum et sanctis moribus adornatum, complacuit in illo anime sue, ut ei accito daret locum supra memoratum."

27. Bourdieu, *Language and Symbolic Power*, 163–70; Philippe Buc, "Conversion of Objects," *Viator* 28 (1997): 99–143.

28. Perron, "Metropolitan Might," 207, n. 114; Latour, *Reassembling the Social*, 70–82.
29. Lars Hermanson, "Discourses of Communion: Abbot William of Æbelholt and Saxo Grammaticus: Imagining the Christian Danish Community, Early Thirteenth Century," in *Imagined Communities*, 59–87; Brian Patrick McGuire, "Absalon's Spirituality: A Man Attached to Holy Men," in *Archbishop Absalon of Lund and His World*, ed. Karsten Friis-Jensen and Inge Skovgaard-Petersen (Roskilde, 2000), 71–87 at 81–83; Sverre Bagge, "Nordic Students at Foreign Universities until 1660," *Scandinavian Journal of History* 9, no. 1 (1984): 1–29; Anti Selart, *Livonia, Rus' and the Baltic Crusades in the Thirteenth Century*, trans. Fiona Robb (Leiden, 2015), 47–50; Tore Nyberg, *Monasticism in North-Western Europe, 800–1200* (Aldershot, 2000), 194–96, 221–22, 238–41.
30. DD 1.3.96, 103.
31. E.g. DD 1.3.96, 140–41, 223, 225, 246, 253; See also Absalon's testament: DD 1.4.32; Erik Ulsig, "The Estates of Absalon and the Hvide Family," in *Archbishop Absalon of Lund*, 89–101; McGuire, "Absalon's Spirituality," 74–81; Perron, "Metropolitan Might," 188–89; Hermanson, *Släkt, vänner och makt*, 5–8, 11, 89–92; more generally: Barbara H. Rosenwein, *Negotiating Space: Power, Restraint, and Privileges of Immunity in Early Medieval Europe* (Manchester, 1999).
32. DD 1.3.100, 138, 218, 241; Herluf Nielsen, "The Papal Confirmations for Archbishop Absalon, Especially Concerning the Castle of Havn (Copenhagen)," in *Archbishop Absalon of Lund*, 103–11.
33. DD 1.3.78–79, 95, 203.
34. E.g. DD 1.3.103, 114, 115: "Hanc nostre confirmationis cartulam quecunque ecclesiastica secularisue persona attemptare instinctu nefario presumpserit. indissolubili anathematis uinculo innodata. a communione corporis sanguinisque dominici ni condigna penitudine resipuerit sequestretur. post obitum gehenne suppliciis eternaliter condempnanda"; 140: "Si quis autem huic nostre confirmationi scienter contraire presumpserit maledictionem et iram dei omnipotentis se nouerit incursurum nisi reatum suum condigna satisfactione correxerit"; 164.
35. DD 1.3.100, 118, 122, 137: "Si quis autem [attemptare presumpserit indignationem omnipotentis] dei et beatorum Petri et Pauli apostolorum eius se nouerit incursurum," 138, 142.
36. Brigitte M. Bedos-Rezak, *When Ego Was Imago: Signs of Identity in the Middle Ages* (Leiden, 2011), 18–19, 98–99.
37. Michael Burger, *Bishops, Clerks, and Diocesan Governance in Thirteenth-Century England: Reward and Punishment* (Cambridge, 2012), 141–46.
38. E.g. DD 1.3.175: "Prefatum uero ducem. et quoslibet alios quos in episcopum impsum temerarias manus iniecisse constiterit. tamdiu sine appelationis obstaculo singulis diebus sollempnibus per totum regnum nunciari facias sicut excommunicatos ab omnibus artius euitandos. donec ecclesie dei . . . Ceterum quod Wrm Ripensis. Petrus Selandiensis. Azcer Wibergiensis . . . et si eos super tanto f[acin]ore culpabiles esse cognoueris. ab episcopali officio. cessante appelatione suspendas"; see also letters:176–77; Hermanson, *Släkt, vänner och makt*, 240.
39. DD 1.3.131.
40. Nielsen, "*Vicarius Christi*," 24–27; Birger Munk Olsen, "Anders Sunesen og Paris," in *Anders Sunesen: stormand, teolog, administrator, digter: femten studier*, ed. Sten Ebbesen (Copenhagen, 1985), 75–97.
41. Iben Fonnesberg-Schmidt, *The Popes and the Baltic Crusades, 1147–1254* (Leiden, 2006), 86–89; Torben K. Nielsen, "The Missionary Man:

Archbishop Anders Sunesen and the Baltic Crusade, 1206–1221," in *The Clash of Cultures on the Medieval Baltic Border*, ed. Alan V. Murray (Farnham, 2009), 95–117.
42. Fonnesberg-Schmidt, *Popes*, 86, n. 30.
43. Saxo, Praefatio 1.1, 72–73: "[Anders] cuius fertilissimum scientię pectus ac uenerabilium doctrinarum abundantia instructum ueluti quoddam cęlestium opum sacrarium exisitmandum est. Tu Galliam Italiamque cum Britannia percipiendę literarum discipline colligendęque earum copię scholę regimen appręhendisti"; Inge Skovgaard-Petersen, "Saxo og Anders Sunesen," in *Anders Sunesen*, 55–74; Jørgen Raasted, "Dogmatik och bibelfortolkning i Anders Sunesens Hexaemeron," in *Anders Sunesen*, 151–69.
44. Pierre Bourdieu, "The Forms of Capital," in *Handbook of Theory of Research for the Sociology of Education*, ed. John E. Richardson and trans. Richard Nice (Westport, CT, 1986), 241–58.
45. DD 1.4.96: "concedimus, ut in Lundensi et Upsallensi archiepiscopatibus, vice nostra evellas, et destruas, disperdas, et dissipes, edifices et plantes sicut ad honorum dei, exaltationem ecclesie ac salutem populi tibi commissi videris expedire," with a clear hint at Jer. 1:10.
46. Nielsen, "*Vicarius Christi*," 17–23; Perron, "Metropolitan Might," 198.
47. DD 1.5.13: "de probitate ac honestate tuam fiduciam obtinemus . . . Cum igitur christiane fidei zelo succensus ad convertendum circonstantes paganos . . . et adhuc laborare disponas ut hoc plenius et efficacius exequaris nos tibi vices nostras."
48. Bysted et al., *Jerusalem in the North*, 195–204; Nielsen, "Missionary Man," 103–10; Jonathan Lindström, *Biskopen och korståget 1206: Om krig, kolonisation och Guds man i Norden* (Stockholm, 2015).
49. Fonnesberg-Schmidt, *Popes*, 126–27.
50. Bysted et al., *Jerusalem in the North*, 232–34.
51. DD 1.5.28: "quendam falsarium in vinculis detinere qui sedis apostolice mentiens se legatum nomine ac officio episcopi usurpatis in multis pontificale presumpsit officium exercere."
52. Bysted et al., *Jerusalem in the North*, 234, and n. 414; Skwierczyński, *Recepcja idei gregoriańskich*, 291–94.
53. *Svenskt Diplomatariums huvudkartotek*, 613, ed. Riksarkivet, https://sok.riksarkivet.se/sdhk?SDHK=613&postid=sdhk_613: "in sueciam inuenimus regnum illud temporaliter & spiritualiter fere per totum mirabiliter & miserabiliter conturbatum. Erat siquidem guerra satis dura inter regem & quosdam nobiles, ex qua homicidia & incendia multa contigerant & rapine. spiritualiter autem eo quod fere omnes sacerdotes erant presbiterorum filii patrum uestigiis inherentes contrahendo sollempniter matrimonia uel publice concubinas habendo in sacris ordinibus constituti."
54. Nielsen, "*Vicarius Christi*," 15–18; Blomkvist et al., "Kingdom of Sweden," 201; These regulations were in no way unique to Scandinavia. During similar legatine synods in neighboring Poland – particularly the coterminous synod in Wrocław in 1248 presided over by Jacob of Liège – papal legates went to much greater lengths and provided more detailed regulations regarding access to church offices, the traffic between ecclesiastical and secular elites, and the forms of hospitality for bishops. Against this background the Skänninge provisions appear much more general and very moderate, which reveals both the limits of William's ambitions and the differences in the complexity of the ecclesiastical structure between these two regions: Wojciech Góralski, "Statuty synodalne legata Jakuba z Leodium," *Prawo kanoniczne* 27 (1984): 149–71.
55. Ingrid Gustin, "Kvinnan, tornet och makten i Bjälbo," in *Triangulering: historisk arkeologi vidgar fälten*, ed. Mats Mogren (Lund, 2009), 111–27.

56. Blomkvist et al., "Kingdom of Sweden," 201; Olesen, "Swedish Expeditions," 260–62.
57. *Svenskt Diplomatariums huvudkartotek*, 613.
58. Ibid.
59. Ibid: "seu in sacerdotes uel domesticos eorum manus iniciendo uiolentas, exceptis personis domini Regis & ducis, sentenciam excommunicacionis incurrant."
60. In the preceding three months William had issued at least six letters of indulgence to support the Dominican monasteries in Sigtuna and Skänninge (*Svenskt Diplomatariums huvudkartotek*, 593, 594, 595, 596, 597, and 598).
61. *Svenskt Diplomatariums huvudkartotek*, 612; more on Bishop Thomas in: Olesen, "Swedish Expeditions," 260–62.
62. Heikkilä, *Sankt Henrikslegenden*, 62; Blomkvist et al., "Kingdom of Sweden," 188–89, 201; Thomas Lindkvist, "Crusades and Crusading Ideology in the Political History of Sweden, 1140–1500," in *Crusade and Conversion on the Baltic Frontier 1150–1400*, ed. Alan V. Murray (Aldershot, 2001), 119–30 at 122–23; Bysted et al., *Jerusalem in the North*, 260–62.
63. Perron, "Metropolitan Might," 211–12; Nielsen, "*Vicarius Christi*"; Morris, *Papal Monarchy*, 432–38, 573–74.
64. Pierre Bourdieu, *Distinction: A Social Critique of the Judgment of Taste*, trans. Richard Nice (Cambridge, MA, 1996), 444.
65. Franz Blatt, "Ministerium – Mysterium," *Archivum latinitatis medii aevi* 4 (1928): 80–81; Kantorowicz, *King's Two Bodies*, 101; Agamben, *Kingdom and the Glory*, 158–59; Bourdieu, *Language and Symbolic Power*, 248; Pierre Bourdieu, "The Mystery of the Ministry: From Particular Wills to the General Will," in *Pierre Bourdieu and Democratic Politics: The Mystery of Ministry*, ed. Loïc Wacquant (Cambridge, 2005), 55–63 at 58–61.

Dedicated Bibliography

Agamben, Giorgio. *The Kingdom and the Glory: For a Theological Genealogy of Economy and Government*. Translated by Lorenzo Chiesa and Matteo Mandarini. Stanford, 2011.

Arnold von Lübeck. *Chronica Slavorum*, MGH Scriptores in folio 38. Edited by Johann M. Lappenberg. Hannover, 1868.

Bagge, Sverre. "Nordic Students at Foreign Universities Until 1660." *Scandinavian Journal of History* 9 (1984): 1–29.

Bedos-Rezak, Brigitte M. *When Ego Was Imago: Signs of Identity in the Middle Ages*. Leiden, 2011.

Blatt, Franz. "Ministerium – Mysterium." *Archivum Latinitatis Medii Aevi* 4 (1928): 80–81.

Blomkvist, Nils, Stefan Brink, and Thomas Lindkvist. "The Kingdom of Sweden." In *Christianization and the Rise of Christian Monarchy: Scandinavia, Central Europe and Rus' c. 900–1200*, edited by Nora Berend, 167–213. Cambridge, 2007.

Bourdieu, Pierre. "The Forms of Capital." In *Handbook of Theory of Research for the Sociology of Education*, edited by John E. Richardson and translated by Richard Nice, 241–58. Westport, CT, 1986.

Bourdieu, Pierre. *Language and Symbolic Power*. Edited by John B. Thompson. Cambridge, MA, 1991.

Bourdieu, Pierre. *Distinction: A Social Critique of the Judgment of Taste*. Translated by Richard Nice. Cambridge, MA, 1996.
Bourdieu, Pierre. "The Mystery of the Ministry: From Particular Wills to the General Will." In *Pierre Bourdieu and Democratic Politics: The Mystery of Ministry*, edited by Loïc Wacquant, 55–63. Cambridge, 2005.
Brégaint, David. *Vox Regis: Royal Communication in High Medieval Norway*. Leiden, 2016.
Burger, Michael. *Bishops, Clerks, and Diocesan Governance in Thirteenth-Century England: Reward and Punishment*. Cambridge, 2012.
Bysted, Ane L., Carsten Selch Jensen, Kurt Villads Jensen, and John H. Lind. *Jerusalem in the North: Denmark and the Baltic Crusades, 1100–1552*. Translated by Sarah Pedersen and Fredrik Pedersen. Turnhout, 2012.
Carocci, Sandro. "Popes as Princes? The Papal States (1000–1300)." In *A Companion to the Medieval Papacy: Growth of an Ideology and Institution*, edited by Keith Sisson and Atria A. Larson, 66–84. Boston, 2016.
Christensen, Tom, Inge Skovgaard-Petersen, and Frank A. Birkebæk, eds. *Absalon: fædrelandets fader*. Roskilde, 1996.
Elliott, John Huxtable. "A Europe of Composite Monarchies." *Past & Present* 137 (1992): 48–71.
Fonnesberg-Schmidt, Iben. *The Popes and the Baltic Crusades, 1147–1254*. Leiden, 2006.
Gelting, Michael H. "The Kingdom of Denmark." In *Christianization and the Rise of Christian Monarchy: Scandinavia, Central Europe and Rus' c. 900–1200*, edited by Nora Berend, 73–120. Cambridge, 2007.
Gustin, Ingrid. "Kvinnan, tornet och makten i Bjälbo." In *Triangulering: historisk arkeologi vidgar fälten*, edited by Mats Mogren, 111–27. Lund, 2009.
Heikkilä, Tuomas. *Sankt Henrikslegenden*. Translated by Rainer Knapas. Helsinki, 2009.
Heikkilä, Tuomas. "An Imaginary Saint for an Imagined Community: St. Henry and the Creation of Christian Identity in Finland, Thirteenth–Fifteenth Centuries." In *Imagined Communities on the Baltic Rim, from the Eleventh to Fifteenth Centuries*, edited by Wojtek Jezierski and Lars Hermanson, 223–52. Amsterdam, 2016.
Heinrich von Lettland. *Chronicon Livoniae/Livländische Chronik*. Edited and translated by Albert Bauer. Darmstadt, 1959.
Henricus Lettus. *The Chronicle of Henry of Livonia*. Translated by James A. Brundage. New York, 2003.
Hermanson, Lars. *Släkt, vänner och makt: En studie av elitens politiska kultur i 1100-talets Danmark*. Gothenburg, 2000.
Hermanson, Lars. "How to Legitimate Rebellion and Condemn Usurpation of the Crown: Discourses of Fidelity and Treason in the *Gesta Danorum* of Saxo Grammaticus." In *Disputing Strategies in Medieval Scandinavia*, edited by Kim Esmark, Lars Hermanson, Hans Jacob Orning, and Helle Vogt, 107–40. Leiden, 2013.
Hermanson, Lars. "Discourses of Communion: Abbot William of Æbelholt and Saxo Grammaticus: Imagining the Christian Danish Community, Early Thirteenth Century." In *Imagined Communities on the Baltic Rim, from the Eleventh to Fifteenth Centuries*, edited by Wojtek Jezierski and Lars Hermanson, 59–87. Amsterdam, 2016.

Inge Skovgaard-Petersen, Inge. "Saxo og Anders Sunesen." In *Anders Sunesen: Stormand, Teolog, Administrator, Digter: Femten Studier*, edited by Sten Ebbesen, 55–75. Copenhagen, 1985.

Jakobsen, Johnny Grandjean Gøgsig. "Friars Preachers in Frontier Provinces of Medieval Europe." In *Medieval East-Central Europe in a Comparative Perspective: From Frontier Zones to Lands in Focus*, edited by Gerhard Jaritz and Katalin Szende, 123–36. London, 2016.

Jensen, Kurt Villads. "Martyrs, Total War, and Heavenly Horses: Scandinavia as Centre and Periphery in the Expansion of Medieval Christendom." In *Medieval Christianity in the North: New Studies*, edited by Kirsi Salonen, Kurt Villads Jensen, and Torstein Jørgensen, 89–120. Turnhout, 2013.

Jónsson, Karl. *Sverris saga etter AM 327,4to*. Edited by Gustav Storm. Oslo, 1981 [1920].

Kalous, Antonín. "Biskupské a legatské rituály a ceremonie." In *Slavnosti, ceremonie a rituály v pozdním středověku*, edited by Martin Nodl and František Šmahel, 315–67. Prague, 2014.

Kantorowicz, Ernst H. *The King's Two Bodies: A Study in Mediaeval Political Theology*. Princeton, 1997.

Latour, Bruno. *Reassembling the Social: An Introduction to Actor-Network-Theory*. Oxford, 2005.

Lindkvist, Thomas. "Crusades and Crusading Ideology in the Political History of Sweden, 1140–1500." In *Crusade and Conversion on the Baltic Frontier 1150–1400*, edited by Alan V. Murray, 119–30. Aldershot, 2001.

Lindström, Jonathan. *Biskopen och korståget 1206: Om krig, kolonisation och Guds man i Norden*. Stockholm, 2015.

Line, Philip. "Sweden's Conquest of Finland: A Clash of Cultures?" In *The North-Eastern Frontiers of Medieval Europe: The Expansion of Latin Christendom in the Baltic Lands*, edited by Alan V. Murray, 57–99. Farnham, 2014.

Liv- Esth- und Curlandisches Urkundenbuch nebst Regesten. Edited by Friedrich Georg von Bunge and Hermann Hildebrand. Reval (Tallin), 1853.

Mäesalu, Mihkel. "Päpstliche und kaiserliche Machtansprüche im livländischen Kreuzzugsgebiet im 13. Jahrhundert." *Zeitschrift für Ostmitteleuropa-Forschung* 62 (2013): 472–89.

McGuire, Brian Patrick. "Absalon's Spirituality: A Man Attached to Holy Men." In *Archbishop Absalon of Lund and his World*, edited by Karsten Friis-Jensen and Inge Skovgaard-Petersen, 71–87. Roskilde, 2000.

Miller, Maureen C. "Beyond National Narratives: Culture, States, and Reframing 'Gregorian' Reform." Keynote lecture, *International Medieval Congress*, Leeds, UK, July 6, 2015.

Morris, Colin. *The Papal Monarchy: The Western Church from 1050 to 1250*. Oxford, 1989.

Müller, Harald. "The Omnipresent Pope: Legates and Judges Delegate." In *A Companion to the Medieval Papacy: Growth of an Ideology and Institution*, edited by Keith Sisson and Atria A. Larson, 199–221. Boston, 2016.

Münster-Swendsen, Mia. "Educating the Danes: Anglo-Danish Connections in the Formative Period of the Danish Church, c. 1000–1150." In *Friendship and Social Networks in Scandinavia c.1000–1800*, edited by Jón Viðar Sigurðsson and Thomas Småberg, 153–73. Turnhout, 2013.

Nielsen, Herluf. "The Papal Confirmations for Archbishop Absalon, Especially Concerning the Castle of Havn (Copenhagen)." In *Archbishop Absalon of*

Lund and His World, edited by Karsten Friis-Jensen and Inge Skovgaard-Petersen, 103–11. Roskilde, 2000.
Nielsen, Torben K. "*Vicarius Christi, Plenitudo Potestatis* og *Causae Maiores*: Teologi og jura hos Pave Innocens III (1198–1216) og Ærkebiskop Anders Sunesen (1201–1223)." *Historisk tidsskrift* (D) 94 (1994): 1–29.
Nielsen, Torben K. "The Missionary Man: Archbishop Anders Sunesen and the Baltic Crusade, 1206–1221." In *The Clash of Cultures on the Medieval Baltic Border*, edited by Alan V. Murray, 95–117. Farnham, 2009.
Nyberg, Tore. *Monasticism in North-Western Europe, 800–1200*. Aldershot, 2000.
Olesen, Jens E. "The Swedish Expeditions ('Crusades') Towards Finland Reconsidered." In *Church and Belief in the Middle Ages: Popes, Saints, and Crusaders*, edited by Kirsi Salonen and Sari Katajala-Peltomaa, 251–67. Amsterdam, 2016.
Olsen, Birger Munk. "Anders Sunesen og Paris." In *Anders Sunesen: stormand, teolog, administrator, digter: femten studier*, edited by Sten Ebbesen, 75–97. Copenhagen, 1985.
Perron, Anthony. "Metropolitan Might and Papal Power on the Latin-Christian Frontier: Transforming the Danish Church around the Time of the Fourth Lateran Council." *The Catholic Historical Review* 89 (2003): 182–212.
Raasted, Jørgen. "Dogmatik och bibelfortolkning i Anders Sunesens Hexaemeron." In *Anders Sunesen: Stormand, Teolog, Administrator, Digter: Femten Studier*, edited by Sten Ebbesen, 151–69. Copenhagen, 1985.
Rosenwein, Barbara H. *Negotiating Space: Power, Restraint, and Privileges of Immunity in Early Medieval Europe*. Manchester, 1999.
"Sancti Willelmi Abbatis Vita et Miracula." In *Vitae Sanctorum Danorum*, edited by M. Cl. Gertz, 300–77. Copenhagen, 1908–12.
Selart, Anti. *Livonia, Rus' and the Baltic Crusades in the Thirteenth Century*. Translated by Fiona Robb. Leiden, 2015.
Skwierczyński, Krzysztof. *Recepcja idei gregoriańskich w Polsce do początku XIII wieku*. Wrocław, 2005.
Smith, Thomas William. "Pope Honorius III and the Holy Land Crusades, 1216–1227: A Study in Responsive Papal Government." PhD diss., Royal Holloway, University of London, 2013.
Spejlborg, Marie Bønløkke. "Anglo-Danish Connections and the Organisation of the Early Danish Church: Contribution to a Debate." *Networks and Neighbours* 2 (2014): 71–86.
Thomas Becket. *The Correspondence of Thomas Becket, Archbishop of Canterbury, 1162–1170*. Edited and translated by Anne Duggan. Oxford, 2000.
Ulsig, Erik. "The Estates of Absalon and the Hvide Family." In *Archbishop Absalon of Lund and his World*, edited by Karsten Friis-Jensen and Inge Skovgaard-Petersen, 89–101. Roskilde, 2000.

10 Social Friendships Between the Dominican Order and Elite Groups in Thirteenth-Century Scandinavia

Johnny Grandjean Gøgsig Jakobsen

The Dominican Order was founded in 1216. In 1220 the first Dominican Friars Preachers were sent to Scandinavia, and in 1222 the order's first (lasting) convent in Scandinavia was founded in Lund. By 1250, eighteen male and female convents had been established within the Dominican province of Dacia, i.e., Scandinavia and northern Estonia, and by 1300, the number of houses had reached twenty-six.[1] Because the Dominican Order was without the financial means to implement this process itself, its rapid dissemination and growth depended on significant support from various elite groups already present in Scandinavian society. The same could, of course, be argued for all monastic institutions of the Middle Ages, but the need for several and continuous friendships with influential groups in the surrounding society was particularly outspoken for the mendicant orders, who were forbidden by their own constitutions to hold large amounts of income-generating property, and therefore, unlike e.g., the Benedictines and Cistercians, could not survive for generations on landed donations acquired from just one generous founder in the initial years of the monastery. The mendicant friars needed to nourish and expand their friendships in the outside world continuously in order to maintain their existence. In this chapter I will focus on elite friendships between the Friars Preachers and influential families, groups, and institutions in thirteenth-century Scandinavia, with the hope of clarifying possible motives, expectations, and outcomes for both sides in such more or less formalized relationships. The chapter aims to show how the success of the Friars Preachers was not least based on their ability to establish and maintain a complex set of many-sided and internally overlapping social ties – a heterogeneous and dynamic network of friendships, which mirrored the growing social complexity of the urban environment of thirteenth-century Europe in which the Dominican Order took off.

Founding Friends of the Friars

When planning the establishment of a new Dominican convent, the friars were deeply dependent on a positive reception from a number of

The Dominican Order and Elite Groups 193

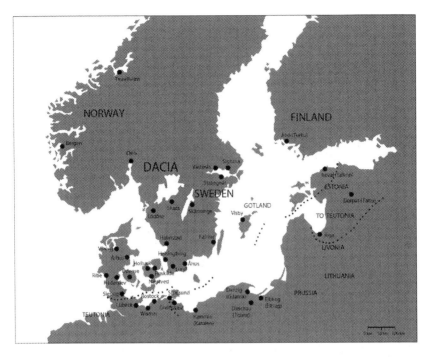

Map 10.1 Dominican convents in the province of Dacia and its immediate surroundings around 1300.
Source: Map by author.

influential groups. Basically, four parties had to agree before a convent could be founded: the order itself had to want and approve it; the bishop of the diocese had to allow it; the magistrate of the home city had to permit it; and somebody had to be willing to pay for it. Among these facilitating parties, one or two were usually the prime initiator(s). Just who took this initiative seems to have changed over the course of the Middle Ages.[2]

Upon their first arrival and until the mid-thirteenth century, Friars Preachers all over Europe were particularly welcomed by the bishops, who must have seen the friars as the answer to the renewed emphasis of the Fourth Lateran Council in 1215 on increasing pastoral efforts towards laypeople (Canon 10) and improving the education of the secular diocesan clergy (Canon 11). In some places the Friars Preachers were not just welcomed by the bishops, they were invited by them. Such explicit invitations are preserved from, among others, Archbishop Albert of Magdeburg (1225), Bishop Hugues of Liège (1229), Bishop Nicolaus of Riga (1234), and Archbishop Juhel of Reims (1246), and explicitly state the need for preachers and clerical teachers.[3] No direct invitations are preserved from Scandinavia, but most Danish, Swedish, and Norwegian bishops seem to have supported Dominican foundations in their dioceses. The Danish archbishop Anders Sunesen himself gave the Friars Preachers a house in central Lund next to the cathedral, which was eventually developed into a friary with its own church.[4] In Sweden, there was a significant shift in favor of the Dominican Order when Archbishop Olof of Uppsala died and was replaced by Jarler in 1236, who not only endorsed the founding of Dominican convents in five Swedish dioceses, but also chose to be buried in the Dominican friary church in Sigtuna.[5] Even in places with no extant written records of the arrival of Friars Preachers, it is possible to deduce a positive and active episcopal involvement.[6] Thus, it was no coincidence that the foundation of Dominican convents in the second quarter of the thirteenth century mainly took place in cathedral cities and other major ecclesiastical centers. With the foundation of a Dominican convent in Strängnäs in 1268, the Order of Preachers was represented in seventeen of the twenty-one dioceses in Scandinavia, in fourteen cases in the very center of the diocese, and then almost always with a friary location in the immediate vicinity of the cathedral chapter. By this time, Dominican convents had also been established in supplementary secular-ecclesiastical centers such as Haderslev, Åhus, Skänninge, Sigtuna, and Visby; in Haderslev, the foundation seems to have coincided with the formation of a local secular collegiate chapter of canons subject to the bishop of Schleswig around 1250.[7] By teaming up with the Friars Preachers, the Scandinavian episcopate not only gained an elite corps of eloquent preachers and theological teachers based near the secular-ecclesiastical centers; they also signaled to the Papal Curia that the implementation of Canons 10 and 11 of the Fourth Lateran Council was well underway. Likewise, for the Friars Preachers, amicable relations with the local episcopal elite were vital: not only did the friars require the bishop's permission to settle in the diocese; without episcopal backing the friars would have had a limited license to preach outside their own churches, and few among the laity and the secular clergy would have recognized their theological authority – and thereby their entire *raison d'être*.

Almost all mendicant friaries were placed in urban areas, either inside the actual town or just outside one of the gates. For such a location to be permitted and to function, the friars needed the acceptance of the town magistrate. In the first half of the thirteenth century, this was not always as easy as one might expect. Unlike their Franciscan colleagues, the Friars Preachers usually set their sights on the bigger towns and cities, but it seems that initially the municipal authorities often failed to see any obvious advantage to letting in yet another ecclesiastical institution which would not pay urban taxes on its property and would generally be placed outside municipal jurisdiction. In Wismar, for instance, the foundation of a Dominican convent was only allowed in 1294 after the friars had entered into a contract with the magistrate that limited their privileges in numerous aspects.[8] Precautions were also taken in Rostock and Elbląg to keep taxable urban land from the hands of the tax-exempt friars.[9] While the urban bourgeoisie of northern Europe, contrary to the impression often given in the literature, generally showed little interest in the mendicant orders before the fifteenth century, from the mid-thirteenth century onwards the town magistrates as institutions gradually began to see the value of housing mendicant convents.[10] A growing part of the lay population apparently enjoyed listening to the sermons of the eloquent mendicant preachers, and as the initially close relations between the episcopate and the mendicants began to cool after 1250, some city magistrates, such as those in Lübeck, found in the Dominicans a new ally against their old episcopal foe.[11] The most positive municipal attitude towards the friars is seen in smaller towns, where the existence of at least one mendicant convent appears to have been an essential element of basic urban identity by the mid-thirteenth century; a town without a friary was not really considered a town![12] From some smaller towns around Europe there are even examples of written invitations from the municipal authorities asking the orders to establish a house with them, "just like you have done in other cities, which now bask in the glory of the friars' sacred house," as stated by the city council of Bern in 1269.[13] Again, no such explicit invitations are preserved from Scandinavia, but it is noteworthy that the Dominican convents in Holbæk, Halmstad, and Vejle – medieval towns which otherwise must have been of little interest to the Dominicans – were founded in the period 1275–1325, when the very same towns appear to have gained their first urban privileges.[14] For the Friars Preachers themselves, the city councils were of course the key lay elite institutions to connect with, since so many practical aspects of the friars' everyday lives would be much easier if the council had a generally positive view of the convent. Moreover, members of the city councils often came to provide the most profitable access to donations, funerals, and chantry foundations from the patriciate families of the city. While smaller towns (like Holbæk, Halmstad, and Vejle) by themselves may have held little attraction for the friars, they could be valuable as geographically well positioned bases for the important rural campaigns (the *terminario*) of the mendicants.[15] In addition, it is very likely that the magistrates of the smaller towns were much more accommodating than they were in the bigger, more reluctant cities. In Vejle, for example, the Dominican convent appears to have owned a significant part of the town by the end of the Middle Ages.[16]

A third and final participant required for the foundation of a mendicant convent was the town lord. With a few exceptions, lordship of all Scandinavian cities in the thirteenth century was administered by princely rulers, i.e., the kings of Denmark, Norway, and Sweden and the duke of Schleswig-Holstein. Temporary regents like Skule Jarl of Norway and Birger Jarl of Sweden can also be placed in this group. Without the acceptance of the local princely lord, it would have been practically impossible for the friars to settle in any Scandinavian town, and thus it would seem that such permissions must have been granted. But, unlike their colleagues elsewhere in Europe, there is hardly any explicit evidence that Scandinavian royalty acted as the prime initiators of the foundation of any Dominican convents in the thirteenth century – with the convent in Oslo, said to have been founded by King Haakon Haakonsson in 1240, being the sole exception.[17] Whereas the Dominican Order generally enjoyed very amicable relations with the ruling princely dynasties of thirteenth-century Europe, often with friars acting as personal confessors and councilors for kings, queens, dukes, and the like, this is a slightly less obvious phenomenon in Scandinavia. Certainly, King Haakon Haakonsson of Norway (r. 1217–63); King Christopher I of Denmark (r. 1252–59), along with his son Erik V Klipping (r. 1259–86) in his youth; and Birger Jarl of Sweden (1248–66) are all known to have made extensive use of select Dominican friars as diplomats, envoys, and court councilors,[18] thereby placing leading Dominican friars in the network of bishops, abbots, and lay lords who enjoyed the king's trust. But these connections seem to have been based on the personal preferences of particular kings rather than an institutional connection. As soon as Haakon, Christopher, and Birger Jarl died, and Erik Klipping came of age (around 1267), the Dominican role at the courts of Scandinavia seems to have vanished. More lasting relationships, beyond those of particular individuals, were formed between Dominican convents and certain families of the highest nobility in northern Europe from the mid-thirteenth century onwards.[19] In both Denmark and Sweden, such Dominican connections to leading noble families are especially evident in the period 1290–1350,[20] but, at least for the Danish Hvide family, we know about their involvement in the foundation of Dominican and especially Franciscan convents from the first half of the thirteenth century.[21] It seems that in the thirteenth and fourteenth centuries it became increasingly popular for leading noble families to manifest themselves with a *memoria* cult program, in which the mendicant convents proved to be highly useful. Many lords and ladies could afford to found mendicant convents – which were significantly cheaper to establish than abbeys of the old monastic orders because the mendicants needed only a house and not a huge landed estate to go with it. The nobles also founded altars and burial places in the mendicant churches, along with perpetual masses to be held on the founders' anniversaries for the benefit of the souls of their entire families.[22] For the friars, close and amicable relations to the ruling lay classes, be it kings or powerful noble families, were attractive for several reasons. They often paid for the construction of priories; they provided a continuous stream of alms and donations after the foundation; they often led to new and beneficial contact with other families who wanted to connect with the initial friends of the friars; and they acted as powerful supporters in legal and political disputes. Finally, and perhaps most importantly, just as with their relationship with the bishops, the public knowledge that the friars had the support of the highest lay elite in the kingdom helped cement the friars' own authority in society: when both the bishop and the local lord openly vouched for them, the sermons of the Friars Preachers had to be worth listening to.

When reading secondary literature, one easily gets the impression that the mendicant orders mainly found their friends and support outside of the established Church. Indeed, the friars are usually portrayed as being in bitter rivalry with both the secular church and other monastic orders. Admittedly, conflicts with the secular clergy and between orders existed, but the truth is that in most places there is significant evidence to the contrary, suggesting that in the majority of cases the friars were welcomed by the cathedral and parish clergy, as well as by other monastic institutions, with whom many friendships and horizontal ties were established.[23] In the following, I will offer a closer look at two of the elite-ecclesiastical friendship groups which included the Dominican Order in mid-thirteenth-century Scandinavia: with canons secular of the cathedral chapters and with nuns of other monastic orders.

Friars Preachers and Canons Secular

Mendicant friars had a somewhat ambivalent relationship with the secular clergy. Numerous scholarly studies have stressed how the friars challenged the pastoral monopoly of the secular church, and evidence of rivalry is indeed abundant, particularly regarding preaching, confession, and funerals. On the other hand, the Friars Preachers were highly dependent on maintaining an amicable relationship with the bishops, canons secular, and parish clergy around Europe if their mission was to have any chance of success. Only with the permission of local bishops, cathedral canons, and parish curators could the friars preach to the lay population, and only with explicit approval from the same secular clergy could the friars hope to be acknowledged by the rest of society as a trustworthy authority on God's will. For the secular clergy, good relations with Dominican friars soon proved to be beneficial in numerous ways as well, first and foremost because the friars provided a theological basis for the secular church to build upon.

More than any other segment within the secular church, the Friars Preachers of Scandinavia, as elsewhere, were closely connected to the canons secular of the cathedral chapters right from the beginning. Indeed, the very first initiative for the Order of Preachers to establish itself in Scandinavia was not taken by any king, bishop, or even the order itself, but by a secular prelate. Provost Gaufred of Sigtuna was a member of the cathedral chapter of Uppsala, and it was probably in this capacity that he was in Rome in 1220, where he became aware of the newly established order. Gaufred allegedly approached the founder of the order, St Dominic, and asked him to let some of his brethren follow him back to Sweden, where he would see to the foundation of a house for them in Sigtuna. Dominic complied and sent two recently admitted friars, Nicolaus Lundensis and Simon de Suecia, but their plans were blocked by Archbishop Olof Basatömir.[24] The first lasting foundation of the Dominican Order in Scandinavia took place in Lund in 1222. As the basis for a friary, the friars were given a house that had formerly been the residence of a Magister Johannes at the cathedral chapter, and the Dominican friary in Lund was therefore situated next to the cathedral chapterhouse.[25] Rano, the first friar appointed to lead the Dominican province of Dacia (i.e., Scandinavia), which was formed in the mid-1220s, had himself begun as a canon secular. He reached the rank of dean at the cathedral chapter in Roskilde before deciding upon a mendicant career path during a stay at the University of Paris.[26]

Rano was far from the only former canon secular in Scandinavia to become a Friar Preacher. In fact, of the admittedly small number of cases in which sources allow for a glimpse into the pre-Dominican life of a Scandinavian friar, several appear to have found their way to the friary via a cathedral chapter – especially within the first hundred years of the order's existence. These include Fr. Boecius, prior of the convent in Roskilde in 1267 and formerly a provost at the nearby cathedral chapter,[27] and Fr. Israel Erlandi, who was to become lector and prior of the convent in Sigtuna as well as one of the most esteemed theologians in Scandinavia of his time, and who started out as canon secular at the cathedral chapter in Uppsala before joining the order around 1281.[28] Similar career changes are commonly recorded for friars elsewhere in northern and central Europe, just as with St Dominic himself, who had initially been an Augustinian canon at the cathedral chapter of Osma in Spain. Even when friars had not once been secular prelates themselves, they are often found to have had brothers and uncles who were, suggesting that Friars Preachers were frequently recruited from the same families that gave sons to the cathedral chapters.

Indeed, close contact between Friars Preachers and cathedral canons seems to have been the goal of numerous Dominican foundations, especially in the period 1220–50, so as to comply with Canon 11 of the Fourth Lateran Council about improving the education of parish clergy. This was to be achieved by the newly established diocese schools at the cathedral chapters, administered by the canons, but even where such cathedral chapters were established (a process which was still incomplete in many dioceses of thirteenth-century Scandinavia), only a few canons secular could be expected to have received university training in anything but the arts and canon law.[29] Thus, expertise in theology was often better found in the monastic orders. For most canons secular, Dominican supervision of theology was apparently not seen as an enforced nuisance. In one case in Skara, the initiative for a Dominican foundation may even have been taken by the canons secular, as the local convent of Friars Preachers was founded in 1239 during an episcopal interregnum from 1238 to 1240–41.[30] The extent to which Friars Preachers actually taught at cathedral schools is uncertain, but I have found no evidence for it anywhere in northern Europe. Despite this, numerous studies suggest that the Dominican Order had a profound influence on the theological and pastoral training of secular clergy at the cathedral schools all over thirteenth- and fourteenth-century Scandinavia, which can only have happened via the canons secular in charge of the teaching.[31]

One way for canons secular to benefit from Dominican teaching and wisdom was through books. Dominican books were fundamentally meant for the order's own brethren, but eventually they became at least as widespread and influential among the secular clergy. Cathedral chapters all over northern Europe, especially in the fourteenth century, appear to have been richly equipped with Dominican textbooks on theology, not least on the matters of preaching and hearing confession; examples of this are also abundant in Scandinavia.[32] While most of this Dominican literature was imported, mainly from France and Italy, some Scandinavian friars are known to have contributed to the genre themselves. The Norwegian Fr. Hjalm, for instance, wrote "in his own hand" a small *missale* and a *breviarium portatile*, which King Haakon V donated to the cathedral of Oslo in 1312–19. The *missale* was to be used for the common good of all priests of the chapter when traveling and celebrating mass outside the cathedral.[33]

Furthermore, it is noteworthy that in most diocese centers with Dominican foundations, the physical location of the friary was next to the local cathedral chapter.[34] This proximity of the two ecclesiastical institutions was hardly coincidental. When Bishop Nicolaus of Riga gave the Friars Preachers a site with a stone house near the cathedral precinct in Riga in 1234, it was explicitly stressed that this was where the friars were to settle.[35] There were similar friary–cathedral proximities for all four convents in Norway,[36] for the first friary in Tallinn,[37] and for five out of seven Dominican convents in the cathedral cities of Denmark.[38] For some unknown reason, however, this was *not* the case in Sweden. Even though Dominican houses were established in most diocesan centers here as well, none of them were adjacent to the cathedral chapters or other major secular churches.[39] Instead, the Swedish Friars Preachers were more often placed near local royal castles.

Another way to search for network contacts of an ecclesiastical institution in the Middle Ages is by looking at its financial benefactors. Of the 268 recorded donations made to the Dominican Order in the province of Dacia in the period 1220–1349, seventy-two (27%) came from ecclesiastical donors. The biggest number of donations within this group came from the canons secular, who accounted for 16%. If we add donations made by the bishops, who usually originated from cathedral canonry, a total of 21% of all known donations made to the Friars Preachers in Scandinavia came from acting or former canons secular. Whereas this percentage remained unaltered throughout the period in question, there were significant differences between the various cathedral chapters: of the forty-two donating canons secular in question, sixteen came from Lund, ten from Uppsala, and seven from Linköping. In connection to the previously mentioned question of physical proximity, it is thus worth noting that two of the three cathedral chapters most generous towards Dominican convents in Scandinavia (i.e., Uppsala and Linköping) were not in the same city as the endowed friars. Apparently, the friars could maintain amicable contacts with cathedral chapters without living close by.

This picture of friendly and mutually beneficial relations between Friars Preachers and canons secular would probably strike some readers as quite contrary to the impression often provided by literature on the topic, especially older literature. Here, the friars of the mendicant orders are usually portrayed as unwelcome rivals to and competitors with the secular clergy, depriving the latter of its pastoral authority and, not least, of its income derived from offerings, donations, and burials. It is indeed true that such issues began to emerge from the middle of the thirteenth century, creating a mendicant–secular gap within the intellectual circles at

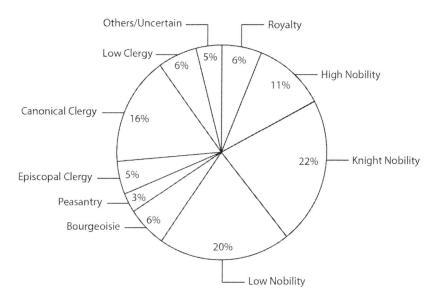

Figure 10.1 The social mix of donors behind the 268 recorded donations to the Friars Preachers in the province of Dacia in the period 1220–1349.

the University of Paris in particular, which eventually led to the infamous bull *Super cathedram* issued by Pope Boniface VIII in 1300 in which the pastoral privileges of the mendicant orders were explicitly settled.[40] This generally hostile picture is often backed by colorful case studies, such as one from Bergen, where the Dominican friary was, as in most other places, built next to the cathedral chapterhouse. In this case, however, it never became a friendly relationship. Indeed, the very first record we have of the Friars Preachers in Bergen is from 1247, when a papal legate severely reprimanded the canons for putting a line of toilets on top of a slope leading down to the cemetery and church of their Dominican neighbors; obviously with the deliberate purpose of harassing the friars and keeping the citizens of Bergen away from their church.[41] Although papal legates, bishops, and kings tried to settle the strife, it apparently continued for centuries. In an attempted settlement from around 1328–30, the reasons listed for the dispute are the usual ones known from elsewhere in Europe (times for preaching, the right to hear confession, economic compensation for burials, etc.),[42] but since these issues were apparently so much harder to settle in Bergen than elsewhere in Scandinavia the true core of the disagreement should perhaps be sought elsewhere. I have suggested that it may have to do with the pervasive presence of foreigners in Bergen, especially the Hansa merchants, who often seem to have ignored the ecclesiastical authority of the canons and the secular church in favor of the local Dominicans who spoke their languages and whose customs they were familiar with from back home.[43] In Tallinn, too, canons and friars never seem to have been on even remotely friendly terms,[44] but for the province of Dacia as a whole, these are the only two exceptions to the apparently amicable relationships between convents and chapters. This was also the case in the vast majority of cathedral cities around northern Europe, in spite of the few, but frequently presented, cases to the contrary.

It was indeed an explicit aim of the Dominican Order to keep their relations with the cathedral chapters as good as possible. This was also stressed for the friars in Dacia, who at their provincial chapter held in Lund in 1254 were informed about several regulations decided at the General Chapter, among them an admonition that all friars should act humbly towards secular prelates and abstain from provoking complaints.[45] It would appear that, perhaps apart from the convent in Bergen, the Dacian friars generally managed to comply with this instruction, as there is plenty of evidence that Scandinavian Dominicans and canons secular worked together. In numerous cases, Friars Preachers acted as witnesses to letters along with cathedral canonry or sometimes even testified in favor of the canons or vice versa.[46]

Finally, friars and canons secular could intercede for each other posthumously. To increase the synergic value of prayers and thereby shorten the stay in purgatory for the souls of late brethren and sisters, ecclesiastical communities entered more or less formalized confraternities with one another early on. These groups included the names of deceased members of other religious communities in their *libri memoriales* to be read out and prayed for by the friars during the daily memorial services. Such a *necrologium* is preserved for the cathedral chapter of canons secular in Lund, which, in a section covering the thirteenth century, in addition to confraternities with the Benedictine monks of All Saints Abbey in Lund and the Augustinian canons regular in Dalby, includes the names of twenty-one deceased Friars Preachers, predominantly from the neighboring convent in Lund, who were to be prayed for by the canons.[47] Undoubtedly, the Lund Dominicans did the same for their secular *confratres* at the neighboring cathedral. The Order of Preachers also made *libri memoriales* with lists of those to be remembered. In Scandinavia, extracts of such Dominican necrologies are preserved from the convents in Ribe and Oslo, but none of these contain notes on confraternities. The reason for this may be that for the mendicant orders such arrangements often went beyond the individual convent to include the entire province. It was decided at the Dominican and Franciscan provincial chapters for whom all the convents were to pray. Such provincial chapter acts for the Friars Preachers in Dacia are preserved for a few years in the second half of the thirteenth century, and although they do not explicitly use the term "confraternity," something of the kind seems to have been in place; for instance, the acts of 1291 describe how all convents of the province were to say a daily mass to intercede for the Cistercian nuns of Sko Abbey in Sweden.[48] The Cistercian sisters in Sko had several confraternal friends, who, besides the Friars Preachers, later came to include the Friars Minor and Hospitallers of St Anthony in all of Scandinavia, the Brigittines in Vadstena, the Carthusians in Mariefred, and the Hospital of the Holy Ghost in Linköping.[49] This rich circle of interceding friends should, however, not diminish the fact that the white nuns of Sko had extraordinarily close relations to the black friars of the Dominicans.

Friars Preachers and (Non-Dominican) Nuns

Women generally appear to have constituted a significant segment of the pastoral audience of mendicant friars. Medieval men and women may have been attracted to slightly different sides of religious life, and Christianity in the shape and content preached and performed by friars of the mendicant orders, both the Franciscans and the Dominicans, does appear to have had a special appeal to many women of the time. Individual laywomen of the upper social strata and communities of beguines often developed close contact with Dominican friars and convents. Even within the Church, the Friars Preachers not only attended to the pastoral needs of the Dominican Sisters (i.e., the female branch of the order), they were – perhaps not least in northern Europe – also quite involved with female religious communities of other monastic orders. For instance, the provincial chapter acts of Dacia in 1252 made it clear that no friar was allowed to hear the confession of nuns, *moniales*, without being explicitly appointed for the task, and even then he was only to enter a nunnery with specific permission from his prior and in the company of a *socius*.[50] It is particularly noteworthy that this was stated in the Dacian Dominican chapter acts eleven years before the foundation of the first Dominican nunnery in the province – and seven years before the order allowed for such nunneries to be admitted at all. Thus, it must have concerned female religious communities of other orders. In England many bishops at this time seem to have insisted that confessors for nuns, regardless of their orderly affiliation, should be Dominican or at least mendicant friars, and certainly not be chosen from among the secular clergy.[51]

When looking at northern Europe as a whole, it is not possible to pick out any particular orders to whose female convents the Friars Preachers appear especially connected, but this often changes when taking a more national or regional perspective. In Sweden, for instance, we can observe very close relations with the Cistercian nunneries; in the western part of Denmark, it was predominantly Benedictine nunneries; whereas in Bohemia, the Dominican friars of the entire province had entered into a confraternity of prayers with the Premonstratensian nuns.[52] Also, in the province of Dacia individual Dominican convents, as well as the province as a whole, frequently entered into confraternities with intercessory prayers for particular nuns or entire female convents from outside orders. At the provincial chapter in Dacia in 1253, intercessory prayers were prescribed in all convents for a number of recently deceased lay persons and clergy. Amongst them are listed three anonymous mothers superior of female convents belonging to other monastic orders: the Cistercian nunneries of Sko and Vreta, and the Benedictine nunnery of Ribe. Generally, it seems as if the intercession program consisted of one mass celebrated by the initiated priests, one psalter to be sung by the uninitiated clerical friars, and a number of paternosters to be said by the lay brothers; an extra effort was prescribed for the archbishop (three masses) and the mothers superior (a Sunday mass).[53] Again at the provincial chapter held in Västerås in 1291, commemorational prayers for the living were prescribed for the abbesses of the Cistercian and Benedictine nunneries in Vreta, Askeby, Risaberga, Gudum, Ø, Ring, Randers, Dalum, and Vissing, and for the whole convent of the Cistercian nunnery in Sko; prayers for the deceased were prescribed for Abbess Elena and Prioress Elena of Sko.[54] The orderly division by nation of abbesses to be prayed for is noteworthy: all four Swedish abbesses of Vreta, Askeby, Riseberga, and Sko were Cistercian; all six Danish abbesses of Gudum, Ø, Ring, Randers, Dalum, and Vissing were Benedictine. The list could have included Cistercian abbesses in Denmark as well (in Roskilde and Slangerup), but this is not the case.

It is difficult to identify any particular reason for the Dominican–Cistercian connection in Sweden, but a key role may have been played by the Cistercian nuns in Sko. Sko Abbey was situated in a rather remote area between Stockholm and Uppsala, about 10 kilometers from the nearest urban community in Sigtuna, which also housed their nearest monastic neighbor: the convent of the Friars Preachers. The Dominican sense of brotherhood with their Cistercian sisters in nearby Sko apparently exceeded mere neighborly relations. Not only was special memorial devotion to the nuns in Sko repeatedly prescribed by the provincial chapters of the thirteenth century for the entire province, Fr. Israel Erlandi, the highly esteemed lector at the convent in Sigtuna, witnessed and co-sealed some beneficial letters for the neighboring nunnery in 1291 and 1293.[55] Much later, in the 1490s, leading friars of the Dominican convents in Stockholm and Strängnäs also gave special attention to the Cistercian nuns in Sko.[56] Given that no male Cistercian monastery was situated anywhere near the nunnery in Sko, it is quite plausible that visiting Friars Preachers from the convents in Sigtuna, Strängnäs, and Stockholm – including the renowned lector Israel Erlandi – also took care of the Cistercian sisters' *cura animarum* as their preachers and confessors.

It may have been through their close connections to the nuns in Sko that the amicable attention of the Friars Preachers eventually spread to other female Cistercian houses in Sweden. Certainly, the institutional friendship between the black friars and the white nuns in Sweden appears too prominent to be coincidental. For instance, in 1292 Prior Olavus of the Friars Preachers in Skara witnessed the admission of Katarina Matsdotter into the Cistercian nunnery of Gudhem;[57] in 1302, Prior Nicolaus of the Dominican convent in Skänninge witnessed and co-sealed a large donation for the Cistercian nunnery of Vreta;[58] in 1370, his successor as prior in Skänninge helped authorize admission of a widow among the Cistercian sisters of Vreta because the abbess lacked a seal of her own;[59] and, finally, in 1486 the Dominican prior provincial of Dacia, Fr. Nicolaus Christierni, issued a letter of confraternity to the Cistercian nuns in Vårfruberga Abbey.[60] A similar inter-order relationship cannot, to my knowledge, be identified for any other religious orders in medieval Scandinavia. The Swedish Dominican male devotion to female Cistercians is, however, not completely unequaled elsewhere in Europe. In thirteenth-century Flanders, for instance, the Dominican Fr. Thomas de Cantimpré wrote an extremely popular hagiography on the life of the Cistercian nun Lutgard de Aywières;[61] such an edition must have required a number of Dominican visits to the Cistercian nunnery.

Just as for the priors provincial's appointment of priests for the Dominican nunneries, it would appear that the Dominican Order mainly picked the older and – and at least potentially – most reliable friars for this external *cura monialium*. The pastoral role of the friars in these "extra-order" nunneries seems to have been the same as in beguine houses and in the Dominican nunneries, that is, as preachers, confessors, and mass-celebrating priests, and perhaps as more general spiritual supervisors. For the more literate female convents, where book studies were incorporated as part of their spiritual work, the visiting friars may also have acted as academic supervisors and "study group" teachers for the nuns, providing them with suitable literature.

Some friars were undoubtedly more positive about such tasks than others, but either way the friars would be financially compensated for their assistance, since the nunneries often had a rental income from one or two tenant farms allocated to pay for such pastoral services. A further motive for the convent, and the order as a whole, to build amicable relationships with nuns of other orders was that, not least in the case of the Cistercians, the women who had taken the white habit usually came from the leading aristocratic families of the region, whom the friars generally liked to engage with – a network which already by the late thirteenth century was seen in many convents, particularly Sigtuna. Also, on an individual level, the company of female religious may have held a special personal motivation for some friars. Besides the unavoidable carnal attraction between the sexes that even St Dominic had to admit having felt,[62] some friars also had a purely spiritual fascination with religious women, whose inner spirituality they eagerly studied and described at length in texts. A common feature of these studies is the friars' belief that female religious, regardless of their orderly affiliation, were better equipped spiritually to come closer to Christ due to the physical weakness of their gender.[63]

Still, some Dominican involvement with outside female convents appears to have been rather tedious and unacceptably time-consuming. In 1515, long after the period dealt with here, Fr. Laurentius, prior provincial for the Dominican province of Dacia, was enjoined by the Danish king to judge a dispute between the prioress and the nuns of the Cistercian nunnery in Roskilde. After three days of negotiations, the prior provincial reported back to the king that he did not know what to do, since neither the prioress nor the nuns were willing to respect his authority – or indeed to let anyone else settle the affair.[64] Thus, although the friendship of Friars Preachers was often desired by female religious communities in high and late medieval northern Europe, some affairs were obviously better left for the women to solve themselves.

Conclusion

Everyone needs friends. This universal claim certainly held true for the Friars Preachers of the Dominican Order in the Middle Ages. Whereas monastic communities of the old orders – such as Benedictines and Cistercians – to some extent could survive for a long time on just one or a few good friends in the founding phase of their existence, the mendicant orders – such as Dominicans and Franciscans – who were not allowed by their own constitutions to hold any income-generating possessions, were in continuous need of friends in the outside world. When Dominican convents were founded in most major towns around thirteenth-century Scandinavia, every single foundation needed to be accepted by at least four parties: the order itself, the local bishop, the town lord (usually the king), and the town magistrate. In addition, someone was needed to donate a site, a house, and/or some money for the construction of a friary. While the bishops appear to have been the primary initiators of Dominican convent foundations in the first half of the thirteenth century, the role of town magistrates and high-ranking noble families seems to have increased in the following century. Apart from the core financial and legislative help needed to establish a convent in the first place, the public display of acceptance from these "founding friends" helped the friars to be recognized in society in general as elite preachers and the highest local authority on theology. In return, the bishops with the friars received the necessary means to comply with Canons 10 and 11 of the Fourth Lateran Council; the magistrates received the "mendicant proof" needed for their town to be recognized as a true urban settlement; and the noble families found an affordable way to boost their own elite identities as founders of monasteries with family *memoria* cults.

Within the Church, it was not just the bishops but also the cathedral canonry that soon formed amicable relationships with the Dominicans. Often, canons secular and Friars Preachers seem to have originated from the same social strata and even the same families; others may have attended the same schools around Europe. Although canon–Dominican relations are known to have been hostile in a few places, such as in Bergen, ties between the two institutions were normally extremely harmonious. The friars gave the canons the theological and pedagogical basis they needed to improve learning at the cathedral schools, and by receiving the Dominican assistance the cathedral canonry helped to cement the friars' authority as preachers among the parish clergy. Moreover, these inter-ecclesiastical relationships went beyond the temporal world, as friars and canons entered confraternities of prayers to help the souls of their deceased brethren.

Finally, the Dominican friars entered into institutional friendships with female religious institutions outside their own order early on. In Scandinavia, this is particularly evident for Cistercian nunneries. In places with no male Cistercian presence nearby, Dominican priests may have been the preferred preachers and confessors for the white nuns, who often came from the leading noble families of the region and with whom the Friars Preachers liked to connect. Furthermore, ardently devout women were particularly interesting to certain Dominican friars, as such women were believed to be closer to Christ than what the friars could ever hope to be themselves.

In modern literature it has often been stated the success of the mendicant orders in thirteenth-century Europe was not least based on the friars' close ties to the growing social class of urban bourgeoisie. A closer look, however, will usually show that merchants and other mercantile groups of urban society hardly played any role at all in the life of most Dominican convents throughout the thirteenth and early fourteenth centuries. The friars were, nevertheless, capable of both making and keeping long-lasting friendships to several other influential groups in society – also in perhaps less obvious circles, such as among canons secular and non-Dominican nuns.

Notes

1. Whereas "convent" in present-day Anglo-American language is commonly perceived to be synonymous with "nunnery," the term is here used in its medieval meaning, applying to both male and female monastic communities. Within monastic studies, the term "convent" in a male context is traditionally used to distinguish mendicant houses from monasteries of the "old orders" (i.e., Benedictines, Cistercians, and Augustinians). The term "friary" will be used as a reference to the actual buildings of a male mendicant convent.
2. Johnny Grandjean Gøgsig Jakobsen, "Who Ordered the Dominicans? Initiators Behind Dominican Convent Foundations in Northern Europe, c. 1216–1350," in *Monastic Culture: The Long Thirteenth Century*, ed. Lars Bisgaard et al. (Odense, 2014), 240–67.
3. Ibid., 244–45.
4. DOPD 1222 22/5; Johnny Grandjean Gøgsig Jakobsen, "Venerunt Fratres Predicatores: Notes on Datings of the First Dominican Convent Foundations in Scandinavia," *Collegium Medievale: Interdisciplinary Journal for Medieval Research* 24 (2011): 5–22 at 9–14.
5. Jarl Gallén, *La Province de Dacie de l'ordre des Frères Prêcheurs* (Helsinki and Rome, 1946), 38–41.
6. Jakobsen, "Who Ordered," 245.
7. Johnny Grandjean Gøgsig Jakobsen, "Hvornår oprettedes dominikanerklosteret i Haderslev?" *Kirkehistoriske Samlinger* (2010): 197–204.
8. MUB vol. 3, no. 2291; Rudolf Kleiminger, *Das Schwarze Kloster in Seestadt Wismar* (München, 1938), 15–20.
9. MUB vol. 3, no. 1722; Edward Carstenn, *Geschichte der Hansestadt Elbing* (Elbing (Elbląg), 1937), 18.
10. Jakobsen, "Who Ordered," 260–62.
11. Ingo Ulpts, "Zur Rolle der Mendikanten in städtischen Konflikten des Mittelalters: Ausgewählte Beispiele aus Bremen, Hamburg und Lübeck," in *Bettelorden und Stadt*, ed. Dieter Berg (Werl, 1992), 131–51 at 141–45. For additional case references, see Johnny Grandjean Gøgsig Jakobsen, "*What Jesus Means Is . . .* : The Dominican Order as Theological Authority for Laity and Clergy in Medieval Northern Europe," in *Authorities in the Middle Ages: Influence, Legitimacy, and Power in Medieval Society*, ed. Siri Kangas et al. (Berlin, 2013), 123–44 at 131–32.
12. Jacques Le Goff, "Apostolat mendiant et fait urbain dans la France médiévale: l'implantation des ordres mendiants," *Annales Economies-Sociétés-Civilisations* 23 (1968): 335–52 at 337; John B. Freed, *The Friars*

and *German Society in the Thirteenth Century* (Cambridge, 1977), 46, 53; Anders Andrén, *Den urbana scenen: städer och samhälle i det medeltida Danmark* (Malmö, 1985), 133 with note 216.
13. Freed, *Friars*, 46 (Bern); Clifford Hugh Lawrence, *The Friars: The Impact of the Early Mendicant Movement on Western Society* (London and New York, 1994), 104.
14. Johnny Grandjean Gøgsig Jakobsen, "Prædikebrødrenes samfundsrolle i middelalderens Danmark" (PhD diss., University of Southern Denmark, 2008), 184–86.
15. Johnny Grandjean Gøgsig Jakobsen, "*Them Friars Dash About*: Mendicant *Terminario* in Medieval Scandinavia," in *Travels and Mobilities in the Middle Ages: From the Atlantic to the Black Sea*, ed. Marianne O'Doherty and Felicitas Schmieder (Turnhout, 2015), 3–29.
16. DOPD 1473. Jakobsen, "Prædikebrødrenes samfundsrolle," 223, 228–29.
17. DOPD 1240 (Oslo). Jakobsen, "Who Ordered," 252–58.
18. For source references, see Jakobsen, "Who Ordered," 255–56.
19. Ibid., 258–60.
20. Gallén, *La Province de Dacie*, 80–81, 114–20; Christian Oertel, "Aristocratic Networks and Monastic Communities: The Case of the Dominican Convent of Sigtuna, Sweden, and the Nobles of Uppland (Late Thirteenth – Early Fourteenth Centuries)," *Journal of Medieval Monastic Studies* 5 (2016): 93–112.
21. DOPD 1232; DOPD 1257. On early Franciscan relations with the Hvide family see Jørgen Nyboe Rasmussen, *Die Franziskaner in den nordischen Ländern im Mittelalter* (Kevelaer, 2002), 59–62, 333–34.
22. Christian Oertel's recent studies of such aristocratic relations with the Friars Preachers in Sigtuna have shown just how extensive, long-lasting, and financially important these networks were to the friars. Oertel, "Aristocratic Networks."
23. Jakobsen, "Prædikebrødrenes samfundsrolle," 138–56; Jakobsen, "*What Jesus Means Is . . .* ," 127–34.
24. HOPD.
25. HOPD; DOPD 1222 22/5; DOPD 1222 16/6.
26. HOPD.
27. DOPD 1255 14/3; DOPD 1267 10/9.
28. DOPD 1281 2/10 (with biographical note).
29. Jarl Gallén, "De religiösa ordnarnas, särskilt Dominikanordens, studier i Skandinavien under medeltiden," in *Historica IV – Föredrag vid det XVIII Nordiska historikermötet Jyväskylä 1981* (Jyväskylä, 1983), 13–28 at 23.
30. DOPD 1239.
31. E.g. Jakobsen, "Prædikebrødrenes samfundsrolle," 145–46; Knut Helle, *Norge blir en stat, 1130–1319* (Kristianssand, 1964), 168, 172; Sten Lindroth, *Svensk lärdomshistoria*, vol. 1 (Stockholm, 1975), 42.
32. Jakobsen, "Prædikebrødrenes samfundsrolle," 53–54; Jakobsen, "*What Jesus Means Is . . .* ," 129–31.
33. DOPD 1312–19.
34. E.g. Le Goff, "Apostolat mendicant," 337; Johnny Grandjean Gøgsig Jakobsen, "At Blackfriars Priory: Dominican Priories Within Urban Geography in Medieval Scandinavia," in *Monastic Europe AD 1100–1700: Landscape and Settlement*, ed. Keith Smith et al. (forthcoming).
35. Gertrud von Walther-Wittenheim, *Die Dominikaner in Livland – Die natio Livoniae* (Rome, 1938), 6–7.
36. Christian C. A. Lange, *De norske Klostres Historie* (Christiania (Oslo), 1856), 51.

The Dominican Order and Elite Groups 209

37. Walther-Wittenheim, *Die Dominikaner*, 8–10.
38. Only the ones in Århus and Odense were situated at considerable distance from the cathedral district.
39. Jakobsen, "At Blackfriars Priory." It should, however, be noted that the first Dominican friary in Finland, founded in 1249, was most likely placed adjacent to the episcopal residence in Koroinen, and that, even after having moved to Turku along with the bishop around 1286, the friars may have first resided in the cathedral precinct before moving to their final location in the south of Turku around the mid-fourteenth century. Johnny Grandjean Gøgsig Jakobsen and Marika Räsänen, "Dominikaanien vaikutus Koroisissa" (forthcoming).
40. Lawrence, *The Friars*, 134, 152–53, 158–59. Contrary to common presentation in literature, mendicant privileges were not limited as such by the bull, but rather made more explicit for both parties.
41. DOPD 1247 13/8.
42. DOPD 1328–30.
43. Jakobsen, "Prædikebrødrenes samfundsrolle," 153–54.
44. Walther-Wittenheim, *Die Dominikaner*, 67–78.
45. DOPD 1254 8/9.
46. E.g. DOPD 1264 1/7; DOPD 1281 14/3; DOPD 1309 16/2; DOPD 1309 22/9.
47. Johnny Grandjean Gøgsig Jakobsen, "Dominikanerne i Lund og augustinerne i Dalby – Mulige forbindelser," in *Locus Celebris – Dalby kyrka, kloster och gård*, ed. Stephan Borgehammar and Jes Wienberg (Gothenburg and Stockholm, 2012), 327–33.
48. DOPD 1291 22/8.
49. Johnny Grandjean Gøgsig Jakobsen, "Friends of the Friars: Confraternal Relations of the Dominican Order in Medieval Scandinavia," in *Bractwa religijne w średniowieczu i w okresie nowożytnym – Religious Confraternities in the Middle Ages and the Modern Era*, ed. Dominika Burdzy and Beata Wojciechowska (Kielce, 2014), 53–68 at 56.
50. DOPD 1252 AugSep.
51. William A. Hinnebusch, *The Early English Friars Preachers* (Rome, 1951), 325.
52. Jakobsen, "Friends of the Friars," 56–57.
53. DOPD 1253 AugSep.
54. DOPD 1291 22/8.
55. DOPD 1291 19/5; DOPD 1293 6/1.
56. DOPD 1496 [29/8–19/9]; SDHK sok.riksarkivet.se/sdhk, no. 33619.
57. DOPD 1292 27/2.
58. DOPD 1302 5/12.
59. DOPD 1370 4/6.
60. SDHK, no. 31684.
61. John W. Coakley, *Women, Men, and Spiritual Power: Female Saints and Their Male Collaborators* (New York, 2006), 11.
62. As stated on his deathbed: "Right to this moment has divine mercy kept me in the purity of the flesh. But still I have to confess that I have not avoided the imperfection of letting the company of young women affect my heart more strongly than conversation with the older ones." Jordanus de Saxonia OP, "Libellus de principiis ordinis predicatorum," in *Monumenta Ordinis Fratrum Praedicatorum Historica*, vol. 16, ed. H. C. Scheeben (Rome, 1935), 92–94 (my translation).
63. Coakley, *Women*, 9, 11, 89, 98–99.
64. DOPD 1515 31/8.

Dedicated Bibliography

Andrén, Anders. *Den urbana scenen: städer och samhälle i det medeltida Danmark*. Malmö, 1985.
Carstenn, Edward. *Geschichte der Hansestadt Elbing*. Elbing (Elbląg), 1937.
Coakley, John W. *Women, Men, and Spiritual Power: Female Saints and Their Male Collaborators*. New York, 2006.
Freed, John B. *The Friars and German Society in the Thirteenth Century*. Cambridge, MA, 1977.
Gallén, Jarl. *La Province de Dacie de l'ordre des Frères Prêcheurs*. Helsinki and Rome, 1946.
Gallén, Jarl. "De religiösa ordnarnas, särskilt Dominikanordens, studier i Skandinavien under medeltiden." In *Historica IV – Föredrag vid det XVIII Nordiska historikermötet Jyväskylä 1981*, 13–28. Jyväskylä, 1983.
Helle, Knut. *Norge blir en stat, 1130–1319*. Kristiansand, 1964.
Hinnebusch, William A. *The Early English Friars Preachers*. Rome, 1951.
Jakobsen, Johnny Grandjean Gøgsig. "Prædikebrødrenes samfundsrolle i middelalderens Danmark." PhD diss., University of Southern Denmark, 2008.
Jakobsen, Johnny Grandjean Gøgsig. "Hvornår oprettedes dominikanerklosteret i Haderslev?" *Kirkehistoriske Samlinger* (2010): 197–204.
Jakobsen, Johnny Grandjean Gøgsig. "Venerunt fratres predicatores: Notes on Datings of the First Dominican Convent Foundations in Scandinavia." *Collegium Medievale: Interdisciplinary Journal for Medieval Research* 24 (2011): 5–22.
Jakobsen, Johnny Grandjean Gøgsig. "Dominikanerne i Lund og augustinerne i Dalby – Mulige forbindelser." In *Locus Celebris – Dalby kyrka, kloster och gård*, edited by Stephan Borgehammar and Jes Wienberg, 327–33. Gothenburg and Stockholm, 2012.
Jakobsen, Johnny Grandjean Gøgsig. "*What Jesus Means Is*: The Dominican Order as Theological Authority for Laity and Clergy in Medieval Northern Europe." In *Authorities in the Middle Ages: Influence, Legitimacy, and Power in Medieval Society*, edited by Siri Kangas, Mia Korpiola, and Tuija Ainonen, 123–44. Berlin, 2013.
Jakobsen, Johnny Grandjean Gøgsig. "Friends of the Friars: Confraternal Relations of the Dominican Order in Medieval Scandinavia." In *Bractwa religijne w średniowieczu i w okresie nowożytnym – Religious confraternities in the Middle Ages and the Modern Era*, edited by Dominika Burdzy and Beata Wojciechowska, 53–68. Kielce, 2014.
Jakobsen, Johnny Grandjean Gøgsig. "Who Ordered the Dominicans? Initiators Behind Dominican Convent Foundations in Northern Europe, c. 1216–1350." In *Monastic Culture: The Long Thirteenth Century*, edited by Lars Bisgaard, Sigga Engsbro, Kurt Villads Jensen, and Tore Nyberg, 240–67. Odense, 2014.
Jakobsen, Johnny Grandjean Gøgsig. "At Blackfriars Priory: Dominican Priories Within Urban Geography in Medieval Scandinavia." In *Monastic Europe AD 1100–1700: Landscape and Settlement*, edited by Keith Smith et al. (forthcoming).
Jakobsen, Johnny Grandjean Gøgsig, and Marika Räsänen. "Dominikaanien vaikutus Koroisissa." (forthcoming).
Jordanus de Saxonia OP. "Libellus de principiis ordinis predicatorum." In *Monumenta Ordinis Fratrum Praedicatorum Historica*, vol. 16, edited by H. C. Scheeben. Rome, 1935.

Kleiminger, Rudolf. *Das Schwarze Kloster in Seestadt Wismar*. Munich, 1938.

Lange, Christian C. A. *De norske Klostres Historie*. Christiania (Oslo), 1856.

Lawrence, Clifford Hugh. *The Friars: The Impact of the Early Mendicant Movement on Western Society*. London and New York, 1994.

Le Goff, Jacques. "Apostolat mendiant et fait urbain dans la France médiévale: l'implantation des ordres mendiants." *Annales Economies-Sociétés-Civilisations* 23 (1968): 335–52.

Lindroth, Sten. *Svensk lärdomshistoria*, vol. 1. Stockholm, 1975.

Oertel, Christian. "Aristocratic Networks and Monastic Communities: The Case of the Dominican Convent of Sigtuna, Sweden, and the Nobles of Uppland (Late Thirteenth–Early Fourteenth Centuries)." *Journal of Medieval Monastic Studies* 5 (2016): 93–112.

Rasmussen, Jørgen Nyboe. *Die Franziskaner in den nordischen Ländern im Mittelalter*. Kevelaer, 2002.

Svenskt Diplomatariums Huvudkartotek. Edited by Riksarkivet. sok.riksarkivet. se/sdhk>, no. 33619 and 31684.

Ulpts, Ingo. "Zur Rolle der Mendikanten in städtischen Konflikten des Mittelalters: Ausgewählte Beispiele aus Bremen, Hamburg und Lübeck." In *Bettelorden und Stadt*, edited by Dieter Berg, 131–51. Werl, 1992.

Walther-Wittenheim, Gertrud von. *Die Dominikaner in Livland – Die natio Livoniae*. Rome, 1938.

Section III
Networks in Action

11 Friends, Foes, and Followers
Power, Networks, and
Intimacy in Medieval Iceland

Auður Magnúsdóttir

Introduction

The political significance of marriage in medieval Europe is uncontested. Not only did it establish bonds of kinship; among the privileged groups of society it included economic transactions and agreements of political support in future conflicts. However, modern research on kinship structures as well as on alternative ways of establishing political relations have considerably *nuanced* our understanding of the political efficacy of marriage in the Middle Ages. In order to secure one's position, one needed loyal followers and reliable alliances. These relations were established in various ways; they were of both a horizontal and a vertical nature; and they complemented each other.[1]

In twelfth- and thirteenth-century Iceland, the vertical bond created through concubinage could prove to be a more long-lasting and reliable bond than the horizontal bond established through marriage.[2] But the consolidation of the Church and the promulgation of its doctrine of monogamous and indissoluble marriage led to gradual changes in forms of cohabitation, so that being married and simultaneously having one or more concubines became impossible over the course of the thirteenth century. Hence, it might be maintained that the political importance of well-organized marriages slowly increased throughout this period, even if concubinage continued to be politically significant.

In Iceland the epoch between 1180 and 1262/64 was characterized by social and political turbulence including concentration of power, consolidation of religious institutions, and ultimately, subordination to the Norwegian crown. In the following my focus will be on the connection between social and political change and the role of marriage in the power struggles of this period.

In order to illustrate the correlation between these changes and the political role of marriage I have chosen to take a closer look at a few of the most prominent chieftains (*goðar*) in thirteenth-century Iceland.[3] All of these men belonged to the same family, the Sturlungar. The specific focus is on the politician and writer Snorri Sturluson and his two elder brothers, Thordr and Sighvatr. All three brothers utilized marriage to secure their position. However, even if all three strove to attain a powerful position, their strategies were somewhat dissimilar. As I will show, this was in accordance with their political aims.

The most powerful of the brothers was Snorri Sturluson. Even though he managed to enrich himself enormously through marriage, both his own and those of his children, his efforts to create solid alliances through these relationships continuously failed. Five years after his death his nephew, Sighvatr's son Thordr kakali, arrived in Iceland. Although politically active in separate periods, the two men had several things in common. Both became members of the Norwegian king's *hirð*, his group of retainers. Both accepted an assignment from the king to bring Iceland under his control. Both men had the ambition to become the most powerful man in the country, and both of them used marriage strategically to reach their goals. In contrast to Snorri, however, Thordr kakali managed to create strong and long-lasting alliances through his match-making. In the following I will scrutinize their different strategies and offer possible explanations as to why Thordr kakali managed to utilize marriage as a social resource, and Snorri did not. Our point of departure will be how Snorri and his brothers made use of marriage and other sexual relationships to build up their power-base, and consequently managed to establish the Sturlungar among the most influential families in Iceland. However, before going further a brief overview of the political landscape in which they were active is necessary.

Power and Politics in Thirteenth-Century Iceland

During the twelfth century Icelandic society and power structures underwent significant changes. Characteristic of the period was the concentration of power, the development from a society ruled by many equally powerful (in theory) chieftains, to the one we see in the beginning of the thirteenth century, when all of the power was in the hands of five families. This development included an important shift in the base of power: the chieftaincies (*goðorð*) that had been based on power over men, and not districts, had become territorial domains (*ríki*).[4] The period c. 1220–64 can in rough terms be defined as a time of civil war, with constant power-struggles and battles between and within the dominant families in the country. However, although landholding as well as economic resources in general grew continuously in importance, power could be upheld only with the support of allies.[5] Thus, although – or perhaps because – power now was concentrated into the hands of a few, the competition for key allies grew even stronger. As we shall see, this became particularly evident in the case of Thordr kakali.

Despite the social and political changes leading towards the acceptance of Norwegian supremacy in 1262/64, the main principles of the political game remained consistent, including the need for allies. Another prerequisite was economic resources.[6] As in other societies with a redistributive economy, assets were distributed amongst friends and followers in the form of feasts and gifts, but even more importantly through marriage and inheritance. And as elsewhere in Europe, marriage, concubinage, and friendship were important political instruments and as such were highly interrelated.

All these types of bonds entailed some form of economic transaction. Marriage included a more or less statutory economic transaction. Concubinage established bonds of friendship and accordingly included gifts, one of which was the concubine herself.[7] Furthermore, illegitimate children often inherited from their father, and a father could inherit from his children, whether they were legitimate or not.[8] Even friendship had to be maintained and strengthened through feasts and gift-giving.[9] However, friendship established without the exchange of women lacked one important feature of marriage and concubinage, namely reproduction.[10] In order to secure their political position, the chieftains had to command reliable supporters. Therefore, it was a benefit to have many children. Sons became loyal supporters of their fathers, and daughters could be given away in marriage and thus be used to establish, maintain, or strengthen friendship-relations.[11]

In order to secure numerous children Icelandic chieftains frequently had long-lasting relationships with concubines in addition to being married. However, childbearing was not the only purpose of long-lasting sexual relationships such as marriage and concubinage; both types of relationships were politically important. Marriage generated political and economic obligations between the families involved, and it was a relationship between equals; a horizontal bond between two independent political actors. Concubinage, on the other hand, was a vertical relationship, since the woman's social status, while not insignificant, was generally lower than her lover's. Among the elites concubinage was established after negotiations, i.e., the woman was handed over to the chieftain with the consent of her guardian. Influential and affluent farmers became important allies during the thirteenth century, and instead of marrying off their daughters with equals these men could choose to use them to create bonds with chieftains. The relationship was beneficial to both parties; the chieftain gained loyal followers, and the concubine's father and brothers could attain a more powerful position than otherwise. Furthermore, because children inherited their father's social position, one could therefore conclude that concubinage enabled a social mobility that was otherwise nearly impossible during this period. However, in contrast to the parties involved in marriage, the concubine's male relatives became dependent on the chieftain, as they owed their new position to him. Thus, the relationship had considerable similarities with patron-client relationships. If these men betrayed their "patron," they ran the risk of losing everything. This, in turn, meant that these relationships often proved to be stronger than marriage, politically speaking.[12]

To sum up, women were an important social resource, exchanged to create bonds of friendship and loyalty between men, and they were of course necessary to secure numerous offspring. Furthermore, by combining marriage with concubinage chieftains not only assured successors; they could also take advantage of both horizontal and vertical bonds.

However, combining marriage with extramarital relationships was obviously not in line with the Christian doctrine of monogamous marriage. Because extramarital relationships were prohibited, concubinage gradually became more unusual among married men. Instead, it seems that they had to choose between the two forms of cohabitation.[13] One consequence of this development was that the economic and political importance of forming successful marriages clearly increased. This development can be followed through the marriage strategies of the Sturlungar.

Snorri and His Brothers

Our knowledge of Thordr, Sighvatr, and Snorri Sturluson's economic and political career is largely based on *Íslendinga saga* and *Hákonar saga Hákonarsonar*. The author of both works was Sturla Thordarson, one of Thordr Sturluson's illegitimate children.[14] Although the two sagas' accounts of the conflicts during the thirteenth century diverge at times, Sturla's account of his father and uncles' marriages and extramarital relations is consistent. However, this does not mean that Sturla's text is without bias. He was a loyal supporter of his father, and as he eventually became a powerful chieftain in his own right, he was deeply involved in many of the conflicts he describes. As a young man Sturla spent much time in Reykholt with Snorri, and thus supposedly had good knowledge of Snorri and his household. Although of high social standing, none of the brothers had resources enough to match their political ambitions. Nevertheless, all three managed to secure their economic, and thereby their political, position through their relationships with women. It can be maintained that their political ambitions differed, however, which in turn may explain their somewhat dissimilar marriage strategies.

Thordr, Sighvatr, and Snorri were the only legitimate sons of the chieftain Sturla Thordarson by his second wife, Gudny Boedvarsdottir.[15] At Sturla's death in 1183, Gudny was in her late thirties and was left with five children, of whom only her eldest son, Thordr, was of age. Sighvatr was thirteen and Snorri, the youngest, only four years old. As a widow and the mother of five children Gudny became more autonomous than she had been during her marriage. She continued to run the farm at Hvammur. Obviously, she had concerns for her children and presumably she also was in need of male protection. This she found in Ari sterki ("the strong"), with whom she had an affair.[16] When the couple later decided to travel abroad, they made practical arrangements to take care of their interests in Iceland. Gudny found a man to take care of her farm, and Ari sterki married off his daughter Helga Aradottir to Gudny's eldest son, Thordr. He was to take over Ari's farm and manage his affairs during his absence.

As Ari's sole heir, Helga seemingly was a desirable consort, and indeed when Ari died in 1188 Thordr and Helga inherited from him. Thordr might also have had political motives for marrying her, since Helga's maternal grandfather was Gissur Hallsson from the Haukdælir family, and he and his sons could prove to be important allies. However, the marriage was an unhappy one, and the couple divorced shortly after Ari's death.[17] Interestingly, Thordr continued to control Ari's estate and to live at his farm, whereas we get no information about Helga's fate. Thus, from an economic point of view the marriage had been a prosperous arrangement, which most likely formed a basis for Thordr's future position and might have created bonds of friendship between him and Helga's maternal family.

After his divorce from Helga, Thordr had a relationship with Hrodny Thordardottir, wife of Bersi inn auðgi ("the rich") Vermundarson and "their friendship lasted for a long time."[18] It is tempting to assume that Thordr attained control over Hrodny's assets – and the connection was, as we shall see, important, not only for him but for his brother Snorri as well. However, three years later Thordr obviously found himself a suitable candidate to marry: the widow Gudrun Bjarnadottir. This time the marriage proved to have crucial significance for Thordr's position. Thus, when describing his father's second marriage Sturla specifically mentions the importance of the relationship: "Thordr Sturluson married Gudrun . . . she brought abundant property with her. Thordr then became a *höfðingi*."[19] By this time, Thordr had reached the age of twenty-six. With his first marriage, he had laid a foundation for a future position; with his second he established his power and secured a position he seemed content with.

Thordr's brother Sighvatr Sturluson had now reached the age of twenty-one. Our author, Sturla, is keen on informing his readers that his father and Sighvatr were close during this time, and Sighvatr even seems to have had a relationship with his sister-in-law Gudrun's sister, Helga Bjarnadottir, with whom he had a daughter. Helga, on the other hand, may not have been as wealthy as her widowed sister, which may explain why Sighvatr chose not to marry her. Instead he bided his time. Sighvatr's tactics were somewhat different from Thordr's. His mind seems to have been set on connecting with the powerful families in Iceland through marriage. While he waited for an appropriate candidate for his wife, Sighvatr administered his resources cleverly.[20]

Sturla informs us that Sighvatr established his own household at the prosperous farm Hjarðarholt in the west of Iceland. Sighvatr used his patrimony as initial capital, speculated with landed property, and invested some of his assets. Sighvatr is also said to have had a friend in yet another Helga, Helga Gydudottir, whose nephew was married to Sighvatr's sister Vigdis. Helga's civil status is not revealed, only that she had inherited from her brother, and that she "did not have much livestock, but plenty of land" ("hafði búfé fátt, en lendur góðar"). Sighvatr supported her financially, and in return he was allowed to use her land as much as he pleased. This in turn enriched him profoundly.[21]

Presumably his success also increased his value in the marriage market. In 1197, at the age of twenty-seven, he was ready to propose marriage to Halldora Tumadottir. Her family, the Ásbirningar family, was one of the most powerful families in Iceland at the time.[22] This was a politically important union, and the marriage proved to be a success. Together with Halldora, Sighvatr had seven sons and one daughter, all loyal supporters of their father.[23] Through his skillful economic maneuvering and marriage Sighvatr established his domain. The Ásbirningar controlled Skagafjörður and parts of the Húnavatn region in the north of Iceland. Furthermore, after the death of Halldora's father Tumi, her mother, herself a member of the powerful Haukdælir family, had remarried into the family of Svinfellingar in the east part of Iceland. Thus, Sighvatr not only established an important network with Halldora's biological family; he also formed a relationship with her stepfather and his family as well. He thereby expanded his social network outside the domain that he and his brother Thordr controlled.

In *Íslendinga saga* both Sighvatr and Thordr are described as contemplative and wise, and as mentioned previously, our author Sturla is keen to emphasize the brothers' closeness to one another.[24] However, they did not share political ambitions. Judging from the saga, Thordr had no ambition to expand his power outside his domain.[25] Although Thordr had enriched himself immensely through his marriages, one could argue that at least his second marriage was of slight political significance. Helgi Þorláksson claims that Thordr would have obtained a prominent position irrespective of his second marriage. The importance of that union, he claims, was that it enabled Thordr to exercise power in a way appropriate to his social position, including giving grandiose feasts and distributing gifts among his friends.[26] Given Thordr's ambition to maintain – and not expand – his power, this may well be the case. For his purposes, a wealthy widow suited perfectly as second wife, even if the union didn't bring him significant political allies. That Thordr had little interest in increasing his power becomes even clearer after Gudrun's death. This time he did not have the need to arrange a new profitable marriage or connect with politically important networks. Instead of remarrying, he established a long-lasting relationship with a concubine named Thora. He had six children with her, among them our author, Sturla, from whom we have this information. The fact that Sturla does not reveal his mother's parentage suggests that she was of humble birth. Therefore, it's unlikely that her relationship with his father had political implications. The same can be said about Thordr's third marriage. After Thora's death he married Valgerdr Arnadottir. Given that nothing is mentioned about her family relations, one might conclude that her relatives were insignificant.[27] All in all, with his marriages, Thordr strove to secure his economic situation, and thereby strengthen his political position *locally*. Thordr wasn't interested in extending his domain to a wider area, and it could, on good grounds, be maintained that he strove to keep himself away from the power struggles of his time.[28] That he was uninterested in expanding his domain is confirmed by the slight political significance of his own intimate relationships. Additionally, in contrast to his brothers, he didn't strive to arrange his children's marriages according to his own political needs.

As mentioned, Sighvatr used different financial tactics to provide himself with a solid economic ground *before* getting married, and his proposal and marriage to Halldora Tumadottir in 1197 played an important part in his political agenda. In time Sighvatr consolidated his power in the western region of Dalir. However, in 1215 he chose to move to the farm Grund i Eyjafjörður in the North Quarter of Iceland. Although unpopular in the beginning, being an outsider in the domain, he managed to establish his position even here. Among his sons he seems to have favored his second-born, Sturla Sighvatsson, who soon after his father's move to Grund took over his former farm in Sauðafell. By then Sturla was eighteen and a promising young man. He had proved to be a strong supporter of his father, and together they continued the effort of strengthening the family's position.

Sturla entered a relationship with Vigdis Gisldottir, who became his concubine and lived with him at the farm until his marriage. The relationship had strong political implications. Vigdis's father, Gisl Bergsson, was a significant farmer (*stórbóndi*) in Miðfjörður, a district in which Sturla (and his father) wished to strengthen their political position. By taking Gisl's daughter as his concubine, Sturla not only established a bond between the two families, he even gained access to Gisl's own social networks, mainly comprising important farmers in Miðfjörður.[29] As with marriage, the concubinage relationship was supposed to benefit both parties. Sturla himself got the support and loyalty of several farmers, including Gisl's five sons, his nephew, and his niece's husband. Their loyalty to Sturla and his father, Sighvatr, continued even after Sturla got married and the relationship to Vigdis was broken. The association with Sturla was important to Gisl and his sons. Through their relationship they moved upwards in the social hierarchy, which in turn affected their power position. But the relationship was different from similar bonds through marriage. Gisl and his sons were indeed members of Sturla's network, but at the same time they were dependent on him. If they opposed him, or failed in their support, they ran the risk of being excluded from the network and thereby losing the benefits they had gained through this vertical – and hierarchical – relationship. As it happened, the alliance would prove to be more reliable than the one Sturla created through marriage.[30]

Sighvatr saw to it that Sturla became head of his own household, and that he thus could pursue his own political ambitions. By moving to the north of Iceland, and yet – through his son – keeping hold of his power base in the west of the country, Sighvatr also managed to expand his own position geographically. In 1223 a marriage was arranged between Sturla and Solveig Sæmundardottir from the powerful Oddaverjar family. By this means, father and son established a network in the southern part of Iceland as well. Obviously, Sighvatr did not lack ambition. However, neither he nor his brother Thordr would claim the same power position as did their youngest brother, Snorri. And in contrast to the latter, neither of them sought to become a member of the Norwegian court.

Snorri Sturluson was fostered by the chieftain Jon Loptsson in the cultural center Oddi in south Iceland at the age of three, and received his education there.[31] Jon Loptsson, a member of the Oddaverjar family, was one of the most influential and respected chieftains of his time. He was a frequently summoned mediator, well versed in law and a clever politician. When Jon died, Snorri was eighteen years old, a young man of high birth and learning.[32] His fostering had created important bonds with the Oddaverjar family, but now that the time had come for him to establish himself he found himself to be "penniless" (*félauss*), as his mother had spent his patrimony.[33] Hence, though he certainly had good connections, he was without economic resources.

Under these circumstances the "friendship" of Snorri's brother Thordr with Hrodny Thordardottir came in handy. Appropriately enough, Hrodny and her husband Bersi's only daughter, Herdis, was marriageable. With Thordr and Snorri's foster brother Sæmundr Jonsson as intermediaries, a marriage was arranged between the young couple. With his mother's economic support Snorri was enabled to pay bride wealth, but as Herdis was her father's sole heir, the marriage would bring him great financial gain.[34] Obviously this was a practical arrangement, although no information is given as to how much say Herdis had in its planning. When his father-in-law Bersi died 1202, Snorri inherited from him. He had two children with Herdis, but when he moved to Reykholt around the year 1206 he left her behind.[35] While Sturla is not explicit about this, it seems that a separation was arranged.

According to Sturla, Snorri was a clever financier, but also a real womanizer: "Snorri had very good financial skills, he was promiscuous, and he had children by women other than Herdis."[36] Apart from Snorri's legitimate children, Hallbera and Jon, he had at least three illegitimate children who reached adulthood, a son called Orækja and two daughters, Ingibjorg and Thordis. We have little knowledge about two of Snorri's concubines, whereas we are able to ascertain more about his relationship to the third one, Gudrun Hreinsdottir. Gudrun was Thordr Bodvarsson's stepdaughter. From Thordr, Snorri attained the chieftaincy Lundamannagoðorð in 1202, the same year he acquired the farm Reykholt. Additionally, Snorri acquired the farm in Stafholt from Gudrun's mother. It is highly probable that Gudrun became his concubine in connection with these arrangements, and thus the relationship can be seen as a part of a political and economic settlement between the parties.[37]

In a short time, Snorri had managed to improve his situation enormously. He controlled his own chieftaincy; he controlled important farms; and he had several children. It would, however, take several more years before he reached the top of his power. By then his children were of marriageable age and thus had become available resources for him to make use of.

Snorri and His Daughters

In the 1220s the political landscape in Iceland underwent some significant changes. In 1222 the leader of the Oddaverjar family and Snorri's foster brother, the previously mentioned Sæmundr Jonsson, died. Among his many sons there were no obvious successors, but on the other hand Snorri Sturluson presumably had harbored ambitions to walk in his footsteps for a long time. In 1219 Snorri had traveled to Norway. There he became a retainer of King Haakon IV Haakonsson and Earl Skule. Before his return to Iceland he accepted the task of bringing Iceland under the power of the Norwegian king.

Between 1222 and 1230 Snorri was the most powerful man in the country. This position was not obtained without turbulence, or as Jón Viðar Sigurðsson states, "It was Snorri Sturluson who started the power struggles in Iceland in the 1220s."[38] However, Snorri was more interested in expanding his own domain than in carrying out the mission he had accepted from the king. He managed to get hold of chieftaincies in several parts of the country. From *Íslendinga saga* it becomes obvious that Snorri intended to place himself in a dominant position among his countrymen. In order to secure his position, he created bonds of kinship with the families that constituted his potential challengers. The marriages he arranged for his daughters clearly illustrate this.

By around the time of Snorri's return from Norway in 1220 almost all chieftaincies in Iceland were in the hands of four families in addition to the Sturlungar. Additionally, the family of Vatnsfirdingar held a powerful position in the Vestfirðir. Between 1224 and 1228 Snorri managed to ally himself with four of these five families.[39] His first foray into matchmaking, however, came when he married off his eldest daughter Hallbera to Arni Magnusson before his trip to Norway.[40] Arni was indeed a man of good birth, but he was a comparatively weak chieftain.[41] It thus seems likely that the union was of more importance for Arni than for Snorri himself, and perhaps was a way for Snorri to get rid of his daughter, who according to the saga was not stable.[42] However, the marriage was a failure, and it was dissolved five years later. By then Arni had been abroad for three years. Upon his return, and even before reuniting with his wife, Arni met up with Snorri and negotiated the terms of the divorce, a clear economic benefit for Snorri.[43]

In 1224 Snorri started creating new alliances. He married off his youngest daughter, Thordis, to Thorvaldr Snorrason from the family of Vatnsfirdingar. The same year he and his friend Thorvaldr Gissurarson from the Haukdælir family arranged a marriage between Snorri's daughter Ingibjorg and Thorvaldr's youngest son, Gissur. Included in the settlement was an agreement that Thorvaldr would see to it that his daughter-in-law, the widowed Hallveig Ormsdottir from the Oddaverjar family and by far the richest woman in the country, would form a *helmingafélag* with Snorri.[44]

The marriage between Ingibjorg and Gissur was arranged by the two fathers and was supposed to validate their friendship. It was a politically important union. Snorri's relationship to Hallveig not only improved his economic situation immensely; their relationship confirmed the ties he had to the family of Oddaverjar. He took custody over Hallveig and her sons' assets, and Sturla states that Snorri now had much more property than anyone else in Iceland.[45] According to Jón Viðar Sigurðsson's estimations, Snorri's assets now corresponded to the value of about 130 average farms.[46]

Four years later, in 1228, the up-and-coming chieftain Kolbeinn ungi Arnorsson, from the family of Ásbirningar, asked for Snorri's divorced daughter Hallbera's hand in marriage.[47] The union was clearly important to both men. By this time Snorri's nephew, Sturla Sighvatsson, was seizing power and thus had begun to constitute a serious threat to Snorri. Sturla and Kolbeinn were cousins and therefore connected to each other through kin. With Kolbeinn as son-in-law Snorri could maintain the same bonds to Kolbeinn as Sturla could, and in that way undermine Sturla's possibilities to claim support from his cousin. However, the couple did not get along at all. Nor was that the only problem with their marriage. The following summer Hallbera accompanied her husband to the Althing. "It was obvious," writes Sturla, "that she was not well."[48] After her death in 1231 Snorri and Kolbeinn had a bitter dispute about Hallbera's inheritance that ended in a settlement clearly favorable to Snorri.[49]

Snorri's strategy had been to establish strong horizontal relationships within Iceland. When he returned to Iceland in 1220, he presumed that his position there had been strengthened through his bond to the Norwegian king and the mission he had promised to undertake on his behalf. By creating bonds with nearly all other important families in the country he strove to confirm and consolidate his position as primus inter pares – and failed. Thorvaldr Vatnsfirding died in 1228, whereby Snorri's alliance with his family was dissolved. Ingibjorg and Gissur were divorced in 1231, the same year that Hallbera died. Neither Kolbeinn nor Gissur maintained his friendship with Snorri. All these relationships – and divorces – had been economically profitable. But Snorri's sons-in-law did not turn out to be his loyal followers, either during or after their marriages. On the contrary, both turned against him and became his enemies. So did his stepsons.

Snorri undoubtedly overestimated his own position and the importance of being the Norwegian king's ally among the local elite in Iceland. His mistake was to misjudge the ambitions of competitors and their willingness to accept his supremacy. As a consequence, he came into conflict with his own brother, his nephew, and ultimately, two of his sons-in-law and both stepsons. Sons usually were loyal supporters of their fathers; they worked for the benefit of their own nearest kin. However, as social equals and independent leaders of other alliances, sons-in-law could have ambitions that in many cases were not congruent with those of their fathers-in-law. Hence, if the son-in-law had his own political goals and alternative networks, he had the possibility of standing on his own feet, and if necessary for his goals, of opposing his father-in-law. In Snorri's case this meant that he couldn't even be sure of support from two of his most powerful sons-in-law, Gissur Thorvaldsson and Kolbeinn ungi. Thus, Kolbeinn as a son-in-law to Snorri, but blood-related to Sturla, chose to support the latter when Snorri and Sturla came into conflict.[50]

The horizontal bonds established through marriage were indeed a bond of dependence, but if the interests of the two families came into collision, each of them had the possibility of acting independently. It wasn't even certain that the two families had the same network as their basis of power. This is one of the explanations of the frailty of the system. In contrast to vertical bonds, horizontal ties could result in difficult conflicts between the members of the network, as the actors in many cases had the same social standing but irreconcilable political aims.[51] This together with the bilateral kinship system, where you not only had different roles as son, brother, grandson, nephew, uncle, son-in-law, and/or brother-in-law, but also had obligations to your relatives on both sides, made marriage an unsure way of establishing lasting and loyal bonds. As we have seen, the chieftains had been able to utilize complementary vertical bonds in addition to the horizontal ones. Friendship was one such bond; another alternative had been concubinage. During the thirteenth century, at the same time as the culmination of the power-struggle, it had become more difficult to disregard the Christian doctrine of marriage. Hence, it had become increasingly more difficult to make strategic use of marriage and concubinage simultaneously, or more specifically, to have multiple partners. Whether in marriage or other types of cohabitation, monogamy was presumed. This called for new strategies.

In 1235 Snorri's nephew Sturla Sighvatsson arrived in Iceland. During his stay in Norway he, like Snorri, had become a member of the king's retinue. And as Snorri had not succeeded in his task of bringing Iceland under Norwegian control, the king had designated Sturla to make a new try. It took Sturla only a short time to gain control over Snorri's domain, and in 1237 he forced Snorri and his son, Oraekja, to go to Norway. After neutralizing Snorri, Sturla turned against Snorri's former sons-in-law, Kolbeinn ungi and Gissur. In their last battle, at Örlygsstaðir 1238, Sturla and his father were defeated and killed, together with Sturla's three brothers. After returning to Iceland, Snorri himself was killed in Reykholt in 1241. For some time, it seemed that the Sturlungar's powerful position had been erased. However, in 1242 Sturla's younger brother, Thordr kakali, made his way to Iceland.

Thordr kakali isn't very present in *Íslendinga saga*.[52] However, the few glimpses we get of him imply that his father regarded him as promising. He is regularly mentioned among his father's followers, and in 1236 Sighvatr temporarily entrusted Thordr with a chieftaincy.[53] However, a year later Thordr went to Norway.[54] No explanation is given for his decision, but it is highly probable that his position as a younger son with as yet no household of his own promoted him to seek honor and prominence abroad. In 1239, he became a member of the king's retinue, and he stayed at his court until he returned to Iceland to confront his father's and brothers' assassins in 1242.[55]

New Men – New Strategies

Since the battle in Örlygsstaðir the power had been in the hands of two men, Sturla Sighvatsson's main antagonists, Kolbeinn ungi and Gissur Thorvaldsson.[56] Kolbeinn had taken control of Sighvatr's chieftancy in the north of Iceland and claimed possession of his property. He thereby managed to exclude Sighvatr's heirs from their paternal heritage. According to the sources, friends, relatives, and followers of Sighvatr and Sturla were forced under oath to obey Kolbeinn no matter who he might come into conflict with.[57] In that way Kolbeinn tried to eliminate any future support to Sighvatr and Sturla's family members. Thus, when Sighvatr's son, Thordr kakali, returned to Iceland in 1242 to avenge his father and brothers and claim his inheritance, his chances of succeeding were minimal. Not only was he destitute; the prospects of allying himself with chieftains of his own standing were remote. Despite this Kolbeinn regarded him as a dangerous enemy. His misgivings were not unwarranted. Within four years Thordr had regained his father's position, and in time he became the most powerful man in the country.

Thordr's first priority was to claim his father's domain in the north of Iceland, which Kolbeinn had confiscated. Their struggles went on for three years without either of them winning a decisive victory or managing to negotiate a settlement. However, before Kolbeinn died in 1245, he divided his domain between his kinsman Brandr Kolbeinsson and Thordr. Although this did not satisfy Thordr, he had attained a certain compensation. Furthermore, he had obtained economic resources that enabled him to act as the chieftain he considered himself to be, e.g., to give feasts and distribute gifts. In 1246, he killed Brandr and took over his domain, thereby achieving control over the entire Northern Quarter as well as over Vestfirðir. This in turn forced his other main enemy, Gissur, to act. In the face of yet another armed battle, an agreement was made between the two men. Both were retainers of the Norwegian king, and according to the settlement they were to go to Norway and let King Haakon settle their dispute. The king judged in Thordr's favor and put him in charge of the whole country. When Thordr arrived back in Iceland in 1247 his mission was to persuade the Icelanders to accept Norwegian subordination and pay taxes to the king.[58] Thordr was now without doubt the most powerful man in the country. He had not only achieved compensation for his losses but had challenged his enemies and built up a network of allies who unconditionally supported him. Given the circumstances, Thordr's rise to power was remarkable. His advancement and political strategies are therefore worth a closer look.

Although a skillful politician Thordr initially found it difficult to persuade his closest relatives to support him. Instead he found allies among the farmers in the region of Vestfirðir, among them one Bardr Thorkelsson who, recognizing that Thordr was without resources and literally homeless, handed over his farm to him. The author of *Þórðar saga kakala* comments laconically on this: "Thordr took over the farm. This was considered very generous."[59] Later Thordr returned Bardr's favor by giving him Svefneyjar in the west of Iceland. This land was worth much more than Bardr's former farm. As Jón Viðar Sigurðsson has pointed out, Thordr's gift turned Bardr into a big farmer. It was a gift he could never return but would forever be indebted for. Or as Jón Viðar Sigurðsson puts it:

> Bardr's help led to Thord having to show his generosity, but the help was so insignificant compared to the gift that Bardr apparently became completely dependent on Thord's will. The only way in which Bardr could reciprocate such a gift was to perform more services for Thordr.[60]

Thordr's chances of forming horizontal alliances were minimal, as his equals had subordinated themselves to Kolbeinn by oath. Hence, if he was to regain his former position, he obviously had to apply new strategies. Although involving neither marriage nor concubinage, his way of ensuring himself of Bardr's support can be seen as typical of the tactics he now adopted. In contrast to his uncle Snorri, Thordr established his strongest networks by using vertical relationships and generously rewarding his closest allies.

Thordr was thoroughly conversant with the instruments of the political order in which he acted. He knew that generous chieftains attained honor and attracted followers. Hence, his gift to Bardr not only secured his support, but also signaled Thordr's abilities as a capable and bountiful chieftain. Notably, Thordr's gift was different from the mutual economic transactions that changed hands, e.g., in connection with marriage negotiations. These transactions were indeed intended to strengthen or confirm alliances, but they were exchanged between social equals and were supposed to be comparable in worth. The obvious, and important, difference between these exchanges and Thordr's gift to Bardr is twofold. Firstly, the distribution of wealth in Thordr and Bardr's case moved downwards in society.[61] Bardr's economic profit changed his social position and thereby provided him with new possibilities. However, due to the vertical character of the relationship, it also created a bond of dependency in which Thordr was the stronger part. Thordr's gift could be considered a reward for Bardr's original friendly maneuver, and it also confirmed bonds of friendship between the two men. Yet the terms of the connection were Thordr's. The similarities between this liaison and a patron-client relationship can hardly be overlooked.

Within a short time Thordr had attracted loyal followers. Thordr's closest supporters were sons of farmers. They were young and ambitious, without a birth right to control chieftaincies but interested in advancing politically.[62] Besides, their relatively low social position meant that none of them had obligations toward Thordr's enemies through kinship or marriage. Their relationship to him was a bond of dependence, but provided that Thordr succeeded in pursuing his claims, it could prove nonetheless to be beneficial for both parties. However, although most of his followers joined him of their own free will, there also were examples of the opposite.

In 1243 Thordr and his men paid a visit to the farmer Thorsteinn Jonsson in Skagafjörður. Thorsteinn was one of Kolbeinn ungi's followers and had fought on his side in the battle of Örlygsstaðir. Thus, Thordr saw him as deeply involved in the assassination of his father and brothers. Thorsteinn was an influential, popular, and wealthy farmer, and Thordr's men were reluctant to attack him. Thordr, in contrast, found Thorsteinn to be the man most "worthy" of his revenge.[63] One early August morning, just before sunrise, Thordr and his men forced entry to Thorsteinn's farm at Hvammur. Whereas Thorsteinn's son managed to escape, Thorsteinn himself was captured, two men were killed, and several injured. Now a mediation between the two men took place, resulting in Thorsteinn changing sides and becoming one of Thordr's allies. Before Thordr's departure Thorsteinn's subordination was consolidated through oath. A friendship was established. As a confirmation of this relationship Thorsteinn's son, Eyjolfr ofsi, became Thordr's follower, and – as it would turn out – one of his most loyal supporters. Eyjolfr's sister, Kolfinna, became Thordr's concubine.[64]

Although without an economic transaction, this strategy follows a traditional pattern of creating bonds or confirming reconciliations between equals. But this relationship was vertical. Thorsteinn's subordination to Thordr was not only confirmed by oath; he also "transferred" his children to Thordr. In this case Thordr gained followers by force, and one might even suggest that Thorsteinn's children were hostages. In time Eyjolfr would be rewarded for his loyal services. The other young men who had joined Thordr on their own initiative also served him well and gained prominent positions amongst his followers. In order to complement and consolidate his ties to his followers, Thordr created bonds of kinship with those men closest to him.

In 1245, after having regained his father's domain, Thordr "strongly encouraged" the marriage between one of his most reliable followers, the farmer's son Hrafn Oddsson, and Thordr's niece, Sturla Sighvatsson's legitimate daughter Thuridr.[65] Hrafn's marriage to Thuridr and Thordr's strong support for it can be seen as a reward for Hrafn's faithful service and friendship, and it is unlikely that Hrafn would have had the possibility to marry upwards without Thordr's influence. Similar to his gift to Bardr, Thordr had presented a gift to Hrafn too significant for him to reciprocate. Instead, the marriage between Hrafn and Thuridr assured Thordr of Hrafn's loyalty and strengthened the bonds between them.

The strategic use of marriage between his followers and his female relatives was something Thordr was to continue to make use of. In that way he not only confirmed the bonds of friendship with his closest men but created ties of kinship as well. In 1246, he arranged the marriage between the previously mentioned Eyjolfr ofsi and Sturla Sighvatsson's illegitimate daughter, Thuridr.[66] Her legitimate half-sister, Gudny, was married to Vigfus Gunnsteinsson, and Nikulas Oddsson married another of Thordr's nieces, Gyda Solmundardottir.[67]

Due to their relationship to and support of Thordr, all these men obtained powerful positions otherwise not attainable for men of their social position. Helgi Þorláksson has highlighted how "new men" made their entry in the political landscape of Iceland during the thirteenth century. During this turbulent century they came to distinguish themselves as permanent followers of chieftains, becoming members of a chieftain's household, or taking care of a household on his behalf. As Helgi Þorláksson points out, these were young men, who although descended from wealthy farmers, had no birth right to chieftaincies, but high ambitions to obtain power.[68] Given Thordr kakali's circumstances on his return to Iceland in 1242, these men obviously constituted an important resource – and he made the best of it.

As mentioned earlier, King Haakon had assigned Thordr the task of persuading the Icelanders to pay taxes to him. On his arrival in Iceland, however, Thordr instead focused on gaining control over the country. Accordingly, the king became displeased with his actions, and summoned him to Norway again. As the king's retainer, Thordr was obliged to obey his orders. Before he left in 1249 he divided his domain among his friends and relatives. Thus, Hrafn Oddsson received authority over Vestfirðir and Eyjolfr ofsi was to manage Eyjafjörður. In time Hrafn became a chieftain in his own right.

Thordr never returned to Iceland, but his followers remained loyal to him. As Helgi Þorláksson has pointed out, Thordr's choice to create vertical bonds might be explained by the fact that there was a lack of chieftains to ally with. However, as he maintains, Thordr´s strategies were caused by other more important factors. The men he surrounded himself with were below him in status. They owed their advancement to him, and as a consequence they were indebted to him and thus unconditionally loyal.

Thordr had distributed his female relatives among his followers. He had witnessed that among the networks his older brother, Sturla, had established, the vertical ones were the most reliable. Thus, he exclusively chose to establish vertical relationships. But whereas his own relationship to his concubine/s followed the traditional pattern of the man being of higher social standing than the woman, the marriages he arranged on behalf of his female relatives were with men of lower social standing. Although a recompense for loyal service, Thordr's use of marriage to reward the men closest to him illustrates important political and social changes in medieval Iceland: the rise of "new men" and the coming formation of a new aristocracy.[69]

Concluding Remarks

During the period in which Snorri, his brothers, and their sons were politically active, Icelandic society underwent significant changes. What had been possible during the twelfth century – when powerful, married chieftains were able to establish intimate and vertical extramarital relationships without intervention from the Church – became considerably more difficult during the thirteenth century. Moreover, even unmarried men who chose concubinage before marriage were supposed to be monogamous. Thus, the political importance of well-organized marriages slowly increased throughout this period. Yet the political significance and need for vertical relations remained consistent.

All three Sturlung brothers, Thordr, Sighvatr, and Snorri, began without adequate material means, and all managed to establish themselves among the most powerful chieftains in the country. Their first step was to ensure themselves of one of the main bases of power: economic resources. Both Thordr and Snorri "married for money" and could thereby establish themselves as chieftains. Sighvatr instead used different strategies of investing his assets and getting hold of properties *before* getting married. Thus, he was able to propose to a woman belonging to one of the most powerful families in the country, a relationship with clear political implications. Irrespective of their choice of strategies, all three men's marriages were important for their future position. However, in contrast to his two brothers, Thordr did not strive to arrange alliances with the other powerful families in the country, but rather concentrated on managing his position locally and maintaining a diplomatic relationship with other chieftains. Snorri would in time become the richest man in Iceland, and undoubtedly he strove to become the most powerful man as well, a primus inter pares. His method of securing his position was to marry off his children with his presumptive competitors and thereby create horizontal bonds. As it turned out, however, none of his networks lasted. Sighvatr expanded his power geographically and managed to consolidate his position in collaboration with his son, Sturla. They effectively utilized vertical friendship relationships, as well as strategic marriage arrangements. Yet in the end Sturla's relationship to his concubine's male relatives would prove to be the most reliable.

Whereas the Sturlung brothers had lacked economic resources to match their social position, Thordr kakali was both destitute and without functioning social networks when he started his impossible mission in 1242. A scrutiny of the political landscape in Iceland showed him that he would have problems obtaining support among his family members and former friends. Thordr concentrated on gathering men who were able and willing to fight. Almost exclusively he concentrated on creating vertical bonds and rewarding his followers generously. Among his available resources were his nieces, who were distributed – in marriage – among his closest men. Although this strategy might have been forced upon him by the circumstances, there is reason to believe that his strategies should be interpreted as the plot of a political mastermind.[70] The vertical relationship was a bond of dependency, but compared to horizontal bonds it was more reliable. And as I have shown, it was beneficial for both parties.

The internal conflicts among the dominant families during the thirteenth century had severely weakened the power-base of the former elites in Iceland. Instead, "new men" entered the stage. Despite these political and social changes, marriage continued to be an important instrument. But whereas farmers previously had established relationships with chieftains by handing over their daughters as concubines, their sons now created the same kind of bonds by marrying women from the former elites.

Notes

1. This field of research is very comprehensive. Here I limit myself to mentioning works of specific interest for my studies on intimate relations, kinship, and friendship, of which this chapter is a part: Gerd Althoff, *Verwandte,*

Freunde und Getreue: Zum politischen Stellenwert der Gruppenbidnungen im früheren Mittelalter (Darmstadt, 1990); Jesse L. Byock, "Valdatafl og vinfengi," *Skírnir* 162 (1988): 127–37; Lars Hermanson, *Släkt, vänner och makt: En studie av elitens politiska kultur i 1100-talets Danmark* (Gothenburg, 2000). Jón Viðar Sigurðsson has published pioneering work on friendship in medieval Iceland: see specifically his *Chieftains and Power in the Icelandic Commonwealth*, trans. Jean Lundskær-Nielsen (Odense, 1999); *Den vennlige vikingen: Vennskapets makt i Norge og på Island ca. 900–1300* (Oslo, 2010); "The Changing Role of Friendship in Iceland, c. 900–1300," in *Friendship and Social Networks in Scandinavia, c. 1000–1800*, ed. Jón Viðar Sigurðsson and Thomas Småberg (Turnhout, 2013), 43–64.
2. This was the focus of my dissertation: see Auður Magnúsdóttir, *Frillor och fruar: Politik och samlevnad på Island 1120–1400* (Gothenburg, 2001). Aspects of the study have been published in several articles. For an English introduction to these theses see Auður Magnúsdóttir, "Women and Sexual Politics," in *The Routledge Worlds: The Viking World*, ed. Stefan Brink and Neil Price (London and New York, 2008).
3. Each *goði* ruled over a so-called *goðorð* (the term is both singular and plural). These terms will be translated as "chieftain" and "chieftancy," respectively.
4. On this development see Sigurðsson, *Chieftains and Power*.
5. For a short but comprehensive account of the Sturlung Age, see Helgi Þorláksson, "Sturlung Age," in *Medieval Scandinavia: An Encyclopedia*, ed. Philip Pulsiano (New York, 1993), 615–16.
6. On the importance of resources and the redistributive nature of the economy in medieval Iceland see Helgi Þorláksson, *Vaðmál og verðlag: Vaðmál í utanlandsviðskiptum og búskap Íslendinga á 13. og 14. öld* (Reykjavik, 1991), 178–90; Sigurðsson, *Chieftains and Power*, 101–19; Auður G. Magnúsdóttir, "Islänningarna och arvsrätten 1264–1281," in *Arverettens handlingsrom: Strategier, relasjoner og historisk utvikling, 1100–2000*, ed. Per Andersen, Speculum Boreale 15 (Stamsund, 2011), 30–31.
7. Magnúsdóttir, *Frillor och fruar*, 77–97.
8. See Thyra Nors's study on illegitimate children in Denmark and their highborn mothers. However, according to Nors, fathers could only inherit from their illegitimate children after having publicly acknowledged them. See Thyra Nors, "Illegitimate Children and Their High-Born Mothers," *Scandinavian Journal of History* 21, no. 1 (1996): 17–37, 19.
9. On friendship in medieval Scandinavia and Iceland see Jón Viðar Sigurðsson, *Viking Friendship: The Social Bond in Iceland and Norway, c. 900–1300* (Ithaca, NY, 2017); Lars Hermanson, *Bärande band: Vänskap, kärlek och brödraskap i det medeltida Nordeuropa, ca 1000–1200* (Lund, 2009).
10. Jack Goody underlines the role of concubinage as a strategy used for securing offspring. See Jack Goody, *The Development of Family and Marriage in Europe* (Cambridge, 1983), 39; Margaret Clunies Ross comes to the same conclusion in her article "Concubinage in Anglo-Saxon England," *Past and Present* 108 (1985): 3–34. This fits well with the information we have about Icelandic medieval society, but in addition to the important role of securing offspring, and given the political development in Iceland during the twelfth and thirteenth centuries, the political importance of concubinage as a means of creating networks increased during the High Middle Ages.
11. Similarly, as Robert I. Moore points out, French lords were principally leaders of warrior bands, and therefore benefited from having many children. See Robert I. Moore, *The First European Revolution 970–1215* (Oxford, 2000), 90.

12. Magnúsdóttir, *Frillor och fruar*, 80–88. See the contribution by Hermanson and Orning on patron-client relationships in chapter 3 in this volume.
13. This development is related to the Christian definitions of marriage and "adultery." An unmarried man had not taken the vows of holy matrimony and therefore, strictly speaking, he did not commit a sin if he was living with one or more concubines, whereas a married man ran the risk of being excommunicated for the same thing.
14. Sturla was born in 1214 and died in 1284. *Hákonar saga Hákonarsonar* is assumed to have been written during the years 1264–65. *Íslendinga* saga is thought to have been composed during Sturla's last years. See Guðrún Ása Grímsdóttir, "The Works of Sturla Þórðarson," in *Sturla Þórðarson: Skald, Chieftain and Lawman*, ed. Jón Viðar Sigurðsson and Sverrir Jakobsson (Leiden and Boston, 2017), 8–19.
15. Sturla Thordarson had fourteen children that we know of, eight daughters and six sons. All six daughters were legitimate and were strategically married off. However, it was his three sons with his second wife, Gudny, who inherited his power position. On this see Sverrir Jakobsson, "Konur og völd í Breiðafirði á miðöldum," *Skírnir* (2013): 161–75, 187.
16. "Ari in sterki [vanði] ferðir sínar í Hvamm, ok gerðust með þeim Guðnýju kærleikar miklir." *Sturl.* I, 229. All translations from *Sturlunga saga* are my own. In this case I assume that Ari's wife was still alive, even if Sturla is not precise about it. However, according to the Church, remarriage was comparable to bigamy, even if it was preferable to fornication. Interestingly this doesn't prevent Sturla from revealing the affair. On the Church and remarriage of widows/widowers see Conor McCarthy, *Marriage in Medieval England: Law, Literature and Practice* (Woodbridge, 2004), 148–50. On the political dimension of this liaison see Jakobsson, "Konur og völd," 161–75.
17. Sturl I, 231.
18. Ibid. "ok helzt þeirra vinátta lengi." The saga is not explicit in explaining this relationship. Bersi was still alive when Thordr and Hrodny began the liaison, and using the term *vinátta* ("friendship") to describe its nature is slightly ambiguous. On the other hand, Sturla is clear that Hrodny moved into Thordr's household and that it was an intimate affair.
19. "Þórðr Sturluson fékk Guðrúnar . . . Tók hann við henni mikit fé. Gerðist Þórðr þá höfðingi," *Sturl* I, 232. The term *höfðingi* has no precise translation in English, but it signifies a man who is prominent among his equals.
20. Sturl I, 234.
21. Sturl I, 235.
22. Sturl I, 234–35.
23. And as it would turn out, Sighvatr also supported his sons, especially his successor, Sturla.
24. Sturl I, 231–32.
25. Sturl I, 303. See Helgi Þorláksson, "Stéttir, auður og völd á 12. og 13. öld," *Saga. Tímarit Sögufélags* 20 (1982): 63–113, 74.
26. Helgi Þorláksson, "Stéttir, auður og völd á 12. og 13. öld," 73–74.
27. Sturl I, 303.
28. Helle Vogt and Jón Viðar Sigurðsson, "Inheritance and Transfer of Landed Property: The Material Fundament of the Elites," in *Nordic Elites in Transformation, c. 1050–1250 Volume I: Material Resources*, ed. Bjørn Poulsen, Helle Vogt, and Jón Viðar Sigurðsson (New York, 2019), 107–29.
29. Magnúsdóttir, "Women and Sexual Politics," 44.
30. Ibid.
31. Sturl I, 113–14.

32. *Íslendinga saga* is inconsistent regarding Snorri's age. Here I rely on the information from annals, according to which he was born in 1179. See Sturl I, 555, n. 1.
33. Sturl I, 237.
34. Sigurðsson, *Chieftains and Power*, 115.
35. Sturl I, 240.
36. Sturl I, 242. "Snorri var inn mesti fjárgæzlumaðr, fjöllyndr ok átti börn við fleium konum en Herdísi."
37. Magnúsdóttir, *Frillor och fruar*, 68.
38. Sigurðsson, *Chieftains and Power*, 71.
39. The family of Svinfellingar in the Eastern Quarter managed to keep a distance from the disputes of this period. Therefore, Snorri may have been less interested in connecting with them.
40. Sturl I, 271.
41. Sigurðsson, *Chieftains and Power*, 137.
42. Sturl I, 271. At least, she was not ready to take care of her own household, nor to stay away from her family – as the author of the saga states: "That summer, before Snorri went abroad, he married his daughter Hallbera to Arni, the son of Magnus Asmundsson. Their wedding took place in Reykholt . . . The following year they spent most of their time at Reykholt because she was miserable if they were not there." ("Þat sumar, áðr Snorri fór útan, gifti hann Hallberu, dóttur sína, Árna, syni Magnúss Ásmundssonar. Var brúðlaup þeira í Reykjaholti . . . Váru þau í Reykjaholti lengstum þau missiri, því at ekki nýtti af henni um samvistur, ef þau váru eigi þar.")
43. Sturl I, 304. According to *Íslendinga saga* Árni not only returned Hallbera's bridewealth, but Snorri claimed Árni's farm Brautarholt as well.
44. Sturl I, 302. A *helmingafélag* was a joint company with equal rights to the assets. However, in accordance with law and tradition, Snorri became Hallveig's guardian. On *helmingafélag* in Iceland see Hrefna Róbertsdóttir, "Helmingafélög hjóna á miðöldum," *Sagnir: Tímarit um söguleg efni* 7 (1986): 31–40; Agnes S. Arnórsdóttir, *Property and Virginity: The Christianization of Marriage in Medieval Iceland* (Aarhus, 2009).
45. Sturl I, 304.
46. Sigurðsson, *Chieftains and Power*, 115.
47. Sturl I, 319.
48. Sturl I, 333. "Ok var þá auðsætt á henni, at hana firrðist heilsa."
49. Sturl I, 347, 358.
50. Sturl I, 333.
51. Magnúsdóttir, "Women and Sexual Politics," 43–44.
52. Our main information on Thordr and his political achievements comes from *Þórðar saga kakala*. The saga is preserved in only one of the versions of the *Sturlunga saga* compilation, and the beginning and the end of the saga are missing. See Úlfar Bragason, *Ætt og saga: Um frásagnarfræði Sturlungu eða Íslendinga sögu hinnar miklu* (Reykjavik, 2010), 9–104. The saga was probably written during the period 1262–1300. See Guðrún Nordal, "Sagnarit um innlend efni – Sturlunga saga," in *Íslensk bókmenntasaga*, vol. I, ed. Vésteinn Ólason (Reykjavik, 1992), 309–44 at 315.
53. Sturl I, 362, 372, 392.
54. Sturl I, 408.
55. Sturl II, 1.
56. As previously mentioned, Sturla and Kolbeinn ungi were blood-related (as cousins), and Kolbeinn had supported Sturla against Snorri Sturluson. During the subsequent political developments and struggles for power, however,

they became enemies. Thus, the two men who had been Snorri's sons-in-law and had later turned against him also became the main antagonists against Snorri's enemy Sturla.
57. Sturl II, 1–3.
58. For a more detailed overview of this development see Sigurðsson, *Chieftains and Power*, 72–74.
59. Sturl II, 11. "Þórðr tók við búinu. Þótti þetta geysistórmannligt."
60. Sigurðsson, *Chieftains and Power*, 91.
61. Ibid.
62. See Helgi Þorláksson, "Stórbændur gegn goðum: Hugleiðingar um goðavald, konungsvald og sjálfræðishug bænda um miðbik 13. aldar," in *Söguslóðir: Afmælisrit helgað Ólafi Hanssyni sjötugum 18 september 1979*, ed. Bergsteinn Jónsson, Einar Laxness, and Heimir Þorleifsson (Reykjavik, 1979), 241–42.
63. Sturl II, 37.
64. Sturl II, 73, 85; Magnúsdóttir, *Frillor och fruar*, 84–85.
65. Sturl II, 70.
66. Sturl II, 20.
67. Sturl II, 84.
68. Helgi Þorláksson, "Stórbændur gegn goðum," 242.
69. On the political strategies of the Norwegian king and the formation of a new aristocracy after the Icelanders were subordinated to Norway in 1262/64 see Sigríður Beck, *I kungens frånvaro: Formeringen av en isländsk aristokrati 1281–1387* (Gothenberg, 2011).
70. Sturl I, 242.

Dedicated Bibliography

Althoff, Gerd. *Verwandte, Freunde und Getreue: Zum politischen Stellenwert der Gruppenbindungen im früheren Mittelalter*. Darmstadt, 1990.

Arnórsdóttir, Agnes S. *Property and Virginity: The Christianization of Marriage in Medieval Iceland*. Aarhus, 2009.

Beck, Sigríður. *I kungens frånvaro: Formeringen av en isländsk aristokrati 1281–1387*. Gothenberg, 2011.

Bragason, Úlfar. *Ætt og saga: Um frásagnarfræði Sturlungu eða Íslendinga sögu hinnar miklu*. Reykjavík, 2010.

Byock, Jesse L. "Valdatafl og vinfengi." *Skírnir* 162 (1988): 127–38.

Goody, Jack. *The Development of Family and Marriage in Europe*. Cambridge, 1983.

Grímsdóttir, Guðrún Ása. "The Works of Sturla Þórðarson." In *Sturla Þórðarson: Skald, Chieftain and Lawman*, edited by Jón Viðar Sigurðsson and Sverrir Jakobsson, 8–19. Leiden and Boston, 2017.

Hermanson, Lars. *Släkt, vänner och makt. En studie av elitens politiska kultur i 1100-talets Danmark*. Gothenburg, 2000.

Hermanson, Lars. *Bärande band: Vänskap, kärlek och brödraskap i det medeltida Nordeuropa, ca 1000–1200*. Lund, 2009.

Jakobsson, Sverrir. "Konur og völd í Breiðafirði á miðöldum." *Skírnir* 187 (2013): 161–75.

Magnúsdóttir, Auður. *Frillor och fruar: politik och samlevnad på Island 1120–1400*. Gothenburg, 2001.

Magnúsdóttir, Auður. "Women and Sexual Politics." In *The Routledge Worlds: The Viking World*, edited by Stefan Brink and Neil Price. London and New York, 2008.
Magnúsdóttir, Auður. "Islänningarna och arvsrätten 1264–1281." In *Arverettens handlingsrom. Strategier, relasjoner og historisk utvikling, 1100–2000*, edited by Per Andersen, Speculum Boreale nr. 15. Stamsund, 2011.
McCarthy, Conor. *Marriage in Medieval England: Law, Literature and Practice.* Woodbridge, 2004.
Moore, Robert I. *The First European Revolution 970–1215.* Oxford, 2000.
Nordal, Guðrún. "Sagnarit um innlend efni – Sturlunga saga." In *Íslensk bókmenntasaga*, vol. I, edited by Vésteinn Ólason, 309–44. Reykjavik, 1992.
Nors, Thyra. "Illegitimate Children and Their High-born Mothers: Changes in the Perception of Illegitimacy in Medieval Denmark." *Scandinavian Journal of History* 21 (2008): 17–37.
Róbertsdóttir, Hrefna. "Helmingafélög hjóna á miðöldum." *Sagnir: Tímarit um söguleg efni* 7 (1986): 31–40.
Ross, Margaret Clunies. "Concubinage in Anglo-Saxon England." *Past and Present* 108 (1985): 3–34.
Sigurðsson, Jón Viðar. *Chieftains and Power in the Icelandic Commonwealth.* Translated by Jean Lundskær-Nielsen. Odense, 1999 [1993].
Sigurðsson, Jón Viðar. *Den vennlige vikingen: Vennskapets makt i Norge og på Island ca. 900–1300.* Oslo, 2010.
Sigurðsson, Jón Viðar. "The Changing Role of Friendship in Iceland, c. 900–1300." In *Friendship and Social Networks in Scandinavia, c. 1000–1800*, edited by Jón Viðar Sigurðsson and Thomas Småberg, 43–64. Turnhout, 2013.
Sigurðsson, Jón Viðar. *Viking Friendship: The Social Bond in Iceland and Norway, c. 900–1300.* Ithaca, NY, 2017.
Þorláksson, Helgi. "Stórbændur gegn goðum: Hugleiðingar um goðavald, konungsvald og sjálfræðishug bænda um miðbik 13. aldar." In *Söguslóðir: Afmælisrit helgað Ólafi Hanssyni sjötugum 18 september 1979*, edited by Bergsteinn Jónsson, Einar Laxness, and Heimir Þorleifsson, 241–42. Reykjavik, 1979.
Þorláksson, Helgi. "Stéttir, auður og völd á 12. og 13. öld." *Saga: Tímarit Sögufélags* 20 (1982): 63–113.
Þorláksson, Helgi. *Vaðmál og verðlag: Vaðmál í utanlandsviðskiptum og búskap Íslendinga á 13. og 14. öld.* Reykjavik, 1991.
Þorláksson, Helgi. "Sturlung Age." In *Medieval Scandinavia: An Encyclopedia*, edited by Philip Pulsiano. New York, 1993.
Vogt, Helle, and Jón Viðar Sigurðsson. "Inheritance and Transfer of Landed Property: The Material Fundament of the Elites." In *Nordic Elites in Transformation, c. 1050–1250, Vol I: Material Resources*, edited by Bjørn Poulsen, Helle Vogt, and Jón Viðar Sigurðsson. New York, 2019.

12 Forming Bonds With Followers in Medieval Iceland
The Cases of Thordr kakali and Thorgils skarði

Viðar Pálsson

Feasts and Gifts as Modes of Social and Political Communication in Medieval Iceland: Historiographical Context

This chapter discusses the ideas and practices of chieftain–follower relationships in late Free State politics in Iceland, as described in *Sturlunga saga* and other relevant sources, through case studies of two prominent political characters of the era, Thordr kakali (*Þórðar saga kakala, The saga of Thordr kakali*) and Thorgils skarði ("harelip") (*Þorgils saga skarða, The saga of Thorgils skarði*). In particular, the role of feasts (*veizlur*) and gifts as demonstrative modes of communicating power and bonds, and how they circumscribed leader–follower relationships commonly labeled friendship (*vinfengi* or *vinátta*), will be analyzed.

The prolific scholarship on gift-giving in medieval and pre-modern cultures of power has undergone considerable revision in recent years.[1] Initially, the topic of feasting and, in particular, gift-giving was brought to the fore within medieval studies as a part of a wider reorientation in social and political history. This reorientation saw a departure from the traditional legal and constitutional approaches that dominated political histories in the nineteenth and early twentieth centuries, which focused on legal and administrative institutions and highlighted a distinction between private and public spheres of power. From such a vantage point, gift-giving belonged primarily to the private sphere, whereas the emphasis of political history was overwhelmingly placed on tracing the medieval origins of the modern state, a quintessentially "public" phenomenon. In contrast, historians of the post–World War II era, in many ways following Otto Brunner's groundbreaking study on power and violence in medieval Austria and Bavaria,[2] merged political and social history to a greater degree by extending the field of political history to include the various ways in which power was exercised outside of formal institutions and "public" platforms, most significantly through networking on a broad scale. This drew attention to cultures of bonds encompassing private and public spheres alike (the distinction thus becoming anachronistic if applied too rigidly) and the means by which they were established and maintained.

The social implications of exchange and its central role within cultures of networking had, however, already been explored by the founding fathers of modern sociology and anthropology, most famously and influentially by Marcel Mauss in the 1920s. Mauss recognized the double-faced nature of the gift as simultaneously facilitating social stability through formal bonds of obligations, and potentially breeding hostility in these same relationships by incurring social and political debt. Nevertheless, it was predominantly the integrative and stabilizing aspects of the Maussian gift that were stressed by medieval historians as they introduced early sociological concepts into their analyses of medieval cultures of bonds in the 1950s, 1960s, and onwards. Well into the 1990s, therefore, gift-giving and formal acts of exchange were primarily studied as producers of "social glue"; that is, friendship and bonds that in the pre-modern absence of statehood functioned as basic social and political structures.

There were many factors that directed gift-giving studies on this trajectory. One was the previously mentioned turn away from viewing pre-modern cultures of power through the modern lens of statehood, generating questions on what then, if not a state, framed and glued medieval society together? Those substituting cultures of bonds as an alternative for the state felt that friendship and gift-giving ran deep in medieval social and political constructions. Another related factor was the frequent juxtaposition of "gift economy" and "profit economy," seen as central characteristics of pre-modern and modern societies, respectively. Together, both factors invited a notion of friendship and gift-giving as prominent and rather generally applicable phenomena in medieval sociopolitical cultures (largely analogous to the archaic societies from which "the gift" as an analytical concept was drawn to begin with), although none suggested, of course, that they structured society from top to bottom: It is the political arena broadly perceived that remains in focus.

Recent revisions in gift-giving scholarship have recast if not rejected this interpretation, voicing skepticism about the utility and applicability of the concept of a "gift economy" when analyzing pre-modern political bonds, especially friendship (*amicitia*) and its primary media of expression – feasts and gifts. Whereas the contractual function of exchange, the backbone of traditional gift-giving scholarship, has not been cast into doubt, there is growing distrust in the idea that friendship was applied as frequently and generally among the political elites of medieval Europe, and their immediate followers, as previously assumed. In terms of horizontal and vertical relationships, this is to say that friendship was applied primarily in political relations among peers and near-peers but rather sparingly in relations between lords and their political inferiors. Thus, recent scholarship emphasizes an exclusive rather than an inclusive function of friendship, feast, and gifts among the politically competent.[3]

This preliminary sketch is prerequisite for the context of the present case study and the questions it seeks to answer. Following the anthropological and sociological turn in medieval studies in the 1970s and 1980s, proactive networking and friendship as a formal, sociopolitical institution came to the fore as an important topic within Icelandic and Scandinavian studies, as it did elsewhere. Gift exchange and social ties among early Scandinavians had been explored already in 1968 by Aaron Gurevich, who, in tune with early anthropologically inspired scholarship, stressed the integrative function of gift-giving rather than its destabilizing potential and competitive impulses. In the 1980s and 1990s, the topic of friendship continued to be pursued within medieval Icelandic studies, but most frequently in the context of feud and conflict management rather than as a subject *per se*. In the decades bracketing the millennium, however, friendship and its role in the sociopolitical culture of stateless Iceland was explored more systematically and comprehensively than before by Jón Viðar Sigurðsson.[4] Most recently, his interpretation of friendship and gifts in the political culture of twelfth- and thirteenth-century Iceland is synthesized in *Den vennlige vikingen* (2010).[5]

Jón Viðar argues that friendship (proactive and fictive kinship vis-à-vis kinship by blood, *ætt*) was "the most important social bond between chieftains and householders" throughout the Free State era; moreover, that it "defined relations" between chieftains, between chieftains and householders, and among householders themselves. It was an all-encompassing social pattern, "the fundamental bond that tied society together." Prior to the ascent of royal power in the closing decades of the thirteenth century, which introduced the local elites to new sources of power from above and thus lessened their need for befriending "downwards," friendship remained pervasive in the sociopolitical culture and characteristic of the bonds between chieftains and their followers. By extension, feasts and gifts were common expressions among them, creating and cementing such bonds. "The chieftains were to protect the householders and their households, organize feasts for them, and give them gifts."[6] Similar notions are echoed in current scholarly literature on medieval Iceland and in saga studies.

However, in my own *Language of Power* (2016), primarily a study of feasting and gift-giving, but also of friendship, I argue for a modification of this view, believing it to be too strongly indebted to previous emphases on integration and "social glue" and not attentive enough to the aristocratic, restrictive, exclusive, and most often *ad hoc* application of feasts and gifts in medieval Iceland and its sagas. They were never a free and spontaneous practice, even within the political sphere, nor do they appear to have been practiced on a wide scale among chieftains and followers.

Obviously, this is not a question of whether chieftains in the Free State practiced unreserved largesse, kept an "open table," or strove to establish ties of friendship through feasting and gift-giving with their *þingmenn* (and potential followers) without limits. Rather, it is a question of how far they reached in establishing ties of friendship with followers, and how frequently or regularly they cemented such relations by means of formal hospitality and exchange. Friendship was formal and public. Its implications of equality or near-equality among its participants made it readily applicable to alliance-making or settlements between peers or near-peers among the politically competent, i.e., horizontally. In the case of vertical bonds, however, its application was bound to be more restricted and tightly framed by the given circumstances. The contemporary sagas that narrate the events of the Free State era abound in the former relationship, but the following case study deals primarily with the latter.

Even though Jón Viðar argues for a more general application of friendship in medieval Iceland than I have done, he nevertheless accepts that friendship must have become more restrictedly applied when political and social stratification became more pronounced, as chieftaincies evolved into territorial lordship during the final phases of the Free State. It is worthwhile, therefore, to examine the case of two chieftains toward the end of the Free State era who did form friendships with their followers through feasts and gifts: It is beneficial not only to conduct a close reading in this particular context, but also to perform a more general assessment against other evidence in the corpus.

The Historical and Textual Context of *Þórðar saga kakala* and *Þorgils saga skarða* – The Concepts of Feasts and Gifts

Among the politically competent, friendship, feasts, and gifts constituted the double nature of generating cohesiveness while simultaneously serving as social markers and public expressions of elite status (or the aspiration for it). This double nature – or perhaps better, "double function," since it is a matter of complexity rather than opposites – is underscored in the cases of Thordr kakali and Thorgils skarði.

The question which inevitably rises, though, is whether this impression of feasts and gifts as an aristocratic and exclusive language of power among the uppermost layers of society is due to the nature of our sources, i.e., the fact that the historical narratives on which we base our analysis were composed by people of that class about their own lives and politics. Would they not look different if our sources covered society as a whole, high and low alike, and would we not find them at all levels and working in similar ways? Answering this question lies at the heart of *Language of Power*, the title of which is descriptive of its conclusions. Whatever forms of sociability people of lower ranks may have enjoyed, and whatever kinds of bonds they may have formed among themselves, the abundant examples of formal friendship, feasts, and gifts throughout the saga corpus make it clear that within the saga world these were perceived to be expressions of power and status. Aside from the fact that they were no less ambiguous and contested expressions than they were a stabilizing force – feast and gifts repeatedly went wrong for all sorts of different reasons, often with violent consequences – they are hardly portrayed as a "social glue," tying society together. They belong to the political sphere, and primarily to its uppermost layers.[7]

The historical context of the chieftains Thordr kakali and Thorgils skarði is that of the final phase of the Free State era in Iceland, the so-called *Sturlungaöld*, the "Sturlung Age" (c. 1220–62/64). During the twelfth and thirteenth centuries, power became concentrated in the hands of a few strong individuals or families, who not only became the sole owners of the original thirty-nine chieftaincies (*goðorð* – initially, these may have been more numerous than thirteenth-century legal sources suggest)[8] but also transformed their power into territorial lordships or regional domains of sorts (*ríki*). The situation was further complicated by the growing involvement of the Norwegian king, emerging powerfully in the first decades of the thirteenth century after nearly a century of civil wars at home.

It was a violent age to be sure, with competition between rival lords leading to military confrontation on an unprecedented scale, yet the separation of this era from the culture of violence and struggle for power that had characterized the earlier Free State should not be exaggerated. Among other things, the language of feasts and gifts remained applicable to the management of bonds among the political elite. This held true at least until the Norwegian king became Iceland's sole chieftain through the submission of the Icelanders in 1262–64 (he claimed chieftaincies earlier still, notably those of his courtier Snorri Sturluson, who had betrayed his lord before being killed in 1241), which paved the way for the country's legal and administrative incorporation into the Norwegian realm from the 1270s onward. During the era of Thordr kakali and Thorgils skarði, therefore, the major players in Icelandic politics were the king's men as members of the court and under the king's command. This did not, however, prevent them from pursuing their political interests in Iceland quite independently, to the king's annoyance.[9]

The narrative of local politics in which Thordr and Thorgils took part is crowded and complex as it has come down to us in the so-called contemporary sagas, a subgenre of the Icelandic sagas. The political events of the Sturlung Age are narrated in *Sturlunga saga*, a saga compilation made around 1300, most likely by Lawman Thordr Narfason (d. 1308) at Skarð in western Iceland. It exists in two main redactions, *Króksfjarðarbók* and *Reykjarfjarðarbók*. Both manuscripts are dated to the second half of the fourteenth century, although *Króksfjarðarbók* is believed to be slightly older than *Reykjarfjarðarbók* and closer to the original. With only one exception, the individual sagas collated are lost to us in their original, separate thirteenth-century versions. This is the case for *Þórðar saga kakala*, the surviving text of which is dispersed within Sturla Thordarson's *Íslendinga saga*, the compilation's central piece. *Þorgils saga skarða*, however, was not initially a part of *Sturlunga saga* and only survives as an addition to the *Reykjarfjarðarbók* redaction.[10]

The author of *Þórðar saga* is unknown, but the saga must have been composed sometime after 1271. It describes the career of Thordr kakali Sighvatsson of the Sturlungar family and his struggle for political establishment in Iceland as the king's man in 1242–49. In 1250, he returned to Norway on the king's orders and died there six years later. Thorgils skarði Boedvarsson, also of the Sturlungar family and the king's man, pursued his political ambitions most energetically and aggressively upon his arrival from the Norwegian court in 1252 until his death in 1258. During their short careers, both men became major chieftains in Iceland. The author of *Þorgils saga* is unknown as well, but the saga is assumed to have been originally composed c. 1275–80, possibly by Thordr Hítnesingr, a prominent farmer in western Iceland and one of Thorgils's loyal followers.

Some of the details of the narrative about how Thorgils became accepted as a chieftain in Skagafjörður and Thordr in Eyjafjörður in northern Iceland (both set out from bases in the West) feature later on together with the examples of feasts and gifts that appear at its center. Two aspects of the political environment in which these events are set should be discussed in advance, though: social stratification and the concepts of feasts and gifts.

The social composition of Free State Iceland and its development from the Viking Age until the close of the thirteenth century remains a perennial topic of debate among historians. There is general consensus, however, that during the Sturlung Age, a class of prominent farmers either emerged or became more distinguished, the so-called *stórbændur* ("major farmers"), whose unique position within their local communities was marked by their economic, social, and political preeminence. Their presence is unmistakable in both *Þórðar saga* and *Þorgils saga*, in which the descriptions of feasts, gifts, and friendships principally refer to them and to their respective chieftains. Rather than posing a political threat to the major farmers, the acceptance of a chieftain might provide opportunities to further accentuate their status – in *Þorgils saga* the major farmers of Skagafjörður consider not recognizing a chieftain at all before taking Thorgils on in that role.

The feasts and gifts the sagas speak of are readily identifiable through stock phrases and labels. Gift is *gjǫf*, from the verb *gefa*, "to give," and a feast is *veizla*, from the verb *veita*, "to grant" or "confer" (used interchangeably with a handful of other terms, most notably *boð*, "an invitation," and derivations thereof). Both concepts defy the modern notion of gifts and feasts, however, since formal exchange in pre-modern societies such as Free State Iceland was rarely without social and political implications. Whereas modern gifts and feasts are thought of as being principally free and voluntary acts, their medieval counterparts were not. This is especially true of *veizla*, which encompassed formal hospitality ranging from that freely given (*Gastfreundschaft*) to the forced and obligatory gesture toward a superior (*Herrschaftsgastung*). These are opposite poles of a wide spectrum, and the feasts and gifts of the sagas are situated along it. The term *veizla* receives its most dynamic expressions in the kings' sagas, where itinerant kingship and its limits are explored in depth. In that context it eventually became a legal concept, "a grant" or "a benefice" held of the king, usually in the form of land earmarked for local maintenance of the king and his itinerant court through formal hospitality and upkeep.[11] This makes for an interesting comparison between the political cultures of Iceland and Norway more generally, for *veizlur* had, for a variety of reasons, a stronger presence in the latter than the former.

Forging Elite Ties in *Þorgils saga skarða* and *Þórðar saga kakala*

Before Thorgils skarði won favor among the farmers in Skagafjörður in 1255 and became their chieftain through feasts and gifts, he fought hard to establish himself in western Iceland. He arrived there in 1252 from the Norwegian court, assigned with the task of advancing royal authority in Iceland (along with another courtier, Gissur Thorvaldsson, head of the Haukdælir family). At first, he struggled for recognition in Snorri Sturluson's old domain, Borgarfjörður – which, as previously noted, the king now claimed as his own – but he was reluctantly received. He then moved on to the Snæfellsnes peninsula in the West, his own family's area, where he continued his campaign to gain respect and acknowledgment.

The saga vividly describes Thorgils's strong-arm measures as he exacted gifts and hospitality from prominent farmers in these two areas, sometimes very violently.[12] The impression given by the saga is that he was not driven by financial need in these exploits so much as by a desire for recognition of his political standing through formal acts of exchange (called *gjafir*, "gifts"). On the one hand, these descriptions are akin to various instances in *Sturlunga saga* describing enforced levies or contributions in kind collected by chieftains during the Sturlung Age. The rise of territorial lordship in the thirteenth century, and the conflicts it generated, fostered a culture of enforced contributions of various sorts (*sauðakvaðir, tillǫgur, efla*, or *gera bú*), and these were sometimes dressed up as gifts or otherwise made out to be voluntary to some degree. Sometimes they were acts of outright seizure.[13] On the other hand, they bear a resemblance to the systematically enforced hospitality practiced by itinerant lords such as the Norwegian king. However, the sagas clearly demonstrate that Icelandic chieftains never practiced itinerant lordship of that kind as a constant feature of their leadership, probably because of the lack of both need and ability. For all we can see, measures such as Thorgils's remained spasmodic modes of political violence in the Free State, practiced when called for or allowed by their circumstances.[14]

The descriptions of Thorgils's measures in Borgarfjörður and on the Snæfellsnes peninsula stand in contrast to his reception in Skagafjörður in the North. Read as a whole, his saga neatly captures the conceptual range of the terms in question. A handful of examples may serve to illuminate the vocabulary and its flexible application. In Borgarfjörður, it was key for Thorgils to ally himself at the outset with the important magnates and brothers Thorleifr at Garðar and Boedvarr at Bær Thordarsynir, who were also his kinsmen. The saga makes it clear that their negotiations did not go as smoothly as Thorgils had wished and that Thorleifr remained unsympathetic to his cause. Thorgils did manage, however, to persuade Boedvarr to become his friend and ally, sealing the bond with a generous gift (*gefa*) of a gilded red shield and two brown horses.[15] It is significant, of course, that Thorgils is the giver but not the recipient in this scenario, as it underscores the relative political status of the participants at that given moment. Thorgils could afford to approach most others less cautiously. Thus, Haukr of Álftanes was put under great pressure when Thorgils paid him a visit and terrorized his household, having one unfortunate member of it beaten up to stress the gravity of his demands (Thorgils's initial greeting was "Where is that devil Haukr?" (Hvar er Haukr djöfullinn?)). Haukr had no choice but to give in, and his submission to Thorgils's political will was subsequently dressed up as friendship via ritualistic expressions of mutual affection: Haukr gave (*gaf*) malt, grain, and "a great axe which Thorleifr at Garðar had given him. Groa [Haukr's wife] gave Thorgils a finger ring" (öxi mikla, er Þorleifr í Görðum hafði gefit Hauki. Gróa gaf Þorgilsi fingrgull). The formality of the exchange is further emphasized by the author's comment that once Thorgils had been granted self-judgment he got "a proper reception" (*viðtökr góðar*) from his host, although apparently it was not at the level of a *veizla*. The observation that Thorgils, Haukr, and Groa "parted decorously" (Skilðu þau lagliga) serves the same purpose.[16]

The demands for gifts and contributions combined fiscal and political needs to various degrees. The goods and objects exchanged between Thorgils and Haukr are noteworthy in this respect because of how they apparently combine these elements. While the malt and grain are clearly akin to other contributions in kind, the axe and the ring are not. There is considerable weight in the axe's "biography," since gifts were commonly

Forming Bonds With Followers in Iceland 245

recirculated in pre-modern cultures of power with the explicit notion that there was a venerable and meaningful history of exchange behind them.[17] The fact that Haukr chose to give, or was made to give, a weapon that he himself had received from another magnate (presumably in a political context) made it clear that a political alliance was being created.

The saga makes a general reference to Thorgils's subsequent experiences in Hítarnes and Snæfellsnes, noting tersely that he "was hosted by the leading farmers, and they all gave him gifts" (gisti at inna meiri bónda, ok gáfu allir honum gjafir).[18] A fuller range of concepts is applied, however, in a detailed description of how Thorgils subjugated Egill Solmundarson in Reykholt in Borgarfjörður in the summer of 1255 through an enforced *veizla* and the exchange of gifts. Before feasting merrily and exchanging gifts with Egill as friends, Thorgils witnessed Egill, startled by his unexpected guest, running naked for the farm church and locking himself in. Judging from the subsequent exchange of words in front of and through the church door, this appears to have been a most sensible reaction on Egill's part. Once self-judgment and a truce had been negotiated, however, a "finest *veizla*" (veizla í bezta) was made to celebrate their friendship. The political obligations involved were then spelled out in typically generic terms for pre-modern friendship and with the concepts of kinship and friendship applied: "From now on they should remain kinsmen and fast friends" (En þaðan af skyldi þeir fella saman frændsemi þeira ok fulla vináttu). They parted with *kærleikar* ("cordially" or "with affection") and with Egill submissively presenting his new friend with two brown horses as a gift (*gefa*).[19]

It was altogether different when Thorgils arrived in Skagafjörður, sharing feasts and gifts with his followers. What makes these scenes intriguing, together with those of *Þórðar saga kakala*, is not their typicality but their exceptionality in the corpus. Indeed, the contemporary sagas only contain a few examples, albeit important ones, of chieftains engaging rather broadly in feasting and gift exchange with their followers and forming friendships with them. Significantly, these relate to only two chieftains, Thorgils skarði and Thordr kakali. Chieftains such as Snorri Sturluson, whose political career is described in greater detail in *Sturlunga* than that of most others and who is portrayed as being extremely ambitious in advancing his political cause and tending his network of influence, is never shown exchanging gifts with inferiors or followers. His only gift in Iceland on record was made to his brother Sighvatr for the sake of reconciliation.[20] Apart from chieftaincies given to him in whole or in part, Snorri is only recorded as having accepted gifts from foreign notables. He is also among the most distinguished hosts of feasts in *Sturlunga saga*, yet he never hosted followers or *þingmenn* in any great number, only notables and those closest to him.

Thorgils had a rocky start in Skagafjörður, as he was caught in a fierce dispute with Bishop Heinrekr at Hólar over issues of local authority.

Having reconciled through feasts and gifts, however, Thorgils embarked on a cycle of exchange with his followers in the autumn of 1256:

> Thorgils held another *veizla* in the autumn. He invited the foremost of the local farmers. There was a huge *veizla*, hosted most generously. Also, there were great gifts at the time of parting, and none of those invited left without one. Thorgils was greatly honored by the farmers for this *veizla*.[21]

The farmers reciprocated in the winter by hosting Thorgils in return:

> Most of the farmers invited him thereafter, and during the winter he attended *veizlur* throughout the area, accepting most honorable gifts from them. The district was filled with joy, and the farmers felt they had almost arrived in heaven, having secured such a leader.[22]

Thorgils had previously accrued alliances with notables and kinsmen in the West through feasts and gifts. Once he had become better established:

> Many in the west invited him home, each receiving him with the best provisions available. Sturla, his kinsman, invited him to Hítardalur. It was a most honorable *veizla*. Thorgils was accompanied by many men. . . . Sturla gave Thorgils, his kinsman, great gifts, and they parted with great cordiality. Thorgils went home north, having collected many friends and much honor.[23]

Finally, Thorgils closed the cycle of hospitality with the leading farmers in the region by inviting them to a Christmas feast in 1257 and distributing gifts among them:

> He hosted great *veizlur* and a great Christmas feast. He invited many major farmers and gave them fine gifts. It was a most lavish occasion in terms of numbers and accommodation.[24]

Whether this exchange of hospitality was intended to be a continuing pattern or meant to come to a close is not entirely clear. The end came suddenly, when Thorgils was killed shortly afterwards, in January 1258, by Thorvardr Thorarinsson, a prominent political competitor of the Svinfellingar family.

As noted, the only comparable scenes in the corpus are those of Thordr kakali feasting with his followers and giving them gifts in *Þórðar saga kakala*. While they do not fully match those of Thorgils and the farmers in Skagafjörður they do show a chieftain hosting his followers and establishing friendships with them through gifts. Unlike the case in *Þorgils saga*, the farmers are not shown hosting Thordr in return for his hospitality and gifts.

Thordr invited his followers to two magnificent feasts, the first being a Christmas feast at Mýrar in Dýrafjörður in Vestfirðir in 1243. Thordr had returned from Norway the previous year but faced great opposition from Kolbeinn ungi, the head of the Ásbirningar family in Skagafjörður and a dominant figure in the north, where Thord intended to make his claim for power. He thus set about recruiting men and support in Vestfirðir, the most destitute part of the country. Once he had succeeded there he established friendship with some of his followers through a feast and gifts:

> He invited all the best men in Vestfirðir to his home at Christmas, and hosted a great *veizla* at Mýrar. . . . And when they left, he gave many of them gifts. All were now greater friends of his than before.[25]

A somewhat similar scene is described when Thordr successfully came to his father's domain in Eyjafjörður in the North two years later, although the description's terseness offers little detail: "He hosted a splendid *veizla* on the Mass of St Mary [at Grund in Eyjafjörður], and gave great gifts to those accompanying him north" (Hann hafði veizlu fagra á Maríumessu ok gaf stórgjafir þeim, er honum höfðu norðr fylgt).[26]

Two things stand out in these scenes from *Þorgils saga skarða* and *Þórðar saga kakala* with regard to both the application of friendship to chieftain-follower relationships and, correspondingly, the purpose of feasts and gifts. Firstly, feasting and gift-giving were not routine practices of political leadership but strategically and purposefully deployed expressions of loyalty. In both instances, the ritualized expressions of friendship are tightly framed by political events in which a pretender overcomes great obstacles through the recruitment of reluctant supporters. Thorgils's pleas in Skagafjörður were initially turned down by the farmers before they accepted him, and so it comes as no surprise that subsequent bonding between them was felt to be appropriately expressed in the ritualized and intense form it assumed. *Þórðar saga* is even more dramatic in this respect, describing Thordr's rise to power as a heroic tale of success against all odds. Both his feasts follow landmark events in his political career, at the most logical moments for reinforcing the ties with those closest to him and rewarding their loyalty and support.

Secondly, there is emphasis on exclusivity, as both sagas dutifully underscore that only major farmers were involved. Thorgils invited only *heraðsbændr inir beztu* ("the best farmers of the region") and then *margir stórbændr* ("many major farmers"). The *flestir bændr* ("most of the farmers") who reciprocated by hosting him in return are self-evidently those who had been his guests. The brief description of Thordr's feast at Grund does not disclose whether local farmers were among his guests – it only notes that his accompanying followers were there. As for his Christmas feast at Mýrar, the saga carefully notes that it was only for the *optimates* of Vestfirðir, *allir inir beztu menn* ("all the best men").

Concluding Remarks

Many of the basic assumptions underlying the interpretation of feasting and gift-giving in medieval Iceland and its sagas briefly sketched in this chapter, and principally discussed in relation to two sets of examples from *Sturlunga saga*, are laid out more fully in my *Language of Power*. Its treatment extends to the saga corpus as a whole (as well as to diplomatic material, poetry, law, and other relevant texts), not least the king's sagas and the sagas of the early Icelanders (*Íslendingasögur*). Suffice it to say that the notion of feasts and gifts in medieval Iceland as being primarily an aristocratic, exclusive, and *ad hoc* language of power draws strength from this wider treatment.

Ambiguity is a central theme in the history of feasting and gift-giving, in medieval Iceland and in pre-modern cultures generally. Just as these practices could spell harmony, social cohesion, and stability, they also expressed and fueled competition, strife, and violence. Indeed, an important theme in current revisions of twentieth-century gift-giving scholarship is the growing appreciation of feasts and gifts as a subjective discourse of power rather than as an objective expression of it.[27] As with any language, demonstrative action was subject to interpretation. Its eventual meaning and outcome were thereby highly contextual, subject to circumstances and the sociopolitical negotiation of actors and audience. This notion is central to understanding the function of feasts and gifts both in medieval Iceland and its sagas and in pre-modern cultures of power more generally. Although this aspect may not be central to the present examples from *Þórðar saga kakala* and *Þorgils saga skarða*, it is nevertheless necessary for their full appreciation. This refers especially to the generosity or largesse of Thorgils skarði as a host, which the saga explicitly presents as the result of negotiation between those involved rather than as an objective measure of the transfer of resources from one hand to another. The saga directly states that Thorgils arrived in Skagafjörður "with empty pockets" (tvær hendr tómar) before hosting those who had supported him "most generously," and that in return he was "greatly honored" by his guests.[28]

Notes

1. Main trends in gift-giving scholarship are surveyed with references in Viðar Pálsson, *Language of Power: Feasting and Gift-Giving in Medieval Iceland and Its Sagas* (Ithaca, NY, 2016), 3–44. See also Arnoud-Jan A. Bijsterveld, "The Medieval Gift as Agent of Social Bonding and Power with Afterword: The Study of Gift Giving Since the 1990s," in *Do ut des: Gift Giving, Memoria, and Conflict Management in the Medieval Low Countries*, ed. Arnoud-Jan Bijsterveld (Hilversum, 2007 [2001]), 17–50.
2. Otto Brunner, *Land and Lordship: Structures of Governance in Medieval Austria*, trans. Howard Kaminsky and James Van Horn Melton, rev. 4th ed. (Philadelphia, 1992 [1939]).

Forming Bonds With Followers in Iceland 249

3. For example, Gerd Althoff's studies on the use of *amicitia* in the political cultures of early France and Germany have underscored how restrictedly and strategically *amicitia* was used by kings and major lords and how circumscribed its vertical application was by circumstances and occasion. Interpreting *amicitia* in medieval political culture as primarily an aristocratic social marker is echoed in Florin Curta's rejection of a "gift economy" in relation to Merovingian and Carolingian aristocratic and courtly culture, to give another example. See principally Gerd Althoff, *Family, Friends and Followers: Political and Social Bonds in Early Medieval Europe*, trans. Christopher Carroll (Cambridge, 2004 [1990]); Gerd Althoff, *Amicitiae und Pacta: Bündnis, Einung, Politik und Gebetsgedenken im beginnenden 10. Jahrhundert* (Hannover, 1992); Florin Curta, "Merovingian and Carolingian Gift Giving," *Speculum* 81, no. 3 (2006): 671–99.
4. Jón Viðar Sigurðsson, *Chieftains and Power in the Icelandic Commonwealth*, trans. Jean Lundskær-Nielsen (Odense, 1999 [1993]).
5. Translated and revised as Jón Viðar Sigurðsson, *Viking Friendship: The Social Bond in Iceland and Norway, c. 900–1300* (Ithaca, NY, 2017).
6. Ibid., 11–12.
7. The cases of Thordr kakali and Thorgils skarði are treated in greater depth and wider context than possible here in Pálsson, *Language of Power*, 167–88, esp. 175–84.
8. See Sigurðsson, *Chieftains and Power*, 39–62; Gunnar Karlsson, *Goðamenning: Staða og áhrif goðorðsmanna í þjóðveldi Íslendinga* (Reykjavík, 2004), 63–86.
9. For a recent treatment and overview, see Sverrir Jakobsson's introduction to Íslenzk fornrit, vols. 31–32, *Hákonar saga Hákonarsonar, Bǫglunga saga, Magnúss saga lagabœtis*, ed. Sverrir Jakobsson, Þorleifur Hauksson, and Tor Ulset (Reykjavík, 2013). More on the protagonists in Auður Magnúsdóttir's contribution in chapter 11 in this volume.
10. See Úlfar Bragason, *Ætt og saga: Um frásagnarfræði Sturlungu eða Íslendinga sögu hinnar miklu* (Reykjavík, 2010), 187–262; Stephen N. Tranter, *Sturlunga Saga: The Rôle of the Creative Compiler* (Frankfurt am Main, 1987); Helgi Þorláksson, "*Sturlunga* – tilurð og markmið," *Gripla* 23 (2012): 53–92.
11. The terminology and definitions of feasts and gifts are surveyed in Pálsson, *Language of Power*, 57–67, *passim*. For the dynamics of *veizlur* in the king's sagas and its legal meaning, see ibid., 57–119.
12. Sturl II, 120–25, cf. also 170–76.
13. On chieftains and finances, see, e.g., Jesse Byock, *Medieval Iceland* (Berkeley, 1988), 77–102; Sigurðsson, *Chieftains and Power*, 101–19; Karlsson, *Goðamenning*, 166–78, 316–33. On contributions and levies in the context of gift-giving and hospitality, see Pálsson, *Language of Power*, 170–75.
14. Pálsson, *Language of Power*, 170–73.
15. Sturl II, 122.
16. Sturl II, 123–25, quoted from 123, 124, and 125 successively. Translations are my own throughout. *Sturlunga saga* is available in English translation: *Sturlunga saga*, 2 vols., trans. Julia H. McGrew (New York, 1970–74).
17. Pálsson, *Language of Power*, 197–98.
18. Sturl II, 125.
19. Sturl II, 170–76, quoted from 172, 173, and 176, successively.
20. Sturl II, 362.
21. "Aðra veizlu hafði Þorgils um haustit. Bauð hann þá til sín heraðsbóndum inum beztum. Var þá veizla fjölmenn ok veitt með inni mestu rausn. Váru ok

gjafir stórar at útlausnum, ok engi fór gjaflaust í brott, sá er boðit hafði verit. Af þessari veizlu fekk Þorgils mikla virðing af bóndum." Sturl II, 207.
22. "Buðu flestir bændr honum þá heim, ok fór hann at veizlum um vetrinn um allt herað ok þá af bóndum inar sæmiligstu gjafir. Var nú í heraði gleði mikil, ok þóttust bændr þá hafa náliga himin höndum tekit, er þeir hafa fengit slíkan höfðingja." Sturl II, 207.
23. "Buðu margir menn honum heim vestr þar, ok tók hverr við honum eftir föngum inum beztum. Þá bauð honum Sturla heim, frændi hans, í Hítardal. Var þar veizla in virðuligsta. Var þar margt manna með Þorgilsi. . . . Gaf Sturla gjafir góðar Þorgilsi, frænda sínum, ok skilðu þeir með kærleikum miklum. Fór Þorgils þá heim norðr, ok hafði hann aflat sér vini marga ok mikla sæmð." Sturl II, 207.
24. "hafði veizlur miklar og jólaboð mikit. Bauð hann þá til sín mörgum stórbóndum ok gaf þeim stórgjafir. Var þar in mesta rausn bæði sakir fjölmennis ok hýbýla." Sturl II, 216–17.
25. "En at jólum bauð hann til sín öllum [inum] beztum mönnum ór Vestfjörðum. Hafði hann þá veizlu mikla á Mýrum. . . . En er menn fóru í brott, veitti hann mörgum mönnum gjafir. Váru þá allir meiri vinir hans en áðr." Sturl II, 40.
26. Sturl II, 70.
27. For medieval Iceland, see Pálsson, *Language of Power*. For medieval Europe, see *Negotiating the Gift: Premodern Figurations of Exchange*, ed. Gadi Algazi, Valentin Groebner, and Bernhard Jussen (Göttingen, 2003).
28. Sturl II, 196.

Dedicated Bibliography

Algazi, Gadi, Valentin Groebner, and Bernhard Jussen, eds. *Negotiating the Gift: Premodern Figurations of Exchange*, Veröffentlichungen des Max-Planck-Instituts für Geschichte 188. Göttingen, 2003.

Althoff, Gerd. *Amicitiae und Pacta: Bündnis, Einung, Politik und Gebetsgedenken im beginnenden 10. Jahrhundert*, Schriften der Monumenta Germaniae Historica 37. Hannover, 1992.

Althoff, Gerd. *Family, Friends and Followers: Political and Social Bonds in Medieval Europe* [*Verwandte, Freunde und Getreue: Zum politischen Stellenwert der Gruppenbindungen im früheren Mittelalter*]. Translated by Christopher Carroll. Cambridge, 2004.

Bijsterveld, Arnoud-Jan A. "The Medieval Gift as Agent of Social Bonding and Power with Afterword: The Study of Gift Giving Since the 1990s." In *Do ut des: Gift Giving, Memoria, and Conflict Management in the Medieval Low Countries*, edited by Arnoud-Jan Bijsterveld, 17–50. Hilversum, 2007 [2001].

Bragason, Úlfar. *Ætt og saga: Um frásagnarfræði Sturlungu eða Íslendinga sögu hinnar miklu*. Reykjavík, 2010.

Brunner, Otto. *Land and Lordship: Structures of Governance in Medieval Austria*. Translated by Howard Kaminsky and James Van Horn Melton. Rev. 4th ed. Philadelphia, 1992 [1939].

Byock, Jesse L. *Medieval Iceland*. Berkeley, 1988.

Curta, Florin. "Merovingian and Carolingian Gift Giving." *Speculum* 81, no. 3 (2006): 671–99.

Jakobsson, Sverrir. "Introduction." In *Hákonar saga Hákonarsonar, Bǫglunga saga, Magnúss saga lagabœtis*, edited by Sverrir Jakobsson, Þorleifur Hauksson, and Tor Ulset Íslenzk fornrit, 1: v–lxvii, 2: v–lxvi, 31–32. Reykjavík, 2013.

Pálsson, Viðar. *Language of Power: Feasting and Gift-Giving in Medieval Iceland and Its Sagas.* Ithaca, NY, 2016.

Sigurðsson, Jón Viðar. *Chieftains and Power in the Icelandic Commonwealth.* Translated by Jean Lundskær-Nielsen. Odense, 1999 [1993].

Sigurðsson, Jón Viðar. *Viking Friendship: The Social Bond in Iceland and Norway, c. 900–1300.* Ithaca, NY, 2017.

Sturlunga Saga, 2 vols. Translated by Julia H. McGrew. New York, 1970–74.

Þorláksson, Helgi. "*Sturlunga* – tilurð og markmið." *Gripla* 23 (2012): 53–92.

Tranter, Stephen N. *Sturlunga Saga: The Rôle of the Creative Compiler*, Europäische Hochschulschriften 1. Deutsche Sprache und Literatur 941. Frankfurt, 1987.

13 Strength Through Weakness
Regent Elites Under Kings Inge, Sigurd, and Magnus Haraldsson

Ian Peter Grohse

In 1137 Magnus IV the Blind, the deposed and embittered king of Norway, traveled abroad to Sweden and Denmark seeking allies in his struggle to reclaim the crown. There he professed that

> Norway would lie open to grabs if any great leaders wanted to go for it, as there was no king over the country and the government of the realm was in the hands of landed men, while those landed men that were first appointed as rulers had all fallen out with each other because of their jealousy.[1]

His claims were half-truths. The title of king in fact belonged to three dynasts, Inge, Sigurd, and Magnus Haraldsson, each of whom had been acclaimed at regional assemblies (*things*) while still in infancy or adolescence the previous year. Nonetheless, Magnus IV's claim casts light on the precarious state of Norwegian politics, in which kings, the notional doyens of political authority, were mere weaklings, and magnates, their nominal servants, were the *de facto* elites of monarchical governance.

Incidences of royal minority were remarkably frequent in twelfth-century Norway, where no fewer than seven underage candidates were thrust forth for succession, often simultaneously and under dubious pretexts.[2] Paradigms of succession that increasingly prioritized heredity over merit positioned these youths in line for the throne although they lacked the cognitive and physical capacities to direct affairs of state.[3] With no obvious demarcation between guardianship of the king and regency of the kingdom,[4] nor between personal and political spheres,[5] those closest to the royal person readily assumed positions over these frail monarchs, seizing shares of government, harvesting benefices of land, or securing royal sponsorship for their own political campaigns in the process.[6]

The following examines some of the strategies by which members of Norway's political elite exploited underage kings to attain authority in the twelfth century. The early reigns of kings Inge, Sigurd, and Magnus Haraldsson (1136–c.1155), which are especially well documented, will serve as the primary cases for analysis.[7] Under the fictitious pretext that these kings could assess and consent to counsel, royal caretakers readily pushed their own agendas and elevated themselves to higher echelons of governmental authority. Scrutinizing these strategies can shed light on caretakers' changing status as "elites," those "members of a society who hold a socially elevated position, whether in terms of wealth, political power, cultural prestige, social networks, knowledge, or some other relevant asset, and who are recognized by others as legitimately possessing such a position in a certain context" (see the introduction to this volume). The discussion will focus on three avenues – maternity, fosterage, and council – by which elites advocated themselves as legitimate custodians of royal governance.

As a secondary aim, this chapter will also address the consequences of these strategies. Magnus IV's assertion that the absence of a capable monarch weakened the kingdom by engendering rivalry among Norway's political elites is frequently implied in modern surveys, which view royal minorities as inherently contentious.[8] Before King Haakon V Magnusson (r. 1299–1319) introduced formal conventions for regency in the early fourteenth century,[9] the succession of children enabled intervention from a range of social and political elites with self-serving and, at times competing, interests. At the same time, the absence of a forceful and unifying ruler could widen political fissures by allowing elites to forge separate, rival factions around the different royal figureheads. In this vein, elites' exploitation of underage kings is often viewed as an expression of the political fragmentation and volatility that characterized the so-called civil wars (1130–1240) in Norwegian history.[10]

The cases in focus may nuance this view by highlighting moments of stability. The simultaneous ascension of multiple elites during the minorities of kings Inge, Sigurd, and Magnus Haraldsson suggests that the succession of weak monarchs could prompt a fruitful redistribution and balancing of power across a broad political plane. The following thus advances Hans Jacob Orning's critique of the centralist and institutional tendencies in research on high medieval Norway.[11] Whereas scholars have often viewed the lack of a functional central executive and the resulting dispersal of power as digressions from state development and occasions for disorder, the following supports the thesis that division could facilitate stability by hindering despotism and by satiating demands for authority and wealth among a range of political elites.

Maternity

Mothers of underage dynasts were unable to assume custody of the royal estate, yet they could exploit their maternal role to exert informal influence over royal governance.[12] This is witnessed in the political enterprises of Ingrid Rognvaldsdottir, mother to the young King Inge. Ingrid was a poster child for the transnational brand of networking practiced among elites in the medieval Nordic kingdoms.[13] The daughter of Prince Rognvald Roundhead of Sweden, Ingrid was unhappily married to Henrik Brokeleg, son of King Svend Estridsen of Denmark, before her betrothal to King Harald Gille of Norway soon after her first husband's death in 1134.[14] While Ingrid's elite *social* status was well established prior to giving birth to a presumptive heir in Norway, she only emerged as a *political* force by vigorously promoting her son as royal successor in the wake of King Harald's death in 1136. Ingrid convened with magnates and the late king's retainers in Bergen before personally traveling to her two-year-old son, who was in fosterage in eastern Norway (see later in the chapter). There she prompted speakers of the regional assembly to acclaim Inge as their king, and although sagas are silent regarding Ingrid's function at that convention, we may speculate that, given her role in initiating the process, she also commanded an audience there.[15] Her status as royal consort to King Harald positioned Ingrid near the heart of political affairs, but it was her relationship to the late king's son that facilitated her participation in governance.

However, Ingrid's political success could not have been based solely on her maternal relationship to Inge, for her influence extended beyond that biological line. In addition to orchestrating her own son's acclamation, she also initiated the succession of Inge's four-year-old half-brother, Sigurd, another royal claimant born of King Harald and his concubine, Tora Guthormsdottir. Prior to departing for eastern Norway, Ingrid and the late king's retainers dispatched an envoy to central Norway to urge the people there to accept Sigurd as king.[16] In contrast to Ingrid, Sigurd's mother Tora remained inconsequential in a political sense, demonstrating that maternity alone did not enhance one's political influence. These women's wider social networks may explain this discrepancy.[17] Ingrid inherited an exceptionally elevated status among Scandinavia's social elite. She was the product of a royal house and was, from her first marriage, mother to Magnus Henriksson, a Danish potentate with a strong claim to his grandfather's Swedish throne.[18] Whereas Ingrid's social network spanned the widest and highest echelons of Scandinavian society, Tora's was comparatively circumscribed. The daughter of Guttorm Greybeard, a prominent landowner in central Norway, Tora represented a link between the elites of her home region and the royal house, but she had no apparent relevance on a national or transnational stage.[19]

The extramarital nature of Tora's relationship with King Harald may also have diminished her political influence in a formal sense. Prior to the late twelfth century, Norwegian customs of succession showed equal deference to the claims of royal children born in and out of wedlock.[20] However, in an age in which legitimate birth, and thus marriage, was gaining political relevance in the eyes of the Church, the concubine Tora was perhaps less well suited for affairs of state.[21] This was also the case for Bjadok, a concubine of the late King Harald prior to his emigration to

Norway from Britain in the 1120s. The mother of Oystein Haraldsson, the purported offspring of that affair, Bjadok journeyed across the North Sea in connection with her son's campaign for succession in 1142.[22] Her role, however, was notably passive. Invited by three Norwegian magnates, Bjadok merely corroborated Oystein's claims of royal descent, and did not meddle in the dynast's executive actions.

Whereas neither Tora nor Bjadok counseled or served in their sons' regency councils, Ingrid ensured herself a more permanent station within monarchical governance, later marrying Ottar Birting, a rising star in Norwegian politics and counselor to kings Inge and Sigurd during their minorities (see later in the chapter), and providing personal advice to King Inge in the early years of his adult reign.[23] Ingrid's reappearance in this capacity suggests that she continued to act as a trusted, if informal, member of the young king's network of *de facto* regents. This is witnessed by her intervention in Inge's troubled relations with his half-brother following the murder of Inge's retainer at the hands of Sigurd's men in 1155. Scolding her son for his failure to retaliate, she explained that he would remain a feeble king if he stood idle while enemies slaughtered his men like swine. Although Inge initially argued with his mother, he was eventually convinced to take action by his most trusted counselor, Gregorius, who intervened in support of Ingrid.[24] Although brief, this glimpse into Ingrid's role in the most intimate of royal councils demonstrates her continued relevance as a member of the governing elite: as a doting mother, a calculating strategist, and a respected, albeit informal, associate of royal council.

In reflecting on her political agency, it is the latter point – her cooperation with magnates in royal councils – that deserves the most attention. Both at the outset of the child kings' regency in 1136 and in the later episode from 1155, Ingrid's power was not sovereign, but willingly shared with other members of Norway's elite. By encouraging the participation of magnates in regency, Ingrid facilitated a degree of political accord that had eluded an earlier queen, Alfiva, mother and regent of the young king Svend Alfivason between 1030 and 1035. Whereas Alfiva's monopoly on power made "the people of the country . . . great enemies of hers, both at that time and for ever after,"[25] Ingrid enjoyed the respect of magnates, encouraged the distribution of power, and facilitated consensus among multiple members of Norway's elite.

Fosterage

Artificial bonds of kinship provided other avenues for elites to exert influence over underage dynasts. Fosterage, a form of adoptive kinship common throughout northern Europe in the Middle Ages, was a particularly expedient means by which elites with no biological relation to the royal house might improve their social and political stations.[26] At least three of King Harald Gille's children – Sigurd, Inge, and Magnus – were fostered by regional magnates after the king's death in 1136. While the magnates' authority was limited to their respective home regions prior to their nomination as royal fosterers, their assumption of pseudo-parental authority over the young kings enabled them to expand their influence across a wider political landscape and determine the delegation of fiefs and benefices.[27]

Fosterage enabled unrelated families to substitute artificial bonds for biological ones, engendering in both parties a sense of devotion that could equal or surpass natal relationships in strength and socio-political relevance.[28] It was a basis for mutually beneficial commitments, "integrating both families in networks of protection and prestige."[29] Whereas lateral arrangements between families of similar status served as a mechanism of alliance-building in minimally stratified societies, vertical forms articulated lordship by emphasizing the socio-political standing of individuals and families on an ascending plane.[30] Situations involving royal children almost always entailed some understanding of the biological family's superiority, and an acceptance of the fostering family's deference.[31]

Multiple references to incidents of royal fosterage in *Heimskringla* suggest that Norway's kings were customarily raised in some form of adoptive care and that the practice of fosterage was pivotal for young kings cultivating their social and political affiliations both at home and abroad.[32] If obtaining favor with the royal house drove families to shoulder the burden of child-rearing, pragmatism may have motivated kings to deliver their children into fosterage. The ambulant nature of kingship and the expectation that rulers would personally oversee the execution of justice and military campaigns left little room for child-care. The high number and equal status of royal offspring presented further challenges, as heirs of extramarital unions demanded the same degree of attention as those born in wedlock. It was thus expedient to distribute the demands of child-rearing among loyal cohorts outside the nuclear household.[33]

Fathering at least eight children, including four male successors, in various regions of the Norse world, King Harald Gille was unable to oversee the upbringing of his offspring. His three youngest sons were placed in the care of baronial fosterers in central, eastern, and western Norway before his death in 1136. These men appear to have commanded a degree of political influence in their own regions prior to assuming custody of the young kings. Sigurd's foster father, Sada-Gyrd Baardsson, first appears on record as the young dynast's surrogate caretaker in 1136, although his own sons, Sigurd and Philip Gyrdsson, are recorded as two of the magnates who defended Norway against Wendish assaults in 1135.[34] Inge's foster father, Amund Gyrdsson, is referred to in the sagas as "a grandson of Logbersason," a prominent lawman in eastern Norway during the reign of King Olav Haraldsson (1067–93).[35] Magnus's foster father, Kyrping-Orm Sveinsson, was a member of the prominent

Støðle dynasty of chieftains of Sunnhordland, western Norway, and was the great-grandson of Erlend of Gjerde, a leader in the free-farmer opposition to King Olav Haraldsson in 1030.[36] Although these men enjoyed social prestige in their respective regions, and presumably some previous association with the crown, none are recorded in narratives prior to their nomination as royal fosterers. Like Ingrid Rognvaldsdottir, they enhanced their initial elite standing through exploitation of "kinship," however contrived, with the underage kings.

We know nothing about the political maneuvers of King Magnus's foster father, Kyrping-Orm, who retired from the political spotlight with the death of his foster son in or around 1141.[37] However, he established a precedent of association with the royal house – his sons, Ogmund Denger and Erling Skakke, became central members of kings Inge and Sigurd's councils in later years.[38] We know slightly more about the political fortunes of Sada-Gyrd and Amund. Despite their ascension to the ambit of royal governance, the influence of these fosterers did not initially expand beyond their home regions. This is due in part to the immediate disorder caused by crippling military assaults by rival pretenders to the throne, Sigurd Slembe and Magnus Sigurdsson. King Inge's foster father, Amund, worked closely with Tjostolv Aalason, a former retainer of King Harald Gille and one of the other men who supported Inge's acclamation, to quell the threat in the eastern part of the country.[39] King Sigurd's foster father, Sada-Gyrd, was comparatively passive in central Norway prior to a series of raids along Norway's western coasts that prompted him to organize a pursuit of the raiders.[40] Their elevation on a "national" stage came in 1139, when their respective parties joined forces to create a centralized regency coalition (see later in the chapter). Remarkably, neither of these men used their status as fosterers to claim superior positions within that coalition. Rather, they formed part of a wider elite body that successfully controlled Norway's political landscape for over a decade.

Friendship and Counsel

Elites with no familial or pseudo-familial ties to the royal line could advance their political standing by feigning service as the kings' friends and counselors. Despite their theoretical sovereignty, in practice infant and adolescent monarchs were incapable of freely recruiting their advisors or passing judgment on their counsel.[41] Those with access to a young king could thus make a show of subservience whilst dictating strategies to their own advantage. In addition to Inge's foster father, the "council" (*ráði*) that supported his acclamation included Tjostolv Aalason and "many other great leaders" (*margir aðrir stórir höfðingjar*).[42] Similarly, the council that acclaimed Sigurd comprised several regional magnates, including Ottar Birting, Peter Sauda-Ulfsson, Guttorm Asolfsson, and

Ottar Balli, as well as "a large number of other leaders" (*fjǫldi annarra hǫfðingja*).[43]

Rather than unabashedly executing governance over the heads of their nominal rulers, these men sought legitimacy for their activities by staging sessions of council with the young kings. This reflected reverence for contemporary ideals of monarchical governance, in which counsel was seen as a feature of just rule.[44] In order to feign the king's authority, and mask or rebrand their practical domination of royal affairs, caretakers employed "fictions of adult rule" that simulated mediation between capable commanders (the kings) and their cabinets of trusted advisors (their magnate supporters).[45] Two episodes exemplify how fictional devices served to secure royal sanction for the establishment of a unified regency council in 1139. In the first episode, King Inge's "counselors" composed a letter to King Sigurd and his men to pitch a potential coalition:

> King Haraldr's son King Ingi sends God's and his own greetings to his brother King Sigurðr and to Sáða-Gyrðr, Ǫgmundr sviptir (Loss), Óttarr birtingr and all landed men, followers and housecarls and all the common people, rich and poor, young and old. All are acquainted with the problems that we have and also with our youth, that you are reckoned to be five winters old, and I three winters. We can undertake nothing except what we do with the help of our friends and kind people. It seems to me that now I and my friends are more afflicted with the trouble and distress that we both suffer than you or your friends. Now be so kind as to go to see me as soon as possible and with as many men as possible, and let us be both together whatever happens. Now he is our greatest friend who continues to ensure that we may be always on the best of terms and treated in as equal a manner as possible in everything.[46]

By presenting the three-year-old Inge in the first person, counselors reinforced the fiction that Inge consented to their proposals and endorsed his "friends'" dominance of executive governance. Friendship in medieval societies connoted "informal patron-client relationships that were personal, voluntary and asymmetrical, yet nonetheless clearly reciprocal," and was expressed by exchanging gifts and support.[47] Although young kings could scarcely enter into reciprocal relationships on their own terms, the document refers to "friends" five times, suggesting that the magnates were eager to access gifts of political authority and wealth through a fictitious contract with the toddler.[48]

Ottar Birting, a leading member of King Sigurd's regency council[49] and the stepfather of King Inge by way of his recent marriage to Ingrid Rognvaldsdottir,[50] was instrumental in initiating the coalition. At a staged session of council in central Norway, Ottar sought to obtain the young

Sigurd's approval, first reading the letter aloud before directing his counsel to the young king:

> Now I will make known to you my mind and find out whether the wishes of King Sigurðr and other men of the ruling class are in accordance with it, that you, King Sigurðr, should also make ready such force as is willing to follow you to defend your land and go with as large numbers as are available to meet your brother King Ingi as soon as you can, and that each of you should support the other in all useful matters, and may almighty God [support] both of you. Now we wish to hear what you have to say, king.[51]

Sigurd was borne into the room by Peter Sauda-Ulfsson, a warrior and another of the child's early supporters.[52] Although the five-year-old was presumably capable of entering unaided, such a mundane entrance by an unimposing figure would have diminished the weight of his declarations, particularly as they concerned matters of war, a man's affair. By hoisting the king into the arms of a warrior, the magnates enhanced the king's position, placing him at eye level with his men, while illustrating the role of his caretakers-cum-counselors in bearing the king and shouldering important matters of state.[53] Prompted by his instructors, Sigurd proclaimed that "if I have my way I shall go to see my brother King Ingi as soon as I can."[54]

These performances bolstered the magnates' control of governance, allowing them to enhance not only their political, but also their economic, status. Narratives emphasize this aspect of performance with respect to King Inge, the weaker of the two brothers. *Heimskringla* recounts that Inge, physically handicapped and with a mild disposition, was "cheerful of speech and pleasant with his friends, generous with wealth, mostly letting leading men make decisions about the government with him."[55] This is strikingly similar to the epitaph of his late father, King Harald, whom *Heimskringla* describes as

> affable, cheerful, playful, humble, generous, so that he spared nothing for his friends, open to advice, so that he let others make decisions with him on anything they wanted. All this brought him friendship and praise. Many men of the ruling class then came to be on good terms with him.[56]

Unlike his father, whose disparaged legacy as a weak individual in scholarship is unmerited,[57] Inge's generosity was, to some degree, born of personal weakness. His delegation of authority was coerced, rather than willed, and he remained dependent on counselors throughout his life.[58]

Beyond illustrating the rhetorical and ritualistic devices for staging royal consent, these episodes demonstrate the willingness of magnates from different regions, pursing different personal economic and political interests, to share rather than monopolize power. Inge and Sigurd's correspondence in 1139 marked the end of a period of factional regency, when separate constellations of magnates dealt independently with executive and military contingencies in their respective regions, and the beginning of a single, conglomerated council for the entire kingdom (*landráðum*).[59] Many of the "friends" named or alluded to in these episodes remained in control of governance and presided over a period of peace for over a decade until the kings reached adulthood in the mid-1150s. This consensual and broad partition of authority would be contrasted two decades later, when Erling Skakke, father to the underage King Magnus Erlingsson, monopolized regency in his son's name. His ascension to power correlated to an intensification of political unrest, and while multiple factors may have contributed to these tensions, the despotic nature of his government, which precluded the participation of co-regents, may have spurred resistance by frustrating the advancement of other elites.[60]

Conclusion

It is seductive to study medieval monarchies through the prism of individual kings, to scrutinize the nature of kingship in respect to the successes and failures of charismatic (adult) rulers. However, in the shadows of these accomplished rulers were other, less capable monarchs who relied on adept men and women to negotiate the highest tiers of executive governance. The preceding discussion therefore underscores the fruitfulness of an alternative approach to monarchical rule, one that seeks the sources of elite power vis-à-vis the weakest of rulers. This compels us to look at other actors who capitalized on that weakness for their own political gain. Moving beyond the royal person, we see which members of Norwegian society accessed and represented underage kings in political arenas, and on what authority. By scrutinizing the avenues, mechanisms, and consequences for political ascension during royal minorities, our aim was to shed light on less celebrated, yet more influential, segments of Norway's governing elites.

While all the men and women who gained access to kings Inge, Sigurd, and Magnus during their minorities were elites in terms of the definition in the introduction to the present volume, they pursued different avenues for advancing and legitimizing their status. As the daughter of a Scandinavian dynast and the consort of the late King Harald Gille, Ingrid Rognvaldsdottir already enjoyed cultural and social prestige and extensive social networks. It was not until the death of her husband, however, that she used her status as mother to a royal heir, Inge, to participate in executive activities. Similarly, while those who fostered the kings were regional potentates, their influence did not extend beyond their home arenas prior to their nomination as the kings' primary caretakers.[61] It was only as the kings' parental surrogates that they reached the highest tiers of monarchical governance. Still others advanced their political station by "befriending" kings, professing to "help" their infantile monarchs whilst practically seizing the reigns of executive authority.

The different avenues through which men and women obtained political power and cultural prestige demonstrate the mutability of royal governance in twelfth-century Norway, where the inchoate nature of monarchical institutions created a wide playing field for political advancement. Aspirations to political influence could prompt conflict between rival elites and, as is often advanced in scholarship on twelfth-century Norway, precipitate a destabilizing scramble for power. Indeed, perspectives that evaluate the stability of governance through the strength of kings invariably view the absence of strong royal executives as a prelude to political turmoil. However, the preceding examples offer evidence to the contrary. While the elites examined here hailed from different regions, occupied different social stations, and pursued different personal agendas, their cooperative efforts to govern Norway on the behalf of underage kings leveled the playing field and created a degree of stability for over a decade between 1139 and 1155. In this respect, the weakness of kings provided elites with opportunities for mutual strength.

Notes

1. *Heimskringla*, 1–3 vols., trans. Alison Finlay and Anthony Faulkes (London, 2011–15), here, vol. 3, 187–88. Hkr 3, 306: "Nóregr mundi liggja lauss fyrir, ef nǫkkurir stórir hǫfðingjar vildi til sækja, er engi var konungr yfir landinu ok lendra manna forrád var þar yfir ríkinu, en þeir lendir menn, er fyrst váru til forráða teknir, þá var nú hverr ósáttr við annan fyrir ǫfundar sakir." Cf. Msk vol. 2, 182–83.
2. These included Inge I, Sigurd II, and Magnus Haraldsson, Haakon II Sigurdsson, Magnus V Erlingsson, Sigurd Markusfoster, and Guttorm Sigurdsson. Hereditary succession in Norway was neither automatic nor exclusive in the twelfth century. All male offspring of a king, legitimate and illegitimate, had an equal hereditary right to claim kingship. Although activation of a claim often presupposed some merit, many feeble kings held royal title. See e.g., Knut Helle, "The Norwegian Kingdom: Succession Disputes and Consolidation," in *The Cambridge History of Scandinavia, Vol. 1, Prehistory to 1520*, ed. Knut Helle (Cambridge, 2003), 369–91 at 370–73. On joint rule see Narve Bjørgo, "Samkongedøme kontra einekongedøme," *Historisk tidsskrift* (N) 49 (1970): 1–33; Sverre Bagge, "Samkongedømme og enekongedømme," *Historisk tidsskrift* (N) 54 (1975): 239–74.
3. Sverre Bagge, *From Viking Stronghold to Christian Kingdom: State Formation in Norway, c. 900–1350* (Copenhagen, 2010), 46. Norway was not unique in this respect, as royal minority was a feature of most medieval monarchical societies. Charles Beem, "Woe to Thee, O Land! The Introduction," in *The Royal Minorities of Medieval and Early Modern England*, ed. Charles Beem (New York, 2008), 1–16; Thilo Offergeld, *Reges pueri: Das Königtum Minderjähriger im frühen Mittelalter* (Hannover, 2001); Theo Kölzer, "Das Königtum Minderjähriger im fränkisch-deutschen Mittelalter:

Eine Skizze," *Historische Zeitschrift* 251 (1990): 291–323; Mark Ormrod, "Coming to Kingship: Boy Kings and the Passage to Power in Fourteenth-Century England," in *Rites of Passage: Cultures of Transition in the Fourteenth Century*, ed. Nicola McDonald and Mark Ormrod (York, 2004), 31–50. Pauline Puppel distinguishes between proxies (*Stellvertretungen*), established at the behest of the reigning monarch or prince, and regencies (*Regentschaft*), arranged without the consent of the monarch or prince. See Pauline Puppel, *Regentin: Vormundschaftliche Herrschaft in Hessen 1500–1700* (Frankfurt am Main and New York, 2004), 35–36. The tenth-century Bishop Salomon of Constance decried royal minorities when, in referring to the young East Frankish King Louis III (also known as "Louis the Child"), he complained that "For a long time the weakness of the child even now acting with the authority of a king has robbed us of a leader. His age is neither suited to war nor capable in law." ("Principe destituit multo nos tempore languor / Infantilis adhuc perfungens nomine regis: Aetas nec pugne est habilis nec legibus apta."), quoted and translated into German in Kölzer, "Das Königtum Minderjährige," 291. Retranslated here from the Latin.
4. On the king's two bodies (natural and political), see Ernst Kantorowicz, *The King's Two Bodies: A Study in Mediaeval Political Theology* (Princeton, 1958); John Watts, *Henry VI and the Politics of Kingship* (Cambridge, 1996), 28–32, 106. In theory, the unmitigated agency of kings precluded others from legitimately claiming surrogacy of royal governance, although practical concerns demanded some form of regency for the kingdom. See Puppel, *Regentin*, 37; Anders Laudage, "Das Problem der Vormundschaft über Otto III," in *Kaiserin Theophanu: Begegnung des Ostens und Westens um die Wende des ersten Jahrtausends. Gedenkschrift zum 1000: Todesjahr der Kaiserin*, ed. Anton v. Euw and Peter Schreiner (Cologne, 1991), 271–76; Kölzer, "Das Königtum Minderjähriger," 323, who distinguishes between the political ideals and practical realities of regency.
5. For intersections of social, familial, and political spheres see e.g., Gerd Althoff, *Verwandte, Freunde und Getreue: Zum politischen Stellenwert der Gruppenbindungen im früheren Mittelalter* (Darmstadt, 1990); Gerhard Lubich, *Verwandtsein: Lesearten einer politisch-sozialen Beziehung im Frühmittelalter (6.-11. Jahrhundert)* (Cologne, Weimar and Vienna, 2008); Lars Hermansson, *Släkt, vänner och makt: En studie av elitens politiska kultur i 1100-talets Danmark* (Gothenburg, 2000).
6. Bagge, "Samkongedømme og enekongedømme," 252; Sverre Bagge, "The Structure of the Political Factions in the Internal Struggles of Scandinavian Countries During the High Middle Ages," *Scandinavian Journal of History* 24 (1999): 299–320 at 303; Bagge, *Viking Stronghold*, 47–48.
7. A lost kings' saga called *Hryggjarstykki*, a near-contemporary account, served as the main source for accounts of their reigns in four surviving narratives: *Heimskringla*, *Morkinskinna*, *Fagrskinna*, and *Ágrip*. See Tommy Danielsson, *Sagorna om Norges kungar fran Magnús góði till Magnús Erlingsson* (Ludvika, 2002). For a previous study with a different focus, see Ian Peter Grohse, "Fra småbarns munn: Myte og propaganda under kongene Inge og Sigurd Haraldsson c. 1136–1139," *Historisk tidsskrift* (N) 95 (2016): 473–91.
8. In discussing regencies in the late thirteenth and early fourteenth centuries, Bagge comments that "periods of regency show greater vacillation which in turn indicates that the absence of a firm authority gave room for a greater variety of interests." Bagge, *Viking Stronghold*, 356.
9. In 1302, King Haakon stipulated that twelve men should share the regency for kings who were minors, each with specific duties and obligations and all

subject to annual evaluations. See NGL vol. 3, 45–55, here 45: "huorso rikis stiorn skal fara medan konongr er i barndome."
10. Factional loyalties to different royal figureheads are said to have engendered sharper divisions and animosity between magnates, e.g., by Jón Viðar Sigurðsson and Anne Irene Riisøy, *Norsk Historie 800–1536* (Oslo, 2011), 99. See also Claus Krag, *Norges historie fram til 1319* (Oslo, 2000), 105–6; Bagge, *Viking Stronghold*, 46.
11. Introduction to Hans Jacob Orning, *Unpredictability and Presence: Norwegian Kingship in the High Middle Ages* (Leiden, 2008), 1–50; Hans Jacob Orning, "Conflict and Social (Dis)order in Norway c. 1030–1160," in *Disputing Strategies in Medieval Scandinavia*, ed. Kim Esmark et al. (Leiden, 2013), 45–82; Hans Jacob Orning, "Borgerkrig og statsutvikling i Norge i middelalderen – en revurdering," *Historisk tidsskrift* (N) 93 (2014): 193–216. Cf. Sverre Bagge, "Borgerkrig og statsutvikling – svar til Hans Jacob Orning," *Historisk tidsskrift* (N) 94 (2015): 91–110.
12. Although females were not regents in a legal sense, we witness "irregular, interim de-facto regencies that serve to support, rather than substitute." (Author's translation of Kölzer, "Das Königtum Minderjähriger," 314.) See also François L. Ganshof, "Le statut de la femme dans la monarchie franque," *Recueils de la Société Jean Bodin* 12 (1962): 5–58. While medieval sources are silent on queens' legal authority as regents (Puppel, *Regentin*, 36), they could exert informal influence over the monarch and the wider political arena. See Ingvild Øye, "Kvinner, kjønn og samfunn: Fra vikingtid til reformasjon," in *Med kjønnsperspektiv på norsk historie*, ed. Ida Blom and Sølvi Sogner (Oslo, 2005), 19–102 at 92–93. Their capacity to influence the upbringing of their children as well as the management of their children's estates demonstrates the interdependence of lordship and kinship in medieval politics. See Bettina Elpers, *Regieren, Erziehen, Bewahren: Mütterliche Regentschaften im Hochmittelalter* (Frankfurt am Main, 2003), 2–3.
13. Birgit Sawyer, "The 'Civil Wars' Revisited," *Historisk tidsskrift* (N) 82 (2003): 43–73 at 44–53, 63–69; Bagge, *Viking Stronghold*, 48–50. See also the contribution by Ole-Albert Rønning in chapter 14 in this volume.
14. Edvard Bull, "Ingerid Ragnvaldsdatter," in *Norsk biografisk leksikon*, vol. 6, ed. Einar Jansen (Oslo, 1934), 522; Halvdan Koht, *Norske dronningar* (Oslo, 1926), 23–25; Bagge, *Viking Stronghold*, 48–49.
15. Hkr 3, 303; Cf. Msk, 179.
16. Ibid.
17. On the social capital of women see e.g., *Aristocratic Women in Medieval France*, ed. Theodore Evergates (Philadelphia, 1999); Jo Ann McNamara, "Women and Power through the Family Revisited," in *Gendering the Master Narrative: Women and Power in the Middle Ages*, ed. Mary Erler and Maryanne Kowaleski (Ithaca, NY and London, 2003), 17–30; Jennifer Ward, *Women in Medieval Europe, 1200–1500*, 2nd rev. ed. (London and New York, 2016), esp. 1–14, 29–80; Sverre Bagge, *Society and Politics in Snorri Sturluson's Heimskringla* (Berkeley, 1991), 117–21.
18. Bagge, *Viking Stronghold*, 49 (n. 58). Magnus fulfilled his claim to Swedish kingship, which he derived through his maternal line, through the regicide of King Sverker I in 1156, and again of King Eric IX in 1160, although he too was deposed the following year.
19. Little is known about the man, but *Heimskringla* reports that his sons, Einar and Andreas, were "men of high lineage and well off" (kynstórir menn ok fjáðir vel), with "*odel* and all its property" ("*óðul ok eignir allar*") in Oppland, central Norway (Hkr 3, 334).

20. Of the forty-six royal candidates during the period of domestic struggle, only twelve or thirteen were born of a legitimate Christian marriage. The determining factor in older traditions was the child's relation to the father rather than the mother, with little concern for the legitimacy of the parents' union. See Øye, "Kvinner, kjønn og samfunn," 95; Krag, *Norges historie*, 114–15. A formal change came with the 1163 law of succession, which gave priority to the first-born son of a legitimate marriage. See *Norske middelalderdokumenter i utvalg*, ed. Sverre Bagge, Synnøve Holstad Smedsdal, and Knut Helle (Bergen, Oslo, Tromsø, 1973), 32–34.
21. Although legitimate birth (and thus the associated marriage) was not yet a prerequisite for royal succession, the Church's preference for King Inge implies that it had political relevance: Andreas Holmsen, *Norges historie: fra de eldste tider til 1660* (Oslo, 1977), 194. See also Inger Ekrem, *Nytt lys over Historia Norvegica: Mot en løsning i debatten om dens alder* (Bergen, 1998), 18–19; Bagge, *Viking Stronghold*, 47; Thyra Nors, "Illegitimate Children and Their High-born Mothers: Changes in the Perception of Illegitimacy in Medieval Denmark," *Scandinavian Journal of History* 21 (2008): 17–37 at 17–19.
22. Hkr 3, 321.
23. Orning, "Conflict and Social (Dis)order," 54.
24. Hkr 3, 339, Msk, 232.
25. Finlay and Faulkes, vol. 2, 274. Hkr 2, 417: "ok váru landzmenn hennar miklir óvinir hennar, bæði þá ok jafnan síðan."
26. Fosterage in medieval Iceland is particularly well studied. See e.g., William Miller, *Bloodtaking and Peacemaking: Feud, Law and Society in Saga Iceland* (Chicago, 1990), 123–24; Gunnar Karlsson, "Barnfóstur á Íslandi að Fornu," in *Miðaldabörn*, ed. Ármann Jakobsson and Torfi Tulinius (Reykjavik, 2005), 37–61; Anna Hansen, "Fosterage and Dependency in Medieval Iceland and Its Significance in Gísla Saga," in *Youth and Age in the Medieval North*, ed. Shannon Lewis-Simpson (Leiden, 2008), 73–86; Gert Kreutzer, *Kindheit und Jugend in der altnordischen Literatur* (Münster, 1987), 221–34; Magnús Már Lárusson, "Fostring," *KLNM* 4, cols. 544–45.
27. Bente Opheim, "Med stønad frå frendar og vener: Slektskap og venskap som partidannande faktorar i den norske innbyrdesstriden 1130–1208" (MA thesis, University of Bergen, 1996), 38; Vidar Alne Paulsen, "Stormenn og elite i perioden 1030–1157" (MA thesis, University of Bergen, 2006), 89.
28. Thomas Charles-Edwards, *Early Christian Ireland* (Cambridge, 2004), 82–177, 221; Llinos Beverley Smith, "Fosterage, Adoption and God-Parenthood: Ritual and Fictive Kingship in Medieval Wales," *Welsh History Review* 16 (1992–3): 1–35 at 4.
29. Adam Kosto, *Hostages in the Middle Ages* (Oxford, 2012), 76. For a theoretical discussion of fosterage or "pro-parentage" arrangements in the development of political alliances between hierarchically ordered kin groups see e.g., Esther Goody, *Parenthood and Social Reproduction* (Cambridge, 1982), 114; Peter Parkes, "Fostering Fealty: A Comparative Analysis of Tributary Allegiances of Adoptive Kinship," *Comparative Studies in Society and History* 45, no. 4 (2003): 741–82.
30. Fosterage was often "an articulation of lordship" between higher- and lower-status families (Kosto, *Hostages*, 76), but could also strengthen lateral alliances (Steve Murdoch, *Network North: Scottish Kin, Commercial and Covert Associations in Europe, 1603–1746* (Leiden, 2006), 33–34).
31. Fosterage was a mechanism of clientage in medieval Ireland, where children were delegated to subordinates alongside the grant of a fief in exchange for the fostering client's allegiance. See Peter Parks, "Celtic Fosterage: Adoptive

Kinship and Clientage in Northwest Europe," *Comparative Studies in Society and History* 48, no. 2 (2006): 359–95 at 363. In the Nordic context, the author of *Heimskringla* also comments that "it is a common saying that a person who fosters a child for someone is of lower rank" (því at þat er mál manna, at sá væri ótígnari er ǫðrum fǫstraði barn) (Finlay and Faulkes, vol. 1, 85; Hkr 1, 145).
32. E.g., King Haakon the Good, also known as Aðalsteinsfóstri ("fostered by [the King of England] Athelstan"). Other examples of royal fosterers include Kalv Arnesson and Einar Tambeskjelvar, who fostered and governed for King Magnus the Good, and Tore Tordsson of Steig, foster father of King Haakon Magnusson Þórisfóstra ("fostered by Tore").
33. In Celtic societies, natal parents paid for their children's upkeep, but delegated the practical responsibilities of child-rearing to fosterers. See e.g., Bronagh Ní Chonaill, "Fosterage in Ireland and Wales," *Celtic Culture: A Historical Encyclopedia*, vol. 1, ed. John Koch (Santa Barbara, 2006), 771–73; Lisa Bitel, *Land of Women: Tales of Sex and Gender from Early Ireland* (Ithaca, NY and London, 1996), 93.
34. Hkr 3, 292.
35. NGL vol. 1, 365. Cf. *Sturlunga Saga – Including the Islendinga Saga of Lawman Sturla Thordsson and Other Works*, vol. 1, ed. Gudbrand Vigfusson (Oxford, 1878), ccvii.
36. Fredrik Paasche, "Erling Skakke," in *Norsk biografisk leksikon*, vol. 3, ed. Edvard Bull and Einar Jansen (Oslo, 1926), 571–72.
37. Hkr 3, 321.
38. Hkr 3, 330; Paulsen, "Stormenn og elite," 89–91.
39. Hkr 3, 306, 318, 330. Cf. Msk, 154, 179–84, 189.
40. Hkr 3, 312. Cf. Msk, 198. King Inge complains of Sada-Gyrd's passivity in a letter in 1139 (see later on in the chapter).
41. Beem, "Woe to Thee, O Land!," 4. This reality has been emphasized, for example, in the case of King Richard II of England, who "was immature and therefore unsuited to exercising authority without the 'help' of advisors" (Gwilym Dodd, "Richard II and the Fiction of Majority Rule," in *The Royal Minorities of Medieval and Early Modern England*, ed. Charles Beem (New York, 2008), 106).
42. Hkr 3, 303. Cf. Msk, 179.
43. Ibid.
44. See e.g., Gerd Althoff, "Colloquium familiare – colloquium secretum – colloquium pulicum. Beratung im politischen Leben des frühen Mittelalters," *Frühmittelalterliche Studien* 24 (1990): 145–67; Bagge, *Viking Stronghold*, 338–39.
45. Christian Hillen and Frank Wiswall, "The Minority of Henry III in the Context of Europe," in *The Royal Minorities of Medieval and Early Modern England*, ed. Charles Beem (New York, 2008), 17–66 at 24; Ormrod, "Coming to Kingship," 40–41; Charles Beem, "Woe to Thee, O Land? Some Final Thoughts," in *The Royal Minorities of Medieval and Early Modern England*, ed. Charles Beem (New York, 2008), 249–54 at 252.
46. Finlay and Faulkes, vol. 3, 193. Hkr 3, 314: "Ingi konungr, son Haralds konungs, sendir kveðju Sigurði konungi, bróður sínum, ok Sáða-Gyrði, Ǫgmundi svipti, Óttari birtingi, ok ǫllum lendum mǫnnum, hirðmǫnnum ok húskǫrlum, ok allri alþýðu, sælum ok veslum, ungum ok gǫmlum, guðs ok sína. Ǫllum monnum eru kunnug vandræði þau, er vét hǫfum, ok svá œska, at þú heitir fimm vetra gamall, en ek þrévetr. Megum vit ekki at fœrask, nema þat, er vit njótum vina okkarra ok góðra manna. Nú þykkjumst ek ok mínir vinir vera nærr staddir vandkvæði ok nauðsyn beggja okkarra en

þú eða þínir vinir. Nú gerðu svá vel, at þú far til fundar míns sem fyrst ok fjǫlmennastr, ok verum báðir saman, hvat sem í gerisk. Nú er sá okkarr mestr vinr, er til þess heldr, at vit sém æ sem sáttastir ok jafnast haldnir í ǫllum hlutum" Cf. Msk, 199.

47. Author's translation of Hans Jacob Orning, "En ideologisk revolusjon: Introduksjon av en ny type underordning basert på lydighet og tjeneste i Norge på 1100- og 1200-tallet," in *Frå Volda til verda: Fjerne og nære kulturmøte*, ed. Atle Døssland et al. (Trondheim, 2012), 97–118 at 98. See also Ernest Gellner, "Patrons and Clients," in *Patrons and Clients in Mediterranean Societies*, ed. Ernest Gellner and John Waterbury (London, 1977), 1–6; Althoff, "Colloquium familiar"; Jón Viðar Sigurðsson, *Det norrøne samfunnet* (Oslo, 2008), 78–92; Jón Viðar Sigurðsson, *Den vennlige vikingen: Vennskapets makt i Norge og på Island ca. 900–1300* (Oslo, 2010), 65–90.
48. Grohse, "Frå småbarns munn," 487–88.
49. Hkr 3, 303. Cf. Msk, 179.
50. Hkr 3, 322. Cf. Msk, 212.
51. Finlay and Faulkes, vol. 3, 193. Hkr 3, 314: "Nú vil ek lýsa yfir mínu skapi ok heyra, hvárt þar fylgi vili Sigurðar konungs eða annarra ríkismanna, at þú, Sigurðr konungr, búisk ok þat lið, er þér vill fylgja, at verja land þitt, ok far sem fjǫlmennastr á fund Inga konungs, bróður þins, sem fyrst máttu, ok styrki hvárr ykkarr annan í ǫllum farsælligum hlutum, en almáttigr guðs báða ykkr. Nú viljum vér heyra orð þín, konungr." Cf. Msk, 200.
52. Hkr 3, 315. Cf. Msk, 208; Hkr 3, 303. Cf. Msk, 200.
53. Grohse, "Frå småbarns munn," 489. The king's presence was paramount for the legitimacy of political events in the Middle Ages, when the visualization of power, "also in the body of the king," substantiated the ideal of the king's two bodies (natural and political) as distinct but inseparable. See e.g., Tanja Michalsky, *Memoria und Repräsentation: Grabmäler des Königshauses Anjou in Italien* (Göttingen, 2000), 29–30; Bernd Thum, "Öffentlich-Machen, Öffentlichkeit, Recht: Zu den Grundlagen und Verfahren der politischen Publizistik im Spätmittelalter," *Zeitschrift für Literaturwissenschaft und Linguistik* 10 (1980): 12–69; Gerd Althoff, "Demonstration und Inszenierung: Spielregeln der Kommunikation in mittelalterlicher Öffentlichkeit," *Frühmittelalterliche Studien* 27 (1993): 27–50. Peter's ceremonial role also demonstrated his political role vis-à-vis the king, for he is said to have received the byname "bearing-servant" (*byrðarsveinn*).
54. Finlay and Faulkes, vol. 3, 194. Hkr 3, 315: "vitu þat allir menn, ef ek skal ráða, at ek vil fara á fund Inga konungs, bróður mins, sem fyrst má ek." Cf. Msk, 200.
55. Finlay and Faulkes, vol. 3, 204. Hkr 3, 331: "blíðmæltr ok dæll vinum sínum, ǫrr af fé ok lét mjǫk hǫfðingja ráða með sér landráðum, vinsæll við alþýðu, ok dró þat allt saman mjǫk undir hann ríki ok fjǫlmenni"; Msk. 221.
56. Finlay and Faulkes, vol. 3, 170. Hkr 3, 278: "léttlátr, kátr ok leikinn, lítillátr, ǫrr, svá at hann sparði ekki við vini sína, ráðþægr, svá at hann lét aðra ráða með sér ǫllu því er vildu. Slíkt alt dró honum til vinsælda ok orðlofs. Þýddust hann þá margir ríkismenn."
57. Knut Arstad, "'han var svag af Charakteer og uden ringeste Herskergaver, hvilket også fremgaar af hele hans Historie': En undersøkelse av Harald Gilles ettermæle," *Historisk tidsskrift* (N) 78 (1999): 435–60.
58. Although Inge's generosity is portrayed as a positive attribute, perhaps even an essential aspect of rule in *Heimskringla* (Bagge, *Viking Stronghold*, 44), other excerpts from the same work suggest that Inge's counselors manipulated him. This is particularly apparent in the behavior of his principal advisor, Gregorius Dagsson, who goaded the king into conflicts. On Gregorius

see e.g., Bagge, "Samkongedømme og enekongedømme," 253; Paulsen, "Stormenn og elite," 83–87.
59. Ágr: 51–52; Hkr 3, 330.
60. On Erling's regency see Bagge, *Viking Stronghold*, 44–52, esp. 50–51; cf. Orning, "Conflict and Social (Dis)order," 74–79.
61. This supports Bagge's view that Norway's domestic struggles transformed magnates from local potentates to royal servants of a centralized, albeit embryotic monarchical state. See e.g., Bagge, *Society and Politics*, 237–40. Royal servants could, however, retain their local standing (ibid., 307). See also Orning, *Unpredictability and Presence*, 32.

Dedicated Bibliography

Althoff, Gerd. "Colloquium familiare – colloquium secretum – colloquium pulicum: Beratung im politischen Leben des frühen Mittelalters." *Frühmittelalterliche Studien* 24 (1990): 145–67.

Althoff, Gerd. *Verwandte, Freunde und Getreue: Zum politischen Stellenwert der Gruppenbindungen im früheren Mittelalter*. Darmstadt, 1990.

Althoff, Gerd. "Demonstration und Inszenierung. Spielregeln der Kommunikation in mittelalterlicher Öffentlichkeit." *Frühmittelalterliche Studien* 27 (1993): 27–50.

Arstad, Knut. "'Han var svag af Charakteer og uden ringeste Herskergaver, hvilket også fremgaar af hele hans Historie': En undersøkelse av Harald Gilles ettermæle." *Historisk tidsskrift* (N) 78 (1999): 435–60.

Bagge, Sverre. "Samkongedømme og enekongedømme." *Historisk tidsskrift* (N) 54 (1975): 239–74.

Bagge, Sverre. *Society and Politics in Snorri Sturluson's Heimskringla*. Berkeley, 1991.

Bagge, Sverre. "The Structure of the Political Factions in the Internal Struggles of the Scandinavian Countries During the High Middle Ages." *Scandinavian Journal of History* 24 (1999): 299–320.

Bagge, Sverre. *From Viking Stronghold to Christian Kingdom: State Formation in Norway, c. 900–1350*. Copenhagen, 2010.

Bagge, Sverre. "Borgerkrig og statsutvikling – svar til Hans Jacob Orning." *Historisk tidsskrift* (N) 94 (2015): 91–110.

Beem, Charles. "Woe to Thee, O Land! The Introduction." In *The Royal Minorities of Medieval and Early Modern England*, edited by Charles Beem, 1–16. New York, 2008.

Beem, Charles. "Woe to Thee, O Land? Some Final Thoughts." In *The Royal Minorities of Medieval and Early Modern England*, edited by Charles Beem, 249–54. New York, 2008.

Bitel, Lisa. *Land of Women: Tales of Sex and Gender from Early Ireland*. Ithaca, NY and London, 1996.

Bjørgo, Narve. "Samkongedøme kontra einekongedøme." *Historisk tidsskrift* (N) 49 (1970): 1–33.

Bull, Edvard. "Ingerid Ragnvaldsdatter." In *Norsk biografisk leksikon*, vol. 6, edited by Einar Jansen, 522. Oslo, 1934.

Charles-Edwards, Thomas. *Early Christian Ireland*. Cambridge, 2004.

Chonaill, Bronagh Ní. "Fosterage in Ireland and Wales." In *Celtic Culture: A Historical Encyclopedia*, vol. 1, edited by John Koch, 771–73. Santa Barbara, 2006.

Danielsson, Tommy. *Sagorna om Norges kungar från Magnús góði till Magnús Erlingsson.* Ludvika, 2002.
Dodd, Gwilym. "Richard II and the Fiction of Majority Rule." In *The Royal Minorities of Medieval and Early Modern England,* edited by Charles Beem, 103–59. New York, 2008.
Ekrem, Inger. *Nytt lys over Historia Norvegica: Mot en løsning i debatten om dens alder.* Bergen, 1998.
Elpers, Bettina. *Regieren, Erziehen, Bewahren: Mütterliche Regentschaften im Hochmittelalter.* Frankfurt am Main, 2003.
Evergates, Theodore, ed. *Aristocratic Women in Medieval France.* Philadelphia, 1999.
Ganshof, François L. "Le statut de la femme dans la monarchie franque." *Recueils de la Société Jean Bodin* 12 (1962): 5–58.
Gellner, Ernest. "Patrons and Clients." In *Patrons and Clients in Mediterranean Societies,* edited by Ernest Geller and John Waterbury, 1–6. London, 1977.
Goody, Esther. *Parenthood and Social Reproduction.* Cambridge, 1982.
Grohse, Ian Peter. "Fra småbarns munn: Myte og propaganda under kongene Inge og Sigurd Haraldsson c. 1136–1139." *Historisk tidsskrift* (N) 95 (2016): 473–91.
Hansen, Anna. "Fosterage and Dependency in Medieval Iceland and Its Significance in Gísla Saga." In *Youth and Age in the Medieval North,* edited by Shannon Lewis-Simpson, 73–86. Leiden, 2008.
Heimskringla, vols. 1–3. Edited and translated by Alison Finlay and Anthony Faulkes. London, 2011–15.
Helle, Knut. "The Norwegian Kingdom: Succession Disputes and Consolidation." In *The Cambridge History of Scandinavia, Vol. 1, Prehistory to 1520,* edited by Knut Helle, 369–91. Cambridge, 2003.
Hermanson, Lars. *Släkt, vänner och makt: En studie av elitens politiska kultur i 1100-talets Danmark.* Gothenburg, 2000.
Hillen, Christian, and Frank Wiswall. "The Minority of Henry III in the Context of Europe." In *The Royal Minorities of Medieval and Early Modern England,* edited by Charles Beem, 17–66. New York, 2008.
Holmsen, Andreas. *Norges historie. fra de eldste tider til 1660.* Oslo, 1977.
Kantorowicz, Ernst H. *The King's Two Bodies: A Study in Mediaeval Political Theology.* Princeton, 1958.
Karlsson, Gunnar. "Barnfóstur á Íslandi að Fornu." In *Miðaldabörn,* edited by Ármann Jakobsson and Torfi Tulinius, 37–61. Reykjavik, 2005.
Koht, Halvdan. *Norske dronningar.* Oslo, 1926.
Kölzer, Theo. "Das Königtum Minderjähriger im fränkisch-deutschen Mittelalter: Eine Skizze." *Historische Zeitschrift* 251 (1990): 291–323.
Kosto, Adam. *Hostages in the Middle Ages.* Oxford, 2012.
Krag, Claus. *Norges historie fram til 1319.* Oslo, 2000.
Laudage, Anders. "Das Problem der Vormundschaft über Otto III." In *Kaiserin Theophanu: Begegnung des Ostens und Westens um die Wende des ersten Jahrtausends: Gedenkschrift zum 1000. Todesjahr der Kaiserin,* edited by Anton v. Euw and Peter Schreiner, 271–76. Cologne, 1991.
Lubich, Gerhard. *Verwandtsein: Lesarten einer politisch-sozialen Beziehung im Frühmittelalter (6.-11. Jahrhundert).* Cologne, Weimar and Vienna, 2008.

McNamara, Jo Ann. "Women and Power Through the Family Revisited." In *Gendering the Master Narrative: Women and Power in the Middle Ages*, edited by Mary Erler and Maryanne Kowaleski, 17–30. Ithaca, NY and London, 2003.
Michalsky, Tanja. *Memoria und Repräsentation. Grabmäler des Königshauses Anjou in Italien*. Göttingen, 2000.
Miller, William Ian. *Bloodtaking and Peacemaking: Feud, Law and Society in Saga Iceland*. Chicago, 1990.
Murdoch, Steve. *Network North: Scottish Kin, Commercial and Covert Associations in Europe, 1603–1746*. Leiden, 2006.
Nors, Thyra. "Illegitimate Children and Their High-born Mothers: Changes in the Perception of Illegitimacy in Medieval Denmark." *Scandinavian Journal of History* 21 (2008): 17–37.
Norske middelalderdokumenter i utvalg. Edited by Sverre Bagge, Synnøve Holstad Smedsdal, and Knut Helle. Bergen, Oslo, Tromsø, 1973.
Offergeld, Thilo. *Reges pueri: Das Königtum Minderjähriger im frühen Mittelalter*. Hannover, 2001.
Opheim, Bente. "Med stønad frå frendar og vener: Slektskap og venskap som partidannande faktorar i den norske innbyrdesstriden 1130–1208." MA thesis, University of Bergen, 1996.
Ormrod, Mark. "Coming to Kingship: Boy Kings and the Passage to Power in Fourteenth-Century England." In *Rites of Passage: Cultures of Transition in the Fourteenth Century*, edited by Nicola McDonald and Mark Ormrod, 31–50. York, 2004.
Orning, Hans Jacob. *Unpredictability and Presence: Norwegian Kingship in the High Middle Ages*. Translated by Alan Crozier. Leiden, 2008.
Orning, Hans Jacob. "En ideologisk revolusjon: Introduksjon av en ny type underordning basert på lydighet og tjeneste i Norge på 1100- og 1200-tallet." In *Frå Volda til verda: Fjerne og nære kulturmøte*, edited by Atle Døssland et al., 97–118. Trondheim, 2012.
Orning, Hans Jacob. "Conflict and Social (Dis)order in Norway c. 1030–1160." In *Disputing Strategies in Medieval Scandinavia*, edited by Kim Esmark, Lars Hermanson, Hans Jacob Orning, and Helle Vogt, 45–82. Leiden, 2013.
Orning, Hans Jacob. "Borgerkrig og statsutvikling i Norge i middelalderen – en revurdering." *Historisk tidsskrift* (N) 93 (2014): 193–216.
Øye, Ingvild. "Kvinner, kjønn og samfunn: Fra vikingtid til reformasjon." In *Med kjønnsperspektiv på norsk historie*, edited by Ida Blom and Sølvi Sogner, 19–102. Oslo, 2005.
Paasche, Fredrik. "Erling Skakke." In *Norsk biografisk leksikon*, vol. 3, edited by Edvard Bull and Einar Jansen, 571–72. Oslo, 1926.
Parkes, Peter. "Fostering Fealty: A Comparative Analysis of Tributary Allegiances of Adoptive Kinship." *Comparative Studies in Society and History* 45 (2003): 741–82.
Parkes, Peter. "Celtic Fosterage: Adoptive Kinship and Clientage in Northwest Europe." *Comparative Studies in Society and History* 48 (2006): 359–95.
Paulsen, Vidar Alne. "Stormenn og elite i perioden 1030–1157." MA thesis, University of Bergen, 2006.
Puppel, Pauline. *Regentin: Vormundschaftliche Herrschaft in Hessen 1500–1700*. Frankfurt am Main and New York, 2004.

Sawyer, Birgit. "The 'Civil Wars' Revisited." *Historisk Tidsskrift* (N) 82, no. 1 (2003): 43–73.
Sigurðsson, Jón Viðar. *Det norrøne samfunnet*. Oslo, 2008.
Sigurðsson, Jón Viðar. *Den vennlige vikingen: Vennskapets makt i Norge og på Island ca. 900–1300*. Oslo, 2010.
Sigurðsson, Jón Viðar, and Anne Irene Riisøy. *Norsk historie 800–1536: Frå krigerske bønder til lydige undersåttar*. Oslo, 2011.
Smith, Llinos Beverley. "Fosterage, Adoption and God-Parenthood: Ritual and Fictive Kingship in Medieval Wales." *Welsh History Review* 16 (1992–3): 1–35.
Sturlunga Saga – Including the Islendinga Saga of Lawman Sturla Thordsson and Other Works, vol. 1. Edited by Gudbrand Vigfusson. Oxford, 1878.
Thum, Bernd. "Öffentlich-Machen, Öffentlichkeit, Recht: Zu den Grundlagen und Verfahren der politischen Publizistik im Spätmittelalter." *Zeitschrift für Literaturwissenschaft und Linguistik* 10 (1980): 12–69.
Ward, Jennifer. *Women in Medieval Europe, 1200–1500*. 2nd. Rev. ed. London and New York, 2016.
Watts, John. *Henry VI and the Politics of Kingship*. Cambridge, 1996.

14 The Politics of Exile in Northern Europe
The Case of Knud V of Denmark

Ole-Albert Rønning

Medieval Scandinavian elites frequently sought aid and support outside of their own kingdoms when they faced problems at home. Narrative sources like the kings' sagas or chronicles like Saxo's *Gesta Danorum* contain numerous examples of political actors, usually kings, going into exile abroad when they met with military defeat or great opposition at home. This practice was especially prevalent in periods of internal struggle, as in the years between 1131 and 1157 in Denmark, and 1130–1240 in Norway.[1] Examining it raises interesting questions about the use and fluidity of social bonds, and the interplay between norms and practices: How did personal relationships among the Scandinavian elites determine where political actors sought aid? Did obligations involved in such relationships determine whether hosts abroad gave aid, or do we have to look to more cynical, political motivations? Were different social bonds used in different ways? Were constructed bonds like friendship or marital ties more likely to ensure support than kinship? If political interests were more important than social obligations, what kind of interests are we dealing with? I would argue that the practice whereby kings and other medieval political actors fled in search of resources with which to defeat their enemies at home provides us with a promising opportunity to study the dynamic use of socio-political resources. It also gives us the chance to investigate how this practice functioned across the Nordic region as a whole, and to what extent this region can be said to have been socially and politically integrated.

When using terms like "exile" and "abroad," we do, however, face the risk of accepting certain premises about how we should understand medieval society and political culture. Firstly, the terms seem to imply the existence of clearly delineated kingdoms with obvious borders for political actors to cross. This is almost certainly anachronistic, as we are dealing with a period in which lordship over land and people was continually contested and overlapping. Secondly, to the modern reader, "exile" can easily be associated with something out of the ordinary, an extreme, perhaps with connotations of the exiled governments of the twentieth century. In the Middle Ages, on the other hand, seeking aid from distant friends or kinsmen seems to have been well within the realm of ordinary political practice.

If the basic terms used to describe the subject of this chapter are potentially so misleading, how should we begin to conceptualize it? A good start might be to think in terms of dynastic, rather than state, politics. Thus, if a Danish political actor seeks help from a relative in Germany, we should understand it as an example of that actor using his *dynastic network*, which could stretch all across northern Europe and beyond, rather than as something that involves crossing national or regional borders. The advantage of such an approach is that we integrate the practice of so-called exile into an understanding of political culture based on networks and personal relationships rather than on states and institutions. The problem is that it does not capture what we might call the geographical aspect of studying exile, in that it does not distinguish between taking advantage of networks "at home" and networks that were farther away. To incorporate this aspect, while avoiding using nationally infused terminology, it is perhaps most effective to think in terms of political actors taking advantage of *near and distant networks or bonds*. We can also apply this terminology to the instances where there was no apparent pre-existing relationship between the political actors and those from whom they sought help. We shall see that in these cases new bonds were created, which in turn can be classified as belonging somewhere on the scale between *near* and *distant*.

The language we use to describe political interactions in the Middle Ages is infused with modern connotations, and it is easy to get tied up in knots trying to escape a terminology that is to some extent inescapable. So while I shall keep on using the term "exile," it should be understood that I am applying it to a culture that lacks both well-established institutions and clear frontiers between polities. We should therefore think of political exiles in the Middle Ages as refugees who used their social resources to get their hands on military or economic resources in hopes of returning, rather than as refugees in the modern sense, fundamentally removed from their political homeland. For medieval political actors, exile is a continuation of politics, in which they sometimes use their dynastic networks, and sometimes not. Sometimes they take action far away from their political centre, and other times this takes place much closer to home. The crucial point is that exile is very much a part of the political culture of medieval Nordic elites, and displaced kings and magnates operated within the framework of that culture. They used and established personal networks that were not contained by regnal boundaries, for the purpose of getting an upper hand in dynastic power struggles. This practice, and what it can tell us about the socio-political resources of the Nordic elites, is the subject of this chapter.

For our purposes, no case study is better than that of King Knud V Magnussen of Denmark (r. 1146–57). Knud was one of the pretenders

The Politics of Exile in Northern Europe 273

to the Danish throne who sprang up after the abdication of Erik III Lam ("the Lamb," r. 1137–46), and his career is very interesting, in particular because of his exile from 1151 to 1152. During this time, Knud tried and repeatedly failed to procure aid from outside of Denmark with which to defeat his rival for the throne, Svend III Grathe (r. 1146–57). Knud tried to take advantage of several different social bonds, including kinship, marital ties, and lordship; and he also sought help from princes, both secular and ecclesiastical, with whom he had no previous relationship. Looking at the different outcomes of Knud's attempts can therefore tell us something about how these relationships functioned in relation to the practice of giving economic and military aid to political refugees.

Knud Magnussen is also interesting because the account of his exile comes down to us in several different sources. The most important is of course Saxo Grammaticus's chronicle, *Gesta Danorum*, but Knud also figures prominently in Helmold of Bosau's *Chronica Slavorum*, and there is a somewhat later account in *Knýtlinga saga*. We also have a letter written by Knud to the German king Conrad III in 1151, in which he asks for help in taking back Denmark. Additionally, there are several very brief mentions of Knud's exile and return in a number of Danish annals. Not all these sources are independent of each other, however. Saxo might have been aware of Helmold's work, and the annals build on each other, as well as on Saxo.

In this chapter, I will primarily deal with one aspect of Knud's exile, namely the ways in which he tried to obtain economic and military resources from foreign patrons. Consequently, I will not go into the cause of Knud's exile in much detail, and I will only briefly deal with his return to Denmark. Instead, I want to follow the Danish king on his journey, first looking at how he tried to take advantage of his existing social network, before turning to the instances where he more consciously played to his hosts' interests.

The Unreliability of Social Bonds

When King Erik III abdicated the Danish throne without leaving an obvious heir in 1146, the result was dynastic conflict. According to Saxo, Svend, son of King Erik II (r. 1134–37), was elected king in Zealand and garnered additional support from Scania. Knud, son of Magnus Nielsen and grandson of King Niels (r. 1104–34), was elected in Jutland.[2] Knud and Svend were the most important players at the beginning of the conflict, but in the background lurked Valdemar, son of Duke Knud Lavard, whose murder in 1131 had set off the Danish internal conflicts to begin with. Saxo writes that Valdemar had little patience for Knud, the son of his father's killer, and thus aligned himself with Svend.[3] In the following conflict, we hear of a number of battles and encounters, none of which

I will go into in much detail here. The turning point came in 1151, when Knud was decisively defeated by Svend in a battle near Viborg in Jutland.

It makes sense that it was Knud's defeat at Viborg which pushed him into exile. A military defeat represented a loss of vital military resources, and petitioning other rulers for men or money was a way to compensate for such a loss. This point seems obvious, but losses on the battlefield were also a considerable drain on political resources. Medieval Scandinavian kings ruled through their aristocratic alliances, so when high-status allies died or switched sides in the wake of a defeat, it directly harmed a king's ability to amass resources, recruit new men, and continue the fight against a rival. Saxo, who recounts Knud's defeat at Viborg in the most detail, makes this connection, as he tells of how many of Knud's men swore allegiance to Svend after the battle.[4] This general point is made in similar narrative accounts as well, such as the kings' saga story of the great number of followers and magnate allies Harald Gille lost at the battle of Fyrileiv in 1134, forcing him to seek the aid of King Erik II in Denmark.[5] The cause of Knud's exile is thus both logical, and, as far as we can know, quite typical.

Both Saxo and Helmold note that Knud had to go abroad as a result of Svend's military victories, but beyond that the two accounts are very different. Prior to chronicling Knud's exile, Helmold writes that the two Danish kings competed for the support of Count Adolf of Holstein, an event we find no trace of in *Gesta Danorum*.[6] While interesting as an example of political actors finding support abroad, I will not discuss Knud's relationship to Adolf here, as it is not really presented by Helmold as a result of exile – although it is no doubt striking that Helmold makes no mention of Knud seeking Adolf's support in his account.

Gesta Danorum and *Chronica Slavorum* also differ in their descriptions of where Knud travelled. According to Helmold, the king was first taken in by Hartwig, the archbishop of Hamburg-Bremen, while in Saxo's version of events Hartwig comes in somewhat later. Saxo claims that Knud first fled to Sweden, where his mother, Rikissa of Poland, was married to King Sverker.[7] According to the Danish historian John Lind, the marriage alliance was a result of Rikissa's wanting to ensure her son a Scandinavian power base outside of Denmark.[8] Here we have the first instance of the exiled Knud trying to take advantage of a social bond, and the question, then, is how strong this bond was. Could Knud count on his stepfather when he was forced to leave Denmark, as his mother had perhaps hoped?

The answer we get from *Gesta Danorum* is a resounding no; "Despite Cnut's being initially welcome to his stepfather in Sweden, after a short time he began to be considered a burden, with the result that he had to put up for sale all the estates he had owned in that region to provide himself with food" (At Kanutus apud Suetiam primum uitrico optatu, mox onustus haberi coepit, ita ut pro comparandis alimentis, quicquid illic prędiorum possederat, uenditaret).⁹ Sick of the mistreatment, Knud eventually bought a boat and set sail for Poland, home to his mother's kin. Thus, the relationship between stepfather and son is depicted not only as one where support is absent, but even as actively hostile. If the Swedish king was unwilling to provide his stepson with food, it seems highly unlikely that he would provide him with money or soldiers. How do we explain this hostility?

Saxo's own explanation is clearly unsatisfactory, as he simply claims of the Swedes that "[t]here is no race readier to take in outcasts, and none that rejects them more easily" (Neque enim ulla gens exules aut promptius recipit aut facilius respuit).¹⁰ *Knýtlinga saga* can perhaps provide us with a more nuanced way of understanding Knud's exile in Sweden. Unlike Saxo, the anonymous author of the saga does not mention that Knud owned any property in Sweden. Instead, he writes that King Sverker offered to grant his stepson land in Sweden in return for Knud's right to the Danish throne. Knud supposedly refused and had to leave.¹¹ While this explanation could have something to it, it seems far-fetched to believe that Knud could transfer his claim to the Danish throne to his stepfather, and we have to keep in mind that *Knýtlinga saga* was written considerably later than the other sources we have for the civil wars of the twelfth century.

The best way to understand the fraught relationship between Knud and Sverker might be to look to Knud's lineage. His grandmother, Margrete Fredkulla, was the daughter of the Swedish king Inge Stenkilsson, making Knud a direct descendant of a Swedish monarch. Furthermore, his father, Magnus Nielsen, had been elected king of Götaland in the 1120s. It is therefore not unlikely that Knud was perceived to have a legitimate claim to the Swedish throne, which would have made him a serious threat to Sverker. Thus, I think Saxo's version of Knud's exile in Sweden is an example of political self-interest trumping social obligation. According to the Danish chronicler, dynastic security was more important to King Sverker than supporting his stepson.

This dynamic would repeat itself when Knud left Sweden for Poland. Saxo writes that Knud's Piast relatives "imagined that, reliant on his maternal connections, he was aiming at partnership in the kingdom, and, although they received him in every other place, they would not let him be admitted to any fortified locations" (Quem illi maternę rei nomine regni consortionem appetere rati cęteris in locis admissum munimentis excipere passi non sunt.)¹² Here Saxo explicitly expresses the problem we saw earlier: Knud is a threat to his relatives because he has a claim to their inheritance, and thus they cannot risk helping him. This frustrates Saxo, as he clearly perceives the Poles as having obligations towards their maternal relative, "to whom they owe charity as a kinsman" (cum propinquo charitatem deberent).¹³ In both of these examples, then, we see that not only do Knud's social bonds to foreign rulers fail to help him, they are in fact a disadvantage. Knud's bonds of kinship entail a right to inheritance and a claim to political power that make the Danish royal refugee a threat to his hosts.

The Importance of Interests

So far, we have seen how a host's interests could outweigh their perceived social obligations. This leaves us with the question of what kind of interests we are dealing with. What role did they play, and how could a refugee like Knud use the political interests of a host to his advantage? Again, Knud's exile at the beginning of the 1150s provides us with examples that let us explore these problems.

According to Saxo, Knud traveled from Poland to the duke of Saxony, Henry the Lion. The Danish chronicler's account of this meeting is very short, simply noting that Knud "had less luck with him than he had hoped" (apud quem minorem spe sua fortunam).[14] We do not get any explanation for why the duke would not be welcoming or supportive towards Knud, but we can make some assumptions. Henry often shows up in *Gesta Danorum* as a prince whose support has to be bought,[15] and his biographer Karl Jordan writes that "He made use of his wealth to achieve political ends, and did his best to increase it by exacting a financial price for political or military aid."[16] It is therefore not unlikely that in exile, Knud simply did not have the necessary resources to recruit Henry the Lion to his cause.[17] Here, then, we see one way in which interests played a role when political actors sought refuge abroad: Their hosts might demand compensation, economic or otherwise, in return for political support. Another prominent example of this is King Valdemar I the Great, who, according to *Fagrskinna* and *Heimskringla*, demanded control of the region of Viken in return for helping the exiled Norwegian magnate Erling Skakke and his son, King Magnus V.[18]

Following his short visit to Duke Henry, Knud is supposed to have sought out the archbishop of Hamburg-Bremen, and it is at this point Helmold finally joins in the narrative. Unfortunately he does not go into much detail, simply noting that Knud was forced into exile with Archbishop Hartwig in Saxony due to King Svend's "repeated victories" (*crebris victoriis*).[19] Nonetheless, the fact that we have two independent accounts of Knud's interaction with Hartwig does make the event more credible than the previous stops on Knud's journey, where we have only Saxo to rely on.

As far as we are aware, there was no social bond between the Danish king and the German archbishop. If there was no such bond, what did Knud have going for him? What leverage could he use to obtain military or economic aid? Saxo's answer to this is unusually clear. Hartwig was, he writes, "a person hostile to the Danes, owing to their removal, long before, from the jurisdiction of his archiepiscopate" (iampridem Danis iurisdictioni sue exemptis infensum).[20] The archbishops of Hamburg-Bremen had for a long time held authority over the church in the Nordic kingdoms and the Western Isles, but this changed when the archbishopric of Lund was established in 1104. The Danish historian Carsten Breengaard has argued that it was crucial for the German archbishops to regain jurisdiction in the North if Hamburg-Bremen was to hold onto its status as an archiepiscopal see,[21] and Saxo gives us the impression that Hartwig wanted to achieve this by helping Knud take the Danish throne. In other words, Knud and Hartwig shared political interests. Knud could offer the promise that, as king, he would reinstate the primacy of Hamburg-Bremen, and in return, Hartwig could offer Knud what he needed the most: economic and military resources with which to defeat Svend. On this occasion, Saxo's account agrees with Helmold's, and we read that Hartwig lent Knud resources which the Danish king used to stage an invasion of Jutland.[22] Thus, it seems that Knud's first success as a political refugee, his first successful attempt at procuring military and financial aid abroad, came when he sought shelter with a man with whom he had no previous relationship, no established social bond. Instead, the two shared political interests, and this looks like the determining factor in their relationship.

Lone Liljefalk and Stefan Pajung have offered a different interpretation of the relationship between Knud and Archbishop Hartwig in a recent article where they discuss Helmold of Bosau as a source for Danish history. They argue that Hartwig's support for Knud was not related to ecclesiastical jurisdiction, but rather came because of a conflict between the archbishop and Duke Henry the Lion. The two had long been in conflict over the appointment of bishops, in addition to some land Henry had allegedly confiscated from Hartwig's family.[23] While I would argue that in Saxo's interpretation it seems clearer what the archbishop would stand to gain from investing resources in a Danish royal refugee, Pajung and Liljefalk's perspective is certainly a conceivable alternative. Irrespective of what interpretation we choose to rely on, however, the account of refuge in and support from abroad stays the same: Knud and Hartwig came together because they both had something to offer each other, not because they had a personal relationship which obligated them to. Not only that, we also get a first hint of how interests and bonds interact, and how interest can form the basis for new bonds. That Knud and Hartwig needed each other caused both of their networks to expand. New relationships were made by political necessity. This dynamic became even more apparent as Knud continued his journey.

Knud's German invasion of Denmark does not seem to have gone according to plan. Saxo offers an extensive description of the ensuing battle between the two Danish kings, which Knud supposedly lost, despite the best efforts of his German cavalry.[24] The chronicler goes on to write that after this defeat Knud returned to Saxony, and if Saxo's chronology is roughly in order it must have been at this point that he sent a letter to the German king Conrad III asking for assistance. Interestingly, the letter is not recorded in any narrative sources, but it has survived, and tells of a third way in which refugees could play to a foreign patron's interest in order to obtain his support. In the letter, Knud addresses the German king as emperor (*Romanorum imperatori augusto*) and king of kings (*rex regum*), even though Conrad was never crowned as such. He also describes himself as a child, while Conrad is a just father (*pater iusticie*). It seems clear that what Knud is doing in the letter is putting himself in an inferior position to the German ruler,[25] but for what purpose? The answer comes further down, where Knud laments how he has been robbed of his kingdom and his patrimony. Because of this, he continues, he has sought refuge in the Roman Empire, in the hope that he will find counsel and support (*consilium et auxilium*). Knud asks Conrad to help him by lending him his "sharp sword" (*gladii uestri seueritate*), so that he can win back what has been taken from him. Knud, in short, is asking for military aid. In return, we read, he will always obey the German king's instruction (*precepta*).[26]

Here we see Knud playing to Conrad's interests by taking a clearly subordinate position in relation to him. If Conrad was willing to help, Knud was offering the future loyalty of a Danish king and by extension the Danish kingdom. This is interesting because it reveals a kind of intersection between the two aspects of political exile we have been looking at so far: obligations to social relationships on the one hand and political self-interest on the other. Knud was attempting to establish a social relation, a bond of lordship, between himself and King Conrad, and it seems like he was doing so for two reasons. Firstly, it would create a kind of obligation on Conrad's part to protect his vassal, to help him regain his kingdom and his patrimony. Secondly, it would increase the German ruler's power and prestige, thus serving not only Knud's interests but Conrad's as well. In short, with his letter Knud is trying to establish what we might call a bond of shared political interest by establishing a bond of lordship. Again, there are striking similarities between Knud's political strategy and that of other members of the Scandinavian elite, suggesting that Knud's behaviour should be understood as a well-established part of medieval political culture. A couple of decades after Knud's exile, a conflict raged between the Norwegian magnate and regent Erling Skakke and the Danish king Valdemar I over control of the region of Viken, around the Oslo fjord. The conflict was finally settled in 1170, when it was agreed that Erling would rule Viken as Valdemar's earl and vassal.[27] In return, this relationship ensured Danish political support not only for Erling himself, but also for his son and grandsons.[28]

Thus, we see how social relationships are built on political interests, and that these social relationships in turn are used for political gain. Knud, Erling, and other kings and magnates like them, establish bonds because it is in their interest to do so. Networks thus grow naturally out of competition for power and influence, and interests in such conflicts are expressed through social relationships. Where there are no bonds, they are created.

The Aftermath

The attempt to involve Conrad in the Danish civil war proved unsuccessful. The reason was most likely that King Svend sent a very similar letter to the German ruler, perhaps as a direct response to Knud's.[29] Svend used the same kind of politically and symbolically charged language as his rival, with the crucial difference being that Svend did not ask for Conrad's intervention. To the contrary, he wanted him to stay out of Danish affairs.[30] Svend also had the advantage of having a personal relationship with Conrad, as he had supposedly served in his retinue.[31] Conrad's decision on whom to support must therefore have been quite easy, as there was really nothing new Knud could offer. The German king already had a kind of vassal on the Danish throne, and there was no good reason to spend valuable resources replacing him.

What followed was the Diet of Merseburg, an assembly in the German Empire attended by both Knud and Svend, and covered not only by Saxo and Helmold's chronicles and *Knýtlinga saga*, but also by Bishop Otto of Freising's *Gesta Friderici Imperatoris*.[32] These narratives differ somewhat in their portrayals of the assembly, but on the general points they are in concord. At the Diet it was decided, probably by some of the leading men of the German realm with the understanding of King Frederick Barbarossa,[33] that Knud would renounce his claim to the throne and recognize Svend as his king and overlord, and in return he would receive land in Denmark.[34] Then, in rituals which are vividly described by Otto of Freising and notably ignored by Saxo, Svend, now sole king of Denmark, paid homage to Frederick Barbarossa.[35]

After his long exile and several unsuccessful attempts to return to Denmark by force, the Diet of Merseburg proved to be Knud's ticket home. While it would be interesting to try to track how Knud was able to re-establish his network and regain his resources when he came back to Denmark, the sources make this difficult. Saxo is the only author with any interest in the aftermath of Merseburg, and even he is relatively brief. We hear that upon Knud's return, Svend did not want to honour his agreement with Knud. Instead of giving Knud control over Zealand, Svend handed over smaller fiefs (*beneficia*) in Jutland, Zealand, and Scania, in the belief that this would leave Knud in a weaker position.[36] We should be careful about accepting this account, however, as it is in part Svend's unwillingness to keep to his word that legitimizes Valdemar, one of the heroes of Saxo's story, in his decision to abandon Svend and ally with Knud. This alliance must be considered as one of the high points of

Knud's political career, but it is doubtful whether it has any connection to Knud's exile or the Diet of Merseburg, as it was allegedly established a couple of years after these events.[37]

We do, however, get some hints elsewhere in the sources as to how Knud might have re-established a network – specifically, in Saxo's account of the invasion of Jutland, when he was helped by Archbishop Hartwig of Hamburg-Bremen, as discussed earlier. We have seen that when Knud fled Denmark after the battle of Viborg in 1151, many of his followers supposedly switched sides and joined Svend.[38] Saxo writes that prior to his invasion, Knud "sent a secret mission to test the loyalty of his soldiers back home." He goes on, "The reply came that they would all be prepared to switch to his side at a moment's notice and would transfer the fealty given to Sven back to their former lord" (domesticorum militum fidem tacita legatione pertentat. Responsum est omnes ad eum ocissime transituros, datamque Suenoni fidem pristina mutaturos.)[39] Saxo does not give us much of an explanation as to why this was so, but we do get the sense that Knud's ability to re-establish a political network in Denmark largely depended on the resources he could assemble. It seems likely that what compelled Knud's original followers to rejoin him was not simply sentimental loyalty, although that certainly could have played a part, but more importantly the fact that the king was returning with a Saxon army. The perception that he had a winning hand, new and substantial political resources, must have helped Knud reconstruct his network.[40] We are reminded of Sverre Bagge's now-famous description of medieval political culture: "nothing succeeds like success."[41]

If we apply these conclusions to Knud's situation in 1152, it is not unlikely that his newfound control of land in Denmark gave him the opportunity to reconnect with old friends and clients, as well as to establish new alliances. Property was a tangible economic resource which could be translated into political capital, arguably with greater ease than the invasions Knud had attempted to leverage during his exile. However we choose to interpret the aftermath of Knud's exile, we are faced with what seems to be the historical reality that following the Diet of Merseburg in 1152, Knud re-established himself as a viable candidate for the Danish throne, and a couple of years later it was Svend, not Knud, who had to seek refuge in Germany.[42] It is unclear how Knud was able to regain his network and his power base; what seems certain is that he did.

Knud's career came to an abrupt end in 1157, when he, Valdemar, and Svend met at Roskilde, following Svend's three-year exile in Germany and repeated attempts to come home at the head of an army. The purpose of the meeting was to celebrate that a settlement had been reached between the three, but it ended in a bloodbath when Svend, according to the official version of the story, attempted to murder his two colleagues. Valdemar got away, and would eventually defeat and kill Svend at the battle of Grathe Heath, rule until 1182, and establish a dynasty. Knud was not able to make such a mark on history. He was killed at the feast in Roskilde.

Conclusion

Knud cannot be considered a particularly successful refugee. All but one of his attempts to procure economic and military aid abroad proved to be dead ends, and when he eventually got his hands on an army, he squandered it. However, it is by no means only the successful attempts at procuring support abroad which can tell us something useful about the practice. So what do our sources' portrayals of Knud's troublesome exile tell us about the interplay between obligations and interests in the interactions between twelfth-century political refugees and their hosts?

We are clearly dealing with a political culture in which the bonds established between people by blood, marriage, or lordship carry great significance. If they did not, there would be no reason for Saxo to emphasize Knud's hope of getting support from his Swedish and Polish relatives, and certainly no reason to lament when he was unsuccessful. Pre-established social bonds, then, were a central feature of medieval elite exile, seemingly able to determine where a refugee could and would seek support. This insight is neither new nor especially revealing, as the limited scholarship on the interconnected networks of the Scandinavian elites of the Middle Ages has emphasized precisely these bonds. Too often, however, they are taken either as proof of political integration,[43] or as equivalent to political alliances.[44] Knud's fate reveals a more complex picture.

Knud's exile forces us to take the point of view of a host housing a refugee like Knud, and thus consider how obligations to social relations like kinsmen and in-laws could be in conflict with one's own interests. Refugees could pose a serious threat to their hosts' political and economic resources, precisely because they were part of interconnected elite networks which could entitle them to inheritance, or perhaps even a throne. A social bond, then, was a double-edged sword. Again and again we see how Knud's attempts at procuring aid fail when he is relying on social bonds to a host whose interests are in conflict with his own. It is significant that in the one instance where Knud does in fact receive material support, he has no previously established social relationship with his patron, Hartwig; and it is obvious how the archbishop stands to gain from being generous.

So is it all about interests? Do the social relationships so carefully emphasized by the sources carry no practical significance? Here too, we run the risk of oversimplifying. Instead of interests making social bonds irrelevant, we should think of personal relationships as mediums through which interests operated and were articulated. Where there are no bonds between political actors who share interests in the moment, such a bond can be created, as Knud attempted to do in his appeal to the German king Conrad III. Thus, a social bond can be a bearer of the interests of the individuals connected by that bond. As a case study, then, King Knud V of Denmark serves to underline the complexity of the Nordic elites and their use of social resources. His career reveals how important interests were, but also shows that these interests were constituted in bonds between people, bonds of marriage, friendship, and lordship.

Notes

1. This chapter is based on my 2015 master's thesis from the University of Oslo. More details and analyses can be found there: Ole-Albert Rønning, "Beyond Borders: Material Support from Abroad in the Scandinavian Civil Wars, 1130–1180" (University of Oslo, 2015). For more on exile as a form of contact between the elites of Scandinavia and England, see the contribution by Marie Bønløkke Missuno in chapter 7 in this volume.
2. Saxo, 14.3.1. All quotes in English are from Peter Fisher's translation in the same publication.
3. Saxo, 14.4.1.
4. Saxo, 14.4.9.
5. Snorri Sturluson, "Magnúss saga Blinda ok Haralds Gilla," in *Íslenzk Fornrit* 28, ed. Bjarni Aðalbjarnarson (Reykjavík, 1951), 278–302.
6. Helmold of Bosau, *Helmoldi Presbyteri Bozoviensis Chronica Slavorum*, ed. Johann M. Lappenberg and Bernhard Schmeidler (Hannover, 1909), ch. 67.
7. Saxo, 14.4.9. Knud's exile in Sweden, and the subsequent one in Poland, are mentioned in a number of Danish annals, but many of these base their entries on Saxo's chronicle. See *Danmarks Middelalderlige Annaler*, ed. Erik Kroman (Copenhagen, 1980), 18, 58, 90, 109, 46, 65, 269, 307.
8. John Lind, "De russiske ægteskaber: Dynasti- og alliancepolitik i 1130ernes danske borgerkrig," *Historisk Tidsskrift* (D) 92, no. 2 (1992): 225–61 at 251. For more on Scandinavian contacts in the East, see the contribution by John Lind in chapter 6 in this volume.
9. Saxo, 14.5.2.
10. Ibid.
11. KS, ch. 108.
12. Saxo, 14.5.3.
13. Ibid.
14. Saxo, 14.5.4.
15. Later in the Danish civil wars, King Svend bought Henry's support (Saxo, 14.17.1), and King Valdemar allegedly had to pay him to ensure his aid against the Wends (Saxo, 14.24.4).
16. Karl Jordan, *Henry the Lion: A Biography*, trans. Paul Stephen Falla (Oxford, 1986), 217.
17. Svend was also in exile when he recruited Henry to his cause, but he came to the duke after an extended stay with his father-in-law, Conrad of Meissen, who might have provided him with the necessary resources to bribe Henry.
18. It could be argued that Valdemar is different from Henry the Lion because his demand is for political control, rather than cash. This can certainly be a useful distinction, but for our purposes the important point is that both demanded specific, substantial compensation for their investment in a refugee.
19. Helmold of Bosau, *Helmoldi Presbyteri Bozoviensis Chronica Slavorum*, ch. 67. English excerpts from CS (see abbreviations).

The Politics of Exile in Northern Europe   283

20. Saxo, 14.5.4.
21. Carsten Breengaard, *Muren om Israels hus: regnum og sacerdotium i Danmark 1050–1170* (Copenhagen, 1982), 176.
22. Saxo, 14.4.5.
23. Lone Liljefalk and Stefan Pajung, "Helmolds Slaverkrønike som kilde til Danmarks, Vendens og Nordtysklands historie," *Historisk Tidsskrift* (D) 113, no. 1 (2014): 1–38 at 26–27.
24. Saxo, 14.5.5–9.
25. Cf. Gerd Althoff, *Family, Friends and Followers: Political and Social Bonds in Medieval Europe* (Cambridge, 2004), 106.
26. DD 1.2.104.
27. Snorri Sturluson, "Magnúss saga Erlingssonar," in *Íslenzk Fornrit XXVIII*, ed. Bjarni Aðalbjarnarson (Reykjavík, 1951), ch. 30; Saxo, 14.41.3.
28. Jón Viðar Sigurðsson has argued that vertical bonds were more durable and long lasting than horizontal bonds between more or less equal political actors. See Jón Viðar Sigurðsson, *Den vennlige vikingen: vennskapets makt i Norge og på Island 900–1300* (Oslo, 2010), 150.
29. Breengaard, *Muren om Israels hus*, 249.
30. DD 1.2.103.
31. Lars Hermanson, *Släkt, vänner och makt: en studie av elitens politiska kultur i 1100-talets Danmark* (Göteborg, 2000), 212.
32. Saxo, 14.8.1–3; CS ch. 73; KS, ch. 109; Otto of Freising, *Ottonis et Rahewini: Gesta Friderici I. Imperatoris*, ed. Georg Waitz (Hannover and Leipzig, 1912), book II, ch. 5.
33. Conrad III had died in 1152 and been succeeded by his nephew, Frederick.
34. Both *Gesta Danorum* and *Knýtlinga saga* specify that Knud would receive Zealand as some kind of fief. Saxo uses the term *beneficium* (Saxo, 14.8.2) while the author of *Knýtlinga saga* writes *til forraði* (KS, ch. 109). Otto is more general, writing that Knud received "some provinces" (*quibusdam provinciis*, Gesta, book II, ch. 5), while Helmold does not mention the subject at all.
35. Carsten Breengaard has argued that the precedent for the Diet of Merseburg was set in the letters sent by Knud and Svend to Conrad III, where Knud stresses his loss of *patrimonium*, and Svend reveals his willingness to submit to a German king: Breengaard, *Muren om Israels hus*, 249.
36. Saxo, 14.8.5.
37. Saxo, 14.14.1. For more on Valdemar's change of allegiance, see the contribution by Kim Esmark in chapter 15 in this volume.
38. Saxo, 14.4.9.
39. Saxo, 14.5.4.
40. We get some additional sense of how this might have worked from the Norwegian provincial Frostathing Law. Here, we read that if a magnate (*lendr maðr*) attacked someone in his own home, and was lucky enough to escape, he should never return to the country "except in the train of a king who comes to conquer the land" (nema með konunge þeim er siálfr ryðr land fyrir ser). "Den ældre Frostathings-Lov," in NGL vol. 1, 173. English translation in *The Earliest Norwegian Laws: Being the Gulathing Law and the Frostathing Law*, trans. Laurence M. Larson (New York, 1935), 278.
41. Sverre Bagge, *Society and Politics in Snorri Sturluson's Heimskringla* (Berkeley, 1991), 96.
42. We can be fairly certain that this event took place, as it is recounted in both *Gesta Danorum* and *Chronica Slavorum*. Saxo, 14.17.1; Helmold of Bosau, *Helmoldi Presbyteri Bozoviensis Chronica Slavorum*, 85.

43. Birgit Sawyer, "The 'Civil Wars' Revisited," *Historisk Tidsskrift* (N) 82, no. 1 (2003): 43–73 at 71.
44. Esben Albrectsen, "Konger og Krige, 700–1523," in *Dansk udenrigspolitiks historie*, ed. Carsten Due-Nielsen, Ole Feldbæk, and Nikolaj Petersen (Copenhagen, 2001), 83.

Dedicated Bibliography

Albrectsen, Esben. "Konger og Krige, 700–1523." In *Dansk udenrigspolitiks historie*, edited by Carsten Due-Nielsen, Ole Feldbæk, and Nikolaj Petersen, 13–215. Copenhagen, 2001.
Althoff, Gerd. *Family, Friends and Followers: Political and Social Bonds in Medieval Europe*. Cambridge, 2004.
Bagge, Sverre. *Society and Politics in Snorri Sturluson's Heimskringla*. Berkeley, 1991.
Breengaard, Carsten. *Muren om Israels hus: regnum og sacerdotium i Danmark 1050–1170*. Copenhagen, 1982.
Helmold von Bosau. *Helmoldi Presbyteri Bozoviensis Chronica Slavorum*. Edited by Johann M. Lappenberg and Bernhard Schmeidler. Hannover, 1909.
Hermanson, Lars. *Släkt, vänner och makt: En studie av elitens politiska kultur i 1100-talets Danmark*. Gothenburg, 2000.
Jordan, Karl. *Henry the Lion: A Biography*. Translated by Paul Stephen Falla. Oxford, 1986.
Kroman, Erik, ed. *Danmarks Middelalderlige Annaler*. Copenhagen, 1980.
Larson, Laurence M., trans. *The Earliest Norwegian Laws: Being the Gulathing Law and the Frostathing Law*. New York, 1935.
Liljefalk, Lone, and Stefan Pajung. "Helmolds Slaverkrønike som kilde til Danmarks, Vendens og Nordtysklands historie." *Historisk Tidsskrift* (D) 113, no. 1 (2014): 1–38.
Lind, John. "De russiske ægteskaber: Dynasti- og alliancepolitiki 1130'ernes danske borgerkrig." *Historisk Tidsskrift* (D) 92 (1992): 225–63.
Otto of Freising. *Ottonis et Rahewini: Gesta Friderici I. Imperatoris*. Edited by Georg Waitz. Hannover and Leipzig, 1912.
Rønning, Ole-Albert. "Beyond Borders: Material Support from Abroad in the Scandinavian Civil Wars, 1130–1180." MA thesis, University of Oslo, 2015.
Sawyer, Birgit. "The 'Civil Wars' revisited." *Historisk Tidsskrift* (N) 82, no. 1 (2003): 43–73.
Sigurðsson, Jón Viðar. *Den vennlige vikingen: Vennskapets makt i Norge og på Island ca. 900–1300*. Oslo, 2010.
Snorri Sturluson. "Magnúss Saga Blinda Ok Haralds Gilla." In *Íslenzk Fornrit XXVIII*, edited by Bjarni Aðalbjarnarson, 278–302. Reykjavík, 1951.
Snorri Sturluson. "Magnúss Saga Erlingssonar." In *Íslenzk Fornrit XXVIII*, edited by Bjarni Aðalbjarnarson, 372–417. Reykjavík, 1951.

15 Social Power and Conversion of Capital
Sune Ebbesen of Zealand

Kim Esmark

In a recent discussion of sociologist Michael Mann's typology of sources of social power and its relevance in a medieval context, Arnoud-Jan Bijsterveld proposes to complement Mann's notions of economic, ideological, military, and political power with a category called "social power in the narrow sense."[1] By constructing this category – pointing specifically to "the ability to establish and control social networks of mutually obliging relations through social mechanisms"[2] (i.e., gift exchange, marriage, dispute settlement, etc.) – Bijsterveld aims to highlight the fact that in medieval society, networks of social relations were the key to all other power assets. Without social power it was impossible to work and protect landed resources and control distribution of goods (economic power, the focus of volume 1 in this series), to form cultural meaning and shape public opinion (ideological power, the subject of volume 3), to mobilize armed forces on the basis of service and dependence (military power), or to command institutionalized means of regulation and coercion (political power). Applying the terminology of another sociologist, Pierre Bourdieu, "social power" may thus be seen as the basic binding material that enabled medieval elites to realize, integrate, or convert various forms of economic, political, symbolic, and other forms of *capital*.[3]

The sources for Danish medieval history only permit sporadic reconstruction of specific elite networks. While it is possible to discern some general patterns, only a few individuals (or groups of individuals) outside the royal families have left sufficient traces to provide a detailed impression of the actual workings of social power. One rare example is Sune Ebbesen (c. 1125?–86), a wealthy landowner, war leader, and trusted friend of three successive kings. Sune Ebbesen figures in charters and donation records; he has a prominent place in Saxo's *Gesta Danorum* (commissioned by Sune's cousin, Archbishop Absalon); and his name and fame were so great that his death was recorded in monastic annals – at that time an exceptional sign of honor for a layman.[4]

Sune Ebbesen operated in the twelfth century, a period during which the structure and *Spielregeln*, "rules of the game," of the power field underwent perceptible changes. Agrarian and commercial growth, sharpening of social boundaries, dynastic feuding, Church reform, centralization of authority, incipient clericalization of courts and law, and new cultural attributes all combined to open up new ways for elites to create, acquire, and employ social power. Speaking once again in sociological terms, the period saw an increasing *differentiation* as well as *concentration* of the forms of capital that structured positions and hierarchies among society's dominant groups.

How, then, did individual members of the elite in Denmark navigate those processes of transformation that were at once the context for and the outcome of their actions and strategies? How was social power produced and applied in the competition for status and resources? And how did traditional assets and practices translate into new forms of capital? These are the questions that will guide the following review of Sune Ebbesen's trajectory in the twelfth-century field of power.

Family and Inherited Capital

Sune Ebbesen was born – most likely sometime in the 1120s – into an important family, which was based in western Zealand between Ringsted and the lakes of Sorø and is referred to by modern historians as the "Hvide family" or "Skjalm clan."[5] As a member of this kin group he inherited not only landed wealth, but also fame and a tightly knit network of cognates and friends which extended to the royal family.

Sune's grandfather, Skjalm Hvide (d. c. 1113), was a prominent war leader under King Erik I the Good (r. 1095–1103), who entrusted him with the regional leadership of Zealand and the newly conquered island of Rügen.[6] According to Saxo, Skjalm succeeded in persuading the entire fleet of Zealand to follow him on a private campaign of revenge.[7] Sune's father, Ebbe, was one of Skjalm's five children. Ebbe resided with his wife Ragnhild, Sune's mother, at the manorial complex of Bjernede, but also held substantial possessions in northeastern Zealand, including the massive tower of Bastrup.[8] Sune himself grew up at Bjernede with two brothers and a sister. Less than five kilometers from Bjernede lay the manor of Fjenneslev, Skjalm's burial place and the home of Sune's paternal uncle Asser Rig. Two other uncles, Toke and Sune, resided in the same area, as did Sune's aunt Cecilia, who was married to Peter Torstensen, lord of Pedersborg Castle just north of Sorø Lake.[9]

Within this local family network Sune developed a particularly close relationship with Asser's sons, Absalon and Esbern Snare. The durability of this family tie is attested by the three cousins' later socio-political cooperation. A perhaps more sentimental expression of their lifelong bond is the mention in Absalon's will, drawn up shortly before his death in 1201, of a silver cup, once presented as a gift from Sune to Absalon and now bequeathed to Sune's son Anders, who came to succeed Absalon at the archepiscopal seat in Lund.[10]

Social Power and Conversion of Capital 287

During Sune's youth, prominent kin-groups in Zealand started to build family monasteries, *Hausklöster*. Land, farms, and watermills were converted into altars, prayers, and commemoration. To the south, the mighty Peder Bodilsen and his brothers founded an abbey in Næstved in 1135, while a donation from the king made the church of Ringsted into a royal cult center. Esrum Abbey in northern Zealand, established in the 1140s by Archbishop Eskil of the Trugund family, was probably also intended to be a *Hauskloster*. In the late 1140s the young Sune Ebbesen saw his father and uncles follow suit with the erection of a small Benedictine house on the island of Sorø – a testimony to the solidarity and aspirations of the family, even if the endowment did not compare to those of Næstved, Ringsted, or Esrum.[11]

In this period the power of the Skjalm clan was probably overshadowed by the Trugund faction, holders of the metropolitan see of Lund from 1103 to 1177, and by the Bodil family, headed by the previously mentioned Peder Bodilsen, who is said to have held particular authority among the Zealanders,[12] and who in 1137 singlehandedly decided the elections of the two most important bishoprics of the realm.[13]

In terms of social power or capital the Skjalm group's prime asset was its link to Erik the Good's branch of the royal line. Around 1100 King Erik had placed his son and heir, Knud Lavard, in Skjalm's custody,[14] and this bond of fosterage continued in the succeeding generation as Knud Lavard's son Valdemar (1131–82) spent at least some of his childhood years in the household of Fjenneslev with Sune's cousins Absalon and Esbern Snare.[15] Sune (and his father Ebbe before him) evidently shared these bonds with a line of potential royal claimants. The relationship would prove decisive for Sune during the dynastic wars, which came to

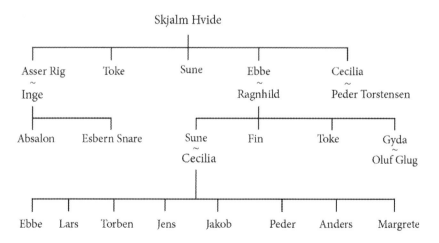

Figure 15.1 Selective genealogy of descendants of Skjalm Hvide.

involve his father and uncles right from their outbreak in 1131 and outlast his own entrance into the power field.

Bellum sociale, 1131–57: Loyalty, Defection, and New Deals

The dynastic wars began after years of increasing tension between competing candidates for the throne and their crisscrossing magnate networks. Skjalm Hvide's foster son Knud Lavard was suspected of aspiring to kingship and was killed in an ambush by his cousin Magnus, son and heir to the aging King Niels.[16] The assassination was obviously a tremendous blow to the prospects of Knud Lavards's foster brothers, who, as Saxo observed, had been very close to Knud through their upbringing together.[17] They called for revenge and rallied with other Zealand magnates behind Knud Lavard's half-brother Erik to start a rebellion.

We will not dwell upon the *histoire événementielle* of the wars that followed, but in the course of twenty-odd years various members of the royal lineage, backed up – or prompted – by shifting constellations of magnates, fought each other in a series of interrelated feuds.[18] The strife continued with varying intensity, occasionally interrupted by negotiations and periods of temporary peace or interstice. As the conflict wore on, rival parties sought to mobilize members of their existing networks – kinsmen, friends, patrons, and clients, at home and abroad – while also trying to build new relationships through gift-giving and marriage. Loyalties were tested, the prospects of each alliance evaluated. Loosely knit groups gained coherence, while other, supposedly close-bound factions split under pressure. Lords strove to identify potential defectors and worked to lure their rivals' supporters into their own camps, while lesser men and dependents, often cleverly investing in multiple loyalties, attempted to anticipate the rise and fall of those on top. Important people were killed, leaving positions to be occupied by new men. Land was confiscated and redistributed, strongholds built and/or destroyed, local social landscapes were changed, and regional power balances were transformed. It was these struggles that made Sune Ebbesen.

Initially, the fighting did not do much to alter the position of the Skjalm clan. Sune's father and uncles invested heavily in mobilizing support for Erik's revenge feud, but when Erik won the crown at the battle of Hamar (Fodevig) in 1134, where most of the Danish bishops were slain, they did not receive any of the vacant sees. Three years later Erik (now known as King Erik II Emune, "the Unforgettable") was killed by one of his own retainers at a public assembly. He was succeeded by Knud Lavard's nephew Erik III Lam ("the Lamb"), who spent years fighting his rebellious cousin Oluf, and once again there is no evidence of any particular gain for the Skjalm group.

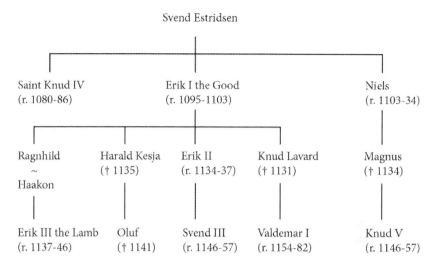

Figure 15.2 Selective genealogy of the royal kindred.

Erik the Lamb's abdication in 1146 created an opportunity for a fresh generation of contenders. Knud, son of Knud Lavard's murderer Magnus, was elected king by the magnates of Jutland. In the provinces of Zealand and Scania the leading men opted for Svend, son of Erik II and nephew of Knud Lavard, and had him acclaimed by the provincial assemblies. War soon resumed, and Svend quickly emerged as the stronger of the two kings. After the battle of Viborg in 1151, Knud saw his men swear allegiance to Svend and, before being finished off completely, he went into exile.[19]

Young Valdemar, son of Knud Lavard and foster child of Sune's uncle Asser Rig, was a natural ally of King Svend, and so was the Skjalm clan. Sune's father Ebbe in particular ranked among Svend's most loyal and trusted men. Saxo tells us that Svend was completely dependent on Ebbe's judgment in both public and private affairs.[20] Other identifiable magnates close to King Svend were the Jutlandic magnate Ulf of Ribe and Peder Torstensen, husband of Sune's aunt Cecilia.[21]

Sune himself reached manhood around this time and must have been part of Svend's retinue as well. When his father died in 1151, at the height of Svend's power, and was buried at the newly founded family sepulcher at Sorø, Sune may have hoped to inherit Ebbe's position. According to Saxo the news of Ebbe's death absolutely shocked Svend,[22] but the king does not seem to have had the same confidence in his friend's son, choosing instead to rely on Peder Torstensen, Ulf of Ribe, and other men.[23] It is even possible that Svend took back some of the lands that Ebbe had been awarded and thus deprived Sune of the means to sustain his own retinue – Sune later complained that his paternal estate had been taken from him.[24]

At Pentecost in 1152, Svend, Knud, and Valdemar gathered before the German king (later emperor) Frederick Barbarossa, Denmark's feudal overlord, at the Diet of Merseburg in order to negotiate a peace settlement. Svend's kingship was confirmed, Knud renounced his claim and contented himself with receiving the province of Zealand (although he ended up having to settle for scattered *beneficiae* in all three provinces), while Valdemar was acknowledged as duke of Schleswig. The agreement did not provide lasting peace, however, but rather prepared the way for new maneuvering. Having returned from exile, Knud somehow managed to rebuild a power base and soon initiated a process of rapprochement with Valdemar, who had gradually positioned himself as a sort of middleman and now cooperated with the son of his father's murderer.[25] The shift of alliance was sealed in 1154 when Valdemar, supposedly on the counsel of his own men, arranged to marry Knud's sister Sofia.[26] The two former enemies agreed on a dowry of no less than one-third of Knud's patrimony "as warrant of friendship and concord,"[27] and soon had themselves proclaimed co-kings at an assembly in Jutland.

This alliance evidently threatened Svend's position. It also provided an opportunity for Sune to reconsider his own options. The situation was not uncomplicated, and not everybody related to the Skjalm network followed the same course. The mighty Peder Torstensen, husband of Sune's aunt Cecilia, stayed loyal to King Svend, but as foster father of Valdemar's bastard child he maintained ties to both sides.[28] In the end Sune made the decisive choice to join his cousins' royal foster brother and leave Svend's camp.[29] His ousting from the king's inner circle had left him with few prospects there anyway. Perhaps the Skjalm network had even co-orchestrated Valdemar's move from the start?[30]

Sune's defection is vividly recounted by Saxo. Feeling his position progressively undermined, King Svend gathered his men in Odense before the relics of the saintly King Knud IV, who had been martyred in 1086 by revolting nobles and peasants and subsequently canonized – a powerful symbol of royal legitimacy and God's criminalization of rebellion.[31] Svend then ordered his men to confirm their loyalty to him on these holy bones. Sune, however, refused to perform the oath and walked out. The others tried to call him back and Svend even promised to restore his lands, but Sune was determined to retract his loyalty. Invoking cultural notions of good/bad lordship and obligations towards family, friends, and shared history, he pointed to the king's wrongdoings and to the bonds of his own father and grandfather which connected him to Valdemar.[32]

Svend's popularity was probably already waning when he lost the support of Valdemar, Sune, and their faction. According to the Saxon chronicler Helmold of Bosau, it was precisely when Knud realized that people had started to grumble about their king that he decided to approach

Valdemar.³³ After Merseburg, Saxo claims, Svend had become greedy and unjust. To demonstrate his power the king supplanted renowned nobles with lower-born upstarts and neglected to reward those who had helped him to secure his kingship, he introduced foreign courtly culture in the royal halls – paid for by rising taxes – and he interfered with local jurisdiction and treated the public assemblies with contempt.³⁴

Saxo's critique of Svend's regime may reflect actual changes at the royal court, but it is first and foremost a justifying narrative, intended to retrospectively *officialize* Sune's potentially dishonorable act of defection.³⁵ In any case, the fractionalization of Svend's network created a domino effect as more and more magnates lost faith in Svend and withdrew their loyalty. Without suffering a military defeat, Svend lost his social power, his ability to attract and control enough important men to maintain his kingship. Considerably weakened, he soon had to leave the country.

In late 1156 the wars came to a finale when Svend returned, aided by neighboring princes and local Danish networks. Negotiations were initiated, mediated by lay and ecclesiastical magnates with ties to both sides, and a new division of power between the three kings was agreed upon. In August 1157 the various parties gathered in Roskilde to celebrate the concord, but during the banquet violence broke out and Knud was killed. Valdemar, who escaped, quickly married Knud's sister in order to secure the loyalty of those men who had just lost their lord. On 23 October the armies of Svend and Valdemar clashed at Grathe Heath in northern Jutland. Svend was slain and Valdemar was recognized as sole king of Denmark.

Königsnähe, 1157–86: Spoils of War and Royal Friendship

The freshly crowned Valdemar was under pressure from Knud's men, who expected him to avenge their deceased lord. The new ruler, however, proceeded with discretion. Some of Svend's close associates, like Ulf of Ribe, were executed, but many others were offered a place in the reconfigured power field. Among them was Sune's cognate, Peder Torstensen, who seems to have merged smoothly into Valdemar's entourage. A certain Thorbern, who had been connected to Svend through bonds of fosterage, was exiled at first, but then became royal castellan – presumably thanks to his bonds to Sune and Absalon.³⁶ Members of the royal kin, who might pose a future threat, enjoyed prominent positions during the early years of Valdemar's reign, only to be purged later on.

For Sune and his kinsmen and friends, Valdemar's victory meant they were now able to truly share in the spoils of kingship, and to establish themselves as members of the uppermost stratum within the elite. First of all, they finally got hold of a high clerical office when Valdemar installed his foster brother Absalon as bishop of Roskilde in 1158.³⁷ Absalon had only just returned from his studies in Paris – he may have been the first Dane to study there – and quickly made his mark on Valdemar's *regnum*.[38] Sune himself profited enormously from the extensive redistribution of land that accompanied the shift of power. The paternal estates he claimed to have lost after the death of his father were now restored. Moreover, like Valdemar's other supporters, he was granted a considerable share of the possessions that were confiscated from the war's losing parties.[39] Thus, he gradually grew to become one of the wealthiest landowners in the kingdom. Historians have estimated that at his death in 1186 he left an inheritance of perhaps 50,000 acres of land (c. 200 km²), the equivalent of no fewer than 750 farms. The worth of the accompanying movables, valuables, and cash is impossible to calculate.[40]

Sune may have inherited some of his land from his wife, Cecilia, who seems to have died before him,[41] and some of it may have been purchased with money and goods acquired through plunder. The decades following the end of the dynastic wars saw continual Danish military activity against the pagan Wends. Sune took a leading role as commander in these campaigns along with his cognates Absalon, Esbern Snare, and Peder Torstensen. According to Saxo, it was Sune and Esbern Snare who, after the conquest of Rügen in 1169, took charge of the ritual destruction of Svantevit, the Wendish idol.[42] The raids against the Wends took place under some kind of crusading umbrella, and after almost three decades of strife the campaigns no doubt contributed to internal pacification.[43] Magnates and their retainers and dependents could unite in a just war against exterior enemies and earn "booty, cattle, corn and slaves" from plunder or from tribute paid in exchange for peace.[44]

The political power of Sune and his associates gradually increased, and they came to be involved in most of the decisions and achievements of King Valdemar and his son and successor, King Knud VI (r. 1182–1202). Saxo, our main source for the political history of the period, probably exaggerates the influence of Skjalm's descendants – after all, Absalon was Saxo's patron – but royal charters confirm that Sune and Absalon belonged to King Valdemar's entourage right from the start of his reign. As attested by these same charters, however, Sune and Absalon shared their *Königsnähe* (lit. "nearness to the king") with other nobles, whose names are mostly passed over by Saxo. The Bodil family, old rivals of the Skjalm clan in southern Zealand, also figured at the Valdemarian court.[45]

The Skjalm group's fortunes increased when Valdemar's infant son Knud was acclaimed by the army in 1166 and formally crowned four years later in Ringsted, and when potential rivals to the throne, allied to other magnate networks, came to be eliminated.[46] The decisive turning point occurred in 1177, when Absalon was made archbishop of Lund (ousting the elderly Eskil of the Trugund family) *and* allowed to keep the see of Roskilde. Along with Absalon, the recipient of this most exceptional dual-bishopric, Sune, Esbern Snare, and other men from their circle of *familiares* were awarded lucrative posts as royal officials (*umbuthsmen*) in the wealthy province of Scania.[47] Informal bonds of friendship were thus given a more formal, institutionalized shape. In their capacity of "public" officials, Sune and his companions inadvertently contributed to the centralizing efforts of the *regnum*. However, as noted by Michael Kræmmer, medieval magnates regarded royal and ecclesiastical offices as perfectly legitimate sources for private enrichment,[48] and Sune and his fellow *umbuthsmen* from Zealand certainly had no objection to imposing harsh taxes and labor duties as well as violating traditional rights. Their stern measures spawned resistance among the Scanians, who wanted Sune and the others – all "born outside Scania" – removed,[49] but violent uprisings in 1178–82 were crushed by the combined forces of the king and archbishop.[50]

King Valdemar's death in May 1182 might have put the position of Sune and his cognates at risk. Their position depended on the succession of Valdemar's teenaged son Knud, which could not be taken for granted despite his formal acclamation and coronation as a boy. If we are to believe Saxo, it was Sune who first recognized the potential crisis and initiated plans to promote the cause of the young protégé.[51] To get a grip on the kingdom, says Saxo, it was imperative to act swiftly. On the counsel of Sune and his friends, Knud therefore hurried to Jutland immediately after Valdemar's funeral to have the late king's knights (*milites*) swear fealty to him.[52] In the following years young Knud ruled under the strong influence of his father's circle of advisors. When Sune himself died in 1186, his cousin, the archbishop Absalon, and his faction seem to have been virtual co-rulers of the kingdom.

Conversion of Capital

Skillful use of social relationships (and the inevitable element of chance) had brought Sune immense wealth and power. Economic and political capital, however, also translated back into social power, as it meant that Sune was able to distribute benefits (land, gifts, positions, privileges) on a steadily expanding scale. Regrettably, the sources do not allow us to explore the structure of Sune's household or wider entourage in detail,[53] but he obviously benefitted from a nearly unrivaled capacity to attract men and to maintain what must have been a vast network of oath-sworn retainers, stewards, clerks, friends, and dependents. As for any lay lord of the time, it was this structure of relationships which constituted Sune's essential power base and provided him with the means to operate as a member of the elite.

A further look at Sune's trajectory reveals the workings of conversion strategies with regard to two other aspects of elite status: symbolic legitimation and social reproduction. As noted by Max Weber, social elites privileged through existing structures of domination are never content to exert power in its naked form. Instead, they wish "to see their positions transformed from purely factual power relations into a cosmos of acquired rights, and to know that they are thus sanctified."[54] In the twelfth century such symbolic justification consisted above all in "the close association of secular and religious power."[55]

Sune Ebbesen is a perfect example in this respect. Around 1170 he decided to replace the old wooden manorial church that had been built by his parents at the paternal estate in Bjernede with a new, spectacular (and costly) round church of made of bricks and granite blocks. The peculiar plan of the building in itself served as a manifest display of the founder's elevated status.[56] The inscription above the entrance door – "Ebbe, son of Skjalm, and his wife Ragnhild constructed a church here, which his son Sune later raised in stone in honor of God and St Mary and St Laurentius"[57] – pointed to the nexus between place, history, family lineage, and otherworldly authorities. St Laurentius was one of the most popular saints among Danish church builders, and Sune had one of his sons named after the martyr. St Mary was of course the special patroness of the Cistercians, who at this time were embraced by the Danish elite, including Sune's own kindred. Thus, in 1161, Absalon, Esbern Snare, and Sune undertook a fundamental reorganization of the monastery founded by their fathers at Sorø. Determined to create a *sepultura cognitionis* worthy of the family's newly won fame and fortune, they replaced the Benedictine community with monks from the Cistercian order, pulled down the old wooden structure to make way for a grand new abbey church in Fontenay style, and initiated the expansion of a much richer endowment. A wide circle of kinsmen and friends joined the project, eager to associate themselves with the cultic center of a family headed by men close to the king, and contributed pious gifts of land, watermills, forests, and fishing ponds from all over Zealand.[58]

Sune made considerable grants himself. At some point in the 1170s he took a joint vow with his cousins to leave Sorø Abbey one half-lot of inheritance when he died (the maximum limit allowed by law for post-mortem gifts).[59] Before that he had already made another joint donation with Thorbern, the royal castellan mentioned earlier.[60] Sune's mother Ragnhild, his brother Toke, and his sister Gyda all contributed gifts as well.[61] His aunt Cecilia also wished to make a donation, but the size of her grant was restricted by her husband, Peder Torstensen, who once again resisted the dominant trend within the network.[62]

Sune was buried at Sorø Abbey with his wife, Cecilia. Most of the other donors would come to rest there too (despite the Cistercian prohibitions against lay burials) and have their names memorialized in holy prayer. By this time Sorø Abbey was rapidly becoming one of the wealthiest and most prestigious religious houses in Denmark, a sacred *memoria* of the status and history of its patrons – or, in sociological terms, a "deposit" of their accumulated symbolic capital.[63] Moreover, the monastery's network of benefactors was a living testimony to the Skjalm faction's *zusammengehörigskeitsgefühl*, and, hence, to the social power of the group's leading men.[64]

Elites don't just worry about legitimacy; they also concern themselves with preserving and promoting the standing of the next generation. Sune and his wife Cecilia had one daughter and seven sons. Margrete, the daughter, married well. Her husband is unknown, but her grandchildren include Archbishop Jakob Erlandsen (d. 1274) and other high-ranking nobles. As for the sons, five of them followed closely in the footsteps of their father, grandfather, and great-grandfather: Ebbe, the firstborn, was named after his grandfather (the name being a significant carrier of symbolic capital) and seems to have inherited Sune's position at the royal court.[65] He died in battle along with his brother Lars in a failed attempt to reinstate his son-in-law as king of Sweden.[66] Torben was killed in 1198 on a military expedition in northern Germany and Jens died a few years later on a pilgrimage or crusade to Jerusalem, while Jakob, who for years ranked among the foremost lay nobles of the realm, lived on until 1246.[67]

With regard to reproduction strategies, however, it is Sune's sons Peder and Anders who attract attention. In the second half of the twelfth century, intellectual capital obtained through formal education was rapidly becoming an ever more relevant asset amongst the elite. The educational requirements for entering high clerical offices were growing, the king was building a proper chancellery on the model of Church bureaucracy, and even some lay lords would staff their households with a scribe.[68]

Access to schooling depended on both money and international connections, and Sune had both. Peder and Anders, both born in the early 1160s, were taught Latin either by a teacher at home or in Sorø or Roskilde.[69] Around the age of fifteen they were then dispatched to Paris, Europe's foremost center of learning at the time, probably inspired by the example of their cognate Absalon, and certainly with the benefit of his contacts within the French intellectual milieu. During his own stay in Paris Absalon had formed a friendship with William, regular canon of the renowned Abbey of Ste Geneviève. Later, as bishop of Roskilde, Absalon invited William to Denmark, where he became abbot of the Augustinian community at Æbelholt in northern Zealand.[70] Absalon had also befriended the famous Stephen of Tournai, who was elected abbot of the same Ste Geneviève Abbey in 1176. It was thanks to these connections that Peder came to study at Ste Geneviève in the 1180s. Extant letters show how both William and Stephen involved themselves wholeheartedly in the young man's education and career.[71] Æbelholt Abbey benefitted from Sune's (and later his son Ebbe's) patronage, and this relationship clearly furthered William's commitment to helping Peder.[72]

Abbot Stephen praised Peder's untiring efforts and exemplary conduct as a student. But Peder was also the self-conscious offspring of the mighty Sune Ebbesen of Zealand and, despite his fragile health, he reportedly received a stream of acquaintances and friends in Paris, the costs of which concerned his father back home. At one point Peder apparently wanted to give up his studies, and had William plead his case to Sune, but to no avail, as, according to the abbot, it was impermissible "to go against your father's will and wise counsel."[73] Peder's brother Anders also studied in Paris and even traveled to Bologna and Oxford, returning home in the early 1190s as a member of the intellectual and ecclesiastical elite of Latin Europe, as described in more detail in Wojtek Jezierski's chapter.[74]

Sune's investments paid off. Within the domestic elite most rival factions controlled lands and people, but not many possessed credentials from Christianity's foremost schools. The process of converting traditional sources of wealth and social power into objectified educational capital not only transformed the composition of the family capital, it also made it more exclusive, and hence more valuable. To profit from this investment, however, social power – networks, connections, patrons – was once again necessary. Thus, upon his return in 1187/88 Peder was welcomed by Absalon, who first made him canon at his see of Lund, and then, in 1192, let him take over the bishopric of Roskilde. From 1202 Peder also acted as royal chancellor. When Anders returned home he started off by serving as provost at his brother's church in Roskilde. Around 1194 he became royal chancellor, and in 1202 he succeeded Absalon as archbishop. His highly learned Latin paraphrase of the Law of Scania was a key achievement in the emergent judicial field. Both Peder and Anders evidently came to exert even greater power than their secular brothers. Like them, however, the two ordained Sunesens also embraced the more traditional aspects of elite life. As prelates they both followed the example of Absalon and other episcopal predecessors and personally commanded a series of military expeditions in northern Germany and the Baltics. In the "list of brothers," an enigmatic catalogue of Danish magnates from around 1200, Peder and Anders are grouped together with all their secular brothers (except Jakob) as a single exclusive band.[75]

Conclusion

Sune Ebbesen of Zealand was the high-born inheritor of landed wealth, ancestral reputation, family ties, and bonds of fictive kinship to a potentially important branch of the royal family. During the upheaval of the dynastic feuds of the 1150s, as well as the subsequent years of peace, he was able, with his cognates and friends, to bring these assets successfully into play. Displaying, as far as we can judge, a keen sense for anticipating movements within the power field, he managed to carve out a truly dominant position among the elites.

In the course of his lifetime the structure and *Spielregeln* of the power field grew progressively more complex. Adapting to this transformation through various strategies of capital conversion, Sune and his group not

Social Power and Conversion of Capital 297

only managed to maintain and even reinforce their position: In the kind of self-propelling circularity that drives every historical transformation process, they also *created* the very changes they strove to adapt to by co-promoting centralized authority and increasing the relative value of religious and educational capital. All along the way, however, social power – defined in this chapter as the capacity to establish and control social relations and networks – remained the necessary key converter in the competition of the elites.[76]

William of Æbelholt's often-quoted laudatory portrait of Sune Ebbesen as "a man of wise counsel, mighty of action and speech" was obviously meant to ingratiate the abbot with his generous, but also paternalistic and occasionally quarrelsome, benefactor.[77] William, however, may not have been quite off target, provided his words are read, not as an evaluation of one particular magnate's individual character, but as a generic description of the social habitus of a successful member of the medieval Danish elite.

Notes

1. Michael Mann, *The Sources of Social Power*, 4 vols., 2nd ed. (Cambridge, 2012); Arnoud-Jan Bijsterveld, "Memoria and Nobility Research in the Netherlands," in *Verortete Herrschaft*, ed. Jens Lieven, Bert Thissen, and Ronald Wientjes (Bielefeld, 2014), 211–30 at 227–30.
2. Bijsterveld, "Memoria," 229.
3. Pierre Bourdieu, "The Forms of Capital," in *Handbook of Theory of Research for the Sociology of Education*, ed. John E. Richardson and trans. Richard Nice (Westport, CT, 1986), 241–58; Pierre Bourdieu, *Distinction: A Social Critique of the Judgement of Taste*, trans. Richard Nice (Cambridge, MA, 1984), 125–68; *The State Nobility*, trans. Lauretta C. Clough (Oxford, 1996), 272–99.
4. AD, 91, 137, 145, 195.
5. Marianne Johansen and Helle Halding, *Thi de var af stor slægt: Om Hvideslægten og kongemagt i dansk højmiddelalder* (Gylling, 2001); Michael Kræmmer, *Den hvide klan: Absalon, hans slægt og hans tid* (Viborg, 1999). Some historians have suggested that Skjalm's ancestry might be traced back to an old royal family from before the unification of the Danish realm: see Anne Nissen Jaubert, "Un ou plusieurs royaumes danois?" in *Les élites et leurs espaces*, ed. Phillipe Depreux, François Bougard, and Regine Le Jan (Turnhout, 2007), 135–54.
6. Saxo, 11.5.3, 12.6.5. Saxo's term is *procuratio*, which suggests that Skjalm, who presumably had made the Rügians tributary himself, carried the title of *jarl*.
7. Saxo, 12.4.1. Most historians suspect Saxo of exaggerating Skjalm's actual power in order to glorify his descendants. See Lars Hermanson, *Släkt, vänner och makt: en studie av elitens politiska kultur i 1100-talets Danmark* (Gothenburg, 2000), 151.
8. DD 1.2.34; Erik Ulsig, *Danske adelsgodser i middelalderen* (Copenhagen, 1968), 40.
9. Michael Kræmmer, "Peder Torstensen af Borg," in *Årbog for Historisk samfund for Sorø Amt* 88 (2001): 21–35.

10. DD 1.4.32. In his will Absalon also forgave Sune's sons an unpaid debt of 130 marks of silver, which Sune had not paid before he died.
11. Tore Nyberg, *Monasticism in North-Western Europe, 800–1200* (Aldershot, 2000), 99–109, 117–18, 136, 145; Thomas Hill, *Könige, Fürsten und Klöster: Studien zu den dänischen Klostergründungen des 12. Jahrhunderts* (Frankfurt am Main, 1992), 125–57, 183–205; Poul Nørlund, "Klostret og dets gods," in *Sorø: Klostret, skolen, akademiet gennem tiderne*, 2 vols., vol. I, ed. Mouritz Mackeprang and William Norvin (Copenhagen, 1924–3153–131 at 53–56.
12. Saxo, 14.1.11.
13. Lone Liljefalk and Stefan Pajung, "Bodil-slægten – en sydsjællandsk gåde," *Personalhistorisk tidsskrift* 1 (2013): 46–60; Hermanson, *Släkt, vänner och makt*, 154–59; Michael H. Gelting, "Da Eskil ville være ærkebiskop af Roskilde: Roskildekrøniken, *Liber daticus Lundensis* og det danske ærkesædes ophævelse 1133–1138," in *Ett annat 1100-tal*, ed. Peter Carelli, Lars Hermanson, and Hanne Sanders (Gothenburg, 2004), 181–229.
14. Saxo, 12.6.5.
15. John Lind, "De russiske ægteskaber: Dynasti- og alliancepolitik i 1130'ernes danske borgerkrig," *Historisk Tidsskrift* (D) 92 (1992): 225–63.
16. For a detailed analysis of the tensions that led to the killing of Knud Lavard see Hermanson, *Släkt, vänner och makt*, 92–147. On the political aims of the Skjalm clan in particular, see John Danstrup, "Træk af den politiske kamp 1131–82," in *Festskrift til Erik Arup den 22. November 1946*, ed. Astrid Friis and Albert Olsen (Copenhagen, 1946), 67–87; Niels Skyum-Nielsen, *Kvinde og slave* (Copenhagen, 1971), 241.
17. Saxo, 13.7.1: "quibus multa ad eum ex educationis communione familiaritas erat."
18. For some useful standard overviews, see Carsten Breengaard, *Muren om Israels hus* (Copenhagen, 1982), 203–62; Ole Fenger, *Kirker bygges alle vegne: 1050–1250*, 2nd ed. (Copenhagen, 2002), 71–76, 126–43; Hermanson, *Släkt, vänner och makt*, is by far the most thorough work on the prosopographical intricacies of the conflicts, but see also Danstrup, "Træk af den politiske kamp"; Birgit Sawyer, "The 'Civil Wars' Revisited," *Historisk Tidsskrift* (D) 82 (2003): 43–73.
19. Saxo, 14.4.9. On Knud's exile see the contribution by Ole-Albert Rønning in chapter 14 in this volume.
20. Saxo, 14.4.3; cf. also *Knytlinge Saga*, trans. Jens Peter Ægidius (Copenhagen, 1977), 141.
21. Saxo, 1.2.101; Saxo, 14.7.5.
22. Saxo, 14.4.3.
23. Danstrup, "Træk af den politiske kamp," 74; Breengaard, *Muren om Israels hus*, 248.
24. Saxo, 14.16.5.
25. Sven Aggesen, *Brevis historia regum Dacie*, in SM I, ch. XVI, 136: "medius illis alternum impendebat subsidium."
26. Saxo, 14.14.2. The alliance also seems to have incorporated the network of Peder Bodilsen, whose niece was Knud's sister's fosterer: Hermanson, *Släkt, vänner och makt*, 220.
27. Ægidius, *Knytlinge Saga*, 144.
28. Kræmmer, "Peder Torstensen på Borg," 27–28.
29. As for Sune's cousins, we must surmise that Esbern Snare followed him in leaving Svend. Absalon was studying in Paris at the time.
30. Kræmmer, *Den hvide klan*, 75; Danstrup, "Træk af den politiske kamp," 74.

Social Power and Conversion of Capital   299

31. King Knud IV received papal canonization in 1101. For the symbolic meaning of his martyrdom and sanctification, see Kim Esmark, "Spinning the Revolt: The Assassination and Sanctification of an 11th-Century Danish King," in *Rebellion and Resistance*, ed. Henrik Jensen (Pisa, 2009), 15–32.
32. Saxo, 14.16.4–5.
33. Helmold von Bosau, *Chronica Slavorum/Slawenchronik*, ed. and trans. Heinz Stoob (Darmstadt, 1973), ch. 85, 298–99.
34. Saxo, 14.9.1–4.
35. Pierre Bourdieu, *The Logic of Practice*, trans. Richard Nice (Cambridge, 1990), 108–9; Kim Esmark, "Just Rituals: Masquerade, Manipulation, and Officializing Strategies in Saxo's *Gesta Danorum*," in *Rituals, Performatives, and Political Order in Northern Europe, c. 650–1350*, ed. Wojtek Jezierski, Lars Hermanson, Hans Jacob Orning, and Thomas Småberg (Turnhout, 2015), 237–68 at 244–45; Lars Hermanson, "How to Legitimate Rebellion and Condemn Usurpation of the Crown: Discourses of Fidelity and Treason in the *Gesta Danorum* of Saxo Grammaticus," in *Disputing Strategies in Medieval Scandinavia*, ed. Kim Esmark et al. (Leiden, 2013), 107–40.
36. Hermanson, *Släkt, vänner och makt*, 152, 229–32; Danstrup, "Træk af den politiske magt," 80–81.
37. At the time of Absalon's appointment, lay investiture was still considered perfectly in line with prevailing norms and practices. See Breengaard, *Muren om Israels hus*, 272–75.
38. On the achievements of Absalon as a Danish Church official, see *Archbishop Absalon of Lund and His World*, ed. Karsten Friis-Jensen and Inge Skovgaard-Petersen (Roskilde, 2000); and the contribution by Wojtek Jezierski in chapter 9 in this volume.
39. Hermanson, *Släkt, vänner och makt*, 245.
40. Poul Nørlund, "Jorddrotter paa Valdemarstiden," in *Festskrift til Kristian Erslev*, ed. Poul Nørlund (Copenhagen, 1927), 141–70; Tage E. Christiansen, "Sune Ebbesens halve hovedlod," *Historisk Tidsskrift* (D) 81 (1981): 183–92; Ulsig, *Danske adelsgodser*, 25, 40; Skyum-Nielsen, *Kvinde og slave*, 240, describes Sune as "a landed potentate of gruesome dimensions."
41. Christiansen, "Sune Ebbesens halve hovedlod," 183–84.
42. Saxo, 14.39.31; Esmark, "Just Rituals," 246–47.
43. Breengaard, *Muren om Israels hus*, 303; Ane L. Bysted, Carsten Selch Jensen, Kurt Villads Jensen, and John H. Lind, *Jerusalem in the North: Denmark and the Baltic Crusades, 1100–1522*, trans. Sarah Pedersen and Fredrik Pedersen (Turnhout, 2012).
44. Skyum-Nielsen, *Kvinde og slave*, 151; Kræmmer, *Den hvide klan*, 136.
45. DD 1.2.120, 1.2.122, 1.2.128–131, 1.3.45, 1.3.49, 1.3.55, 1.3.62, 1.3.89; Danstrup, "Træk af den politiske kamp," 75–76, 82; Hermanson, *Släkt, vänner och makt*, 199–200.
46. Hermanson, *Släkt, vänner och makt*, 236–41; Hermanson, "How to Legitimate Rebellion," 120–34.
47. Exactly which titles or offices the Zealand magnates held in Scania is not clear and may not be important to their functions of power (Saxo, 15.4.1, 1454–55. Saxo refers to royal *questores* and *prefecti*, while the *Vetus chronica Sialandie*, in SM II, 52, speaks of *exactores*). According to Skyum-Nielsen, *Kvinde og slave*, 175, Sune Ebbesen also carried the title of *marascallus* in the 1180s, but the royal marshal seems to have been his nephew Gunne: cf. DD 1.3.135.
48. Kræmmer, *Den hvide klan*, 108.

49. Saxo, 15.4.11: "Saxonem, Achonem, Sunonem et Esbernum, homines extra Scaniam ortos."
50. Poul Holm, "De skånsk-hallandske bondeoprør 1180–82," in *Til kamp for friheden: Sociale oprør i nordisk middelalder*, ed. Anders Bøgh, Jørgen Würtz Sørensen, and Lars Tvede-Jensen, 72–89 (Aalborg, 1988); Hermanson, *Släkt, vänner och makt*, 241–45.
51. Saxo, 15.6.8.
52. Saxo, 16.1.1.
53. General observations on twelfth-century lay and ecclesiastical households in Skyum-Nielsen, *Kvinde og slave*, 178–80.
54. H. Gerth and C. Wright Mills, *From Max Weber: Essays in Sociology* (Oxford, 1946), 157.
55. Bijsterveld, "Memoria," 228.
56. Christiansen, "Sune Ebbesens halve hovedlod," 191.
57. *Danmarks kirker V: Sorø Amt*, 2 vols., vol. I, ed. Victor Hermansen and Poul Nørlund (Copenhagen, 1936–38), 352: "Ebbo filius Scelmonis et uxor eius Rachanild construxerunt hic ecclesiam quam postea filius eius Suno erexit lapideam in onore Dei et Sce. Marie et Sci. Laurenci."
58. SRD IV, 467–74; Nørlund, "Klostret og dets gods," 56–71; Kim Esmark, "Religious Patronage and Family Consciousness: Sorø Abbey and the 'Hvide family,' c. 1150–1250," in *Religious and Laity in Western Europe, 1000–1400: Interaction, Negotiation, and Power*, ed. E. Jamroziak and J. E. Burton (Turnhout, 2006), 110.
59. SRD IV, 473. The pledge was corroborated in a papal charter of 1182: see DD 1.3.100.
60. SRD IV, 470.
61. SRD IV, 467–69.
62. SRD IV, 467. Peder Torstensen may simply have prioritized his own lineage – virtually left in the dark by the sources – over that of his wife's.
63. Cf. Karl-J. Hölkeskamp, *Reconstructing the Roman Republic: An Ancient Political Culture and Modern Research*, trans. Henry Heitmann-Gordon (Princeton and Oxford, 2010), 107–24.
64. The family even got its own saint: In the 1170s Margrete, a close relative (*consanguina*) of Sune's sons, was killed by her husband and unjustly accused of suicide, but proved innocent by heavenly wonders and enshrined by Absalon in the episcopal church of Roskilde (*De S. Margareta Roskildensi*, VSD, 389–90).
65. DD 1.3.179 and 1.3.216.
66. In the annals, Ebbe and Lars were styled "bravest of warriors, sons of lord Sune of Zealand from Knardrup" (fortissimus pugnatoribus, filiis domini Sunonis Sialandici de Knarretorp): see AD, 139 (also 134, 146).
67. Skyum-Nielsen, *Kvinde og slave*, 240–44; Michael Kræmmer, *Kongemordernes slægt* (Copenhagen, 2007), 27–33; Esmark, "Religious Patronage," 104–5.
68. Fenger, *Kirker bygges alle vegne*, 216–21; *Dansk forvaltningshistorie I*, ed. Leon Jespersen, E. Ladewig Petersen, and Ditlev Tamm (Copenhagen, 2000), 3–48; Skyum-Nielsen, *Kvinde og slave*, 176–78.
69. Sten Ebbesen, "To lærde ærkebiskopper," in *Lund – medeltida kyrkometropol*, ed. Per Olov Ahrén and Anders Jarlert (Lund, 2004), 145–70 at 148.
70. Cf. the contribution by Wojtek Jezierski in chapter 9 in this volume.
71. DD 1.3.128–133, 1.3.153–154; *Epistolæ abbatis Wiilelmi de Paraclito*, DD 1.3.II.30.
72. DD 1.3.I.39, 1.3.II.19, 1.3.II.30, and 1.3.II.73. William also acted as the king's foremost spokesman in communications with foreign princes.

73. DD 1.3.II.30: "patris tui uolentati sanisque consiliis . . . obuiare non licuit." More on Ste Geneviève and Peder's stay in Paris in Gudrun Hastrup and Birger Munk Olsen, "Paris, Philip August og Peder Sunesen – En dansker i Paris i 1180'erne," in *AIGIS Supplementum II: Festskrift til Adam Bülow-Jakobsen* (Institut for Græsk og Latin, Københavns Universitet, 2013), http://aigis.igl.ku.dk/aigis/AB-J/GH.BMO.pdf..
74. Sten Ebbesen, ed., *Anders Sunesen: stormand, teolog, administrator, digter: femten studier* (Copenhagen, 1985); Kræmmer, *Kongemordernes slægt*, 48–60.
75. *Kong Valdemars Jordebog*, ed. Svend Aakjær, 3 vols. (Copenhagen, 1926–45, repr. 1980), I, 86. The purpose and editorial principle behind the "list of brothers" remains a matter of scholarly dispute. See most recently Janus Møller Jensen, ed., *Broderliste, broderskab, korstog: bidrag til opklaringen af en gåde fra dansk højmiddelalder* (Odense, 2006).
76. Cf. Régine le Jan on European elites of the same period, who "developed strategies of reproduction within open networks based on ties of cognatic kinship, friendship and fidelity, by mobilizing all their human capital, male and female, clerical and lay." ("ont su développer des stratégies de reproduction à l'intérieur de réseaux ouverts qui réposaient sur des liens de parenté cognatique, d'ámitié et de fidélité, en mobilisant tout leur capital humain, masculin et féminin, clérical et laïque"). Régine le Jan, "Les élites au haut moyen âge: approche sociologique et anthropologique," in *Théorie et pratiques des élites au Haut Moyen Age: Conception, perception et réalisation sociale*, ed. F. Bougard, H-W. Goetz, and R. Le Jan (Turnhout, 2011), 69–99 at 98.
77. DD 1.3.II.30: "Uir siquidem consilii est, potens in opere et sermone."

Dedicated Bibliography

Aakjær, Svend, ed. *Kong Valdemars Jordebog*, 3 vols. Copenhagen, 1926–45, reprinted 1980.
Archbishop Absalon of Lund and his World. Edited by Karsten Friis-Jensen and Inge Skovgaard-Petersen. Roskilde, 2000.
Bijsterveld, Arnoud-Jan A. "Memoria and Nobility Research in the Netherlands." In *Verortete Herrschaft*, edited by Jens Lieven, Bert Thissen, and Ronald Wientjes, 211–30. Bielefeld, 2014.
Bourdieu, Pierre. *Distinction: A Social Critique of the Judgement of Taste*. Translated by Richard Nice. Cambridge, MA, 1984.
Bourdieu, Pierre. "The Forms of Capital." In *Handbook of Theory of Research for the Sociology of Education*, edited by John E. Richardson and translated by Richard Nice, 241–58. Westport, CT, 1986.
Bourdieu, Pierre. *The Logic of Practice*. Translated by Richard Nice. Cambridge, 1990.
Bourdieu, Pierre. *The State Nobility*. Translated by Lauretta C. Clough. Oxford, 1996.
Breengaard, Carsten. *Muren om Israels hus: regnum og sacerdotium i Danmark 1050–1170*. Copenhagen, 1982.
Bysted, Ane L., Carsten Selch Jensen, Kurt Villads Jensen, and John H. Lind. *Jerusalem in the North: Denmark and the Baltic Crusades, 1100–1552*. Translated by Sarah Pedersen and Fredrik Pedersen. Turnhout, 2012.

Christiansen, Tage E. "Sune Ebbesens halve hovedlod." *Historisk Tidsskrift* (D) 81 (1981): 183–92.
Danstrup, John. "Træk af den politiske kamp 1131–82." In *Festskrift til Erik Arup den 22. November 1946*, edited by Astrid Friis and Albert Olsen. Copenhagen, 1946.
Ebbesen, Sten, ed. *Anders Sunesen: Stormand, Teolog, Administrator, Digter: Femten Studier*. Copenhagen, 1985.
Ebbesen, Sten. "To lærde ærkebiskopper." In *Lund – medeltida kyrkometropol*, edited by Per Olov Ahrén and Anders Jarlert, 145–70. Lund, 2004.
Esmark, Kim. "Religious Patronage and Family Consciousness: Sorø Abbey and the 'Hvide family', c. 1150–1250." In *Religious and Laity in Western Europe 1000–1400: Interaction, Negotiation, and Power*, edited by Emilia Jamroziak and Janet Burton, 93–110. Turnhout, 2006.
Esmark, Kim. "Spinning the Revolt: The Assassination and Sanctification of an 11th-Century Danish King." In *Rebellion and Resistance*, edited by Henrik Jensen, 15–32. Pisa, 2009.
Esmark, Kim. "Just Rituals: Masquerade, Manipulation, and Officializing Strategies in Saxo's *Gesta Danorum*." In *Rituals, Performatives, and Political Order in Northern Europe, c. 650–1350*, edited by Wojtek Jezierski, Lars Hermanson, Hans Jacob Orning, and Thomas Småberg, 237–68. Turnhout, 2015.
Fenger, Ole. *Kirker bygges alle vegne: 1050–1250*. 2nd ed. Copenhagen, 2002.
Gelting, Michael H. "Da Eskil ville være ærkebiskop af Roskilde. Roskildekrøniken, *Liber daticus Lundensis* og det danske ærkesædes ophævelse 1133–1138." In *Ett annat 1100-tal*, edited by Peter Carelli, Lars Hermanson, and Hanne Sanders, 181–229. Gothenburg, 2004.
Gerth, H., and C. Wright Mills. *From Max Weber: Essays in Sociology*. Oxford, 1946.
Helmold von Bosau. *Chronica Slavorum/Slawenchronik*. Edited and translated by Heinz Stoob. Darmstadt, 1973.
Hermansen, Victor, and Poul Nørlund, eds. *Danmarks kirker V: Sorø Amt*. 2 vols. Copenhagen, 1936–38.
Hermanson, Lars. *Släkt, vänner och makt. En studie av elitens politiska kultur i 1100-talets Danmark*. Gothenburg, 2000.
Hermanson, Lars. "How to Legitimate Rebellion and Condemn Usurpation of the Crown: Discourses of Fidelity and Treason in the *Gesta Danorum* of Saxo Grammaticus." In *Disputing Strategies in Medieval Scandinavia*, edited by Kim Esmark, Lars Hermanson, Hans Jacob Orning, and Helle Vogt, 107–40. Leiden, 2013.
Hill, Thomas. *Könige, Fürsten und Klöster. Studien zu den dänischen Klostergründungen des 12. Jahrhunderts*. Frankfurt, 1992.
Hölkeskamp, Karl-J. *Reconstructing the Roman Republic: An Ancient Political Culture and Modern Research*. Translated by Henry Heitmann-Gordon. Princeton and Oxford, 2010.
Holm, Poul. "De skånsk-hallandske bondeoprør 1180–82." In *Til kamp for friheden: Sociale oprør i nordisk middelalder*, edited by Anders Bøgh, Jørgen Würtz Sørensen, and Lars Tvede-Jensen, 72–89. Aalborg, 1988.
Jaubert, Anne Nissen. "Un ou plusieurs royaumes danois?" In *Les élites et leurs espaces*, edited by Philippe Depreux, François Bougard, and Régine Le Jan, 135–54. Turnhout, 2007.

Jensen, Janus Møller, ed. *Broderliste, broderskab, korstog: bidrag til opklaringen af en gåde fra dansk højmiddelalder*. Odense, 2006.
Jespersen, Leon, Erling Ladewig Petersen, and Ditlev Tamm, eds. *Dansk forvaltningshistorie I*. Copenhagen, 2000.
Johansen, Marianne, and Helle Halding. *Thi de var af stor slægt: Om Hvideslægten og kongemagt i dansk højmiddelalder*. Gylling, 2001.
Knytlinge Saga. Translated by Jens Peter Ægidius. Copenhagen, 1977.
Kræmmer, Michael. *Den hvide klan: Absalon, hans slægt og hans tid*. Copenhagen, 1999.
Kræmmer, Michael. "Peder Torstensen af Borg." *Årbog for Historisk Samfund for Sorø Amt* 88 (2001): 21–35.
Kræmmer, Michael. *Kongemordernes slægt*. Copenhagen, 2007.
Le Jan, Régine. "Les élites au haut moyen âge: approche sociologique et anthropologique." In *Théorie et pratiques des élites au Haut Moyen Age. Conception, perception et réalisation sociale*, edited by François Bougard, Hans-Werner Goetz, and Régine Le Jan, 69–99. Turnhout, 2011.
Liljefalk, Lone, and Stefan Pajung. "Bodil-slægten – en sydsjællandsk gåde." *Personalhistorisk tidsskrift* 1 (2013): 46–60.
Lind, John H. "De russiske ægteskaber: Dynasti- og alliancepolitiki 1130'ernes danske borgerkrig." *Historisk Tidsskrift* (D) 92 (1992): 225–63.
Mann, Michael. *The Sources of Social Power*, 4 vols. 2nd ed. Cambridge, 2012.
Nørlund, Poul. "Jorddrotter paa Valdemarstiden." In *Festskrift til Kristian Erslev*, edited by Poul Nørlund, 141–70. Copenhagen, 1927.
Nørlund, Poul. "Klostret og dets gods." In *Sorø: Klostret, skolen, akademiet gennem tiderne*, vol. I, 2 vols, edited by Mouritz Mackeprang and William Norvin, 53–131. Copenhagen, 1924–31.
Nyberg, Tore. *Monasticism in North-Western Europe, 800–1200*. Aldershot, 2000.
Sawyer, Birgit. "The 'Civil Wars' Revisited." *Historisk Tidsskrift* (N) 82, no. 1 (2003): 43–73.
Skyum-Nielsen, Niels. *Kvinde og slave*. Copenhagen, 1971.
Ulsig, Erik. *Danske adelsgodser i middelalderen*. Copenhagen, 1968.

16 Constructing the Friendships and Hierarchies of the Clerical Elite

A Case Study of the Relationship Between Øm Abbey and Bishop Tyge

Sveinung K. Boye

The breakthrough of political and legal institutions throughout Europe during the High Middle Ages led to a change in how power was constructed and disputes were settled. Face-to-face-relationships, informal power, and social networks became less important for the outcome of disputes and power struggles, and were replaced by political institutions, formalized hierarchies, and legal procedures as the hegemonic ideals for structuring society. In Scandinavia, the mid-thirteenth century is often seen as a high point in this development. However, recent studies, inspired by "dispute studies" and "legal anthropology," have indicated that the change was not as quick and uncomplicated as much of the older research suggested. For instance, in his study of kingship in the Norwegian kings' sagas, Hans Jacob Orning concluded that although the idea of the *rex iustus* was an important ideal in the mid-thirteenth century, in practice the institutional power of the Norwegian kings was limited; their power was still largely informal, personal, and dependent on their individual relationships with members of the lay and clerical elite. This also meant that kings had to act pragmatically when dealing with disloyal behavior, and tailor their responses to each situation rather than acting according to legal principles.[1] Another Scandinavian historian, Kim Esmark, has analyzed the conflicts between the Danish Cistercian monastery of Sorø and members of the local lay elite in the thirteenth and fourteenth centuries. His conclusion is that a strengthening of institutionalized power and formal law did not lead to a change from "one set of legal attitudes to another," but rather broadened the field of strategies and ways of reasoning available to the disputants.[2]

Perspectives from legal anthropology have inspired these and other scholars to consider elements like "threats, promises, negotiation, out-of-court mediation, rituals, emotional posturing, violence, [and] feuding" (among others) as mechanisms for handling conflict, which complemented the formal channels of law and litigation.[3] Through an anthropological approach to the study of power and conflict resolution, scholars have begun depicting the changes in thirteenth-century Scandinavia in more moderate and nuanced ways, but the understanding of relationships and conflicts within the clerical elite has been influenced to a lesser extent.

This chapter is thus an attempt to apply anthropological perspectives to an analysis of the power relations between members of the Danish clerical elite in the mid-thirteenth century. In this particular case that means analyzing power through the concept of "friendship" (*amicita*), rather than through law and formalized hierarchies alone. The conflict that took place in the 1260s between the Cistercian abbey of Øm in Jutland in Denmark and Bishop Tyge of Aarhus (bishop 1262–72) will be used as a case study in order to reveal how relationships between abbeys and bishops could be perceived, and how power and hierarchy could be constructed within such relationships. Studying how clerical "friendships" were constructed, negotiated, articulated, and restructured can give us some indication of how the power of the clerical elite could function and change through the use of such bonds.[4]

The conflict in question was recorded by the Øm monks in *Exordium Monasterii Carae Insulae* (the *Øm Abbey Chronicle*). It is a history of the abbey, about half of which concerns the conflict with Bishop Tyge of Aarhus, and half the formation of the abbey, its relationships with former bishops, important land transactions, the rights and privileges the abbey had received, information about abbots, and so on. The account of the conflict was written in the 1260s, while some parts of the chronicle were written in the early thirteenth century, including details about the abbey's friendship with Bishop Svend, one of Tyge's predecessors. This relationship is echoed in the Øm monks' view of their relationship with Tyge more than half a century later, giving a longer perspective to this inquiry that really addresses questions relevant to the entire thirteenth century.

The two most influential scholarly works on the chronicle – Niels Skyum-Nielsen's *Kirkekampen* (1963) and Brian Patrick McGuire's *Conflict and Continuity at Øm Abbey* (1976) – both predate the introduction of methodical approaches associated with legal anthropology to the study of medieval Scandinavian conflicts. Skyum-Nielsen's approach is very different from my own in that it is more or less exclusively focused on the judicial aspects of the conflict. He treats the chronicle with a great deal of skepticism and hostility, as evidenced by the quite contemptuous language he uses to describe the monks, their account of the conflict, and their strategies.[5] Skyum-Nielsen was concerned with identifying judicial as well as moral rights and wrongs. Critical of the monks' account and eager to expose the source as untruthful, he chose not to take the monks' understanding of the conflict seriously. The chronicle is indeed biased, and constructs heroes and villains; however, that does not mean it cannot provide interesting and relevant knowledge about how conflicts between members of the clerical elite were fought and perceived.

I also take a somewhat different approach from Brian Patrick McGuire's analysis. McGuire's description of the conflict is admirably thorough and packed with bright observations, but his book deals little with the structural mechanics, *Spielregeln* (the "rules of the game," in Gerd Althoff's formulation), and perceptions of the conflict, and does not really discuss the continuity or changes in the logics of the power relationships in any depth. Admittedly, he notes that the monks were dreaming of returning "to the good old days . . . when debts and obligations were not so clearly defined,"[6] but in this chapter I aim to help clarify how the monks used concepts like friendship, donations, and gift exchanges to define their ideal relationship with a local bishop, and in this way tried to shake off their bishop's claims.

Two Types of "Friendship"

The conflict between Bishop Tyge and Øm Abbey arose when the newly appointed bishop demanded *procurationes* (essentially the right to board and lodging) at the abbey for himself and his men for three weeks during Lent every year, the same rights he claimed his predecessors had enjoyed. The Øm monks, spearheaded by Bo, their abbot, dramatically stated that they would rather die than grant this request, and a long and exceptionally bitter conflict ensued.[7]

Bishop Tyge's demands would mean a considerable financial burden for the abbey, but there was even more at stake. Behind Tyge's seemingly simple requirements was the bigger question of what the relationship between the abbey and the bishop should be like. Accepting Tyge's terms would have meant that the monks had given up their ambition for an informal and fluid friendship in favor of a strictly hierarchical relationship. Tyge and the monks both described the relationship they wanted by using the word "friendship" (*amicita*),[8] but they could not agree on the specific terms, duties, and rules that such a relationship entailed. It seems that the bishop demanded a formalized and hierarchical relationship, in which he would enjoy clearly defined rights and privileges. He wanted the abbey and himself to become "good friends" – but on his terms.

The monks, on the other hand, used the flexible concept of "benevolence" (*benevolentia*) to promote an informal relationship in which their obligations to the bishop were dependent on what they could receive in return – in other words, a kind of gift economy of favors and generosity. They based their ideal friendship with Tyge on the relationships they had enjoyed with some of the previous Aarhus bishops, which the chronicle principally portrays, not as regulated by canon law and formalized church hierarchies, but rather as characterized by exchanges of land, favors, privileges, and other gifts, and articulates by using the concept of "benevolence." We learn that Bishop Eskil (1157–65) founded the monastery, generously helped the monks, and offered them gifts.[9]

A more thorough description is given of the abbey's relationship with his successor, Bishop Svend (1165–91), who would eventually become the monastery's best and most charitable friend, but initially harbored some hostility towards the monks, "on account of his predecessor's generosity, through which the diocesan property had apparently diminished."[10] His mind is said to have been changed as a result of two incidents in his life: a rough voyage home from England and a later life-threatening illness convinced him to support the abbey in order to thank God for his survival and to save his soul.[11] He started helping the abbey in every way, and gave to it everything that he could.[12]

The chronicler frames Svend's change of heart as a religiously motivated choice: helping the monastery was the best way for him to save his soul. Svend's grave would eventually be placed in the abbey because of his generosity (a good pathway to salvation), and the monks would also have contributed to the salvation of the abbey's benefactor through intercessory prayer.

There is, however, no doubt that there was a strong social dimension to the exchange of gifts and land between the bishop and the abbey. This is perhaps most clearly articulated in the passages recording land transactions. According to Timothy Reuter, land in the Middle Ages can be seen as "a medium through which relations of friendship, kinship and enmity, as well as of patronage and deference, can find public and often highly ritualized expression precisely at those points at which rights in it are being granted away or modified."[13] This is, as we will see, a key to understanding how the relationships between Øm Abbey and the Aarhus bishops were constructed and negotiated throughout the abbey's history. About Bishop Svend's donations we are told that because:

> the bishop now having been made placable in all things, forgetting the bitterness of his displeasure which he had held against them, they transferred Småenge to him so that they might have the more favor from him.... Receiving this favorably, and having been aroused by their benevolence to greater love toward them, he kept it for a short while and afterwards gave it back to the brethren, accepting from them a dwelling place in Karlby, which had belonged to Veng; but that too, along with other properties that he had conveyed to the monastery, he restored with all piety. The diocese was at that time very poor and modest, but he enlarged it by extending its wealth and reputation, and whatever he gave to the monastery were from his own patrimony and from those things that he was able to acquire from the surplus of his *mensa* in his episcopate.[14]

These donations and exchanges of land had a function with many parallels throughout medieval Europe. Historians like Barbara H. Rosenwein and Stephen D. White – both writing about relations between monasteries and the lay elite in medieval France – have shown that land donations and exchanges were ways of creating and maintaining social relationships.[15] In this particular case the transactions were clearly bound up in a gift economy, and in his interaction with Øm Abbey, Bishop Svend was thus using a language of gifts and friendly gestures that he shared with the lay elite. The "friendship" between Svend and Øm Abbey entailed informal reciprocal benevolence, rather than a strict hierarchical bond of service and subordination.

The chronicle goes on to tell how much Svend loved the Øm monks, and says that he gave them everything the poor and newly established monastery needed.[16] Amongst other things, he freed the abbey from the obligation of paying tithes and wrote a will bequeathing it even more land, including an area called Djursland (which would later be brought up in the conflict with Bishop Tyge); and he added to these material gifts his staunch protection of the monastery. This last point was arguably the most important aspect of the relationship from the abbey's point of view, as it meant that

> never once did any abbot who led [the abbey] in [Svend's] days have to attend secular law assemblies for any reason whatsoever, because both clerics and laymen held the brethren in the greatest reverence, seeing that the bishop always and everywhere stood firm on their behalf.[17]

By contrast, the conflict with Tyge meant that the monks could "never achieve any justice over those who did injustice against [them]."[18] In other words, the episcopal protection was vital for the abbey's honor and local standing, as well as for their legal security.

The friendship between Bishop Svend and Øm Abbey was not a horizontal relationship, but neither was it a formalized bond of service. It was a fluid, reciprocal friendship based on the logics of a gift economy. Excessive gift-giving was, of course, not always a sign of love and respect; it could be a powerful weapon used to create debt – and thus to establish a power relation – so the degree to which "friendships" were voluntary for both parties could vary.[19] However, the chronicler presents this particular friendship as one of genuine mutual benevolence and goodwill. The friendship was vertical, but it was also informal and had the appearance of a certain equality. Both parties showered each other with gifts, but the monks seem to have received more than they could reciprocate (at least in material value). A large part of Svend's kindness (or *benevolentia*) was that he did not cash in on the abbey's debt of generosity when he didn't have to.

In sharp contrast, Bishop Tyge demanded clearly defined rights if he should agree to be the friend of Øm Abbey. This meant that he insisted that his visits at the abbey should be considered as a kind of tax, rather than as a gift or an informal gesture in an exchange of gifts and favors. The differences between the two views of what a friendship should entail are quite clearly articulated in the chronicle. For instance, at one point Abbot Bo confronts Bishop Tyge, saying, "If you wish to come as a guest, you will be given everything you need, but if you come for the purpose of procuring the lodging as a tax or debt nothing will be given to you,"[20] indicating that the monks were happy to receive the bishop as their guest as long as the meaning of the visit conformed to their understanding of the relationship. Similarly, when Tyge refused Abbot Bo's vague offer that "if we shall have seen your benevolence, we are willing to serve you,"[21] he refused the reciprocal gift-logic of such an informal friendship. He was equally unimpressed by Bo's related claim that "by reason of your high office and your dignity, we wish to serve you as much as any abbey in Denmark serves its bishop that does not receive more from their bishopric than we do; and we will serve you even more if you shall have shown us and our people your full benevolence."[22]

On what grounds then did Tyge make his demands for a relationship with clearly defined rights and privileges?

The Ambivalence of the Land Donation

Since the Council of Chalcedon (AD 451) the canonical position had been that bishops had the right and duty to supervise all religious houses within their dioceses. Their specific rights within the monasteries included overseeing and confirming the election of abbots and priors, and, crucially in the case of the Øm conflict, the right to make periodic visitations. During these visitations a bishop was entitled to board and lodging for himself and his entourage. In the wake of the Gregorian reform, however, an increasing number of monasteries succeeded in negotiating exemption from episcopal supervision, and were placed directly under the pope's authority instead. The Cistercian order managed to negotiate exemption from episcopal authority for all the monasteries of the order, and the loss of episcopal jurisdiction led to conflicts between bishops and monasteries in twelfth- and early thirteenth-century Europe.[23]

Tyge's demands for lodging rights at Øm echo the traditional episcopal visitation rights, but the claim goes much further, as the usual duration of an episcopal visitation was only one day and one night.[24] Skyum-Nielsen confronted this issue in his analyses of the conflict. On the one hand, he argued that the monks' use of papal letters confirming their exemption from episcopal visitations was a misunderstanding, because the demands for three weeks' board and lodging had to do with repayment for donations rather than visitation rights. His argument was that a visitation could legally never last for three weeks.[25] On the other hand, he claimed that the origin of the episcopal demands (one of Tyge's predecessors, Peder Elavsen (1224–46), used to stay at the abbey in his time as bishop) lay in the necessity of visitation. He claimed that although the bishop had no formal visitation rights, it was only natural to intervene when the proper authorities were kept unaware of severe violations of the monastic rule.[26] Skyum-Nielsen is vague on this point, and disregards the understanding conveyed in the chronicle. Rather than revealing the monks' poor juridical understanding, the two quite different (and more or less mutually exclusive) views seem to be examples of the fluid interpretations of legal and moral principles available to disputing parties in mid- to late thirteenth-century Denmark. In the interpretation of the bishop's demands, the lines between visitation, patron rights, and other forms of *herrshaftsgastung* are blurred, and both sides in the dispute draw on different interpretations that served their purpose. Throughout the chronicle Tyge's demands are referred to as *procurationes* but also as *visitatio*. Tyge refers to his forced visit at Øm as a duty (probably a visitation duty), a custom, a repayment for the donations of previous bishops, and as a seigneurial right, while the counterarguments of the monks were that they were legally freed from episcopal visitation, that the previous donations were personal gifts for the souls of individual bishops, and that the abbey could not be placed under the bishop's jurisdiction.[27] Kim Esmark has underlined that what might seem like straightforward legal claims were often entangled in competing discourses on legal, moral, religious, and cultural norms, which could all be used to legitimize claims and counterclaims. This was done by using what Pierre Bourdieu termed "officializing strategies"; that is, branding one's own interests as an expression of collectively shared, commendable values.[28]

Having no formalized authority over the abbey, Tyge had to look for justification of a hierarchical bond which would allow him three weeks lodging at Øm. His main way of dealing with the problem was to reinterpret the meaning of land donated to Øm generations earlier by his predecessor Bishop Svend. At the heart of his argument lay the ambiguity of the social meaning of land donations, which was hugely relevant in determining which type of bond would govern the relationship between Tyge and Øm.

In her study of "the social meaning" of Cluny's landed properties in the period 909–1049, Barbara H. Rosenwein discovered changing perceptions of land transactions and ownership. Throughout the tenth century, she claims, the predominant interpretation of land donations, exchanges, and even sales was that they were social acts given meaning through the logics of a gift economy, rather than impersonal economic transactions. This meant that land was constantly changing hands, functioning as "social glue." Interpretations of land transactions and ownership gradually changed, however, as a different discourse through which meaning was assigned emerged in the eleventh century. On the one hand, land transactions were now seen as more purely economic acts, and the land that had been constantly changing hands in order to create and maintain social relationships was accumulating in the hands of Cluny as their patrimony. On the other hand, as the social dimension of ownership was disappearing, Cluny's patrimony took on the form of "a seigneurie of grand dimensions."[29] This meant that land could be used to create hierarchical bonds of lordship, and that the monastery's properties thus "became the seat of economic and political power."[30]

Rather than representing a complete shift, the two models coexisted throughout the Middle Ages. Stephen D. White has noted a similar change much later, in the thirteenth century, in his study of donations to the French abbeys of Saint Aubin of Angers, Marmoutier, Saint Mary of Noyers, La Trinité of Vendôme, and Saint Vincent of Le Mans,[31] and in the second half of the thirteenth century the ambiguity of the meaning of land donations and ownership was a key line of argumentation in the Øm conflict. As the dispute over the episcopal lodging-rights escalated, Tyge argued that if the monks were not prepared to grant him visitation at the abbey because it was an old custom, they at least owed it to him because of the landed properties they had received in Djursland.[32] He also wrote a letter to the monks adding that it was well known that their monastery had been founded by his predecessor Eskil and richly endowed with gifts from Bishop Svend, and used this as an argument for his right to lodge at the monastery with his entourage.[33] Øm Abbey's properties in Djursland had been given to them by their generous friend Bishop Svend, but Tyge's and the monks' interpretations of what the gift meant were widely different. Tyge saw the land donation as, for lack of a better term, a "feudal" transaction (this is clearly stated: "*qui tamen pretextu uisitationis in feodis procurationes ab eis exigere*"),[34] which secured certain clearly defined seigneurial rights (i.e., lodging privileges at Øm) for *all* successive Aarhus bishops. The episcopal office – his institutional position – was crucial in his line of argumentation, but the monks saw their relationships with individual bishops as strictly personal, and donations as gifts confirming a personal friendship. The chronicler stresses several times that everything Svend had given them was "from his own *mensa*" and patrimony (rather than being the property of the diocese), and has Abbot Bo claim:

> Nor did he [Bishop Svend] retain for himself and his successors by reason of possession, with respect to the aforementioned lodging rights, those things that he conveyed to us in Djursland as you claim; but from his own patrimony he utterly relinquished them to us with the consent and favor of the best men in Denmark and as a remedy for his soul.[35]

The episcopal office was clearly becoming an institutionalized factor in the bishop's relationships with local elites, but the monks connected the ownership (and prior ownership) of a gift or donation to its social meaning, and underlined the personal aspects of their relationships to the Aarhus bishops.

Restructuring Friendships Through Conflict

A closer analysis of the conflict structure reveals further aspects of the power dynamic. Since bishops had no specific, clearly defined rights within the Cistercian monasteries in their dioceses, the relationships between Øm Abbey and the Aarhus bishops were essentially based on power rather than law. Brian Patrick McGuire has indeed noted that law was not a dominant factor in the dispute, and that although both parties occasionally tried to introduce legal arguments, "when either side tried to formulate or go against a theoretical basis for such a custom [i.e., the right to stay at the abbey for three weeks], neither could come up with any sufficient answer."[36] Even though both Bishop Tyge and the Øm monks had to justify their positions by combining references to customs and cultural norms with a legal argumentation, the decisive factor was ultimately power. This meant that a negotiation could take place locally, and the social networks in the local community were mobilized on both sides. As key aspects of the two parties' power in the local community, social networks were an important factor in the negotiations to decide which claims each side could and could not force upon the other.

Almost immediately after becoming bishop, Tyge made it clear that he was not currently a friend of the monastery. The chronicler claims that just after the bishop returned from Rome, a lay brother from Øm was attacked and severely wounded, but when Abbot Bo talked to Tyge about this injustice, the bishop brought the culprits to work on his estates, thus placing them under his protection and jurisdiction.[37] This was a powerful symbolic act, unambiguously signaling to the monks that "his soul was not with [them]."[38]

Demonstrative acts of hostility like this were common features in the political cultures of medieval Europe, used to instigate conflicts that could alter power relationships. Patrick Geary writes that

> the forms taken by dramatic outbreaks of conflict in this society [i.e., a medieval society with only rudimentary state formation] are far from random. They often include violent seizure of property, the killing or capturing of opponents, and the real or ritual exercise of power over persons or things in dispute.[39]

Displaying anger or performing conspicuous acts of hostility were ways of signaling to someone that they had broken the terms of a relationship or that the terms had to be renegotiated for the relationship to be reestablished.[40] Historical research approaching the study of disputes from a legal-anthropological perspective has shown that rather than threatening social order, conflicts (even violent ones) were regulated events used to establish, demonstrate, maintain, and negotiate structure and hierarchy.

In the Øm chronicle the term "friendship" (*amicita*) seems to indicate an agreement between two parties to treat each other with goodwill, and to help, support, and protect each other. However, the demands of each party, and their definitions of benevolence, were negotiable, and therefore to a large extent a question of power, which may be actualized through conflict and cemented in the following settlement. Tyge's hostility and the conflict itself can thus be seen as part of the process of challenging and renegotiating the terms of his relationship with the abbey. That a conflict like this should occur almost immediately after a new bishop had taken episcopal office is fairly typical, although this particular conflict was unusually difficult to resolve. Both parties could potentially benefit from testing the limits of their rights and authority in the newly inherited relationship, which at that point was fragile and moldable. Similarly, research has shown that new heads of elite families would demonstratively break agreements their predecessors had with local monasteries, and dispute land donations they had made, not to crush the monasteries or create lasting enmity, but to renegotiate the terms of the bonds between them.[41]

The Øm conflict would eventually evolve from a local power struggle into high politics. However, in its early phases both parties expected the conflict to be resolved locally. They anticipated that local power and social networks would be as influential in defining the relationship between the bishop and the abbey as the formal hierarchies and legal frameworks of the church organization. It was the task of the local community to help facilitate a compromise that satisfied the honor of both parties, and to take sides in a way that confirmed their own relationships with the disputants. Jens Kanne, a knight and friend of the monastery (*miles et amicus claustri*), was convinced that he and "other friends of the monastery (*aliis amicis claustra*) would mediate a good settlement between the abbot and the bishop."[42] When the conflict had become particularly bitter, Jens approached Abbot Bo and asked him to meet with Tyge in the cathedral church in Aarhus. Friends and supporters of both sides were present in the settlement meetings, and when negotiations began to fail, Abbot Bo told all the tenant farmers and laborers from the abbey's estates to arm themselves and hurry to the church where the meeting was held, ready to resist if the bishop should use violence.[43] Ultimately local social networks and manpower had a significant influence on which claims could be forced upon each party by the other.

The dispute was a local matter, involving more or less the entire local community. Everyone wanted to restore the harmony of friendship between the bishop and the abbey, as they were all connected to the conflict through bonds with the disputing parties which made neutrality impossible.

The Local Use of Excommunication

The local character of the conflict (in this phase) is even illustrated in the disputing parties' attitudes towards papal letters, and the bishop's use of excommunication. What were seemingly programmatic papal letters were only used as an instrument of negotiation in a local setting,[44] and excommunication (a seemingly formalized instrument of power) was used in the local context to force negotiations with the abbot and to diminish the abbey's power by crushing its social networks. Tyge started harassing the abbey's tenant farmers and laborers – their *familia* – and had his bailiffs proclaim to them that: "Each and every one of you shall return to your homes and be under interdict, because till now you have served the monks of Øm, and if you have not stopped serving them soon, we will undoubtedly excommunicate you all!"[45] Frightened, they came "crying and wailing to the abbey,"[46] hoping that the abbot would hear their pleas and settle his differences with the bishop. Though the abbot tried to calm his tenants, nearly all of them wanted to free themselves from the abbey's service when the bishop's bailiffs summoned them again and again, placed them under interdict, and extorted money from them.[47]

When Tyge placed Øm's *familia* under interdict and had his bailiffs extort money from them, it was clearly a strategic move – a clever way of dismantling the local network of the monastery, and thereby gaining an edge in the dispute. Nearly all of Øm's farmers and laborers wanted to free themselves from the abbey's service when it became clear that it could not protect them from the bishop. Protection had obviously been a defining aspect of their relationship in the first place. This weakened the abbey's position in the local power struggle.

As Patrick Geary has pointed out, excommunications "were intended not to destroy the enemies of the Church but to bring about negotiations."[48] When Abbot Bo himself was excommunicated, he was thus being pressured to renegotiate the terms of the friendship, and to admit to less favorable terms than he was comfortable with. When he and all his supporters were excommunicated, some of the abbot's friends took him aside, and said, "You cannot endure your bishop's anger, and it is not fitting for you or anybody else to stand against your bishop. Go to him and offer him satisfaction (*satisfactionem*), and you will become good friends (*boni amici*)."[49] This underlines the fact that the power relationship was constructed, not primarily by the formalized hierarchies of the church, but by the bonds of what they termed "friendship." The enmity could easily be turned into an affectionate friendship when the terms for such a relationship were agreed upon, and institutionalized instruments of power, such as excommunication, were used to force negotiations and favorable terms.

"We excommunicate you for calling yourself abbot," said the bishop, "we excommunicate your brotherhood for calling you their abbot, and anyone claiming that you are an abbot, we excommunicate."[50] Excommunication placed the target outside of the Christian community, which meant that he or she was denied access to the churches and the rituals that could secure their salvation. But the abbot's answer illustrates how the effects of excommunications were also dependent on the local setting, for he merely stood up and proclaimed that: "Just as easily as you have excommunicated my subordinates, I absolve them"[51] In practice, the question of who could legitimately excommunicate and absolve was often decided locally, so this too could be part of a local power struggle. Even though some misdeeds automatically warranted an excommunication, in effect there were few universally accepted rules and restrictions, making excommunication a remarkably flexible instrument of power.

The Changing Character of the Dispute

In their comparative study of conflicts that the monasteries of Cluny, Fleury, and Marmoutier had with local lay and ecclesiastical elites in the tenth to early twelfth centuries, Barbara H. Rosenwein, Thomas Head, and Sharon Farmer merge the seemingly incompatible concepts of friendship and enmity into the analytical concept of "friend/enemy," when describing disputes similar to the Øm conflict. The term communicates that friendship and enmity were fragile, and usually temporary, states of a relationship. Enemies of the monasteries were usually former friends and would often become even closer friends when their conflict had been resolved through compromise.[52] From this perspective conflicts are seen, as indicated previously, as the process through which friendships and their terms were challenged, renegotiated, restructured, and eventually confirmed.[53] According to the study this was a typical trait of the relationships and disputes in periods and geographical areas with weak central power. However, when central powers were strong, the two sides of a conflict tended to demand decisive winners and losers rather than honorable compromises, and there was a clearer line between friendship and enmity. The decisive factor in this other kind of conflict was not the local networks, but friendly powers outside of the local elite who could determine absolute winners and losers.[54]

The Øm conflict, which started out as what we might call a friend/enemy conflict, was about to change into something similar to the second kind of dispute. It seems that neither the bishop nor the abbey had the power to win a complete victory locally, and their inability to reach a compromise lifted the conflict out of its local setting. It then developed into high politics when top Danish and European ecclesiastical and lay elites got involved as both sides called for their support.

Having powerful friends outside the local community was important for abbeys and abbots, particularly in situations like the one facing Øm Abbey. This was probably why the monks decided that they needed a new abbot, and chose a man named Ture as Bo's replacement. Ture had previously been abbot of Vitskøl and Esrum, and is described by the chronicler as "a man of noble birth and wisdom, well known by all the best men (*melioribus*) in the kingdom of Denmark."[55] His elite background and social networks seems to have been the reason why the Øm monks wanted him as their leader. Of course, these were aspects that had always been important when choosing abbots, and when a few lines in the chronicle are given to sum up each of the former abbots, many of them are recognized for their noble birth and relationships with powerful men. Abbot Vilhelm (1189–94) is described as "deeply loved by King Valdemar";[56] Abbot Brandan (1194–98) as "loved and honored by everyone";[57] and Abbot Mikkel (1235–46) as "deeply loved by King Erik as well as other leading men and nobles in the land."[58] Henrik, the abbot of Vitskøl at the time when Øm Abbey was established, was, according to the chronicler, "a man of venerable character, deeply loved as much by the king as by all of the leading men of the realm because of their reverence for the grace of God that shone in his face, as well as for the eloquence of the stream of mellifluous words that came from his mouth."[59] The cultural mechanics linking love with piety and eloquent speech are somewhat unclear, but maybe people gravitated towards him as a man they trusted to protect their souls effectively. In a later addition to the manuscript that contains the chronicle, subsequent abbots are described: Abbot Asgod is said to have been "a generous and friendly man"[60] (probably indicating a good network builder), whereas Abbot Conrad was "a generous and extravagant man" who "because of his benign and friendly spirit had a good relationship with his convent."[61] The abbots' networks of friends seem to have been a defining aspect of their ability to run and protect the monastery.

It was the disputing parties' connections with powerful people inside and outside Denmark, as well as the political context in Denmark at the time, which allowed the local dispute to become big politics. The most important context was the "Church Strife," a conflict between the king and some of the Danish bishops, which saw the archbishop of Lund and the bishops of Odense and Roskilde exiled from Denmark. The Danish clerical elite were divided on the matter, and Tyge was one of the king's supporters even though he was a bishop. The strife became important for the Øm conflict mainly because Tyge and the abbey were calling on different sides to aid them in their cause. Øm Abbey, like the other Danish Cistercian monasteries, supported the archbishop and called mainly on him and church officials who supported him, while Tyge's close relationship with the king would eventually lead to his final victory.

The character of the dispute really started changing when Abbot Bo appealed to Bishop Niels of Viborg (the king's chancellor) and the king's marshal Jens Kalf, and had them try to influence Bishop Tyge. It was useless. They approached the bishop and said that he could not destroy the abbey without reason, but he would not budge. Then, using a communal letter, the Danish Cistercians tried to get the pope involved, and the Øm monks also appealed to the exiled Archbishop Jakob Erlandsen. Abbot Bo, acknowledging his own shortcomings, then resigned his post, was replaced by Abbot Ture, and went to Rome and got a papal letter which also failed to have an effect. The conflict finally seemed to have reached an end when Bishop Esger of Ribe and Niels of Schleswig were asked to step in as arbiters. A settlement was reached, based on the former Aarhus bishop Peder Elavsen's concordance with Øm: He was never to bring more than four clerks and five laymen on Ash Wednesday, and never stay more than three weeks. Tyge gave an oath to respect these conditions, but the following Lent he broke them spectacularly by showing up with what the monks considered a ridiculous number of men.

The Øm monks then asked for the help of Guido, a papal legate who was in Denmark trying to sort out the conflict between the king and the archbishop. Their hopes were high, partly because of Guido's Cistercian background, but even though Guido tried to help the monks, he was unsuccessful.[62] Tyge refused to meet the legate every time he was summoned, and he also refused to show up to court proceedings when Guido made Bishop Bonde of Schleswig the judge of the case. He was therefore excommunicated *in absentia* and sentenced to pay the abbey's expenses in the case. This had no practical effect.

It was Tyge's connections with the young King Erik V Klipping and his mother and guardian, Margrete Sambiria, that would eventually determine the outcome. According to the chronicler, Tyge had served them lies about Øm Abbey throughout the conflict in order to create enmity. The abbey's appeals to the archbishop and the papal legate (who had excommunicated the king for chasing the archbishop out of Denmark), and the fact that the monks had obtained the protection of King Erik's antagonistic cousin Duke Erik, greatly helped Tyge to turn the king against the monks, and thus to make the Øm dispute part of a much bigger conflict.

In the end the monks couldn't withstand the pressure when they received threats of incarceration and looting, and of being chased from their monastery if they did not submit to Tyge. The chronicle ends in a tone of quiet resignation, describing the hardship and poverty of their new existence.

A Tragedy of Personal Relationships?

The *Øm Abbey Cronicle* may seem like a symbolic tragedy, where the fall of the old social order is symbolized by the fall of the abbey, and the institutionalized understanding of power which replaces it is personified in the antagonistic bishop. The monks viewed their relationship with the local bishop as an informal, personal, and reciprocal friendship, but were eventually forced to accept a strict, hierarchical relationship in which the bishop had the right to board with them for three weeks as a kind of tax. However, as the analysis in this chapter has indicated, this is an oversimplified interpretation. Rather than legitimizing their claims by using legal principles, the bishop and the monks used many different kinds of arguments to their advantage, in a tangled web of legal, moral, and cultural norms. This allowed for the validity of several coexisting but competing claims regarding both visiting rights and the meaning of land donations. And even though Bishop Tyge and the Øm monks had completely different views of what their relationship should be like, the conflict structure reveals that formalized hierarchies and legal procedures were marginal aspects of both the bishop's and the monks' understanding of the disagreement. It was rather a local, feud-like dispute (which eventually grew out of its local frame) – a negotiation over the terms of a "friendship" – in which law was secondary to power, and social networks just as important as formal hierarchies.

Both parties initially wanted to settle the dispute locally on the basis of local networks and power, rather than in a court setting. Although appeals would be made to higher powers within the church hierarchy (including the archbishop, the papal legate, and the pope himself), and a court solution was eventually tried, these strategies were only employed when the dispute could not be settled by other means, and they ultimately proved unsuccessful. When the conflict grew out of its local context, both parties sought support wherever it could be found, and even when the king intimidated the monks into submission it can hardly be said that the dispute was solved through the formalized channels of the kingdom.

The power relation between the abbey and the bishop was, simply put, constructed more within the framework of their concepts of friendship than the formalized church hierarchies. The influence of ideas about institutionalized power can clearly be seen in Tyge's ambition to turn his relationship with the abbey into a hierarchical bond of service rather than a reciprocal bond based on a gift economy, but the bishop still used a friend/enemy type feud to construct such a power relation. Rather than promoting his role as church leader, he emphasized his seigneurial right (which, of course, was not a new concept) to land donated to the abbey, and although he explicitly tied these rights to his office rather than to his person, he did not use his formal position as a church leader as his main argument.

Notes

1. Hans Jacob Orning, *Unpredictability and Presence: Norwegian Kingship in the High Middle Ages* (Leiden, 2008).
2. Kim Esmark, "Disputing Property in Zealand: The Records of the Sorø Donation Book," in *Disputing Strategies in Medieval Scandinavia*, ed. Kim Esmark et al. (Leiden, 2013), 181–219.

Friendships of the Clerical Elite 319

3. Kim Esmark and Hans Jacob Orning, "General Introduction," in *Disputing Strategies in Medieval Scandinavia*, ed. Kim Esmark et al. (Leiden, 2013), 1–28 at 4.
4. In an article, Brian Patrick McGuire has discussed how the elite identity of the Scandinavian Cistercians developed. When the order came to Scandinavia in the twelfth century the Cistercian self-understanding was marked by their ideal of poverty and humility. They received support and donations from the secular elite, but did not themselves identify with the elite collective. McGuire goes on to explain that after a period of growth, the Danish Cistercians were turned against by their former benefactors in the secular elite, and thus had to defend the rights and privileges they had acquired, which also meant they "had to give up their claims to be downtrodden and underprivileged. Instead they asserted their 'birthright' as part of a privileged elite." (Brian Patrick McGuire, "The Cistercians as a Scandinavian Elite," in *Les Élites Nordiques et L'Europe Occidentale (XIIe–XVe siècle)*, ed. Tuomas M. S. Lehtonen and Élisabeth Mornet (Paris, 2007), 113–26 at 116.
5. His reference to the monks' "hypocrisy and fraud" and his assessment of the Øm abbots as "foolish" (*taabelig*) and "mad" (*vanvittig*) are representative. (Niels Skyum-Nielsen, *Kirkekampen i Danmark, 1241–1290: Jakob Erlandsen, samtid og eftertid* (Copenhagen, 1963), 189–90).
6. Brian Patrick McGuire, *Conflict and Continuity at Øm Abbey: A Cistercian Experience in Medieval Denmark* (Copenhagen, 1976), 100.
7. "Vnusquisque respondit se malle mori quam ei tam indebitas procurationes exibere." (*Exordium Monasterii Carae Insulae*. In SM, 211. Hereafter cited as *Exordium*.
8. When Abbot Bo met with Tyge to gain his friendship, the bishop answered, "Yes, we will be good friends (*amici*) – when what is ours is given to us." (Bene erimus amici, si nobis dantur que nostra sunt.) (*Exordium*, ch. 36, p. 209). All translations from Latin into English are the author's, in part aided by the Danish translation in Jørgen Olrik, Jacob Isager, and H. N. Garner, ed., *Øm klosters krønike* (Øm, 1997).
9. *Exordium*, ch. 1, p. 160.
10. "propter largitionem predecessoris sui, eo quod uideretur episcopatus possessionibus esse inminutus." (*Exordium*, ch. 1, p. 161).
11. *Exordium*, ch. 1, p. 161, ch. 22, p. 178.
12. Ibid., ch. 22, p. 178.
13. Timothy Reuter, "Property Transactions and Social Relations Between Rulers, Bishops and Nobles in Early Eleventh-Century Saxony: The Evidence of Vita Meinwerci," in *Property and Power in the Early Middle Ages*, ed. Wendy Davis and Paul Fouracre (Cambridge, 2002), 165–99 at 172.
14. " et electus eis per omnia placabilis factus esset, obliuiscens funditus amaritudinem indignationis sue, quam contra eos habuerat, ut maiorem gratiam ipsius haberent, concesserunt ei Smaheng. . . . Quod ille, benigne suscipiens et de beniuolentia eorum maiori erga eos amore accensus, paruo tempore sibi retinuit et postea fratribus resignauit, accipiens ab eis mansionem Karlebu, que ad Weng pertinebat; sed et ipsam cum alijs bonis, que claustro contulerat, cum omni deuotione restituit. Erat autem episcopatus tunc ualde tenuis et pauper, sed ipse eum dilatando diuitijs et honoribus ampliauit, et quecunque claustro dedit, de proprio patrimonio fuerunt et de his, que de superfluitate mense sue in episcopatu acquirere potuit." (*Exordium* ch. 2, p. 162).
15. Barbara H. Rosenwein, *To Be the Neighbor of Saint Peter: The Social Meaning of Cluny's Property, 909–1049* (Ithaca, NY, 1989); Stephen D. White, *Custom, Kinship, and Gifts to Saints: The* Laudatio Parentum *in Western*

France, 1050–1150 (Chapel Hill, 1988). Kim Esmark has remarked that land donations to and patronage of monasteries were ways of constructing a unified kin-group in twelfth- and thirteenth-century Denmark (Kim Esmark, "Religious Patronage and Family Consciousness: Sorø Abbey and the 'Hvide Family', c. 1150–1250," in *Religious and Laity in Western Europe, 1000–1400: Interaction, Negotiation and Power*, ed. Emilia Jamroziak and Janet E. Burton, 93–110 (Turnhout, 2006)).

16. *Exordium*, ch. 22, pp. 178–79.
17. "nunquam aliquis abbatum, qui in diebus eius prefuerunt, necesse haberet pro quacunque causa uel semel ad commune placitum secularum uenire, quia tam clerici quam laici in summe ueneratione fratres habebant, uidentes episcopum pro eis semper et ubique firmiter stare." (*Exordium*, ch. 22, p. 188).
18. "Interim quicunque nobis iniuriam fecit, nullam adepti sumus iusticiam de ipso." (*Exordium*, p. 208).
19. Lars Hermanson, "Statsbildning och vänskap i 1100-talets Norden," in *Statsutvikling i Skandinavia i middelalderen*, ed. Sverre Bagge et al. (Oslo, 2012), 119–43 at 122.
20. "Si gratia hospitandi uultis uenire, uobis dabuntur omnia necessaria; si causa procurationis uel debiti, nichil omnino administratur uobis." (*Exordium*, ch. 36, p. 216).
21. "si uestram senserimus beniuolenciam, uelle deseruire." (*Exordium*, ch. 36, p. 209).
22. "propter honorem et reuerenciam uestram uolumus in tanto seruire uobis sicut aliqua abbacia in Dacia seruit episcopo suo, que non habet plus de episcopatu, quam nos habemus; et eciam plus uolumus seruire, si perfectam perspexerimus uestram erga nos et nostros beniuolenciam." (*Exordium*, ch. 36, p. 211).
23. Clifford Hugh Lawrence, *Medieval Monasticism: Forms of Religious Life in Western Europe in the Middle Ages* (Harlow, 2001 [1984]), 132.
24. Skyum-Nielsen, *Kirkekampen*, 187.
25. Ibid.
26. Ibid., 184.
27. *Exordium*, ch. 36, p. 210–11, 213, 248, 250.
28. Kim Esmark, "Godsgaver, calumniae og retsantropologi," in *Ett annat 1100-tal*, ed. Peter Carelli, Lars Hermanson, and Hanne Sanders (Gothenburg, 2004), 143–80 at 165–66; Pierre Bourdieu, *Outline of a Theory of Practice*, trans. Richard Nice (Cambridge, 1977), 40. In a study of inheritance and fiefs in twelfth-century France, Stephen D. White has argued for "the existence of a more malleable and internally contradictory legal culture or discourse that included several different models of what a fief was, and by implication, how it should pass from one person to another." (Stephen D. White, "The Discourse of Inheritance in Twelfth-Century France: Alternative Modes of Fief in Raoul de Cambrai," in *Law and Government in Medieval England and Normandy: Essays in Honour of Sir James Holt*, ed. G. Garnett and J. Hudson (Cambridge, 1994), 173–97 at 177).
29. Rosenwein, *To Be the Neighbor*, 205. Other researchers have arrived at similar conclusions about donations to European monasteries in the High and Late Middle Ages, pointing out that when the social meaning of the donations diminished, they were no longer primarily reserved for the local aristocracy (Catharina Andersson, "Kloster och aristokrati, Nunnor, munkar och gåvor i det svenska samhället till 1300-talets mitt" (PhD diss., University of Gothenburg, 2006), 61–65).
30. Rosenwein, *To Be the Neighbor*, 206. Danish historians like Kim Esmark and Helge Paludan have remarked that competing discourses of land transactions

Friendships of the Clerical Elite 321

were an important factor in conflicts between the Cistercian monastery of Esrum and the lay aristocracy in Zealand. The main argument promoted by the lay aristocracy was that the land could not be alienated from the owner's family, and that land donated by, for example, their forefathers could thus be reclaimed. The monasteries usually retorted by promoting the equally valid ideal of the pious gift, which *could* be alienated from its former owner. Esmark has shown how dispute cases (*calumniate*) at Esrum were remarkably similar to conflicts in other parts of Western Europe, where a similar field of competing discourses, norms, and legal and moral principles were invoked (Esmark, "Godsgaver, calumniae og retsantropologi," 143–80; Helge Paludan, *Familia og familie: To europæiske kulturelementers mødes højmiddelalderens Danmark* (Aarhus, 1995), 88–93. For a French perspective see White, *Custom, Kinship, and Gifts to Saints*).

31. White, *Custom, Kinship, and Gifts to Saints*, 192–95.
32. "Si non uultis dare nobis ratione consuetudinis, oportet uos dare nobis ratione possessionum in Dyursø, quod omnino denegare non potestis." (*Exordium*, ch. 36, p. 213).
33. *Exordium*, ch. 36, p. 213.
34. Ibid., p. 246. Also noted by McGuire in *Conflict and Continuity at Øm Abbey*, 98.
35. "Nec ratione possessionum, quas nobis in Dyursæ contulit, [ad] predictas procurationes sibi et suis successoribus retinuit, ut dicitis, sed ex suo patrimonio nobis eas totaliter cum consensu meliorum Dacie ac fauore pro remedio anime sue dereliquit." (*Exordium*, ch. 36, p. 215).
36. McGuire, *Conflict and Continuity at Øm Abbey*, 85.
37. For more about the legal aspects of protection in late thirteenth-century Denmark see Michael H. Gelting, "The Problem of Danish 'Feudalism': Military, Legal and Social Change in the Twelfth and Thirteenth Centuries," in *Feudalism: New Landscapes of Debate*, ed. Sverre Bagge, Michael H. Gelting, and Thomas Lindkvist (Turnhout, 2011), 159–84 at 175–76.
38. "animus eius non erat nobiscum" (*Exordium*, ch. 36. p. 209).
39. Patrick J. Geary, "Living with Conflicts in Stateless France: A Typology of Conflict Management Mechanisms, 1000–1200," in *Living with the Dead in the Middle Ages*, ed. Patrick J. Geary (Ithaca, NY, 1994), 125–60 at 140.
40. For the political functions of anger see Richard E. Barton, "'Zealous Anger' and the Renegotiation of Aristocratic Relationships in Eleventh- and Twelfth-Century France," in *Angers Past: The Social Uses of an Emotion in the Middle Ages*, ed. Barbara H. Rosenwein (Ithaca, NY, 1998), 153–70; Sveinung K. Boye, "Chronicling Angry Bishops: On the Use and Perceptions of Episcopal Anger in 13th-Century Scandinavian Narratives," *Collegium Medievale* 28 (2015): 5–36; Stephen D. White, "The Politics of Anger," in *Angers Past*, 127–52.
41. See Esmark, "Godsgaver, calumniae og retsantropologi"; Henk Teunis, *The Appeal to the Original Status: Social Justice in Anjou in the Eleventh Century* (Hilversum, 2006), 136.
42. "cum alijs amicis claustra faceret concordiam bonam inter ipsum abbatem et episcopum" (*Exordium*, 218).
43. *Exordium*, ch. 36, p. 219.
44. Rosenwein has noted the same about the role of papal letters in conflicts concerning Cluny (Barbara H. Rosenwein, Thomas Head, and Sharon Farmer, "Monks and Their Enemies: A Comparative Approach," *Speculum* 66, no. 4 (1991): 764–96 at 775.)
45. "Reuertimini unusquisque ad loca sua, et estote sub interdictu, quia actenus monachis de Øm seruiuistis; et si non cito de eorum ministerio recesseritis, omnes nos proculdubio excommunicabimus." (*Exordium*, ch. 36, p. 220).

46. "plorantes et ululantes" ibid.
47. Ibid.
48. Geary, "Living with Conflicts," 150. See also my own article: Boye, "Chronicling Angry Bishops."
49. "Tu non uales sustinere iram episcopi tui; nec tibi nec alijs conuenit resistere episcopo suo. Accede ad eum et exibe ei satisfactionem, et eritis bon amici." (*Exordium*, ch. 36, p. 220).
50. "Nos excommunicamus te, quia dicis te esse abbatem, excommunicamus conuentum tuum, eo quod nominant te abbatem; et omnes illos, qui abbatem appellant, excommunicamus." (*Exordium*, ch. 36, p. 220).
51. "Eadem facilitate, qua uos subditos meos excommunicatis, eadem facilitate ego eos absoluo." (*Exordium*, ch. 36, p. 220).
52. Rosenwein et al., "Monks and Their Enemies."
53. Ibid. Stephen D. White similarly claims that in eleventh-century western France, conflict resolutions had the appearance of a formalized court procedure, but the conflicts were in reality settled by compromise. Authority figures who seemed to be judges were in fact no more than arbiters. (Stephen D. White, "'*Pactum . . . legem vincit et amor judicum*': The Settlement of Disputes by Compromise in Eleventh-Century Western France," *American Journal of Legal History* 22, no. 4 (1978): 281–308; Stephen D. White, "Inheritance and Legal Arguments in Western France, 1050–1150," *Traditio* 43 (1987): 55–103.)
54. Rosenwein et al., "Monks and Their Enemies."
55. "nobilis persona et sapiens, et bene notus ab omnibus melioribus regni Dacie" (*Exordium*, 229).
56. "rege Waldemaro multum dilectus" (ibid., 192).
57. "ad omnibus dilectas et honoratus" (ibid., 191).
58. "multum a rege Erico nec non et alijs pricipibus et nobilibus terre dilectus" (ibid., 196).
59. "uir uite uenerabilis et tam rege quam a cunctis principibus regni pro reuerentia gratie dei que lucebat in uultu eius, et facundia riuuli sermonis melliflui qui exibat de ore eius, ualde dilectus" (*Exordium*, ch. 1, p. 161).
60. *Øm klosters krønike*, 79.
61. Ibid.
62. For more on papal legates in Scandinavia, see the contribution by Wojtek Jezierski in chapter 9 in this volume.

Dedicated Bibliography

Andersson, Catharina. "Kloster och aristokrati, Nunnor, munkar och gåvor i det svenska samhället till 1300-talets mitt." PhD diss., University of Gothenburg, 2006.

Barton, Richard E. "'Zealous Anger' and the Renegotiation of Aristocratic Relationships in Eleventh- and Twelfth-Century France." In *Anger's Past: The Social Uses of an Emotion in the Middle Ages*, edited by Barbara H. Rosenwein, 153–70. Ithaca, NY, 1998.

Bourdieu, Pierre. *Outline of a Theory of Practice*. Translated by Richard Nice. Cambridge, 1977.

Boye, Sveinung K. "Chronicling Angry Bishops: On the Use and Perceptions of Episcopal Anger in 13th Century Scandinavian Narratives." *Collegium Medievale* 28 (2015): 5–36.

Esmark, Kim. "Godsgaver, *calumniae* og retsantropologi. Esrum kloster og dets naboer, ca. 1150–1250." In *Ett annat 1100-tal. Individ, kollektiv och kulturella mönster i medeltidens Danmark*, edited by Peter Carelli, Lars Hermanson, and Hanne Sanders, 143–80. Gothenburg, 2004.

Esmark, Kim. "Religious Patronage and Family Consciousness: Sorø Abbey and the 'Hvide Family', *c.* 1150–1250." In *Religious and Laity in Western Europe 1000–1400: Interaction, Negotiation, and Power*, edited by Emilia Jamroziak and Janet Burton, 93–110. Turnhout, 2006.

Esmark, Kim. "Disputing Property in Zealand: The Records of Sorø Donation Book." In *Disputing Strategies in Medieval Scandinavia*, edited by Kim Esmark, Lars Hermanson, Hans Jacob Orning, and Helle Vogt, 181–218. Leiden, 2013.

Esmark, Kim, and Hans Jacob Orning. "General Introduction." In *Disputing Strategies in Medieval Scandinavia*, edited by Kim Esmark, Lars Hermanson, Hans Jacob Orning, and Helle Vogt, 1–28. Leiden, 2013.

"Exordium Monasterii Carae Insulae." In SM.

Geary, Patrick J. "Living with Conflicts in Stateless France: A Typology of Conflict Management Mechanisms." In *Living with the Dead in the Middle Ages*, edited by Patrick J. Geary, 125–60. Ithaca, NY, 1994.

Gelting, Michael H. "The Problem of Danish 'Feudalism': Military, Legal and Social Change in the Twelfth and Thirteenth Centuries." In *Feudalism: New Landscapes of Debate*, edited by Sverre Bagge, Michael H. Gelting, and Thomas Lindkvist, 159–84. Turnhout, 2011.

Hermanson, Lars. "Statsbildning och vänskap i 1100-talets Norden." In *Statsutvikling i Skandinavia i middelalderen*, edited by Sverre Bagge, Michael H. Gelting, Frode Hervik, Thomas Lindkvist, and Bjørn Poulsen, 119–43. Oslo, 2012.

Lawrence, Clifford Hugh. *Medieval Monasticism: Forms of Religious Life in Western Europe in the Middle Ages*. Harlow, 2001 [1984].

McGuire, Brian Patrick. *Conflict and Continuity at Øm Abbey: A Cistercian Experience in Medieval Denmark*. Copenhagen, 1976.

McGuire, Brian Patrick. "The Cistercians as a Scandinavian Elite." In *Les Élites Nordiques et L'Europe Occidentale (XIIe – XVe siècle)*, edited by Tuomas M. S. Lehtonen and Élisabeth Mornet, 113–26. Paris, 2007.

Olrik, Jørgen, Jacob Isager, and Holger N. Garner, eds. *Øm klosters krønike*. Øm, 1997.

Orning, Hans Jacob. *Unpredictability and Presence: Norwegian Kingship in the High Middle Ages*. Leiden, 2008.

Paludan, Helge. *Familia og familie: To europæiske kulturelementers møde i højmiddelalderens Danmark*. Aarhus, 1995.

Reuter, Timothy. "Property Transactions and Social Relations Between Rulers, Bishops and Nobles in Early Eleventh-Century Saxony: The Evidence of Vita Meinwerci." In *Property and Power in the Early Middle Ages*, edited by Wendy Davis and Paul Fouracre, 165–99. Cambridge, 2002.

Rosenwein, Barbara H. *To Be the Neighbour of Saint Peter: The Social Meaning of Cluny's Property, 909–1049*. Ithaca, NY, 1989.

Rosenwein, Barbara H., Thomas Head, and Sharon Farmer. "Monks and Their Enemies: A Comparative Approach." *Speculum* 66, no. 4 (1991): 764–96.

Skyum-Nielsen, Niels. *Kirkekampen i Danmark, 1241–1290: Jakob Erlandsen, samtid og eftertid*. Copenhagen, 1963.

Teunis, Henk. *The Appeal to the Original Status: Social Justice in Anjou in the Eleventh Century*. Hilversum, 2006.
White, Stephen D. "*Pactum . . . legem vincit et amor judicum*: The Settlement of Disputes by Compromise in Eleventh-Century Western France." *American Journal of Legal History* 22, no. 4 (1978): 281–308.
White, Stephen D. "Inheritance and Legal Arguments in Western France, 1050–1150." *Traditio* 43 (1987): 55–103.
White, Stephen D. *Custom, Kinship, and Gifts to Saints: The Laudatio Parentum in Western France 1050–1150*. Chapel Hill, 1988.
White, Stephen D. "The Discourse of Inheritance in Twelfth-Century France: Alternative Modes of Fief in Raoul de Cambrai." In *Law and Government in Medieval England and Normandy: Essays in Honour of Sir James Holt*, edited by G. Garnett and J. Hudson, 173–97. Cambridge, 1994.

17 Elites and Social Bonds – How Nordic Were the Nordic Medieval Elites?

Arnoud-Jan Bijsterveld, Kim Esmark, and Hans Jacob Orning

This anthology has addressed the question of how Nordic elites, both lay and clerical, established and maintained status through forming, negotiating, and using various social bonds (kinship, friendship, patronage, etc.). The book has adopted a bottom-up perspective, viewing authority primarily as a result of the control and appropriation of informal social resources in the form of networks of interpersonal relationships. The point of applying a bottom-up perspective is not that power was built only from below, but that it did not emanate primarily from one particular (royal) center either. Rather, power was constructed and negotiated by multiple agents around multiple positions in the power field, both vertically and horizontally, by such means as gift exchange, offers of protection and service, friendship and alliance. At the same time, to speak of social resources as "informal" does not imply that they were "private" or "hidden," as in fact they might be demonstrably "public" (as with an important noble marriage or honorable friendship, for instance) and regulated by collectively shared and sometimes heavily binding norms. Yet social resources in the sense described here were not controlled by formal laws and institutions or ordered from a singular privileged point in social space. In Weberian terms, they had a traditional or patrimonial rather than a legal or bureaucratic character. Also, their extent and structure did not necessarily align with the borders of kingdoms or administrative units. The bottom-up approach thus also entails an ambition to analyze networks on a variety of geographical scales, ranging from local through regnal and trans-regnal to trans-Nordic ones.

This afterword, then, has a twofold aim: to sum up some main results of the studies in the volume, and to expand the scope of the endeavor by drawing on a wider European context, partly by discussing interaction between Scandinavia and the rest of Europe, and partly through comparison of similarities and differences between Scandinavia and wider Europe, including intra-Scandinavian variations. It will do so by discussing the key themes of elite networks and social resources, the "Nordicness" of the Nordic elites, and, finally, the issue of historical transformation.

Fuzzy Families, Flexible Friendships: The Strength of Social Networks

The general conclusion from the foregoing chapters is that social resources were a key component and converter of power and rank among Nordic medieval elites. In a highly competitive, multipolar power field, elite status basically rested on the ability to create, maintain, and manipulate social ties, placing Althoff's axiomatic "family, friends, and followers" at the center of all socio-politics.[1]

In one way or another, kinship stands at the heart of many contributions in the volume. Belonging to a prominent lineage was a precondition for participation in high politics, as most Nordic magnates came from powerful interrelated families. Here, marriage was a key institution, assigning women a central position as connecting links between groups. At least among the top echelons of society the networks that were thus constructed on the basis of family, affinity, and descent frequently transcended distinctions between royal and non-royal blood, as well as borders between kingdoms (see in particular Lind, Missuno, Auður Magnúsdóttir, Grohse, Rønning).

Family ties within the elites, however, were complex. In the Nordic world the "kinship system" was always bilateral, and thus structurally open; and as shown throughout the book the *practical use* (as opposed to official norms and rules) of blood relations and affines made kin a rather fluid and malleable concept. Family bonds often blended with other non-genealogical ties, and in the end their strength was determined by common interests. Kinship as it appears in the studies here was perhaps first of all a socio-cultural framework for formulating issues of affiliation, identity, and loyalty, and for raising claims and mobilizing support. The moral obligations potentially implied by kinship could and would be invoked strategically, but alliances constructed through blood and marriage rarely stood the test if pivotal interests worked in other directions (Rønning, Auður Magnúsdóttir).

If prominent ancestry and useful kinsmen were mandatory resources for elites, so in no smaller measure were relations of friendship and patronage. In fact, political alliances, built on notions of friendship (*vinátta*, *amicitia*), between members of the elite were probably the most important vehicles for creating and sustaining power in the Nordic region, where "informal" horizontal networks and action groups rather than any kind of state, church, or institutionalized orders constituted the context for political competition. Positions and hierarchies were relatively fluid and dependent upon personal qualities and abilities to maneuver in the political game. Just like kinship groups, horizontal factions and alliances were rarely permanent or close-knit units.[2] Especially when tested in situations of contest and conflict, such groups were regularly exposed to defection, side-switching, and reconfigurations (Esmark, Rønning).

Moreover, as distinctions between horizontal and vertical bonds were often blurred, an important bone of contention between parties was precisely how to define their relationship. Boye's chapter demonstrates how clerical agents in a situation of conflicting interests played on discourses of both equality/symmetry and hierarchy/subordination. The same goes with magnates' relationships with kings and ecclesiastical princes or institutions: Such relationships came to constitute important assets and also represented an augmentation of socio-political resources available to members of the elite.[3] However, this kind of tie did not transform the rivalry among elite members in any crucial manner, but merely served to increase competition and to refine and differentiate the means and methods necessary to prosper and succeed.

For all their fragility, elite factions (or "elite collectives")[4] and their constant rivalry and alliance-making are thus everywhere in the present book. In Källström's study, Swedish runic inscriptions bear witness to local and regional elite networks in early medieval Uppland. Grohse shows that competing elite networks were also at work within a monarchical context, while Rønning describes the workings of alliance-making in royal dynastic strife. The apparent lability of horizontal bonds should not be seen as a fatal weakness. Those bonds clearly mattered, even if they were broken, adjusted, ignored, or exaggerated in various contexts. Actually, one could argue that it was precisely the flexibility and fluidity of alliances that made them adaptable, and thus workable, means for elites in political power struggles. Securing success required skills and pragmatism more than blind adherence to norms, or rather, it required the ability to bend and represent one's actions by way of "officializing strategies" so that they appeared as adhering to social norms.[5]

A precondition for elite status was the command of necessary economic resources (the subject of the first volume of this series). The limitations of sources unfortunately make it difficult to explore local authority in medieval Scandinavia. Historians are hardly allowed insights into specific local patrimonial structures, such as the bonds of patronage and clientelism between aristocratic lords and lesser men, peasants, and dependents. Exactly how elite networks extended downwards into the lower strata of society – from which they extracted their wealth, and with whose members they also needed to cultivate social ties – therefore remains largely hidden. However, Iceland provides an exception in this respect, as the detailed accounts in the sagas do shed light on local power relations. Viðar Pálsson in his chapter thus shows how Icelandic chieftains used gifts and feasts as strategic weapons in order to maintain local personal bonds and strengthen power, in particular at crucial moments of power shifts. Saga narratives also permit unusually detailed analyses of marriage strategies (Auður Magnúsdóttir) as well as quantitative analyses and comparisons of the structure and extent of local networks (Kenna and MacCarron). To what degree specific Icelandic conditions may serve as a model for the wider Nordic world remains a point of debate.

Even if for some definite purposes members of the clergy might mobilize as a distinct faction, the studies in this volume confirm the futility of distinguishing too strictly between secular and clerical elites in medieval Scandinavia. First, lay magnates and bishops and abbots originated from the same families, and the distribution of clerical offices largely depended on family and friendship connections. Boye's analysis of a strictly intra-ecclesiastical dispute demonstrates how heavily it was enmeshed in secular concerns and mechanisms of conflict resolution. Second, Nordic elites used religious resources to enhance power, for instance when founding and endowing *Hausklöster*, sacred loci for commemoration and celebration as well as centers for concentration of economic wealth. Third, social resources from one field could be converted into resources in other fields, and this was increasingly done by elites sensitive to new developments. As demonstrated by Esmark, secular elites showed no hesitation in pursuing ecclesiastical offices when these became steadily more important during the twelfth century. Jakobsen and Jezierski show that the introduction of new forms of religious capital in a Scandinavian context – ties with and offices in monastic and papal circles – implied entering into a dialogue with secular society. Even if the Church was an institution with a formalized delegative hierarchy, holders of clerical offices were enmeshed in webs of family, friends, and followers like any other member of the elites, and basically played the same game.

Expanding the view to Western Europe between the tenth and thirteenth centuries, the same points could be made, namely that elite networks were the building blocks for gaining and maintaining power. Here, too, secular and ecclesiastical elite networks were fully intertwined and encompassed powerful men and women, from local and regional *potentes* up to and including rulers and kings. Indeed, social bonds of various kinds, including kinship, horizontal alliances, and vertical patron-client bonds, should be regarded as a main source of power in the emerging European societies. As mentioned in the introduction to this book, this is also the conclusion of the 2002–2009 international collaborative project on the European elites of the High Middle Ages, according to which the history of medieval elites is essentially a history of connections and networks.[6]

In the book *The Sources of Social Power*, the sociologist Michael Mann distinguished several sources of what he calls social power (defined as "mastery over other people" as exercised by rulers, states, and other institutions), namely ideological, economic, military, and political power.[7] However, somewhat surprisingly considering the title of his book, Mann did not include *social* power as a dimension in his analysis. Yet the ability to establish and control social networks through mechanisms such as gift exchange, marriage, and other alliances, as well as offers of protection and service, constituted the foundation of elite power in the High Middle Ages. One could also argue that the emergence of "feudal" kingdoms in late eleventh- and twelfth-century Western Europe rested on the same mechanisms. Even if kings tried to – and to some extent succeeded in – centralizing jurisdiction, legislation, public administration, and the use of force, the underlying alternative forms of order with their focus on rituals of peace-making and the maintenance of networks of allegiance and fidelity remained as crucial as ever. Kings and prelates must to a large degree be considered players at the same level as other elite members of society, in that for them, too, the establishment and continuity of power depended on the creation and maintenance of horizontal social bonds and amicable relations.[8]

In Western Europe, too, kinship in the broad sense permeated all associations, bonds, dependencies, and so on, as can be seen in the general use of terms of consanguinity – such as *nepos* (cousin or nephew) and *parentes* or *propinqui* (relatives) – to denote relationships in all of these, be they of a "feudal" or ecclesiastical kind. The terminology of kinship was activated even in cases where the parties were only distantly related or related in spiritual or symbolic terms (for instance as spiritual or sworn brothers), testifying that kinship was not denoting primarily a "natural" or "biological" bond, but what Esmark calls a "fluid and multiform product of varied strategies and representations, which were continuously negotiated and adapted to different contexts and practical needs."[9]

With time, there appears to have developed a gradual shift in Western European elites from rather loosely defined cognatic structures which involved large kinship groups, to more demarcated patrilineal and agnatic structures focused on the possession of a family patrimony including one or more strongholds, one of which would typically lend its name to the family as a "house."[10] Yet this tendency was not absolute, as cognatic kinship retained much of its power as a compelling source of affiliation, identity, and loyalty and remained a strategic bond which could be, and indeed had to be, invoked actively as an obligation for mobilizing support.[11] In the Church, too, kinship constituted a driving force behind the creation of power alliances between bishops and secular *potentes* (who were often recruited from the same elite families), as well as in the establishment of monasteries within elite families, where they often functioned as *Hausklöster* and as a means to keep together and control the family patrimony.[12] As such, family networks were deeply enmeshed in ecclesiastical and spiritual networks.

In addition to building their power on kinship groups, Western European elites maintained their positions through establishing horizontal alliances of various kinds. High medieval elite culture can be envisioned as a community that was built on an apparent paradox of fierce antagonism and shared values. Particularly in France, epic poems promoted a culture of competition among a warrior elite united nonetheless around a shared ideology of martial and Christian values. By "romancing the past" French vernacular historiography and chivalric romances made a strong case for the importance and value of elite networks, which also constituted a hedge against the king in response to the latter's assuming a more authoritative position in society.[13] Even though the emerging central monarchies and Church teachings highlighted the prominence of vertical, authoritative bonds and the importance of a political ideology based on embracing the Roman principles of statehood and legitimacy, horizontal bonds at "state" level remained crucially important well into the thirteenth century.[14] "Public authority" continued to be founded on a ruler's dynamic network of personal alliances established, restored, and maintained through gift-giving. As an integral part of these horizontal bonds, secular elites in Western Europe from c. 1100 revealed themselves willing to incorporate a rhetoric of religious penance and a readiness to offer satisfaction to offended religious parties into their modes of conflict management, thus showing an impetus toward consensus rather than polarization.[15] Moreover, the Crusades provided an occasion for what has been termed the amalgamation of secular and spiritual values into the warrior elite.[16] In the twelfth century, in a time of religious renewal, collectives of members of the lay elites joined forces and operated together in founding and endowing monasteries of the new orders.[17]

Patron-client relationships in medieval Europe are traditionally associated with feudalism. Even if this concept has been contested in the last decades, the importance for elites of establishing vertical bonds of dependence at a local level has not been seriously questioned. Service was generally seen as socially degrading and marking positions of subservience.[18] However, in the High Middle Ages, military and spiritual service came to be seen as elevating in status and, as a result, was taken up as a way of defining bonds of mutual loyalty. One example of this is the *ministeriales* in certain parts of Western Europe.[19] These "servants" were raised to positions of power and responsibility, serving as knights and financial aides to anyone holding power and property, of either ecclesiastical or secular status. Even at the lowest level of the elite, these men constituted the immediate and loyal entourage of owners of strongholds. When the local count Folcold, who owned a castle and landed property in the central Dutch river area in the 1120s and 1130s, was fighting his feuds with neighboring lords, he could not but operate together with what are called his *cognati et amici* and his band of *famuli* and *clientes* who defended his castle.[20] Their loyal service eventually would raise them to elite status as knights.

Although for the sake of analysis we can distinguish between vertical and horizontal bonds, such as between the kings and his followers or a lord and his retinue, there is no way of seeing vertical and horizontal relations as fully institutionalized or exclusively formalized in Western

Europe any more than we can in the Nordic region. What we are actually observing is a mixture or joint appearance of vertical and horizontal elements. Even in the case of vertical, patron-client or "feudal" bonds, the horizontal bonding remained an integral part. Fredric L. Cheyette, describing the society of southern France in the twelfth century, replaced a vertical interpretation of vassalage by conceptualizing a culture of fidelity instead: that is, a culture of emotional as well as political bonding based on oath-taking between members of the social elites. According to Cheyette, "the oath that the great aristocrats took to each other did not mark subservience."[21] Instead, based on the principle of honor and shared values, the oath of fidelity bound them to each other, creating coherence next to or in spite of vertical arrangements. Thus, the distinction between vertical and horizontal becomes blurred. A similar blurring can be observed in the way in which the ninth- and tenth-century West Frankish kings and members of the high aristocracy, in their private commemorative foundations, tried to reciprocally associate themselves with the spiritual rewards of the liturgical services they established, thus hoping to perpetuate their networks of fidelity and friendship in the hereafter.[22] In so doing, they reinforced their reciprocal bonds while at the same time underlining their social distinction, the horizontal and vertical going hand in hand.

All in all, the social and political impact of establishing and maintaining status through forming and using social bonds of various kinds, above all kinship, horizontal alliances, and vertical patron-client bonds, was certainly not limited to the geographic area which is the focus of this volume but remained central to high medieval Western Europe as well. Recent historiography appears to highlight just that.

Challenging the Singularity and the Alterity of Nordic Elites

How interconnected were Nordic elites with one another, and to what degree can we draw a division between the Nordic elites and elites outside Scandinavia? Nordic elites have often been presented in terms of contrasts, for instance, between sheep-herding Icelandic chieftains living in a stateless society at the margins of the European orbit on the one hand, and on the other, Danish magnates positioned in an established kingdom close to Europe with a soil resembling the classic feudal manor. In this anthology, the Danish Sune Ebbesen (d. 1186; see Esmark) and the Icelander Snorri Sturluson (d. 1241; see Auður Magnúsdóttir) can serve as examples of these differences. Sune could build on a complex web of networks and resources; he was tightly integrated into the monarchical power structure through both bonds of fosterage and close cooperation with the kings; and he seems to have enjoyed a firm position as a local and regional leader, without experiencing any problems or challenges from his family or from rival contenders. Snorri, inversely, was primarily a secular leader who lived far from kings and correspondingly closer to recalcitrant relatives and peasants. But how illuminating is such a contrast? Adopting a bottom-up perspective with a focus on informal bonds and strategies makes these differences less pronounced. Snorri had a number of resources at his disposal, including socio-political (being born into and fostered by elite families), cultural (through his authorship of sagas and mythology), as well as *Königsnähe* (membership in the Norwegian king's retinue).[23] Moreover, he did not live in a "stateless" society, as the Norwegian king was deeply enmeshed in Icelandic politics and most Icelandic elites (including Snorri himself) were bound to the king as retainers.[24] Finally, the fact that Snorri experienced more troubles than Sune in his local leadership need not be attributed to historical differences, but could equally well be a result of genre divergences, as the Icelandic sagas depicted rivalries at a local scale in a manner far more detailed, and probably also far less biased, than Danish (and some Norwegian) Latin sources.

If Nordic elites were more similar than has been assumed, they still did not constitute a unified "class," as their position vis-à-vis one another was characterized no less by rivalry than by cooperation.[25] Elites all over the Nordic area competed for power and influence, applying social bonds flexibly in order to achieve their aims. In cases where we can study the local or regional power bases of Nordic elite members, they appear highly interconnected, as exemplified by Iceland (Kenna and MacCarron) and Sweden (Källström).

Studying politics in terms of networks does not imply that regnal borders were of no importance whatsoever. Divisions into realms had a strong topographical component, and a central asset in elite competition was obviously to control or influence kings, kingship, and – by implication – kingdoms. Grohse's contribution demonstrates how the royal court functioned as a locus for rival elite networks, one whose success depended on its ability to balance various factions against one another. Thus, the existence of monarchies in no way erased the importance of informal elite networks as a basis of power and dominance in society, but rather these monarchies functioned as foci for channeling network resources. However, a focus on elite networks turns the issue of territorial borders into a more fuzzy variable than when approaching things from a more institutional angle. As demonstrated in this anthology, elite networks could extend widely across regnal and indeed Nordic borders into the Baltic (Lind), England (Missuno), and Germany (Rønning). The Church played an important role in extending international networks, as seen with regard to Dominican Friars (Jakobsen), in connection with papal legates (Jezierski), and for English contacts (Missuno).

This implies that the drawing of firm borders between Scandinavia and Europe also needs to be questioned. When viewed from a non-Scandinavian perspective, an often-overlooked aspect is the close relations which the Carolingian and post-Carolingian world continued to foster and promote with the Nordic world. This is evident, first of all, from the frequent marriage arrangements between Scandinavian royal dynasties and European kings and rulers from the ninth century onwards. As examples from England, Flanders, and France attest, such marriages served as a social and political glue of the highest political relevance, creating and binding allies, or securing military aid or succession in the High Middle Ages.[26] A map recently drawn by Johannes Preiser-Kapeller of the marriage network of high medieval Europe between AD 1000 and 1200, based on two hundred selected marriages between members of royal and not-royal houses and families across Europe, shows the remarkable interconnectedness of the Scandinavian kingdoms with Europe as a whole.[27]

Intellectual networks and the exchange of high-ranking churchmen (cf. Jezierski) clearly show a similar pattern of ongoing connections between Scandinavia and the rest of Europe. This communication was not one-sided, but "needs to be understood as a reciprocal culture of cross-fertilization and exchange that involved both individuals . . . and collectives or institutions," as argued in a recent anthology on the cultural relationship between England and Scandinavia in the twelfth century.[28]

The intense commercial relations between the two "worlds," starting in the Viking Age and continuing all through the Middle Ages, show that trade between the post-Carolingian and the Nordic world must have been a regular phenomenon.[29] As Timothy Reuter demonstrated, the transition between trade, plunder, and tribute was not always clear-cut in post-Carolingian Europe, and this attests to a far greater familiarity and indeed similarity between "Vikings" and "Europeans" than the sources normally present.[30] Commercial contacts between Scandinavia and Europe have often been presumed to dwindle after the Viking Age, only to resurge with the Hanseatic merchants from the thirteenth century onwards. However, archaeologists and historians have argued recently that the reciprocal trade relations between the Nordic world and Viking Age *emporia* and *portus* evolved uninterruptedly into the trade network between market towns along the coast from the Baltic to the North Sea, and inland areas that appear in *Hanse* sources from the middle of the thirteenth century.[31]

It is hard to generalize about the king's role in elite networks in Europe, because royal power varied substantially from area to area. In so-called feudal Europe, where kings often held only nominal power, "political power was claimed and negotiated through the collective action of a series of overlapping and interleaving groups on a hierarchy of public stages," as formulated by Matthew Innes.[32] The count of Flanders is a case in point: although a liege man of the French king, the Flemish count managed to engage in political and marriage alliances with the kings of England and Denmark, the count of Holland, and the duke of Saxony in the eleventh and twelfth centuries.[33] In the German realm, in the course of the eleventh and twelfth centuries, dukes and counts (and even bishops) typically managed to establish social and territorial footholds in territories not their own.[34] For instance, demesnes and strongholds received in dowry or as a material reward for an office often served to create such a bridgehead beyond one's own territory, as physical nodes of power. How such bonds also transected the borders of Nordic and European polities is exemplified by the Danish magnate Knud Lavard (d. 1131), who held the earldom of Schleswig from the Danish king while also being a vassal of King Lothar of Germany, who furthermore conferred on him the title of lord of the West Slavic Obodrites.[35] This dispersion of power might look like "feudal anarchy," but in fact it marks an opportunistic, yet clever way to expand networks and to spread strategic interests.

However, even in England – which after the Norman conquest represents the best example of royal power capable of asserting itself in a top-down manner – it can be hard to distinguish between the king as official head of the state and his role as a grand patron. Robert Bartlett considers the latter function to be the primary one:

> The patronage that the king had to offer was of very varied types. The rarest, and most painful to the giver, was a grant of royal land. Offices could also be granted, with tenure for life or a term. A more flexible and less draining source of patronage could be found in the wardships and marriages that the king had at his disposal.[36]

Also in a context of strong monarchs as in England, secular and ecclesiastical elites were able to or at least strove to assert for themselves room to maneuver: "Power, if it was to be effective, had to come to terms with the modalities of local power, with aristocratic regional power bases."[37] To create a certain level of autonomy, even the closest vassals hedged their bets, establishing social bonds beyond the limits of their overlords' territory.

So, in conclusion, we might say that the Nordic world, despite the similarities in the way social bonds served to attain power and control from Iceland to Denmark, was neither a homogeneously organized world of its own nor closed off from socio-political, religious, cultural, and commercial interaction and exchange with the rest of Europe: quite the contrary. This once again suggests that the salience of informal social resources and networks as a basis of power is not to be regarded as something specifically Scandinavian but, as least in principle, as a pan-European phenomenon.

However, what may to a great extent explain the difference in the representation of the Nordic world vs. Western Europe as painted in historiography is that this scholarship reproduces the viewpoint of the sources, which might blur our view. Western European written sources were produced almost exclusively by clerics and churchmen associated with or unambiguously supporting royal power, and therefore carry a heavy ideological stamp. Western Europe lacks the rich contextual information about aristocratic interactions provided by the sagas that are so prominent in the preceding chapters. As a result, historians investigating power and authority in Western Europe may have been biased too in almost automatically looking from a top-down perspective, as if only "state" and Church institutions and regulations determined the political relations on the ground. This approach might be excusable in a historiography aiming to determine the historical legitimacy of the nineteenth-century nation-state, as has been the implicit and explicit aim of most medieval history being done in Western European countries ever since, but it should be challenged and revised in any contemporary academic writing.[38] Likewise, it is about time to challenge the distinction between a "civilized" and culturally dominant center – i.e., the Carolingian world and its "successor states" France and the Holy Roman Empire, as well as England after 1066 – and a backward, uncultured periphery. This issue will be dealt with in the last section.

Transformation as Formalization: Statehood and Alternative Orders

Several authors in this book refer to a process of *formalization* in Scandinavia between c. 1050 and 1250. Formalization in this context may be loosely defined as a gradual development towards more institutionalized (impersonal, routinized) forms of lordship on the one hand, and *Verrechtlichung* of social relations on the other. Less ambiguity, ritual, and negotiation; more structure, codification, and authority. State and Church have traditionally been considered prime movers of this process, as kings and bishops propounded progressive societal reforms in the face of reactionary aristocratic opposition.[39] While elements supporting such interpretations are surely identifiable in the period, the question remains to what extent – and at what time – new impulses actually changed the nature of power and politics. Looking at formalization from the perspective adopted in this book – e.g., elite networks and actual political practice – the factitious separation between monarchy, Church, and aristocracy, and the strict classificatory distinction between "private" and "public" are of limited use as analytical tools. In the chapters of the present volume, formalization is apparent as a property that was constructed or activated in situations where it represented a useful strategy for specific elite actors facing specific challenges (see in particular Rønning, Esmark, Boye). From this point of view, the socio-political dynamics of networks were not merely the backdrop for supposedly more progressive centralist endeavors, but rather a constant and continuing condition, which formalization efforts had to adjust to and indeed build upon. It is beyond the scope of this anthology to give a conclusive answer to the question of how deeply medieval Nordic politics were thus transformed, but it is hoped the book's perspective and methodology have opened a new avenue for studying these issues in a way which is less biased by institutional concerns and anachronistic divisions between "progressive" and "backward-looking" forces.

Moving back once again to wider Europe, the bottom-up perspective according to which power is constructed and negotiated by multiple agents – including but not exclusively kings – may seem at odds with the centralist and state-oriented model most often assumed to have been in place in most Western European kingdoms and principalities.[40] To be sure, the legacy of the ideal of the state, which we could call a Carolingian ideal, continued to play a key role in the theory and practice of how power was exercised in the emerging kingdoms there. As Charles West aptly observes, "the Carolingians are imagined as the heirs (or the creators) of a properly public state."[41] This model entailed a strictly hierarchical "system" of lordship consisting of vertical bonds based on "feudal" ties, in which the king promised protection and material rewards in exchange for his vassals' aid and counsel. West summarizes the Carolingian endeavor as "a formalisation of interaction across the entire social spectrum" and observes this in the "relative centralised system of government" with "structures of authority" and in a "more formalised understanding of the nature of power"; that is, the reification and institutionalization of power shaped as "property relations" and jurisdiction. He sees this, moreover, in the "heightened reliance on the written word" and in the creation of "a language of politics infused with a liturgised theology," resulting in "liturgical kingship" and a close association of "secular" and "spiritual" power.[42]

Yet next to "formal institutions," West observes in the Carolingian and post-Carolingian world the salience of "alternative forms of order and solidarity," oriented to practice, not norms, and to "lordship, not the state," especially among the secular elite, "a loose grouping defined by behavioural patterns, kinship networks, and a ready resort to violence."[43] This means that although the emerging central monarchies and Church teachings highlighted the prominence of vertical, authoritative bonds, and the importance of a political ideology based on embracing the Roman principles of statehood and legitimacy, horizontal bonds at "state" level remained crucially important. So-called public authority was and remained founded on a ruler's dynamic network of personal alliances which were established, restored, and maintained through gift-giving. Hence, even in the "ideal" of a formalized, centralized state, "pre-institutionalized" structures were much less "dis-orderly" than is often assumed. In fact, medieval societies all contained a mix of the two. Rather than distinguishing between horizontal and vertical power strategies and between bottom-up and top-down dynamics in social networking, historians should keep a keen eye on their indivisibility.[44] This looking for a balance and displaying the significance of an "alternative order" is exactly what is done in the chapters in this volume, thus presenting a historiographical practice to be followed while assessing anew the formation of "state" power in the remainder of continental Europe.

Geographically, medieval Scandinavia was situated on the outskirts of Europe. It had no Carolingian (or Roman) heritage to boast of, and its political processes of state formation and Christianization started later than in Carolingian areas. Should high medieval Scandinavia be considered as just a latecomer on the European stage, as a more "primitive" area, or was it more similar to Europe than is usually assumed? In older textbooks, Scandinavia was simply excluded when Europe was described in the High Middle Ages, at best figuring as a nest for Viking expansion, the "second wave of migration" threatening Europe in the ninth and tenth centuries, and after that constituting a periphery hardly worthy of mention when discussing the expansion of Christian European culture.[45]

A more nuanced view emerged in Robert Bartlett's *The Making of Europe* from 1993, where the subtitle "Conquest, Colonization and Cultural Change 950–1350" hints at a broader conception of Europe than the Carolingian heartlands.[46] In Bartlett's book, the dominating figure was one of diffusion. The peripheries of Europe, foremost eastern and northern Europe, were colonized from the "core" of Europe ("Frankish Europe"), and this process was one of "replication, not differentiation," resulting in a homogenizing "Europeanization of Europe."[47] That this was primarily a one-way process of diffusion emerges clearly from Bartlett's adoption of the chronicler Arnold of Lübeck's formulation c. 1200 concerning the Danes: they "adjusted themselves to other nations."[48] In the course of this process, Europe became more homogenized, diversity giving way to uniformity. Bartlett's thesis represented a watershed in including the peripheries in Europe within the grand narrative of European history, and also by turning the attention from kings to a "knightly-clerical-mercantile consortium" as the driving forces behind this process of Europeanization.[49] However, according to Bartlett's view Scandinavia remained a copy of the core, a latecomer to a culture which had already found its form. As such, it allowed little interaction or two-way communication to take place, leaving central Europe unaffected by the expansion movement in the High Middle Ages.[50]

Chris Wickham offered an alternative perspective on this relationship in his *Framing the Early Middle Ages* of 2005, where he argues that a precondition for state formation in peripheral Europe was a transition from "tribal" to "aristocratic" societies. This happened in England, but not in Denmark (which is his primary example from Scandinavia), where "aristocratic dominance over peasant neighbours was not established" before the millennium.[51] When a "unitary state" emerged around 1000, it was the result of an indigenous development, not of an expansion from the center of Europe. Instead, Denmark was characterized by "[r]itual/ political, tribal, leadership by local-level 'chieftains' over autonomous peasants," with the Icelandic *goði-þingmaðr* relationship known from the Icelandic Free State before 1262/64 serving as a more plausible model.[52]

Bartlett and Wickham have done a lot to make the otherwise peripheral north part of the general history of medieval Europe. The mere inclusion of Scandinavia in their works is one thing, but they also demonstrate how discussions of the relationship between the northerners and the Franks, the Germans, and others need not lapse into old tropes of "primitivity" vs. "civilization." Nevertheless, to some extent both still tend to treat Scandinavia as inherently *special*, either as a latecomer to mainstream standards (Bartlett) or following its own independent course (Wickham). In the present volume we have explored a somewhat different picture. Digging below and beyond the standard Nordic historiographical objects of kingdom, church, and institution to focus instead on the dynamics of social networks and resources among elites, it appears, first, that Scandinavia might be more internally diverse than assumed when viewed from the outside (differences between, say, Zealand and Iceland being in some respects bigger than between Zealand and Saxony). Second, rather than positing Denmark, Norway, Sweden, and Iceland in an adjunct world of their own, the studies presented here propose a picture of similarity and integration: Common practices, communication, and reciprocal exchanges (socio-political, but also religious, cultural, and mercantile) bound Scandinavian elites up with their European counterparts. The northern world – or parts of it – seem to have shared too many similarities with other European regions to be dealt with in isolation.[53]

Notes

1. Gerd Althoff, *Family, Friends and Followers: Political and Social Bonds in Medieval Europe* [*Verwandte, Freunde und Getreue: Zum politischen Stellenwert der Gruppenbindungen im früheren Mittelalter*], trans. Christopher Carroll (Cambridge, 2004).
2. Vertically formed bonds appear to have had more permanence. See Jón Viðar Sigurðsson, *Chieftains and Power in the Icelandic Commonwealth*, vol. 12, The Viking Collection 12 (Odense, 1999).
3. See, for instance, Chris Wickham, *Courts and Conflict in Twelfth-Century Tuscany* (Oxford, 2003) on the revival of Roman law in Tuscany.
4. Lars Hermanson, *Släkt, vänner och makt: En studie av elitens politiska kultur i 1100-talets Danmark* (Gothenburg, 2000).
5. Pierre Bourdieu, *The Logic of Practice* (Cambridge, 1990), 109.
6. Geneviève Bührer-Thierry, "Connaître les élites au haut moyen âge," in *Théorie et pratiques des élites au Haut Moyen Age: Conception, perception et réalisation sociale*, ed. François Bougard, Hans-Werner Goetz, and Régine Le Jan (Turnhout, 2011), 373–84.
7. Michael Mann, *The Sources of Social Power: I. The History of Power from the Beginning to A.D. 1760* (Cambridge, 1986).
8. Rees Davies, "The Medieval State: The Tyranny of a Concept?" *Journal of Historical Sociology* 16, no. 2 (2003): 289–90 (critical response in Susan

How Nordic Were the Nordic Medieval Elites? 339

Reynolds, "There Were States in Medieval Europe: A Response to Rees Davies," *Journal of Historical Sociology* 16, no. 4 (2003)); Arnoud-Jan A. Bijsterveld, *Do ut des: Gift Giving, Memoria, and Conflict Management in the Medieval Low Countries* (Hilversum, 2007), 49; Arnoud-Jan Bijsterveld, "Aristocratic Identities and Power Strategies in Lower Lotharingia: The Case of the Rode Lineage (Eleventh and Twelfth Centuries)," in *La Lotharingie en question: Identités, oppositions, intégration: Lotharingische Identitäten im Spannungsfeld zwischen integrativen und partikularen Kräften*, ed. Michel Margue and Hérold Pettiau (Luxembourg, 2018), 315–61. Cf. the contribution by Kim Esmark in chapter 15 in this volume.

9. Kim Esmark, "Religious Patronage and Family Consciousness: Sorø Abbey and the 'Hvide family', *c*. 1150–1250," in *Religious and Laity in Western Europe 1000–1400: Interaction, Negotiation, and Power*, ed. Emilia Jamroziak and Janet Burton (Turnhout, 2006), 93–110 at 109.
10. Constance B. Bouchard, "Family Structure and Family Consciousness Among the Aristocracy in the Ninth to Eleventh Centuries," *Francia* 14 (1986): 639–58; Benjamin Arnold, *Princes and Territories in Medieval Germany* (Cambridge, 1991), 141–51; Thomas Zotz, "Die Situation des Adels im 11. und frühen 12. Jahrhundert," in *Vom Umbruch zur Erneuerung? Das 11. und 12. Jahrhundert: Positionen der Forschung*, ed. Jorg Jarnut and Matthias Wemhoff, MittelalterStudien 13 (München, 2006), 341–55.
11. Amy Livingstone, *Out of Love for My Kin: Aristocratic Family Life in the Lands of the Loire* (Ithaca, NY, 2010); Constance B. Bouchard, *Those of My Blood: Constructing Noble Families in Medieval Francia* (Philadelphia, 2003).
12. Benjamin Arnold, *Count and Bishop in Medieval Germany: A Study of Regional Power, 1100–1350* (Philadelphia, 1991).
13. Joachim Bumke, *Höfische Kultur: Literatur und Gesellschaft im hohen Mittelalter* (München, 1986), transl. as *Courtly Culture: Literature and Society in the High Middle Ages* (Berkeley CA, 1991); Gabrielle Spiegel, *Romancing the Past: The Rise of Vernacular Prose Historiography in Thirteenth-Century France* (New York, 1993); Stephen D. White, "The Discourse of Inheritance in Twelfth-Century France: Alternative Models of the Fief in *Raoul de Cambrai*," in *Law and Government in Medieval England and Normandy: Essays in Honour of Sir James Holt*, ed. George Garnett and John Hudson (Cambridge, 1994), 173–97.
14. See Jenny Benham, *Peacemaking in the Middle Ages: Principles and Practice* (Manchester, 2011) on medieval "diplomatics."
15. Steven Vanderputten and Arnoud-Jan Bijsterveld, "Penitential Discourse and Conflict Management in the Late-Eleventh- and Early-Twelfth-Century Southern Low Countries," *Revue belge de Philologie et d'Histoire: Belgisch Tijdschrift voor Filologie en Geschiedenis* 90 (2012): 471–92.
16. Marcus Bull, *Knightly Piety and the Lay Response to the First Crusade: The Limousin and Gascony c.970–c.1130* (Oxford, 1993).
17. Bijsterveld, *Do ut des*, 104–6.
18. Marc Bloch, *Feudal Society*, vol. 1 (London, 1975).
19. Arnold, *Princes and Territories*, 120, 180–81, 183.
20. As described in Bijsterveld, *Do ut des*, 215–18.
21. Fredric L. Cheyette, *Ermengard of Narbonne and the World of the Troubadours* (Ithaca, NY and London, 2004), 192.
22. Philippe Depreux, "La dimension 'publique' de certaines dispositions 'privées'. Fondations pieuses et memoria en Francie occidentale aux IXe et Xe siècles," in *Sauver son âme et se perpétuer: Transmission du patrimoine et mémoire au haut Moyen Âge*, ed. François Bougard, Cristina La Rocca, and Régine Le Jan (Rome, 2005), 332–78, 527.

23. Torfi H. Tulinius, "Capital, Field, Illusio: Can Bourdieu's Sociology Help Us Understand the Development of Literature in Medieval Iceland?" in *Sagas and Societies, International Conference at Borgarnes, Iceland, 2002*, ed. Stefanie Würth, Tunno Jonuks, and Axel Kristinsson (Tübingen, 2004).
24. One could actually argue that the Norwegian king played a more dominant role in Icelandic politics in the first half of the thirteenth century than in Norway, since he actively summoned chieftains to and from Norway in a way that decisively influenced the power game. Hans Jacob Orning, *Unpredictability and Presence: Norwegian Kingship in the High Middle Ages*, trans. Alan Crozier (Leiden, 2008).
25. The issue of whether the elites constituted a "class" in the Marxist sense, even if "class consciousness" may only have been incipient, has been much discussed in Norway (Kåre Lunden, *Norge under Sverreætten, 1177–1319: Høymiddelalder, Norges Historie* (Oslo, 1976).
26. Kerstin Hundahl, Lars Kjær, and Niels Lund, eds., *Denmark and Europe in the Middle Ages, C.1000–1525: Essays in Honour of Professor Michael H. Gelting* (London, 2016); John Lind, "De russiske ægteskaber: Dynasti- og alliancepolitiki 1130'ernes danske borgerkrig," *Historisk Tidsskrift* (D) 92 (1992); Kurt Villads Jensen, *Korstog ved verdens yderste rand: Danmark og Portugal ca. 1000 til ca. 1250* (Odense, 2011).
27. Johannes Preiser-Kapeller, "Marriage Network of High Medieval Europe (1000–1200 AD)," www.academia.edu/37090935/The_marriage_network_of_high_medieval_Europe_1000-1200_AD_.
28. Mia Münster-Swendsen, Thomas K. Heebøll-Holm, and Sigbjørn Olsen Sønnesyn, ed., *Historical and Intellectual Culture in the Long Twelfth Century: The Scandinavian Connections*, Durham Medieval and Renaissance Monographs and Essays 5 (Toronto, 2016), 91–103; Quotation from the review by Benjamin Pohl in *The Medieval Review* (TMR) 18.09.09. See also Sif Rikhardsdottir, *Medieval Translations and Cultural Discourse: The Movement of Texts in England, France and Scandinavia* (Cambridge, 2012), 17–18. More generally, the dynamic and reciprocal relationship between Scandinavia and the rest of Europe has been the theme of two major research projects during the last decades, with the Centre for Medieval Studies in Bergen focusing on the political and religious relationship (see www.uib.no/cms/) and the project "Translation, Transmission and Transformation. Old Norse Romantic Fiction and Scandinavian Vernacular Literacy 1200–1500" in Oslo addressing the literary and cultural relationship (see www.hf.uio.no/iln/english/research/projects/ttt/).
29. Frans Theuws and Arnoud-Jan Bijsterveld, "Early Town Formation in the Northern Low Countries: Roman Heritage, Carolingian Impulses, and a New Take-Off in the Twelfth Century," in *Town and Country in Medieval North Western Europe: Dynamic Interactions*, ed. Alexis Wilkin, John Naylor, Derek Keene, and Arnoud-Jan Bijsterveld, The Medieval Countryside 11 (Turnhout, 2015), 87–118, 92. See also Rudolf Simek and Ulrike Engel, ed., *Vikings on the Rhine: Recent Research on Early Medieval Relations Between the Rhinelands and Scandinavia*, Studia Medievalia Septentrionalia 11 (Vienna, 2004).
30. Timothy Reuter, "Plunder and Tribute in the Carolingian Empire," *Transactions of the Royal Historical Society* 35 (1985).
31. Brian Ayers, *The German Ocean: Medieval Europe around the North Sea* (Sheffield and Bristol, 2016); Justyna Wubs-Mrozewicz, *Traders, Ties and Tensions: The Interactions of Lübeckers, Overijsslers and Hollanders in Late Medieval Bergen* (Hilversum, 2008).

32. Matthew Innes, *State and Society in the Early Middle Ages: The Middle Rhine Valley, 400–1000*, Cambridge Studies in Medieval Life and Thought, 4th ser., 47 (Cambridge, 2000), 140.
33. Georges Declercq, "Entre mémoire dynastique et représentation politique: Les sépultures des comtes et comtesses de Flandre (879–1128)," in *Sépulture, mort et symbolique du pouvoir au moyen âge: Tod, Grabmal und Herrschaftsrepräsentation in Mittelalter: Actes des 11es Journées Lotharingiennes. 26–29 septembre 2000*, ed. Michel Margue (Luxembourg, 2006), 321–72.
34. Arnold, *Princes and Territories*, 136 (see more generally on this issue the entire chapter 8, "From consanguinity to dynasty?" 135–51).
35. John H. Lind, "Knes Kanutus: Knud Lavard's Political Project," in *Of Chronicles and Kings: National Saints and the Emergence of Nation States in the High Middle Ages*, ed. John Bergsagel, David Hiley, and Thomas Riis (Copenhagen, 2015), 103–28.
36. Robert Bartlett, *England Under the Norman and Angevin Kings, 1075–1225*, The New Oxford History of England (Oxford, 2000), 31.
37. Davies, "The Medieval State," 290.
38. Patrick J. Geary, *The Myth of Nations: The Origins of Europe* (Princeton, 2002); Davies, "The Medieval State," 287.
39. For the Nordic historiography, see examples in Hermanson, "*Släkt, vänner och makt.*"
40. Davies, "The Medieval State," 288–89.
41. Charles West, *Reframing the Feudal Revolution: Political and Social Transformation Between Marne and Moselle, c. 800-c. 1100* (Cambridge, 2013), 5.
42. Ibid., 19, 47, 98, 259–60, 263.
43. Ibid., 49–50.
44. As is also the main claim of Susan Reynolds, *Kingdoms and Communities in Western Europe 900–1300* (Oxford, 1984).
45. See for instance C. Warren Hollister, *Medieval Europe: A Short History*, 8th ed. (Boston, 1998), with the telling headings "The New Invasions" and "Europe Survives the Siege."
46. Robert Bartlett, *The Making of Europe: Conquest, Colonization and Cultural Change 950–1350* (London, 1994).
47. Ibid., 20, 307, 269.
48. Ibid., 289.
49. Ibid., 308.
50. Bartlett's book has frequently served as a fruitful starting point for discussions on the relationship between Scandinavia and Europe. Although often targeted for its diffusionist thesis, the book remains unusually "good to think with." See for instance the CMS-project in Bergen referred to in note 28 above.
51. Chris Wickham, *Framing the Early Middle Ages: Europe and the Mediterranean 400–800* (Oxford, 2005), 339, 375.
52. Ibid., 375, 433. This point is reiterated in Wickham's shorter *Medieval Europe* (New Haven, CT, 2016), 305, where he states that coercion of peasants was a precondition for state formation, and that this was slower to develop and lesser pronounced in Denmark than farther south.
53. As for the particular case of Denmark, the socio-political features' similarities with wider Europe and the resulting need for systematic comparative studies have for years been underlined by Michael H. Gelting. See, for instance, "Det komparative perspektiv i dansk middelalderforskning: Om

Familia og familie, Lið, Leding og Landeværn," *Historisk Tidsskrift* (D) 99, no. 1 (1999): 146–88; "Danmark – en del af Europa," in *Middelalderens Danmark: Kultur og samfund fra trosskifte til reformation*, ed. Per Ingesmann, Ulla Kjær, Per Kristian Madsen, and Jens Vellev (Copenhagen, 1999), 334–51.

Dedicated Bibliography

Althoff, Gerd. *Family, Friends and Followers: Political and Social Bonds in Medieval Europe [Verwandte, Freunde und Getreue: Zum politischen Stellenwert der Gruppenbindungen im früheren Mittelalter]*. Translated by Christopher Carroll. Cambridge, 2004.

Arnold, Benjamin. *Count and Bishop in Medieval Germany: A Study of Regional Power, 1100–1350*. Philadelphia, 1991.

Arnold, Benjamin. *Princes and Territories in Medieval Germany*. Cambridge, 1991.

Ayers, Brian. *The German Ocean: Medieval Europe around the North Sea*. Sheffield, 2016.

Bartlett, Robert. *The Making of Europe: Conquest, Colonization and Cultural Change 950–1350*. London, 1994.

Bartlett, Robert. *England under the Norman and Angevin Kings, 1075–1225*. Oxford, 2000.

Benham, Jenny. *Peacemaking in the Middle Ages: Principles and Practice*. Manchester, 2011.

Bijsterveld, Arnoud-Jan A. "Aristocratic Identities and Power Strategies in Lower Lotharingia: The Case of the Rode Lineage (Eleventh and Twelfth Centuries)." In *La Lotharingie en question: identités, oppositions, integration: Lotharingische Identitäten Im Spannungsfeld Zwischen Integrativen Und Partikularen Kräften: Actes Des 14es Journées Lotharingiennes: 10–13 Octobre 2006*, edited by M. Margue and H. Pettiau, 167–207. Luxembourg, 2006.

Bijsterveld, Arnoud-Jan A. *Do Ut Des: Gift Giving, Memoria, and Conflict Management in the Medieval Low Countries*. Hilversum, 2007.

Bouchard, Constance B. "Family Structure and Family Consciousness among the Aristocracy in the Ninth to Eleventh Centuries." *Francia* 14 (1986): 639–58.

Bouchard, Constance B. *Those of My Blood: Constructing Noble Families in Medieval Francia*. Philadelphia, 2003.

Bourdieu, Pierre. *The Logic of Practice*. Translated by Richard Nice. Cambridge, 1990.

Bührer-Thierry, Geneviève. "Connaître les élites au haut moyen âge." In *Théorie et pratiques des élites au Haut Moyen Age: Conception, perception et réalisation sociale*, edited by François Bougard, Hans-Werner Goetz, and Régine Le Jan, 373–84. Turnhout, 2011.

Bull, Marcus. *Knightly Piety and the Lay Response to the First Crusade: The Limousin and Gascony c.970-c.1130*. Oxford, 1993.

Bumke, Joachim. *Höfische Kultur: Literatur und Gesellschaft im hohen Mittelalter*. Translated as Courtly culture. Literature and society in the high Middle Ages. Berkeley CA, 1991 [1986].

Cheyette, Fredric L. *Ermengard of Narbonne and the World of the Troubadours*. Ithaca, NY, 2001.

Davies, Rees. "The Medieval State: The Tyranny of a Concept?" *Journal of Historical Sociology* 16, no. 2 (2003): 280–300.
Declercq, Georges. "Entre mémoire dynastique et représentation politique: Les sépultures des comtes et comtesses de Flandre (879–1128)." In *Sépulture, mort et symbolique du pouvoir au moyen âge: Tod, Grabmal und Herrschaftsrepräsentation in Mittelalter: Actes des 11es Journées Lotharingiennes. 26–29 septembre 2000*, edited by Michel Margue. 321–72. Luxembourg, 2006.
Depreux, Philippe. "La dimension 'publique' de certaines dispositions 'privées': Fondations pieuses et memoria en Francie occidentale aux IXe et Xe siècles." In *Sauver son âme et se perpétuer: Transmission du patrimoine et mémoire au haut Moyen Âge*, edited by François Bougard, Cristina La Rocca, and Régine Le Jan, 332–78. Rome, 2005.
Esmark, Kim. "Religious Patronage and Family Consciousness: Sorø Abbey and the 'Hvide Family', c. 1150–1250." In *Religious and Laity in Western Europe 1000–1400: Interaction, Negotiation, and Power*, edited by Emilia Jamroziak and Janet Burton, 93–110. Turnhout, 2006.
Geary, Patrick J. *The Myth of Nations: The Origins of Europe*. Princeton, 2002.
Gelting, Michael H. "Danmark – en del af Europa." In *Middelalderens Danmark: Kultur og samfund fra trosskifte til reformation*, edited by Per Ingesmann, Ulla Kjær, Per Kristian Madsen, and Jens Vellev, 334–51. Copenhagen, 1999.
Gelting, Michael H. "Det komparative perspektiv i dansk middelalderforskning. Om Familia og familie, Lið, Leding og Landeværn." *Historisk Tidskrift* (D) 99 (1999): 146–88.
Hermanson, Lars. *Släkt, vänner och makt: En studie av elitens politiska kultur i 1100-talets Danmark*. Gothenburg, 2000.
Hollister, C. Warren. *Medieval Europe: A Short History*. 8th ed. Boston, 1998.
Hundahl, Kerstin, Lars Kjær, and Niels Lund, eds. *Denmark and Europe in the Middle Ages, C.1000–1525: Essays in Honour of Professor Michael H. Gelting*. London, 2016.
Innes, Matthew. *State and Society in the Early Middle Ages: The Middle Rhine Valley, 400–1000*. Cambridge Studies in Medieval Life and Thought. 4th Series 47. Cambridge, 2000.
Jensen, Kurt Villads. *Korstog ved verdens yderste rand: Danmark og Portugal ca. 1000 til ca. 1250*. Odense, 2011.
Lind, John H. "De russiske ægteskaber: Dynasti- og alliancepolitiki 1130'ernes danske borgerkrig." *Historisk Tidskrift* (D) 92 (1992): 225–63.
Lind, John H. "Knes Kanutus: Knud Lavard's Political Project." In *Of Chronicles and Kings: National Saints and the Emergence of Nation States in the Early Middle Ages*, edited by John Bergsagel, Thomas Riis, and David Hiley, 113–38. Copenhagen, 2015.
Livingstone, Amy. *Out of Love for My Kin: Aristocratic Family Life in the Lands of the Loire, 1000–1200*. Ithaca, NY, 2010.
Lunden, Kåre. *Norge under Sverreætten, 1177–1319*, vol. 3. Norges Historie. Oslo, 1976.
Mann, Michael. *The Sources of Social Power, Vol I: A History of Power from the Beginning to A.D. 1760*. Cambridge, 1986.
Münster-Swendsen, Mia, Thomas K. Heebøll-Holm, and Sigbjørn Olsen Sønnesyn, eds. *Historical and Intellectual Culture in the Long Twelfth Century:*

The Scandinavian Connections, Durham Medieval and Renaissance Monographs and Essays 5. Toronto, 2016.

Orning, Hans Jacob. *Unpredictability and Presence: Norwegian Kingship in the High Middle Ages*. Translated by Alan Crozier. Leiden, 2008.

Pohl, Benjamin. *The Medieval Review*, September 9, 2018 https://scholarworks.iu.edu/journals/index.php/tmr/article/view/25595.

Preiser-Kapeller, Johannes. "Marriage Network of High Medieval Europe (1000–1200 AD)." www.academia.edu/37090935/The_marriage_network_of_high_medieval_Europe_1000-1200_AD_.

Reuter, Timothy. "Plunder and Tribute in the Carolingian Empire." *Transactions of the Royal Historical Society* 35 (1985): 75–94.

Reynolds, Susan. *Kingdoms and Communities in Western Europe, 900–1300*. Oxford, 1984.

Reynolds, Susan. "There Were States in Medieval Europe: A Response to Rees Davies." *Journal of Historical Sociology* 16, no. 4 (2003): 550–55.

Rikhardsottir, Sif. *Medieval Translations and Cultural Discourse: The Movement of Texts in England, France and Scandinavia*. Cambridge, 2012.

Sigurðsson, Jón Viðar. *Chieftains and Power in the Icelandic Commonwealth*. Translated by Jean Lundskær-Nielsen, The Viking Collection, Studies in Northern Civilization 12. Odense, 1999 [1993].

Simek, Rudolf, and Ulrike Engel. *Vikings on the Rhine: Recent Research on Early Medieval Relations Between the Rhinelands and Scandinavia*, Studia Medievalia Septentrionalia 11. Vienna, 2004.

Spiegel, Gabrielle. *Romancing the Past: The Rise of Vernacular Prose Historiography in Thirteenth-Century France*. New York, 1993.

Theuws, Frans, and Arnoud-Jan Bijsterveld. "Early Town Formation in the Northern Low Countries: Roman Heritage, Carolingian Impulses, and a New Take-Off in the Twelfth Century." In *Town and Country in Medieval North Western Europe: Dynamic Interactions*, The Medieval Countryside 11, edited by Alexis Wilkin, John Naylor, Derek Keene, and Arnoud-Jan Bijsterveld, 87–118. Turnhout, 2015.

Tulinius, Torfi, H. "Capital, Field, Illusio: Can Bourdieu's Sociology Help Us Understand the Development of Literature in Medieval Iceland?" In *Sagas and Societies, International Conference at Borgarnes, Iceland, 2002*, edited by Stefanie Würth, Tunno Jonuks, and Axel Kristinsson, 1–23. Tübingen, 2004.

Vanderputten, Steven, and Arnoud-Jan Bijsterveld. "Penitential Discourse and Conflict Management in the Late-Eleventh- and Early-Twelfth-Century Southern Low Countries." *Revue belge de Philologie et d'Histoire: Belgisch Tijdschrift voor Filologie en Geschiedenis* 90 (2012): 471–92.

West, Charles. *Reframing the Feudal Revolution: Political and Social Transformation Between Marne and Moselle, c. 800–1000*. Cambridge, 2013.

White, Stephen D. "The Discourse of Inheritance in Twelfth-Century France: Alternative Modes of Fief in Raoul de Cambrai." In *Law and Government in Medieval England and Normandy: Essays in Honour of Sir James Holt*, edited by George Garnett and John Hudson, 173–97. Cambridge, 1994.

Wickham, Chris. *Courts and Conflict in Twelfth-Century Tuscany*. Oxford, 2003.

Wickham, Chris. *Framing the Early Middle Ages: Europe and the Mediterranean 400–800*. Oxford, 2005.

Wubs-Mrozewicz, Justyna. *Traders, Ties and Tensions: The Interactions of Lübeckers, Overijsslers and Hollanders in Late Medieval Bergen*. Hilversum, 2008.

Zotz, Thomas. "Die Situation des Adels im 11. und frühen 12. Jahrhundert." In *Vom Umbruch zur Erneuerung? Das 11. und 12. Jahrhundert: Positionen der Forschung*, edited by Jorg Jarnut and Matthias Wemhoff, 341–55. München, 2006.

Contributors

Arnoud-Jan Bijsterveld is Professor of History at Department of Sociology, Tilburg University

Sveinung K. Boye is PhD at Department of Historical Studies, University of Gothenburg

Kim Esmark is Associate Professor at Department of Communication and Arts, Roskilde University

Ian Peter Grohse is Associate Professor of Medieval History at Department of Archaeology, History, Religious Studies and Theology, The Arctic University of Norway

Lars Hermanson is Professor of Medieval History at Department of Historical Studies, University of Gothenburg

Johnny Grandjean Gøgsig Jakobsen is Associate Professor at Department of Nordic Studies and Linguistics, University of Copenhagen

Wojtek Jezierski is Associate Professor, School of Historical and Contemporary Studies Södertörn University and Department of Historical Studies, University of Gothenburg

Magnus Källström is Associate Professor at Swedish National Heritage Board, Department for Conservation, Visby

Ralph Kenna is Professor of Theoretical Physics at Faculty Research Centre in Fluid and Complex Systems, Coventry University

John H. Lind is Professor Emeritus at Centre for Medieval and Renaissance Studies, University of Southern Denmark

Pádraig MacCarron is Dr. with An Foras Feasa, Maynooth University, and Statistical Physics Group, Centre for Fluid and Complex Systems, Coventry University

Auður Magnúsdóttir is Assistant Professor at Department of Historical Studies, University of Gothenburg

Contributors 347

Marie Bønløkke Missuno is PhD at Department of Culture and Society, Aarhus University

Hans Jacob Orning is Professor of Medieval History at Department of Archaeology, Conservation and History, University of Oslo

Viðar Pálsson is Associate Professor of History at Faculty of History and Philosophy, University of Iceland

Ole-Albert Rønning is PhD at Department of Archaeology, Conservation and History, University of Oslo

Jón Viðar Sigurðsson is Professor of Medieval History at Department of Archaeology, Conservation and History, University of Oslo

Helle Vogt is Professor of Legal History at JUR Centre for Interdisciplinary Studies of Law, University of Copenhagen

Index

Aarhus 305–7, 311–13, 317
Åbo 171, 181
Absalon, Archbishop of Lund 37, 60, 64, 171–7, 181–2, 285–7, 291–6
Adam of Bremen, chronicler 79, 97–8, 112–14
Adelsö 82
Adolf, Count of Holstein 274
Æbelholt Abbey 174–6, 295
Æthelred the Unready, King of England 127
ætt (kin group) 11, 13, 15, 20, 22–3, 239
Åhus 194
Ailnoth, chronicler 135–6
Albert, Archbishop of Magdeburg 193
Albert of Buxhoeveden, Bishop of Riga 171
Alexander III, Pope 172
Alfiva, Queen of Norway 255
Althoff, Gerd (historian) 11, 34, 56, 306, 326
amicus 4, 238, 313–14, 326, 330
Amund Gyrdsson 256
Anders Sunesen, Archbishop of Lund 20–1, 171, 173, 176, 178, 181–2, 194
Anund from Russia 98–9
Anund Jakob, King of Sweden 129
Ari sterki 218–19
ármenn 40, 43
Arni Magnusson (philologist) 223–4
Arnold of Lübeck, abbot and chronicler 172–3, 176, 337
Asbirningar family 220, 224
Asbjorn, Danish earl/jarl 134–5
Asgod, Abbot of Ørn 316
assembly 2, 19, 16, 21, 36, 87, 95, 252, 254, 279, 288–91, 308

Asser, Bishop of Viborg 175
Asser Rig 173, 286, 289
Auður Magnúsdóttir (historian) 37, 215, 326–7, 331
Austria 237

Bagge, Sverre (historian) 280
bailiff 2, 43, 85, 314
Baltic 89, 96, 104, 106, 119, 177, 181, 332–3
Bardr Thorkelsson 227–9
Barlow, Frank (historian) 131
Bartlett, Robert (historian) 334, 337–8
Bastrup tower 286
Bavaria 237
Benedictine order 135–6, 172, 174, 192, 202–3, 205, 287, 294
benevolentia (benevolence) 306, 308
Bergen 178, 201, 206, 254
Bern 195
Bernard of Clairvaux, abbot 174
Bersi Vermundarson 219, 222
Bijsterveld, Arnoud-Jan (historian) 56, 285, 325
bilateral kinship 17–18, 225
Birger Magnusson, Swedish earl/jarl 179
Birka 96–7
Bjadok, concubine 254–5
Bjälbo clan 61, 63, 179
Bjernede 286, 294
Björkö 96
Blekinge 14
Bo, Abbot of Øm 306, 309, 311–14, 316–17
Bodil family 287, 292
Boecius, prior 198
Boedvarr at Bær Thordarson 244

Boissevain, Jeremy (anthropologist) 55
Bolesław the Brave, Duke of Poland
  111–12
Bologna 176, 296
Bolton, Timothy (historian) 132
Bonde, Bishop of Schleswig 317
bønder/bóndi 2, 221
Boniface III, Pope 201
Bønløkke Missuno, Marie (historian)
  125, 170
Borg 13, 36
Borgarfjörður 243–5
Borresta 89
Bourdieu, Pierre (sociologist) 14–15,
  20–1, 55, 285, 310
Brandan, Abbot of Øm 316
Brandr Kolbeinsson 227
Breengaard, Carsten (historian) 277
Britain 110, 255
Bromma 87
Bruges 132
Brunner, Otto (historian) 237
bryti/brytber 40, 43, 82, 85
Burckhardt, Jacob (historian) 11
Byzantine emperor 84, 94, 108,
  115–16

camerarius 41
canonical kinship 23–4
Canon law 17, 198, 306
capital (economic, political,
  educational, social, symbolic) 3, 6,
  12, 23, 55, 104, 109, 170–1, 173,
  175–7, 180–2, 220, 280, 285–7,
  293–7, 328
Cecilia, wife of Sune Ebbesen 292,
  294–5
Celestine III, Pope 175–6
celibacy 18, 171
character networks 144
Chernigov 104, 114, 116
Cheyette, Frederic (historian) 4,
  33, 331
Christian, monk/bishop 178
Christopher I, King of Denmark 196
Cistercian order 174–5, 178, 192,
  202–6, 294, 304–5, 309, 312,
  316–17
civil war 44, 58, 61–2, 65, 173, 179,
  216, 241, 275, 279
Clairvaux Abbey 174
Cluny Abbey 310–11, 315
clustering coefficient 149, 154
cognatus 4

Colbatz 178
compensation (ethebot) 20
concubinage 13, 17, 37, 215, 217–18,
  221, 225, 227, 230
Conrad, Abbot of Øm 316
Conrad III, King of Germany 273,
  278–9, 282
Constantine IX Monomachos,
  Byzantine Emperor 115
Constantinople 84, 104, 177
Council of Chalcedon 309
Council of the Realm 68
courtly culture 58, 291

Dacia, Dominican province 192,
  198–205
Dalby 202
Dalir 221
Dalum 203
Devonshire 132
Djursland 308, 311
Dnepr 106
Dominican order 180–1, 192, 194–9,
  201–2, 204–6
drængʀ/dreng 84–5
Durkheim, Émile (sociologist) 11
dux 115, 127–8
Dvina/Daugava 106, 108–9
Dýrafjörður 247

Ebbe Skjalmsen 173, 294
Ebbe Sunesen 286–7, 289
Edmund Ironside, English prince 114
Edward the Confessor, King of
  England 128–30
Egill Solmundarson 245
Eigenkirchenwesen 37
Eirik Ivarsson, Archbishop of
  Nidaros 171
Elbląg 195
Elena, Abbess of Sko 203
Elena, Prioress of Sko 203
Emma, Duchess of Normandy 112
England 83–4, 89, 111–15, 125–36,
  203, 307, 332–5, 337
entrusted men/*trúnaðarmenn* 44
Erik I the Good, King of Denmark
  135–6, 286–7
Erik II Emune, King of Denmark 22,
  61, 116, 273–4, 288–9
Erik III Lam, King of Denmark 273,
  288–9
Erik V Klipping, King of Denmark
  196, 317

Erik IX The Saint, King of Sweden 170–1, 181
Erik X Eriksson, King of Sweden 179
Erik XI Eriksson, King of Sweden 180
Erling Skakke, Norwegian earl/jarl 67, 257, 260, 276, 278
Esbern Snare 175, 286–7, 292, 294
Esger, Bishop of Ribe 317
Eskil, Archbishop of Lund 37, 61, 173–4, 287, 292, 306, 311
Eskil, Bishop of Aarhus 306
Eskilsø 174
Erlend of Gjerde 257
Esmark, Kim (historian) 1, 11, 135, 285, 304, 310, 325–6, 328–9, 331, 335
Esrum Abbey 17, 174, 178, 287, 316
Estonia 169, 171, 192
Estrid, Danish Princess 87, 112–13, 127–9
Eugene III, Pope 174
Evesham 135–6
excommunication 175, 180, 314–15
Exeter 132
exile 110–11, 114–16, 130–1, 134, 171, 271–6, 278–81, 289–90
Eyjafjörður 221, 230, 242, 247
Eyjolfr ofsi Thorsteinnsson 229–30

face-to-face-society 1, 5, 54, 66, 304
familia 314
Farmer, Sharon (historian) 315
feast 6, 39, 57, 62, 135, 217, 220, 227, 237–43, 245–8, 281, 327
félag 57
feud 18, 44, 61, 239, 288, 318
feudalism 33–4, 330
feuding society 19
fief 33
field of power 285, 288, 291, 296, 325–6
Finland 106, 170–1, 177, 179, 181
Fjenneslev 173, 286–7
Flanders 130–4, 204, 333
Fodevig 288
fogd 43
Folcold, Dutch magnate 330
Fonnesberg-Schmidt, Iben (historian) 177
formalization 5, 21, 23–4, 42–3, 45, 64, 66–8, 180–1, 335
fornaldarsögur 43
fosterage, fostering 13, 15, 37, 39, 41, 63–4, 85, 173, 222–3, 243, 253–7, 260, 287–91, 331–3

Fourth Lateran Council 182, 193–4, 198, 206
France 176, 199, 308, 329, 331, 333, 335
Franciscan order 194, 196, 202, 206
Frederick Barbarossa, Emperor of the Holy Roman Empire 67, 279, 290
freeholder 34, 36–7
Freeman, E.A. (historian) 131
Friars priors 5, 180, 192–306
frændi 13, 15–16, 23, 245
Frostathing Law 21
Fyrileiv 274

Gardariki/Garðaríki 94, 110
Gastfreundschaft 243
Gaufred, provost 197–8
Geary, Patrick J. (historian) 33, 312, 314
Georgii Simonovich, Russian Prince/Kniaz 115, 119
Gerlög 87–9, 92
Germany 81, 111, 272, 280, 295–6, 332, 334
gestir 66
giald (payment) 111
gift economy 238, 306, 308, 310, 318
gift exchange 239
gift giving 217, 330, 336
gift theory 54
gildi 86
Gisl Bergsson 221
Gisli the outlaw 159
Gissur Hallsson 219
Gissur Thorvaldsson 225–6, 243
Gluckman, Max (anthropologist) 18
Gniezno 178
Godefrid, Abbot of Lekno 178
goði 338
godparenthood 37, 39
Godwine, English earl/jarl 126–32
good men 17
Gorm, King of Denmark 82
Götaland 16, 275
Grathe Heath 280, 291
Gregorian reform 172, 179, 309
Gregorius de Crescentio, Papal legate 171, 174
Gregory VII, Pope 172
Groa, wife of Hauk 244
Grund 221, 247
Gruppenforschung 56
Gudhem 204
Gudny Boedvarsdottir 218–19
Gudrun Bjarnadottir 219–20

Gudrun Hreinsdottir 223
Gudum 203
Guido, Papal legate 180, 317
guild 2, 57, 62, 66, 86
Guillaume, Canon regular 173–4
Gulathing Law 38
Gunnald 83–4
Gunner, Abbot of Øm 171
Gunnhild, English Countess 128, 132–3
Gurevich, Aaron (historian) 239
Guttorm Asolfsson 257
Guttorm Greybeard 254
Gyda Ebbesen 294
Gyda Solmundardottir 229
Gytha/Gyda, English Countess 112, 115–16, 127–8, 132–3

Haakon IV Haakonsson, King of Norway 178, 196, 223, 227, 230
Haakon V Magnusson, King of Norway 199, 253
Haakon the Blind 104, 114–15
Haakon Eiriksson, Norwegian earl/jarl 114–15
Haakon Röde, King of Sweden 82
Haakon Sigurdsson, Norwegian earl/jarl 110, 113
habitus 21, 297
Haderslev 194
Hadrian IV, Pope 170
hæverska (courtliness) 43
Haki Antonsson (historian) 135
Hallbera Snorradottir 222–5
Halldora Tumadottir 220–1
Hallveig Ormsdottir 224
Halmstad 195
Halsten, King of Sweden 98
Hanseatic merchants 201, 333
Hansen, Lars Ivar (historian) 56
Harald Bluetooth, King of Denmark 82
Harald Fairhair, King of Norway 110
Harald Gille, King of Norway 254, 256–60, 274
Harald Sigurdsson (Hardrada), King of Norway 110, 113, 125, 129–31
Hardeknud, King of England and Denmark 125, 129–30
Harold Godwinson, King of England 116, 128, 131–3
Hartwig, Archbishop of Hamburg-Bremen 274, 276–7, 280–1
Hastings 116, 125, 129, 131
Haukdælir family 2, 19, 220, 243

Haukr of Álftanes 244
Hauskloster 22, 105, 174, 287
Hávamál 57
Head, Thomas (historian) 315
Heinrekr, Bishop of Holar 245
Helga Aradottir 219
Helga Bjarnadottir 219
Helgi Þorláksson (historian) 220, 229–30
Helmold of Bosau, chronicler 273–4, 277, 279, 290
Henrik Brokeleg 254
Henryk Kietlicz, Archbishop of Gniezno 178
Henry of Livonia, chronicler 109
Henry the Lion, Duke of Saxony 276–7
Herdis Bersadottir 222
Hermanson, Lars (historian) 1, 14, 33, 54, 56, 59–61
Herrevadsbro 180
Herrschaftsgastung 243
Hexaëmeron 177
Hildesheim 173
Hillersjö 87, 92, 98
hirð/ hirðmaðr 66, 216
Hítarnes 245
Hjalm, friar 199
Hjarðarholt 219
Hlaðir earls 111, 113–15
Holbæk 195
Holland 333
Holy Roman Empire 34, 335
homage 33, 279
Homer 161
homophily 144, 158
honor 5, 13, 16, 20–1, 39–40, 65, 83, 128, 171, 226, 228, 246, 285, 294, 308, 313, 331
Honorius III, Pope 169, 171, 174
hospitality 180, 240, 243–4, 246
householder 239
Hrafn Oddsson 229–30
Hrodny Thordardottir 219, 222
Hugues, Bishop of Liége 193
Húnavatn 220
Husby-Sjuhundra 92, 99
huskarl 93
Hvammur 218, 228
Hvide family/Skjalm clan 22, 173, 175–6, 196, 286–9, 292

Iliad 161, 164
imagined community 14

352 Index

Ingeborg, Duchess of Denmark 116
Ingeborg, Queen of Denmark 176
Ingegerd, Swedish Princess 113, 115–16
Inge Haraldsson, King of Norway 252–60
Inge Stenkilsson, King of Sweden 61, 116, 275
Ingibjorg Snorradottir 224–5
Ingrid Rognvaldsdottir 253, 257–8, 260
Ingvarr the Far-traveled 84
inheritance 12, 23–4, 81, 87, 217, 224, 226, 275–6, 281, 292, 294
Innes, Matthew (historian) 333
Innocent III, Pope 172, 176–8, 181
interdict 175, 314
Israel Erlandi, friar 198, 204
Iversen, Frode (archaeologist) 36

Jakob Erlandsen, Archbishop of Lund 295–6, 317
Jakob Sunesen 295
Jämtland 81
jarl (earl) 63, 66–7, 83, 113, 115, 126–8, 130, 179–80, 278
Jarlabanke Ingefastsson 85–7
Jarler, Archbishop of Uppsala 179, 194
Jaroslav Vladimirovich, Prince of Novgorod 104, 109, 113–15
Jarrow 136
Jens Kalf 316
Jens Kanne 313
Jens Sunesen 295
Jesch, Judith (philologist) 84, 95
Johannes, magister 198
Johannes, prior 181
Jon Loptsson 222
Jón Viðar Sigurðsson (historian) 11, 35, 37–8, 56, 59–60, 165, 223–4, 227, 239
Juhel, Archbishop of Reims 193
Jutland 94, 134, 273–4, 277, 279–80, 289–91, 293, 305

Karlby 307
Kasin Boye, Sveinung (historian) 180
Katarina Matsdotter 204
Kettering, Sharon (historian) 38
Kiev 104–6, 108, 110–14, 116–17
Kiholm 96

King's Mirror, The 43, 58
kings' sagas 36, 38, 56–7, 109, 133, 243, 271, 304
kinship society 12, 14, 23–4, 60
kniaz/prince 105, 115
Knud IV The Holy, King of Denmark 134–6, 290
Knud V Magnussen, King of Denmark 271–82, 289–91
Knud VI, King of Denmark 173, 175–6, 292–3
Knud Lavard, Danish Duke 65, 116, 273, 287–9, 334
Knud the Great, King of Denmark, Norway and England 44, 67, 111–15, 125–7, 129, 133, 136
Kolbeinn ungi Arnorsson 224–8, 247
Kolfinna Thorsteinsdottir 229
Konghelle 171
Königsnähe 3, 18, 22, 291–2, 332
kotkarl/þjónn 42
Kræmmer, Michael (historian) 293
Kristina, Swedish Princess 116
Kyrping-Orm Sveinsson 256–7

lagman (lawman) 16, 63, 241, 256
Lake Mälar 81, 89, 96
landskyld/land rent 37
landsmaðr 94
Lateran Council 179
Lateran palace 169, 181
laudatio parentum 17
Laurentius, friar 205
Law of Scania 20–1, 296
Law of the Retinue (*Hirðskrá*) 42, 58, 66
legate 169–80, 201, 317–18
Lejre 36
Łękno 178
lendr maðr 40, 94–5
lese-majesty 62
lið 84, 93–4
Liljefalk, Lone (historian) 277
Lind, John H. (historian) 104, 274, 326, 332
Linköping 200, 202
Livonia 169, 172, 181
Logbersason (lawman) 256
Lotario dei Conti di Segni, future Pope Innocent III 176
Lothar, King of Germany 334
løysi (freedman) 85
Lübeck 172, 176, 195, 337
Luhmann, Niklas (sociologist) 54

Lund/Lund Cathedral 17, 19, 94, 170–4, 176–8, 192, 194, 198, 200–202, 277, 286–7, 292, 296, 316
Lutgard de Aywières 204

Magnus I Olavsson, the Good, King of Norway and Denmark 113, 129–30
Magnus III Barefoot, King of Norway 116
Magnus IV the Blind, King of Norway 252–3, 257
Magnus V Erlingsson, King of Norway 61, 260
Magnus Haraldsson, King of Norway 252–3, 256–7, 260
Magnus Henriksson, King of Sweden 254
Magnus Nielsen, Prince of Denmark and King of Götaland 65, 273, 275
mágr, magh, måg (son-in-law) 16, 85
Mälar region 89, 94, 98–9
Malmfrid, Queen of Norway, Queen of Denmark 116
Mann, Michael (sociologist) 56, 285, 328
Margrete Fredkulla, Queen of Denmark 19, 275
Margrete Sambiria, Queen of Denmark 317
Margrete Sunedottir 295
Mariefred 202
Marmoutier Abbey 315
marriage 3–4, 6, 12, 13, 15–19, 21–2, 24, 58–9, 65, 85–7, 89, 106, 108–9, 113, 116, 127–8, 130, 132, 215–22, 224–5, 227–31, 254, 258, 274, 281–2, 285, 288, 325–8, 333
Marx, Karl (sociologist) 33
maternity 253–4
Mauss, Marcel (sociologist) 54, 238
McGuire, Brian Patrick (historian) 305–6
memoria 175, 196, 206, 294
mensa 307, 311
Merseburg 111, 279–80, 290–1
Miðfjörður 221
Mikkel, Abbot of Øm 316
miles 40, 313
Miller, Maureen C. (historian) 172
ministeriales 330
ministerium 182
minority 252

Mstislav-Harald, Prince/kniaz of Novgorod 116
Mstislav Vladimirovich of Chernigov 104, 114
Mýrar 247

Næstved 287
Näsby 96–7
Nicholas Breakspear, Hadrian IV, Papal legate/Pope 170
Nicolaus, Bishop of Riga 193, 199
Nicolaus, prior 204
Nicolaus Christierni, friar 204
Nicolaus Lundensis, friar 198
Nidaros/Nidaros Cathedral 134
Niels, Bishop of Schleswig 317
Niels, Bishop of Viborg 316
Niels Svendsen, King of Denmark 65
Nikolas Arnesson, Norwegian Bishop 37
Nikulas Oddsson 229
Norrtälje 83, 89
Nors, Thyra (historian) 14
North Sea 125, 131, 134, 255, 333
North Sea Empire 114, 125–6
Novgorod 106, 110–12, 114, 116–17

oaths/oath-helpers 16, 22, 33, 36, 42, 44, 55, 65–6
Obodrites 334
Oddaverjar family 61, 222–4
Oddi 222
Odense 134–6, 290, 316
office-holder 40–1
officializing strategies, officialize 291, 310, 327
official kinship 15
Ogmund Denger 257
Öland 94
Olav I Tryggvason, King of Norway 109–10, 113
Olav II Haraldsson, King of Norway 110, 113–15, 129, 256–7
Olav III Kyrre, King of Norway 131, 133
Olavus, Prior 204
Olof, Archbishop of Uppsala 194
Olof Skötkonung, King of Sweden 113, 118
Olsen, Olaf (historian) 129
Øm Abbey 171, 180, 304–8, 311–12, 315–17
Omer, Bishop of Ribe 175
Orækja Snorrason 222, 226

Orderic Vitalis, chronicler 130, 132
Örlygsstaðir 65, 226, 228
Orning, Hans Jacob (historian) 1, 33, 54, 253, 304, 325
Oslo 196, 199, 202, 278
Osma 198
Ottar Balli 258
Ottar Birting 255, 257–8
Otto of Freising, chronicler 279
ownership 16, 37, 310–11
Oxford 176, 296
Oystein, Archbishop of Norway 37, 134
Oystein Haraldsson, King of Norway 255

Pajung, Stefan (historian) 277
Paris 171–3, 176, 198, 201, 292, 295–6
Paterikon 104–5, 114
patron-client relationship 5, 33–45, 56, 60, 62–4, 67, 83, 128, 217, 228, 258, 328, 331
Peder Bodilsen 287
Peder Elavsen, Bishop of Aarhus 309, 317
Pedersborg Castle 286
Peder Sunesen, Bishop of Roskilde 176
Peder Torstensen 22, 289–92, 294
Perron, Anthony (historian) 171, 181
Peter Sauda-Ulfsson 257, 259
Philip Augustus, King of France 176
Philip Gyrdsson 256
Poland 111–12, 178, 274–6
political culture 34, 59, 239, 271–2, 278, 280–1
Polotsk 106, 108–9
Pomerelia 178
Powell, Walther W. (historian) 54–5
practical kinship 14–15, 20, 24
Preiser-Kapeller, Johannes (historian) 333
protection racket 44, 67
provincial laws 85
provisores 40
Prussia 169, 178
Pskov 106

Ragnhild, wife of Ebbe Skjalmson 92, 286, 294
Randers 203
Rano, friar 198
reproduction 17, 176, 217, 293, 295

retinue 34, 40, 42, 58, 62, 66, 170, 180, 226, 279, 289–90, 330, 332
Reuter, Timothy (historian) 307, 333
rex iustus 304
Reykholt 218, 222–3, 226, 245
Reynolds, Susan (historian) 56
Ribe 202–3, 289, 291, 317
Richard, Duke of Normandy 112
Rikissa, Polish Princess 274
Rikissa Birgersdotter, Queen consort of Norway 180, 274
Rimbo 92, 98–9
Ringsted 286–7, 292
Risaberga 203
ritual 33, 135, 292, 312, 335
Riurikids 105, 109, 112, 115–16
Rognvald Roundhead 254
Roman curia 58, 66
Roman Empire 278
Rome 64, 170–2, 174–6, 178, 181–2, 198, 312, 317
Rønning, Ole-Albert (historian) 44, 271, 326–7, 332, 335
Rosenwein, Barbara H. (historian) 307, 310, 315
Roskilde 113, 129, 176, 198, 203, 205, 280–1, 291–2, 295–6, 316
Rostock 195
royal saints 62, 136
Rügen 174, 286, 292
Rus 5, 94, 104–6, 108–17, 119

Sada-Gyrd Baardsson 256
Sæmundr Jonsson 222–3
Saint Aubin of Angers, Abbey 311
Saint Mary of Noyers, Abbey 311
Saint Vincent of Le Mans, Abbey 311
Sauðafell 221
Sawyer, Birgit (historian) 81
Saxo Grammaticus 19, 56, 60, 63, 65, 132, 271, 273–7, 279–81, 285–6, 288–93
Saxony 276
Scania 17, 94, 97, 273, 279, 289, 293
Schleswig 175, 194, 196, 290, 317, 334
Schmid, Karl (historian) 56
Searle, Eleanor (historian) 14
service/servant/ *þjónn*/ *þjónustumaðr* 3, 5, 39–41, 43–4, 57, 62, 84–5, 94, 104–5, 115, 179–80, 229–30, 257, 285, 308, 314, 318, 325, 329–30
Severn 132

Sighvatr Sturluson 216, 218–22, 226, 230–1, 245
Sigtuna 97, 180–1, 194, 197–8, 204–5
Sigurd I Jorsalfare, King of Norway 116
Sigurd II Haraldsson, King of Norway 252, 254–6, 258
Sigurd Slembe 257
Simon de Suecia, friar 198
Skagafjörður 220, 228, 242–8
Skålhamra 89
Skänninge 178–81, 194, 204
Skara 199, 204
Skarð 241
skenkjari/pincerna regis 41
Skjalm clan *see* Hvide family
Skjalm Hvide 286–8, 292
Sko Abbey 202, 204
Skule Bårdsson, Norwegian earl/jarl 196, 223
Skultuna 83
Skyum-Nielsen, Niels (historian) 305, 309–10
Slangerup 203
Småenge 307
Snæfellsnes 243–5
Snorri Sturluson, chronicler 18, 56, 60, 63, 113, 130–1, 133, 215–16, 218–19, 222–7, 230–1, 241, 243, 245, 331–2
social power 285, 328
Södermanland 79, 81, 84–5, 92, 95
Södertälje 92, 95–7
Solveig Sæmundardottir 222
Sophia Volodarevna, Queen of Denmark 109
Sorø Abbey 173–5, 286–7, 289, 294–5, 304
Spielregeln (rules of the game) 56, 285, 296, 306
stabularius 40
Stafholt 223
St Alban 134–6
Stamford Bridge 125, 129–31
Staraia Ladoga 106
state formation 43, 55, 68, 81, 312, 337
statehood 238, 330, 335–6
St Dominic 171, 198, 205
Ste Geneviève Abbey 173
Stenkil, King of Sweden 98
Stephen of Tournai, abbot 295

St Henry 170–1, 181
St Laurentius 294
St Mary 247, 294
Stødle family 257
Stockholm 96, 204
St Oswald 135
Strängnäs 194, 204
Sturla Sighvatsson 65, 221–2, 224–6, 229–31
Sturla Thordarson, chronicler 218–20, 222, 224, 242, 246
Sturlung Age 58, 241–3
Sturlung family 58, 61, 215–16, 218, 223, 226, 230–1, 242
Sune Ebbesen 175, 285–8, 294–7, 331
Sune Skjalmsen 286–7
Sunnhordland 257
Svantevit 292
Svefneyjar 227
Svend, Bishop of Aarhus 305, 307–8, 310–11
Svend I Forkbeard, King of Denmark 115
Svend II Estridsen 112–13, 116, 129–30, 132, 254
Svend III Grathe, King of Denmark 273–4, 276–7, 279–80, 289–91
Svend Alfivason, King of Norway 255
Sverker, King of Sweden 274–5
Sverre Sigurdsson, King of Norway 58, 60–1, 65, 171
Svinfellingar family 220, 246
Sword Brethren, Order of the 169, 171
sýslumaðr 40, 43

Tabula Othiniensis 134
Täby 86–7, 89
Tallinn 199, 201
tax 1, 37, 43, 194–5, 227, 230, 291, 293, 308–9, 318
tenant 205, 313–14
þegn/thegn, 84–5, 130
Theodoricus Monachus 22
Thietmar of Merseburg, chronicler 111
þingmaðr 240, 245, 338
Thomas, Bishop of Åbo 181
Thomas de Cantimpré, Dominican friar 204
Thora Guthormsdottir 220
Thorbern, royal castellan 291, 294

Thordis Snorradottir 222, 224
Thordr Hítnesingr 242
Thordr kakali 216, 226–31, 237, 240–2, 245–7
Thordr Narfason 241
Thordr Sturluson 218–23, 230–1
Thorgils skarði Boedvarsson 237, 240–8
Thorleifr at Garðar 244
Thorsteinn Jonsson 228–9
Thorvaldr Vatnsfirding 18, 225
Thorvardr Thorarinsson 246
thrall (slave) 36–7, 39, 83, 85
Thuridr Sturludottir 229
þættir (short tales) 144–8, 158, 161, 164
Tiber 182
Tissø 36
tithe 37, 175, 308
Tjostolv Aalason 257
Toke Ebbesen 286
Toke Skjalmsen 286–7
Tönnies, Ferdinand (sociologist) 11
Torben Sunesen 295
Torbjörn Skald 89, 92, 96
Tostig, English earl/jarl 112, 128, 130–1, 133
Trinité de Vendôme, Abbey 311
Trondheim 170
Trugund family 287, 292
Trund clan 61
Trust/*fides* 66
Ture, Abbot of Øm 316–17
Turinge stone 92–7, 99
Tyge, Bishop of Aarhus 304–6, 308–14, 316–18

Ulf, Danish earl/jarl 13
Ulf of Ribe 289, 291
Ulv of Borresta 89
umbuthsman (royal official) 293
Uppland 81–4, 86–7, 89, 92–4, 98, 327
Uppsala 170, 179, 194, 198, 200, 204

Vadstena 202
Vaksala 98
Valdemar, Bishop of Schleswig 175
Valdemar I the Great, King of Denmark 64, 67, 109, 117, 173–4, 273, 276, 278–80, 287, 289–93
Valdemar II the Victorious, King of Denmark 175–6, 178
Valdemar Birgersson, King of Sweden 180

Valgerdr Arnadottir 221
Vallentuna 87
Varangian guard 84, 104, 109–15
Vårfruberga Abbey 204
Vartislaw, Pomeranian Prince 65
vassal/vassalage/vassus/vassallus 3, 33–4, 40, 108, 278–9, 331, 334
Västerås 203
Västmanland 83
Vatnsfirdingar family 223–4
veizla (feast) 242–7
Vejle 195
Vestfirðir 223, 227, 230, 247
Viborg 171, 274, 280, 289
Vigdis Gisldottir 221
Vigdis Sturludottir 220–1
Vigfus Gunnsteinsson 229
Viken 276, 278
Vilhelm, Abbot of Øm 316
villicus 40
vinátta/ vinr 23, 38–40, 86, 237, 326
Visby 194
Vissing 203
Vita Ædwardi 127, 130
Vita Ansgarii 79
Vitskøl Abbey 316
Vladimir Monomakh, Prince of Kiev 105, 115–17
Vladimir Sviatoslavich, Prince of Novgorod and Grand Prince of Kiev 106, 108–9, 111, 113–14
Vreta 203–4

Wearmouth 136
Weber, Max (sociologist) 2, 293, 325
Wends 110, 256, 292
Wessén, Elias (philologist) 92, 94–5
West, Charles (historian) 336
White, Stephen D. (historian) 3, 33, 307, 311
Wickham, Chris (historian) 2, 337–8
William of Æbelholt, abbot 174, 176, 295–7
William of Jumièges, chronicler 131
William of Sabina/William of Modena, Papal legate 169–70, 172, 178–81
William the Bastard, Duke of Normandy and King of England 126, 129, 131–3
Wismar 194

York 134–6

Zealand 173–5, 273, 279, 285–90, 292–6, 338

Printed in the United States
By Bookmasters